Corporations and Human Rights

SCHRIFTEN
zum internationalen und zum öffentlichen
RECHT
Herausgegeben von Gilbert Gornig

Band 81

PETER LANG
Frankfurt am Main · Berlin · Bern · Bruxelles · New York · Oxford · Wien

Niels Beisinghoff

Corporations and Human Rights

An Analysis of ATCA Litigation against Corporations

PETER LANG
Internationaler Verlag der Wissenschaften

Bibliographic Information published by the Deutsche Nationalbibliothek
The Deutsche Nationalbibliothek lists this publication in the Deutsche Nationalbibliografie; detailed bibliographic data is available in the internet at <http://www.d-nb.de>.

Zugl.: Frankfurt (Main), Univ., Diss., 2008

D 30
ISSN 0943-173X
ISBN 978-3-631-58418-7

Printed in Germany 1 2 3 4 5 6 7

www.peterlang.de

For my parents

Barbara and Rudolf Beisinghoff

Preface

I embarked upon the idea of writing this thesis during a lecture on human rights at the University of Sydney in 2004. The Alien Tort Claims Act (ATCA)[1] was mentioned. Nigerian children were subjected to medical experimentation by the U.S. pharmaceutical company Pfizer without informed consent of their parents and without authorization by the Nigerian government.[2] Pfizer carried out a test with Trovan, a drug which had not received official approval as a drug by the U.S. Food and Drug Administration and had very dangerous side effects. The parents desperately struggled for compensation. The *International Covenant on Civil and Political Rights* provides in Article 7: "No one shall be subjected to torture or to cruel, inhuman or degrading treatment or punishment. In particular, no one shall be subjected without his free consent to medical or scientific experimentation."[3] The Nigerian victims brought a suit pursuant to ATCA for violation of their human rights.[4] The underlying question that has always captured my interest was: Can humans enforce their human rights? Can they also enforce human rights against a transnational corporation (TNC)?

There have been some moments when I was not entirely sure whether I would be able to finish this work. It has been finally possible, also thanks to many people. There are four persons whom I owe my most special thanks. First, I would like to thank my supervisor, Prof. Dr. Dr. Rainer Hofmann from the Johann Wolfgang Goethe-University in Frankfurt for his support, patience, grand cordiality, and encouragement. He has been a great PhD supervisor and is an admirable person. Second, I would like to thank Edward Santow, Senior Lecturer at the University of New South Wales in Sydney/Australia. It was especially his academic and personal support, assistance and encouragement that was immeasurably important to me and this work. Lastly, I would like to thank my parents Rudolf and Barbara, who have encouraged and supported me to become the first male Dr. Beisinghoff of all times and therefore the PhD is dedicated to them.

I would also like to thank Prof. Dr. Stefan Kadelbach for his second opinion. The great human rights lawyer Paul Hoffmann invited me to visit him at his

---

1 ATCA is also sometimes referred to as the Alien Tort Statute (ATS) or Alien Tort Act (ATA).

2 J Stephens, 'Panel Faults Pfizer in '96 Clinical Trial in Nigeria' *Washington Post* 2006) A01.

3 International Covenant on Civil and Political Rights (ICCPR) GA Res 2200A (XXI), UN Doc A/6316, adopted and opened for signature, ratification and accession by General Assembly resolution 2200A (XXI) of 16 December 1966,entered into force Mar 23, 1976 (1966).

4 *Abdullahi v. Pfizer*, No 01 Civ 8118, 2002 US Dist LEXIS 17436, 2002 WL 31082956, D.C. S.D. N.Y. (2002) The case was dismissed on the ground of *forum non conveniens*, but Pfizer was forced to appear in a Nigerian court.

Californian law firm Schonbrun DeSimone Seplow Harris & Hoffman LLP in Venice Beach, Los Angeles/USA and assisted me in understanding the U.S. human rights litigation. Many other human rights experts have given me important advice, such as Dr. Karsten Nowrot from Martin-Luther University Halle Wittenberg, Tyler Giannini from Harvard University, Dr. Claudia Hailer, Professor Michael J. Bazyler from Whittier Law School, Professor William Dodge from University of California Hastings College of Law and Professor Beth Stephens from Rutgers School of Law. Mindy Rosemann from the Human Rights Program at Harvard University enabled my research at Harvard University.

This thesis was mostly written at the Max-Planck Institute for International Law in Heidelberg, Germany; at Harvard University, USA; at the University of Sydney, Australia and at the Johann Wolfgang Goethe University in Frankfurt, Germany.

I would also like to specially thank the Friedrich Naumann Foundation for Freedom and the German Federal Ministry of Education and Research for the scholarship which financially enabled me to write this PhD. Also, the Naumann Foundation provided the platform for many seminars that I have attended and organized. Through and with the Foundation I could co-found the non-governmental organization Lebenschancen Malawi.

To all those that have helped me and supported me I wish to say: "*Danke!*"

Abu Dhabi / Frankfurt, 5. Dezember 2008

Niels Beisinghoff

Table of Contents

List of Abbreviations

ACHR	American Convention on Human Rights
ACJ	African Court of Justice
ACoHPR	African Commission on Human and Peoples' Rights
ACtHPR	African Court on Human and Peoples' Rights
AI	Amnesty International
ALI	American Law Institute
ATCA	Alien Tort Claims Act
ATS	Alien Tort Statute
AU	African Union
BDP	Business Partners for Development
BGB	Bürgerliche Gesetzbuch – German Civil Code
BGH	Bundesgerichtshof
BIT	Bilateral investment treaty
C.A.	Court of Appeals
Cal.	California
CalCCP	California Code of Civil Procedure
CAT	Convention against Torture and Other Cruel, Inhuman or Degrading Treatment or Punishment
CCAIL	German Code of Crimes against International Law
C.D.	Central District
CEDAW	Convention on the Elimination of All Forms of Discrimination against Women
CEO	Chief Executive Officer
CERD	Convention on the Elimination of All Forms of Racial Discrimination
CIA	Central Intelligence Agency
CMW	Convention on the Protection of the Rights of All Migrant Workers and Members of Their Families
CSR	Corporate Social Responsibility
Cth	Commonwealth
D.C.	District Court
D.C.	District of Columbia
DSB	Dispute Settlement Body
EC	European Communities
ECHR	European Court of Human Rights
ECJ	The Court of Justice of the European Communities

ECHR	European Convention on Human Rights
ECtHR	European Court of Human Rights
ECOSOC	Economic and Social Council
ECR	European Court Reports
ED	Eastern District
EEC	European Economic Community
EU	European Union
FCC	German Federal Constitutional Court
FDI	Foreign direct investment
FLA	Fair Labor Association
Fla.	Florida
FSIA	Foreign Sovereign Immunities Act
GA	General Assembly
Ga.	Georgia
GAOR	General Assembly Official Record
GATS	General Agreement on Trade in Services
GATT	General Agreement on Tariffs and Trade
GDP	Gross Domestic Product
GG	Grundgesetz – German Basic Law
GRI	Global Reporting Initiative
HRL	Human Rights Litigation
HRW	Human Rights Watch
IACoHR	Inter-American Commission on Human Rights
IACtHR	Inter-American Court of Human Rights
IBRD	International Bank for Reconstruction and Development
ICC	International Criminal Court
ICC	International Chamber of Commerce
ICCPR	International Covenant on Civil and Political Rights
ICESCR	International Covenant on Economic, Social and Cultural Rights
ICJ	International Court of Justice
ICRC	International Committee of the Red Cross
ICSID	International Center for Settlement of Investment Disputes
ICTR	International Criminal Tribunal for Rwanda
ICTY	International Criminal Tribunal for the former Yugoslavia
IDA	International Development Association
IFC	International Finance Corporation
IGO	International Governmental Organization
ILC	International Law Commission

I.L.M.	International Legal Materials
ILO	International Labour Organization
ILR	International Law Reports
ILRF	International Labor Rights Fund
IMF	International Monetary Fund
IMO	International Maritime Organization
IMT	International Military Tribunal
INGO	International Non-Governmental Organization
IPEC	International Programme on the Elimination of Child Labour
ITU	International Telecommunication Union
IUOTO	International Union of Official Travel Organizations
La.	Louisiana
Mass.	Massachusetts
Md.	Maryland
M.D.	Middle District
Mercosur	Mercado Común del Sur
MIGA	Multilateral Investment Guarantee Agency
MNC	Multinational corporation
MOGE	Myanmar Oil and Gas Enterprise
MOSOP	Movement for the Survival of Ogoni People
NAFTA	North American Free Trade Agreement
NATO	North Atlantic Treaty Organisation
NCP	Organisation for Economic Co-operation and Development National Contact Points
N.D.	Northern District
NGO	Non-governmental organization
NIF	National Islamic Front
N.J.	New Jersey
N.Mar.	Northern Mariana Islands
N.Y.	New York
OAS	Organization of American States
OECD	Organisation for Economic Co-operation and Development
Pa.	Pennsylvania
PLO	Palestine Liberation Organization
PNG	Papua New Guinea
Res.	Resolution
RICO	Racketeer Influenced and Corrupt Organizations Act
SC	Security Council

SCR	Security Council Resolution
S.Ct.	Supreme Court
S.D.	Southern District
SPLA	Sudan People's Liberation Army
SRI	Socially responsible investing
SRSG	UN Special Representative for Business and Human Rights
Tex.	Texas
TNC	Transnational corporation
TRIPS	Agreement on Trade Related Aspects of Intellectual Property Rights
TVPA	Torture Victim Protection Act
UDHR	Universal Declaration of Human Rights
UK	United Kingdom
UN	United Nations
UNCLOS	United Nations Convention on the Law of the Sea
UNCTAD	United Nations Conference on Trade and Development
UNEP	UN Environment Programme
UNHCR	UN High Commissioner for Refugees
UNICEF	UN Children's Fund
UNSCR	United Nations Security Council Resolution
UNTS	United Nations Treaty Series
UNWTO	United Nations World Tourism Organization
UPU	Universal Postal Union
US	United States of America
Va.	Virginia
Wash.	Washington
WHO	World Health Organization
WIPO	World Intellectual Property Organization
WTO	World Trade Organization
WTO DSB	World Trade Organization Dispute Settlement Body

Introductory notes

I. Choice of thesis

Why this topic? Despite remarkable normative and institutional developments since World War II and the creation of the *Universal Declaration of Human Rights (UDHR)* the world remains mired in widespread violations of human rights.[5] Although there are promising trends toward democratic governance and the alleviation of poverty worldwide, there remain massive abuses of human rights. Genocidal episodes have scarred the conscience of the world again and again – even in the twenty-first century, Sudan being a prime example. Enforcement remains the weakest component of the international human rights system.[6] There is a disjuncture between the theoretical recognition of a broad spectrum of rights vested in every individual and a reality in which those rights are too frequently curtailed or denied and individuals are left with inadequate mechanisms of enforcing their rights. This inconsistency between rights and reality also forms the basis of this thesis. The nations of the world have enthusiastically embraced the articulation of human rights in legally binding international treaties. We now must ask: how can those rights be enforced?

Traditional international human rights treaties have been framed to address human rights violations by nation states. But since the adoption of many of those treaties the international political and cultural setting has fundamentally changed. The process of Globalization has reduced the influence of nation states and increased the influence of transnational corporations in almost every facet of our lives.[7] The question arises whether there are legal instruments to safeguard individuals against human rights violations by transnational corporations (TNCs) and, if so, how these rights can be enforced.

Corporations have violated human rights in numerous cases and many might still believe that corporations cannot be punished for these human rights violations. The Alien Tort Claims Act (ATCA) litigation taught them differently. In most of these cases, especially in countries with weak rule of law, the victims have no way to seek justice, because their host countries may be corrupt or controlled by the same people who are involved in those human rights violations.[8]

---

5 Universal Declaration of Human Rights GA Res 217 A(III), UN Doc A/810 at 71 (1948).

6 See DL Donoho, 'Human Rights Enforcement in the 21st Century' (2006) <http:// law.bepress.com / cgi / viewcontent.cgi ? article = 6113 & context = expresso > (March 14, 2007).

7 UN Special Representative of the Secretary-General on human rights and transnational corporations and other business enterprises, 'E/CN.4/2006/97- Interim report of the Special Representative of the Secretary-General on the issue of human rights and transnational corporations and other business enterprises' (2006) <http:// daccess -ods .un. org / access.nsf / Get ? Open&DS =E / CN.4/2006 / 97&Lang=E> (May 23, 2007) at para 9-12.

8 As one of many examples: PC Aka, 'Prospects for IGBO human rights in Nigeria in the new

The host country is the country where the TNC is doing business in contrast to the country where the TNC is based, which is called the home country. Home countries often fail to control the activities of their TNCs abroad. International law seemed ill-equipped to regulate TNCs. Since the mid-1990s, many human rights cases against TNCs have been litigated in US courts. Many corporations have been held responsible for egregious human rights violations and they will continue to be held liable. The ATCA seems to be the answer to the weakest component in the human rights system. The ATCA provides a missing link: the mechanism by which to hold TNCs to account for human rights violations of which they are wholly or partly culpable.

The ATCA provides the first avenue in the world to seek civil damages for human rights violations. It appears to be a potent instrument to enforce human rights against private actors and, in this sense, it symbolizes a revolution in human rights law. Most international human rights treaties did not provide for the possibility for an individual to enforce human rights, only states had the right to sue against human rights breaches.[9] The ATCA provides an interesting example of how international law, and especially international human rights law, is patriated into domestic law; it may also be seen as an example of how international "soft law" (*OECD Guidelines for Multinational Enterprises, UN Norms on the Responsibilities of Transnational Corporations and Other Business Enterprises with Regard to Human Rights*) develops into "hard law" (as transnational law based on universal jurisdiction).

---

century' 48 Howard Law Journal 165 (2004).

9 At the UN level, individual complaint mechanisms are found under five conventions: in the First Optional Protocol to the International Covenant on Civil and Political Rights (ICCPR) GA Res 2200A (XXI), UN Doc A/6316, adopted and opened for signature, ratification and accession by General Assembly resolution 2200A (XXI) of 16 December 1966,entered into force Mar 23, 1976 (1966); Article 22 Convention Against Torture and Other Cruel Inhuman or Degrading Treatment or Punishment 10 December 1984, 1465 UNTS 85 (entered into force 26 June 1987) (1984); Optional Protocol to the CEDAW; Article 14 International Convention on the Elimination of All Forms of Racial Discrimination (adopted December 21, 1965, entered into force January 4, 1969) 660 UNTS 195 (1965). Individual complaints under one of the above-mentioned treaties can be brought only against a state that has recognized the competence of the committee established under the relevant treaty or become party to the relevant optional protocols. Article 34 European Convention of Human Rights and Fundamental Freedoms ETS No5 (1950) allows individual complaints. While under the old system, covered by Article 25 of the European Convention, the individual complaint mechanism was optional for state parties, under the new system, established by Protocol No. 11, entered into force in 1998, the mechanism is compulsory for all states parties to the Convention. For more information see: Icelandic Human Rights Centre, 'International Supervisory Mechanism for Human Rights' (2007) <http:// www. humanrights. is/ the-human-rights- project/ humanrightscasesandmaterials/ human rights concepts ideas and fora/ the concepts of human rights an introduction / international supervisory mechanism for human rights/> (May 29, 2007).

For many reasons, it is interesting to analyze US human rights litigation. One of these reasons is that the United States possibly stands as the country that, since 1919, has had the most profound impact on the development of international law. In the historiography of international law, some authors, most notably among them Wilhelm Grewe, have argued that several periods can be distinguished, such as the Spanish era (1494-1648), the French era (1648-1789/1815), the English era (1789/1815-1919) and the predominantly American era since 1919, especially since 1989 when the US became the only remaining Superpower.[10] This Superpower had rather exceptional human rights records, both in violation and in defense of most basic human rights.[11] Nevertheless, the US also offers a legal instrument to enforce human rights against TNCs that is more progressive than any other instrument worldwide, which is the ATCA litigation. According to the authors view this litigation against TNCs for human rights violations represents a progressive approach to international law, which will soon be followed by other jurisdictions and masterminds the establishment of human rights accountability of TNCs in international law. The ATCA litigation therefore appears to stand as evidence supporting Grewe's histography of international law.

The ATCA is been used as a "chief weapon in a 21st-century battle over corporate responsibility in an age of Globalization."[12] The ATCA human rights litigation against individuals has been largely affirmed by the *Sosa* decision of the US Supreme Court. The next big test will possibly be whether the ATCA can be used against TNCs as well as individuals.[13] No comprehensive study has been done on comparing the ATCA litigation to international law in terms of corporate liability for human rights violations. The ATCA litigation often refers to the "law of nations," but does the understanding of the US litigation of international law really reflect international law? This study attempts to be a small contribution to this field of research.

This thesis may also help humans in enforcing their rights. In the event that the ATCA litigation were abolished or limited, surely, inventive lawyers would pursue the same ends of holding corporations accountable for violations of human rights through different means. Finding and strengthening these new means may also rely on research such as this. This work could be used as background for the understanding of the role of TNCs in international law. It documents the status of the

---

10 WG Grewe and M Byers, *The Epochs of International Law* (Walter de Gruyter, Berlin; New York 2000).

11 HH Koh, 'On American Exceptionalism' 55 Stanford Law Review 1479 (2003).

12 P Waldmeir, 'An Abuse of Power: US Courts Should not Punish Companies for Human Rights Violations Committed Overseas' *Financial Times* (March 14, 2003) 12 at 12; See also S Gul, 'The Supreme Court Giveth and the Supreme Court Taketh Away: An Assessment of Corporate Liability Under § 1350' 109 West Virginia Law Review 379 (2007) at 379.

13 S Gul, 'The Supreme Court Giveth and the Supreme Court Taketh Away: An Assessment of Corporate Liability Under § 1350' 109 West Virginia Law Review 379 (2007) at 401.

ATCA provisions, their interpretation and also some of ATCA's weaknesses and strengths.

II. Methodology of the thesis

According to the *Corpus Juris Civilis*, the foundational work on Roman law, justice is the constant and perpetual desire to give to one another that to which one is entitled.[14] Law must constantly strive to achieve a just balance between the interests of all parties involved. This basic idea is also fundamental to the methodology of any legal research. This research views at US Common law litigation from the German civil law perspective.

A. Montesquieu and the separation of powers

Montesquieu and Locke pioneered the concept of the separation of powers, as between the legislature, the judiciary and the executive. This concept has been incorporated differently into the US Common law and German civil law systems. The Roman-Germanic tradition would rather look at the legislation in the form of statutory provisions and the legislative history to those provisions to fill in the current lacunae. It appears to have a more textual approach that may have been more strongly influence by legal positivism.

In his work *The Spirit of Law*, Montesquieu stated: "There is no liberty if the judiciary power be not separated from the legislative and executive. Were it joined with the legislative, the life and liberty of the subject would be exposed to arbitrary control; for the judge would be then the legislator. Were it joined to the executive power, the judge might behave with violence and oppression."[15] He went on to state that "the law, which is clear sighted in one sense, and blind in another, might, in some cases, be too severe. But as we have already observed, the national judges are no more than the mouth that pronounces the words of the law, mere passive beings, incapable of moderating either its force or rigor."[16] He therefore rejected any interpretative role for the independent judiciary. Consigned to a strictly interpretative role, Montesquieu's judges roles are highly formalistic, with a mechanical method of jurisprudence, reduced to mere "subsumption automatons."[17] As the mere

---

14 Civil law (*corpus juris civilis*), The Enactments of Justinian I, The Institutes, Book I, Title I, Concerning Justice and Law, in AM Scott, *The Civil Law* (The Central Trust Company, Cincinnati 1932).

15 CdS Montesquieu and others, *The Spirit of Laws* (Clarke, Cincinnati 1873), Bk XI ch VI at 173.

16 *Ibid.* at Bk XI, ch VI at 182.

17 MP Bergman, 'Montesquieu's Theory of Government and the Framing of the American Constitution' 18 Pepperdine Law Review 1 (1990) at 16. The term "subsumption automatons" goes back to Ehrlich, Kantorowisz, Fuchs and the Free Lawyers. The Free Lawyers called attention to sources of law other than the statutory texts in the early decades of 19th Century, when the all-encompassing new German codes, combined with a thoroughgoing legal positivism, threatened to reduce judges to "subsumption automatons" without regard for individual justice or community interests. See MD Dubber, 'The German Jury and the Metaphysical Volk: From Romantic Idealism to Nazi Ideology' 43 American Journal of

mouthpieces of the law, the courts are not in a position to "check" the acts of the other two branches.[18]

B. US Common law methodology

The US Common law, in contrast to the Roman-Germanic civil law tradition, often appears to have a more flexible and dynamic approach in interpreting legislation and appears less textual and dogmatic. The US Common law system seems to adapt more quickly to current legal issues, whereas a judge in the German civil law tradition is more likely to "wait" for the legislator to address a new legal problem.

An outstanding example of this greater flexibility is the ATCA litigation. In the *Exxon* decision the bench discussed and denied corporate liability: "It is also highly unfair to corporations operating in states with potentially problematic human rights records which under the color of law rule may (or may not) be subject to liability for doing business there and benefiting from the state's infrastructure."

In the *Eastman Kodak* decision the District Court for the Southern District of Florida found that "as a matter of initial impression, the Court believes that it would be a strange tort system that imposed liability on state actors but not on those who conspired with them to perpetrate illegal acts through the coercive use of state power. Although the negative prohibitions of our own Constitution generally extend only to state action, those who conspire with state actors to invade the constitutional rights of others may be held liable along with the state actors."[19] There are many further examples of the wide jurisdiction of US courts in ATCA litigation.[20]

Comparative Law 227 (1995) at 258.

18 MP Bergman, 'Montesquieu's Theory of Government and the Framing of the American Constitution' 18 Pepperdine Law Review 1 (1990) at 17.

19 *Eastman Kodak Co. v. Kavlin*, 978 FSupp 1078, D.C. S.D. Fla. (1997) at 1091, citing *Dennis v. Sparks*, 449 US 24, 27-28, 101 SCt 183, 185-87, 66 LEd2d 185 US S.Ct (1980).

20 Some examples from ATCA litigation showing the US American flexibility of judiciary:
- Discussing the requirement of exhaustion of remedies in ATCA litigation: "Considerations of equity and consistency also recommend this approach since otherwise American victims of torture would be bound by an exhaustion requirement under the TVPA and foreign plaintiffs could avoid such strictures by pleading under the ATCA." From *Sarei v. Rio Tinto*, 456 F3d 1069, C.A. 9 (2006) at 1090;
- "It is not unfair that a plaintiff's conclusory claims of social injustice in the foreign nation where she deliberately chose to live, work, and transact the business out of which the litigation arises should be accorded less than controlling weight in the selection of a judicial forum for the related litigation." from *Eastman Kodak Co. v. Kavlin*, 978 FSupp 1078, D.C. S.D. Fla. (1997) at 1085;
- Discussing the principle of international comity: "Put more simply, federal courts will not review foreign judgements unless the parties challenging that judgement demonstrate that it was unfair. While the instant case does not involve a judgement against either Plaintiffs or Defendants, a similar principle of fairness should guide the Court in deciding whether to dismiss this case on grounds of international comity." From *Mujica v. Occidental Petroleum Corp.*, 381 F Supp 2d 1134, D.C. C.D. Cal. (2005) at 1163.

Historically, TNCs abused human rights in countries with weak legal systems, but the US judiciary, through ATCA litigation addressed this problem. The ATCA was enacted by the US Congress in 1789 as a one-sentence law, but the human rights litigation has been largely developed by the US judiciary in the 20th and 21st century. This took seed with the *Filártiga* decision, and has been developing over the course of nearly 30 years. Its scope and limits have been refined by numerous court decisions.[21] The case law reveals how loopholes were addressed by the US judiciary, which seems to have large competence to develop the law.

This judicial freedom appears to be almost guaranteed by the legislative body of the US. The US Senate acknowledged ATCA litigation and wrote in the legislative report to the Torture Victim Protection Act (TVPA): "In the case of *Filártiga v. Pena-Irala*, the Second Circuit Court of Appeals recognized a right of action against foreign torturers under the rarely invoked Alien Tort Claims Act. […] The 'appellate' court unanimously acknowledged that although torture of one's own citizens was not recognized as a violation of the law of nations in 1789, when the Alien Tort Claims Act was enacted, the universal prohibition of torture had ripened into a rule of customary international law, thereby bringing torture squarely within the language of the statute."[22]

Furthermore, the US Senate also authorized the judiciary to carry out further development. The US Senate Judiciary Committee suggested that courts should consider "unfairness of the judicial system, unfair procedures, and lack of competence" of judiciaries in different countries.[23] "Although the inquiry is complex, legislators were confident that the principle could be applied by courts as it was generally consistent with common-law principles of exhaustion as applied by courts in the United States."[24]

C. German civil law methodology

The differences between the German civil law and the US Common law methodology can be also witnessed in contract or tort law, the latter being also the basis for ATCA litigation. In the Anglo-American legal tradition, contract and tort law are, for the

- Discussing if US district courts may address questions of universal jurisdiction: "In short, plaintiffs' imaginative view of this Court's power must face the reality that United States district courts are courts of limited jurisdiction. While their power within those limits is substantial, it does not include a general writ to right the world's wrongs." From *Aguinda v. Texaco*, 945 FSupp 625, D.C. S.D.N.Y. (1996) at 628.

21 *Filártiga v. Peña-Irala*, 630 F2d 876, C.A. 2 (1980). The further development is outlined in chapter III.

22 U.S. House of Representatives, *P.L. 102-256, Torture Victim Protection Act of 1991, H.R. REP. NO. 102-367 (I), November 25* (1991), pt. 1, p. 3.

23 S. REP. NO. 102-249, pt. 4, at 10 (1991).

24 *Sarei v. Rio Tinto*, 456 F3d 1069, C.A. 9 (2006).

most part, a product of Common law development. Germany treats contract law, in theory, as being wholly governed by its statutory provisions in the civil code of the *Bürgerliche Gesetzbuch* (BGB) of 1900. Motivated, at least in part, by the positivist tendency towards all-encompassing codifications, Germany passed the BGB into law in 1900, whereas in Great Britain and the United States the law grew organically from case to case.

William Ewald has pointed out the differences in the authoritativeness of sources in those two systems. The status of the German judge within the legal system is subtle and complex, and although twentieth-century German private-law judges are more powerful than nineteenth-century German private-law judges, neither they nor the academic jurists in universities play quite the same institutional role as their common-law counterparts.[25] In part, this is attributable to tradition and, in particular, to the Roman-law tradition, which always paid greater respect to the scholar than to the judge.[26] On the other hand, this is also attributable to the form of a modern German private-law judicial opinion. Even the decisions of the Federal Supreme Court, the Bundesgerichtshof (BGH) are delivered without dissenting opinions. The Court always speaks with a single voice, stating its reading of the code, and referring to earlier cases and to the scholarly literature, but not, in general, embarking on a complex analysis of the arguments for and against its conclusion.[27] "The power to decide is one thing, but individual prestige and influence another; and in some ways the private-law decisions of the German Supreme Court bear a greater resemblance to the decisions of relatively anonymous agencies like the IRS[28] than they do to the decisions of the United States Supreme Court. In contrast to what one finds in the common-law world, the most famous names in twentieth-century German law belong to jurists and not to judges."[29]

However, if Montesquieu's extreme view of the judicial role as being merely mechanical interpretation of law is right, then it cannot explain the fact that, even though there have been only small changes of the BGB since 1900, the BGB has outlived the legal systems of five completely different political systems. The BGB outlived monarchy until the end of World War I, then the democratic Weimar Republic until 1933, the Nazi Third Reich until 1945, the first years of Communism in the German Democratic Republic (GDR) and remains applicable up to this day in the Federal Republic of Germany.

---

25 W Ewald, 'Comparative Jurisprudence (I): What was it like to Try a Rat?' 143 University of Pennsylvania Law Review 1889 (1995) at 2086.

26 A Watson, *The Making of the Civil Law* (Harvard University Press, Cambridge 1981) at 83.

27 W Ewald, 'Comparative Jurisprudence (I): What was it like to Try a Rat?' 143 University of Pennsylvania Law Review 1889 (1995) at 2087.

28 The Internal Revenue Service (IRS) is the United States federal government agency that collects taxes.

29 W Ewald, 'Comparative Jurisprudence (I): What was it like to Try a Rat?' 143 University of Pennsylvania Law Review 1889 (1995) at 2087.

Therefore, Laurence Claus seems to be correct when he states that "resolving disputes may require judicial exposition of existing law. Exposition is elaboration. Elaboration is lawmaking. [...] The mission of law is to control the exercise of power through words; if one adds to the words, one adds to the law." [30] This finding holds true for both systems.

D. Methodological approach in this thesis

This thesis approaches the US human rights litigation from the perspective of the more formalistic and also highly systematic Roman-Germanic civil law tradition. In the field of international law, the US Common law approach may have advantages, since in international law judicial decisions also have a more authorative function. Judicial decisions of international courts are a "most important factor in the development of international law."[31] Bearing in mind the particularities of the US Common law, it may be more amenable to finding legal answers to problems of international law, as it did in the case of corporate violations of human rights through ATCA litigation.

Greater flexibility can also be witnessed in US legal academia. The ATCA human rights discussion in legal academia splits people into warring camps. The articles and books published on this subject have titles like "Awakening Monster"[32] or "The Current Illegitimacy of International Human Rights Litigation;"[33] the other side contains titles including "The Amorality of Profit,"[34] "Her Body is a Battlefield"[35] and "Our Business is People (Even if it Kills Them)."[36] Some articles that were written on the human rights litigation were rather driven by political agendas and have the effect of mystifying the ATCA. The ATCA litigation is rife with ambiguity and inconsistency, especially in the first years after *Filártiga*. This work tries to separate myth from reality and analyze the litigation and legal discussion objectively.

---

30 L Claus, 'Montesquieu's Mistakes and the True Meaning of Separation' 25 Oxford Journal of Legal Studies 419 (2005) at 432.

31 L Oppenheim, RY Jennings and A Watts, *Oppenheim's International Law* (9th edn, Longman, Harlow 1992) at 41. Also the European Court of Justice is also seen as the motor of the European integration, see, e.g. Av Bogdandy, 'Zweierlei Verfassungsrecht - Europäisierung als Gefährdung des gesellschaftlichen Grundkonsenses?' 39 Der Staat 163 (2000) at 178.

32 GC Hufbauer and NK Mitrokostas, *Awakening Monster: The Alien Tort Statute of 1789* (Policy analyses in international economics 70, Institute for International Economics, Washington, D.C. 2003).

33 CA Bradley and JL Goldsmith, 'The current illegitimacy of international human rights litigation' 66 Fordham Law Review 317 (1997).

34 B Stephens, 'The Amorality of Profit: Transnational Corporations and Human Rights' 20 Berkeley Journal of International Law 45 (2000).

35 GC Spencer, 'Her body is a battlefield: The applicability of the alien tort statute to corporate human rights abuses in Juarez, Mexico' 40 Gonzaga Law Review 503 (2004-5).

36 S Kabel, 'Our Business Is People (Even If It Kills Them): The Contribution of Multinational Enterprises to the Conflict in the Democratic Republic of Congo' 12 Tulane Journal of International and Comparative Law 461 (2004).

It attempts to be a helpful contribution to the theoretical discussion and a guideline for litigants.

To write this thesis without incorporating his own views, the author would need to be superhuman – or perhaps, even worse, he would need to subjugate his natural, human reactions to the impact on other humans of TNCs. Especially in such an evolving field of law with considerable uncertainty, the allegation of idealizing this highly contested and political field of law can easily be made. Especially in the field of international law, opinions widely vary and it is more challenging to determine the current law since there is no ultimate judicial or legislative body that can rule definitively on the state of the law. Nevertheless, it is the author's intention to examine impartially and objectively.

III. Other works in this field of research

This thesis centers on a rapidly evolving field of international law. Many law journals, newspaper and other articles have been written on the subject of the ATCA and the emerging field of international human rights litigation in the United States. However, most of these articles just briefly outline the basis of the ATCA and the litigation, without delving into more advanced questions, such as the question of human rights responsibilities of TNCs. There are only few monographs that could be used as principal resources for research in the field of the ATCA and TNCs, such as the books by the Australian Professor Sarah Joseph, the Dutch dissertation of Nicola Jägers, the German dissertations of Claudia Hailer and Karsten Nowrot and the soon to be published dissertation by Michael Köbele.[37] Whereas Hailer's dissertation mainly focuses on the ATCA litigation generally, the publications of Köbele and Joseph focus on the litigation against TNCs. Joseph's work also includes other jurisdictions, such as Australia, Canada and the UK, and it looks at different methods of holding corporations liable. Köbele focuses strongly on the obstacles for human rights litigation against TNCs in the US. A seminal 1000 page-dissertation on the influence of TNCs on international law was written by Nowrot. Jägers has written mostly on the international law concerning TNCs. The examination in this thesis will center on the US litigation against TNCs and their human rights responsibilities.

---

37 S Joseph, *Corporations and Transnational Human Rights Litigation* (Human rights law in perspective, Hart Publishing, Oxford 2004); N Jägers, *Corporate Human Rights Obligations: In Search of Accountability* (Intersentia, Antwerpen 2002); C Hailer, *Menschenrechte vor Zivilgerichten - die Human Rights Litigation in den USA* (Duncker & Humblot, Berlin 2006); K Nowrot, *Normative Ordnungsstruktur und private Wirkungsmacht - Konsequenzen der Beteiligung transnationaler Unternehmen an den Rechtssetzungsprozessen im internationalen Wirtschaftssystem* (BWV Berliner Wissenschafts-Verlag, Berlin 2006) and Köbele's work is not published as yet.

IV. Risk of ATCA litigation

"Three rectifying words from the legislator and whole libraries become waste paper."[38] So said the German jurist, Julius Herrmann von Kirchmann, in 1848 in the context of questioning whether legal studies can be seen as scientific. He questioned legal research, especially in areas of law that may be subject to a sudden change to the relevant rule simply by operation of an act of the legislature. Legal research that has been conducted on a statutory provision that is later superseded may not hold the same value in terms of current relevance as before the statutory amendment, but does this also mean that it turns into mere "waste paper?"

In October 2005, Senator Dianne Feinstein of California introduced a bill called the Alien Tort Statute Reform Act.[39] Specifically, the measure would have stated that federal courts shouldn't proceed with tort claims when the President adequately certifies that such exercise of jurisdiction will have a negative impact on the foreign policy interests of the US. However, it did not ask for an abolishment of the ATCA litigation, but rather asked for codification of many aspects of the law and was also not directed against the human rights litigation of TNCs. After pressure by human right activists, Feinstein informally withdrew the bill by asking the Chair of the Judiciary Committee, Senator Arlen Specter, not to schedule a hearing. She stated, "I believe the present legislation calls for refinement in light of concerns raised by human rights activists."[40] Over the previous decades of human rights litigation the US House of Representatives has now refrained from invalidating or limiting the ATCA and the threat of invalidation though legislation seems to be not the most immediate, even though many authors have asked for legislative guidance.[41] In the words of the *Sosa* decision: "Congress, however, has not only expressed no disagreement with our view of the proper exercise of the judicial power, but has responded to its most notable instance by enacting legislation supplementing the judicial determination."[42]

Rather, there is a danger that ATCA human rights litigation *against corporations* will be abolished, by invalidation through the US Supreme Court. The Supreme Court

---

38 "Drei berichtigende Worte des Gesetzgebers und ganze Bibliotheken werden zur Makulatur." in: JHv Kirchmann, *Die Wertlosigkeit der Jurisprudenz als Wissenschaft* (2nd edn, Manutius-Verl., Heidelberg 2000) at 1.

39 D Feinstein, 'Senator Feinstein Seeks to Clarify Adjudication of Foreign Lawsuits in US Federal Court' (2005) <http://feinstein.senate.gov/ 05releases/ r-alientort.htm> (August 23, 2007).

40 International Law Committee of the Association of the Bar of the City of New York, 'The Making of Filártiga v. Peña: The Alien Tort Claims Act after Twenty-Five Years' 9 New York City Law Review 249 (2006) at 274.

41 See, e.g., P-Y Hsu, 'Should Congress Repeal the Alien Tort Claims Act?' 28 Southern Illinois University Law Journal 579 (2004) at 597; GC Hufbauer and NK Mitrokostas, *Awakening Monster: The Alien Tort Statute of 1789* (Policy analyses in international economics 70, Institute for International Economics, Washington, D.C. 2003) at 55.

42 *Sosa v. Alvarez-Machain* (03-339) 542 US 2739, US S.Ct. (2004) at 2765.

recently affirmed the constitutional validity of the ATCA litigation in *Sosa v Alvarez-Machain*.[43] It found that the door for human rights claims is "still ajar."[44] The threat of a complete abolition of the ATCA litigation at the hands of the judiciary has, therefore, diminished. However, the US Supreme Court only acknowledged human rights litigation on the basis of ATCA *against individuals* and has addressed corporations only in a cryptic footnote, which indicates the tendency to treat individuals and corporations alike.[45] It could still find, in a later case in which the Court is asked to consider the ATCA, that the ATCA cannot be used to claim damages *against corporations* in respect of breaches of human rights by corporations. Bearing in mind the nomination of the Judges John Roberts and Samuel Alito by George W. Bush to the US Supreme Court in 2005, a more "conservative" US Supreme Court might subject human rights litigation against corporations to possible restrictions. Since the question of the ATCA claims *against TNCs* seems to be not completely resolved, this thesis might be useful for defining the status of TNCs in US law and in international law.

V. Outline of the thesis

The entire topic of TNCs and human rights is highly topical. The amount of literature written on that topic is hardly manageable. Already in 1982, the United Nations Centre on Transnational Corporations had compiled a 426 page bibliography on the subject.[46] Afterwards the amount of writing on the subject grew steadily, quickly and exponentially. Within this flood of literature, it is necessary to narrow the analysis. The work is limited to US human rights litigation against corporations, which is mostly comprised of the ATCA litigation. The ATCA cases against state officials and individuals will not be examined. This thesis can only be seen as a first step towards this task and will mainly focus on the most fundamental question of the scope of liability. It may be the starting point for further research that will look more closely at questions like which human rights responsibilities TNCs have under international law.

In Chapter I, this doctoral thesis sets the framework for the better understanding of the work. Chapter II represents the first focus of the thesis and outlines the avenues that are taken to enforce human rights as against TNCs. Chapter III describes the

43 *Ibid.*

44 *Ibid.* at 2764.

45 *Ibid.* at 2766 ("A related consideration is whether international law extends the scope of liability for a violation of a given norm to the perpetrator being sued, if the defendant is a private actor such as a corporation or individual. Compare *Tel-Oren v. Libyan Arab Republic*, 726 F.2d 774, 791-795 (C.A.D.C.1984) (Edwards, J., concurring) (insufficient consensus in 1984 that torture by private actors violates international law), with *Kadic v . Karadzic*, 70 F.3d 232, 239-241 (C.A.2 1995) (sufficient consensus in 1995 that genocide by private actors violates international.")

46 CD Wallace, *Legal Control of the Multinational Enterprise: National Regulatory Techniques and the Prospects for International Controls* (M.Nijhoff, The Hague 1983) at VII.

ATCA. Chapter IV outlines the most significant ATCA cases against TNCs. Chapter V represents a second focus of this thesis and examines the question of the corporate scope of liability for human rights in US law. Chapter VI examines the US understanding of international law. Chapter VII presents the understanding of international law in ATCA litigation. Finally, the conclusion presents a summary of the arguments.

For clarity, a few notes about the diction are briefly mentioned here. The citations and footnotes follow the Oxford Standard for Citation of Legal Authorities (OSCOLA). The punctuation and spelling are following the rules of American English. The word "American" in this document refers to the United States of America. I apologize for this geographically incorrect, though common, use of that term. The symbol $, without further specification, refers to US Dollars. Since the author of this thesis does not have English as his mother tongue, he must ask the reader to be patient with some German-accented eccentricities.

Chapter I. Setting the stage – Current legal setting of human rights accountability of TNCs

I. Idea and history of human rights

The idea behind human rights is to protect the citizens from abuse of power, whether it is the abuse of power by nation states or by TNCs or by other individuals. The concept of human rights refers to the proposition that humans have universal rights, regardless of religion, nationality or other categorization with which they identify or are identified. Human rights generally include rights concerning: 1) the well being of individuals; 2) the freedom and autonomy of individuals; and 3) the representation of the human interest in government. Important human rights are the right to life, freedom from torture, freedom of religion and of expression, freedom of movement, right to justice, right to an adequate standard of living and the right to self-determination.

International human rights law is a relatively new field of learning. One widely used and philosophical approach to justify the concept of human rights is the natural law theories, which are based on the "natural" moral order. This "natural order" is based on understandings of justice. Modern human rights emerged during the Enlightenment, as "reason began to triumph over religion."[47] On August 26, 1789, the French National Assembly passed the "Déclaration des droits de l'Homme et du citoyen." Later that year, the United States passed the Bill of Rights. The cradle of human rights law was natural law. It then became accepted that positive law and human rights law could be submerged within domestic jurisdiction. Totalitarian regimes like the Soviet Union restricted the political rights of their citizens, made widespread use of terror tactics and caused the deaths of several million people – for example, during the Ukrainian famine, which was caused by the Soviet Government under Josef Stalin in the 1930s.[48] Internationally, these events were seen as internal issues to be addressed under domestic law.

This concept changed with the Nuremberg War Crimes Tribunal where it was presumed that there is a set of norms, which are applicable to all human beings internationally.[49] In the history of international law, the atrocities of WWII changed the positivist approach. Gustav Radbruch, a former positivist, phrased it in the well-known Radbruch formula: "The conflict between justice and legal certainty may well be resolved in this way: The positive law, secured by legislation and power, takes

---

47 K Sellars, *The Rise and Rise of Human Rights* (Sutton, Stroud 2002) at viii.

48 R Conquest, *The Harvest of Sorrow: Soviet Collectivization and the Terror-Famine* (Hutchinson, London 1986); F Pigido-Pravoberezhny, *The Stalin Famine: Ukraine in the year 1933* (Ukrainian Youth Association in Great Britain, London 1953).

49 RG Patman, 'International Human Rights' in RG Patman (ed) *Universal Human Rights?* (St. Martin's Press, New York 2000) at 2.

precedence even when its content is unjust and fails to benefit the people, unless the conflict between statute and justice reaches such an intolerable degree that the statute, as 'flawed law,' must yield to justice."[50]

The Nuremberg and Tokyo Tribunals represented an important victory for international human rights law. In the stirring words of Robert Jackson, the Chief Counsel of the United States in Nuremberg: "That four great nations, flushed with victory and stung with injury stay the hand of vengeance and voluntarily submit their captive enemies to the judgment of the law is one of the most significant tributes that power has ever paid to reason."[51] Defendants were prosecuted under the Nuremberg Charter for three types of crimes: crimes against peace (focusing on unlawful international aggression), war crimes (focusing on unnecessary killing and destruction), and crimes against humanity (focusing on the genocide of the Holocaust).

Further progress of human rights was slowed down by the tense international climate during the Cold War. The General Assembly of the United Nations adopted and proclaimed the *UDHR* on December 10, 1948. It was passed simply as a resolution of the UN General Assembly. While this document was not legally binding, the two human rights covenants, the *International Covenant on Civil and Political Rights* (*ICCPR*) and the *International Covenant on Economic, Social and Cultural Rights* (*ICESCR*), are binding.[52] These two covenants have been ratified by the vast majority of the UN's member states.[53] Both covenants entered into force in 1976. In 1977, Amnesty International (AI) was awarded with the Nobel Peace Prize, which provided

---

50 G Radbruch, 'Gesetzliches Unrecht und übergesetzliches Recht' 1 Süddeutsche Juristenzeitung 105 (1946) translated in G Radbruch, 'Statutory Lawlessness and Supra-Statutory Law' 26 Oxford Journal of Legal Studies 1 (2006) Contrast this with Radbruch's statement in 1932: "It is the professional duty of the judge to validate the law's claim to validity, to sacrifice his own sense of the right to the authoritative command of the law, to ask only what is legal and not if it is also just." E Lask, *The Legal Philosophies of Lask, Radbruch, and Dabin* (Harvard University Press, Cambridge 1950) at 119. This seems a world away from Radbruch's 1946 "formula," above.

51 *The United States of America, the French Republic, the United Kingdom of Great Britain and Northern Ireland, and the Union of Soviet Socialist Republics v. Hermann Wilhelm Göring, et al.- Opening Statement*, http:// wwwroberthjacksonorg/ Man/ theman2-7-8-1/, International Military Tribunal (1945).

52 International Covenant on Civil and Political Rights (ICCPR) GA Res 2200A (XXI), UN Doc A/6316, adopted and opened for signature, ratification and accession by General Assembly resolution 2200A (XXI) of 16 December 1966,entered into force Mar 23, 1976 (1966); International Covenant on Economic, Social and Cultural Rights (ICESCR) GA Res 2200, UN Doc A/6316, adopted and opened for signature, ratification and accession by General Assembly resolution 2200A (XXI) of 16 December 1966, entered into force Jan 3, 1976 (1966).

53 The *ICCPR* was ratified by 152 states and the *ICESCR* was ratified by 149 states; Office of the UN High Commissioner for Human Rights, 'Status of ratifications of the principal international human rights treaties, As of 09 June 2004' (2004) <http:// www.unhchr.ch/ pdf/ report.pdf> (March 24, 2006).

human rights activist worldwide with recognition.[54] Several conventions have been passed in the aftermath of World War II, such as the *Convention on the Prevention and Punishment of the Crime of Genocide* (entry into force 1951), the *Convention on the Elimination of All Forms of Discrimination Against Women* (1981), the *Convention against Torture* (1984), and the *Convention of the Rights of the Child* (1989).[55]

Only with the end of the Cold War did it appear that international law would flourish. This period started with the promise of a new world order. In the 1990s, a wave of democratization and liberalization swept the world. The years between 1989 and 2001 saw a more rapid growth in the human rights movement than at any time since the Nuremberg Tribunal. The international community launched several UN-led humanitarian interventions,[56] set up international tribunals for war crimes committed in Yugoslavia and Rwanda and recently established the International Criminal Court (ICC).

After the terrorist attacks on September 11, 2001, and the second US led invasion in Iraq, the promise of a new world order has faded significantly. The importance of international law and human rights had to be redefined and many countries have sought to balance the need to recognize human rights principles with the need to combat terrorism.

Nevertheless, huge progress has been made in the development of international and human rights law. At the beginning of the human rights movement, international human rights was a dream, now it has become the *lingua franca* of modern political discourse.[57] Human rights were and are on the rise. The sovereignty of states is on the demise. As Judge Higgins of the ICJ has pointed out, "Sovereignty is a relative concept in international affairs that changes through time, and it has become

---

54 W Osiatynski, 'Human Rights for the 21st Century' 2000 Saint Louis-Warsaw Transantlantic Law Journal 29 (2000) at 34.

55 Convention on the Prevention and Punishment of the Crime of Genocide December 9, 1948, 78 UNTS 277, approved and proposed for signature and ratification or accession by General Assembly resolution 260 A (III) of 9 December 1948, entered into force Jan 12, 1951 (Genocide Convention) (1948); Convention on the Elimination of All Forms of Discrimination against Women 1249 UNTS 13, adopted and opened for signature, ratification and accession by General Assembly resolution 34/180 of December 18, 1979, entered into force September 3, 1981 (1979)Convention Against Torture and Other Cruel Inhuman or Degrading Treatment or Punishment 10 December 1984, 1465 UNTS 85 (entered into force 26 June 1987) (1984); Convention on the Rights of the Child November 20, 1989, UNGA Res 44/25 (entered into force 2 September 1990) (1989).

56 UNOSOM in Somalia from 1992-95, UNMIK in Kosovo from 1999, UNMIBH in Bosnia and Herzegovina from 1995- 2002, UNOMUR and UNAMIR in Rwanda from 1993-96, UNMIH, UNSMIH, UNTMIH, MIPONUH in Haiti from 1993-2000 and UNAMET, UNTAET, UMISET, UNMIT in East Timor from 1999- 2006.

57 K Sellars, *The Rise and Rise of Human Rights* (Sutton, Stroud 2002)*at* 197.

common-place to say that there has been tremendous erosion in the concept of sovereignty, relating particularly to the areas of human rights and now possibly humanitarian interventions."[58]

The signs for the future of international law and human rights law are promising. In March 2004, China, one of the most repressive countries with widespread human rights violations and a former opponent to the concept of human rights amended its constitution to include a promise to ensure human rights. In Article 33 it now includes the promise: "The state respects and safeguards human rights."[59] Although the constitution is not directly enforceable in China, the amendment might signal a growing acknowledgment of human rights. Human rights and humanitarian law have reached a position of unprecedented importance.[60] As the International Council on Human Rights Policy has written, international human rights law "is the only existing internationally-agreed expression of the minimum conditions that everyone should enjoy if they are to live with dignity as human beings."[61] Therefore, human rights and international law are on the rise. Even though human rights can now assume a position of unprecedented importance, they are unfortunately still violated in a myriad of cases all around the world.

II. Relativity of human rights

This work could be confronted with the accusation of being another part of the campaign of Western value imperialism. During the 1993 World Conference on Human Rights, the Bangkok Declaration was passed by various states, which stated that in assessing human rights "the significance of national and regional particularities and various historical, cultural and religious backgrounds" (Article 8) must be borne in mind.[62] It took a relativistic stand towards human rights, as opposed to a universalistic stand. The universalist claims that the general content of human rights must be the same everywhere, albeit that implementation can be culturally influenced, as for example a fair trial need not necessarily involve a jury. The relativist says that notions of right and wrong differ throughout the world, because

---

58 R Higgins, 'The End of Sovereignty' in ASoI Law (ed) *ASIL Proceedings, Panel IV of the 88th Annual Meeting* (1994) at 73.

59 D Yunhu, 'Inclusion of human rights in the Constitution- An Important Milestone in China's Human Rights Development' <http:// www.humanrights.cn/ zt/ magazine/ 200402004921101 215. htm> (March 24, 2006).

60 See for example: R Klein, 'Cultural Relativism, Economic Development and International Human Rights in the Asian Context ' 9 Touro International Law Review 1 (2001) at 66; B Stephens, 'Human Rights Accountability: Congress, Federalism and international law' 6 ILSA Journal of International and Comparative Law 277 (2000).

61 International Council on Human Rights Policy, 'Beyond Voluntarism, Human Rights and the Developing International Legal Obligations of Companies' (2002)*at* 15.

62 Vienna Declaration and Programme of Action, U.N. GAOR, World Conference on Human Rights, 48th Sess., U.N. Doc. A/Conf.157/24(1993).

the world has divergent views about right and wrong and these views are linked to the underlying culture.[63]

Even though there were numerous signatories to the Bangkok Declaration, the underlying arguments of these states were quite diverse. Many Islamic states rejected the universalist idea of human rights, because they perceive Sharia as the divine law. Other states, mostly Asian, argued that economic development may necessitate favoring social and economical rights over civil and political rights.[64] Also, the relativistic view could also be used to mask human rights abuses.

The notion of human rights, as it was given voice in the West during the Enlightment, articulates thoughts to promote individual freedom. Their European origin does not mean that it is not applicable to other states. Communist thought for example is based on the German philosophers Karl Marx and Friedrich Engels, which did not hinder Communist countries throughout the world to apply it to their nation. Furthermore, the *UDHR* was signed and drafted by nations from the whole world, including states from Asia, South America and Africa. There is a strong argument that individual rights are no hindrance to economic development, but rather support economic development.[65] There has been no substantial famine in a democratic country, whereas the dictatorial Soviet Union in the 1930s, China of the 1960s and North Korea during the 1990s experienced devastating famines.

Kofi Annan delivered his first human rights speech as UN Secretary General in Africa, deliberately addressing those African rulers who used cultural relativism as a shield behind which to resist the soft power of human rights. Illustrating the core insight of what ultimately constitutes the foundation of human rights, Annan asked: "Do not African mothers weep when their sons or daughters are killed or maimed by agents of repressive rule? Are not African fathers saddened when their children are unjustly jailed or tortured? Is not Africa as a whole impoverished when even one of its brilliant voices is silenced? We cannot afford to lose one life, spare one idea, relinquish one hope, if we are to succeed on our chosen course. So I say this to you, my brothers and sisters, that human rights are African rights, and I call upon you to ensure that all Africans are able fully to enjoy them."[66]

---

63 HJ Steiner and P Alston, *International Human Rights in Context: Law, Politics, Morals* (2nd edn, Oxford University Press, Oxford 2000) at 367.

64 MA Santoro, *Profits and Principles: Global Capitalism and Human Rights in China* (Cornell University Press, Ithaca 2000) at 131.

65 A Sen, 'Human Rights and Economic Achievements' in D Bell and JR Bauer (eds) *The East Asian Challenge for Human Rights* (Cambridge University Press, Cambridge; New York 1999).

66 K Annan, 'Secretary-General Calls for Efforts to Unleash African "Third Wave" Based on Democracy, Human Rights, and Sustainable Development; Address given on June 2, 1997 by Secretary-General Kofi Annan to the Annual Assembly of Heads of State and Government of the Organization of African Unity (OAU) in Harare.' (1997) <http:// www.un.org/ ecosocdev/ geninfo/ afrec/ vol11no1/ sgoau.htm> (December 1, 2007).

The resolution of the complex and multi-faceted debate on universalism and relativism of human rights will not be achieved in this work, but it cannot be concealed that this thesis does support the international and universalistic view towards human rights, especially in relation to the most egregious human rights abuses. It shall not be argued that human rights shall be the pretext to dictate how other countries have to govern their country. It should be recognized that there can be regional and transitional differences in human rights policies.

The universalist versus relativist debate is "dauntingly complex, requiring consideration of fundamental, and perhaps irresolvable, issues regarding morals, the nature of rights and the philosophical foundations of human rights."[67] The decisive question might therefore be: "How can the international community develop human rights standards of universal application while maintaining respect for the cultural values and practices of the world's diverse societies?"[68]

For the ATCA litigation this neither means that the US Court have to completely refrain from adjudicating human rights violations abroad, nor does it mean that the US jurisdiction may be involved with every domestic issue, but should apply the political question doctrine, the *forum non conveniens* principle, the international comity doctrine and the principles of immunity, where applicable.

III. Globalization

According to some scholars the term "Globalization" originates from the management boards of TNCs in the 1970s and 1980s.[69] And throughout the 1990s to

---

67 D Vagts and DL Donoho, 'Book Review: International Human Rights. Universalism versus Relativism. By Alison Dundes Renteln' 85 American Journal of International Law 416 (1991).

68 See e.g., AD Renteln, *International Human Rights: Universalism versus Relativism* (Sage, Newsbury Park 1990).

69 G Walter, *Globales Netz und globale Politik: Politische Antworten auf Globalisierung am Beispiel des Internet* (1st edn, Weltpolitik im 21 Jahrhundert Bd 12, Nomos, Baden-Baden 2005); CCv Weizsäcker, *Logik der Globalisierung* (3rd edn, Vandenhoeck und Ruprecht, Göttingen 2003) at 47; CCv Weizsäcker, *Logik der Globalisierung* (3rd edn, Vandenhoeck und Ruprecht, Göttingen 2003)R Müller, 'The Multinational Corporation and the Exercise of Power: Latin America' in A Said and LR Simmons (eds) *The New Sovereigns - Multinational Corporations as World Powers* (Spectrum Books, Englewood Cliggs 1975) at 22 ("the globalization of the world's largest private enterprises"); J Galtung, 'What is Wrong with Transnational Corporations - And what can we do about it?' in W Däubler and K Wohlmut (eds) *Transnationale Konzerne und Weltwirtschaftsordnung* (Nomos, Baden-Baden 1978) at 73 ("Globalization of the major world corporations"); T Levitt, *The Globalization of Markets* (Division of Research Graduate School of Business Administration Harvard University, Boston 1982); TJ Noyelle, *New York's Financial Markets: The Challenges of Globalization* (Conservation of Human Resources studies in the new economy, Westview Press, Boulder 1989); K Ohmae, *Triad Power: The Coming Shape of Global Competition* (Free Press, New York; London 1985); K Ohmae, *The End of the Nation State: The Rise of Regional Economies* (Free Press, New York 1995).

this day it has become one of the most "fashionable" words.[70] Globalization is a worldwide process that affects nearly every aspect of life.[71] Globalization is the term used to describe the changes in societies and the world economy that result from dramatically international trade and cultural exchange.[72] Globalization has specifically strong influence on the economy, the communication and media sector, the environment, security and terrorism, and it has important implications for the sovereignty and democratic legitimacy of nation states. State borders formed a rigid pattern on the global society. These borders are increasingly being dismantled. Since the end of the Cold War in 1991, most states have reduced trade barriers for the trade of goods and services. The end of the Cold War also helped make the market economy the dominant economic order and helped Globalization gain even more momentum.

The world has become a more level playing field in terms of a globalized market economy.[73] Production and services are being outsourced. For example, in 2005 roughly 400,000 US tax returns were completed in India.[74] Many thousands of American school children have e-tutoring teachers many time zones away in India, supplying their services for much cheaper prices.[75] Germany's 80 biggest corporations, that are included in market indexes DAX and MDAX, earn two thirds of their revenue outside Germany and more than half of their employees work outside Germany.[76] This strong foreign involvement is similar in smaller German companies.[77]

Globalization means that the world population became interdependent more than ever before. It means that we face common problems and threats on one hand, and common opportunities on the other. A significant threat that the world is facing is the problem of global warming. Other threats are the population explosion, poverty, the international spread of diseases, such as HIV/AIDS and Avian Influenza, and the

---

70 RJ Barnet and J Cavanagh, *Global Dreams: Imperial Corporations and the New World Order* (Simon & Schuster, New York 1994) ("'Globalization' is the most fashionable word of the 1990s, so portentous and wonderfully patient as to puzzle Alice in Wonderland and thrill the Red Queen because it means precisely whatever the user says it means."); It has been one of the top 10 words of the year in Germany in 1996, see Gesellschaft für deutsche Sprache, 'Wörter des Jahres' (2007) <http:// www.gfds.de/ index.php?id=11> (June 30, 2007).

71 R Bahdi, 'Globalization of Judgement: Transjudicialism and the Five Faces of International Law in Domestic Courts' 34 The Geroge Washington Law Review 555 (2002) at 602.

72 S Danailov, 'The Accountability of Non-State Actors for Human Rights Violations: the Special Case of Transnational Corporationa' (1998) <http:// www.humanrights.ch/ cms/ upload/ pdf/ 000303_ danailov_ studie.pdf> (January 12, 2006) at 3.

73 TL Friedman, *The World is Flat: A Brief History of the Twenty-First Century* (1st edn, Farrar Straus and Giroux, New York 2006) at 7.

74 *Ibid.* at 12-13.

75 *Ibid.* at 42-43.

76 U Sommer, 'Konzerne wachsen stark im Ausland' *Handelsblatt* (December 27, 2006) 1.

77 *Ibid.*

problems in the developing world, especially Sub-Saharan Africa. There are numerous other global problems and it has become increasingly evident that these problems can only be solved internationally.

Globalization has certainly affected law, jurisprudence and legal research. Globalization also had a significant effect on this doctoral thesis, which was largely written in Germany. It was possible to write about US litigation and US law with access to worldwide resources like the internet and various legal databases such as Westlaw, which has greatly facilitated research for this thesis. The German dissertation by Alfried Heidbrink on the ATCA in 1989 was written without access to the Internet and these databases.[78]

Globalization will lead to a greater convergence in legal research and jurisprudence. Globalization may eventually also lead to a greater conversion in the different legal systems worldwide. Globalization also definitely changes the face of international law. Globalization and the power of private actors might stand as the biggest change to international law since its inception in 1648 through the Westphalian treaties.[79] "Historians may well look back on the first years of the 21st century as a decisive moment in the human story."[80] Today, the different societies that make up the human family are interconnected as never before. They face threats that no nation can hope to master by acting alone and opportunities that can be better exploited if all nations work together. Globalization, together with the progress in information technology, might be seen as the greatest revolutionary force of our times.

Globalization has led to the problem that the state that before could watch and regulate also ethical behavior of "its" corporations, has now become less powerful. At the same time coporations became more powerful which is problematic.[81] The decisive question is therefore: "How can we combine market and ethics again?"[82]

---

78 A Heidbrink, *Der Alien Tort Claims Act (28 U.S.C. § 1350), Schadensersatzklagen vor US-amerikanischen Gerichten wegen Verletzungen des Völkerrechts* (München 1989).

79 K Nowrot, *Normative Ordnungsstruktur und private Wirkungsmacht - Konsequenzen der Beteiligung transnationaler Unternehmen an den Rechtssetzungsprozessen im internationalen Wirtschaftssystem* (BWV Berliner Wissenschafts-Verlag, Berlin 2006) at 699, number 38.

80 GD Triggs, *International Law- Contemporary Principles and Practices* (Butterworths, Chattswood 2006) at 1; UN Secretary General, 'A more secure world: Our shared Responsibility, Report of the Secretary-General's High-Level Panel on Threats, Challenges and Change' (2004) <www.un.org/ secureworld> (December 1, 2006).

81 H Ruh, 'Ethik und Erfolg verbünden sich: Ein neues Bündnis' in H Ruh and KM Leisinger (eds) *Ethik im Management: Ethik und Erfolg verbünden sich* (Orell Füssli, Zürich 2004) at 17 ("Die aktuelle Globalisierung hat nun aber zu einem ethischen Vakuum geführt, eben aus dem Grunde, weil auf globaler Ebene keine griffigen Institutionen zur ethischen Steuerung entwickelt worden sind. Dass dieses Manko zu schwerwiegenden, aus ethischer Sicht negativen Folgen führen musste, war Kennern der Ökonomiegeschichte immer klar [...] Da ist einmal die gigantische Umweltzerstörung [...] die Schere zwischen Arm und Reich [...] Working Poor [...] Arbeitslosigkeit [...] ").

82 *Ibid.* at 17.

Stefan Kadelbach concluded that there are different layers of ethical governance.[83] The international level may provide for elementary ("thin") ethics, and the surrounding society may provide for "thick" ethics.

IV. Transnational corporations

The transnational corporation and foreign direct investment (FDI) are the most important conduits of Globalization.[84] Globalization has been largely driven by TNCs.[85] TNCs have integrated the world. It is widely recognized that one of the most significant changes in international economics and, consequently, international relations and politics in recent decades has been the dramatic growth of TNCs.[86]

A. History of TNCs

Only a few centuries ago, privately owned for-profit corporations barely existed as organizational institutions. Early examples of privately owned for-profit organizations were the Hanseatic League from the Late Middle Ages,[87] or the transnational operations of the Fugger family that had a worldwide monopoly on copper trading.[88] The Princely house of Thurn and Taxis controlled the postal service from the 16th to late 19th century, during which time it made more than 1,000 bilateral and multilateral contracts.[89]

At the beginning of the 19th century business was still mostly organized in proprietorships and partnerships. In 1776, the eminent economist Adam Smith in his book, "Wealth of nations," opined that the business corporation or joint stock corporation will not succeed as an organizational institution.[90] At that time there were about fifty such corporations, such as the Royal African Company, the Hudson Bay Company, the South Sea Company, the British East India Company, and the United

---

83 S Kadelbach, 'Ethik des Völkerrechts unter Bedingungen der Globalisierung' 64 Zeitschrift für ausländisches öffentliches Recht und Völkerrecht 1 (2004) at page 19.

84 MA Santoro, *Profits and Principles: Global Capitalism and Human Rights in China* (Cornell University Press, Ithaca 2000) at xiv.

85 JJ Savitzky and SJ Burki, 'Globalization and the multinational corporation' <http://www.iadb.org/ int/ jpn/ English/ support_files/ GLB% 203% 20Glob.and% 20Multinational% 20Corporation.pdf> at 46.

86 CD Wallace, *Legal Control of the Multinational Enterprise: National Regulatory Techniques and the Prospects for International Controls* (M.Nijhoff, The Hague 1983) at 1.

87 P Fischer, 'Das transnationale Unternehmen als Phänomen in der Völkerrechtsgeschichte '*Völkerrecht und Rechtsphilosophie, Internationale Festschrift für Stephan Verosta* (Duncker & Humblot, Berlin 1980) at 348.

88 *Ibid.* at 356.

89 *Ibid.* at 364.

90 A Smith, *An inquiry into the nature and causes of the wealth of nations* (Whitestone, Dublin 1776), other paragraphs are on the corporation of towns, universities and countries, see Book V, chapter1, part 3 or Book II, chapter 2, para 79; see also T Donaldson and TW Dunfee, *Ties That Bind: A Social Contracts Approach to Business Ethics* (Harvard Business School Press, Boston 1999) at 273.

Company of Merchants trading to the East Indies. Smith thought that business corporations would only be of importance for the banking sector and the sector of navigable canals. He mistrusted business corporations, because of negligence of directors and the division of ownership and control. Today, however, corporations are the dominant form of business organizations.[91] The rationale for the rise of corporations lies in: (1) limited liability for investors; (2) free transferability of investor interests; (3) legal personality; and (4) centralized management.[92] Smith's distrust in the diversion of ownership and responsibility remains however a serious problem and is one reason for the exploitation of humans by corporations.

Prior to World War II, with the exception of some corporations engaged in extractive industries, most international economic transactions were essentially limited to export and import operations. Following World War II, TNCs began to invest to a great extent in manufacturing facilities in developed nations and in extraction industries in developing nations. In the 1960s, TNCs began to invest in manufacturing facilities in developing nations as well. In the last decades, TNCs have moved to invest across all sectors.[93]

B. Definition of TNCs

What is a transnational corporation (TNC)? A TNC is often referred to synonymously as a "multinational corporation" or "multinational enterprise."[94] There are many definitions, such as the one in the UN Norms on the Responsibilities of Transnational Corporations, the UN Draft Code of Conduct on Transnational Corporations or in the *OECD Guidelines*.[95] For the purposes of this examination, TNCs are defined as

91 RC Clark, *Corporate Law* (Little, Brown, Boston 1986) at 1.

92 *Ibid.* at 2.

93 HS Pérez Loose, *Changing the International Regime for Multinational Corporations through Codes of Conduct from Harsh words to "Soft Law"; Doctoral thesis, Harvard Law School* (Cambridge 1988) at 5.

94 Some try to differentiate: UN Committee on Trade and Development, 'Multinational corporations (MNCs) in least developed countries (LDCs) ' <http:// www.globalpolicy.org/ reform/ 2002/ modelun.pdf> , 'Multinational Business Enterprises' 12 Yearbook of International Organizations 1189 (1968-9).

95 See for example:
1. UN Commission on Human Rights, 'E/CN.4/Sub.2/2003/12/Rev.2 - Norms on the Responsibilities of Transnational Corporations and Other Business Enterprises with Regard to Human Rights' (2003) <http://www1.umn.edu/humanrts/links/norms-Aug2003.html> :
"The term 'transnational corporation' refers to an economic entity operating in more than one country or a cluster of economic entities operating in two or more countries - whatever their legal form, whether in their home country or country of activity, and whether taken individually or collectively.";
2. UN Draft Code of Conduct on Transnational Corporations UN Doc E/1988/39/Add1 (1988):
"This Code is universally applicable to enterprises, irrespective of their country of origin and their ownership, including private, public or mixed, comprising entities in two or more countries, regardless of the legal form and fields of activity of these entities, which operate under a system of decision-making, permitting coherent policies and a common strategy

incorporated enterprises comprising a parent enterprise and its foreign affiliates, following the UNCTAD definition.[96] A "parent enterprise" is defined as an enterprise that directly or indirectly controls assets of other entities in countries other than its home country, usually by owning an equity capital stake.[97] A foreign affiliate is an incorporated enterprise in which an investor, who is a resident in another economy, owns a stake that permits a lasting interest in the management of that enterprise. A foreign affiliate can be a subsidiary, an associate or a branch.[98] The control is centralized, but the decision-making is decentralized, resulting in a kind of "unity in diversity."[99] In this dissertation the definition of TNCs does not play a crucial role, since it deals mainly with US human rights litigation, which addresses TNCs as well as other corporations.

---

through one or more decision-making centres, in which the entities are so linked, by ownership or otherwise, that one or more of them may be able to exercise a significant influence over the activities of others and, in particular, to share knowledge, resources and responsibilities with the others.";
3. Working definition of the UN Intergovernmental Working Group on a Code of Conduct on TNCs: A transnational corporation is an enterprise (a) comprising entities in two or more countries, regardless of legal form and fields of those entities; (b) which operates under a system of decision-making permitting coherent policies and a common strategy through one or more decision-making centers; (c) in which the entities are so linked by ownership or otherwise, that one or more of them may be able to exercise a significant influence over the activities of others and, in particular, to share knowledge, resources and responsibilities with others. See PE Bondzi-Simpson, *The International Regulation of Relationships between Transnational Corporations and Host States: Conceptual Analyses and an Inquiry into Attempts at Codification and Control* (University of Toronto, Toronto 1991) at 24.
4. OECD Guidelines for Multinational Enterprises June 27, 2000, ILM 40 (2000), 237 (2000): "A precise definition of multinational enterprises is not required for the purposes of the Guidelines. These usually comprise companies or other entities established in more than one country and so linked that they may co-ordinate their operations in various ways. While one or more of these entities may be able to exercise a significant influence over the activities of others, their degree of autonomy within the enterprise may vary widely from one multinational enterprise to another. Ownership may be private, state or mixed. The Guidelines are addressed to all the entities within the multinational enterprise (parent companies and/or local entities). According to the actual distribution of responsibilities among them, the different entities are expected to co-operate and to assist one another to facilitate observance of the Guidelines."
For a very thorough discussion of the different definitions, see K Nowrot, *Normative Ordnungsstruktur und private Wirkungsmacht - Konsequenzen der Beteiligung transnationaler Unternehmen an den Rechtssetzungsprozessen im internationalen Wirtschaftssystem* (BWV Berliner Wissenschafts-Verlag, Berlin 2006) at 39- 98.

96 UNCTAD, 'UNCTAD World Investment Report 2005, Transnational corporations and the Internationalization of R&D' (2005) <http:// www.unctad.org/ Templates/ WebFlyer.asp? intItemID = 3489& lang=1> at 297.

97 This capital stake is normally 10 % of the shares or voting power, see *Ibid.* at 297.

98 For a definition of these corporate forms see *Ibid.* at 297.

99 CD Wallace, *Legal Control of the Multinational Enterprise: National Regulatory Techniques and the Prospects for International Controls* (M.Nijhoff, The Hague 1983) at 20.

C. Only "powerful" TNCs

Hillemann's view that only the "global players" should be included in the definition of TNC, because of their state-like potential to influence human rights, is a common misunderstanding that should be repudiated.[100] Very small companies also have the potential to impact significantly on the enjoyment of human rights. There are numerous examples of small corporations that have seriously violated human rights. A historic example is the small company, Degesch GmbH, which supplied the gas that was used in the gas chambers during the Holocaust.[101] Numbers of the Chinese "sweatshops," accused of workplace-related human rights violations, are owned by small Taiwanese companies.[102] The corporations, that fight on the side of the United States in the military conflict in Iraq, are often small and medium sized-business companies, such as AEGIS Defense Services Ltd; AMTI Operation; MPRI, Inc.; SCG International, LLC; Special Operations Consulting-Security Management Group (SOC-SMG); Trojan Securities and many others.[103]

D. Corporations with state participation

Aside from the classic TNC, there are two other special forms of TNCs: the state-owned corporation and the intergovernmental corporation. These two special forms often show that there is no bright line between a private TNC and a corporation that is endowed with some sovereign rights. A state-owned corporation is a legal entity separate from the state. Even though its influence is decreasing, the influence is often still very high, especially in countries that have recently moved to a market economy, such as China and Russia.

Inter-governmental corporations are relatively rare but, for the purposes of international law, they are especially interesting. It is a private enterprise that is incorporated by different governments. The need to institutionalize co-operation led international law to borrow the institution of the corporation from civil law.[104] When states established the first of these entities – including for international river

---

100 C Hillemanns, *Transnationale Unternehmen und Menschenrechte- Eine Studie zu den ersten beiden Prinzipien des Global Compact* (Zürich 2004) at 19 and 185.

101 Zyklon B, 'Website' (2007) <http://www.zyklon-b.info> (April 18, 2007).

102 DK Brown, AV Deardorff and RM Stern, 'The Effects of Multinational Production on Wages and Working Conditions in Developing Countries' (2002) <http:// www.econ.kuleuven.be/ internationale. economie/ home/ WorkingGroupSeminars/ Files/ Deardorff.pdf> at 178, MA Santoro, *Profits and Principles: Global Capitalism and Human Rights in China* (Cornell University Press, Ithaca 2000) at footnote 7, page 21.

103 A list of these and about one hundred further small and medium-sized private military companies can be found at F Schreier and M Caparini, 'Privatizing Security: Law, Practice and Governance of Private Military and Security Companies' (2005) <http:// www.dcaf.ch/ _docs/ op06_ privatising- security. pdf> (August 21, 2007), Annex 1 at 143 et *seq.*

104 I Seidl-Hohenveldern, C University of and L Research Centre for International, *Corporations In and Under International Law* (Hersch Lauterpacht memorial lectures 6, Grotius, Cambridge 1987) at 70.

commissions,[105] administrative unions[106] and other international organizations – they endowed these organizations with rights that were previously vested in the state. The International Telecommunications Satellite Consortium (INTELSAT), established in 1964, is an example. Other examples are the broadcasting channel Eurovision or European Company for the Financing of Railroad Rolling Stock (Eurofima).

V. Power of corporations

It is difficult to compare the power of a state to that of a corporation. Many academic articles cite the Institute for Policy Studies in Washington.[107] It compares the GDP of countries to the sales of corporations and concludes that 52 of the top 100 "economies" were corporations.[108] "General Motors is now bigger than Denmark and DaimlerChrysler is bigger than Poland."[109] However, this comparison is misleading because these two measures of economic output are structurally very different.

The GDP measures only the value added through production and services within the borders of a country. The sales measures the total amount of money a corporation receives through its activities. In order to find a comparable measure in corporate finance to the measure of the national GDP one would need to refer to the corporate value added, which can be found by reducing the intermediate consumption. The intermediate consumption again consists of the total monetary value of goods and services consumed or used up as inputs in production by enterprises, including raw materials and various other expenses. For example, the value added by General Motors in 2000 was US$ 42 billion and the total sales were $185 billion.[110] The value added is roughly about 20 to 30 percent of the sales, dependent on the industry. Comparing the value added by countries and TNCs only two of the top 50 "economies" and 37 of the top 100 are TNCs.[111] There is a study that argues that the

105 Rhine commission established in 1815; European Commission of the Danube established in 1856.

106 The first such "administrative union" was the International Telecommunication Union, established in 1865.

107 As small excerpt from many, see for example M Weschka, 'Human Rights and Multinational Enterprises: How can Multinational Enterprises be Held Responsible for Human Rights Violations Committed Abroad?' 66 Zeitschrift für ausländisches öffentliches Recht und Völkerrecht 625 (2006) at footnote 2; AA Dhir, 'Realigning the Corporate Building Blocks: Shareholder Proposals as a Vehicle for Achieving Corporate Social and Human Rights ' 43 American Business Law Journal 365 (2006) at footnote 6, P Pillai, 'From Corporate Social Responsibility to International Legal Responsibility- An Overview' 7 Faculteit der Rechtsgeleerdheid, Vrije Universiteit Amsterdam, Griffin's View 97 (2006) at footnote 2.

108 S Anderson, 'Corporate vs. Country Economic Clout, The Top 100' (2003) <http://www.ips-dc.org/ global_ econ/ top_ 100. pdf> ; S Anderson and J Cavanagh, "'Top 200- The rise of corporate global power", Institute for Policy Studies' (2001) <http://www.ips-dc.org/downloads/Top_200.pdf>.

109 S Anderson and J Cavanagh, "'Top 200- The rise of corporate global power", Institute for Policy Studies' (2001) <http://www.ips- dc.org/ downloads/ Top_200. pdf> *at* 3.

110 M Wolf, 'Countries still rule the world' *Financial Times* (February 6, 2002).

111 *Ibid.*

value added by the largest TNCs in comparison to that of nation states declined between 1980 and 2000.[112]

Moreover, the power of states and corporations is difficult to compare since they are conceptually very different. States have coercive powers in that they make and enforce the law. States can force TNCs to comply with the law, whereas the inverse is generally impossible. Even economically weak states may force their nationals, possibly millions of people, to do certain things, whereas corporations do not possess such a coercive power. For example, even though, economically speaking, North Korea may be weak, it has a military force of approximately 1.2 million armed personnel.

Nevertheless, it is fair to say that since the emergence of corporations in the 19th century, TNCs have become increasingly important and powerful. Increasing trade and open borders widened the potential of corporations and limited state power.[113] Some large TNCs, global players, have amassed fortunes of such magnitudes that enable them to accrue power once only known to states. Their effective power often permits them to negotiate and contract as equals with national governments.[114] In the words of Simon Chesterman, "The fact that the largest multinationals now dwarf the economies of many countries is suggestive of their importance."[115]

Furthermore, in the worldwide process of privatization, TNCs are increasingly performing tasks that have been traditionally performed by states.[116] TNCs are working in fields of public interest, such as water and energy supply, health services and education. Most sensitive for violations of human rights are corporations that work as private security companies, private military firms or prison administration firms.[117]

The power and impact of TNCs are continuously growing. In the event that, at some point, TNCs accrue a state-like potential to impact on human rights, it will be important to protect human rights against TNCs, even though they may be non-state

---

112 P De Grauwe and F Camerman, 'How big are the big Multinational Companies?' <http:// www. econ. kuleuven.be/ ew/ academic/ intecon/ Degrauwe/ PDG- Publications_ abstracts.htm>.

113 M Wolf, 'Countries still rule the world' *Financial Times* (February 6, 2002).

114 HM Kindred, *International law, chiefly as interpreted and applied in Canada* (6th edn, Emond Montgomery, Toronto 2000) at 51.

115 S Chesterman, 'Oil and Water: Regulating the Behavior of Multinational Corporations Through Law' 36 New York University School of Law - Journal of International Law and Politics 265 (2004) at 307.

116 See also U Di Fabio, *Das Recht offener Staaten: Grundlinien einer Staats- und Rechtstheorie* (Mohr Siebeck, Tübingen 1998) at 60: "Insofern könnte in Bezug auf die Inhalte der modernen Staatsidee von einer Entstaatlichung der öffentlichen Gewalt gesprochen werden."

117 See for example H Carney, 'Prosecuting the Lawless: Human Rights Abuses and Private Military Firms' 74 George Washington Law Review 317 (2006).

actors.[118] International law has traditionally been directed towards states, but it is gradually shifting towards individual and corporate liability to protect individuals' human rights. This stresses the importance of the question of how to make TNCs accountable in cases of human rights abuses.

VI. Effect of TNCs and Globalization

As Lord Chancellor Thurlow in the late 19th century stated, "corporations have neither bodies to be punished, nor souls to be condemned. They therefore do as they like."[119] This famous statement suggests that the corporate model often leads to a dilution of responsibility and has also led to numerous unpunished corporate crimes. It is difficult to write about the effect of corporations on human rights. Opinions are often diametrically opposed and the subject is sensitive. The general picture of corporations is often negative.[120] The assumption is often that corporations exploit humans for profit. Some see them as imperialistic forces, generating wealth only for the small elite at the expense of natural resources, cultural identity and impoverished labor of developing nations.

A. Sweatshops

The pejorative term "sweatshop" is often closely associated with TNCs and their human rights practices. A sweatshop describes a place of production, where people work for minimal wages and under harsh working conditions, often in the developing world and sometimes using child labor. It arouses many feelings. From a humanitarian point of view, all should have the right to safe working conditions with adequate remuneration. From a realistic point of view, however, it should be noted that an immediate abolition of sweatshops would often punish those who are meant to be relieved, since workers would lose their jobs.

The opinion that sweatshops should be preserved might sound cynical at first; however, it is not completely without reason. This is also evidenced by the fact that various scholars have advocated this position, including the most prominent academic of international development, Jeffrey Sachs.[121] Also the human rights organization,

---

118 Similar: U Di Fabio, *Das Recht offener Staaten: Grundlinien einer Staats- und Rechtstheorie* (Mohr Siebeck, Tübingen 1998) at 65.

119 E First Baron and Lord Chancellor Thurlow, 'The Oxford Dictionary of Quotations 550 (3d ed. 1979).' ; A Ramasastry, 'Corporate Complicity: From Nuremberg to Rangoon An Examination of Forced Labor Cases and Their Impact on MNC Liability' 20 Berkeley Journal of International Law 91 (2002) at 91.

120 MA Santoro, *Profits and Principles: Global Capitalism and Human Rights in China* (Cornell University Press, Ithaca 2000) at 1; P De Grauwe and F Camerman, 'How big are the big Multinational Companies?' <http:// www. econ. kuleuven.be/ ew/ academic/ intecon/ Degrauwe/ PDG- Publications_ abstracts. htm> at 1 and 2.

121 Jeffrey Sachs was named one of the 100 most influential persons in 2004 by Time magazine and is director of the UN Millennium project to end poverty; His view on sweatshops: Lifeonline, 'The Seattle Syndrom' <http://www.tve.org/ lifeonline/ index.cfm? aid= 1206> (February 8, 2006); See also MA Santoro, *Profits and Principles: Global Capitalism and*

Human Rights Watch (HRW), acknowledges that "simply firing children who are found to be working in hazardous occupations is not an effective strategy. Efforts to achieve compliance with labor laws should be complemented by programs and services that give children realistic alternatives to hazardous labor. [...] Lacking other options, they and their families are dependent on the income they receive from hazardous labor, using this income to pay for their school fees and for basic necessities such as food, clothing, and medication."[122]

Even though working in a sweatshop is miserable, it is often better than a life without work and income. Although sweatshop-life is a bleak life prospect, it often represents an improvement on the situation that would most likely arise were there no employment at all. In Chan's examination of life in Chinese sweatshops, the workers most often remit money home, which supports the assertion that sweatshop workers often have more money than people in rural China.[123] A recent study on sweat shops in 13 typical sweat shops countries, supported by the US libertarian think tank Independent Institute, has found that TNCs and also their national subcontractors pay higher wages in sweat shops than the national average income.[124]

Nevertheless, the goal should be to improve the situation of workers all over the globe. Only since the protests of consumers concerned with the ethics of sweatshop products have TNCs started to improve the situation in these sweatshops, as seen in the change of business ethics in the Nike corporation for example.

B. Responsibility and ownership

Corporations are often seen as institutionalized systems that diffuse responsibility and are therefore impersonal faceless entities.[125] One of countless examples might be the environmental disaster on the Danube River that was caused by a spill of 100 tones of cyanide from a mining operation in Romania. 300 tones of fish died as result of the spill. The local fishing industry lost their livelihood. The spill was caused by the mining joint venture, AURUL, which stands for "Australian-Romanian." 50 percent of AURUL was owned by a small Australian mining corporation, Esmeralda Exploration Ltd. Brett Montgomery, chairman of Esmeralda, denied any liability. The

---

Human Rights in China (Cornell University Press, Ithaca 2000) at 98.

122 Human Rights Watch, 'Turning a Blind Eye- Hazardous Child Labour in El Salvador's Sugarcane Cultivation' (2004) <http:// hrw.org/ reports/ 2004/ elsalvador0604/> (May 28, 2007) at 70.

123 A Chan, 'The Culture of Survival: Lives of Migrant Workers through the Prism of Private Letters' in EP Link, R Madsen and P Pickowicz (eds) *Popular China: Unofficial Culture in a Globalizing Society* (Rowman & Littlefield Publishers, Lanham 2002) at 178.

124 B Powell and D Skarbeg, 'Sweatshop and Third World Living Standards: Are the Jobs Worth the Sweat?' (2004) <http:// www. independent.org/ pdf/ working_papers/ 53_sweatshop.pdf> at 13.

125 'Klare Regeln, Wer trägt in globalisierten Unternehmen die Verantwortung?; Antworten von Ulrich Steger, Professor am IMD in Lausanne und früher selbst Manager' *Brand Eins Online Magazin* (October 2004).

Minister for the Environment in Australia stated: "I don't believe that we have a moral obligation – this is a private matter for the company involved." The other 50 percent of the joint venture was owned by the Romanian government, which also denied any responsibility.[126] Therefore, often nobody remains to be blamed, since each of the relevant actors only bears a small part of the responsibility and points to the others.

C. Benefits of TNCs and Globalization

Despite the dark side of corporations and the examples of human rights violations by TNCs, the author's underlying view is that the overall effect of TNCs on humankind and human rights has been and remains positive. Their economic success contributes to overall public prosperity. Only with the vehicle of corporations is it possible to build long-lasting relationships between institutions that are not related to individuals. Only with the vehicle of corporations is it possible to separate ownership and control. Some people have the means to participate as shareholders; others want to control the activities of the corporation. Only via the organizational mechanism of incorporation is it possible to achieve some of the most important progress seen in recent history, such as railways, automobiles, aircrafts, air-carriers and information technology.

Risky business models would not have been endeavored, if a natural person were to bear all the risk personally. Arguing that TNCs or, more generally, corporations are generally negative for the society and should be abolished is as misguided as arguing that earlier forms of corporations, such as cities, universities and nation states should be abolished as well. Not desiring any form of delegation of power to an institution or organization is not desirable in any society.

TNCs have profited from Globalization and spread around the globe. TNCs are often targets of the anti-Globalization movement. One of the allegations against them is that Globalization only profits those with money and that the poor are left behind. Interestingly, however, research indicates that, especially those people from the poorest nations think that global trade and TNCs have a positive effect on their country. In a survey by Pew Global Attitudes Project majorities in 33 of 44 countries, including every surveyed nation in Africa, are of the opinion that foreign companies have a generally positive influence.[127]

Often the number of the poor is said to be on decline because of TNCs and Globalization. Looking at the number of people living in absolute or extreme poverty,

---

126 I Nadisan, 'Comments on Baia Mare Pollution- Flagelul poluare la Baia Mare, Eventimentul AURUL, Vasile Gordis University Press ' (2001) <www. zpok.hu/ cyanide/ baiamare/ nadisan.htm> G Draffan, 'Endgame Directory of Transnational Corporations' (2006) <http:// www. endgame. org/ dtc/ e.html> (July 27, 2006).

127 Pew Global Attitudes Project, 'World publics approve increased international trade, But concern for problems of global economy' (2003) <http:// pewglobal.org/ commentary/ display. php? AnalysisID=68> .

being the first of the UN Millennium Development Goals, some positive trends might be identified. Whereas poverty remains one of the largest problems worldwide,[128] the number of people globally living from less than a dollar has declined between 20 and 40% in the time between 1981 and 2001.[129] However, if one focuses on the developing world outside China then the number of poor by the less than US$ 1 per day standard has changed rather little.[130] Also, the number of people living with less than $2 per day has changed little.[131] Ten years after the 1996 Rome World Food Summit, the number of undernourished people in the world remains high.

In 2001–03, Food and Agriculture Organization of the UN (FAO) estimates there were still 854 million undernourished people worldwide. Virtually no progress has been made towards the target of halving the number of undernourished people by 2015.[132] Therefore one may conclude that Globalization and TNCs have not had a positive effect on the right to food. However, the abovementioned positive development in China, can aside from many national political reasons also be traced back to the large capital inflow through TNCs. China is the third largest recipient of foreign direct investment (FDI) in the world, behind the UK and the US. As UNCTAD has concluded: "FDI can assist host developing countries in a number of ways, including adding to financial resources and productive capacity, supporting export activity, creating employment and transferring technology."[133]

Globalization and TNCs are also connected with many environmental and social problems. However, it is far beyond the scope of this essay to draw a conclusion to the consequences of Globalization and TNCs. It seems obvious however that Globalization does include opportunities and threats to humankind.[134]

D. Analysis

TNCs are often presented as being exploitive of workers and nature. The ultimate question of the value of TNCs is not for this thesis to answer. TNCs tend to raise the

---

128 UN Millennium Development Summit, 'UN Millennium Development Goals' (2000) <http:// www.un.org/ millenniumgoals/ background.html> (August 18, 2007).

129 S Chen and M Ravallion, 'How did the wold's poorest fare since the early 1980's' (2001) <http://www.worldbank.org/ research/ povmonitor/ MartinPapers/ How_ have_ the_ poorest_ fared_ since_ the_ early_ 1980s. pdf> (August 18, 2007) at 22.

130 *Ibid.* at 22.

131 *Ibid.* at 22.

132 FAO, 'The State of Food Insecurity in the world- Eradicating World Hunger - Taking Stock Ten Years after the World Food Summit' (2006) <ftp:// ftp. fao. org/ docrep/ fao/ 009/ a0750e/ a0750e00.pdf> (September 3, 2007) at 4.

133 UNCTAD, 'World Investment Report' (2006) <www.unctad.org/ en/ docs/ wir2006_en .pdf > (September 4, 2007) at 245.

134 See , e.g., JE Stiglitz, *Globalization and its Discontents* (W.W. Norton, New York 2002); JE Stiglitz, *Making Globalization Work* (W.W. Norton, New York 2006); J Norberg, 'Globalization and the poor' (2004) <http:// medienbibliothek. fnst. de/ uploads/ medienbibliothek/ occasional1. pdf>.

wages by raising the labor productivity and the scope of production.[135] In authoritarian and dictatorial regimes they often contribute to democratization.[136] In sum, the impact of TNCs is both positive and negative. This thesis will look at the negative side, in particular, the human rights violations committed by TNCs and the possibilities to address these.

VII. Examples of human rights violations by TNCs

A. History of human rights violations by TNCs

The allegation that TNCs are connected with human rights violations can be traced back to the very beginning of the history of corporations. The British East India Company faced allegations that, by smuggling opium to China, it participated in the decline of Chinese society.[137] Most egregious human rights violations occurred during World War II. Beneficiaries of these human rights violations were mainly German and Japanese corporations, but some Swiss, Austrian, Italian, American and other corporations also profited from these human rights violations.

There are further human rights abuses where corporations were involved, including, but not limited to the insurance claims from the Armenian massacre,[138] enslavement during colonization,[139] victims of Apartheid[140] and Herero genocide.[141] There is ample evidence that the US telecommunications corporation ITT had supported the coup of General Augusto Pinochet against Salvador Allende in Chile in 1973. They have paid sums as high as US$ 1 million and lobbied the US government, including former Secretary of State Henry Kissinger to instigate US interventions with violent means through the CIA, after ITT's assets had been nationalized.[142] A multitude of TNCs from West Germany, the United States, the United Kingdom, France, China, Singapore, the Netherlands, Egypt and India have been involved in the production of

---

135 DK Brown, AV Deardorff and RM Stern, 'The Effects of Multinational Production on Wages and Working Conditions in Developing Countries' (2002) <http:// www. econ. kuleuven. be/ internationale. economie/ home/ WorkingGroupSeminars/ Files/ Deardorff.pdf> at 45.

136 MA Santoro, *Profits and Principles: Global Capitalism and Human Rights in China* (Cornell University Press, Ithaca 2000).

137 DA Levy, 'The Opium Trade' (2000) <http:// www.maritimeheritage.org/ newtale/ opium.html> (July 25, 2006).

138 MJ Bazyler, *Holocaust Justice: The Battle for Restitution in America's Courts* (New York University Press, New York 2003) at 317.

139 *Ibid.* at 328.

140 J Sarkin, 'Reparation For Past Wrongs: Using Domestic Courts Around The World, Especially The United States, to Pursue African Human Rights Claims' 32 International Journal of Legal Information 426 (2004) at 455.

141 *Ibid.* at 452.

142 See A Sampson, *Weltmacht ITT: Die politischen Geschäfte eines multinationalen Konzerns* (Rowohlt Verlag, Reinbek 1975); or P Jensen, *The Garotte: the United States and Chile, 1970-1973* (Aarhus University Press, Aarhus 1988).

the chemical weapons in Iraq in the 1980s, where the toxic gas produced was latter used for the genocidal attacks on the Kurds in the North of Iraq.[143]

B. Current situation of human rights violations by TNCs

Human rights violations of TNCs have not only occurred in the past. Recently, human rights violations by TNCs have occurred, especially, in countries with weak governance.[144] TNCs can be involved in any human rights violations, from genocide to violation of the right to leisure time. At this point human rights violations of TNCs concerning militarized commerce, slave labor and child labor shall be briefly highlighted.

1. Militarized commerce

In countries with severe civil unrest, some TNCs work together with local armies or unofficial paramilitary forces. Professor Forcese refers to them as "militarized commerce."[145] The issue of "militarized commerce" is and was of particular concern in Myanmar, Indonesia, Papua New Guinea, Nigeria, Sudan, Sierra Leone and Colombia. Oil exploring companies directly profited from certain human rights violations and murders during the Sudanese civil war between the Northern Arabs and the Southern Christian population in which more than 1.9 million civilians died. Foreign TNCs, such as China National Petroleum Corporation (CNPC), Petronas Carigali Overseas Sdn Bhd, Malaysia and Sudapet Ltd, Sudan, provided the infrastructure for military attacks on civilians and profited by having a *cordon sanitaire* for the oil explorations.[146] Another example of current egregious human

---

[143] T Paterson, 'Leaked Report Says German and US Firms Supplied Arms to Saddam ' *The Independent* (December 18, 2002); T Zülch, *Völkermord an den Kurden - Eine Dokumentation der Gesellschaft für bedrohte Völker* (Luchterhand Literaturverlag, Frankfurt am Main 1991) at 117 et *seq.*; D Jehl, 'Who Armed Iraq? Answers the West Didn't Want to Hear' *New York Times* (July 18, 1993) E 5.

[144] JG Ruggie, 'National Roundtable on Corporate Social Responsibility and the Canadian Extractive Industry in Developing Countries, Montreal, November 14, 2006, Remarks at Public Session' (2006) <http:// www. ksg. harvard. edu/ m-rcbg/ CSRI/ publications/ other_ Ruggie_ Montreal . pdf> (August 17, 2007) ("For my interim report last spring I examined 65 cases of the worst human rights abuses reported by NGOs over the previous few years. Two-thirds were in the extractive sector. What else was striking? The 65 cases took place in 27 countries, of which all but two were low-income countries; all scored low on governance and rule of law indicators; all scored high on corruption. Clearly, there is a negative symbiosis between weak governance and the worst corporate human rights abuses.")

[145] C Forcese, 'Deterring "Militarized Commerce": The Prospect of Liability for "Privatized" Human Rights Abuses' 31 Ottawa Law Review 171 (2000) at 173; C Forcese, 'A definition of militarized commerce: Invitation to join new Coalition on Militarized Commerce (CMC), May 15, 2000,' (2000) <http:// www.peace.ca/ invitationtojoinnewcoalition. htm> (January 18, 2006).

[146] J Harker, 'Human security in Sudan: The report of a Canadian assessment mission; Prepared for the Minister of Foreign Affairs' (2000) <http:// www. reliefweb. int/ library/ documents/ cansudan2. pdf> and J Arunga, *The devil's footpath (Film)* (2004); a list of the companies can be found on Vital Statistics: Oil Companies Operating in Sudan(2001) <http:// www.moles.org/

rights violations is the suppression of the Ogoni people in Nigeria by Shell.[147] The forced labor in Myanmar, where the petroleum companies Unocal, US, Total S.A., France, PTT, Thailand and Myanmar Oil and Gas Enterprise (MOGE), Myanmar held equities.[148]

The importance of private military corporations has been highlighted by the American War on Terror. Many military functions, especially in Iraq, were supplied by private military companies and they have been involved in many deadly shootings – to this day, no one of these private security personnel has been sentenced.[149] The C.I.A. has used private airplane companies to transport agents and captives from and to Afghanistan, Guantánamo Bay detainment camp and other places.[150] Furthermore numerous private corporations have been contracted by the US government for the military conflict in Iraq. "Private military firms and their employees [...] tend to fall through the cracks of current legal codes, which sharply distinguish civilians from soldiers. Contractors are not quite civilians, given that they often carry and use weapons, interrogate prisoners, load bombs and fulfill other critical military roles. Yet they are not quite soldiers, either."[151] This shines a light on the need for international regulation for these corporations.

2. Slave labor

Other examples of human rights violations by TNCs include bonded or forced labor, which violates the prohibition of slavery.[152] Slavery involves severe economic exploitation; the absence of any framework of human rights; and the maintenance of control of one person over another with the prospect or reality of violence.[153] According to an investigative journalist the products of slave labor are also processed

---

ProjectUnderground/ drillbits/ 6_02/ vs.html> (January 16, 2006).

147 *Wiwa v. Royal Dutch Petroleum Co.*, No 96 Civ 8386, 1998 US, Dist LEXIS 23064 D.C. S.D. N.Y. (1998) and on appeal *Wiwa v. Royal Dutch Petroleum Co.*, 226 F3d 88, C.A.2 (2000).

148 *Doe v. Unocal (Unocal I)*, 963 F Supp 880, D.C.C.D. Cal. (1997), on appeal *Doe v. Unocal*, 27 F Supp 2d 1174, D.C. C.D. Cal. (1998); *Doe v. Unocal*, 248 F 3d 915 D.C. C.D. Cal. (2001); *Doe v. Unocal (Unocal II)*, 110 F Supp 2d 1294, D.C. C.D.Cal. (2000); *Doe v. Unocal*, 2002 US App LEXIS 19263, C.A. 9 (2002); *Doe v. Unocal*, 2003 WL 359787, C.A. 9 (2003).

149 J Scahill, 'A Very Private War' *Guardian* (August 1, 2007).

150 S Shane, S Grey and M Williams, 'C.I.A. Expanding Terror Battle Under Guise of Charter Flights' *The New York Times* (May 31, 2005).

151 P Singer, 'Outsourcing War' *Foreign Affairs* (March 1, 2005).

152 Stipulated in Article 4 Universal Declaration of Human Rights GA Res 217 A(III), UN Doc A/810 at 71 (1948), Article 8 International Covenant on Civil and Political Rights (ICCPR) GA Res 2200A (XXI), UN Doc A/6316, adopted and opened for signature, ratification and accession by General Assembly resolution 2200A (XXI) of 16 December 1966,entered into force Mar 23, 1976 (1966); International Convention to Suppress the Slave Trade and Slavery 25 September, 1926, ATS 11 (entered into force 9 March 1927) (1926); Protocol Amending the Convention to Suppress the Slave Trade and Slavery 7 December 1953, 182 UNTS 51 (entered into force 7 December 1953) (1953).

153 G Craig and others, *Contemporary slavery in the UK* (Joseph Rowntree Foundation, York 2007) at 12.

by TNCs, such as Nucor Corp., the second-largest US steel company.[154] It allegedly buys pig iron made with charcoal produced by slaves in Brazil. This steel is then used in cars and trucks made by Ford Motor Co., General Motors Corp., Nissan Motor Co. and Toyota Motor Corp.[155]

3. Child labor

The prohibition of child labor is stipulated in Article 10(3) of the *ICESCR*.[156] The International Labour Organization (ILO) has estimated that 250 million children between the ages of 5 and 14 work in developing countries – at least 120 million on a full time basis.[157] 61 percent of these are in Asia, 32 percent in Africa, and seven percent in Latin America. Most working children in rural areas are found in agriculture; many children work as domestics; urban children work in trade and services, with fewer in manufacturing and construction. The reasons to employ children are obvious. They are very compliant, are often seen as more efficient workers and do not demand minimum wages or create a union.

A worldwide scandal concerning TNCs and child labor emerged before the Soccer World Cup in 1998, when Adidas and Nike were in the headlines for producing their soccer balls in Pakistan through child labor.[158] In Indian silk industry children are sometimes bonded to work at the age of seven and are subject to beatings.[159] A detailed HRW investigative report has found that children as young as 8, have been found cultivating and harvesting sugar cane (with machetes) under dangerous conditions.[160] The sugar is then sold directly to Coca-Cola.[161] Even though the German TNCs Bayer and the US-American Monsanto have started to address the issue of child labor in their cotton seed supply chain, in 2005-2006 a report compiled

---

[154] M Smith and D Voreacos, 'The Secret World of Modern Slavery' *Bloomberg Markets December* 2006) 46 at 48.

[155] *Ibid.* at 48.

[156] International Covenant on Economic, Social and Cultural Rights (ICESCR) GA Res 2200, UN Doc A/6316, adopted and opened for signature, ratification and accession by General Assembly resolution 2200A (XXI) of 16 December 1966, entered into force Jan 3, 1976 (1966).

[157] Human Rights Watch, 'Child Labor' (2007) <http:// hrw.org/ children/ labor.htm> (May 15, 2007).

[158] S Toor, 'Child Labor in Pakistan: Coming of Age in the New World Order' 575 Annals of the American Academy of Political and Social Science 194 (2001) at 201.

[159] Yeramma S., eleven years old, bonded at around age seven for Rs. 1,700 (US$ 35) Karnataka, March 27, 2002; Human Rights Watch, 'Small Change- Bonded Child Labor in the Indian Silk Industries' (2003) <http://www.hrw.org/ reports/2003/india/India0103-03.htm> (May 15, 2007) at footnote 93.

[160] Human Rights Watch, 'Turning a Blind Eye- Hazardous Child Labour in El Salvador's Sugarcane Cultivation' (2004) <http://hrw.org/ reports/2004/elsalvador0604/> (May 28, 2007) at 15; See also K Sullivan, 'El Salvador Scarred by Child Labor, Subsistence Work in Sugar Cane Leads to Injuries, Continuing Poverty' *Washington Post* (June 10, 2004) A08.

[161] Human Rights Watch, 'Turning a Blind Eye- Hazardous Child Labour in El Salvador's Sugarcane Cultivation' (2004) <http://hrw.org/reports/2004/elsalvador0604/> (May 28, 2007) at 58.

by different NGOs alleged that around 20% of the workers on Bayer's and 10% of the workers on Monsanto's cotton seed suppliers in Andhra Pradesh, India, were children under 15.[162]

4. Other corporate human rights violations

The right to a minimum level of remuneration is violated frequently. [163] In the Shenzhen region in China wages are sometimes as low as US$ 8 per month, even though the Chinese minimum wage was set at $34.[164] A Filipino worker, making shirts sold in Wal-Mart stores, reports that she has to work for a 24 hours period with only an hour or two for breaks. She earns as little as $0.46 an hour.[165]

In 2001, more than 11,000 workers were killed in industrial accidents in China, as officially recorded; however, the official number is thought to represent only a fraction of the real number.[166] Workers in the Chinese mining industry are asked to sign a waiver in case of an accident or fatality. These contracts are called life-and-death contract (*sheng si zhuang*).[167]

---

162 D Venkateswarlu, *OECD Watch, Deutsche Welthungerhilfe, India Committee of the Netherlands, Eine Welt Netz NRW, International Labor Rights Fund, Seeds of Change- Impact of Interventions by Bayer and Monsanto on the Elimination of Child Labour on Farms Producing Hybrid Cottonseed in India* (2007).

163 Article 7(a)(ii) of the *ICESCR* guarantees the right to remuneration that provides for dignified living conditions for workers and their families.

164 A Chan, 'The Culture of Survival: Lives of Migrant Workers through the Prism of Private Letters' in EP Link, R Madsen and P Pickowicz (eds) *Popular China: Unofficial Culture in a Globalizing Society* (Rowman & Littlefield Publishers, Lanham 2002). However, the Chinese regulations concerning minimum wages are not binding, but solely recommendations: "Wages paid to labourers by the employing unit shall not be lower than the local standards on minimum wages." see The Labour Law of the People's Republic of China adopted at the Eighth Meeting of the Standing Committee of the Eighth National People's Congress of the People's Republic of China on July 5, online at http://wwwacftuorgcn/ labourlawhtm (September 4, 2007) (1994). And often the minimum wage provisions are ignored by employers and the local authorities, see Y-J Choi, 'Post-Mao Institutional Transformation and SOE Reform in China' (2003) <http:// journals2. iranscience.net: 800/ mcel. pacificu.edu/ mcel. pacificu.edu/ easpac/ esterline.php3> (September 4, 2007).

165 International Labor Rights Fund, 'Wal-Mart speaking tour' (2006) <http:// www. unionvoice.org/ laborrights/ notice-description.tcl? newsletter_id= 1571224> (August 25, 2006); S Raman, 'Wal-Mart workers critique labor conditions' (2006) <http:// media. www. browndailyherald.com/ media/ storage/ paper472/ news/ 2006/ 02/ 08/ CampusNews/ WalMart. Workers. Critique. Labor. Conditions- 1603789. shtml? sourcedomain =www. browndailyherald. com& MIIHost= media. collegepublisher. com> (August 25).

166 W-Y Leung, 'What can be done for the largest but deadliest manufacturing center in the world?' China Labour Bulletin (2002) at 1.

167 *Ibid.* at 1.

The right to leisure time[168] is regularly violated throughout the world.[169] Wal-Mart has often been accused of failing to respond to anti-union violence and many harsh human rights violations in supplier factories.[170] In the Philippines, the Korean-owned garment factory, Chong Won Fashion Inc., a major supplier for Wal-Mart, is alleged to have violated workers' freedom of association, forced workers to adopt 24 hour shifts, and do not allow workers to drink water or go to the bathroom during work hours.[171] Other frequent violations of TNCs are in the area of non-discrimination, women' rights and the right to information.[172] The right to bargain collectively and to strike[173] is violated in many cases, such as in Columbia and Guatemala.[174] Rights of indigenous peoples have been violated, for instance, in the cases of Freeport-McMoran in Irian Jaya, Indonesia, or Texaco in Ecuador.[175]

C. Analysis

A full survey of human rights violations of TNCs is beyond the reach of this work. It is sufficient to say that principally TNCs can be and also have been involved in violations of a whole range of human rights. Most human rights violations by TNCs occur in the area of economic rights, such as the right to adequate remuneration and to bargain collectively, but in some cases TNCs have also interfered with civil and political rights, such as prohibition of arbitrary detention, torture and the right to life and fair trial.[176]

---

168 Stipulated in Article 7 International Covenant on Economic, Social and Cultural Rights (ICESCR) GA Res 2200, UN Doc A/6316, adopted and opened for signature, ratification and accession by General Assembly resolution 2200A (XXI) of 16 December 1966, entered into force Jan 3, 1976 (1966) and Article 23 Universal Declaration of Human Rights GA Res 217 A(III), UN Doc A/810 at 71 (1948).

169 For example, A Chan, 'The Culture of Survival: Lives of Migrant Workers through the Prism of Private Letters' in EP Link, R Madsen and P Pickowicz (eds) *Popular China: Unofficial Culture in a Globalizing Society* (Rowman & Littlefield Publishers, Lanham 2002) at 185.

170 K Kolben, 'Integrative Linkage: Combining Public and Private Regulatory Approaches in the Design of Trade and Labor Regimes' 48 Harvard International Law Journal 203 (2007) at 230; Senate Commerce Science and Transportation, *Congressional Testimony via FDCH by Charles Kernaghan, 2007 WLNR 3068941* (2007).

171 International Labor Rights Fund, 'Give 'em an inch, and they'll take a mile.' (2006) <http://www.unionvoice.org/ campaign/ChongWon> (November 5, 2006).

172 For an overview see International Council on Human Rights Policy, 'Beyond Voluntarism, Human Rights and the Developing International Legal Obligations of Companies' (2002) *at* 2145.

173 Stipulated in Article 8 d.) International Covenant on Economic, Social and Cultural Rights (ICESCR) GA Res 2200, UN Doc A/6316, adopted and opened for signature, ratification and accession by General Assembly resolution 2200A (XXI) of 16 December 1966, entered into force Jan 3, 1976 (1966).

174 *Sinaltrainal v. Coca-Cola Co.*, 256 F Supp 2d 1345, D.C. S.D. Fla. (2003); *Villeda Aldana v. Fresh Del Monte Produce, Inc.*, 305 F Supp 2d 1285, D.C. S.D. Fla. (2003).

175 S Anderes, *Fremde im eigenen Land- Die Haftbarkeit transnationaler Unternehmen für Menschenrechtsverletzungen an indigenen Völkern* (Zürich 2001) at 14-35.

176 'Corporate Liability for Violations of International Human Rights Law' 114 Harvard Law Review 2025 (2001).

Looking at the multitude of human rights violations of TNCs, one could be forgiven for concluding that corporations are the worst offenders against human rights, but this is not true. The idea of human rights arose from the struggle of the individual against the state. Comparing the human rights violations in North Korea, Myanmar, Iran, Sudan and Zimbabwe to those of the current corporate human rights violations by PetroChina for its possible involvement in the genocide in Sudan, Coca-Cola for alleged involvement in killing trade unionists in Colombia the state seems to be a greater threat to the enjoyment of human rights.

VIII. History of legal accountability of TNCs for human rights violations

Attempts to hold TNCs legally accountable for human rights abuses have been, until recently, rare and mainly limited to a few post-World War II criminal trials against individual board members.

A. Subsequent Nuremberg Trials of the US Military Tribunal

The first times that human rights were brought into litigation against corporations were three trials from leading industrialists in Nazi Germany. They were the industrialist cases and were not held in the International Military Tribunal (IMT) as the trials against the major war criminals, but by the US Military tribunal in the same rooms as the IMT in the US occupied zone in Nuremberg, Germany. These trials did not hold corporations as such liable. The Tribunal did not have jurisdiction over legal persons and therefore it could not render a verdict against the corporations itself.[177] Only the directors were criminally prosecuted.

1. *Flick* case

The first case was the *Flick* case.[178] The defendants in this trial were Friedrich Flick and five other high-ranking directors of the Flick limited partnership, which was one of the biggest corporate groups in the world of its time and it largely expanded by profiting from confiscated property in the east and by using slave labor. Three of the six accused were sentenced to prison terms between two and a half and seven years for crimes against humanity through enslavement, plunder and other charges.[179] Flick was convicted and served three years of a seven year prison sentence. He went on to rebuild his business empire, becoming one of the world's wealthiest people by the time of his death in 1972. His son, Karl Friedrich Flick, inherited the company and sold it in the 1970s. It was assumed that K.F. Flick was worth around 6 billion Euros.

177 A Ramasastry, 'Corporate Complicity: From Nuremberg to Rangoon An Examination of Forced Labor Cases and Their Impact on MNC Liability' 20 Berkeley Journal of International Law 91 (2002) at 107.

178 *The United States of America vs. Friedrich Flick, et. al.*, Trials of War Criminals before the Nuernberg Military Tribunals Under Control Council Law no 10, Washington, DC, Microcard Editions, 1971, International Military Tribunal (1947).

179 Further information on S Jung, *Die Rechtsprobleme der Nürnberger Prozesse- Dargestellt am Verfahren gegen Friedrich Flick* (Mohr, Tübingen 1992).

Even though this wealth was amassed also from the exploitation of Jews, Flick has always refused to pay any compensation to the forced labor victims, also to the foundation “Remembrance, Responsibility and Future.”[180]

2. IG Farben case

The second case was the *IG Farben* case.[181] IG Farben (short for Interessengemeinschaft Farbenindustrie AG) was a conglomerate of chemical companies, formed in 1925. It played a major role in financing Hitler’s government. The corporation built a production site next to Auschwitz so as to use the inmates as slave labor workers. At its peak, the company employed up to 83,000 slave laborers. The 23 defendants in this case were all directors of IG Farben. The charges were centered around the complicity in waging an aggressive war, but also plunder and slave labor. The Court found that Farben seized property in an unlawful way. It violated Article 47 of the Hague Convention IV, which states: “Pillage is formally forbidden.”[182] Ten defendants were indicted to prison for up to eight years.

Interestingly Judge Herbert gave a dissenting judgment, finding that all defendants were guilty on the count of crimes against humanity through participation in the enslavement and deportation to slave labor. He stated “criminal responsibility goes beyond the actual immediate participants at Auschwitz. It includes other Farben plant-managers and embraces all who knowingly participated in the shaping of the corporate policy.”[183] Due to the severity of the war crimes committed by IG Farben during World War II, the company was considered to be too corrupt to be allowed to continue to exist. In 1951 the company was split up into the original constituent companies. The four largest quickly bought the smaller ones, and today only Agfa, BASF, and Bayer remain, while Hoechst merged with the French Rhône-Poulenc Rorer to form Aventis.

---

180 R Isermann, 'Friedrich Karl Flick: Der die Republik verkaufte' *DIE ZEIT online* (October 6, 2006). For further information on the foundation see subheading “III. German forced labor litigation succeeded“ at footnote 690.

181 *The United States of America vs. Carl Krauch, et.*, Trials of War Criminals before the Nuernberg Military Tribunals Under Control Council Law no 10, Washington, DC, Microcard Editions, 1971, International Military Tribunal (1947).

182 Convention (IV) respecting the Laws and Customs of War on Land and its annex: Regulations concerning the Laws and Customs of War on Land. The Hague October 18, 1907, 36 Stat 2277, TS No 539 (1907).

183 *The United States of America vs. Carl Krauch, et.*, Trials of War Criminals before the Nuernberg Military Tribunals Under Control Council Law no 10, Washington, DC, Microcard Editions, 1971, International Military Tribunal (1947).

3. *Krupp* case

The third case was litigated against 12 former directors of the Krupp group.[184] The Friedrich Krupp corporation was turned into a privately owned company of Alfried Krupp during the war. The company owned mines, steel and armament plants, shipyards and a machinery factory.[185] Krupp used up to 100,000 men in the forced labor program. The Court found that the confiscation of property in occupied countries constituted a violation of Article 46 of the Hague Convention,[186] which requires that private property in an occupied territory to be respected.

The United States Military Tribunal held that the Krupp firm actively sought to engage in plunder. The tribunal thereby repeatedly referred to the collective intent of the firm.[187] The Court rejected the argument of necessity. It proved that it was up to the German private business enterprises to put in requests for slave labor. The *Krupp* case underscores the possibility that in certain instances, it is the actions of the enterprise rather than the individual defendant that appears criminal.[188] The defendants were charged with war crimes and crimes against humanity. One defendant was acquitted, the others received prison sentences between 3 and 12 years. The main defendant, Alfried Krupp, was sentenced to 12 years and was ordered to sell all his property. Nevertheless, he was released in 1951, was allowed to resume his office as CEO of Krupp and regained his former property in 1953.

4. Other cases

In the Ministries case, the last of the 12 US trials known as the Subsequent Nuremberg Trials, one of the defendants was a director of the Dresdner Bank. Dresdner Bank provided large sums of money in loans to SS enterprises that employed huge numbers of inmates in various concentration camps. The question arose whether it is a crime to make a loan to an enterprise knowing or having the belief that its actions constituted violations of international law. The Court stated: "We cannot go so far as to enunciate the proposition that the official of a loaning bank is chargeable with the illegal operations alleged to have resulted from the loans

---

184 *The United States of America vs. Alfried Krupp, et. al.*, Trials of War Criminals before the Nuernberg Military Tribunals Under Control Council Law no 10, Washington, DC, Microcard Editions, 1971, International Military Tribunal (1947).

185 *Ibid.*

186 Convention (IV) respecting the Laws and Customs of War on Land and its annex: Regulations concerning the Laws and Customs of War on Land. The Hague October 18, 1907, 36 Stat 2277, TS No 539 (1907): "Family honour and rights, the lives of persons, and private property, as well as religious convictions and practice, must be respected. Private property cannot be confiscated."

187 A Ramasastry, 'Corporate Complicity: From Nuremberg to Rangoon An Examination of Forced Labor Cases and Their Impact on MNC Liability' 20 Berkeley Journal of International Law 91 (2002) at 110.

188 *Ibid.* at 108.

or which may have been contemplated by the borrower."[189] In the French and British zone of occupation other industrialists, such as Bruno Tesch and Hermann and Ernst Roechling, were found guilty of war crimes.[190]

B. Kinkaseki Mine Trial

A corporate case that is less well known is the case of the Japanese Nippon Mining Company for their actions at the Kinkaseki Mine in Formosa (now Taiwan) during World War II.[191] The trial was held in front of the British War Crimes Court in Hong Kong in May 1947. The two main legal issues were: (1) whether the Army or the Nippon Mining Company was responsible for accidents and mistreatment of prisoners of war; and (2) whether the working conditions in the mines were adequate. Even though the mining director did not directly participate in the mistreatment of the prisoners, he was found guilty. The arguments of the defendants reflected the arguments presented by the German industrialists. They claimed that they had accepted slave labor because they were not in a position to refuse the Japanese government's requests. The managers denied knowledge of the beatings. The Court found eight of the nine accused guilty.

C. Wollheim case

In Germany there were a few cases in which damages were claimed for unjust enrichment on the grounds of slave labor. In 1953, Norbert Wollheim won his case against IG Farben, which had to pay 10,000 Deutsche Mark. The Court stated: "The fundamental principles of equality, justice and humanity must have been known to all civilized persons, and the IG corporation cannot evade its responsibility any more than can an individual [...] They must have known of the 'selections' for it was their human duty to know the conditions of their employees. Their alleged total lack of knowledge merely confirms their lack of interest in the lives of the Jewish prisoners for whom they had a duty of care, at least during the time inmates were in their power. There was a duty to do what they could to protect the life, body and health of the plaintiff, and not even the SS could free them from that duty – which they failed to carry out. For that failure, which was at least negligent, the company is liable."[192]

---

189 *United States v. von Weizsaecker (Ministries Case)* Trials of War Criminals before the Nuernberg Military Tribunals Under Control Council Law no 10, Washington, DC, Microcard Editions, 1971, International Military Tribunals, XIV Trials of War Criminals (1952) at 854, cited in A Ramasastry, 'Corporate Complicity: From Nuremberg to Rangoon An Examination of Forced Labor Cases and Their Impact on MNC Liability' 20 Berkeley Journal of International Law 91 (2002) at 113, footnote 97.

190 *Trials of Bruno Tesch and two others*, March 1-8, 1946, British Military Court Hamburg (1946).

191 A Ramasastry, 'Corporate Complicity: From Nuremberg to Rangoon An Examination of Forced Labor Cases and Their Impact on MNC Liability' 20 Berkeley Journal of International Law 91 (2002) at 113 et. *seq.*

192 *Beschluss vom 21.6.1954*, 2/3 OH 12/54, German Regional Court (Landgericht) (1954)cited from: FAFO, 'Business and International Crimes, Category II: Forced Labor/Enslavement'

D. Analysis to the history of legal accountability of TNCs

In conclusion, those early cases concerning the accountability of TNCs and their directors provide the first precedents in which a court imposed liability on a group of individuals who were in charge of a company. The cases show the difficulty of assessing the responsibility of the board of directors for human rights violations that occurred in connection with their business activities. A mere loan was not deemed to be sufficient, whereas the request for forced labor was sufficient in some cases. The defense of necessity was only applicable in the case that the defendants could demonstrate that they feared for the loss of life as opposed to property.

There are two major differences to the cases above and those that will be examined in this work. First, the historic cases were mostly cases against individuals. Second, the historic cases were criminal prosecutions, whereas in contemporary American litigation victims claim civil damages. So the "corporate Rubicon"[193] was crossed the first time with the ATCA litigation, where for the first time a *corporate actor* itself was held liable for human rights violations, and not the individuals that sat in the board of directors.

IX. Concluding remarks to Chapter I

Human rights are an achievement of enlightened thought. The importance of human rights is on the rise. Only few state or non-state actors continue to question the universality of human rights. TNCs as non-state actors are very powerful and they increasingly venture into areas that were previously the exclusive domain of states. Human rights were originally thought to defend humans against the state. Now that the state devolves its power to other non-state actors, spurred by the process of Globalization and privatization, it is most important to maintain the same standard of human rights protection. Humans have been exposed to fierce human rights violations by TNCs. Nevertheless, the corporate form in general can be seen as a great achievement in human history. Corporations have had and still have a positive impact on our lives.

The negative side of corporate behavior, such as moral free riding and human rights violations needs to be regulated. The regulation so far is insufficient. Law needs to react to social changes. Overall, it can be noted that the structural divergence of the territoriality of states and the trans-territoriality of economic relations has created legal loopholes that were and still are being used by TNCs. It is one of the biggest challenges for the current legal profession to address this shortcoming. The transnational activities of TNCs can only be effectively regulated by law that also transgresses national borders – international law, also in the form of transnational litigation.

<http:// www.fafo.no/ liabilities/part_II-2forc-lab.htm> (January 20, 2006).

193 Term was first used by EJ Schrage, 'Judging Corporate Accountability in the Global Economy' 42 Columbia Journal of Transnational Law 13 (2003) at 158, footnote 22.

Chapter II. Enforcing human rights law against TNCs – Avenues to hold TNCs accountable

How can human rights be enforced against TNCs? Who can adjudicate alleged human rights violations of TNCs? Which avenues are most promising? In some countries, it remains very difficult to obtain meaningful, substantive remedies for violations of human rights. This chapter considers how to enforce human rights as against TNCs. It reviews some possibilities, but it can certainly not be seen as-comprehensive enumeration of avenues of enforcement of human rights law against TNCs.[194]

I. Enforcing international law

The relative success of any attempt to enforce a law is intimately connected with the lawful means available to compel compliance with that law. No law can be perfectly enforced, but the degree of enforcement can vary greatly. The Autobahn, the German highway, is widely known for not having any speed limit. However, on some parts of the Autobahn there is a speed limit, for example whenever there is a construction site the speed limit might be 100 kilometers per hour. But not everyone always complies with this traffic rule. Many people tend to drive at 110 kilometers per hour, some drive even faster. Is it then possible to say that the speed limit is enforced?

The attitudes and reasoning by various drivers towards law enforcement should be considered. Some drivers obey the rule solely because it is indicated by signs. Some obey the rule because they understand the rationale behind it and do not want to endanger construction workers nor traffic accidents. Some may obey the rule solely because they cannot physically overtake as a result of heavy traffic flows. Some obey the rule because they fear being caught by the police and do not wish to pay the speeding ticket. Some fear to lose their driver's license if they drive faster than 140 kilometers per hour. Some obey the rule because, in any event, they do not drive more than 100 kilometers. Some drivers obey the rule by routine; that is, they have internalized this rule into their personal system of ethics. In the end, most people obey the rule, but not everybody. Consequently, the speed limit may not be universally enforced, but it is still enforced to a degree.[195]

The critical question is whether the *level* of enforcement is adequate. The main criteria to be considered are: (1) whether a sufficient number of speeding drivers are caught to make the roads safer because enough of the dangerous drivers have been taken off the roads; (2) whether the level of enforcement changes society's behavior by, for instance, deterring people from driving too fast (or, in other words, unsafely);

---

194 For further avenues on the possibilities to enforce human rights, see e.g., N Jägers, *Corporate Human Rights Obligations: In Search of Accountability* (Intersentia, Antwerpen 2002).

195 This example is based on the example of the US highway speed limit from HH Koh, 'Transnational Legal Process' 75 Nebraska Law Review 181 (1996) at 194.

and (3) how high the probability is that the ones that drive more than 100 kilometers get caught.

This situation regarding enforcement in domestic law is comparable to the situation in international law. Professor Koh calls this the "transnational legal process." Given that there is a "complex combination of rational self-interest, transnational interaction, norm-internalization, and identity formation, international law becomes a factor driving their international relations."[196] Even the most isolated rogue states follow some international rules since they must also interact with other nations.

International law "may be under enforced, it may be imperfectly enforced, but it is enforced, not by a simple domestic process of legislation, adjudication, and executive action, but by a variety of enforcement mechanisms that transpire in a variety of public and private *fora*, under a variety of domestic and international laws, triggered by a variety of governmental and nongovernmental actors. In short, international law is enforced by the transnational legal process, which is triggered not just by the United States and Russia, but other actors, including, but not limited to the Security Council, the WTO, Exxon, Greenpeace, the Paris Club, AI, and the Lowenstein International Human Rights Clinic at Yale Law School."[197] Similarly, Professor Louis Henkin asserted in an oft-quoted phrase from his book, 'How Nations Behave,' "almost all nations observe almost all principles of international law and almost all of their obligations almost all of the time."[198] Does this finding of general compliance with international law also apply to human rights law? How does the enforcement of international human rights work for TNCs?

II. Differentiating between avenues of enforcement

In the following review, the avenues of enforcement are subdivided into approaches of international law, European Union (EU) law, national law, business approaches, NGO approaches and consumer approaches. This distinction is not always clear-cut, because many of them are multi stakeholder approaches. The Voluntary Principles on Security and Human Rights in the Extractive Sectors, for example, were set up by the governments of the United States, the United Kingdom, various companies and NGOs.

Alternatively, the various avenues of enforcement could be categorized by their enforcement mechanisms – such as voluntary codes of conduct, soft law, labeling schemes, reporting, campaigning, auditing, monitoring, economic sanctioning, and "hard law." However, in practice, there is no clear line between some of the avenues of enforcement. For example reporting and labeling standards are often enforced by

---

196 *Ibid.* at 205.

197 *Ibid.* at 194.

198 L Henkin, *How Nations Behave: Law and Foreign Policy* (2nd edn, Published for the Council on Foreign Relations by Columbia University Press, New York 1979) at 47.

"hard law." In the case of *Kasky v. Nike*,[199] the method for enforcing human rights was by a combination of business reporting, consumer and NGO pressure and municipal law enforcement. In that case, Nike was ordered to change its reporting, because it had made false statements and material omissions of fact in its social responsibility reports on working conditions in its factories.

III. International law

"While non-state actors were building the Global village, we were busy with yesterday's issues and concepts."[200] International law is often confronted with the accusation that it is slow in reacting to international problems since it relies largely on the consensus of states either by treaties or by customary law. Therefore, how does international law help to enforce human rights as against TNCs?

A. United Nations

1. UN Bill of Rights

The UDHR,[201] the International Covenant on Economic, Social, and Cultural Rights (ICESCR),[202] the International Covenant on Civil and Political Rights (ICCPR)[203] and the two Optional Protocols are sometimes recognized as the UN Bill of Rights.[204] The UDHR was a declaration adopted by the United Nation General Assembly on December 10, 1948 describing basic human rights. As a mere resolution it is not legally binding on states, but it served and still serves as an important authority for international human rights law and articulates common standards for all peoples and all nations. Still it is a contested question if the entire declaration acquired the status of customary law.[205] Even so, many of the provisions of the UDHR have become part of international customary law binding on all states.[206]

---

199 *Kasky v. Nike*, 24 Cal 4th 939, US SCt. Cal. (2002).

200 P Alston, 'The Myopia of the Handmaidens: International Lawyers and Globalization' 8 (3) European Journal of International Law 435 (1997) at 447.

201 Universal Declaration of Human Rights GA Res 217 A(III), UN Doc A/810 at 71 (1948).

202 International Covenant on Economic, Social and Cultural Rights (ICESCR) GA Res 2200, UN Doc A/6316, adopted and opened for signature, ratification and accession by General Assembly resolution 2200A (XXI) of 16 December 1966, entered into force Jan 3, 1976 (1966).

203 International Covenant on Civil and Political Rights (ICCPR) GA Res 2200A (XXI), UN Doc A/6316, adopted and opened for signature, ratification and accession by General Assembly resolution 2200A (XXI) of 16 December 1966,entered into force Mar 23, 1976 (1966).

204 See, e.g. UN GA, 'Observance of the International Day for the Eradication of Poverty - Report of the Secretary-General' (2006) <http:// www.un.org/ esa/ socdev/ poverty/ documents/ SG_ Poverty_ 2006_ final.pdf>.

205 Riedel in B Simma and others, *The Charter of the United Nations - A Commentary* (2nd edn, Oxford University Press, Oxford; New York 2002), Volume 2, Article 55, footnote 30; K Hailbronner, 'Der Staat und der Einzelne als Völkerrechtssubjekte' in WG Vitzthum (ed) *Völkerrecht* (de Gruyter, Berlin 2004) at 214.

206 See, e.g.; KJ Partsch, 'Human Rights in General' in R Wolfrum and C Philipp (eds) *United Nations: Law, Policies and Practice* (Beck, München 1995) at 609; In the Restatement (Third) of Foreign Relations Law (1987), § 702 the following human rights violations are recognized

Although it was primarily directed at the behavior of states, it also addresses non-state actors. In its preamble, the *UDHR* states that "every individual and every organ of society" shall promote this declaration as a common standard for all people. Given that this statement appears in the preamble, it is aspirational, and still remains somewhat ambiguous. Article 29 specifies that everyone has duties to the community. Article 30 prohibits "any State, group or person" from engaging in any activity or performing any act aimed at the destruction of any of the rights and freedoms in the *Declaration*. The *ICCPR* and the *ICESCR* both describe the individual as having "duties to other individuals and to the community to which he belongs" and states that he "is under a responsibility to strive for the promotion and observance of the rights recognized in the present *Covenant*." The *Declaration* and *Covenants* leave no doubt that corporations are also addressed. Nevertheless, one has to say that these international agreements were meant to be binding only for states.[207]

The *ICESCR* does not have a similar mechanism. Its provisions may only be addressed by the Human Rights Council, which will be discussed later. Decisions of the Human Rights Council can be seen as an analysis of a quasi-judicial body on the interpretation on the merits of a case. However, its decisions are not binding on any member state who is a subject of a complaint.[208]

In summary, the *UDHR* does include obligations that apply to TNCs. The obligations have moral persuasive authority, but they are not directly enforceable. Even if the provisions of Articles 29 and 30 are found to represent customary international law, the *UDHR* provides no mechanism for enforcement. John Ruggie, the UN Special Representative on the issue of human rights and business once stated that there

---

as customary international law: (a) genocide, (b) slavery or slave trade, (c) the murder or causing the disappearance of individuals, (d) torture or other cruel, inhuman and degrading treatment or punishment, (e) prolonged arbitrary detention, (f) systematic racial discrimination, or (g) a consistent pattern of gross violations of internationally recognized human rights).

207 CM Vázquez, 'Direct vs. Indirect Obligations of Corporations Under International Law' 43 Columbia Journal of Transnational Law 927 (2005) at 942 ("In sum, the Norms go considerably further than existing international law in imposing human rights obligations on private corporations. They require private corporations to respect some rights that, under existing international law, are either (a) not widely recognized, (b) unprotected from private infringement, or (c) intended to be protected from private infringement through the domestic laws of the states-parties. With respect to economic and social rights, it is unclear how the rights could translate into obligations of private corporations. Even courts and commentators sympathetic to the project of direct application of international law to private corporations recognize that very few human rights norms apply directly to non-state actors under international law as it exists today."); K Nowrot, *Normative Ordnungsstruktur und private Wirkungsmacht - Konsequenzen der Beteiligung transnationaler Unternehmen an den Rechtssetzungsprozessen im internationalen Wirtschaftssystem* (BWV Berliner Wissenschafts-Verlag, Berlin 2006) at 543 and 549.

208 D Williams, 'Reforming Human Rights Treaty Bodies' 1999 Australian Journal of Human Rights 30 (1999).

appeared to be little movement that corporations have direct responsibilities under the *UDHR* and related instruments.[209]

2. UN Global Compact

After the UN failed to set up the UN Code of Conduct on Transnational Corporations in the time between 1974 and 1992, the UN under UN Secretary-General Kofi Annan pursued the goal of addressing Transnational Corporations through alternative means. Annan invited consideration of other options to make corporations adhere to human rights standards.[210] In recognition of the growing importance of TNCs and other non-state actors, he wanted to form an alliance of these institutions under the auspices of the United Nations in order to protect human rights.

This resulted in the creation of the UN Global Compact founded in 2001; the UN Norms on the Responsibility of Transnational Corporations (approved in 2003); and the appointment of a UN Special Representative for Business and Human Rights in 2005.

The UN Global Compact was officially launched in 2001. As of January 2007 the Compact had 3,800 participants, including over 2,900 businesses in 100 countries around the world.[211] Corporations that wish to participate are encouraged to adhere to ten principles from the areas of human rights, labor protection, anti-corruption and environmental protection. The human rights principles are: (1) Business should support and respect the protection of international human rights within their sphere of influence;[212] and (2) make sure their own corporations are not complicit in human rights abuses.[213]

The spheres of influence of the company can be divided into those in the workplace and those in the community. The website includes further guidance and materials on how to adhere to the human rights principles.[214] In explaining the second principle, the website also defines and explains how companies can protect their property and how they should formulate contracts with security firms.

---

209 John Ruggie in UN Human Rights Council, 'Press Release- Council Discusses Human Rights and Transnational Corporations, Right to Health and Human Rights Defenders' (2007) <http:// www.unhchr.ch/ huricane/ huricane.nsf/ view01/ 19207DD921EE5D22C12572AC00702E2C? opendocument> (May 23, 2007).

210 UN Global Compact(2007) <http://www.unglobalcompact.org> (September 7, 2007).

211 *Ibid.*

212 For a thorough discussion of the first UN Global Compact principle and of its foundation in international law, see C Hillemanns, *Transnationale Unternehmen und Menschenrechte- Eine Studie zu den ersten beiden Prinzipien des Global Compact* (Zürich 2004) at 37 et *seq.*

213 For a thorough discussion of the second UN Global Compact principle and of its foundation in international law, see *Ibid.* at 144 et *seq.*

214 UN Global Compact, 'Issues- Human Rights' (2006) <http:// www. unglobalcompact. org/ Issues/ human_rights/ index.html> (July 27, 2006).

The wording of the principles manifests in a way that they are not legally binding. However, the participating corporations agreed to submit a communication on progress on an annual basis on the progress the company has made in implementing the ten principles in their business activities. Inactive companies or non-communicating companies are reported on the website of the Global Compact.[215] Furthermore, the Global Compact office has started measures to insure the integrity of the UN Logo Policy and has also provided for a complaint procedure to address abusive corporate behavior.[216]

The opinions on the Global Compact are divergent. Especially at the beginning the UN was strongly criticized.[217] Critics were and are still concerned that there is, as yet, no enforcement or monitoring mechanism to assess whether they live up to the Compact's principles. Other critics say that economic interests impact negatively on the level of compliance with the human rights principles. Others maintain that is also questionable whether the UN's mandate covers the establishment of a partnership with business, such as the Global Compact.[218]

Even the worst human rights malefactors are able to join the UN Global Compact and thereby "bluewash," as distinct from "whitewash," their corporate reputation. Companies such as Shell, Talisman, Occidental, Coca-Cola and Rio Tinto are members of the UN Global Compact and have declared their intention to respect human rights.[219] At the same time, these companies are subject to grave allegations that they have committed significant human rights violations in recent years. Companies can pick and choose which principles they want to follow.

The proponents regard the UN Global Compact as an innovative instrument to educate corporations towards more socially and environmentally responsible behavior. The UN Global Compact has raised awareness and promoted socially

---

215 UN Global Compact, 'Communication on Progress (COP)' (2007) <http:// www. unglobalcompact. org/ CommunicatingProgress/ index.html> (September 23, 2007).

216 UN Global Compact, 'Global Compact Note on Integrity Measures' (2006) <http:// www. unglobalcompact. org/ AboutTheGC/ gc_integrity_mesures.pdf> (September 21, 2007); See also S Deva, 'Global Compact: A Critique of the U.N.'s "Public-Private" Partnership for Promoting Corporate Citizenship' 34 Syracuse Journal of International Law and Commerce 107 (2006) at 119.

217 See, e.g., J Karliner and B Kenny, 'The United Nations Sits In Suspicious Company' *International Herald Tribune* 2000); N Jägers, *Corporate Human Rights Obligations: In Search of Accountability* (Intersentia, Antwerpen 2002) at 129 with further references.

218 Joint written statement by the Centre Europe-Tiers Monde and Others, in A Taylor, 'The UN and the Global Compact' 17 New York Law School Journal of Human Rights 975 (2001) at 980 et *seq.*

219 See criticism for the admission of Rio Tinto to the Global Compact: Asia-Pacific Human Rights Network, 'Associating with the Wrong Company, Rio Tinto's Record and the Global Compact' (2001) <http:// www.minesandcommunities.org/ Company/ rio8.htm> (January 25, 2006).

responsible behavior of corporations. It is a discussion forum that stands as a valuable promoter of human rights for business. It serves as an important vehicle for promoting best practice and opens an important link between business and the United Nations to work together for better corporate responsibility. It also needs to be mentioned that the UN Global Compact office addressed some of the criticism by implementing a reporting mechanism on abuses and issuing a logo policy in order to prevent "bluewashing." Therefore, the Global Compact is a very important tool in addressing and educating business concerning their responsibilities, but fails to provide for a mechanism to enforce human rights.

3. UN Norms on the Responsibilities of Transnational Corporations

On August 13, 2003 Oxfam reported that "Today, a United Nations human rights body in Geneva adopted the first set of comprehensive international human rights norms specifically applying to transnational corporations and other businesses. The nongovernmental organizations joining in this statement come together to welcome the U.N. Human Rights Norms and Commentary, and to urge their supporters and others concerned with human rights, the environment, and development to begin using them to spur greater corporate social responsibility."[220] On that day the United Nations Sub-Commission for the Promotion and Protection of Human Rights unanimously approved the UN Norms on the Responsibilities of Transnational Corporations and Other Business Enterprises with regard to human rights (UN Norms).[221]

The UN Norms provide soft law norms for TNCs to promote and protect human rights on an international scale. These norms may be viewed as a basis for the potential development of a treaty, establishing and confirming the rudimentary obligations of states, individuals and corporations to respect and promote human rights. The UN Norms state: "Within their respective spheres of activity and influence, transnational corporations and other business enterprises have the obligation to promote, secure the fulfillment of, respect, ensure respect of and protect human rights recognized in international as well as national law."[222] It includes the right to equal opportunity and non-discriminatory treatment, rights to security of

220 Oxfam GB, 'Nongovernmental Organizations Welcome the New UN Norms on Transnational Business' (2003) <http://www.humanrightsfirst.org/ workers_ rights/ issues/ norms/ wr_ press_ st _ 081303.htm> (May 5, 2007).

221 E/CN.4/Sub.2/2003/12/Rev.2, August 26, 2003, ECOSOC Commission on Human Rights, Sub-Commission on the Promotion and Protection of Human Rights, Fifty-fifth session; for a discussion on these norms see: C Hillemanns, 'UN Norms on the Responsibilities of Transnational Corporations and Other Business Enterprises with regard to Human Rights' 4 German Law Journal 10 (2003).

222 UN Commission on Human Rights, 'E/CN.4/Sub.2/2003/12/Rev.2 - UN Norms on the Responsibilities of Transnational Corporations and Other Business Enterprises with Regard to Human Rights' (2003) at para 1.

persons, rights of workers, respect for national sovereignty and human rights, obligations with regard to consumer and environmental protection.

It asks business to adopt internal rules that shall be periodically reported and monitored. States should establish the necessary framework to implement these norms domestically. A significant attribute of the UN Norms is that they take a broad approach to human rights as compared to the *ILO Declaration* that focus on labor standards, the *OECD Guidelines* that mention human rights only once, and the Global Compact.[223]

These norms were intended as assistance to companies that want to draft internal codes of conduct. They are a useful summary for corporations which enable them to adopt those obligations instead of looking to the plethora of different human rights treaties. They can be used as a benchmark for corporate conduct. Another very appealing aspect of the UN Norms is that they address TNCs as well as other business entities. This has been a matter of some controversy.[224] As put forward by some participants in the discussion it may be difficult to define TNCs and, as well, the enjoyment of human rights can also be affected by other business entities and therefore they are also included in the final version. The UN Norms set a very helpful benchmark for corporate codes of conduct, but they do not include any enforcement mechanisms.

4. UN Council on Human Rights

The UN Council on Human Rights is another rather recent development in the history of the UN and had its first meeting in June 2006. The Council is the successor of the UN Commission on Human Rights. The UN Commission was a charter-based commission within the overall framework of the UN. It was a subsidiary body of the UN Economic and Social Council (ECOSOC) and is also assisted in its work by the Office of the UN High Commissioner for Human Rights. It was the UN's principal instrument for the promotion and protection of human rights. Its mandate was to examine, monitor and publicly report on human rights situations in specific countries and territories.

It was criticized for the composition of its membership, which includes countries with dubious human rights records, such as Sudan, Cuba and Libya. In addition, its credibility was undermined by its inability to pass a meaningful resolution on the genocide in Darfur, Sudan.[225] It did not regard human rights violations of TNCs as

223 D Weissbrodt, 'Business and Human Rights' 74 University of Cincinnati Law Review 55 (2005) at 66.

224 N Jägers, *Corporate Human Rights Obligations: In Search of Accountability* (Intersentia, Antwerpen 2002) at 127.

225 'Symposium Program, Commentary by ambassadors to the United Nations' 4 Northwestern University Journal of International Human Rights 25 (2005) at 116.

one of its main themes. It had the potential to address and denounce certain human rights violations, but it had no mechanism to enforce compliance.

In an attempt to address some of the shortcomings of the former UN Commission on Human Rights, in April 2006 the UN General Assembly passed GA resolution 60/251 which created the new human rights body, the UN Council on Human Rights. Each member nation of the Council must be approved individually and directly by a majority of 96 of the 191 members of the General Assembly, in a secret ballot. Council membership is limited to two consecutive terms, and any Council member may be suspended by a two-thirds vote of the Assembly. Despite these efforts, the initial members of the Council included numerous states with poor human rights records, such as the People's Republic of China, Cuba, Saudi Arabia, Tunisia, Pakistan and Russia. On International Human Rights Day, December 12, 2006, UN Secretary-General Annan openly criticized the UN Council on Human Rights on the ground that it had not realized the hopes that were put into it. He was worried about the disproportionate focus on Israel and the humanitarian crisis in Darfur was not put into focus until that time.[226]

Furthermore, Annan was worried that some members intended to weaken or abolish the "crown jewel" of the system, the Special Procedures system, which allows the independent reporting on violations of particular kinds, or in specific countries.[227] Special Procedures are carried out either by an individual (called a "Special Rapporteur," "Special Representative of the Secretary-General," "Representative of the Secretary-General," "Representative of the Commission on Human Rights" or "Independent Expert") or a working group that is usually composed of five members. The mandates of the special procedures are established and defined by the resolution creating them. Mandate-holders of the special procedures serve in their personal capacity, and do not receive salaries or any other financial reward for their work. The independent status of the mandate-holders is crucial in order to fulfill their functions impartially.

---

226 "But I am worried by its disproportionate focus on violations by Israel. Not that Israel should be given a free pass. Absolutely not. But the Council should give the same attention to grave violations committed by other states as well." in: K Annan, 'Remarks of the UN Secretary-General on the occasion of the Human Rights Day 2006' (2006) <http:// www.un.org/ events/ humanrights/ 2006/ sg-remarks.shtml> (May 23, 2007).

227 "The Special Procedures are the crown jewel of the system. They, together with the High Commissioner and her staff, provide the independent expertise and judgement which is essential to effective human rights protection. They must not be politicized, or subjected to governmental control." In *Ibid.*

5. UN Secretary General's Special Representative for Business and Human Rights

In April 2005 the UN Human Rights Commission requested the Secretary-General Annan to appoint a Special Representative on the issue of human rights and transnational corporations and other business enterprises.

The Special Representative was given the following mandate: (a) To identify and clarify standards of corporate responsibility and accountability for transnational corporations and other business enterprises with regard to human rights; (b) To elaborate on the role of states in effectively regulating and adjudicating the role of transnational corporations and other business enterprises with regard to human rights, including through international cooperation; (c) To research and clarify the implications for transnational corporations and other business enterprises of concepts such as "complicity" and "sphere of influence;" (d) To develop materials and methodologies for undertaking human rights impact assessments of the activities of transnational corporations and other business enterprises; (e) To compile a compendium of best practices of states and transnational corporations and other business enterprises.[228]

Annan selected John Ruggie as Special Representative. Ruggie has so far issued seven valuable reports on the current status of business and human rights.[229] A brief

228 UN Human Rights Commission Resolution 2005/69 in April 2005.

229 UN Special Representative of the Secretary-General on human rights and transnational corporations and other business enterprises, 'E/CN.4/2006/97- Interim report of the Special Representative of the Secretary-General on the issue of human rights and transnational corporations and other business enterprises' (2006) <http:// daccess-ods. un.org/ access.nsf/ Get? Open& DS=E/ CN.4/ 2006/ 97&Lang=E> (May 23, 2007); UN Special Representative of the Secretary-General on human rights and transnational corporations and other business enterprises, 'A/HRC/4/35/Add.3- Human Rights Policies and Management Practices of Fortune Global 500 Firms: Results of a Survey' (2006) <http:// daccess-ods.un.org/ access.nsf/ Get? Open& DS=A/ HRC /4/ 35/ Add.3&Lang=E> (May 23, 2007); UN Special Representative of the Secretary-General on human rights and transnational corporations and other business enterprises, 'A/HRC/4/35- Report of the Special Representative of the Secretary-General on the issue of human rights and transnational corporations and other business enterprises' (2007) <http:// daccess- ods.un.org/ access.nsf/ Get? Open& DS=A/HRC/ 4/35&Lang =E>; UN Special Representative of the Secretary-General on human rights and transnational corporations and other business enterprises, 'A/HRC/4/35/Add.1- State responsibilities to regulate and adjudicate corporate activities under the UN core human rights treaties: an overview of treaty body commentaries' (2007) <http:// daccess-ods. un.org/ access.nsf/ Get? Open& DS=A/ HRC/ 4/ 35/ Add.1& Lang=E>; UN Special Representative of the Secretary-General on human rights and transnational corporations and other business enterprises, 'A/HRC/4/35/Add.2- Corporate Responsibility under International Law and issues in Extraterritorial Regulation: Summary of Legal Workshops' (2007) <http://daccess-ods.un.org/ access.nsf/ Get? Open&DS= A/ HRC/ 4/ 35/ Add.2& Lang=E> ; UN Special Representative of the Secretary-General on human rights and transnational corporations and other business enterprises, 'A/HRC/4/35/Add.3- Human Rights Policies and Management Practices of Fortune Global 500 Firms: Results of a Survey'

overview of their key findings shall be presented here, since they represent the current state of the art in the research field of business and human rights.

As a first step, Ruggie gathered empirical data with questionnaires that were given to the Fortune Global 500 corporations and governments. Both sets of questionnaires had rather low response rates, but it is still possible to draw some conclusions. It was found that states focus on providing tools for setting up Corporate Social Responsibility (CSR) regimes or promoting human rights. Only the EU goes an important step further and includes human rights provisions in investment and trade treaties.[230] Of the states surveyed only about 30 percent had criminal codes that allow for direct liability of legal entities.[231] However these states do, only in exceptional circumstances, include extraterritorial jurisdiction.[232] Extraterritorial jurisdiction for offences like bribery by legal entities such as TNCs is applicable only under strict conditions in few states.[233]

In his report on state responsibility, Ruggie showed that the state has an obligation to adjudicate private corporate acts as these obligations are recognized in the UN core human rights treaties.[234] Ruggie found that not all state structures appear to have internalized the full meaning of the state duty to protect.[235] Articles 5 and 7 of the Convention against Torture and Other Cruel, Inhuman or Degrading Treatment or Punishment also require parties to exercise extraterritorial jurisdiction; however, in his view, not over legal entities.[236]

(2006) <http:// daccess-ods.un.org/ access.nsf/ Get?Open& DS=A/ HRC/4/ 35/ Add.3&Lang=E> (May 23, 2007); UN Special Representative of the Secretary-General on human rights and transnational corporations and other business enterprises, 'A/HRC/ 4/ 35/ Add.4- Business recognition of human rights: Global patterns, regional and sectoral variations' (2007) <http:// daccess-ods. un.org/ access.nsf/ Get?Open&DS=A/ HRC/ 4/ 35/ Add.4&Lang=E> ; UN Special Representative of the Secretary-General on human rights and transnational corporations and other business enterprises, 'A/HRC/4/74- Report of the Special Representative of the Secretary-General on the issue of human rights and transnational corporations and other business enterprises' (2007) <http:// daccess-ods.un.org/ access.nsf/ Get?Open& DS=A/ HRC/ 4/74 &Lang=E>.

230 UN Special Representative of the Secretary-General on human rights and transnational corporations and other business enterprises, 'A/HRC/4/35/Add.3- Human Rights Policies and Management Practices of Fortune Global 500 Firms: Results of a Survey' (2006) <http://daccess-ods.un.org/ access.nsf/ Get?Open&DS=A/ HRC/ 4/35/ Add.3&Lang=E> (May 23, 2007) at paras. 31 et *seq.*

231 *Ibid.* at para. 35.

232 *Ibid.* at para. 36.

233 *Ibid.* at para 63.

234 UN Special Representative of the Secretary-General on human rights and transnational corporations and other business enterprises, 'A/HRC/4/35/Add.1- State responsibilities to regulate and adjudicate corporate activities under the UN core human rights treaties: an overview of treaty body commentaries' (2007) <http:// daccess-ods. un.org/ access.nsf/ Get?Open&DS=A/ HRC/ 4/35/ Add.1&Lang=E> at para 93.

235 *Ibid.* at paras 7 et *seq.*

236 *Ibid.* at para 92.

The Fortune Global 500 corporations recognize significant obligations toward other stakeholders, but this recognition decreases as the focus moves outward from employees into value chains, communities, countries of operation, and beyond.[237] The corporations used their own website rather than third-party options to report on their human rights situation.[238] Ruggie found that the recognition of responsibility towards human rights in the business community has increased significantly in recent years, but the levels of reporting and monitoring still vary greatly.[239]

Ruggie issued the last report in February 2007[240] which drew conclusions concerning the different areas of his mandate. He found that "no silver bullet can resolve the business and human rights challenge" and a broad array of measures is required by all relevant actors.[241] Ruggie is of the opinion that this can only be seen as a first step.[242] In his view, the most consequential legal development is international human rights litigation in domestic courts reflecting international standards, such as the ATCA litigation.[243] He warns, however, that transnational litigation, like the ATCA litigation, may reflect variations in national practice, which in his view is not an ideal solution.[244]

6. UN General Assembly

The United Nations General Assembly has addressed corporations in some of its resolutions. In its efforts to isolate Apartheid-era South Africa, the General Assembly repeatedly noted that corporations have duties to respect UN sanctions. It called on "corporations and employers" to "withdraw from any commercial operations in South Africa."[245] In 1983, the General Assembly condemned the activities of all foreign

---

237 UN Special Representative of the Secretary-General on human rights and transnational corporations and other business enterprises, 'A/HRC/4/35/Add.3- Human Rights Policies and Management Practices of Fortune Global 500 Firms: Results of a Survey' (2006) <http://daccess-ods.un.org/ access.nsf/ Get?Open&DS=A/ HRC/4/ 35/ Add.3&Lang=E> (May 23, 2007)at para 99.

238 *Ibid.* at para 95.

239 UN Special Representative of the Secretary-General on human rights and transnational corporations and other business enterprises, 'A/HRC/4/35/Add.4- Business recognition of human rights: Global patterns, regional and sectoral variations' (2007) <http://daccess-ods.un.org/ access.nsf/ Get?Open&DS=A/ HRC/4 /35/ Add.4&Lang=E> .

240 UN Special Representative of the Secretary-General on human rights and transnational corporations and other business enterprises, 'A/HRC/4/35- Report of the Special Representative of the Secretary-General on the issue of human rights and transnational corporations and other business enterprises' (2007) <http:// daccess-ods.un.org/ access.nsf/ Get?Open&DS=A/ HRC/ 4/35&Lang=E>.

241 *Ibid.* at para 88.

242 *Ibid.* at para 88.

243 *Ibid.* at para 84.

244 *Ibid.* at para 84.

245 See, e.g., G.A. Res. 2671F, UN GAOR, 25th Sess., Supp. No. 28 at 33, 34, UN Doc. A/8028 (1970) (deploring "the continued co-operation by certain States and foreign economic interests with South Africa...as such co-operation encourages the Government of South Africa in the

economic interests operating in Namibia.[246] However, the power of the General Assembly is limited to discussing, making recommendations to member states and bringing certain matters to the attention of the Security Council, as provided in Articles 10 and 11 of the UN Charter.

7. UN Security Council

The UN Security Council has the power to impose military or non-military sanctions in order to restore international peace and security under chapter VII of the UN Charter. After the end of the Cold War, it has increasingly imposed economic sanctions.[247] Since 1990, it has also included corporate entities as addressees of those economic sanctions. The contentious economic sanctions against Iraq for example, that had also considerable negative humanitarian effects, included 150 parastatal corporations.[248]

With UN Security Council Resolution (UNSCR) 1267 in 1999 and its follow-up resolutions concerning the situation in Afghanistan and the War on Terror, the Council established a comprehensive list of private corporations and individuals that collaborated with Al-Qaida and the Taliban.[249] Thereafter, the UN has passed several

pursuit of its inhuman policies"); Programme of Action Against Apartheid, UN SCOR, 38th Sess., Supp. for Oct.-Dec. 1983 at 58, 63, UN Doc. S/16102 (1983) (calling on "corporations and employers" to "withdraw from any commercial operations in South Africa"); Appeal by Leaders of the African National Congress, the South African Indian Congress and the Liberal Party of South Africa for a Boycott of South African Produce by the British People (Dec. 1959), in UN Dep't of Pub. Info., The United Nations and Apartheid 1948-1994 at 243, UN Doc. DPI/1568, UN Sales No. E.95.I.7 (1994).

246 GA Res 38/36 A (1983), cipher 45: "Strongly condemns the activities of all foreign economic interests operating in Namibia under the illegal South African administration which are illegally exploiting the resources of the Territory and demands that transnational corporations engaged in such exploitation comply with all the relevant resolutions of the United Nations by immediately refraining from any new investment or activities in Namibia, by withdrawing from the Territory and by putting an end to their co-operation with the illegal South African administration.

247 Such sanctions were imposed in response to situations in the Democratic People's Republic of Korea (2006), terrorism in the Middle East (2005), Sudan (2005), Côte d'Ivoire (2004), Congo (2004), Liberia (2003), Iraq (2003), Liberia (2003), Eritrea and Ethiopia (2000), Afghanistan (1999), Republic of Yugoslavia (1998), Sierra Leone (1997), Liberia (1995), Rwanda (1994), Angola (1993), Haiti (1993), Somalia (1992), Libyan Arab Jamahiriya (1992), Republic of Yugoslavia (1991), Iraq (1991), South Africa (1977) and Southern Rhodesia (1968).

248 Concerning the humanitarian effects of the sanctions, see R Geiss, 'Humanitarian Safeguards in Economic Sanctions Regimes: A Call for Automatic Suspension Clauses, Periodic Monitoring, and Follow-Up Assessment of Long-Term Effects' 18 Harvard Human Rights Journal 167 (2005), For the list of the parastatal companies see Foreign Assets Control Regulations for Importers and Exporters (Office of Foreign Assets Control)(2007) or UNSCR 661 in 1990, 1483 from 2003 (Sanctioning persons or and approximately 150 Iraqi parastatal corporations). Parastatal means a company or agency owned or controlled wholly or partly by the government.

249 UNSCR 1333 (2000), 1390 (2002), 1455 (2003), 1526 (2004), 1617 (2005) and 1735 (2006).

resolutions that also impose sanctions on private corporations. Of those resolutions, seven are still in place. Those are the UN sanctions concerning the situations in the Balkans (1999), Liberia (2003), Cote D'Ivoire (2004), Congo (2005), Syria (2005), Sudan (2006) and the Democratic People's Republic of Korea (2006).[250] The UN sanctions are enforced by UN members, such as by the US Office for Foreign Assets Control. These UN sanctions can be seen as groundbreaking in terms of addressing private human rights transgressions. Despite their enforceability and power in the sense that they have been issued as measures under Chapter VII these UN sanctions only address a very small portion of the human rights violations by TNCs.

8. Other UN Regulations

There are a multitude of UN treaties and other international instruments that include regulations on the behavior of non-state actors, including the *Convention on the Prevention and Punishment of the Crime of Genocide*, the *Convention against Torture and Other Cruel, Inhuman or Degrading Treatment or Punishment*, the *Slavery Convention* and the *Supplementary Convention on the Abolition of Slavery, the Slave Trade, and Institutions and Practices Similar to Slavery* and many others.[251]

See also UN SC, 'UN Security Council Sanctions Committees' (2007) <http:// www.un.org/ sc/ committees/ dfp.shtml> (June 6, 2007).

250 Balkans - UNSCR 1244 (1999) (Sanctioning any persons or entity that have committed, or are posing a significant risk of committing, acts of violence that have the purpose or effect of threatening the peace in or diminishing the stability or security of any area or state in the Western Balkans region, undermining the authority, efforts, or objectives of international organizations.); Liberia - UNSCR 1521 (2003), 1532 (2004), (Sanctioning any person or entity that has close relations to former Liberian President Charles Taylor's government and certain other persons and to prevent the import into their territories of all rough diamonds, round logs, and timber products originating in Liberia.); Cote D'Ivoire- UNSCR 1572 (2004)(Sanctioning any person or entity contributing to the political and social unrest in Côte d'Ivoire.); Congo - UNSCR 1596 (2005), 1649 (2005), 1698 (2006) (Sanctioning persons or entities that have materially assisted, sponsored, or provided financial, material, or technological support for, or goods or services in support of, the activities of political or military leaders of a Congolese armed group that impedes the disarmament, demobilization, or reintegration of combatants.); Syria - UNSCR 1636 (2005); (Sanctioning any person or entity that has materially assisted, sponsored, or provided financial, material, or technological support for, or goods or services in support of, any terrorist act, bombing, or assassination attempt, in relation to the terrorist act in Beirut, Lebanon, on February 14, 2005, that resulted in the assassination of former Prime Minister of Lebanon Rafiq Hariri, and the deaths of 22 others, and other bombings or assassination attempts in Lebanon since October 1, 2004, that are related to Hariri's assassination or that implicate the Government of Syria or its officers or agents.); Sudan - UNSCR 1591, 1672 (2006) (Sanctioning any person or entity responsible for the continuing conflict in Darfur/Sudan); Democratic People's Republic of Korea - UNSCR 1718 (2006) (Sanctioning persons or entities that engage in or provide support for DPRK's nuclear-related, other weapons of mass destruction-related and ballistic missile related programmes.)

251 See Convention on the Prevention and Punishment of the Crime of Genocide December 9, 1948, 78 UNTS 277, approved and proposed for signature and ratification or accession by General Assembly resolution 260 A (III) of 9 December 1948, entered into force Jan 12, 1951 (Genocide Convention) (1948); Convention Against Torture and Other Cruel Inhuman or

These UN regulations lay a fundamental framework for human rights law. Their provisions are fundamentally important for the determination of human rights violations, such as in the UN Council on Human Rights, but also for transnational litigation investigating human rights transgressions of TNCs. However, these conventions are not directly enforceable as against TNCs.

B. WTO

The World Trade Organization (WTO) is an international organization that sets the rules for the international trading system and adjudicates disputes relating to these rules.[252] 151 nations are members of the WTO.[253] It has an established and powerful dispute settlement mechanism. It has the potential to provide an enforcement mechanism for human rights, which has been demanded by some.[254]

One problem is that the WTO cannot impose legally binding orders directly on TNCs. This problem could theoretically be met by holding the state responsible for the violations of its TNCs.[255] The second problem is the mandate of the WTO. The WTO's mandate is to ensure that trade flows as smoothly, predictably and freely as possible. It does not include human rights provisions. Article XX of the *GATT* provides that restrictive measures can be taken.[256] Article XX (e) stipulates that nothing in the agreement shall prevent a member state from taking measures against products that were produced by prison labor. Article XX (b) allows trade barriers necessary to protect human, animal or plant life or health. At the present time, however, Article XX (b) is only applied to restrict the importation of final products

---

Degrading Treatment or Punishment 10 December 1984, 1465 UNTS 85 (entered into force 26 June 1987) (1984); International Convention to Suppress the Slave Trade and Slavery 25 September, 1926, ATS 11 (entered into force 9 March 1927) (1926); Supplementary Convention on the Abolition of Slavery, the Slave Trade, and Institutions and Practices Similar to Slavery 226 UNTS 3 (entered into force 30 April 1957) (1956); See also UN Commission on Human Rights, 'E/CN.4/Sub.2/2003/12/Rev.2 - Norms on the Responsibilities of Transnational Corporations and Other Business Enterprises with Regard to Human Rights' (2003) <http://www1.umn.edu/humanrts/links/norms-Aug2003.html> at preamble; SR Ratner, 'Corporations and Human Rights: A Theory of Legal Responsibility' 111 Yale Law Journal 443 (2001) at 467; B Stephens, 'The Amorality of Profit: Transnational Corporations and Human Rights' 20 Berkeley Journal of International Law 45 (2000) at 73.

252 Agreement Establishing the World Trade Organization (Marrakesh Agreement) 33 ILM 1143; April 5, 1994 (entered into force January 1, 1995) (1994).

253 WTO, 'Members and Observers' (2007) <http://www.wto.org/ english/ thewto_e/ whatis_e/ tif_e/ org6_e.htm> (September 7, 2007).

254 See, e.g., D Kinley and J Tadaki, 'From Talk to Walk: The Emergence of Human Rights Responsibilities for Corporations at International Law' 44 Virginia Journal of International Law 931 (2004) at 1006.

255 Concerning the nationality of TNCs see below, subheading "nationality of corporations."

256 General Agreement on Tariffs and Trade (GATT 1947) October 30, 1947, 55 UNTS 194 (1947).

that expose domestic populations to health risks.[257] Article XX (a) allows trade barriers necessary to protect public morals.

Human rights have been used in WTO cases, but only very seldom and rather as a peripheral argument by the parties and are not found in the Panel or Appellate Body findings.[258] In the case *EC – Selected Customs Matters* the question was raised if the EC has provided for mechanisms for the prompt review and correction of administrative action relating to customs matters.[259] The EC argued that the human rights provision in Article 6 of the *ECHR* (Right to a fair trial) together with the ECtHR adjudication would ensure that EC countries would promptly review customs cases. But, without referring to this human rights provision, the Panel found that the United States' claim of violation of the obligation to provide prompt review relating to customs matter in Article X: 3(b) of the *GATT* 1994 was not founded.[260]

There has been the case of the waiver for "blood diamonds" under the Kimberly process. The Kimberley Process Certification Scheme is a process designed to certify the origin of diamonds from sources that are free of conflict.[261] The waiver in the Kimberly process was decided by the WTO Council by way of exception. It allowed trade measures exemptions from *GATT* provisions on most-favored-nation treatment (Article I: 1), elimination of quantitative restrictions (Article XI: 1) and non-discriminatory administration of quantitative restrictions (Article XIII: 1). The blood diamonds waiver is a truly exceptional case, given that the most powerful governments, nearly the whole diamond industry, NGOs and civil society worked together to achieve the waiver.[262] The Kimberley process arose out of a special situation and will probably not provide a WTO model for the enforcement of human rights in general.[263] Furthermore, the WTO obviously pressures less developed states, such as Pakistan, to abide by core labor standards.[264] After accession to the WTO,

---

257 *Report of the Panel, Thailand--Restrictions on Importation of and Internal Taxes on Cigarettes* GATT BISD (37th Supp), WTO (1996); *WTO Appellate Body Report, United States--Standards for Reformulated and Conventional Gasoline (May 20)*, WT/DS2/AB/R, WTO DSB (1996); *WTO Appellate Body Report, European Communities -Measures Affecting Asbestos and Asbestos-Containing Products (Mar. 12)*, WT/DS135/AB/R, WTO DSB (2001); see also D Kinley and J Tadaki, 'From Talk to Walk: The Emergence of Human Rights Responsibilities for Corporations at International Law' 44 Virginia Journal of International Law 931 (2004) at 1012.

258 See, e.g., *United States - Section 211 Omnibus Appropriations Act of 1998 (US - Section 211 Appropriations Act) (1 February)*, WT/DS176/AB/R, WTO DSB (2002) at 71.

259 *EC - Selected Customs Matters (16 June)*, WT/DS315/R, WTO DSB (2006).

260 *Ibid.* at 384.

261 J Pauwelyn, 'WTO Compassion or Superiority Complex?: What to make of the WTO Waiver for "Conflict Diamonds"' 24 Michigan Journal of International Law 1177 (2003) at 1179.

262 *Ibid.* at 1179.

263 *Ibid.* at 1205.

264 A Afzal, 'Pakistan, the WTO, and Labor Reform' 29 Boston College International and Comparative Law Review 107 (2006).

Pakistani companies faced increasing pressure to assure against discriminatory practices.[265]

In the more than 350 panel decisions the term "human rights" was mentioned in 20 documents, mostly in irrelevant considerations of the parties and not as part of the panel decision. And mostly it was embodied in the term "European Convention on Human Rights."[266] The term "economy" on the other hand was mentioned in 352 documents. Considering all these facts, it is fair to say that human rights do not play a role in the WTO. The WTO might have a leveling effect on some global labor standards, but the WTO at its present state cannot be seen as a viable path to enforce human rights violations against TNCs. Also, the incentives for using a trade barrier in the WTO seem small, since the country might risk being the subject to scrutiny of its human rights situation and it could be subject to retaliatory measures and political pressure.

C. World Bank

The World Bank Group is a group of five international organizations responsible for providing finance for the purposes of development and poverty reduction. Its five agencies are the International Bank for Reconstruction and Development (IBRD), the International Development Association (IDA), International Finance Corporation (IFC), Multilateral Investment Guarantee Agency (MIGA) and the International Centre for Settlement of Investment Disputes (ICSID). The IBRD Articles of Agreement stipulate in Article 10(10) the "non-political" mandate of the Bank: "The Bank and its officers shall not interfere in the political affairs of any member; nor shall they be influenced in their decisions by the political character of the member or members concerned. Only economic considerations shall be relevant to their decisions, and these considerations shall be weighed impartially in order to achieve the purposes stated in Article I."[267]

Many scholars argue that the protection and promotion of basic human rights is not off-limits to the World Bank.[268] There are three arguments in favor of including human rights considerations in the activities of the World Bank: (1) human rights are

---

265 *Ibid.* at 112.

266 Search of the ICSID database 'WTO-DEC' on Westlaw on September 7, 2007.

267 International Bank for Reconstruction and Development (IBRD) Articles of Agreement Articles of Agreement of the International Bank for Reconstruction and Development, July 22, 1944, 60 Stat 1440, 2 UNTS 134, amended Dec 16, 1965, UST 1942, 606 UNTS 294 (IBRD Articles of Agreement) (1944).

268 G Brodnig, 'The World Bank and Human Rights: Mission Impossible' (2005) <http:// www. ksg. harvard. edu/ cchrp/ Web%20Working% 20Papers/ BrodnigHR&WorldBank.pdf> (May 25, 2007); D Kinley and J Tadaki, 'From Talk to Walk: The Emergence of Human Rights Responsibilities for Corporations at International Law' 44 Virginia Journal of International Law 931 (2004) at 1006; SR Ratner, 'Corporations and Human Rights: A Theory of Legal Responsibility' 111 Yale Law Journal 443 (2001) at 538.

part of the Bank's mandate, (2) human rights are "economic considerations," and (3) human rights are not "political affairs."

"Well established principles of international law, the gradual adoption of a rights-based approach to development by the international aid community and the growing empirical evidence of economists and other social scientists about the interdependence between economic welfare and human rights make it increasingly difficult for the Bank to cling to a restrictive interpretation of its mandate."[269]

It makes little sense that the World Bank is able to determine that female genital mutilation is an economic issue because of the economic costs associated with it, but that other human rights violations are not.[270] In recent years the work of the World Bank has increasingly qualified the "non-political" mandate by its work on combating corruption and its involvement in the areas of indigenous people's rights, the prohibition of child labor and the prohibition of forced labor. The World Bank's moves towards a greater recognition of human rights reflect the move of development policies towards a rights-based approach. A rights-based approach to development is a conceptual framework for the process of human development that is normatively based on international human rights standards and operationally directed to promoting and protecting human rights.[271]

The legitimacy of this approach may be derived from the fact that the UN Charter stands above the bank's charters obligations.[272] By applying the principle of *"Normenhierachie"* – which derives from the Roman law principle of *"lex superior derogat legi inferiori"* meaning that the higher ranking legal source overrides the lower ranking one – one's attention should be drawn to Article 103 of the UN Charter.[273] It provides: "In the event of a conflict between the obligations of the Members of the United Nations under the present Charter and their obligations under any other international agreement, their obligations under the present Charter shall prevail."

---

269 G Brodnig, 'The World Bank and Human Rights: Mission Impossible' (2005) <http:// www.ksg.harvard.edu/ cchrp/Web% 20Working% 20Papers/BrodnigHR&WorldBank.pdf> (May 25, 2007) at 20.

270 DD Bradlow, 'The World Bank, the IMF, and human rights' 6 Transnational Law & Contemporary Problems 47 (1996).

271 For a Human Rights approach to development politics see AK Sen, *Development as Freedom* (Knopf, New York 2001)AK Sen, *Choice, Welfare, and Measurement* (Harvard University Press, Cambridge 1997), D McGoldrick, 'Sustainable Development and Human Rights: An Integrated Conception ' 45 International and Comparative Law Quarterly 796 (1996) (for an integrated legal approach).

272 M Darrow, *Between Light and Shadow: The World Bank, the International Monetary Fund and International Human Rights Law* (Hart Publishing, Oxford 2003) at 129.

273 Charter of the UN 1945 1 UNTS xvi (1945).

The World Bank announced guidelines for TNCs for the purpose of foreign direct investment (FDI) in 1992. The guidelines basically served as a restatement of the rules and practice that had grown over the years around FDI and TNCs.[274] Cooperating partners of the World Bank are increasingly, and often seriously, punished for corruption offenses; but not, as yet, for human rights violations.[275] Overall it can be noted that the current World Bank policy and regulation gradually increases its support for human rights considerations, but it cannot and will not be seen as an instrument to adjudicate human rights violations of TNCs.

D. ILO and the Tripartite Declaration

The International Labour Organization (ILO) is a specialized agency of the United Nations that deals with labor issues. It seeks to strengthen workers' rights and improve working conditions. Its unique structure, composed of workers, employers and governments predestine it as international organization to regulate the behavior of TNCs. It was also one of the first to establish a set of rules for TNCs in 1977 with the *Tripartite Declaration of Principles concerning Multinational Enterprises and Social Policy.*[276] The *Declaration* addresses employment policies and conditions of work and life. It establishes minimum labor standards, defines the right to organize, sets minimum age requirements and abolishes forced labor. However, the crux of the regulation is that it relies on the voluntary implementation of corporations or governments.

In summary, the *ILO Tripartite Declaration* is a high-level statement of international public policy and its regulations are generally accepted by employer organizations around the world, as well as from trade unions and governments. The ILO's potential to enforce human rights as against TNCs is, however, like so many other non-binding instruments limited to "moral persuasion, publicity, shame, diplomacy and dialogue."[277] Moreover, the *ILO Declaration* fell largely into disuse and its use as point of reference for TNCs has been rather seldom.[278]

---

274 CD Wallace, 'The Legal Framework for Regulating the Global Enterprise Going Into the New WTO Trade Round--A Backward and a Forward Glance' 16 Transnational Lawyer 141 (2002) at 146.

275 As one example the World bank debarred a German engineering firm from further World bank procurement for up to seven years in November 2006. See: World Bank, 'World Bank Sanctions Lahmeyer International for Corrupt Activities in Bank-Financed Projects, Press Release No 129/2007/INT' (2006) <http:// web.worldbank.org/ WBSITE/ EXTERNAL/ NEWS/ 0,,content MDK:21116129~pagePK: 34370~piPK: 34424~theSitePK:4607,00.html> .

276 Tripartite Declaration of Principles concerning Multinational Enterprises and Social Policy Nov 16, 1977, 17 ILM 422 (1977).

277 D Kinley and J Tadaki, 'From Talk to Walk: The Emergence of Human Rights Responsibilities for Corporations at International Law' 44 Virginia Journal of International Law 931 (2004) at 1018, footnote 413.

278 N Jägers, *Corporate Human Rights Obligations: In Search of Accountability* (Intersentia, Antwerpen 2002) at 115.

E. OECD Guidelines

The Organisation for Economic Co-operation and Development (OECD) set up the *Guidelines for Multinational Enterprises*. These are recommendations for corporations, made by the governments of OECD member countries.[279] They were drafted in 1976 and last revised in 2000. Their aim is to ensure that TNCs operate in harmony with the policies of the countries in which they operate. These voluntary standards cover a large proportion of a TNC's operations, including information disclosure, labor relations, its impact on the environment, corruption, consumer protection, science and technology, competition and taxation. Human rights are only addressed obliquely.

The *Guidelines* state that human rights are primarily the responsibility of governments, but corporations should respect the human rights of the people who are affected by their activities. It was decided not to specify the human rights obligations of TNCs on the grounds that it was the primary responsibility of governments to uphold those rights.[280] The *OECD Guidelines* establish National Contact Points (NCPs) that should provide a forum for discussion of the guidelines, but they do not have any formal dispute resolution power. Their role is simply to facilitate and promote the guidelines. As in the case of the *ILO Tripartite Declaration* the *OECD Guidelines* were only rarely referred to by TNCs.[281] The *Guidelines* were drafted at a very early stage and may have contributed to more socially responsible behavior of TNCs. On the other hand and again, they are non-binding and the *Guidelines* supervisory system is not effective.[282]

F. International Criminal Court

Days after the adoption of the *Rome Statute of the International Criminal Court* (ICC) in July 1998, the Financial Times warned that the accomplice liability provision in the treaty could create international criminal liability for employees, officers and directors of corporations.[283] The prosecutor for the ICC, Louis Moreno Ocampo, stated that his office may investigate the effect that multinational businesses

---

[279] OECD Guidelines for Multinational Enterprises June 27, 2000, ILM 40 (2000), 237 (2000); More information: Organisation for Economic Co-operation and Development, *Environment and the OECD Guidelines for Multinational Enterprises: Corporate Tools and Approaches* (Organisation for Economic Co-operation and Development, Paris 2005); Organisation for Economic Co-operation and Development., *OECD Guidelines For Multinational Enterprises: Focus on Responsible Supply Chain Management* (OECD, Paris 2002); R Blanpain, *The OECD Guidelines for Multinational Enterprises and Labour Relations, 1982-1984: Experience and Review* (Kluwer Law and Taxation Publishers, Deventer; Boston 1985).

[280] P Redmond, 'Transnational Enterprise and Human Rights: Options for Standard Setting and Compliance' 37 International Lawyer 69 (2003) at 98.

[281] N Jägers, *Corporate Human Rights Obligations: In Search of Accountability* (Intersentia, Antwerpen 2002) at 108.

[282] *Ibid.* at 108.

[283] M Nyberg, 'At Risk from Complicity with Crime' *Financial Times*, (July 28, 1998).

had on the continuation of the conflict in the Democratic Republic of Congo.[284] The ICC was established in 2002 as a permanent tribunal in which to prosecute individuals for war crimes, genocide and crimes against humanity. The Court can exercise jurisdiction if national courts are unwilling or unable to investigate or prosecute such crimes. It is thus a "court of last resort." It only has jurisdiction over nationals of those countries that have signed the *Rome Statute*.

At the 1998 Rome Diplomatic Conference on the International Court, delegates from France proposed that legal persons should be included in the Court's jurisdiction.[285] The wording of the proposal was: "Without prejudice to any individual criminal responsibility of natural persons under this Statute, the Court may also have jurisdiction over a juridical person for a crime under this Statute. Charges may be filed by the Prosecutor against a juridical person, and the Court may render a judgment over a juridical person for the crime charged, if: […]; (b) The natural person charged was in opposition of control within the juridical person under the national law of the state where the juridical person was registered at the time the crime was committed; and (c) The crime was committed by the natural person acting on behalf of and with the explicit consent of that juridical person and in the course of its activities; and (d) The natural person has been convicted of the crime charged. For the purpose of this Statute, 'juridical person' means a corporation whose concrete, real, or dominant objective is seeking private profit or benefit, and not a state or other public body in the exercise of state authority, a public international body or an organization registered and acting under the national law of a state as a non-profit organization."[286]

However, it proved impossible to reach a consensus about what types of organizations should be included and who represents a legal entity before the Court.[287] Some countries with public corporations, joint ventures and other commercial activities were concerned about the potential risk for the government.[288]

---

284 S Kabel, 'Our Business Is People (Even If It Kills Them): The Contribution of Multinational Enterprises to the Conflict in the Democratic Republic of Congo' 12 Tulane Journal of International and Comparative Law 461 (2004) at 474.

285 See especially C Chiomenti, 'Corporations and the International Criminal Court; Global Law Working Paper 01/05, Symposium - 'Transnational Corporations and Human Rights', Hauser Global Law School Program' (2005) <http:// nyulawglobal.com/ workingpapers/ GLWP0105Chiomenti_ 000.rtf> (September 7, 2007); See also N Jägers, *Corporate Human Rights Obligations: In Search of Accountability* (Intersentia, Antwerpen 2002) at 228 et *seq.*; S Kabel, 'Our Business Is People (Even If It Kills Them): The Contribution of Multinational Enterprises to the Conflict in the Democratic Republic of Congo' 12 Tulane Journal of International and Comparative Law 461 (2004) at 476.

286 A/Conf./183/WGGP/L.5/Rev. 2, 3 July 1998.

287 N Jägers, *Corporate Human Rights Obligations: In Search of Accountability* (Intersentia, Antwerpen 2002) at 228 et *seq.*

288 Clapham, 'The Question of Jurisdiction Under International Criminal Law Over Legal Persons: Lessons from the Rome Conference on an International Criminal Court' in MT Kamminga and

The final stumbling block was the fact that many countries do not recognize criminal liability of corporations.[289] Finally, the French delegation withdrew the proposal and now the ICC has only jurisdiction over natural persons. Therefore, the ICC could only prosecute individuals, such as directors of business entities that were involved in the abovementioned set of serious human rights violations.

So far, the ICC has not investigated against corporate officers. However, by fortifying the duties of individuals under international law, the web of liability for corporate malfeasance may also tighten. Considering the detailed and terrific allegations of the involvement in inhumane acts, the probability is high that the Sudanese Minister, Ahmed Harun, will be convicted.[290] It will be interesting, if a possible conviction will also have an effect on the Sudanese national oil corporation Sudapet (Sudan National Petroleum Corporation) in the consortium of Petrodar Operating Company Ltd. Partners of the consortium include China Petrochemical Corporation (Sinopec Group) and China National Petroleum Corporation (CNPC).[291] However, at this stage, it does appear very unlikely that trials against their corporate officers will be held in front of the ICC. Instead there is a higher, albeit still small, likelihood that they will be held in front of US courts under the ATCA litigation.

Nevertheless, the zone of sanctuary for corporate perpetrators of violations of international criminal law may also become smaller through the establishment of the ICC. Regarding the fact that the idea of criminal liability of corporations on the international level was discussed at length, this might represent (a) A viable path for

---

S Zia-Zarifi (eds) *Liability of Multinational Corporations under International Law* (Kluwer Law International, The Hague 2000) at 156; S Kabel, 'Our Business Is People (Even If It Kills Them): The Contribution of Multinational Enterprises to the Conflict in the Democratic Republic of Congo' 12 Tulane Journal of International and Comparative Law 461 (2004) at 477.

289 N Jägers, *Corporate Human Rights Obligations: In Search of Accountability* (Intersentia, Antwerpen 2002) at 230.

290 *Situation in Darfur, Sudan in the Case of The Prosecutor v. Ahmad Muhammad Harun ("Ahmad Harun") and Ali Muhammad al Abd-Al-Rahman ("Ali Kushayb")*, Pre-Trial Chamber I, No ICC-02/05-01/07, ICC (2007). The case of Darfur was referred to the ICC by the UN Security Council, since Sudan is not a party to the Rome Statute establishing the ICC.

291 See chapter IV at subheading "XI. *Presbyterian Church of Sudan v. Talisman Energy* – Corporations and Sudan genocide" at 154 and in this chapter below at subheading "C. Corporate social responsibility in practice: codes of conduct" at 88. See also W Hawkins, 'China's Role in Genocide' *Washington Times* 2006) A16; Sudan Divestment Task Force, 'PetroChina, CNPC, and Sudan: Perpetuating Genocide' (2007) <http:// www.sudandivestment.org/ docs/ PetroChina_ CNPC_ Sudan.pdf> (September 6, 2007); Yale Law School - The Allard K. Lowenstein International Human Rights Clinic, 'An Analysis of Select Companies' Operations in Sudan: A Resource for Divestment' (2005) <http:// www.inosphere.com/ sudan/ docs/ Yale_ Lowenstein_ Updated_Report.pdf> (July 19, 2007) at 31-36.

the ICC in future and (b) A head-start for national jurisdictions to pursue the approach of criminal liability of corporations for human rights violations.[292]

G. State responsibility

Another avenue of holding states responsible for human rights violations of TNCs in their jurisdiction could be the possibility of state responsibility. Since 9/11 this problem became even more apparent as Al-Quaida was working as a non-state actor from many different countries, with a "safe haven" in Afghanistan. And on the other side the combat in the War on Terror has been largely supported by private military firms.[293] The threat imposed by non-state actors has become comparable to that of state actors in many fields. But how is it possible to address the threats of non-state actors?

1. Nationality of corporations

States could be held liable for actions of "their" TNCs. However, this immediately provokes an anterior question: Which TNCs can the state be held accountable? How can one determine a TNC's "home country?" Is it the TNCs that were incorporated in the relevant state, the TNCs that have their headquarters in that state, TNCs that are listed on the stock exchange, TNCs that are in domestic ownership or control or those that do business in the country or a combination of these categories?

These problems have not yet been resolved at international law.[294] Concerning the right of diplomatic protection, in 1970 the International Court of Justice (ICJ) held in the *Barcelona Traction* case that only the state of incorporation can claim diplomatic protection, not the state of the majority of shareholders.[295] However, this finding may

---

[292] See also, C Chiomenti, 'Corporations and the International Criminal Court; Global Law Working Paper 01/05, Symposium - 'Transnational Corporations and Human Rights', Hauser Global Law School Program' (2005) <http:// nyulawglobal.com/ workingpapers/ GLWP0105 Chiomenti_ 000. rtf> (September 7, 2007) at 30.

[293] See, *inter alia*, F Schreier and M Caparini, 'Privatizing Security: Law, Practice and Governance of Private Military and Security Companies' (2005) <http:// www.dcaf.ch/ _docs/ op06_ privatising- security.pdf> (August 21, 2007).

[294] See UN High Commissioner for Human Rights, 'Workshop on Attributing Corporate Responsibility for Human Rights under International Law- Summary Report' (2006) <Workshop on Attributing Corporate Responsibility for Human Rights under International Law- Summary Report> (March 13, 2007) at 6; LJ Lee, 'Barcelona Traction in the 21st Century: Revising its Customary and Policy Underpinnings 35 Years Later' 42 Stanford Journal of International Law 237 (2006).

[295] *Barcelona Traction, Light and Power Co. (Belgium v. Spain)*, ICJ Reports 1970, 3, ICJ (1970) at para 42: "In allocating corporate entities to states for purposes of diplomatic protection, international law is based, but only to a limited extent, on an analogy with the rules governing the nationality of individuals. The traditional rule attributes the right of diplomatic protection of a corporate entity to the state under the laws of which it is incorporated and in whose territory it has its registered office. These two criteria have been confirmed by long practice and by numerous international instruments."

now be outdated.[296] In the *ELSI* Case the ICJ has also cautiously refrained from its position in *Barcelona Traction* and has made "economic interests rather than legal relationship the operative basis for protection."[297]

Lawrence Lee has thoroughly examined the state practice concerning the nationality of a corporation, finding that developed states have not fully accepted the rule of incorporation as customary law, and developing states prefer a *genuine link* requirement.[298] Overall, "the traditional law of diplomatic protection has been largely replaced by a number of treaty-based dispute settlement procedures."[299] For those rare cases that diplomatic protection will be sought by TNCs, the question of deciding on the nationality of a *multi*-national or *trans*-national corporation is very difficult to assess and seems far from resolved.

2. ILC Articles on Responsibility of States for Wrongful Acts

In 2001 the International Law Commission (ILC) adopted the text of the Articles on Responsibility of States for International Wrongful Acts.[300] It covers the principles governing when and how a state is held responsible for a breach of an international obligation. Essentially, the state is only responsible for its own acts, meaning the acts of the government, any political sub-division of the state, any organ, agency or employee. In order to hold a state accountable for the behavior of an individual or corporation, Articles 5, 8 and 11 are relevant.

Article 5 provides that the conduct of persons or entities exercising elements of governmental authority shall be considered an act of the state under international law, provided the person is acting in that capacity. This provision is intended to take into account the increasingly common phenomenon of para-statal entities, where privatized state institutions take on certain public or regulatory functions.[301]

---

296 See also F Orrego Vicuña, 'Changing approaches to the nationality of claims in the context of diplomatic protection and international dispute settlement' 15 ICSID review 340 (2000).

297 SD Murphy, 'The ELSI Case: An Investment Dispute at the International Court of Justice' 16 Yale Journal of International Law 391 (1991) at 419.

298 LJ Lee, 'Barcelona Traction in the 21st Century: Revising its Customary and Policy Underpinnings 35 Years Later' 42 Stanford Journal of International Law 237 (2006) at 275.

299 J Kokott, 'Interim Report on "The Role of Diplomatic Protection in the Field of the Protection of Foreign Investment," International Law Association: Second Report of the Committee on Diplomatic Protection of Persons and Property' (2002) <http:// www.ilahq.org/ pdf/ DiplomaticProtection/ DiplomaticProtectionSecondReport2002.pdf> (June 6, 2007) at 31.

300 Articles on Responsibility of States for International Wrongful Acts Report of the International Law Commission on the work of its Fifty-Third Session, UN GAOR, 6th Comm, 56th Sess, Supp No 10, at 43-44, UN Doc A/56/10 (2001); with commentary: International Law Commission, 'Commentary on Articles on Responsibility of States for International Wrongful Acts' (2001) <http:// www.un.org/ law/ ilc/ texts/ State_responsibility/ responsibility_ commentaries(e).pdf> (January 30, 2006).

301 International Law Commission, 'Commentary on Articles on Responsibility of States for International Wrongful Acts' (2001) <http://www.un.org/ law/ ilc/ texts/State_responsibility/ responsibility_ commentaries(e).pdf> (January 30, 2006) at chapter IV.E.2.

Under Article 8, the conduct of a person or group of persons shall be considered an act of a state under international law if the person or group of persons is in fact acting on the instructions of, or under the direction or control of, that state in carrying out the conduct. International law acknowledges the separate nature of corporate entities, except in cases where the "corporate veil" is an artificial device or a vehicle for fraud or evasion.

A state may create a state-owned corporation to avoid constitutional rules concerning the state budget, or to facilitate international trade.[302] This was also the position taken, for example, in relation to the *de facto* seizure of property by a state-owned oil company. It was found that the state did not use its ownership interest as a vehicle for directing the company to seize the property.[303] On the other hand, where there was evidence that the corporation was using its ownership interest to achieve a particular result, the conduct in question has been attributed to the state.[304]

Finally, Article 11 stipulates that conduct, which is not attributable to a state under the preceding Articles, shall nevertheless be considered an act of that state under international law to the extent that the state acknowledges and adopts the conduct in question as its own. Article 11, by contrast to the preceding Articles, provides for state conduct that was not or may not have been attributable to it at the time of commission, but which is subsequently acknowledged and adopted by the state as its own.[305]

Article 11 is drawn from state practice and international judicial decisions, to the effect that the conduct of individuals in a state cannot automatically be recognized as an action of the state until the state acknowledges and adopts the conduct in question

302 I Seidl-Hohenveldern, C University of and L Research Centre for International, *Corporations In and Under International Law* (Hersch Lauterpacht memorial lectures 6, Grotius, Cambridge 1987) at 55.

303 *SEDCO, Inc. v. National Iranian Oil Co.* , 15 Iran-United States Claims Tribunal Report 23, Iran-United States Claims Tribunal (1987). See also: *International Technical Products Corp. v. Islamic Republic of Iran*, 9 Iran- United States Claims Tribunal reports 206, Iran- United States Claims Tribunal (1985); *Flexi-Van Leasing, Inc. v. Islamic Republic of Iran*, 12 Iran- United States Claims Tribunal Report 335, Iran- United States Claims Tribunal (1986) at 349; International Law Commission, 'Commentary on Articles on Responsibility of States for International Wrongful Acts' (2001) <http://www.un.org/ law/ ilc/ texts/ State_responsibility/ responsibility_ commentaries(e).pdf> (January 30, 2006) at chapter IV.E.2. at 108.

304 *Hertzberg et al. v. Finland*, UN GAOR Human Rights Comm, 37th Sess, Supp No 40 at 161, para 103, UN Doc A/37/40, Human Rigths Committee (1982) at annex XIV, para 9.1. See also *X v. Ireland, (App. 4125/69)*, 14 Yearbook European Convention on Human Rights 198, European Commission on Human Rights (1971); Young, James and Webster v. United Kingdom, E.C.H.R., Series A, No. 44 (1981).

305 International Law Commission, 'Commentary on Articles on Responsibility of States for International Wrongful Acts' (2001) <http://www.un.org/ law/ ilc/ texts/ State_responsibility/ responsibility_ commentaries(e).pdf> (January 30, 2006) at chapter IV.E.2. at 119.

as its own.[306] Similarly, the law of the sea attributes state responsibility for breaches of international law by vessels flying the relevant state flag.[307]

These principles govern the question of attribution only. Where conduct has been acknowledged to be that of a state, it will still be necessary to consider whether the conduct was internationally wrongful in terms of the ILC provisions. Where an attributable wrongful act has been identified, a court must have jurisdiction to consider the alleged violation of international law. Overall, these articles of attribution of private actions do not cover most human rights violations of TNCs, because they will very often not include any state action.

3. ICJ and ICTY

As stated in Article 93 of the UN Charter, all 192 UN members are automatically parties to the statute of the ICJ. A party to the Court's statute is entitled to participate in cases before the court. However, being a party does not automatically give the Court jurisdiction over disputes. Jurisdiction is often a crucial question for the Court in contentious cases. The key principle is that the ICJ only has jurisdiction on the basis of consent as stipulated in Article 36 of the statute of the ICJ. In interlocutory proceedings, the respondent often raises many objections concerning the justiciability of the case. For instance, the respondent might claim that the requisite consent has not been achieved or that there is not a "legal dispute."

In cases in which the ICJ possesses jurisdiction, the Court provides a ruling that is binding as between the state parties to the dispute. Individuals, corporations, parts of a federal state, non-governmental-organizations (NGOs), UN organs and others do not have standing (*locus standi*) before the ICJ. In spite of these hurdles, there appears to be a growing body of jurisprudence that addresses the question of attribution of private behavior to states. In the *Nicaragua* case, the ICJ held that the United States could be held responsible for the acts of the Contras in their war against the Nicaraguan Government in the 1980s only if it had "effective control of the military or paramilitary operations in the course of which the alleged violations were committed."[308]

---

306 *Ibid.*, chapter IV.E.2. at 119.

307 United Nations Convention on the Law of the Sea December 10, 1982, 1833 UNTS 3 (entered into force November 16, 1994) ("UNCLOS") (1982) Article 194 (2) states: " States shall take all measures necessary to ensure that activities under their jurisdiction or control are so conducted as not to cause damage by pollution to other States and their environment, and that pollution arising from incidents or activities under their jurisdiction or control does not spread beyond the areas where they exercise sovereign rights in accordance with this Convention." The *Agreement to Promote Compliance with International Conservation and Management Measures by Fishing Vessels on the High Seas* (Resolution 15/93), known also as the Compliance Agreement, similarly builds on flag state responsibility for fishing vessels flying its flag (Article III) and operating on the high seas.

308 *Military and Paramilitary Activities in and Against Nicaragua (Nicaragua v. US) (Merits)*, ICJ 14, 98, ICJ (1986) at para 65.

The International Criminal Tribunal for the Former Yugoslavia (ICTY) applied a wider formula. In the case of *Prosecutor v Tadic*, the Tribunal held that a state can be held attributable as long as it "has a role in organizing, coordinating or planning the military actions" of the group, not necessarily controlling its particular operations.[309]

4. ECtHR

The European Court of Human Rights (ECtHR) has been a powerful judicial organ in enforcing the human rights articulated in the *ECHR*. Even though the judgments are binding only for the state that is a party to the dispute, the ECtHR has adopted a sophisticated system of state responsibility and horizontally binding human rights obligations. Horizontal human rights obligation, as opposed to vertical human rights obligation, means that it is not only the state that is bound to respect human rights, but also any non-state actor towards another non-state actor. The ECtHR held, for example, that Spain was accountable for the violation of the right to enjoy private and family life because the Spanish authorities had failed to regulate the operation of a waste treatment plant resulting in interference with respect for the applicants' home, private and family life.[310]

The 800 million individuals who are subject to the jurisdiction of the 47 member states of the European Council have an instrument to address and enforce human rights violations by TNCs by filing a claim to the ECtHR. It is a procedural requisite, however, that an applicant to the ECtHR first must exhaust all the remedies in the state concerned before applying to the ECtHR. This can include appealing to the ultimate appellate court, such as the Supreme Court or constitutional court.

The ECtHR cannot force a member state to comply with its ruling. However, the Committee of Ministers can, as the ultimate sanction, expel a member state from the Council of Europe, thus making it a "pariah" state within Europe, which at this point in time has not occurred.

Moreover, the EU and especially the Court of Justice of the European Communities (ECJ) take a keen interest in the ECtHR and its jurisprudence. In the absence of a formal link between the courts, they have built up a relationship based on informal comity and co-operation.[311] In recent years, the ECJ has increasingly referred to the case law of the ECtHR.[312] Compliance with decisions of the ECtHR varies widely

309 Prosecutor v. Tadic, Case No. IT-94-I-A (1999) (International Criminal Tribunal for Former Yugoslavia Appeals Chamber) at para 137.

310 *Lopez Ostra v Spain*, Ser A No 303-C, ECtHR (1994).

311 ADJ Balfour, *Application of the European Convention on Human Rights by the European Court of Justice* (Harvard Law School Student Scholarship Series, Berkeley Electronic Press (bepress), Berkeley 2005) at 12.

312 *P v S and Cornwall County Council*, ECR I-2143, C-13/94, ECJ (1996) at para 16; *Criminal Proceedings against X*, ECR I-6609, C-74 and 129/95, ECJ (1996) at para25; *Vereingte Familiapress v Heinrich Bauer Verlag*, 3 CMLR 1329, C-368/95, ECJ (1997) at para 26; *Grant*

among the members of the Council of Europe. For instance, the Russian Federations' compliance with the strictures of the *ECHR* has been far from easy.[313]

5. IACtHR and ACoHPR

The Inter-American Court of Human rights (IACtHR) and the Inter-American Commission on Human Rights (IACoHR) provide the human rights protection system of the Organization of American States (OAS). In *Velásquez-Rodriguez*, the IACtHR recognized that the *American Convention on Human Rights* (*ACHR*) had a similar effect to the horizontal effect in the *European Convention.*[314]

It stated: "Thus, in principle, any violation of rights recognized by the Convention carried out by an act of public authority or by persons who use their position of authority is imputable to the State. However, this does not define all the circumstances in which a State is obligated to prevent, investigate and punish human rights violations, or all the cases in which the State might be found responsible for an infringement of those rights. An illegal act which violates human rights and which is initially not directly imputable to a State (for example, because it is the act of a private person or because the person responsible has not been identified) can lead to international responsibility of the State, not because of the act itself, but because of the lack of due diligence to prevent the violation or to respond to it as required by the Convention."[315]

However the IACtHR does not provide a means to bring forth a claim by an individual. Individuals must first lodge their cases with the Commission and have that body rule on the question of admissibility. In contrast to the *ECHR*, only some member states to the OAS have accepted contentious jurisdiction on a blanket basis. To date 17 of 35 members have accepted it.[316] The US did not.

---

v South West Trains, ECR I-621, C-249/96, ECJ (1998) at para 34; *Baustahlgewebe*, ECR I-8417, C-185/95, ECJ (1998) at para 29; *Roquette Freres SA v Directeur General de la Concurrence, de la Consommation et de la Repression des Fraudes*, ECR I-9011, C94/00 ECJ (2002) at para 29 ; *Bernard Connolly*, ECR I-1611, ECJ (2001) at paras 29-49; *Krombach v Bamberksi*, ECR I-1935, C-7/98, ECJ (2000) at para 39.

313 See, e.g., J Kahn, 'Russian Compliance with Articles Five and Six of the European Convention of Human Rights as a Barometer of Legal Reform and Human Rights in Russia' 35 University of Michigan Journal of Law Reform 641 (2002) at 643; 20% of the applications to the ECtHR are directed against Russia, see Registry of the European Court of Human Rights, 'Survey of Activities 2006 of the European Court of Human Rights' (2007) <http:// www. echr. coe.int/ NR/ rdonlyres/ 69564084-9825- 430B-9150- A9137DD22737/ 0/Survey_2006.pdf> (July 17, 2007) at 3.

314 American Convention on Human Rights November 22, 1969, OASTS No 36, 1144 UNTS 123, 9 ILM 673 (entered into force July 18, 1978) (1969a).

315 *Velásquez Rodriguez Case*, Inter-AmCtHR (Ser C) No 4, Inter-American Court of Human Rights (1988).

316 Argentina, Bolivia, Colombia, Costa Rica, Chile, Ecuador, El Salvador, Guatemala, Haiti, Honduras, Nicaragua, Panama, Paraguay, Peru, Suriname, Uruguay, and Venezuela.

The African Commission on Human and Peoples' Rights (ACoHPR) is a supranational body charged with promoting and protecting human rights in the member states of the African Union (AU). It has issued a report in the *Wiwa* case and held that the Nigerian Government violated Articles 5, 6, 7, 9 (2), 10 (1), 11, 16 and 26 of the African Charter on Human and Peoples' Rights (ACHPR).[317] It remained silent on the role of non-state corporate actors in the violation. It remained faithful to its state-centric approach towards the protection of human rights.[318] But it is possible that the African Court on Human and People's Rights (ACtHPR),[319] which will be set up as a merger[320] with the African Court of Justice (ACJ),[321] will take a different approach to the question of state responsibility.

6. Analysis to state responsibility

Establishing liability of TNCs via state responsibility is a viable approach. The ECtHR system is far more advanced than the others. However, it is only an intermediate solution and tedious in enforcing. A direct enforcement against TNCs seems favorable. Two state responsibility problems remain, that it is (1) how to establish the nationality of a corporation and (2) how to bind the TNC directly; only the home state of the TNC is bound by the decision and it might refrain from imposing sanctions on the malfeasant TNC.

H. Analysis to international law approaches

The classical theory of international law focuses on states as its subjects. It is not surprising that *international* law, as suggested by the term, is based on a *state-centric* paradigm. Jeremy Bentham defined international law in 1789 as a legal system that "was exclusively about the rights and obligations of states *inter se* and never about the rights and obligations of individuals."[322]

For the regulation of human rights violations by TNCs, international law provides supposed customary law, treaty obligations and many different forms of soft law in the form of codes of conduct, guidelines, and the compacts. It provides a useful basis for discussion and bringing facts to light, but it still is a long way from providing

---

317 *Ken Saro-Wiwa* ACoHPR (1998) at 62 et *seq.*

318 S Kingah, 'Protecting African People against private violators of human rights: What can the new African Court of Human and Peoples' rights do to check the activities of Transnational corporations (TNCs)?' at 7.

319 Protocol to the African Charter on Human and Peoples' Rights on the Establishment of an African Court on Human and Peoples' Rights June 10, 1998, OAU Doc CAB/LEG/63/3rev 5 (1998).

320 Executive Council Decision on the Merger of the African Court and the Court of Justice of the African Union, January 28, 2005, EX.CL/Dec.165 (VI).

321 Protocol of the Court of Justice of the African Union adopted during the 2nd Ordinary Session of the Assembly of the African Union, Assembly/AU/Dec 25 (II), 2nd Sess, Doc/EX/CL/59 (III) (not yet in force), available at http://wwwafrica-unionorg (2003).

322 MW Janis, 'Jeremy Bentham and the Fashioning of "International Law' 78 American Journal of International Law 405 (1984) at 408-09.

effective legal international enforcement machinery. The enforcement mechanisms are rather meager and often reduced to moral persuasion, diplomacy and dialog.

At present, international law is ill-equipped to enforce human rights against TNCs. It could even be said that international law has failed to provide mechanisms for regulating corporate conduct in the field of human rights.[323] The inability to enforce and protect basic human rights, to hold violators accountable, and offer compensation to victims, is perhaps "the most glaring weakness of international law."[324]

The reasons for this weakness might be the incapacity of international organizations to recognize other entities as subjects of international law and the states' reluctance to relinquish their dominant position in international law.[325] The potential for a legal control system in international law is small.[326] It is striking that this inadequate situation in international law has barely changed within the last decades.[327] There is still no legally enforceable control system in place for TNCs. The international guidelines and international *fora* have assisted to establish an international consensus on the responsibilities of TNCs.

However, international law has also changed considerably since World War II. The discussion on the jurisdiction of legal persons before the ICC can be seen as representative for the position of TNCs at international law. Many countries would welcome it, others are getting used to it. Even though TNCs are increasingly regarded as subjects of international law, international law is still far away from providing strong enforcement mechanisms for the prosecution of human rights violations by TNCs.

IV. EU law

How does EU law allow for the enforcement of human rights as against TNCs?[328] The Council of Europe is an international organization separate from the EU, although all members of the EU are also members of the Council of Europe. Therefore, all EU citizens have the right to seek review of the decisions of their highest courts to the ECtHR, when they claim their human rights have been violated

---

323 'Corporate Liability for Violations of International Human Rights Law' 114 Harvard Law Review 2025 (2001) at 2030.

324 B Stephens, 'The Civil Lawsuit as a Remedy for International Human Rights Violations Against Women' 5 Hastings Women's Law Journal 143 (1994) at 169.

325 F Johns, 'The Invisibility of the Transnational Corporation: An analysis of International Law and Legal Theory' 19 Melbourne University Law Review 893 (1993) at 900.

326 CD Wallace, *Legal Control of the Multinational Enterprise: National Regulatory Techniques and the Prospects for International Controls* (M.Nijhoff, The Hague 1983) at 327.

327 See for example Wallace conclusion in 1982 in *Ibid.* at 327.

328 This work attempts to use the term EC law when referring to the law before the Maastricht Treaty came into force in 1992. For the time after the Treaty it will refer to all EU law (including EC law) as EU law, even though between 1992 and the coming into force of the Treaty of Lisbon technically law from the first pillar of EU law is EC law.

by TNCs or other state- or non-state-actors. With the adoption of an elaborate system of horizontal human rights obligations and far-reaching state responsibility, EU citizens already possess an instrument to address human rights violations by TNCs.

EU law is a unique legal system which operates alongside the laws of member states of the EU. EU law has a direct effect within the legal systems of its member states, and overrides national law in many areas, especially in terms of economic and social policy.[329] The ECJ has jurisdiction over EU law including in relation to the interpretation and application of the Treaties of the EU and of the provisions laid down by the competent European institutions.[330]

The Charter of Fundamental Rights of the EU is a document containing human rights provisions, similar to the *UDHR*.[331] It was solemnly proclaimed by the EU Parliament, the European Council and the EU Commission, the three most powerful EU institutions, in 2000.[332] It was not a binding source of law however.[333]

The treaty establishing a Constitution for Europe, commonly referred to as the European Constitution included the Charter, but was rejected in referenda held in France and the Netherlands and the ratification process for the Constitution ceased.

---

329 See *Costa v. ENEL*, ECR 585, 6/64, ECJ (1964) at 593 ("It follows from all these observations that the law stemming from the treaty, an independent source of law, could not, because of its special and original nature, be overridden by domestic legal provisions, however framed, without being deprived of its character as Union law and without the legal basis of the community itself being called into question.") Many countries' highest courts have stated that Union law takes precedence provided that it continues to respect fundamental constitutional principles of the Member State, the ultimate judge of which will be the Member State (more exactly, the court of that Member State), rather than the European Union institutions themselves. This reflects the idea that Member States remain the "Master of the Treaties", and the basis for EU law's effect. See, e.g. in the U.K., *Factortame Ltd. v Secretary of State for Transport (No. 2)*, 1 AC 603, U.K. House of Lords (1991); in Germany see *Solange II*, BVerfGE 73, 339, German Constitutional Court (Bundesverfassungsgericht) (1986); in Italy see *Frontini v. Ministero delle Finanze*, 2 CMLR 372, Corte Costitutionale Italy (1973); in France see, *Raoul George Nicolo*, 1 CMLR 173 Conseil d'Etat (1990); However, in Ireland Article 29 (4.3.) provides "No provision of this Constitution invalidates laws enacted, acts done or measures adopted by the State necessitated by the obligations of membership of the European Communities or of the Communities or prevents laws enacted, acts done or measures adopted by the European Union or by the Communities, or institutions thereof, or by bodies competent under the Treaties establishing the Communities, from having the force of law in the State."

330 Article 35 Treaty on the European Union, adopted February 7, 1992, entered into force on November 1, 1993 (Maastricht Treaty) ILM 247, 256 (1992).

331 Charter of Fundamental Rights of the European Union 2000-12-18 EN Official Journal of the European Communities C 364 (2000).

332 [2000] OJ C 364/8, December 18, 2000.

333 C McCrudden, 'The Future of the EU Charter of Fundamental Rights, Jean Monnet Working Paper No.10/01' (2001) <http:// www.jeanmonnetprogram.org/ papers/ 01/ 013001.html> (September 6, 2007) at subheading "3. Compromises and ambiguities."

With the EU summit in Berlin in June 2007 it was decided by the European Council to accept the EU Reform Treaty which finally passes the Charter of Fundamental Rights of the EU as legally binding.[334] Most likely the Reform Treaty will be signed in Lisbon in December 2007.

However, EU law had also reflected its obligation to adjudicate with respect to human rights in its provisions before the Lisbon Treaty. The Treaty Establishing the European Economic Community (EEC), the so-called Rome Treaty of 1957, includes provisions in Articles 136 et *seq*. on the improvement of the working environment to protect workers' health and safety, social security, equality between men and women and other provisions that relate to human rights.[335] It includes also the four fundamental freedoms of the EU: the free movement of goods, services, capital and people.[336] The ECJ has developed these freedoms in numerous decisions. An important milestone decision has been *Internationale Handelsgesellschaft* for the protection of fundamental rights.[337] In *Hauer* the Court also articulated the protection of property and the freedom of profession.[338] In *Hoechst* the Court articulated the right to respect for home and in *Panasonic* the right to privacy.[339] The Court recognized the proportionality principle in *Hauer* and in *Deutsche Milchkontor* the principle of protection of confidence and the principle of legal certainty.[340]

The respect for human rights in EU law is also reflected in the oft-cited decisions of the German Constitutional Court concerning the review of European Community Law in its so-called decision "*Solange I*" and "*Solange II*."[341] "*Solange*" means "as

334 As the United Kingdom insisted during the June 2007 summit talks, the Reform Treaty draft and the Charter of Fundamental Rights will include a statement that it will not create new rights for the EU or encroach on law of the United Kingdom. Poland has got a phrase into the mandate of the intergovernmental conference negotiating the Reform Treaty stating the Charter cannot affect national governments' power to legislate in the sphere of "public morality [and] family law." However, the Charter will still be legally binding.

335 Treaty Establishing the European Community Mar 25, 1957, 298 UNTS 11, as amended by Treaty of Amsterdam, Oct 2, 1997, 1997 OJ (C 340) 1, as amended by Treaty of Nice, Feb 26, 2001, 2001 OJ (C 80) 1, consolidated version reprinted in 2002 OJ (C 325) 33 (1957), Title I and III.

336 *Ibid.*, Title I and III.

337 *Internationale Handelsgesellschaft, 1970 ECR 1125, Case 11/70*, (1970) at paras 2,3 and 14.

338 Protection of property: *Hauer v Rheinland-Pfalz*, ECR 3727, 44/79, ECJ (1979) at paras 4-7; Freedom of profession at paras 4 and 16.

339 *Hoechst AG v Commission of the European Communities, September 21, 1989, 46/87 and 227/88*, 1989 ECR 2859, ECJ (1989) at para 2; *National Panasonic (U.K.) Limited v Commission of the European Communities*, 1980 ECR, Case 136/79, ECJ (1980) at para 21.

340 *Hauer v Rheinland-Pfalz*, ECR 3727, 44/79, ECJ (1979) at para 23; *Deutsche Milchkontor GmbH and others v Federal Republic of Germany*, 1983 ECR 2633, ECJ (1983) at paras 6-9 and 26-33.

341 *Solange I*, BVerfGE 37, 271, German Constitutional Court (Bundesverfassungsgericht) (1974) and *Solange II*, BVerfGE 73, 339, German Constitutional Court (Bundesverfassungs-gericht) (1986).

long as" and could also be translated as "to the extent as." In 1974, the German Federal Constitutional Court (FCC) found that it could review European Community (EC) Law, *as long as* the EC does not guarantee human rights. In its decision *Solange II* it revised this position and held that *as long as* the EC guarantees an effective protection of human rights it will refrain from reviewing EC Law.[342] With the *Solange II* decision, the German Federal Constitutional Court did not accede its jurisdiction concerning EC decisions. It only states that it will not exercise the jurisdiction as long as the present conditions as to the protection of fundamental rights by the ECJ prevail.[343] Although the Court questioned this *Solange II* position in the *Maastricht* decision[344] it basically returned to the position of *Solange II* in *Bananenmarkt.*[345]

For decades, the ECJ has now held that "respect for human rights is a condition for the lawfulness of Community acts."[346] EU law has direct effect. Direct effect is a principle of EU law stating that European regulations have direct effect on EU citizens.[347] The ECJ also supports the principle of the horizontal effect of European law. It found that the right to gender-based equal pay directly applies to private entities in key cases in the 1970s.[348] An individual can rely on EU law to enforce fundamental human rights against TNCs on the European territory, especially rights concerning gender discrimination, the right of privacy, the right for home, the freedom of profession.

V. National approaches

In the event of a violation of human rights by a TNC, there are two states that could address the problem: the home state of the TNC[349] or the host state (that is, where the alleged violation occurred). Host states are generally responsible for the conduct of TNCs within their jurisdiction.[350] However, host states with gross human rights

---

342 *Solange II*, BVerfGE 73, 339, German Constitutional Court (Bundesverfassungsgericht) (1986).

343 J Frowein, 'Solange II' 25 Common Market Law Review 201 (1988) at 204.

344 *Maastricht*, BVerfGE 89, 155, German Constitutional Court (Bundesverfassungsgericht) (1993).

345 *Bananenmarktordnung*, BVerfGE 102, 147, German Constitutional Court (Bundesverfassungsgericht) (2000).

346 *Portugal v Council (Opinion by Advocate General La Pergola)*, ECR I-6177, 268/94, ECJ (1996) at para 34.

347 Established in *Van Gend en Loos v Nederlands Administatie der Belastingen*, ECR I, 26/62, ECJ (1963).

348 See, e.g., *Walrave v Association Union Cycliste Internationale*, ECR 1405, 36/74, ECJ (1974); *Defrenne v Societe Anonyme Belge de Navigation Aerienne Sabena*, ECJ Ruling Case 43/75, 1976 ECR 455, ECJ (1976).

349 See concerning the problem of defining the "home state" above at subheading "1. Nationality of corporations" at 64 in this chapter.

350 See e.g., G Fischer, 'Schadensersatzansprüche wegen Menschenrechtsverletzungen im internationalen Privat- und Prozessrecht' in Goydke (ed) *Vertrauen in den Rechtsstaat:*

violations or where rule of law is poorly recognized and protected have often been reluctant to regulate the behavior of TNCs.[351] They might be afraid to lose foreign direct investment or other income, as has been the case with Shell in Nigeria. Litigating in some host nations with grave human rights violations, as occurred with the atrocities that accompanied oil exploration in Sudan, have sometimes ended in "a total failure of justice."[352] Furthermore, TNCs often attain extensive power, complexity and diversion of responsibility through many different layers of international management that a sole country, especially a small country, may either be unwilling or unable to pursue law-breaking TNCs.

In the past home states of TNCs have regarded the activities of their corporations abroad as being not within their judicial or state responsibility. This was the situation with AURUL in Romania, where Romanian fishermen and women sought compensation from the Australian government, which was the home state of the company in the joint venture between the Romanian state and the foreign investor.[353] This means that the victims of such human rights violations by TNCs – here the fishers of the Danube river in Romania had no means of redress. The host country where the violation occurred denied jurisdiction. The home nation of the TNC denied jurisdiction as well.[354]

Festschrift für Walter Remmers (Heymann, Köln; Berlin; Bonn; München 1995) at 447 et *seq.*; Article 40 EGBGB (Introductory Act to the Civil Code) ("Ansprüche aus unerlaubter Handlung unterliegen dem Recht des Staates, in dem der Ersatzpflichtige gehandelt hat. Der Verletzte kann verlangen, daß anstelle dieses Rechts das Recht des Staates angewandt wird, in dem der Erfolg eingetreten ist.")

351 UN Special Representative of the Secretary-General on human rights and transnational corporations and other business enterprises, 'E/CN.4/2006/97- Interim report of the Special Representative of the Secretary-General on the issue of human rights and transnational corporations and other business enterprises' (2006) <http://daccess-ods.un.org/ access.nsf/ Get?Open&DS=E/ CN.4/ 2006/ 97&Lang=E> (May 23, 2007) at para 27.

352 *Presbyterian Church of Sudan et al. v. Talisman Energy, Inc.*, 244 F Supp 2d 289, D.C. S.D. N.Y. (2003) at 335: "Talisman suggests that plaintiffs bring their claims in Sudan. In support of this claim, Talisman includes an affidavit by Dr. Abdel Rahman Ibrahim el Khalifa, an associate professor of law at the University of Khartoum. The affidavit outlines in detail procedures and jurisprudence of the Sudanese judicial system. Notably absent from the affidavit, however, is any statement indicating that the Sudanese judicial system is fair and free from corruption, and that plaintiffs, who are alleging that Sudan committed genocide and war crimes, could get a fair trial. Plaintiffs' expert, Dr. Abdullahi Ahmed An–Na'im addresses this point, and notes that plaintiffs, who are non-Muslims, enjoy greatly reduced rights in Sudan under the system of Islamic law (Sharia) in place. See Affidavit of Dr. Abdullahi Ahmed An–Na'im at 8, 17, and 18. These reduced rights include a total lack of legal personality for plaintiffs who practice traditional African religions, and diminished testimonial competence for Christians. See id. at 17. Dr. An–Na'im concludes that 'the trial of this case in Sudan will result in a total failure of justice.'"

353 See chapter I at subheading "B. Responsibility and ownership" at 28.

354 UN Special Representative of the Secretary-General on human rights and transnational corporations and other business enterprises, 'E/CN.4/2006/97- Interim report of the Special Representative of the Secretary-General on the issue of human rights and transnational

However, there appears to be fewer and fewer host states that deny jurisdiction for gross human rights violations. At the same time, a growing number of home countries are concerned about the behavior of "their" TNCs abroad. This trend is promising, but still leaves loopholes.

A. Drittwirkung

The principle third-party liability or the horizontal effect of human rights was mentioned above as a possible instrument, as reflected especially in the decisions of the ECtHR.[355] Under this principle, a private party has the right to sue other private parties for violations of human rights. It thereby enables victims of human rights violations to enforce their rights against TNCs directly. The principle of horizontal effect of human rights was originally developed in Germany under the term, *Drittwirkung*, in the 1950s.[356] It goes back to the famous *Lüth* decision,[357] which stands as a landmark decision in German constitutional law and also in international human rights law.[358] In that case, the Court found that the human rights laid down in the German constitution (*Grundgesetz – GG*) are not only of importance as subjective rights protecting the individual against state intrusions into the private sphere; they also represent an *objective dimension in representing society's crucial values.*[359] From that point onwards, human rights represent an objective order of values in German law. They are immutable standards that derive from the GG and, as such, cannot be derogated from. Therefore, they govern the entire legal order, including civil law.

Human rights are used for the interpretation of norms, especially general statutes or blanket clauses, meaning clauses with a broad and general provision, for example the provision of good faith in Section 242 of the German Civil Code.[360] Human rights

---

corporations and other business enterprises' (2006) <http://daccess-ods.un.org/ access.nsf/ Get? Open&DS=E/ CN.4/ 2006/97&Lang=E> (May 23, 2007) at para 27 (stating that these countries are often characterized by week governance, corruption and little political freedom).

355 See N Jägers, *Corporate Human Rights Obligations: In Search of Accountability* (Intersentia, Antwerpen 2002) at 36 et *seq* with further references.

356 SR Ratner, 'Corporations and Human Rights: A Theory of Legal Responsibility' 111 Yale Law Journal 443 (2001) at 471, n.104.

357 *Lüth*, BverfGE 7, 198 German Constitutional Court (Bundesverfassungsgericht) (1958)– An English translation of the *Lüth*-decision: B Markesinis, 'Institute of Global Law - German Translated Decisions- BVerfGE 7, 198' <http://www.ucl.ac.uk/ laws/ global_law/ german-cases/ cases_bverg.shtml?15jan1958> (February 1, 2006).

358 See also E Barnert and N Doll, 'Conference Impressions: The persisting riddle of fundamental rights jurisprudence and the role of the Constitutional Court in a Democratic State' 4 (3) German Law Journal (2003).

359 *Lüth*, BverfGE 7, 198 German Constitutional Court (Bundesverfassungsgericht) (1958) at para 27.

360 Section 242 of the German Civil Code provides: "The obligor must perform in a manner consistent with good faith taking into account common usage." The commentary on this provision has more than 300 pages in D Looschelders and D Olzen, '§ 242' in Jv Staudinger and others (eds) *BGB* (Sellier, Berlin 2005) at 65 et *seq*.

have been used in civil law for example in interpreting the norms for the protection of the right to privacy, or in the discussion on "wrongful life" and abortion.[361] In case a court in a civil matter does not properly consider the relevance of human rights in a civil dispute between the parties, the persons involved can file a constitutional complaint to the German Constitutional Court.[362]

The principle of *Drittwirkung* also gave rise to what has become known as a *human rights claim*. German tort law in connection with various human rights from the bill of rights in the German constitution (Articles 1-19 GG) can be used as a human rights claim, meaning a cause of action in the event of a human rights violation.[363] In the *Lüth* decision this human rights claim was used as a protection of the right to freedom of expression.[364] It also protects the right to privacy of the individual or the right of liberty in Article 2 of the GG.[365] Since its articulation by the German Constitutional Court in 1953, other countries have also adopted the principle of horizontal application of human rights. Switzerland, Israel, Canada, South Africa, Ireland and the Netherlands have similar concepts.[366]

The problem of *Drittwirkung* is that it does not have extraterritorial reach.[367] There has as yet been no authoritative curial decision by an international court that human rights also represents an "objective dimension in representing society's crucial values" in the world society, which would make *Drittwirkung* directly enforceable

---

361 B Pieroth and B Schlink, *Grundrechte, Staatsrecht II* (C.F. Müller Heidelberg 2000) at 43 et *seq.*; For the right to privacy- B Pieroth and B Schlink, *Grundrechte, Staatsrecht II* (C.F. Müller Heidelberg 2000) at 87 of the Supreme Court of the German Reich (RGZ 45, 170) concerning the injunctive relief and the right to one's image on the base of Section 1004 Civil Code; Wrongful life- on the basis of Section 847 Civil Code- decision of the Bundesgerichtshof (BGHZ 86, 240) concerning liability of medical malpractice because of unsuccessful abortion; Good faith- on the basis of Section 242 Civil Code and Article 12 of the German constitution (freedom of profession)- decision of the Bundesarbeitsgericht (BAGE 97, 92) concerning job protection in a small company.

362 According to Article 93 paragraph 1 Nr. 4a Grundgesetz.

363 Section 823 et *seq.* of the German civil code (Bürgerliche Gesetzbuch - BGB) in connection with Articles 1 through 19 of the Constitution, the Grundgesetz - GG.

364 *Lüth*, BverfGE 7, 198 German Constitutional Court (Bundesverfassungsgericht) (1958) at paras 33 et *seq.*

365 Grundgesetz - German Basic Law (1949), Article 2 para. 1 provides: "Everyone has the right to the free development of his personality insofar as he does not violate the rights of others or offend against the constitutional order or the moral code."

366 For the Netherlands and Israel see SR Ratner, 'Corporations and Human Rights: A Theory of Legal Responsibility' 111 Yale Law Journal 443 (2001) at 471; Switzerland see E Bucher, 'Drittwirkung der Grundrechte?- Überlegungen zu "Streikrecht" und "Drittwirkung" i.S. von BGE 111 245-259' 83 Schweizerische Juristen-Zeitung 37 (1987).
For Canada, Ireland and South Africa- see S Gardbaum, 'The "Horizontal Effect" of Constitutional Rights' 102 Michigan Law Review 387 (2003) at 398.

367 See B Pieroth and B Schlink, *Grundrechte, Staatsrecht II* (C.F. Müller Heidelberg 2000) at 47; Also N Jägers, *Corporate Human Rights Obligations: In Search of Accountability* (Intersentia, Antwerpen 2002) at 44.

everywhere. It might be a viable option for claimants in some countries, but aside from the ATCA litigation it did not prove to be a viable approach for extraterritorial human rights violations. In conclusion, individuals have very good enforcement mechanisms against TNCs for violations that were undertaken in countries that accept the concept of *Drittwirkung*. Outside of Germany and Europe, only within a few countries horizontally applicable human rights can be seen as a means of enforcing human rights against TNCs.

B. Corporate criminal liability

Of 16 nations surveyed in a study by Ramasastry and Thompson, 11 nations provide legal mechanisms to hold corporations criminally liable.[368] Those 11 nations are Australia, Belgium, Canada, France, India, Japan, the Netherlands, Norway, South Africa, the United Kingdom and the United States.[369] In five countries (Argentina, Germany, Indonesia, Spain and the Ukraine), it is not recognized. Germany however has interesting provisions relating to environmental liability.[370] Section 30 of the *Gesetz über Ordnungswidrigkeiten* (that is, the *Administrative Offenses Act*) provides that a legal person, such as a corporation, can be required to pay the monetary penalty imposed upon one of its representatives.[371]

State practice in many different nations with different legal backgrounds indicates that criminal law has expanded to cover corporate actors.[372] This does not necessarily mean that human rights are enforceable against corporations. It solely means that these countries also hold corporations accountable for violations of criminal law. Criminal law would probably provide for punishment for a number of significant human rights violations, including genocide and torture. The problem, however, is the extraterritorial reach of domestic criminal law. The problem of extraterritorial reach could be addressed by the entry into force of the ICC and the punishment for breaches of serious violations of international humanitarian law. Articles 6, 7 and 8 of the *Rome Statute for the ICC* include punishment for genocide, crimes against humanity and violations of the laws and customs of war, meaning grave breaches of the *Geneva Conventions*. According to the *Rome Statute*, these norms are only complementary to national provisions.[373] The complementary nature of the *Rome*

368 The sixteen countries surveyed include Argentina, Australia, Belgium, Canada, France, Germany, India, Indonesia, Japan, the Netherlands, Norway, South Africa, Spain, Ukraine, the United Kingdom and the United States. Countries recognizing corporate criminal accountability are Australia, Belgium, Canada, France, India, Japan, the Netherlands, Norway, South Africa, the United Kingdom and the United States. See A Ramasastry and RC Thompson, *Commerce, Crime and Conflict* (Fafo New Security Programme, 2006) at 13.

369 See *Ibid.* at 13.

370 *Ibid.* at 13.

371 Bundesrecht, 'Gesetz über Ordnungswidrigkeiten' (2007) <http:// bundesrecht. juris. de/ owig_1968/ __30.html> (June 5, 2007).

372 A Ramasastry and RC Thompson, *Commerce, Crime and Conflict* (Fafo New Security Programme, 2006) at 13.

373 Under the Rome Statute, the ICC is essentially a court of last resort. A case is not admissible if:

Statute has led many jurisdictions to implement the ICC's crimes into domestic legislation.[374]

In conclusion, the web of potential liability for companies is gradually spreading and tightening, also by the mean of corporate criminal liability. One major problem of corporate criminal liability remains, that is the non-recognition of its criminality in many countries. Therefore, it is an avenue that is limited only to certain jurisdictions, as yet.

C. Transnational litigation for TNC human rights liability outside of the US

The problem of denied jurisdiction can be solved via transnational litigation. The vast majority of transnational civil litigation against TNCs for human rights related claims has arisen in the United States. Outside the US there have been less cases of human rights transnational litigation against TNCs.

In countries of the EU the Brussels Regime regulates the allocation of jurisdiction in international legal disputes of a civil or commercial nature involving persons resident in a member state of the EU. The Brussels Regime consists of the *Brussels Convention*, the *Lugano Convention*, and the Brussels I Regulation.[375] Compared to the US jurisdiction courts under the Brussels regulation apply very strict rules for

(1) it is "being investigated or prosecuted by a State which has jurisdiction over it, unless that state is unwilling or unable genuinely to carry out the investigation or prosecution"; (2) it has "been investigated by a State which has jurisdiction over it and the State has decided not to prosecute the person concerned, unless the decision resulted from the unwillingness or inability of the State genuinely to prosecute;" (3) the "person concerned has already been tried for conduct which is the subject of the complaint;" or (4) the "case is not of sufficient gravity to justify further action by the Court." see Article 17 of the Rome Statute.

374 South Africa- Implementation of the Rome Statute of the International Criminal Court Act 27 of 2002; United Kingdom - International Criminal Court Act 2000; Germany - Act to Introduce the German Code of Crimes Against International Law (CCAIL); Australia - International Criminal Court Act 2002 (Cth) and the International Criminal Court Act 2002 (Cth). New Zealand, Canada, France, the Netherlands, Norway, Slovenia and Switzerland have also introduced similar legislation.

375 The Brussels Convention, officially the "Convention of 27 September 1968 on Jurisdiction and the Enforcement of Judgments in Civil and Commercial Matters", (also known as the EEX Convention), was agreed in 1968 by the member states of the EU, with the goal of increasing economic efficiency and promoting the single market by harmonising the rules on jurisdiction and preventing parallel litigation. The Lugano Convention, officially the "Convention of 16 September 1988 on jurisdiction and the enforcement of judgments in civil and commercial matters", (also known as the EVEX Convention), is almost identical, and was agreed in 1988 with the then six members of the European Free Trade Area except for Liechtenstein. The Brussels I Regulation officially the Council Regulation (EC) No 44/2001 of 22 December 2000 on jurisdiction and the recognition and enforcement of judgments in civil and commercial matters (or Council Reg (EC) 44/2001 for short). In the European Union, the two earlier conventions have largely been supplanted by this Regulation which is directly applicable to all EU member states. The Regulation makes some changes to the Brussels Convention, but is generally very similar. The Regulation entered into force on March 1, 2002.

territorial and subject matter jurisdiction and only very few cases of human rights violations of corporations reach the EU courts.

However, if such a case would reach the German courts, the German Constitution provides for the application of human rights. When applying human rights law to those cases the German Constitution, as construed by the German Constitutional Court and the predominant opinion in German doctrine, requires general respect for fundamental principles of foreign legal orders.[376] As Rainer Hofmann has concluded this may however not result in violations of essential principles of the German constitutional order or of the minimum standard in the field of human rights.[377]

There have been transnational cases in other jurisdictions concerning the violation of human rights by corporations, especially in Common law countries.[378] Two of transnational cases can be counted as successful. One of them was the *Lubbe* case in England and the other one was the *Dagi* case in Australia. In *Lubbe v Cape*, 3000 claimants instigated an action against the UK corporation Cape Plc for the negligent failure to adopt safe working practice to prevent illness caused by asbestos exposure in its subsidiary in South Africa.[379] The court in the first and second instance denied jurisdiction on the grounds of *forum non convenience*. The House of Lords reversed the lower courts' decision. The key factor in its decision was that the South African legal forum did not provide a viable option to make use of legal aid or contingency fees.

In the *Dagi* decision, the Australian mining corporation, BHP, was sued for polluting the Ok Tedi River in Papua New Guinea (PNG) and adjacent land, thus prejudicing the plaintiffs' enjoyment of the relevant water and land.[380] The defendants interestingly did not seek a dismissal on the grounds of *forum non conveniens*. The High Court of Australia has adopted a *forum non conveniens* test that is more favorable to plaintiffs. A case is only dismissed if the Australian jurisdiction is "a clearly inappropriate forum."[381] In comparison, the standard for dismissal in the UK is that there exists a "more appropriate forum,"[382] and in the US "a more convenient forum."[383] In these three countries the courts appear to be a more open to becoming a forum for human rights claims in recent years.

---

376 R Hofmann, *Grundrechte und grenzüberschreitende Sachverhalte* (Springer Verlag, Berlin 1994) at 350.

377 *Ibid.* at 350.

378 See e.g., S Joseph, *Corporations and Transnational Human Rights Litigation* (Human rights law in perspective, Hart Publishing, Oxford 2004) at chapter 6 (England, Australia, and Canada); N Jägers, *Corporate Human Rights Obligations: In Search of Accountability* (Intersentia, Antwerpen 2002) at 203 et *seq.*

379 *Lubbe v. Cape plc*, 4 All ER 268 (HL) 277, U.K. House of Lords (2000).

380 *Dagi v BHP*, 1 VR 428, Australia Supreme Court of Victoria (1995).

381 *Voth v Maildra Flour Mill* 171 CLR 538, High Court of Australia (1990).

382 *Spiliada Maritime Corp v. Cansulex*, AC 460 U.K. House of Lords (1987).

383 The American notion of *forum non conveniens* relies on the *Gilbert* and *Piper* decisions: *Gulf*

The *Connelly v RTZ* case involved a throat cancer victim employed at a mine in Namibia. Mr. Connelly contended that he ought to be allowed to proceed with his case in England where he had been granted legal aid, whereas there was effectively no legal aid in Namibia. In July 1997 in a landmark ruling, the House of Lords agreed.[384] There are many further interesting human rights cases.[385] Interestingly, Switzerland, which is a civil law country, also recently allowed a claim against IBM for human rights violations during Second World War, which was finally halted by the Federal Supreme Court of Switzerland.[386]

Overall there appears to be an emerging trend towards recognizing transnational suits for human rights violations by TNCs. The cases in other jurisdictions outside of the US have often been based on tort law. These cases have often focused on preliminary matters such as *forum non conveniens* or choice of law. Other hurdles in these cases have been subject matter jurisdiction and foreign sovereign immunity. Acknowledging the growing number of human rights cases outside of the US, the US still remains the predominant forum for transnational human rights litigation involving TNCs. A very important reason for this role is the existence in the United States of the ATCA.

D. Other national instruments

Governments around the world also make use of other avenues in order to hold TNCs accountable for human rights violations, as for example in bilateral investment treaties, social and environmental reporting and other national legislative and informal activities aimed at holding corporations responsible for human rights.

The US government has utilized legislative and informal policy activities to regulate the operation of US-based corporations in countries with serious human rights issues, as was the case with the *Anti-Apartheid Act* of 1986[387] and the *Burma Freedom and Democracy Act*.[388] The Burma Act sought to prohibit any investment supporting the State Law and Order Restoration Council (SLORC), the military junta that seized

---

Oil Corp. v. Gilbert, 330 US 501, 67 SCt 839, 91 LEd 1055, US S.Ct. (1947) at 508-509 and *Piper Aircraft Co. v. Reyno*, 454 US 235, US S.Ct. (1981).

384 *Connelly v. RTZ, July 24, 1997*, 1998 Law Reports, Appeal Cases 854, U.K. House of Lords (1997).

385 For other cases see S Joseph, *Corporations and Transnational Human Rights Litigation* (Human rights law in perspective, Hart Publishing, Oxford 2004), chapter 6 and MCaHR Castan Centre for Human Rights Law, 'Transnational Human Rights Litigation against Companies' (2004) <http:// www.law.monash.edu.au/ castancentre/ projects/ mchr/ trans-hr-litigation.html> (March 8, 2006).

386 *GIRCA v. IBM*, http://jumpcgibgerch/cgi-bin/JumpCGI?id=14082006_4C113/2006, Federal Supreme Court of Switzerland (2006); A Ramasastry, 'A Swiss Court decides to allow Gypsies' Holocaust Lawsuit to proceed' (2004) <http:// writ. news. findlaw.com/ ramasastry/ 20040708.html> (March 6, 2006).

387 Anti-Apartheid Act of 1986, 22 U.S.C. § 5001 note (2000) (repealed 1994).

388 Burma Freedom and Democracy Act of 1995. H.R. Res. 2892, 104th Cong. (1995).

control of Burma in 1988. Also local governments, such as the City of San Francisco or the State of Massachusetts, have passed laws that prohibit state agencies from doing business in Burma/Myanmar.[389] These laws induced many companies to divest from Myanmar.

The *Anti-Apartheid Act* was a thorough attempt to regulate TNCs in South Africa.[390] Any US national employing more than 25 people in South Africa had to adopt the Sullivan principles. It required the entity to uphold racial non-discrimination in the workplace and supported community investment in order to increase employment opportunities for oppressed racial groups. Furthermore, the Clinton Administration promulgated the Model Business Principles in May 1995, but they have been virtually non-existent since their adoption in the sense that they have not been referred to or applied.[391]

Successful examples of enforcing human rights compliance as against TNCs were the state actions surrounding the Swiss banks Holocaust restitution case.[392] Against the background of the ATCA litigation against Swiss banks the United States government issued a report, written by then Federal Undersecretary of State, Stuart Eizenstat, which sharply criticized Swiss banks for their dealings with Nazi Germany.[393] The New York Banking Senate Committee, headed by Senator Alfonso D'Amoto, began holding hearings on the issue.[394]

Alan Hevesi, the chief financial officer of New York City threatened the Swiss banks with "rolling sanctions."[395] In step 1 he threatened to stop depositing New York short-term investments with the Swiss banks and would bar Swiss banks and investment firms from selling state and city debt unless a settlement was reached by September 1998. In step 2, private investment managers investing for the state and the city would be instructed to cease trading through Swiss firms, and in step 3 other unspecified sanctions would follow.[396] Other state treasurers announced similar

389 D Everett, 'New Concern for Transnational Corporations: Potential Liability for Tortuous Acts Committed by Foreign Partners' 35 San Diego Law Review 1123 (1998) at 1135; concerning the unconstitutionality see MB Baker, 'Flying over the judicial hump: A human rights drama featuring Burma, the Commonwealth of Massachusetts, the WTO, and the federal courts' 32 Law and Policy of international business 51 (2000).

390 L Berat, 'Undoing and Redoing Business in South Africa: The Lifting of the Comprehensive Anti-Apartheid Act of 1986 and the Continuing Validity of State and Local Anti-Apartheid Legislation' 6 Connecticut Journal of International Law 7 (1990) at 25 et *seq*.

391 MB Baker, 'Tightening the Toothless Vise: Codes of Conduct and the American Multinational Enterprise' 20 Wisconsin International Law Journal 555 (2001) at 114.

392 *In re Holocaust Victim Assets Litigation*, 105 FSupp2d 139, D.C. E.D.N.Y. (2000).

393 MJ Bazyler, *Holocaust Justice: The Battle for Restitution in America's Courts* (New York University Press, New York 2003) at 22.

394 *Ibid.* at 13-14.

395 *Ibid.* at 21 et *seq.*

396 *Ibid.* at 23.

plans.[397] The settlement of US$ 1.25 billion came one week after Moody's, the rating agency, published a report stating that UBS might lose its triple-A rating if these state sanctions were imposed.[398]

Owing to their growing role, bilateral investment treaties could be another forceful instrument to implement human rights regulations. They have little influence on customary international law, owing to their lack of *opinio juris* and their *lex specialis* character. Nevertheless, they can provide an important model for legally binding provisions between states.[399] States rarely include human rights considerations in trade and investment treaties. The EU is an exception and includes the language of human rights in trade and investment treaties.[400]

France was the first country to require publicly listed companies to report on the social and environmental impact of their business activities. Under Article 116 of the French New Economic Regulations law (*Nouvelles Régulations Economique*), companies are required to report on several social and environmental issues. 700 listed companies are now subject to this regulation.[401] Other countries, such as Denmark, the Netherlands, Norway and Sweden, require social and environmental reporting from certain types of industries.[402]

E. Analysis to national approaches

A growing number of host states, as well as home states, address the problem of human rights violations of TNCs and establish enforcement mechanisms. Home states often develop reporting mechanisms and model codes of conduct. Some nations include human rights in trade and investment treaties. With the approach of

---

397 *Ibid.* at 23.

398 MJ Bazyler and C Mesa, 'The Holocaust Restitution Movement in Comparative Perspective' 20 Berkeley Journal of International Law 11 (2002) at 17.

399 CD Wallace, 'The Legal Framework for Regulating the Global Enterprise Going Into the New WTO Trade Round--A Backward and a Forward Glance' 16 Transnational Lawyer 141 (2002) at 146.

400 UN Special Representative of the Secretary-General on human rights and transnational corporations and other business enterprises, 'A/HRC/4/35/Add.3- Human Rights Policies and Management Practices of Fortune Global 500 Firms: Results of a Survey' (2006) <http://daccess-ods.un.org/ access.nsf/ Get?Open&DS= A/HRC/4/35/Add.3&Lang=E> (May 23, 2007) at para 60. "The use of human rights provisions in bilateral trade and investment treaties is quite limited, although EU trade and investment treaties now systematically incorporate human rights. Even in the EU framework, human rights clauses are often included only in the preambles of agreements, making their legal enforceability questionable."

401 Forum citoyen pour la responsabilité sociale des entrerprises, 'Increasing corporate social and environmental reporting in France' (2005) <http:// forumcitoyenpourlarse.org/ article.php3?id_article=42> (February 10, 2006).

402 EU, 'European Commission - Employment & Social Affairs - Corporate Social Responsibility: National public policies in the European Union' <http://europa.eu.int/comm/ employment_social/ emplweb/ csr-matrix/ csr_topic_allcountries_en.cfm?field=7> (February 10, 2006).

Drittwirkung, a growing number of states judicially recognize the human rights obligations of private parties towards other private parties. A growing number of states executes extraterritorial jurisdiction, but mostly for individuals. Suing corporations criminally or civilly for extraterritorial human rights violations is still largely underdeveloped, with the exception of the ATCA litigation in the United States.

Generally, a national approach to litigate breaches of international law seems to be subsidiary to an international approach. But as long as international law does not possess any judicial organs to enforce international law as against TNCs, national courts can and should act as "trustees." Otherwise corporate malfeasance will remain unpunished for these sometimes egregious transgressions of international law. The potential of transnational litigation, such as ATCA litigation, seems very promising, since it will take a long time until an international court on non-state actors, such as TNCs, will have jurisdictional authority to sue and enforce international law.

VI. Business approaches

"One industry association official told me that his organization dropped out when the topic of discussion became the shape of the table in the tribunal chamber where companies would be tried," as Ruggie remarked in 2006, when he was laying out his UN mandate to address business and human rights.[403] This concern by that official seems to be still representative of a large proportion of industry thinking. On the other hand, the terms "Corporate Social Responsibility" (CSR), "corporate citizenship" and "corporate governance" are buzzwords of modern corporate practice. Do they really impact human rights practices? Are they an enforcement mechanism for human rights?

A. Sullivan principles

An early example of a business approach towards human rights enforcement was the Sullivan Principles concerning South Africa during the Apartheid era. They were written by an African-American General Motors board member, Leon H. Sullivan, in 1977.[404] The principles stated that whites and non-whites had to share the same work facilities and have equal job opportunities. Initially, 12 of the most prominent American companies agreed to enforce the six principles. In 1984, Sullivan added a seventh principle stating that Apartheid had to be abolished within two years. By 1986, 200 of the 260 American corporations doing business in South Africa had adopted the Sullivan principles.[405] In 1987, Sullivan called on US companies to divest their business in South Africa. In 10 months, 70 companies followed the request.

---

403 JG Ruggie, 'Speech at a Forum on Corporate Social Responsibility in Bamberg/Germany' (2006) <http://www.reports-and-materials.org/ Ruggie- remarks- to- Fair- Labor- Association-and-German- Network- of- Business- Ethics-14-June-2006.pdf> (May 24, 2007).

404 D Hauck, *Two Decades of Debate: The Controversy Over US Companies in South Africa* (Investor Responsibility Research Center, Washington, D.C. 1983) at 155.

405 P Arnold and T Hammond, 'The Role of Accounting in Ideological Conflict: Lessons from the

In 1990, the Apartheid era in South Africa ended. There were, of course, a large number of external and internal factors that contributed to the end of Apartheid, including international pressure as many UN sanctions and also the divestment movement, which contributed towards widespread economic destabilization. The MacBride Principles concerning Northern Ireland had a similar purpose as the Sullivan principles and were intended to secure equal treatment for Catholic and Protestant workers. These principles were not as successful.[406]

B. Corporate social responsibility theory

Beginning in the 1980s and 1990s, many governments presiding over planned economies began deregulating and moving toward market-based economies by allowing the private sector to make the pricing, production, and distribution decisions. The market economy faces deficiencies, such as monopolies, environmental pollution, contribution to climate change, exploitation of resources and the violation of human rights.

CSR refers to a company's obligation to be responsible for its business operations. This takes account of the conflict between social and financial goals. The view that a corporation has responsibilities in the area of human rights and environment and towards other stakeholders is contentious. The entire discussion is deeply rooted in corporate law theory.[407] There are basically two different views: the shareholder and the stakeholder view. The irresponsible view that a corporation does not need to follow any rules whatsoever will not be examined here.[408]

In a now-famous article, which refers to his book Capitalism and Freedom, Milton Friedman outlined the shareholder view. "There is one and only one social responsibility of business – to use its resources and engage in activities designed to increase its profits."[409] Henry Hansmann and Reinier Kraakman, as corporate law theorists, also support a similar shareholder theory of the corporation.[410] It states that corporations have no specific social responsibilities beyond profit-maximizing for the

---

South African Divestment Movement' 19 Accounting Organizations and Society 111 (1994) at 116.

406 Further information on the Sullivan and McBride Principles can be found at J Perez-Lopez, 'Promoting International For Workers Rights Through Business Codes of Conduct' 17 Fordham International Law Journal 1 (1993).

407 For further information see J Sarra, 'Corporate Social Responsibility in the Global Economy: Canadian Domestic Law and Legal Processes as a Vehicle for Creating and Enforcing International Norms' (2003) <http:// www.ciaj-icaj.ca/ english/ publications/ J-Sarra.pdf > (February 7, 2006).

408 For more information see CA Williams, 'Corporate Social Responsibility in an Era of Economic Globalization' 35 UC Davis Law Review 705 (2002) at 715.

409 M Friedman, 'The Social Responsibility of Business is to increase its Profits' *New York Times (Magazine)* (September 13, 1970) 32.

410 H Hansmann and R Kraakman, 'The End of History for Corporate Law' 89 Georgetown Law Journal 439 (2001) at 441.

benefit of shareholders, but that such profit-maximizing must occur within the confines of the law. Following this view, corporations meet their proper social responsibilities by excelling in their economic activities, which then contributes to a well-functioning economy by employing people, paying taxes and contributing to the social welfare system.[411]

The stakeholder view states that a corporation must be responsible to more than solely the shareholder's interests. The corporation should also take into account the interest of its supplier, its employees, its community and the state in which it is operating. It should, in essence, be responsive to the interests of all persons that are affected by its operations. In contrast to the shareholder view, it is not entirely obvious who the stakeholders are and to what degree their interests have to be taken into account. Usually proponents of this view demand higher standards of social and environmental behavior of corporations.

It seems that the two views – the shareholder and stakeholder view – may not be so divergent. Even if a strict shareholder or anti-stakeholder view is taken, there are many compelling arguments for a corporation to behave according to the standards of CSR. According to the shareholder view, the corporation has to reflect the will of the shareholders. There is evidence that a growing number of the world's population and also shareholders do not support the goal of profit-maximization at any cost. They want their corporations to follow environmental and social standards.[412] Since there is a principal-agent relationship between shareholders and corporation, the agent has to reflect the will of the principal. Since a growing number of shareholders wish their share in the corporation to be managed according to certain social and environmental standards, the corporation has to reflect this will.

And even if the shareholders would not be interested in social and environmental performance there is compelling evidence there is a correlation between ethical behavior and financial performance. There may not exactly be harmony between ethical and financial performance in the short term. The principle that ethics pay, based on Aristotle and Kant, still holds true in the long term, according to economic philosophers as Hans Jonas, Thomas Rusche, Hans Ruh and Olaf Karitzki.[413] There is

---

411 CA Williams, 'Corporate Social Responsibility in an Era of Economic Globalization' 35 UC Davis Law Review 705 (2002) at 714.

412 D Monsma and T Olson, 'Muddling through Counterfactual Materiality and Divergent Disclosure: The Necessary Search for a Duty to Disclose Material Non-Financial Information' 26 Stanford Environmental Law Journal 137 (2007) at 159 ("The market is demanding far more social and environmental disclosure today. An expanding number of socially responsible investors, in particular, specifically seek information about company management commitments and SEG performance.")

413 H Jonas, *Das Prinzip Verantwortung - Versuch einer Ethik für die technologische Zivilisation* (Suhrkamp, Frankfurt am Main 1984); H Ruh, 'Ethik und Erfolg verbünden sich: Ein neues Bündnis' in H Ruh and KM Leisinger (eds) *Ethik im Management: Ethik und Erfolg verbünden sich* (Orell Füssli, Zürich 2004) at 18 ("In ausgewählten Bereichen und bei einsichtigen

also strong empirical evidence that ethical behavior will reflect positive on the financial and overall performance of a corporation.[414]

Taking a brief glimpse at the negative correlation of financial performance and ethical behavior: Scandals in which child labor was used by Nike in the production of soccer balls or the Brent Spa oil platform sinking by Shell caused massive public outcries. This damaged the corporation's reputation and its brand image. It can also harm the sales and stock prices of those companies.[415] Therefore, many corporations are aware that they will have a more sustainable growth, when they ensure safe working conditions and social and environmental standards, as was the case with the US TNC Interface Inc. or the German TNC Otto GmbH & Co KG.[416] Even

---

Unternehmern, Aktionären und Managern setzt sich die Idee der Selbstverantwortung, der ethischen Selbstbindung, neu durch. Die genannten Defizite werden wahrgenommen und als Ethikversagen gedeutet. Die Folgerung ist klar: Wenn die Ethik nicht mehr staatlich, nicht mehr von aussen, aber auch nicht mehr von der Kirche durchgesetzt wird, dann müssen die aufgeklärten Unternehmen diese Ethik in freier Verantwortung und Selbstbindung selber durchsetzen."); T Rusche, 'Ethik und Wirtschaft im Dialog: Die Spannung von Moralität und Rentabilität in der kommunikativen Unternehmensethik' in H Ruh and KM Leisinger (eds) *Ethik im Management: Ethik und Erfolg verbünden sich* (Orell Füssli, Zürich 2004) at 50 ("Die Unternehmensethik steuert auch nicht unmittelbar das strategische und operative Handeln, sondern dient der normativen Reflexion und Weiterentwicklung der Unternehmenskultur, die ihrerseits das erfolgsorientierte Handeln der individuellen Akteure in der Unternehmung reguliert."); O Karitzki, 'Hinführung II: Auf dieHaltung kommt es an – über zu viel, zu wenig und falsches Vertrauen' in A Brink and O Karitzki (eds) *Unternehmensethik in turbulenten Zeiten Wirtschaftsführer über Ethik im Management* (Bern; Stuttgart; Wien 2004) at 90 ("Sich ein Unternehmen ohne Ethik vorzustellen ist schwierig: Unternehmen brauchen für die Leistungserstellung Menschen, und Menschen bringen, neben ihren Interessen und Fähigkeiten, auch ihre moralischen Werte in diesen Prozess mit ein. Keine Wertschöpfung ohne Wertetransfer.")

414 See e.g., C Murphy, 'The Profitable Correlation Between Environmental and Financial Performance: A Review of the Research' (2002) <http://www.lightgreen.com/files/pc.pdf> (July 19, 2007) at 14 ("Empirical research on the environmental/financial performance relationship has: 1) tested a wide variety of environmental performance indicators against a range of financial measures; and 2) found that positive environmental performance is linked with positive financial results, and that negative environmental performance leads to negative results.")

415 For the damage caused to Shell see for example: Greenpeace, 'Press Releases and Diaries from the Brent Spar Occupation' (1996) <http:// archive.greenpeace.org/ comms/ brent/ diary.html> (February 7, 2006) and J Hollender and S Fenichell, *What Matters Most: How a Small Group of Pioneers is Teaching Social Responsibility to Big Business, and why Big Business is Listening* (Basic Books, New York 2004).

416 K Brix, B Bromma and J Jaenisch, 'Nachhaltiges Unternehmertum- Diskussion des Konzeptes an Unternehmensbeispielen vom Bionier bis zum sustainable Enterpreneur' (2006) <http:// www. uni- lueneburg. de/ fb4/ institut/ ustrat/ management/ pdf-dateien/ csm_studien/ CSM_Studie_ Nachhaltiges_ Unternehmertum.pdf> (July 18, 2007) at 55 et *seq.*; Five Winds International, 'Policy Framework for Environmental Sustainability Project: Case Studies' (2004) <http:// www.pollutionprobe.org/ whatwedo/ PFR/casestudies.pdf> (July 18, 2007) at 57 et *seq.*; Interface Inc., 'Homepage' (2007) <http://www.interfaceinc.com> (June 5, 2007);

companies that are not that well respected for their human rights and environmental policies such as Wal-Mart have decided to offer organic foods.[417] Ethical and normative management seems to replace solely economic-strategic management theory.

Lastly, even if a strict anti-stakeholder view is followed, corporations have to stay within the "rules of the game,"[418] which also means that they have to comply with legal obligations to follow human rights and environmental policies. Friedman himself as one of their main proponents admits that the goal of profit-maximization can only be pursued as long as the corporation stays "within the rules of the game, which is to say, engages in open and free competition, without deception or fraud."[419] It means that they have to comply with the law. If the law enforced on the business corporation includes human rights and principles of environmental protection, because they represent national and international law, then Friedman's view also includes corporate social responsibility.

C. Corporate social responsibility in practice: codes of conduct

Sometimes just seemingly acknowledging, their responsibility as discussed above, companies increasingly adopt CSR policies and practices voluntarily.[420] The CSR movement has now grown out of its fledgling stages. Whereas in the beginning of the movement (in the 1970s) corporate managers might have neglected any social responsibility and argued that states are responsible for the protection of humans and the environment, this view is uncommon in modern corporate boardrooms.

In the first days of CSR, the term was also sometimes used for charitable donations by the corporation for community projects or art galleries. Now an increasing number of corporations are developing enforceable and elaborated codes of conduct. Codes of Conduct are often seen as an instrument to address human rights and environmental policies. Some corporations mention briefly that they would adhere to human rights in glossy brochures. Others set up regimes to monitor supply chain management combating all forms of child labor and implement standards of work and safety protection. Little of this existed as recently as five years ago.[421] An extensive

---

Otto, 'Homepage' (2007) <http://www.otto.de> (June 5, 2007).

417 A Cantisano, 'Wal-Mart Plans to Move More Aggressively into Organics, Now Its Fastest Growing Category' (2005) <http://www.organicconsumers.org/organic/walmart.cfm> (August 11, 2006); P Gogoi, 'Wal-Mart's Organic Offensive' *Business Week* 2006).

418 M Friedman, 'The Social Responsibility of Business is to increase its Profits' *New York Times (Magazine)* (September 13, 1970) 32 ("there is one and only one social responsibility of business–to use it resources and engage in activities designed to increase its profits so long as it stays within the rules of the game.")

419 *Ibid.*

420 JG Ruggie, 'Prepared Remarks at Clifford Chance, London, 19 February' (2007) .

421 UN Special Representative of the Secretary-General on human rights and transnational corporations and other business enterprises, 'A/HRC/4/74- Report of the Special Representative of the Secretary-General on the issue of human rights and transnational corporations and other

mapping of voluntary standards, as adopted by major corporations and industry initiatives, demonstrated that leading firms today recognize an array of human rights, though often haphazardly, and they have adopted at least rudimentary accountability mechanisms, including internal and external reporting.[422] One of the latest trends seems to combine the corporate competitive advantages with ethical behavior in that field.[423]

Now, almost every major company has some kind of internal code of business ethics, with varying names. Of the corporations in the market index BBC Global 30, comprising the biggest companies from different sectors from Northern America, Europe and Asia all corporations had such a code.[424]

---

business enterprises' (2007) <http://daccess-ods.un.org/ access.nsf/ Get?Open& DS=A/ HRC/ 4/74& Lang=E> at para 66.

422 UN Special Representative of the Secretary-General on human rights and transnational corporations and other business enterprises, 'A/HRC/4/35/Add.3- Human Rights Policies and Management Practices of Fortune Global 500 Firms: Results of a Survey' (2006) <http://daccess-ods.un.org/ access.nsf/ Get?Open&DS= A/HRC/ 4/35/Add.3&Lang=E> (May 23, 2007).

423 See e.g., D O'Brien, 'Integrating Corporate Social Responsibility with Competitive Strategy' (2001) <http://www.angelfire.com/ journal2/ comunicarse/ IntegratingCorporate.pdf> at 20 ("Companies who can convert their core competencies into SACs ['socially anchored competencies'] and integrate them throughout the organization will achieve a competitive advantage by employing competencies to proactively address their stakeholder interests. Companies will benefit from an enhanced reputation that comes from placing the highest value on people and the environment and carrying out actions that are consistent with these values.")

424 BBC News, 'BBC Global 30' (2007) <http:// news.bbc.co.uk/ 1/ hi/ business/ 3701740. stm> (September 6, 2007) British Petroleum (BP), 'Code of Conduct' (2007) <http:// www. bp.com/ liveassets/ bp_internet/ globalbp/ STAGING/ global_assets/ downloads/ C/ coc_ en_ full_ document.pdf> (September 6, 2007)China National Offshore Oil Corporation (CNOOC), 'Sustainable Development Report' (2007) <http:// www.cnooc.com.cn/ zhybg/ % BF% C9% B3% D6% D0% F8% B7% A2% D5% B9% B1% A8% B8% E6% D3% A2% CE% C4% B0% E6% A3% A82005% C4% EA% A3% A9.pdf> (September 6, 2007)Citigroup, 'Code of Conduct' (2007) <http:// www.citigroup.com/ citigroup/ corporategovernance/ codeconduct.htm> (September 6, 2007) ENEL, 'Code of Ethics' (2007) <http:// www.enel.com/ en/ our_company/ code_of_ethics/> (September 6, 2007) ExxonMobil, 'Corporate Citizenship Report' (2007) <http:// www.exxonmobil.com/ Corporate/ Citizenship/ CCR6/index.asp> (September 6, 2007) General Electric, 'Citizenship Report' (2007) <http:// www.ge.com/ company/ citizenship/ index.html> (September 6, 2007)HSBC, 'Corporate Responsibility Report' (2007) (September 6, 2007) Microsoft, 'Citizenship Report' (2007) <http:// download. microsoft.com/ download/7 /5 /4 /7548d2a2- 9d22- 4d2d- 8c13- 2521f6a1c148/ citizenship2006.pdf> (September 6, 2007) NewsCorp, 'Standards of Business Conduct' (2007) <http:// www.newscorp.com/ corp_gov/ sobc.html> (September 6, 2007) Nestlé, 'Corporate Business Principles' (2007) <http:// www.nestle.com/ Resource.axd?Id= 70014B84- A4FC- 4F82- BFA0- 23939DC52E9D> (September 6, 2007) Nokia, 'Sustainability Summary' (2007) <http:// www.nokia.com/ A4359260> (September 6, 2007) Novartis, 'Corporate Citizenship' (2007) <http:// www.corporatecitizenship. novartis.com/ managing-cc/ governance/ code-policies-guidelines. shtml> (September 6, 2007) Pfizer, 'Corporate Responsibility Report' (2007) <http:// www.pfizer.com/ files/ corporate_citizenship/ cc_report_2005.pdf> (September

The standards of reporting differed greatly. Nokia has a differentiated and clearly arranged corporate responsibility website outlining the company's impact (including a sustainability summary), stakeholder performance (including social supply chain management), social projects (including philanthropic projects), environmental reporting (including energy efficiency criteria) and a target chart (with issues, actions and time frames).[425] On the other hand another large TNC, the second largest corporation in terms of employees, China National Petroleum Corporation (CNPC), has issued a Social Responsibility Report in 2004, the newest available.[426] But it is rather cynical. The company proclaims on two pages, illustrating laughing Chinese managers and African children at a water fountain that "CNPC always makes unremitting efforts to care for people and environment, actively support community development, integrate the growth of company with the development of society, and finally realize the common progress." The report includes a few donations to community development mainly in the Chinese north-western region of Xinjiang. At the same time there are gravest allegations that CNPC and their shareholders the People's Republic of China has among other things "helped Sudan build its own factories to manufacture small arms and ammunition, the real weapons of mass destruction in Khartoum's campaign of ethnic cleansing."[427] A report by the Sudan Divestment movement claims that "the implied role of CNPC in the China-Sudan arms trade and the financial support it provides Khartoum through generous production-sharing agreements justifiably place CNPC as a facilitator of Darfur's genocide."[428]

Caterpillar Ltd states in its code of conduct that it "accepts the responsibilities of global citizenship" and recognizes that Caterpillar's "commitment to financial success must also take into account social, economic, political, and environmental

---

6, 2007) Procter and Gamble, 'Global Sustainability and Philanthrophy Report' (2007) <http:// www.pg.com/ content/ pdf/ 01_about_pg/ corporate_citizenship/ sustainability/ reports/ sustainability_ summary_2006.pdf> (September 6, 2007)Siemens, 'Responsibility Performance' (2007) <http:// w1.siemens.com/ en/ corporate- responsibility/> (September 6, 2007).

425 Nokia, 'Sustainability Summary' (2007) <http://www.nokia.com/A4359260> (September 6, 2007).

426 CNPC, 'Corporate Social Responsibility' (2004) <http://www.cnpc.com.cn/ Resource/ eng/ img/ 04AnnualReport/ Corporate_Social.pdf> (September 6, 2007).

427 W Hawkins, 'China's Role in Genocide' *Washington Times* 2006) A16; P Sherwell and P Goff, 'Beijing Courts New Allies with 'Black Gold Diplomacy' US Scrambles to Match China as Battle for Access to World's Oil Reserves Becomes New 'Giant Game'' *Sunday Telegraph* 2006) 28; See also Yale Law School - The Allard K. Lowenstein International Human Rights Clinic, 'An Analysis of Select Companies' Operations in Sudan: A Resource for Divestment' (2005) <http:// www.inosphere.com/ sudan/ docs/ Yale_ Lowenstein_ Updated_ Report.pdf> (July 19, 2007) at 31-36.

428 Sudan Divestment Task Force, 'PetroChina, CNPC, and Sudan: Perpetuating Genocide' (2007) <http:// www.sudandivestment.org/ docs/ PetroChina _CNPC_ Sudan.pdf> (September 6, 2007) at 5.

priorities,"[429] but it delivers machines to the Israeli army to destroy civilian property in violation of the *Fourth Geneva Convention.*[430]

There are numerous examples of such lip service. Wal-Mart has a code of conduct that includes provisions on freedom of association, bathroom breaks, drinking water, pay and work hours. Nevertheless many of their suppliers violate these rights.[431] "Apparently it seems that Wal-Mart's code of conduct is nothing but a public relations tool as once again it has become clear that Wal-Mart has no intentions of enforcing its code in any real way."[432]

As an example from the area of environmental policies, one may look at Shell. Shell claims to understand the challenges of climate change. Its website states "interest in alternatives to fossil fuels is growing rapidly as concerns over climate change and energy security increase. Today, we have one of the broadest alternative energy portfolios of any major energy company. We are working to build a substantial commercial business in at least one alternative source."[433] In reality, Shell has invested in the profitable area of solar panels, which could be done by any medium-sized business.[434] Shell could have easily invested in producing silicon, which is one of the real challenges in the alternative energy sector at the moment and which could only be achieved with huge investments.[435] Shell invests in some wind farms and some biofuels. In total, Shell's investments in, as they call it, "Wind and Solar" make up less than 1% of its total capital investment.[436] Shell extracted 1.3 billion barrels or 206 billion liters of oil in the year 2006.[437] Shell is the second largest explorer and refiner of petroleum. Petroleum usage emits approximately 3000 million tons of carbon dioxide annually. With approximately 43 per cent of total carbon dioxide emissions, petroleum is the largest contributor to global warming, as the CEO John

---

429 Caterpillar, 'Our Values in Action, Caterpillar's Worldwide Code of Conduct' (2005) <http://www.cat.com/ cda/files/89286/7/worldwide_code.pdf> .

430 *Corrie v. Caterpillar, Inc.*, 403 F Supp 2d 1019, D.C. W.D. Wash. (2005).

431 See chapter I "B. Current situation of human rights violations by TNCs" at 32.

432 International Labor Rights Fund, 'Give 'em an inch, and they'll take a mile.' (2006) <http:// www.unionvoice.org/ campaign/ ChongWon> (November 5, 2006).

433 Royal Dutch Shell plc., 'Alternative Energy' (2007) <http:// www.shell.com/ home/ Framework? siteId= envirosoc- en&FC2 =/ envirosoc-en/ html/ iwgen/ leftnavs/ zzz_lhn5_4_0. html& FC3=/ envirosoc-en/ html/ iwgen/ environment/ alternative_energy/ dir_alternative _energy_ 13042007. html> (May 9, 2007).

434 H Thie, 'Verlogene Argumente, vergiftete Köder- Hermann Scheer im Gespräch' (2006) <http:// www.freitag.de/ 2006/ 14/06140301.php> (May 9, 2007).

435 *Ibid.*

436 See their investments in their quarterly results 2006 and 2007 at Royal Dutch Shell plc., 'Investor Centre Quarterly Results' (2007) <http://www.shell.com/ home/ Framework?siteId=investor-en& FC2=/ investor- en/ html/ iwgen/ leftnavs/ zzz_lhn4_1_0.html &FC3=/ investor-en/ html/ iwgen/ quarterlyresults/ 2006/ dir_2006_qresults_index.html> (May 9, 2007).

437 Der Tagesspiegel Online, 'ExxonMobil und Shell 2006 erneut mit Rekordgewinnen' (2007) <http:// www.tagesspiegel.de/ wirtschaft/ nachrichten/ exxonmobil-shell/ 90604.asp>.

Browne of British Petroleum (BP) admits.[438] Furthermore, Shell is one of the largest gas explorers and refiners, which is the second worst contributor to the greenhouse effect.[439] Is Shell's proportionally tiny 1% investment in renewable energies a serious attempt to contribute to corporate social and environmental responsibility? It is not. The problem of carbon dioxide emissions definitely cannot be left to be regulated by voluntary business codes, it urgently needs firmer regulation. A viable approach might be to internalize the costs for the environmental externalities.

As last example of outstanding code of conduct lip service from the area of combat of corruption, one may look at Siemens. Siemens was a corporate member of Transparency International from 1998 until 2006. During this time, Siemens was involved in huge amounts of bribery in many countries. Siemens' own internal investigations have revealed dubious payments amounting to 420 million Euros over the last seven years.[440] Meanwhile, public prosecutors in at least six different countries are conducting criminal investigations.[441] The disappointed founder of Transparency International, Peter Eigen, concluded in April 2007 that Siemens was a member of Transparency International merely for the purpose of window dressing.[442]

Furthermore, there are other codes of conducts that are established by non-corporate entities, such as governments, chambers of commerce and international organizations. They are usually model codes of conduct to guide TNCs in the formulation of their own codes. Multinational corporations are the major addressees of these non-corporate codes of conduct.[443] Although the main objectives of the non-corporate codes aim to create a normative framework for TNCs, they also can contain provisions directed at regulating the role of governments.[444]

The International Chamber of Commerce (ICC) was possibly among the first organization to produce guidelines for corporate behavior, the 1972 *ICC Guidelines*

---

438 J Browne, 'Climate Change Speech' (1997) <http:// www.preen.org/ bpspeech.htm> (May 9, 2007).

439 Carbon Dioxide Information Analysis Center, 'Global CO2 Emmissions from Fossil-Fuels and Cement - Production in million metric tonnes of carbon' (2007) <http:// cdiac.ornl.gov/ trends/ emis/ glo.htm> (May 9, 2007).

440 Tagesschau.de, 'Noch mehr Geld verschwunden als gedacht?' (2006) <http:// www.tagesschau.de/ aktuell/ meldungen/ 0,,OID6175366_REF1,00.html> (May 25, 2007).

441 M Esterl and D Crawford, 'Why Siemens Bribery Probe Slogs On' *The Wall Street Journal* 2007) A12.

442 B Grill, 'Wir sitzen im Glashaus- Der deutsche Antikorruptionskämpfer Peter Eigen über seine Initiative für Entwicklungsländer, den G8-Gipfel und seine große Enttäuschung über Siemens' *DIE ZEIT* 2007).

443 HS Pérez Loose, *Changing the International Regime for Multinational Corporations through Codes of Conduct from Harsh words to "Soft Law"; Doctoral thesis, Harvard Law School* (Cambridge 1988) at 425.

444 *Ibid.* at 437.

for International Investment.[445] Another early example of a code is the Infant Formula Code of the WHO.[446] Most model codes of conduct stem from industry associations such as the International Council of Toy Industries, Worldwide Responsible Apparel Production, Electronic Industry Code of Conduct, the Equator Principles, and the International Council on Mining and Metals. Social Accountability 8000, the Ethical Trade Initiative, and the Fair Labor Association are multi-stakeholder initiatives. Examples from the UN and their agencies are the UN Code on Transnational Corporations,[447] the Code of Conduct for Liner Conferences,[448] the Code on Restrictive Business Practices,[449] and the Code of Conduct on Transfer of Technology.[450] Additionally, some countries have set up model codes of conduct.[451]

One example of a multi-stakeholder Code of Conduct, the "Voluntary Principles on Security and Human Rights," is briefly examined here.[452] This initiative was launched in December 2000 under the leadership of the US Department of State and the UK Foreign Office. The original members of the contact group included Chevron, Shell and BP and NGOs, such as AI and HRW. The participating members now include the Netherlands and Norway as well as other corporations.

The purpose of the Voluntary Principles was to develop specific guidelines for companies on ways they should handle their security arrangements that would be consistent with international standards on human rights. They involve things like performing human rights risk assessments, checking on the human rights records of

---

445 CD Wallace, *Legal Control of the Multinational Enterprise: National Regulatory Techniques and the Prospects for International Controls* (M.Nijhoff, The Hague 1983) at 298.

446 J Baker, 'The International Infant Formula Controversy: A Dilemma in Corporate Social Responsibility' 4 Journal of Business Ethics 181 (1985) at 183.

447 For example HS Pérez Loose, *Changing the International Regime for Multinational Corporations through Codes of Conduct from Harsh words to "Soft Law"; Doctoral thesis, Harvard Law School* (Cambridge 1988) at 300.

448 *Ibid.* at 246.

449 *Ibid.* at 271.

450 *Ibid.* at 321. Other early UN instruments include the United Nations Conference on Trade and Development (UNCTAD) Code of Conduct on the Transfer of Technology Code from 1975 and the UNCTAD Set of Multilaterally Agreed Equitable Principles and Rules for the Control of Restrictive Business Practices from 1980.

451 The Government of the United States promoted a set of five brief "Model Business Principles" that were developed in 1995 after consultation with business, labor and other NGOs. In addition, the administration has fostered the development of industry-based codes as for example, the White House Apparel Industry Partnership program. The Government of the United Kingdom supported the "Ethical Trading Initiative" in 1998 that brought together business, labor and NGOs to discuss standards and monitoring methods that address working condition issues in corporate supply chains. The Government of India cooperated in developing the "Rugmark" label aimed at promoting child labor standards.

452 Voluntary Principles on Security and Human Rights, Welcome available at http:// www.voluntaryprinciples.org/ (September 8, 2007) (2000).

the security forces that are being deployed. The adherence to these principles is as the name suggests entirely voluntary. There is no formal mechanism for monitoring company compliance or auditing performance. Facing the grave human rights violations in the extractive industry sector, especially from some of the members of the Voluntary Principles, one scholar commented that it is hard to see how these concerns can be effectively addressed through voluntary self-regulation.[453]

Even though it has been developing for some decades, the code of conduct movement has not attained legal maturity. There is a need to rearrange and define the responsibilities at the different hierarchical layers and, most importantly, the enforcement of the codes of conduct needs to be improved. Mere lip service to human rights or environmental standards is insufficient. The biggest problem in regards to voluntary codes of conduct is the lack of enforceability. There remain many corporations that claim that they comply with social and environmental values, but do not adhere to them in practice.

Despite all these glaring negative examples, codes of conducts do still have some beneficial effects, when they are appropriately communicated. One of the most important effects is that they have contributed to a worldwide learning process with regard to the ethical operations of TNCs.[454] They have delegitimatized certain practices of TNCs, as with the Infant Formula code of the WHO; or in the recent case of large-scale corruption involving Siemens.[455] They have the effect of legitimizing host state actions as against TNCs.[456] Many companies feel the need to change their overall policies. A progressive model proposed by the German expert on business ethics, Josef Wieland, is partially to determine the remuneration based on qualitative criteria such as ethical behavior.[457]

A new element of the usefulness of codes of conduct was possibly added by the *Nike* case.[458] Nike made public statements in its code of conduct for public relation purposes that it would protect workers' rights and institute safe working conditions in the factories of their suppliers in South East Asia. Nike was sued in California for

---

453 MJ Watts, 'Righteous Oil? Human Rights, the Oil Complex, and Corporate Social Responsibility' 30 Annual Review of Environmental Resources 373 (2005) at 401.

454 HS Pérez Loose, *Changing the International Regime for Multinational Corporations through Codes of Conduct from Harsh words to "Soft Law"; Doctoral thesis, Harvard Law School* (Cambridge 1988) at 457.

455 DH Lamparter, 'Im Visier der Justiz; Siemens, Daimler, VW: In Deutschlands Konzernen werden immer mehr Korruptionsfälle aufgedeckt' *DIE ZEIT* (November 23, 2006) 27.

456 HS Pérez Loose, *Changing the International Regime for Multinational Corporations through Codes of Conduct from Harsh words to "Soft Law"; Doctoral thesis, Harvard Law School* (Cambridge 1988) at 459.

457 DH Lamparter, '"Verpfeifen kommt zuletzt"; Gegen Korruption hilft nur ein radikaler Bruch in der Kultur des Unternehmens, sagt Wirtschaftsethiker Josef Wieland' *DIE ZEIT* (November 23, 2006) 27.

458 *Kasky v. Nike*, 24 Cal 4th 939, US SCt. Cal. (2002).

making false and misleading statements and agreed to settle at US$ 1.5 million to the Fair Labor Association (FLA).[459]

D. Triple bottom line reporting

In the 1980s, some companies started to address human rights and environmental policies, but there has not been any standardized reporting practice. Triple bottom line reporting intends to capture an expanded spectrum of values and criteria for measuring organizational success. In practice, triple bottom line accounting usually means expanding the traditional company reporting framework to take into account not just financial outcomes but also environmental and social performance.

Environmental and social reporting is still developing and there are many open questions and problems. Which issues should be covered? How should they be measured? Who are the key audiences? Even though there are encouraging examples of triple bottom line reporting, such as Interface Inc., the largest carpet manufacturer of the world, the idea has not yet become prevalent in corporate practice.[460] In order to protect the environment and social values triple bottom line reporting appears to be a very promising path. The NGO Sustainability, the rating agency Standard & Poor's and the UN Environment Programme (UNEP) recently surveyed the social and environmental transparency of the leading companies of the world. First ranked was the British company, British Telecom.[461] However, according to the study, the quality of the social and environmental reporting and the criteria still varied widely. The Global Reporting Initiative (GRI) aims to develop and improve sustainability reporting and is currently recognized as the international standard in sustainability reporting.[462] 1000 companies from over 60 countries report according to GRI's reporting framework. In some countries, sustainability reporting is mandatory and auditing is emerging, albeit that this is little used currently.[463]

E. Human rights assessments

Relatively few of the biggest corporations worldwide conduct systematic human rights impact assessments routinely. In the view of Ruggie, the UN Special Representative for Business and Human Rights, no single measure would yield more immediate results in the human rights performance of firms than conducting such assessments routinely where a significant human rights impact could be expected.[464]

---

459 B Egelko, 'Nike settles suit for $ 1,5 million: Shoe giant accused of lying about workers' treatment' *San Francisco Chronicle* (September 13, 2003) B1 at 949.

460 Interface Inc., 'Homepage' (2007) <http://www.interfaceinc.com> (June 5, 2007).

461 S Bergius, 'Investoren fordern Nachhaltigkeit' *Handelsblatt* (February 8, 2006) 27.

462 Global Reporting Initiative, 'Homepage' (2007) <http:// www.globalreporting.org/Home> (September 9, 2007).

463 C Morris, 'The Triple Bottom Line- A talk with Alyson Slator, Communications Director at the Global Reporting Initiative' (2007) <http:// www.heise.de/tp/r4/artikel/24/24531/1.html> (March 2, 2007).

464 John Ruggie in UN Human Rights Council, 'Press Release- Council Discusses Human Rights

F. Analysis to business approaches

The negative side of voluntary approaches was summed up by Engle in the following way: "While codes of conduct are thus not completely useless, believing that corporate self regulation alone will prevent human rights abuses in the name of profits requires either naiveté or disingenuity. Corporate social responsibility is usually nothing other than a public relations exercise, at best intended to improve the image of the corporation and at worst to whitewash corporate exploitation and delay the establishment of binding legal norms. [...] Empirical studies have shown that codes of conduct generally do not influence corporate behavior. [...] For these reasons codes of conduct should be viewed with skepticism."[465]

On the positive side, it can be noted that the practices of business towards human rights are gradually changing. Whereas in the middle of the twentieth century responsibility for the treatment of its employees was often passed on to states, the notion of corporate social responsibility of corporations seems to be accepted now. The enforcement of the Sullivan principles in the 1970s was a successful example of how human rights issues can be addressed and corporations started to revise their thinking. Companies increasingly publish environmental and social reports and even hire independent auditors to monitor the implementation of social and environmental standards. Corporations are often motivated by the deeper insight that sustainable environmental and social policies can lead to more sustainable and profitable business strategies. Rightfully their mantra is: "Doing well while doing good."[466]

VII. NGO approaches

An important role in enforcing human rights as against TNCs is that by non-governmental organizations (NGOs). In the case of NGOs, the addressor and the addressee of the regulation are from the private sector. With the approaches chosen by international law the problem is that they can only succeed when an international or at least multinational consensus is found, which is hard to achieve in this evolving area of law. The problem of national regulation is that they are territorially limited. Business approaches are normally confined to one company or one branch in one country. Approaching the regulation of TNCs by NGOs appears to be promising, because of their internationality and flexibility. NGOs have been active especially in the area of labeling, monitoring, raising publicity and building partnerships with TNCs.

---

and Transnational Corporations, Right to Health and Human Rights Defenders' (2007) <http:// www.unhchr.ch/ huricane/ huricane.nsf/ view01/ 19207DD921EE5D22C12572AC00702E2C? opendocument> (May 23, 2007).

465 EA Engle, *Alien Torts in Europe? Human Rights and Tort in European Law* (Bremen 2005) at page 125.

466 See above in this chapter at subheading "B. Corporate social responsibility theory" at 85.

In the last couple of years, a sophisticated system of monitoring and labeling schemes – involving social and environmental labels – has developed. The social labels can be subdivided into workplace standards and CSR quality management standards.

A successful example of a NGO labeling and monitoring regime in the area of workplace standards is SA 8000, which was launched in 1998 by Social Accountability International (SAI). The SA 8000 standard seeks to ensure that certain benchmarks are applied to workplace practices through accredited and independent third party auditing. It is based on international human right norms, such as core ILO standards, the *UDHR* and the *UN Convention on the Rights of the Child*. It measures the performance of companies in eight areas: child labor, forced labor, health and safety, free association and collective bargaining, discrimination, disciplinary practices, working hours and compensation.[467] Manufacturers and suppliers seeking certification to SA 8000 must adopt and implement a program to pursue SA 8000 certification. Once the auditor has determined that the factory does not have any "major non conformance," a certificate will be issued for a period of three years, during which it will be re-examined. Other social labeling schemes include the Ethical Trading Initiative, Fair Labor Association, Worldwide Responsible Apparel Production, Rugmark and many others.[468]

Codes of conduct were set up by Clean Clothes Campaign Code of Labor Practices, AI, ICFTU Basic Code of Labor Practice and many others.[469] Presently, AI has possibly the most comprehensive and progressive guidelines for regulating the activities of TNCs vis-à-vis human rights. They include: company policy on human rights; security arrangements; respecting the rights of the local community; freedom from discrimination; freedom from slavery; health and safety; freedom of association and the right of collective bargaining; fair working conditions; and credible and periodical mechanisms to monitor effectively all operations' compliance with codes of conduct and international human rights standards.[470]

Social reporting standards were set by the Global Reporting Initiative, AccountAbility AA1000, Association of Chartered Certified Accountants, the International Corporate Sustainability Reporting Site and many others.[471] As noted above, social and environmental reporting has not yet become a prevalent business

467 Social Accountability International(2007) <http://www.sa-intl.org> (June 5, 2007).

468 For more information see EU, 'ABC of the main instruments of Corporate Social Responsibility' (2004) <http:// ec. europa.eu/ employment_ social/ publications/ 2005/ ke1103004_ de.html> (March 1, 2006) at 41 et *seq*.

469 For more information see *Ibid.* at 7 et *seq*.

470 Amnesty International, 'Human Rights Principles for Companies' (1998) <http:// web.amnesty.org/ library/ index/ engACT700011998? open&of =eng-398> (February 10, 2006).

471 For more information see EU, 'ABC of the main instruments of Corporate Social Responsibility' (2004) <http:// ec.europa.eu/ employment_social/ publications/ 2005/ ke1103004_de.html> (March 1, 2006) at 28 et *seq*.

practice. Even in France where it is mandatory many problems are not resolved yet, as for example how to report on internal human resources issues and their wider impact on society.[472] In future, it may become as important as financial reporting.

Important campaigns against human rights violations have been led by HRW, Multinational Monitor, Bonded Labor Liberation Front, the Foul Ball Campaign and many other local and international organizations. An early example of high profile NGO campaigns was the boycott against Nestlé.[473] The reason for the boycott was that allegedly in developing countries infants who are artificially fed are 25 more time at risk of death due to diarrheal disease as compared to those who are breastfed. Nestlé allegedly resorted to improper practices in the marketing of breast milk substitutes directly with pregnant women.[474] The Boycott was initiated by a non-governmental organization in the 1970s and it has led to the adoption of the International Code of Marketing of Breast-milk Substitutes by the WHO. The Code prohibits advertising of infant feeding products to the public and prohibits free samples to mothers or health care workers.[475] Some claim that Nestlé continues to violate these provisions,[476] whereas others claim that Nestlé has not endangered infant health and the activists have used improper scientific methods to prove their allegations.[477]

HRW has set up a special group on human rights and business that has issued numerous detailed reports on human rights violations by corporations. A 159-page report documents how a leading gold mining company, AngloGold Ashanti, developed links with a murderous armed group that committed war crimes in the Democratic Republic of Congo.[478] Another report details the hazardous child labor involved in harvesting sugar cane, which is then purchased by the Coca-Cola

---

472 E Hoffmann, 'Environmental Reporting and Sustainability Reporting in Europe - An Overview of Mandatory Reporting Schemes in the Netherlands and France' (2003) <http:// www.iges.or.jp/ en/ phase2/ be/ pdf/ report7.pdf> (July 18, 2007) at 23.

473 NE Zelman, 'The Nestle Infant Formula Controversy: Restricting the Marketing Practices of Multinational Corporations in the Third World' 3 Transnational Lawyer 697 (1990) at 720 et *seq.*

474 J Baker, 'The International Infant Formula Controversy: A Dilemma in Corporate Social Responsibility' 4 Journal of Business Ethics 181 (1985) at 181 et *seq.*

475 WHO International Code of Marketing of Breastmilk Substitutes WHA Res 3422 Annex, WHO ocl A34/VR/15 (1981).

476 J Wise, 'Baby Milk Companies Accused of Breaching Marketing Code' (1997) <http:// www.bmj.com/ cgi/ content/ full/ 314/ 7075/ 165/e> (July 18, 2007); INFACT Canada, 'Examples of Nestlé's International Code Violations' (2005) <http:// www.infactcanada.ca/ The% 20Nestle%2 0Boycott.pdf> (May 25, 2007).

477 LH Newton, 'Truth is the Daughter of Time: The Real Story of the Nestle Case' 104 Business and Society Review 367 (2000).

478 Human Rights Watch, 'The Curse of Gold' (2005) <http:// hrw.org/ reports/2005/drc0505.> (May 28, 2007).

Company.[479] There are various other appalling accounts of businesses violating human rights.[480]

Another very successful campaign was spearheaded by the American Anti-Slavery Group, which was aimed directly at the major institutional investors holding stock in the Canadian company, Talisman. Talisman was involved in a project in Sudan and the government of Sudan was reliant on oil revenues for its genocidal war efforts.[481] AI, the American Anti-Slavery Group, the Canadian Inter-Church Coalition and many other NGOs joined the tidal wave of protest.[482] The Ontario Teachers' Pension Plan threatened to sell their shares if the company did not pull out of Sudan. Despite large profits from its operations in Sudan, Talisman's stock steadily fell. In 2003, Talisman agreed to withdraw from Sudan.[483] After Talisman and the Austrian company withdrew, other corporations such as the China National Petroleum Corporation (CNPC) and the Indian company ONGC Videsh took over.

Overall, it can be noted that NGOs have played a vital and irreplaceable role in enforcing human rights as against TNCs. They have often played the role of international watchdogs. They have raised publicity and have thereby compelled TNCs to change their behavior regarding human rights. Nestlé, Shell, McDonalds, Coca Cola, Nike and Citigroup are among numerous prominent corporations that have suffered the wrath of high profile negative campaigns.[484] NGOs might possibly play a decisive role in monitoring and enforcing codes of conduct. The problem is that NGOs cannot finally solve the problem of human rights violations of TNCs on a global scale. Corporate rogues or moral free riders can always take over the business practice of those corporations that were forced to comply with human rights, as in the case of Sudan. Another problem of NGOs is that of legitimacy. NGOs are only accountable to their donors and not to all people.[485]

---

479 Human Rights Watch, 'Turning a Blind Eye- Hazardous Child Labour in El Salvador's Sugarcane Cultivation' (2004) <http:// hrw.org/ reports/2004/elsalvador0604/> (May 28, 2007).

480 Human Rights Watch, 'Human Rights and Business Reports' (2007) <http:// hrw.org/ doc/ ?t=corporations_pub> (May 28, 2007).

481 Pub. L. No. 107-245, 116 Stat. 1504, § 6 (2002) (The US Sudan Peace Act included a Congressional finding that the government of Sudan had committed genocide and a finding that the Sudan government would use sales of oil to finance continued military action to regain control of Sudanese territory, the same military action that led to genocide.); HRW, 'Sudan, Oil, and Human Rights' (2003b) <http:// www.hrw.org/ reports/ 2003/ sudan1103/> (September 8, 2007) at subheading "Government Uses Oil Wealth for Arms Imports and Industry" in part III.

482 SJ Kobrin, 'Oil and Politics: Talisman Energy and Sudan' 36 International Law and Politics 425 (2004) at 439.

483 See *Ibid.*

484 See, e.g., for the Shell campaigns, J Lobe, 'Shell under fire from greens, shareholders' *OneWorld US* (December 23, 2004), or for a campaign against Citigroup, S Bergius, 'Banken entdecken die Moral' *Handelsblatt* (December 6, 2005) 30- 10,000 clients run away from Citigroup in 2003 after an appeal by the "Rainforest Action Network."

485 Concerning the legitimating theories see K Nowrot, *Normative Ordnungsstruktur und private Wirkungsmacht - Konsequenzen der Beteiligung transnationaler Unternehmen an den*

VIII. Consumer approaches

Living in a consumer society has given rise to some consumers questioning their consumption choices more thoroughly in recent years. Another trend is that of ethical investment with a growing number of people possessing increasing amounts of money especially in Western society. These two trends, ethical consumption and ethical investment, shall be examined briefly insofar as they relate to the enforcement of human rights as against TNCs. Are these two consumer approaches sufficiently forceful and viable?

A. Ethical consumerism

Ethical consumerism, simply put, means buying things or refraining from buying things on the basis of ethical considerations.[486] A variety of issues are often defined as ethical concerns, including environmental sustainability, health and safety risks, animal welfare, fair trade, labor conditions, and human rights. Ethical consumption is done either by favoring or by avoiding products or companies. Early ethical consumerism can be seen in Gandhi's use of consumer boycotts, the principle of *swadeshi* in the struggle for Indian independence in the early 20th century. The boom time of ethical consumption began in the late 1980s when groups opposed to animal-testing started using consumer boycotts to a significant effect. By 1990, three of the world's four biggest cosmetics companies had been persuaded to abandon at least some types of animal testing.[487]

Surveys show that ethical consumerism is an emerging force. There is a growing interest among consumers to know more about the origins of the food and other products they buy. In a 2004 survey on the US west coast, more than 80 percent of respondents endorsed the idea of food labels as a source of information they are seeking.[488] Europeans are even more committed to the idea of ethical consumption, and regional and local labels are more prevalent there. Phil Howard, a researcher at the University of California, Santa Cruz Center for Agroecology & Sustainable Food Systems, stated: "The fair-trade movement began in Europe and is already changing the production practices of products like coffee and bananas."[489]

Rechtssetzungsprozessen im internationalen Wirtschaftssystem (BWV Berliner Wissenschafts-Verlag, Berlin 2006) at 626 et *seq.* (According to Nowrot we are heading towards a less state-centric and more output-orientated legitimacy in international law.)

486 Women & the economy (A project of UNPAC), 'Ethical consumption' <http:// unpac.ca/ economy/ ethicconsumption.html> (February 13, 2006); A list of companies and countries currently being boycotted can be found on the website: E Consumer, 'Boycotts list' <http:// www.ethicalconsumer.org/ boycotts/ boycotts_list.htm> (February 13, 2006).

487 R Harrison, 'The rise and rise of ethical consumerism' 50 Ethical consumer magazine (1997).

488 J McNulty, 'Consumers eager to know more about the environmental and social impacts of the food they buy, survey finds, January 24, 2005, available at ' (2005) <http:// www.ucsc.edu/ news_events/ press_releases/ text.asp?pid=629> (February 13, 2006).

489 *Ibid.*

In surveys people often express great willingness to pay more for products that comply with high ethical standards. In Howard's survey the median price people were willing to pay more was 71 percent above the regular price for strawberries, which are handpicked according to social standards. "[A] November 1999 study by Marymount University's Center for Ethical Concerns also found that Americans would pay more for non-sweatshop garments. In that poll, 86% said that they would be willing to pay up to US$ 1 more for a $20 garment guaranteed to be made in a legitimate shop."[490]

However, while it should be acknowledged that people being surveyed regularly express greater willingness to pay than they actually do in the marketplace, the results show the potential level of support for ethical consumption. Ethical consumption is rising steadily. Last year, UK consumers spent £25 billion (approximately US$ 43.63 billion) on ethical goods and services – a rise of 15 percent on 2003.[491] Bernd Pischetsrieder, former CEO of BMW and Volkswagen said that as the consumers increasingly base their thoughts on ethical considerations, the company has to reflect those thoughts in their ethics.[492]

B. Socially responsible investment

Another powerful consumer approach to control the activities of TNCs is social investing. Social investing began in the 1920s with churches, which divested themselves of the so-called "sin stocks" – alcohol, tobacco and gambling. Now, the Interfaith Center on Corporate Responsibility (ICCR) is an umbrella organization that helps to orchestrate the activities of 285 responsible investing institutions that collectively control more than US$ 110 billion in investment assets. The idea and concept behind socially responsible investing (SRI) is similar to that of ethical consumerism. There are four kinds of SRI: screening, community investing, shareholders activism, and investment integration. The overall amount of money invested in one or more of the SRI strategies grew to US$ 2.29 trillion in 2005. Nearly one in ten dollars is now invested in SRI. Since 1995, there has been a 258 percent growth in overall SRI investment, which has slightly outpaced the 249

490 Program on International Policy Attitudes (PIPA), 'Americans on Globalization: A Study of US Public Attitudes' (2000) <http:// www.pipa.org/ OnlineReports/ Globalization/ executive_ summary.html> (February 13, 2006) at 37.

491 M Hickmann, 'U.K. market for organic & fair trade clothes & other products growing rapidly' (2005) <http:// www.organicconsumers.org/ btc/market121205.cfm> (February 13, 2006).

492 B Pischetsrieder, 'Konzernwerte als Grundlage ökonomischen Erfolgs – oder: Was hat Transparenz mit Ethik zu tun?' in A Brink and O Karitzki (eds) *Unternehmensethik in turbulenten Zeiten- Wirtschaftsführer über Ethik im Management* (Haupt, Bern; Stuttgart; Wien 2004) at 96: "Und weil Menschen ihr Verhalten an ethischen Grundwerten orientieren, müssen zwangsläufig im Unternehmen Werte gelten, die mit den gesellschaftlichen Werten übereinstimmen und die von den Menschen aus ihrem sozialen Umfeld in das Unternehmen transportiert werden."

percent rise in the overall market.[493] The range of products for social investors is increasingly diversified.[494]

Screening stands for the inclusion or exclusion of stocks and shares in investment portfolios. The most commonly used social screen is the exclusion of tobacco. Some 162 of 201 (that is, 88 percent) socially screened funds in the US use this screen.[495] Recently, a number of SRI and sustainability indices have been introduced, including the Dow Jones Sustainability Index, the FTSE4 Good, the Domini 400 Social Index and the Ethibel Sustainability Index. Some are based on exclusion criteria, while others also look at the overall social and ethical performance. The amount invested in socially responsible investments in Europe has passed €1 trillion. Approximately 15 per cent of total funds under management in Europe now follow socially responsible criteria – a growth of 36 per cent since December 2002.[496]

Community investing involves providing funds to socially beneficial projects, especially those that would otherwise find it difficult to attract capital, including micro credits to small farmers. Of the different types of SRI methods, community investment has grown the most in the last ten years. In 1995 community investing assets totaled US$ 4 billion and has since grown almost 400 percent to $19.6 billion.[497]

Shareholder activism involves engaging with company management to achieve a positive change. It seeks to influence a company's behavior through dialog regarding the company's behavior. In 2002, for example, nearly 33 percent of Unocal's shareholders attending the company's annual meeting approved an activist-led proposal urging the company to follow ILO human rights standards in Myanmar. "This is probably the most successful shareholder resolution ever on human rights."[498] Another example is a shareholder resolution brought forward by New York City's public pension funds on Freeport McMoran's human rights policy and in

---

493 W Baue, 'Social investment forum trends report tracks rises and falls of socially responsible investing' (2006) <http://www.socialfunds.com/ news/ article.cgi/ 1913.html> (February 14, 2006).

494 S Bergius, 'Dachfonds entdecken Nachhaltigkeit' *Handelsblatt* (February 8, 2006) 33.

495 W Baue, 'Social investment forum trends report tracks rises and falls of socially responsible investing' (2006) <http://www.socialfunds.com/ news/ article.cgi/ 1913.html> (February 14, 2006).

496 London Stock Exchange, 'European socially responsible investment reaches €1 trillion' (2006) <http:// www.londonstockexchange.com/en-gb/ pricesnews/ investnews/ article.htm? ArticleID= 17643852> (September 26, 2006).

497 W Baue, 'Social investment forum trends report tracks rises and falls of socially responsible investing' (2006) <http:// www.socialfunds.com/ news/ article.cgi/ 1913.html> (February 14, 2006).

498 David Schilling, director of the Global Corporate Accountability Program of the ICCR in: As you sow, 'Current Initiatives, Human rights abuses by US companies overseas Unocal Corp.' <http:// www.asyousow.org/ unocal.htm> (February 14, 2006).

particular its relationship with the Indonesian army in Papua New Guinea.[499] Even the legendary investor, philanthropist and one of richest persons in the world, Warren Buffet, faces growing criticism, especially from the NGO Sudan Divestment Task Force, for the investment of his fund Berkshire Hathaway with Petro China, a subsidiary of China National Petroleum Corporation (CNPC).[500] Petro China is alleged to be heavily involved in the Sudanese genocide.[501] Whereas Fidelity has sold 90% of its assets of Petrochina, Buffet's Berkshire Hathaway fund has not given in to the steadily growing criticism.[502] The number of social and environmental shareholder resolutions filed increased from 299 in 2003 to 348 in 2005. Assets managed using shareholder advocacy also rose from US$ 448 billion in 2003 to $703 billion in 2005.[503]

Investment integration involves seeking to integrate social and environmental criteria with conventional financial analysis. Several states such as Belgium, Germany, France, Sweden and the UK have adopted disclosure regulations requiring pension funds to state whether they take account of social, environmental and ethical criteria in their investment decisions, and if so, how.[504]

An oft-repeated criticism of SRI is that social investors sacrifice investment return in order to stay in line with their ethical values. This allegation is not supported by the evidence.[505] The Domini Social Index is based on the S&P 500 Index and applies a broad range of social and environmental screening. It outperformed the S&P 500 during its 15-year history. Companies will financially benefit from an enhanced social responsible investment.[506]

---

499 J Sabatini, 'Shareholder Activism, New York City funds push Freeport McMoran to improve human-rights policy' (2003) <http:// www.minesandcommunities.org/ Action/ press108.htm> (February 14, 2006).

500 S Kirchgaessner, 'World News: Darfur activists target US investors' *Financial Times Europe* (September 6, 2007) 6.

501 H Buchter, 'Der gute Mensch und der Völkermord' *Financial Times Deutschland* (April 23, 2007) 1; See also above in this chapter at subheading "VI. Business approaches" at footnote 427.

502 E Ng, 'Fidelity sells down ADR holding in PetroChina' *South China Morning Post* (May 17, 2007).

503 W Baue, 'Social investment forum trends report tracks rises and falls of socially responsible investing' (2006) <http:// www.socialfunds.com/ news/ article.cgi/1913.html> (February 14, 2006).

504 EU, 'ABC of the main instruments of Corporate Social Responsibility' (2004) <http:// ec.europa.eu/ employment_social/ publications/ 2005/ ke1103004_de.html> (March 1, 2006) at 49.

505 See also above in this chapter at subheading "B. Corporate social responsibility theory."

506 See e.g., on the strategic perspective D O'Brien, 'Integrating Corporate Social Responsibility with Competitive Strategy' (2001) <http:// www.angelfire.com/ journal2/ comunicarse/ IntegratingCorporate.pdf> ; On the financial perspective: P Sethi, 'Investing in Socially Responsible Companies is a must for Public Pension Funds - Because there is no Alternative' 56 Journal of Business Ethics 99 (2005).

C. Analysis to consumer approaches

It seems that a growing number of corporations worldwide adhere to human rights and the problem of human rights violations by TNCs might be reduced. Ethical consumerism and SRI have experienced a strong surge in popularity in recent decades. The consumer approach can be said to be the most powerful avenue to enforce human rights. Corporations will respond to the wishes of consumers, because of the mechanics of supply and demand. The case of Talisman showed how investors forced a company to comply with human rights standards. But it also showed that not all consumers and investors care about ethical standards in consumption and investment, as it can be noticed momentarily in the case of Warren Buffett and his fund Berkshire Hathaway that seems to be indifferent about the involvement of CNPC and Petrochina in the Sudanese atrocities in Darfur. Therefore, not all corporations will act ethically; again this highlights the problem of the moral free rider. So there will always be corporations that violate human rights. That is why regulatory avenues for enforcing accountability are necessary.

IX. Concluding remarks to Chapter II

The problem of human rights abuses by TNCs are not yet sufficiently addressed by international law. The level of enforcement is insufficient. There is still a high rate of corporate malfeasance concerning human rights internationally. The perception of human rights has appeared to change gradually, but moral free riders may still get away without being held accountable. Most victims of human rights violations of TNCs are left without redress.

There is a trend of recognition of state responsibility for the acts of non-state actors, but it simply cannot be seen as powerful instrument at the moment. National judicial approaches to the problem of human rights violations of TNCs are of increasing importance, but seldom apply extraterritorially. Business approaches are concentrated around voluntary principles. Principally, it is a positive development that TNCs started to acknowledge their obligations, but voluntary business compliance methods can often be viewed with skepticism. NGOs, the media and consumers play a crucial role in pressing TNCs to adhere to human rights. Nevertheless they cannot replace judicial review of human rights violations of TNCs.

Having reviewed the various instruments, there seem to be three major conclusions. First, the web of corporate liability for human rights violations is gradually tightening. Second, only with a combination of those avenues mentioned above is it possible to address the problem of human rights violations of TNCs. When a human rights clinic or a human rights lawyer is confronted with an alleged human rights violation, they will have to consider all different avenues and select the one that is most likely to result in a successful outcome. Very often the most successful strategy will be an integrated approach. The most viable approaches in addressing human rights violations are litigation, shaming and boycotting campaigns, negotiation, political avenues and fact-finding missions. A prime example of an integrated approach was the Holocaust restitution campaign, where it was possible to threaten litigation and use political negotiation and other approaches in order to achieve a successful restitution outcome. Third, the best possibility to force TNCs to adhere to human rights at the moment is transnational litigation, such as ATCA litigation.

Chapter III. ATCA

"The law of nations generally does not create private causes of action to remedy its violations, but leaves to each nation the task of defining the remedies that are available for international law violations;"[507] this finding from the *Kadic* decision is simple and striking. The United States courts succeeded in creating a viable path to enforce human rights. It stands as one of the most potent human rights enforcement mechanism.[508]

Transnational litigation still stands as the only viable path, because the international courts do not have jurisdiction over TNCs and transnational litigation might fill this gap until such an international judicial forum is created, which might take a long time. It is unjust to provide no mechanism for the adjudication of these breaches of international law, thereby allowing severe corporate crimes to go unpunished. Transnational litigation plays a crucial role in enforcing human rights. Only the threat of litigation is likely to make *all* TNCs comply with human rights law. For example, the threat of US litigation involving the Holocaust cases was critical in inducing the German Government and German corporations to settle the claims of former slave laborers.[509]

There is no other country in the world that has a statute like the ATCA.[510] ATCA is a unique and peculiar provision.[511] Its existence would probably surprise most

---

507 *Kadic v. Karadzic*, 70 F3d 232, C. A. 2 (1995) at 246.

508 See, e.g., T Collingsworth, 'The Key Human Rights Challenge: Developing Enforcement Mechanisms' 15 Harvard Human Rights Journal 183 (2002) at 202 ("[T]he ATCA offers to provide a significant new aspect to human rights law and enforcement efforts by holding private actors accountable for violations."); J Fielding, 'Enforcing International Labor Standards through the Use of the Alien Tort Claims Act' 17 New York International Law Review 77 (2004) at 79 ("Traditionally, the Alien Tort Claims Act(ATCA) has been the vehicle for the enforcement of international human rights law, of which international labor standards are a distinct, and an often underprivileged subset."); I Poullaos, 'The Nature of the Beast: Using the Alien Tort Claims Act to Combat International Human Rights Violations' 80 Washington University Law Quarterly 327 (2002) ("The Alien Tort Claims Act (the ATCA), [FN1] lay nearly dormant for 191 years. Today, the ATCA is at the center of a reformation in the enforcement of international human rights")

509 MJ Bazyler and C Mesa, 'The Holocaust Restitution Movement in Comparative Perspective' 20 Berkeley Journal of International Law 11 (2002) at 25.

510 B Stephens, "Translating Filártiga: A Comparative and International Law Analysis of Domestic Remedies for International Human Rights Violations' ' 27 Yale Journal of International Law 1 (2002) at 32.

511 A Ramasastry and RC Thompson, *Commerce, Crime and Conflict* (Fafo New Security Programme, 2006) at 24; Currently the most thorough analysis of the ATCA litigation can be found in: C Hailer, *Menschenrechte vor Zivilgerichten - die Human Rights Litigation in den USA* (Duncker & Humblot, Berlin 2006).

Americans and also non-Americans.[512] Some other countries recognize international law as part of the national law. Nevertheless cases against TNCs based on extraterritorial breach of international law have been very rare outside of the US, as for example in the UK.[513] Absent from a cause of action on the basis of international law, the only possibility to sue corporate perpetrators of human rights violations abroad would be the so-called "garden-variety of municipal torts,"[514] which usually have no extraterritorial effect and has proven to be useless.[515] The US ATCA statute occupies a central position in providing for the accountability of TNCs where they have committed human rights violations. Many TNCs could only be held accountable on the basis of the ATCA.

The ATCA is codified at 28 U.S.C. Section 1350 and was adopted in 1789. It simply states that "the district courts shall have original jurisdiction of any civil action by an alien for a tort only, committed in violation of the law of nations or a treaty of the United States."[516] ATCA is one of the most widely discussed provisions in modern international law.[517]

Basically, only three requirements have to be satisfied: (a) the plaintiff is an alien, (b) alleging a tort and (c) breaching international law.[518] Since most often the first two requirements are fulfilled, the highly disputed questions in the ATCA litigation is whether plaintiffs have pleaded a breach of international law actionable under the ATCA. In short, the ATCA enables victims of violations of international law from any non-US country to seek damages from defendants from any country for violations of international law. In the words of Judge Bork: American courts rule on "cases premised on actions by foreigners against foreigners on foreign soil."[519] Most

---

512 *Kadic v. Karadzic*, 70 F3d 232, C. A. 2 (1995) at 246.

513 PT Muchlinski, 'Holding Multinational to Account: Recent Developments in English Litigation and the Company Law Review' 23 Company Lawyer 168 (2002).

514 *Xuncax v. Gramajo*, 886 FSupp 162, D.C. Mass. (1995) at 183.

515 See below in this chapter at subheading "VIII. Other Laws for accountability of TNCs in the US" at 124.

516 Aliens Tort Claims Act 1789, 28 U.S.C., § 1350(1789).

517 WS Dodge, 'The Historical Origins of the Alien Tort Statute: A Response to the 'Originalists'' 19 Hastings International and Comparative Law Review 221 (1996) at 221; E Duruigbo, 'The Economic Cost of Alien Tort Litigation: A Response to Awakening Monster: The Alien Tort Statute of 1789' 14 Minnesota Journal of Global Trade 1 (2004) at 1 (few issues command more attention in scholarly, advocacy, and policy circles today than the lawsuits brought in the courts of the United States by foreign claimants seeking redress for international law violations by multinational corporations (MNCs). The principal statutory basis for such suits has been the Alien Tort Statute (ATS), also known as the Alien Tort Claims Act (ATCA)).

518 *Filártiga v. Peña-Irala*, 630 F2d 876, C.A. 2 (1980) at 887, see also *Amerada Hess Shipping Corp. v. Argentine Republic*, 830 F2d 421, C.A. 2 (1987) at 425, *rev'd on other grounds Amerada Hess Shipping Corp. v. Argentine Republic*, 488 US, 109 SCt 683, 102 LEd2d 818, US S.Ct. (1989).

519 RH Bork, 'Judicial Imperialism' *Wall Street Journal* (July 12, 2004) A16.

of the cases that were based on the ATCA were human rights violations.[520] Cases have been brought for torture,[521] religious or ethnic persecution,[522] labor standards,[523] expropriation,[524] environmental abuse,[525] terrorism[526] and other causes. But there are numerous hurdles to these claims, as the Act of State doctrine, principles of international comity, the political question doctrine, sovereign immunity, statute of limitations, *forum non conveniens* and exhaustion of remedies.[527] Over the life of the ATCA, approximately 120 cases have raised claims under ATCA until 2004; 20 of those predated *Filártiga*.[528] The often-cited fear of a tsunami of frivolous claims has not materialized.[529]

I. Debate around ATCA

"This one-sentence law – the Alien Tort Statute of 1789 – could plausibly culminate in a nightmare, more than 200 years after it was enacted. Within the next decade, for example, 100,000 class action Chinese plaintiffs, organized by New York trial lawyers, could sue General Motors, Toyota, Volkswagen, General Electric, Mitsubishi, Siemens, Motorola, NTT, Nokia, and 20 other blue-chip corporations in a federal court for abetting China's denial of political rights, for observing China's restrictions on trade unions, and for impairing the Chinese environment. These plaintiffs might claim actual damages of $6 billion and punitive damages of $20

---

520 For example in the comprehensive list of GC Hufbauer and NK Mitrokostas, *Awakening Monster: The Alien Tort Statute of 1789* (Policy analyses in international economics 70, Institute for International Economics, Washington, D.C. 2003), of the listed 28 ATCA cases against TNCs there is only one case (*Hamid v. Price Waterhouse*, 51 F. 3d 1411), which was not based on human rights violations.

521 See e.g. *In re Estate of Ferdinand Marcos Human Rights Litigation ("Estate I")*, 978 F2d 493 C.A. 9 (1992); *In re Estate of Ferdinand Marcos Human Rights Litigation (Estate II)*, 25 F3d 1467, C.A. 9 (1994); *Xuncax v. Gramajo*, 886 FSupp 162, D.C. Mass. (1995); *Tachiona et al. v. Mugabe et al.*, 169 FSupp2d 259, D.C. S.D. N.Y. (2001); *Tachiona et al. v. Mugabe et al.*, WL230860, D.C. S.D.N.Y. (2002); *Wiwa v. Royal Dutch Shell Petroleum Corp.*, 226 F3d 232, C.A. 2 (2001), cert denied, 532 U.S. 941(2001).

522 See, e.g. *Kadic v. Karadzic*, 70 F3d 232, C. A. 2 (1995), cert denied, 518 U.S. 1004 (1996).

523 See, e.g. *Deutsch v. Turner Corp.*, 317 F3d 1005, C.A. 9 (2003).

524 See, e.g. *Bigio v. Coca-Cola Co.*, 239 F3d 440, C.A. 2 (2001).

525 See, e.g. *Jota v. Texaco, Inc.*, 157 F3d 153, C.A. 2 (1998); *Aguinda v. Texaco, Inc.*, 303 F3d 470, C.A. 2 (2002); *Beanal v. Freeport-McMoran, Inc.*, 197 F3d 161, C.A. 5 (1999);*Flores v. Southern Peru Copper Corp.*, 253 F Supp 2d 510, D.C. S.D. N.Y. (2002); *Sarei v. Rio Tinto PLC*, 221 FSupp2d 1116, D.C. C.D. Cal. (2002); For an overview see also RL Herz, 'Litigating Environmental Abuses Under the Alien Tort Claims Act: A Practical Assessment' 40 Virginia Journal of International Law 545 (2000).

526 See, e.g., *Tel-Oren v. Libyan Arab Republic*, 726 F2d 774, C.A. D.C. (1984).

527 See, e.g., S Gul, 'The Supreme Court Giveth and the Supreme Court Taketh Away: An Assessment of Corporate Liability Under § 1350' 109 West Virginia Law Review 379 (2007) at 409 with further references.

528 B Stephens, 'Upsetting Checks and Balances: The Bush Administration's Efforts to Limit Human Rights Litigation' 17 Harvard Human Rights Journal 169 (2004) at 177.

529 B Stephens, 'Taking Pride in International Human Rights Litigation' 2 Chinese Journal of International Law 485 (2001) at 175.

billion. To minimize their exposure to punitive damages, the corporations could settle for an intermediate amount, such as $10 billion."[530] This assertion stands as the beginning of the monograph "Awakening Monster: The Alien Tort Statute of 1789." It should be acknowledged that not all the hypotheses they discuss are as speculative as this.

The authors of the monograph, Hufbauer and Mitrokostas, did not ask for the abolition of the ATCA, but only for its containment by the US Congress. As one important limitation the causes of action should be reduced to an enumerated list of the most egregious human rights violations.[531] The monograph does not adequately take into account that the ATCA litigation has, since its revival in *Filártiga*, always been very moderate. Only the most egregious human rights violations have been recognized as actionable. ATCA claims have always been subject to numerous obstacles. The example that has been used in their nightmare scenario in the beginning of their monograph would neither have been successful under the ATCA litigation then nor with the current litigation after the Supreme Court decision in *Sosa v. Alvarez-Machain.*[532]

Human rights violations for impairing Chinese environment, political rights and restrictions would most likely not have been categorized as belonging to the actionable human rights before *Sosa* and even less after *Sosa*. Furthermore, such a claim would have been rejected for reasons of the Act of State and political question doctrines. Finally, most of the aforementioned companies would not have passed the stringent test of aiding and abetting these human rights violations. In fact, companies like Motorola can be seen as having a positive role on the human rights situation in their operating environments. Their working conditions rank among the best in all of China and they encourage critical thinking in their corporate structures.[533] There are numerous other flaws in the speculative accounts of their nightmare scenario, which clearly pursue a political agenda, financed by the Peterson Institute in Washington, D.C. One thing, however, remains true: corporations that egregiously exploit human rights might have to stand trial on the basis of ATCA litigation. Calling that an "awakening monster" is curious. The ATCA fights corporations that have behaved like monsters when forsterig torture or genocide. It would be more appropriate to see the ATCA as "taming the monsters."

---

530 GC Hufbauer and NK Mitrokostas, *Awakening Monster: The Alien Tort Statute of 1789* (Policy analyses in international economics 70, Institute for International Economics, Washington, D.C. 2003) at 1.

531 *Ibid.* at 55.

532 *Sosa v. Alvarez-Machain* (03-339) 542 US 2739, US S.Ct. (2004).

533 See MA Santoro, *Profits and Principles: Global Capitalism and Human Rights in China* (Cornell University Press, Ithaca 2000) at 5.

Opponents of a broad interpretation of the ATCA often criticize it as a form of US judicial imperialism that undermines other jurisdictions.[534] Most of the voices critical of the ATCA litigation do not propose complete repeal of the ATCA, but rather a containment of the ATCA.[535] Others claim that the ATCA should be completely abolished, but that mostly before the *Sosa* decision.[536] Often they argue that the separation of powers bars any intrusion from the judiciary. An intrusion could endanger international relations. It could harm the US and world economies by imposing human rights standards on world trade. Some say that foreign litigants should not be imported to the US and thereby undermine other jurisdictions.[537] The question of judicial imperialism in extraterritorial jurisdiction is very interesting and raises the question when such an intrusion into foreign jurisdiction can be seen as lawful or justifiable. However, there is international consensus with the adoption of the *Rome Statute* establishing the ICC that the adjudication of an enumerated set of international crimes may and shall be done extraterritorially.

The Carter, Bush Sr. and Clinton administrations have supported the ATCA.[538] President George H. Bush has signed the TVPA into law, which was a clear affirmation of the ATCA litigation.[539] The State Department under his son George W. Bush departed from this view and had a major influence on the ATCA litigation. It has filed *amicus curiae* in at least seven ATCA lawsuits and has always sided with the alleged violators of human rights.[540] Examples include the cases of *Rio Tinto, Unocal* and twice in respect of *ExxonMobil.*

---

534 See, e.g., RH Bork, 'Judicial Imperialism' *Wall Street Journal* (July 12, 2004) A16; P Waldmeir, 'An Abuse of Power: US Courts Should not Punish Companies for Human Rights Violations Committed Overseas' *Financial Times* (March 14, 2003) 12; T Niles, 'The Very Long Arm of American Law' *Financial Times* (November 6, 2002) 15.

535 See, inter alia, GC Hufbauer and NK Mitrokostas, *Awakening Monster: The Alien Tort Statute of 1789* (Policy analyses in international economics 70, Institute for International Economics, Washington, D.C. 2003).

536 P-Y Hsu, 'Should Congress Repeal the Alien Tort Claims Act?' 28 Southern Illinois University Law Journal 579 (2004) at 597.

537 EJ Schrage, 'Judging Corporate Accountability in the Global Economy' 42 Columbia Journal of Transnational Law 13 (2003) at 175.

538 B Stephens, 'Upsetting Checks and Balances: The Bush Administration's Efforts to Limit Human Rights Litigation' 17 Harvard Human Rights Journal 169 (2004) at 169.

539 *Sosa v. Alvarez-Machain* (03-339) 542 US 2739, US S.Ct. (2004) at 2763-2764.

540 Brief for the United States in Support of Petition for Writ of Certiorari, Sosa v. Alvarez-Machain (No. 03-339) (Sept 2003); Brief for the United States of America as Amicus Curiae, Doe v. Unocal Corp. at 3 (No. 00-56603) (July 14, 2003); Supplemental Statement of interest of the United States of America, Doe v. ExxonMobil Corp., 1-01-CV-1357-LFO (July 14, 2003); Corrected United States' Motion to Vacate October 21, 2002 Order and Statement of Interest, In the Alternative, Suggestion of Immunity Plaintiffs A, et al., v. Jiang Zemin, et al. (Dec. 2002); Doe v. ExxonMobil: Statement of Interest by US Department of State (Jun 29, 2002); Sarei v. Rio Tinto: Statement of Interest of US Department of State (Nov 5, 2001); Doe v. Liu Qi, and Plaintiff A v. Xia Deren: Statement of Interest by Department of State (Sept 25, 2001); a list of these briefs with their sources in the internet can be found at: Center for Justice and Accountability, 'Legal Documents, State Department Briefs' <http:// www.cja.org/

The Bush administration feared that the "Global War on Terror" could be impacted and that the ATCA litigation threatens the separation of powers. The State Department's attempts to undermine ATCA have been widely criticized as being another pointer of the Bush administration's campaign to obtain an expansive field of non-reviewable executive power.[541]

Even though the Bush administration, some legal scholars and considerable parts of the corporate world might favor limiting the ATCA to being just a jurisdictional statute, the predominant view favors the strong interpretation of the ATCA as a right to claim. The group of the ATCA supporters consists of scholars, non-governmental organizations, human rights lawyers and many others.[542] They reach this interpretation by reference to the legislative history, the purpose of the legislator and the statutory wording as clearly indicating that the ATCA was meant to be understood as a right to claim damages. Similarly, when the US Congress enacted the TVPA, it stated that the ATCA has "important uses and should not be replaced."[543] And that is also how the Supreme Court finally decided in *Sosa.*[544]

The EU Commission has not positioned itself on either side, but rather cautioned the *Sosa* Court to determine the limits of the ATCA human rights litigation with care. In an *amicus brief* in the *Sosa* case, the European Commission "respectfully requests this Court, if it holds that the Alien Tort Statute sets forth a cause of action, to define the cause of action by reference to the substantive content and jurisdictional limits of international law. The substantive content of the law of nations requires courts to adhere strictly to the rules for identifying customary international law, while exercising care to avoid retrospective application of newly developed norms."[545]

---

legalResources/ StateDepartmentBriefdocs.shtml> (March 15, 2006).

541 B Stephens, 'Upsetting Checks and Balances: The Bush Administration's Efforts to Limit Human Rights Litigation' 17 Harvard Human Rights Journal 169 (2004) at 203.

542 To name just a few in alphabetical order; *NGOs*: Amnesty International USA, Center for Constitutional Rights, EarthRights International, Human Rights First, International Labor Rights Fund, The Center for Justice and Accountability; *Academics*: William J. Aceves, Anthony D'Amato, Michael Bazyler, Terry Collingsworth, William S. Dodge, Sarah Joseph, Harold Hongju Koh, Jordan J. Paust, Anita Ramasastry, Steven R. Ratner, Ralph Steinhardt, Beth Stephens; *Lawyers*: Judith Chomsky, Michael Hausfeld, Paul L. Hoffman, Dan Stormer.

543 U.S. House of Representatives, *P.L. 102-256, Torture Victim Protection Act of 1991, H.R. REP. NO. 102-367 (I), November 25* (1991); See also S. Rep. (Judiciary Committee) No. 249, 102nd Cong., 1st Sess. (1991).

544 *Sosa v. Alvarez-Machain* (03-339) 542 US 2739, US S.Ct. (2004).

545 EU Commission, 'Brief of Amicus Curiae The European Commission in Support of Neither Party' (2004) <www.nosafehaven.org/_legal/atca_oth_EurComSupportingSosa.pdf> (May 15, 2007).

II. History of the ATCA

The history of the ATCA has been particularly interesting.[546] As to the history of the Alien Tort Act, Judge Friendly famously declared in 1975 this "old but little used section is a kind of legal Lohengrin; although it has been with us since the first Judiciary Act, § 9, 1 Stat. 73, 77 (1789), no one seems to know whence it came."[547]

The ATCA has often been depicted as an obscure provision, often with the purpose to negate its applicability. It is true that it is difficult to establish the rationale for the enactment of the ATCA. There is little formal legislative history, because the ATCA was passed into law in the first session of the US Congress. Nevertheless, thanks to many comprehensive studies on the history of the ATCA and contemporaneous hints on the purpose and meaning, Judge Friendly's statement no longer applies. Today, the identity and purpose of the ATCA is well researched.[548]

---

546 For further information: WS Dodge, 'The Historical Origins of the Alien Tort Statute: A Response to the 'Originalists'' 19 Hastings International and Comparative Law Review 221 (1996).

547 *IIT v. Vencap, Ltd.*, 519 F2d 1001, C.A. 2 (1975), Lohengrin is a legendary figure depicted in the Wagner opera of the same name. It was a mysterious knight who was imbued with mystical powers, and those powers can only be maintained if their nature is kept secret.

548 AA D'Amato, 'Judge Bork's Concept of the Law of Nations is Seriously Mistaken' 79 American Journal of International Law 92 (1985); AA D'Amato, 'The Alien Tort Statute and the Founding of the Constitution' 82 American Journal of International Law 62 (1988); A-M Burley, 'The Alien Tort Statute and the Judiciary Act of 1789: A Badge of Honor' 83 American Journal of International Law 461 (1990); WS Dodge, 'The Historical Origins of the Alien Tort Statute: A Response to the 'Originalists'' 19 Hastings International and Comparative Law Review 221 (1996); J Fitzpatrick, 'The Future of the Alien Tort Claims Act of 1789: Lessons from In re Marcos Human Rights Litigation' 67 St John's Law Review 491 (1993); HH Koh, 'Transnational Public Law Litigation' 100 Yale Law Journal 2347 (1991); RB Lillich, 'Invoking International Human Rights Law in Domestic Courts' 54 University of Cincinnati Law Review 367 (1985); K Randall, 'Federal Jurisdiction over International Law Claims: Inquiries. into the Alien Tort Statute' 18 New York University Journal of International Law and Politics 91 (1985); K Randall, 'Further Inquiries into the Alien Tort Statute and a Recommendation' 18 New York University Journal of International Law and Politics 473 (1986); JM Rogers, 'The Alien Tort Statute and How Individuals "Violate" International Law' 21 Vanderbilt Journal of Transnational Law 47 (1988); SA Rosenberg, 'The Theory of Protective Jurisdiction' 57 New York University Law Review 933 (1982); AP Rubin, 'Professor D'Amato's Concept of American Jurisdiction is Seriously Mistaken' 79 American Journal of International Law 105 (1985); J-M Simon, 'The Alien Tort Claims Act: Justice or Show Trials?' 11 Boston University International Law Journal 1 (1993); RG Steinhardt, 'Fulfilling the Promise of Filártiga: Litigating Human Rights Claims Against the Estate of Ferdinand Marcos' 20 Yale Journal of International Law 65 (1995); B Stephens, 'The Civil Lawsuit as a Remedy for International Human Rights Violations Against Women' 5 Hastings Women's Law Journal 143 (1994); JM Sweeney, 'A Tort Only in Violation of the Law of Nations' 18 Hastings International and Comparative Law Review 445 (1995).

A. Continental Congress 1781

As early as 1781 the Second Continental Congress of the United States passed a resolution recommending that the states provide for a mechanism for the punishment of violations of the law of nations.[549] The treatment of aliens and the respect for the law of nations became a matter of urgency in the following years, because of a number of assaults on foreign diplomats.[550] Finally, in 1789, after the US Constitution was passed and a more centralized federal government had been implemented, the First US Congress did not have to rely on the state governments to pass a law for the protection of the law of nations. The US congress had the power and passed the ATCA with the Judiciary Act of 1789 in its first session.

B. *Marbois* case in 1784

ATCA was enacted during a time of tensions in external affairs, especially between the US and European nations. Against this background the *Marbois* Case was highly influential for the enactment of the ATCA. A French diplomat was attacked in the state of Pennsylvania. The only option available to the federal government was to ask Pennsylvanian courts to prosecute that case, but they could not require these courts to take action. Since the assault or wrongful treatment of foreigners was one of the major reasons for the incitement of war the US federal government decided to remedy this situation.[551] The US was afraid of upsetting the European powers. To prevent any tensions and because the federal legislature was of the opinion that the federal courts would deal with such international issues more sensibly than state courts, they enacted the ATCA.

C. Enactment in 1789

As it was originally enacted the ATCA provided: "That the district courts shall have [...] cognisance [sic], concurrent with the courts of the several States, or the circuit courts, as the case may be, of all causes where an alien sues for a tort only in violation of the law of nations or a treaty of the United States."[552] The question arises what was meant by "law of nations." "Law of nations" at that time was viewed as "a

---

549 21 Journals of the Continental Congress 1774-1789, Library of Congress 1912 at 1136, cited from WS Dodge, 'The Historical Origins of the Alien Tort Statute: A Response to the 'Originalists" 19 Hastings International and Comparative Law Review 221 (1996) at 227.

550 *Ibid.* at 229 et *seq.*

551 AA D'Amato, 'The Alien Tort Statute and the Founding of the Constitution' 82 American Journal of International Law 62 (1988) at 64.

552 The Statute was modified in 1873 to read: "The district courts shall have jurisdiction as follows: Of all suits brought by any alien for a tort 'only' in violation of the law of nations, or of a treaty of the United States." Revised Statutes Title 13, Chapter 3, § 563, para. 16 (1873). It was slightly altered in a 1911 codification to read: "The district courts shall have original jurisdiction as follows:... Of all suits brought by any alien for a tort only, in violation of the laws of nations or of a treaty of the United States." Act of March 3, 1911, Chapter 231, § 24, 36 Stat. 1087, 1093 (1911). The current version of the Statute dates back to a 1948 revision of the Judicial Code.

system of rules, deducible by natural reason, and established by universal consent among the civilized inhabitants of the world."[553] According to Blackstone, the principal offenses against the law of nations were: "1.Violation of safe-conducts; 2. Infringement of the rights of embassadors [sic]; and 3. Piracy."[554]

The main purpose of the ATCA at the time of its inception was possibly the removal of a potential cause for international conflict with the mercantile European powers at a time when the US was still a weaker economic and military power.[555] Alexander Hamilton, one of the most influential founding fathers of the US Constitution, stated that "the peace of the WHOLE [the federal state] ought not to be left at the disposal of a PART [the state]. The Union will undoubtedly be answerable to foreign powers for the conduct of its members. And the responsibility for an injury ought ever to be accompanied with the faculty of preventing it. As the denial or perversion of justice by the sentences of courts, as well as in any other manner, is with reason classed among the just causes of war, it will follow that the federal judiciary ought to have cognizance of all causes in which the citizens of other countries are concerned."[556] This statement might have been based on Emmerich de Vattel. Vattel, as one of the most influential international law scholars of the time, stated that the denial of justice to aliens abroad was a just cause for the initiation of war.[557]

The framers of the ATCA were obviously afraid of what state courts might do in cases involving foreigners. State courts in 1787 were notoriously biased against foreigners.[558] "Thus, the Alien Tort Statute was an important part of a national security interest in 1789."[559]

---

553 4 William Blackstone, Commentaries at 66, cited from WS Dodge, 'The Historical Origins of the Alien Tort Statute: A Response to the 'Originalists'' 19 Hastings International and Comparative Law Review 221 (1996), page 226.

554 4 William Blackstone, Commentaries at 68, cited from *Ibid.* at 226.

555 J Haberstroh, 'The Alien Tort Claims Act & Doe v. Unocal: a Paquete Habana approach to the rescue' 32 Denver Journal of International Law and Policy 231 (2004) at 237.

556 A Hamilton, 'The Federalist No. 80, The Powers of the Judiciary' (1788) <http:// www.constitution.org/ fed/ federa80.htm> (September 5, 2007); See also WS Dodge, 'The Historical Origins of the Alien Tort Statute: A Response to the 'Originalists'' 19 Hastings International and Comparative Law Review 221 (1996) at 233.

557 J Haberstroh, 'The Alien Tort Claims Act & Doe v. Unocal: a Paquete Habana approach to the rescue' 32 Denver Journal of International Law and Policy 231 (2004) at 237, footnote 42 ("Although on this matter he reflected a wide consensus, Vattel was less influential in France and Britain than he was among the militarily weak trading nations.")

558 AA D'Amato, 'The Alien Tort Statute and the Founding of the Constitution' 82 American Journal of International Law 62 (1988) at 65, footnote 12.

559 *Ibid.* at 65.

D. *Bolchos* case 1795

The first action concerning jurisdiction under the ATCA was *Bolchos v. Darrell* in 1795.[560] The case dealt with the restitution of slaves between a French citizen, who had captured slaves from a Spanish vessel, and a defendant, who had mortgaged these slaves in an US port. The Court stated that it had jurisdiction under admiralty law and the ATCA and that the defendant had violated the law of nations. "[T]he law of nations would adjudge neutral property [the slaves], thus circumscribed to be restored to its neutral owner [here the 'mortgagee']; but the 14th Article of the treaty with France [treaty of 'Amity and Commerce' with France[561]] alters that law, by stipulating that the property of friends [here France] found on board the vessels of an enemy [here Spain] shall be forfeited."[562] Therefore the defendant, the agent for the mortgagee, was sentenced to pay restitution to the plaintiff, the French citizen.

E. Sierra Leone case 1795

Another useful incident for a better understanding of the ATCA took place in the same year in 1795. The Attorney General of Pennsylvania was asked to opine on the actions that might be taken against American citizens who aided the French in attacking the British colony of Sierra Leone in violation of a treaty promising US neutrality.[563] He expressed some doubt that the offenders could be held criminally responsible, but he left no doubt that the injured parties from Sierra Leone had a remedy in civil suit in the courts of the United States referring to the ATCA.[564]

F. Analysis

Summing up, it can be concluded that ATCA's original purpose was to incorporate international obligations from treaties and customary law into the national law of the US. The federal legislature was concerned that the states could violate international law and thereby create negative repercussions for the entire nation. Two other aims might stand as a rationale of the enactment of ATCA: a desire for uniformity in the interpretation of the law of nations within the US,[565] and a fear that state courts would be hostile to alien claims.[566]

---

560 *Bolchos v. Darrell*, 3 F Cas 810 (No 1,607), US District of South Dakota (1795); See also K Randall, 'Federal Jurisdiction over International Law Claims: Inquiries. into the Alien Tort Statute' 18 New York University Journal of International Law and Politics 91 (1985).

561 Treaty of Amity and Commerce, Feb 6, 1778, United States-France, 8 Stat 12, TS No 83 (1778).

562 *Bolchos v. Darrell*, 3 F Cas 810 (No 1,607), US District of South Dakota (1795) at 811.

563 WS Dodge, 'The Historical Origins of the Alien Tort Statute: A Response to the 'Originalists'' 19 Hastings International and Comparative Law Review 221 (1996) at 233.

564 See 1 Op. Attorney General 57 (1795), cited from Dodge, Historical, page 234.

565 J Jay, 'The Federalist No. 3' (1787) <http:// www.constitution.org/ fed/ federa03.htm> (September 5, 2007); See also WS Dodge, 'The Historical Origins of the Alien Tort Statute: A Response to the 'Originalists'' 19 Hastings International and Comparative Law Review 221 (1996) at 233.

566 3 The Debates in the Several State Conventions on the Adoption of the Federal Constitution

III. *Filártiga* decision in 1980

The transformation of the ATCA from an obscure and largely obsolete statute to a widely used tool to vindicate human rights violations began with the *Filártiga* decision. In the first 191 years of the statute's existence and until the landmark decision of *Filártiga* the ATCA was rarely invoked, although not as seldom as often assumed. There were 21 cases before *Filártiga* was decided in June 1980 where plaintiffs asserted jurisdiction under the ATCA.[567] In *Filártiga v. Peña-Irala*,[568] the Court of Appeals for the Second Circuit issued the first decision recognizing that the ATCA created a federal cause of action. It was a landmark decision, which set a precedent for US courts for three reasons:
- to punish non-US citizens for breaches of international law,
- to hear claims of non US citizens based on ATCA and
- to apply it to acts outside of the territory of the US.

The seventeen-year old Joelito Filártiga was kidnapped and tortured to death in 1976 by the Police in Asunción, which was led by the Inspector General Americo Norberto Peña-Irala. The Filártigas claim that Joelito was tortured to death in retaliation for the political activities of his father. The murder charges in Paraguay were unsuccessful. Later both the sister of Joelito, Dolly Filártiga, and Peña-Irala moved to the US. When Dolly heard of Peña-Irala's presence in the US she served him with a civil complaint in US courts for wrongful death on the grounds of the ATCA. The trial judge ruled that the "law of nations" did not extend to the treatment by a foreign country towards its own citizens.[569]

The Court of Appeals reversed this ruling and held that the "law of nations" in the ATCA refers to the law of nations as it exists today, not as it existed at the time ATCA was enacted. "Thus it is clear that courts must interpret international law not as it was in 1789, but as it has evolved and exists among the nations of the world today."[570] By ruling that the "law of nations" does not only regulate the behavior of nations vis-à-vis each other, but the conduct of nations towards individuals, the Court

---

583 (J. Elliot ed., 2d ed. 1881); see also WS Dodge, 'The Historical Origins of the Alien Tort Statute: A Response to the 'Originalists" 19 Hastings International and Comparative Law Review 221 (1996) at 233.

567 See K Randall, 'Federal Jurisdiction over International Law Claims: Inquiries. into the Alien Tort Statute' 18 New York University Journal of International Law and Politics 91 (1985) at footnote 15.

568 *Filártiga v. Peña-Irala*, 630 F2d 876, C.A. 2 (1980).

569 *Ibid.*.

570 *Ibid.* at 881.

set the stage for a new era in federal human rights litigation.[571] The Court awarded roughly US$ 10.4 million to the Filártigas.[572]

The *Filártiga* decision is still an intriguing example of the internationalist view in the US judiciary. It ended with a "ringing endorsement"[573] of human rights law: "In the twentieth century the international community has come to recognize the common danger posed by the flagrant disregard of basic human rights and particularly the right to be free of torture. Spurred first by the Great War, and then the Second, civilized nations have banded together to prescribe acceptable norms of international behavior. From the ashes of the Second World War arose the United Nations Organization, amid hopes that an era of peace and cooperation had at last begun. Though many of these aspirations have remained elusive goals that circumstance cannot diminish the true progress that has been made. In the modern age, humanitarian and practical considerations have combined to lead the nations of the world to recognize that respect for fundamental human rights is in their individual and collective interest. Among the rights universally proclaimed by all nations, as we have noted, is the right to be free of physical torture. Indeed, for purposes of civil liability, the torturer has become like the pirate and slave trader before him *hostis humani generis*, an enemy of all mankind. Our holding today, giving effect to a jurisdictional provision enacted by our First Congress, is a small but important step in the fulfillment of the ageless dream to free all people from brutal violence."[574]

The concern that *Filártiga* would unleash a flood of litigation on the federal courts was not confirmed. Following *Filártiga*, two waves of ATCA litigation can be distinguished, bearing in mind that only very few cases have been successful. The first wave of cases was against individual perpetrators, such as former US Secretary of State Henry Kissinger, former US Attorney General John Ashcroft, US President George W. Bush, former Shell Nigeria Managing Director Brian Anderson. Additionally there were numerous cases brought against foreign individual perpetrators, including former Chinese Premier, Li Peng, former Chinese Communist Party General Secretary of Sicuan, Zhou Yongkang, Zimbabwe's President Robert Mugabe, former General, Guillermo Garcia of El Salvador, Indonesian former vice chief of staff, Johny Lumintang, Honduran former military intelligence chief, Juan Evangelista Lopez, former Serbian President Milosevic, former President of the Serbian Republic, Radovan Karadžić and Philippine ex-dictator, Ferdinand Marcos.

---

571 R Thompson, 'A Comparative Survey of Private Sector Liability for Grave Violations of International Law in National Jurisdictions, Surveys of Canada, France, Norway, the United Kingdom, and the United States' (2003) <http://www.fafo.no/ liabilities/nat_surv.htm> at 37.

572 *Filártiga v. Peña-Irala*, 577 F Supp 860, D.C. E.D.N.Y. (1984) at 867.

573 B Stephens, 'Sosa v. Alvarez-Machain: 'The Door Is Still Ajar' for Human Rights Litigation in US Courts' 70 Brooklyn Law Review 533 (2004) at 536.

574 *Filártiga v. Peña-Irala*, 630 F2d 876, C.A. 2 (1980) at 890.

The second wave was brought against corporations. It began with the case brought against Texaco in 1993.[575] Many further cases have been brought against corporations, such as Unocal, Royal Dutch Petroleum, Talisman Energy, Inc, Del Monte Produce Inc, Chevron, DynCorp, ExxonMobil Corp., Coca-Cola Co., Drummond Company, Inc, Citigroup Inc., Barclays National Bank, Bank of America, Societe Nationale Des Chemins De Fer Francais, Southern Peru Copper Corp., Pfizer Inc., United Technologies Corp., Price Waterhouse, Freeport-McMoran Inc, Ford Motor Company, Union Carbide Corp., Texaco Inc., The Gap, Advanced Textile Corp and others.

IV. *Tel-Oren* decision in 1984

In the aftermath to the *Filártiga* decision, there has been essential debate about whether the US is an appropriate forum to decide violations of international law. The disagreement between the "internationalists" and their opponents, including the "originalists,"[576] has been especially apparent in the decision *Tel-Oren v. Libyan Arab Republic*, which was decided in February 1984.[577] The case involved a complaint by survivors of a fierce terrorist attack in Israel in 1978.[578] The claim was brought against the Palestine Liberation Organization (PLO), the Libyan Arab Republic, the Palestine Information Office, the National Association of Arab Americans and the Palestine Congress of North America. The District Court for the District of Columbia dismissed the suit.[579] The Court of Appeals for the District of Columbia Circuit affirmed the dismissal.

The three judges agreed on the result of the decision, but disagreed on the reasons to dismiss–especially, on two questions regarding the ATCA. First, does the ATCA provide for a private right of action or is it merely a procedural statute of jurisdiction? Secondly, does the ATCA address the law of nations as it stood in 1789 or as it stands today? Judge Bork held that the ATCA is merely a procedural statute and dismissed the action for that reason. Judge Edwards disagreed and held that the "law of nations" was to be understood by reference to the general consent of civilized nations as it exists today. Edwards cited the Supreme Court in *The Paquete Habana.*[580] He upheld the dismissal of the action because he regarded only state actors to be bound by international law and the PLO is not a state actor in his view.[581] The third judge, Judge Robb, upheld the dismissal, because the case involved a

575 *Aguinda v. Texaco*, 1993 WL 13148394, D.C. S.D.N.Y. (1993).

576 See, for example, Judge Bork in *Tel-Oren v. Libyan Arab Republic*, 726 F2d 774, C.A. D.C. (1984) (Bork, J., concurring); JM Sweeney, 'A Tort Only in Violation of the Law of Nations' 18 Hastings International and Comparative Law Review 445 (1995) at 477.

577 *Tel-Oren v. Libyan Arab Republic*, 726 F2d 774, C.A. D.C. (1984).

578 For details see AA D'Amato, 'Judge Bork's Concept of the Law of Nations is Seriously Mistaken' 79 American Journal of International Law 92 (1985).

579 *Tel-Oren v. Libyan Arab Republic*, 517 F Supp 542, D.C. D.C. (1981).

580 *The Paquete Habana*, 175 US 677, US S.Ct. (1900).

581 *Tel-Oren v. Libyan Arab Republic*, 726 F2d 774, C.A. D.C. (1984) at 789.

political question and a court decision would represent an intrusion into US foreign policy.[582]

V. *Kadic* decision in 1995

While the *Filártiga* decision stands as the watershed decision to establish that violations of international law are actionable in the United States,[583] the *Kadic* decision stands as the watershed decision of holding individuals liable for violations of international law, also without state participation.[584] The *Kadic* decision includes the famous and often cited finding: "we hold that certain forms of conduct violate the law of nations whether undertaken by those acting under the auspices of a state or only as private individuals."[585] The reach of international law is not confined to the actions of a state, but also regulates the behavior of individuals. Pirates were bound to recognize international law as being *hostis humani generis*, enemies of all mankind.

In the modern era, the hijacker, war criminal and perpetrator of genocide have also come to be considered *hostis humani generis*.[586] The *Kadic* decision is, therefore, at odds with the position taken by Judge Edwards in the *Tel-Oren* decision in that the Court endowed the individual also with international legal personality with direct obligations at international law, which are also enforceable via the ATCA.

VI. *Sosa* decision

Judge Edwards commenced his opinion in the *Tel Oren* decision by stating: "The case deals with an area of the law that cries out for clarification by the Supreme Court."[587] It took not less than 20 years before the Supreme Court decided finally to confront this aspect of human rights litigation in the *Sosa* case.[588] The background to the case is that Francisco Sosa kidnapped Dr. Humberto Alvarez-Machain on behalf of the US Drug Enforcement Agency, because Alvarez was accused of aiding and

---

582 *Ibid.* at 825.

583 *Filártiga v. Peña-Irala*, 630 F2d 876, C.A. 2 (1980).

584 *Kadic v. Karadzic*, 70 F3d 232, C. A. 2 (1995).

585 *Ibid.* at 239.

586 *Ibid.* at 239.

587 *Tel-Oren v. Libyan Arab Republic*, 726 F2d 774, C.A. D.C. (1984) at 775.

588 Discussed in Earthrights, 'In Our Court; ATCA, Sosa and the triumph of human rights; A report about the Alien Tort Claims Act' (2004) <http:// www.earthrights.org/ files/ Reports/ inourcourt.pdf > (March 14, 2006); S Fohn, 'Do DEA Field Agents Have the Power to Unilaterally Execute a Trans-Border Abduction?: The Ninth Circuit's Take on Alvarez-Machain v. United States' 27 Houston Journal of International Law 221 (2004); E Kontorovich, 'Implementing Sosa v. Alvarez-Machain: What Piracy Teaches About the Limits of the Alien Tort Statute ' 80 Notre Dame Law Review 111 (2004); SD Murphy, 'Supreme Court Interpretation of Alien Tort Claims Act' 98 American Journal of International Law 845 (2004); BR Roth, 'Sosa v. Alvarez-Machain; United States v. Alvarez-Machain. 124 S.Ct. 2739. United States Supreme Court, June 29, 2004' 98 American Journal of International Law 798 (2004); B Stephens, 'Sosa v. Alvarez-Machain: 'The Door Is Still Ajar' for Human Rights Litigation in US Courts' 70 Brooklyn Law Review 533 (2004).

abetting the murder of one of its agents. Sosa brought Alvarez-Machain to trial in California on murder charges and lost the case. Alvarez-Machain later sued his kidnapper and won the case in the Court of Appeals of the Ninth Circuit. Sosa appealed to the US Supreme Court. A key issue in Sosa was whether foreign victims may use ATCA as the basis for lawsuits alleging human rights violations abroad. The District Courts have interpreted this question differently. The second and eleventh Circuit Courts had held that it does create a private right of action.[589] The fourth and eleventh Circuit Courts took the opposite view.[590]

The case stands as one of the most important cases in the history of the Supreme Court. The case has sparked an outpouring of support for either side.[591] Many interest groups submitted *amicus briefs*. The EU Commission also submitted an *amicus brief*, because of the extraterritorial impact of the ATCA litigation. It did not support either side, but asked the Supreme Court to exercise great care

The opponents of human rights litigation stated that ATCA is a jurisdictional grant. They made several strong arguments. The Court stated that the ATCA is part of the Judiciary Act, which deals with procedural provisions only. The Court said that most international treaties are non-self-executing, which means that a private right of action did not automatically become a part of domestic US law, without implementation by the US Congress.[592] It said that the ATCA provides no guidance on the scope and limits on rights of actions. As such, courts repeatedly had to invent limits to the ATCA "out of thin air."[593]

Justice Scalia's in his dissenting opinion found it remarkable that the Court of Appeals for the Second Circuit "created" a private cause of action in *Kadic v. Karadzic*, even though the *Genocide Convention Implementation Act of 1987* said that it shall not "be construed as creating any substantive or procedural right

---

589 *Filártiga v. Peña-Irala*, 630 F2d 876, C.A. 2 (1980) at 887 stated: "it is sufficient ... to construe the [ATCA] ... simply as opening the federal courts for adjudication of the rights already recognized by international law;" *In re Estate of Ferdinand Marcos Human Rights Litigation (Estate II)*, 25 F3d 1467, C.A. 9 (1994) at 1474-75; *Abebe-Jira v. Negewo*, 72 F3d 844, C.A. 11 (1996) at 847; also *Flores v. Southern Peru Copper Corp.*, 253 F Supp 2d 510, D.C. S.D. N.Y. (2002) at 13, footnote 17.

590 *Tel-Oren v. Libyan Arab Republic*, 726 F2d 774, C.A. D.C. (1984) at 811 (Bork, J. concurring); *Al Odah v. United States*, 321 F3d 1134, C.A. D.C. (2003) at 1145-47.

591 As a good overview on the proponents and opponents to ATCA see for example: No Safe Haven, 'Legal Documents, Briefs supporting and opposing ATCA' <http:// www.nosafehaven.org/ legal.html> (March 16, 2006).

592 PHF Bekker, *The Treatment of Evidentiary Sources of International Law in US Alien Tort Statute Cases (Europa Instituut of Leiden University)* (Kluwer, 2004) at 163; see also *Wiwa v. Royal Dutch Petroleum Co.*, 226 F3d 88, C.A.2 (2000) at 103.

593 PHF Bekker, *The Treatment of Evidentiary Sources of International Law in US Alien Tort Statute Cases (Europa Instituut of Leiden University)* (Kluwer, 2004) at 165.

enforceable by law by any party in any proceeding."[594] According to Justice Scalia, this represents the intent of the legislature and executive. To the opposite of Justice Scalia's view, in *Kadic*, it was noted that the *executive* branch "has emphatically restated in this litigation its position that private persons may be found liable under the Alien Tort Act for acts of genocide, war crimes, and other violations of international humanitarian law."[595] Therefore, the *Kadic* Court found it could hardly be construed as repealing by implication the cause of action supplied by the ATCA.[596] The *legislature*, in the frequently cited TVPA legislative materials, has authorized the ATCA litigation.[597]

The Supreme Court denied Dr. Alvarez-Machain's right to pursue his claims, but it essentially confirmed the *Filártiga* doctrine and the preceding international human rights litigation. The decision was a victory for human rights.[598] The Court denied the US government's attempts to prevent human rights victims to bring claims in US courts. The fact that *Sosa* can be counted as a success for human rights might also be deduced from the fact that, soon after the *Sosa* decision, Unocal Inc. finally agreed to settle its lawsuit involving allegations of human rights violations during the construction of a pipeline in the 1990s. Since in the *Sosa* decision the US Supreme Court did not invalidate the ATCA as a basis for human rights claims, the oil corporation Unocal must have felt compelled to settle the claim six months after *Sosa*.

The Supreme Court chose a peculiar approach. It declared that the ATCA is solely a jurisdictional statute, but it found that an authorization for a right of action can be found in federal Common law.[599] "We think it would be unreasonable to assume that

594 *Sosa v. Alvarez-Machain* (03-339) 542 US 2739, US S.Ct. (2004) at 2775.

595 *Kadic v. Karadzic*, 70 F3d 232, C. A. 2 (1995) at 239.

596 *Ibid.* at 242.

597 U.S. House of Representatives, *P.L. 102-256, Torture Victim Protection Act of 1991, H.R. REP. NO. 102-367 (I), November 25* (1991) ("The TVPA would establish an unambiguous and modern basis for a cause of action that has been successfully maintained under an existing law, Section 1350 of the Judiciary Act of 1789 (the Alien Tort Claims Act), which permits Federal district courts to hear claims by aliens for torts committed "in violation of the law of nations." (28 U.S.C. sec. 1350). Section 1350 has other important uses and should not be replaced. There should also, however, be a clear and specific remedy, not limited to aliens, for torture and extrajudicial killing. In the case of Filártiga v. Pena-Irala, the Second Circuit Court of Appeals recognized a right of action against foreign torturers under the rarely invoked Alien Tort Claims Act. [...] The Filártiga case met with general approval. [...] The TVPA would provide such a grant, and would also enhance the remedy already available under Section 1350 in an important respect: While the Alien Tort Claims Act provides a remedy to aliens only, the TVPA would extend a civil remedy also to US citizens who may have been tortured abroad.")

598 See Earthrights, 'In Our Court; ATCA, Sosa and the triumph of human rights; A report about the Alien Tort Claims Act' (2004) <http:// www.earthrights.org/ files/ Reports/ inourcourt.pdf> (March 14, 2006).

599 *Sosa v. Alvarez-Machain* (03-339) 542 US 2739, US S.Ct. (2004) at 2761.

the First Congress would have expected federal courts to lose all capacity to recognize enforceable international norms simply because the Common law might lose some metaphysical cachet on the road to modern realism."[600] This finding is criticized for not complying with the *Erie* doctrine, according to which federal courts do not have the power to make up general federal Common law when hearing state law claims under diversity jurisdiction.[601]

Commentators viewed the *Sosa* decision as a species of limited "jurisdiction plus" analysis.[602] According to the *Sosa* decision, actions can be brought directly under the ATCA for a "narrow set"[603] or "very limited set of claims"[604] of violations of customary international law. However, the Court urged federal courts to use "great caution" in creating such new causes of action.[605] It has to satisfy the standard of the historical antecedents. The Supreme Court reveals five approaches in how to exercise the "great caution."[606]

(1) The causes of action need to be sufficiently definite, as was the case for piracy in 1789.[607]
(2) The practical consequences of the creation of a new cause of action have to be kept in mind. The floodgates to many different kinds of claims from other jurisdiction shall not be opened.[608]
(3) The federal courts shall observe "legislative guidance".[609]
(4) The claimant must have exhausted any remedies available in the domestic legal system, and perhaps in other *fora* such as international claims tribunals.[610]
(5) Serious weight shall be given to the interference with the powers of the executive branch concerning foreign affairs.[611]

Eugene Kontorovich argues that the test applied by the Supreme Court to determine whether a particular international law claim can be subject to jurisdiction under the

---

600 *Ibid.* at 2765.

601 *Erie Railroad Co. v. Tompkins*, 304 US 64, US S.Ct. (1938). More information on the importance of the *Erie* doctrine and federal common law for ATCA human rights claims later in chapter VI, subheading "C. International law and the US Supreme Court" at 226.

602 S Gul, 'The Supreme Court Giveth and the Supreme Court Taketh Away: An Assessment of Corporate Liability Under § 1350' 109 West Virginia Law Review 379 (2007) at 399.

603 *Sosa v. Alvarez-Machain* (03-339) 542 US 2739, US S.Ct. (2004) at 2756.

604 *Ibid.* at 2760.

605 *Ibid.* at 2763.

606 Based on C Hailer, 'Die US-amerikanische Human Rights Litigation' 44 Archiv des Völkerrechts 76 (2006) at 87, 88.

607 *Sosa v. Alvarez-Machain* (03-339) 542 US 2739, US S.Ct. (2004) at 2765.

608 *Ibid.* at 2766.

609 *Ibid.* at 2762.

610 *Ibid.* at 2766, footnote 21.

611 *Ibid.* at 2766, footnote 21, as for example in the Apartheid case and South Africa that has chosen a non-adversarial and non-judicial path, the Truth and Reconciliation Commission.

ATCA is therefore historical. It requires a close examination of those "characteristics" of the eighteenth century offences that gave them their special status in Common law and the law of nations.[612] This might become a significant interpretative presumption in future ATCA litigation. "In sum, although the ATCA is a jurisdictional statute creating no new causes of action, the reasonable inference from the historical materials is that the statute was intended to have practical effect the moment it became law. The jurisdictional grant is best read as having been enacted on the understanding that the Common law would provide a cause of action for the modest number of international law violations with a potential for personal liability at the time."[613] The Supreme Court concluded that the door for claims based on international law is still ajar, but subject to vigilant monitoring.[614]

This view of ATCA reflects the approach that was previously taken by the inferior courts. They had also only accepted a set of limited human rights violations as a cause of action. The *Sosa* decision was eagerly expected from all sides: those who were defending its original interpretation and those who were trying to drastically limit it. Some feared that the decision might annul the existing human rights litigation in the United States.[615] Generally speaking, the other side hoped that the decision would put an end to this form of human rights litigation in the United States. That did not happen. The US courts will remain a forum to litigate the most egregious human rights claims.

VII. Analysis to ATCA

The ATCA articulates a most interesting norm. It is the basis of US human rights litigation. The ATCA was originally intended as a commitment to the adherence of international law obligations. It was long forsaken and had its revival around the time of the end of the Cold War. The ATCA survived all the attacks from the administration of President George W. Bush and others who opposed the idea of human rights enforcement in domestic courts. The Supreme Court in *Sosa* affirmed the potential for human rights litigation. The first appellate court decision thereafter, in *Sarei v. Rio Tinto*, incorporated and broadened the scope of the ATCA jurisdiction.[616] ATCA can now provide a basis to enforce a broad array of human rights and also environmental rights, not only *jus cogens* norms. The ATCA may provide the most powerful vehicle to enforce human rights worldwide.

---

612 E Kontorovich, 'Implementing Sosa v. Alvarez-Machain: What Piracy Teaches About the Limits of the Alien Tort Statute ' 80 Notre Dame Law Review 111 (2004) at 113.

613 *Sosa v. Alvarez-Machain* (03-339) 542 US 2739, US S.Ct. (2004) at 2760.

614 *Ibid.* at 2764.

615 See for example: S Joseph, *Corporations and Transnational Human Rights Litigation* (Human rights law in perspective, Hart Publishing, Oxford 2004) at xi.

616 *Sarei v. Rio Tinto*, 456 F3d 1069, C.A. 9 (2006).

VIII. Other Laws for accountability of TNCs in the US

Another mechanism to hold human rights perpetrators liable in the US is the Torture Victim Protection Act (TVPA). It allows actions for extrajudicial killings and torture. It was enacted in 1992 and signed into law by President George Bush, Sr. As the United States House of Representatives has stated in the legislative materials to the TVPA, "it would establish an unambiguous and modern basis for a cause of action that has been successfully maintained under an existing law, section 1350 of the Judiciary Act of 1789 [ATCA]." And "while the Alien Tort Claims Act provides a remedy to aliens only, the TVPA would extend a civil remedy also to US citizens who may have been tortured abroad.[617] As also stated by the House of Representatives ATCA "should remain intact to permit suits based on ... norms [other than torture and summary execution]."[618] It is only possible to apply the TVPA against individuals and not corporations, and this renders it less interesting for this examination, aside from the fact that the legislative materials to the TVPA confirmed the ATCA as a basis for human rights claims, as developed by US courts.

Another avenue to hold corporations accountable in the US is the Racketeer Influenced and Corrupt Organizations (RICO) statute, which prohibits racketeering activity in relation to the collection of unlawful debts. A court can exercise RICO jurisdiction over extraterritorial acts so long as extraterritorial damage was caused by intra-territorial conduct (the conduct test) or such acts have substantial effects inside the US (the effects test). RICO has been successfully used in *Wiwa v. Royal Dutch Petroleum Co.*[619] It was denied in *Unocal.*[620]

Certainly, there is also the potential to apply the so-called garden variety of municipal tort principles. It has been tried various times as in *Unocal*, the *Union Carbide* claim, *Sequihua v. Texaco*, *Aguinda v. Texaco* and Delgado *v. Shell Oil*. But all of these claims were dismissed.[621] The ATCA has various advantages. The tort in the ATCA is classified as a breach of the law of nations. This facilitates the finding of liability in the form of intention or negligence or strict liability. Second, the ATCA applies regardless of whether the conduct is unlawful in the State where the tort arose.

A further method to hold corporations liable for human rights violations might have been opened by the decision in *Kasky v. Nike.*[622] In this case, the US Supreme Court

617 H.R. Rep. No. 367 102d Cong., 2d Sess. at 4 (1991), reprinted in 1992 U.S.C.C.A.N. 84 at 86; See also *Sosa v. Alvarez-Machain* (03-339) 542 US 2739, US S.Ct. (2004) at 2763-2764.

618 *Ibid.*, (explaining that codification of *Filártiga* was necessary in light of skepticism expressed by Judge Bork's concurring opinion in *Tel-Oren*).

619 *Wiwa v. Royal Dutch Petroleum Co.*, No 96 Civ 8386, 2002 US, Dist LEXIS 3293, US D.C. S.D. N.Y. (2002).

620 *Doe v. Unocal*, 2002 US App LEXIS 19263, C.A. 9 (2002).

621 See S Joseph, *Corporations and Transnational Human Rights Litigation* (Human rights law in perspective, Hart Publishing, Oxford 2004), pages 67-77.

622 *Kasky v. Nike*, 24 Cal 4th 939, US SCt. Cal. (2002).

decided that the public relations campaign concerning the human rights treatment of Nike's workers was false commercial speech. This basically means that US corporations will now have to take greater care in making factual statements about their human rights and environmental records in codes of conduct. Summarizing it can be said, that there might be evolving alternatives to the ATCA, but the ATCA remains the main vehicle to hold corporations liable for human rights violations in the US.

IX. Advantages for plaintiffs in the US legal system

There are numerous reasons why human rights actions take place in the US. Americans look to courts instead of the legislature to compensate the victims of tortuous behavior.[623] The American legal system possibly ranks among the most litigious and most plaintiff-friendly systems in the world.[624] As Lord Denning observed in his vivid and often quoted terms: "As a moth is drawn to light, so is a litigant drawn to the United States. If he can only get his case into their courts, he stands to win a fortune. At no cost to himself; and at no risk of having to pay anything to the other side. The lawyers there will conduct the case 'on spec' as we say, or on a 'contingency fee' as they say. The lawyers will charge the litigant nothing for their services but instead they will take 40 percent of the damages, if they win the case in court, or out of court on a settlement."[625] As is the case with the contingent fee, the US is the only advanced legal system in the world that has not in some manner adopted the so-called "English Rule" (meaning that the "loser pay"), which entitles the winner in civil cases to recover his "reasonable" attorney fees from the loser.[626]

The US legal system does present further advantages for plaintiffs in general, as the possibility of class actions, high punitive damages, contingency fees, jury trials,

623 W Tetley, 'A Canadian Looks at American Conflict of Law Theory and Practice, Especially in the Light of the American Legal and Social Systems' 38 Columbia Journal of Transnational Law 299 (1999) at 327.

624 B Stephens, "Translating Filártiga: A Comparative and International Law Analysis of Domestic Remedies for International Human Rights Violations' ' 27 Yale Journal of International Law 1 (2002) at 16; W Tetley, 'A Canadian Looks at American Conflict of Law Theory and Practice, Especially in the Light of the American Legal and Social Systems' 38 Columbia Journal of Transnational Law 299 (1999) at 353.

625 *Smith Kline & French Labs Ltd. v. Bloch*, 1 WLR 730 Ct. App. (England) (1982).

626 WK Davis, 'The International View of Attorney Fees in Civil Suits: Why is the United States the 'Odd Man Out' in How it Pays its Lawyers' 16 Arizona Journal of International and Comparative Law 361 (1999) at 403. (Adopting the 'English Rule' defendants would hold the upper hand "because of the fear of plaintiffs that they may have to pay the costs if they do not prevail. This fear and the underlying risk would likely be worse in America given our higher costs. In short, the English Rule might very well cut down on the rates of litigation and lower overall costs to society as a result, and , in turn, might very well increase the reputation of the legal community. But those with valid claims might be deterred from filing suit, especially those with the most to lose.")

plaintiff-friendly discovery rules, a generally sophisticated legal system and lawyers that are willing to take high-risk cases. Many of these legal characteristics are unique, even in comparison to the cradle of the Common law system, England.[627] To a lawyer trained in the Roman civil law tradition some characteristics of American law seem peculiar and some characteristics seem progressive or exemplary for one's own system.

X. Concluding remarks to Chapter III

The US ATCA is a very powerful instrument to enforce human rights against TNCs. UN Special Representative for Business and Human Rights, Ruggie is of the opinion that transnational litigation, as ATCA, is not the ideal solution.[628] According to Ruggie, the ideal solution would possibly be an international tribunal that could adjudicate on alleged human rights violations by TNCs from all different countries with consistent international standards. This tribunal is a distant prospect.

In the case of criminal liability of individuals according to the *Rome Statute* it is clearly provided that the international court, the ICC, is only complementary to national jurisdiction.[629] Why should that be different for TNCs? For corporate

---

627 B Stephens, "Translating Filártiga: A Comparative and International Law Analysis of Domestic Remedies for International Human Rights Violations' ' 27 Yale Journal of International Law 1 (2002) at footnote 59.

628 UN Special Representative of the Secretary-General on human rights and transnational corporations and other business enterprises, 'A/HRC/4/35- Report of the Special Representative of the Secretary-General on the issue of human rights and transnational corporations and other business enterprises' (2007) <http:// daccess-ods.un.org/ access.nsf/ Get?Open& DS=A/ HRC/ 4/ 35&Lang=E> at para 84.

629 The Preamble of the Rome Statute provides that "the International Criminal Court established under this Statute shall be complementary to national criminal jurisdictions." See also Article 17 of the Statute provides that a case is inadmissible if:
(a) The case is being investigated or prosecuted by a State which has jurisdiction over it, unless the State is unwilling or unable genuinely to carry out the investigation or prosecution;
(b) The case has been investigated by a State which has jurisdiction over it and the State has decided not to prosecute the person concerned, unless the decision resulted from the unwillingness or inability of the State genuinely to prosecute;
(c) The person concerned has already been tried for conduct which is the subject of the complaint, and a trial by the Court is not permitted under Article 20, para 3;
(d) The case is not of sufficient gravity to justify further action by the Court.
Article 20, para 3, specifies that, if a person has already been tried by another court, the ICC cannot try them again for the same conduct unless the proceedings in the other court:
(a) Were for the purpose of shielding the person concerned from criminal responsibility for crimes within the jurisdiction of the Court; or
(b) Otherwise were not conducted independently or impartially in accordance with the norms of due process recognized by international law and were conducted in a manner which, in the circumstances, was inconsistent with an intent to bring the person concerned to justice.'
The U.K.'s implementing legislation, for example, provides that the U.K. courts will have jurisdiction over a person who 'commits acts outside the United Kingdom at a time when he is not a United Kingdom national, a United Kingdom resident or a person subject to U.K. service

liability the ATCA decision in *Unocal* may stand in a similar tradition as the cases of holding individuals liable for breaches of international law that were based on the Nuremberg and the Tokyo trials and continued in trials, such as *Eichmann* and *Pinochet* and *Jean Akayesu*.[630] It would not be inconsistent with international law as established through the criminal liability of individuals to create a mechanism under which the liability of corporations for international crimes could be imposed.

This objective of criminal liability of TNCs may then be pursued either through national jurisdiction or directly through rules and jurisdiction of an international institution such as the ICC.[631] ATCA provides the door into the most progressive transnational human rights litigation worldwide. It seems to provide the only possibility to enforce human rights against TNCs for the time being. International human rights litigation in the US based on ATCA forces TNCs to comply with human rights.

Therefore, the preliminary conclusion is that transnational litigation is an indispensable instrument for the enforcement of human rights as against TNCs. It might stand as the only avenue that offers the following further advantages. First, it addresses all TNCs universally. Second, it is "hard law." Third, it is directly applicable to non-state actors. Fourth, it can be invoked by and against individuals or other private actors, such as TNCs. Fifth, it is possible to hold TNCs accountable in civil jurisdiction for damages and criminally with the concept of corporate criminal liability in those jurisdictions that recognize the concept. Transnational litigation against TNCs would be subsidiary to any international court on human rights violations against corporations that is established in the future. But even if that court were established, transnational litigation involving TNCs would not be replaced, but only complemented. Such is the case with the *Rome Statute for the ICC*. Transnational litigation is therefore an important enforcement avenue and will be discussed in greater detail in the form of international human rights litigation in the US.

There are other nations that apply norms transnationally or extraterritorially, but these norms mostly apply to individual malfeasants, not so much to corporate actors.[632]

---

jurisdiction and who subsequently becomes resident in the United Kingdom', see Section 68(1) of the United Kingdom's International Criminal Court Act 2001.

630 *Doe v. Unocal*, 27 F Supp 2d 1174, D.C. C.D. Cal. (1998); *In re Pinochet*, 38 ILM 430, U.K. House of Lords (1998); *Attorney-Gen. of the Government of Israel v. Eichmann*, 36 ILR 277, Sup. Ct. Israel (1962); *Prosecutor v. Jean-Paul Akayesu*, Case No ICTR-96-4-T, Summary available at 37 ILM 1399, ICTR (1998).

631 C Chiomenti, 'Corporations and the International Criminal Court; Global Law Working Paper 01/05, Symposium - 'Transnational Corporations and Human Rights', Hauser Global Law School Program' (2005) <http:// nyulawglobal.com/ workingpapers/ GLWP0105 Chiomenti_000.rtf> (September 7, 2007) at 30.

632 A Ramasastry and RC Thompson, *Commerce, Crime and Conflict* (Fafo New Security Programme, 2006) at 16.

Those norms that apply to corporations, mostly relate to bribery of public officials, money laundering or the importation of stolen property.[633] The fact that the US ATCA statute also covers human rights violations is unique.[634] The ATCA litigation involving TNCs begun with the *Unocal* decision in 1997.[635]

---

633 *Ibid.* at 16.

634 *Ibid.* at 24.

635 *Doe v. Unocal (Unocal I)*, 963 F Supp 880, D.C.C.D. Cal. (1997).

Chapter IV. Key judicial cases in ATCA litigation against TNCs

This chapter presents a selection of important human rights cases involving TNCs in US litigation. The material facts are drawn from the judgments and additional sources, such as newspaper articles and electronic sources, including human rights activist websites and corporate websites. The aim is to assess some examples of the human rights violations by TNCs within their respective factual contexts. The cases are ordered chronologically by the time when the action was brought to court. The analysis of these cases represents the author's opinion.

I. *Doe v. Unocal* – corporations are subjects of international law

A. Material Facts

Plaintiffs in the case of *Doe v Unocal* were villagers of the Tenasserim region of Myanmar, who alleged that the defendant Unocal, a Californian oil company, directly or indirectly subjected the villagers to forced labor, murder, rape, and torture, when the defendant constructed an oil pipeline through Myanmar. Unocal held a 28% share in the Yadana Oil Pipeline project.[636] The French company, Total S.A., held 31%; Thailand's oil company, PTT, held 25%; and Myanmar Oil and Gas Enterprise (MOGE) held 15%. It is undisputed that the Myanmar military provided security and other services for the project, and that Unocal knew about this.[637] The Myanmar Military set up a force of four battalions of 600 men for the purpose of protecting the project.[638] The Myanmar military built helipads and cleared roads along the proposed pipeline route for the benefit of the project. The plaintiffs testified that they were forced to work as "porters" to work on infrastructure projects for the pipeline project.[639] One of the plaintiffs tried to escape and was shot at.[640] In retaliation the Myanmar Military threw this man's wife and child into a fire: the wife was badly burned and the child died.[641] Several plaintiffs testified that rapes occurred as part of the forced labor program.[642] Furthermore, there are reports that many villages were relocated without compensation to facilitate the construction of the pipeline.[643]

---

636 A Salpukas, 'Burma Project Tests Unocal Resolve' *New York Times* (May 22, 1997) D1; See also HJ Tolley and A Lawrence, 'Doe v. Unocal: Forced Labor and Corporate Liability' (2002) <http:// homepages.uc.edu/ thro/ doe/doe-unocal.htm> (December 9, 2005) at 2.

637 *Doe v. Unocal (Unocal III)*, 395 F3d 932, C.A. 9 (2002) at 937.

638 *Ibid.* at 937.

639 *Ibid.* at 939.

640 *Ibid.* at 939.

641 *Ibid.* at 939-940.

642 *Ibid.* at 940.

643 *Doe v. Unocal (Unocal II)*, 110 F Supp 2d 1294, D.C. C.D.Cal. (2000) at 1298.

The Myanmar government and military have a long and well-documented history of human rights abuses and Unocal was made aware of this before it entered the project. The US Department of State *Country Report on Human Rights Practices* for 1991 states that the "Burmese army has for decades conscripted civilian males to serve as porters."[644] When Unocal was confronted with these allegations in January 1995, Unocal's president, John Imle, said that he would continue the engagement in Myanmar with the military, even though Myanmaris were used as forced labor workers. "If forced labor goes hand and glove with the military yes there will be more forced labor."[645] He also said that he was well aware that these acts might breach human rights, but he refused to take responsibility for the behavior of the military.[646] Imle admitted that their human rights behavior is in a "grey zone."[647] As Paul Hoffman, one of the lead attorneys for the plaintiffs, put it, Unocal made a Faustian deal; a deal with the devil.

B. Litigation

In September 1996, four villagers and the Federation of Trade Unions of Burma and the National Coalition Government of the Union of Burma, the government in exile, brought an action against Unocal and the project, hereinafter called the *Roe* action. In October 1996, a second action was brought by fourteen villagers, who sought to represent a class of all residents of the Tenasserim region who have suffered similar injuries, hereinafter called the *Doe* action. The cases were decided by US District Judge Richard Paez, who was nominated by then President Bill Clinton.[648]

In *Doe*, at first instance, the District Court dismissed the claims against the Myanmar state-owned MOGE pursuant to the Foreign Sovereign Immunities Act (FSIA). The Court dismissed the claims against the French company, Total, for lack of personal jurisdiction, which was later affirmed by the Court of Appeals.[649] The Court at first instance determined that the subject matter jurisdiction was available under the ATCA and that the plaintiffs had pled sufficient facts.

In the *Roe* action the District Court found that the trade unions and the government in exile lacked standing. The other findings were identical to the *Doe* action. In August 2000, the District Court consolidated the *Doe* and *Roe* actions for summary judgment. The plaintiffs of both actions appealed the District Court's decision. The Court of Appeals decided the appeals in September 2002. The principal legal issues

---

644 United States Department of State, *Country Reports on Human Rights Practices for 1991* (U.S. Government Printing Office, Washington, D.C. 1992) at 796.

645 *Doe v. Unocal (Unocal III)*, 395 F3d 932, C.A. 9 (2002) at 941.

646 *Ibid.* at 942.

647 *Ibid.* at 942.

648 HJ Tolley and A Lawrence, 'Doe v. Unocal: Forced Labor and Corporate Liability' (2002) <http:// homepages.uc.edu/ thro/doe/doe-unocal.htm> (December 9, 2005) at 3.

649 *Doe v. Unocal*, 248 F 3d 915 D.C. C.D. Cal. (2001).

in the Unocal Case on the appellate level were: the question of complicity; the necessity of state action; and the choice of law.

On the question of complicity, the Court of Appeals found that "the evidence does suggest that Unocal knew that forced labor was being utilized and that the Joint Venture benefited from that practice."[650] The Court stated that Unocal knew or should have known that its conduct, including the payments to build infrastructure, would assist or encourage the Myanmar military to subject the plaintiffs to forced labor.[651]

In the issue of state action requirement, the Court noted that traditionally in international law only states were bound to human rights. But then the bench referred to decisions of international tribunals, such as the Nuremberg Tribunal, which stated that individuals and corporations can also be held responsible for human rights violations.[652]

It held that the plaintiffs sufficiently alleged violations of the law of nations under the ATCA and that international law had been appropriately applied. Obviously, the defendants were waiting for the US Supreme Court's decision in *Sosa v. Alvarez.*[653] The US Supreme Court affirmed the ATCA as a basis for human rights claims.[654] In April 2005, Unocal agreed to settle and compensate the victims for an undisclosed, but assumedly, large amount.[655] The case was therefore jointly dismissed. It seems likely that the agreement in this case was also expedited by the fact that Chevron took over Unocal. Chevron might have had an interest in eliminating either the risk of high damages or the negative public opinion.[656]

---

650 *Doe v. Unocal (Unocal II)*, 110 F Supp 2d 1294, D.C. C.D.Cal. (2000) at 1310.

651 *Ibid.* at 1310.

652 *Doe v. Unocal (Unocal III)*, 395 F3d 932, C.A. 9 (2002) at 948.

653 *Sosa v. Alvarez-Machain* (03-339) 542 US 2739, US S.Ct. (2004).

654 *Ibid.* at 2761 et *seq.*

655 Earthrights, 'Final Settlement Reached in Doe v. Unocal' (2005) <http:// www.earthrights.org/ legalfeature/ final_settlement_reached_in_doe_v._unocal.html> (September 9, 2007) ("The parties to several lawsuits related to Unocal's energy investment in the Yadana gas pipeline project in Myanmar/Burma announced today that they have settled their suits. Although the terms are confidential, the settlement will compensate plaintiffs and provide funds enabling plaintiffs and their representatives to develop programs to improve living conditions, health care and education and protect the rights of people from the pipeline region. These initiatives will provide substantial assistance to people who may have suffered hardships in the region. Unocal reaffirms its principle that the company respects human rights in all of its activities and commits to enhance its educational programs to further this principle. plaintiffs and their representatives reaffirm their commitment to protecting human rights.")

656 Earth Rights International, 'Historic advance for universal human rights: Unocal to compensate Burmese villagers' (2005) <http:// www.earthrights.org/ legalfeature/ historic_ advance_ for_ universal_ human_ rights_ unocal_ to_ compensate_ burmese_ villagers_2.html> (September 9, 2007).

C. Analysis

The Unocal case stands as one of the cases where a company felt compelled to settle the suit and pay compensation for human right violations. The entire process, from its inception to the settlement of the case took nine years. It is a historic victory for human rights and for the corporate accountability movement. "This case will reverberate in corporate boardrooms around the world and will have a deterrent effect on the worst forms of corporate behavior."[657]

II. Holocaust litigation against Swiss banks

A. Material facts

The other successful ATCA litigation was the litigation concerning the Holocaust. The Holocaust is the name applied to the systematic state-sponsored persecution and genocide of various ethnic, religious and political groups during World War II by Nazi Germany and its collaborators. About 6 million Jews were killed and the total death toll of the Nazi government atrocities (including Slavic people, homosexuals, Sinti and Roma, political opposition) is estimated to be well at around 21 million.[658]

In the context of human rights litigation against TNCs only the three most prominent cases of Holocaust-related ATCA litigation are presented here: the Swiss banks litigation; the German industry litigation; and the Japanese forced labor camps litigation. The former two were successful, the latter was not. For the sake of completeness, the other Holocaust-related ATCA claims are also mentioned here.[659] The claim against French banks was settled at approximately US$ 172.5 million.[660] The claim against the Belgian banks was settled at US$ 55.5 million.[661] Moreover, some of the cases concerning art that was looted during the Holocaust had impressive outcomes. The case of five masterpieces by Gustav Klimt, including the world-famous portrait of Adele Bloch-Baur, was litigated in various US courts. The US Supreme Court ruled that the heirs to the estate of which the picture was a part could sue a foreign sovereign country, Austria. The final decision was announced by an Austrian arbitration panel, which ruled that these works belonged to the heirs.[662] The picture of Adele itself was sold for US$ 135, the highest sum ever paid.[663]

---

657 R Weissman, 'Victories! Justice! The People's Triumphs Over Corporate Power' *Multinational Monitor* (July 1, 2005) 35.

658 RJ Rummel, *"Demozid" - der befohlene Tod: Massenmorde im 20. Jahrhundert; Übersetzung aus dem Englischem* (Lit Verlag, Münster 2003) at 95.

659 For more information see MJ Bazyler, *Holocaust Justice: The Battle for Restitution in America's Courts* (New York University Press, New York 2003) at chapters 3,4 and 5.

660 *Ibid.* at 198.

661 *Ibid.* page 201.

662 *Maria V. Altmann et. al. v. Republik Österreich Schiedsspruch vom 15. Januar 2006*, http:// www.adele.at/ Schiedsspruch/ Schiedsspruchpdf, Arbitration Panel Austria (Schiedsgericht Österreich) (2006).

663 V Noce, 'L'«Adele» de Klimt bat le «Garçon à la pipe» de Picasso; Son portrait d'Adele Bloch-Bauer, à l'histoire tourmentée, est devenu la toile la plus chère au monde' *Liberation* (June 23,

The Swiss banks litigation began the Holocaust litigation and at the heart of its genesis was a coincidence. Ed Fagan, a controversial attorney in New York did some unrelated work for Gizella Weisshauss, an energetic Holocaust survivor.[664] She told Fagan about her various attempts to collect the money deposited by her father in Switzerland before the war. She travelled to Switzerland various times. The Union Bank of Switzerland (UBS) as many other Swiss banking institutions have rejected claimants based on a variety of legalisms. Methods to retain the funds of European Jews dormant bank accounts were not to answer letters of survivors or to ask for death certificates[665] – not issued by Nazi officials – or to ask for tremendous search fees as high as 750 Swiss francs.[666] Furthermore, it has been shown that the Swiss banks systematically destroyed evidence relating to their dealings in World War II.[667]

B. Litigation

In October 1996, Fagan filed the first class action lawsuit against the Swiss banks, seeking US$ 20 billion in damages.[668] It marked the beginning of the Holocaust restitution movement in US courts, which led to one of the highest settlements in human rights cases. The case was joined by three other cases and then consolidated under the master docket, *In re Holocaust victim assets litigation.*[669] The Swiss banks were confronted with two main allegations: (1) they failed to return moneys deposited with them by Jews, (2) they traded in assets looted from the Jews by the Nazis and in assets that were the product of slave labor.[670]

Plaintiffs alleged that the banks collaborated with and aided the Nazi regime in furtherance of war crimes, crimes against humanity, crimes against peace, slave labor

---

2006) 24 ; C Vogel, 'Lauder Pays $ 135, a Record for a Klimt Portrait' *New York Times* (June 19 2006) 12.

664 Ed Fagan should be credited with his dedication to the Holocaust claims and other huge class action claims. At the same time he was criticized by some colleagues because of his sometimes dilettante written submissions, which in the Apartheid claims led to the withdrawal of his mandate. See for example S Howald, 'Globale Gerechtigkeit – Apartheid-Klagen gegen Konzerne, Vortrag an der Kantonschule Trogen AR vom 23. November 2005' (2005) at 12.

665 MJ Bazyler, *Holocaust Justice: The Battle for Restitution in America's Courts* (New York University Press, New York 2003) at 15 (A Jewish heir of a bank account accounts the difficulties she had for many decades to claim her money from the Credit Suisse in Geneva: "It was like dealing with the Gestapo all over again. They insisted I needed a death certificate. I pleaded with them. I told them there were no records from the camps. I started to scream at a bank manager, 'What do you want me to do? Find Hitler and Himmler and ask them to sign my father's death certificate?' They looked at me blankly.")

666 SE Eizenstat, *Imperfect Justice: Looted Assets, Slave Labor, and the Unfinished Business of World War II* (Public Affairs, New York 2003) at 46-51.

667 MJ Bazyler, *Holocaust Justice: The Battle for Restitution in America's Courts* (New York University Press, New York 2003) at 17.

668 *Ibid.* at 7.

669 *In re Holocaust Victim Assets Litigation*, 105 FSupp2d 139, D.C. E.D.N.Y. (2000).

670 MJ Bazyler and C Mesa, 'The Holocaust Restitution Movement in Comparative Perspective' 20 Berkeley Journal of International Law 11 (2002) at 14.

and genocide. Plaintiffs also alleged that defendants breached fiduciary and other duties, breached contracts, converted plaintiffs' property, enriched themselves unjustly, were negligent, violated customary international law and the ATCA, violated Swiss banking law and the Swiss commercial code of obligations, engaged in fraud and conspiracy, and concealed relevant facts from the named plaintiffs and the plaintiff class members in an effort to frustrate the plaintiffs' ability to pursue their claims.[671]

The Swiss banks moved to dismiss on various grounds, including *forum non conveniens*, lack of personal and subject matter jurisdiction, and failure to join indispensable parties. While the motions to dismiss were pending, the parties engaged in a settlement agreement, which made it unnecessary to decide the motions.[672] The Swiss banks settled at US$ 1.25 billion. They were pressured to settle the dispute by various different groups, including US state officials and various investigative reporting articles and books were published.[673] The Special Representative of the President, the Senate and various state governments maintained pressure on the Swiss banks and threatened sanctions.[674]

C. Analysis

Overall, it can be said that this settlement was largely enabled by the cooperation of different groups – most particularly, the media, government, business and the courts. The ATCA and human rights litigation was the initial vehicle for the whole process. They provided the victims of the Holocaust with a forum in which to articulate their claim for restitution in respect of the complicity of private corporations in the atrocities during the Nazi era.[675] Fifty-three years after the end of the Holocaust, the survivors were finally able to obtain their assets that had been lying dormant in Switzerland.

The whole Swiss bank litigation process stands as a significant triumph of justice many years after the terrifying atrocities during the Nazi era. It is interesting that it took such a long time to address the critical issue of Swiss banks' complicity in the Nazi atrocities. The reasons for this delay cannot be resolved here, but it suffices to

---

671 *In re Holocaust Victim Assets Litigation*, 105 FSupp2d 139, D.C. E.D.N.Y. (2000) at 141.

672 *Ibid.* at 142.

673 MJ Bazyler, *Holocaust Justice: The Battle for Restitution in America's Courts* (New York University Press, New York 2003) at 1-3, for example "Nazi Gold: The full story of the fifty year Swiss-Nazi conspiracy to steal billions from Europe's Jews and Holocaust survivors", "The Swiss, the Gold and the Dead: How Swiss bankers helped finance the Nazi war machine," et al.

674 See *Ibid.* at 21 et *seq.*

675 B Neuborne, 'Preliminary Reflections on Aspects of Holocaust-Era Litigation in American Courts' 80 Washington University Quarterly 795 at 815; SM Chelsey and others, 'Sosa v. Alvarez-Machain, US Supreme Court No. 03-339, Brief for the world Jewish Congress and the American Jewish Committee as Amici Curiae in support of respondents' (2005) <www.nosafehaven.org/ _legal/ atca_ pro_wrldJwshCongress.pdf> at 3.

say that momentum has developed in recent years that these types of allegations of historical wrongs merit systematic investigation and resolution. This suggests that other wrongs might also be addressed in the coming years – such as those relating to the Turkish atrocities of the Armenian people in the early 20th century or even US slave trading.[676]

III. German forced labor litigation succeeded

A. Material facts

Since the 1950s, Germany has paid approximately US$ 60 billion to some Jewish victims of the Holocaust.[677] Some Jewish Holocaust victims received small pensions. Germany never paid for victims of slave labor.[678] Between eight and ten million people were forced to work as laborers in factories and camps in Germany, Austria and throughout occupied Europe during World War II. The conditions in these labor camps or concentration camps were horrific. People were essentially worked to death with inadequate rations and in terrible conditions. Many were killed if they were unable to work.[679]

"There was hardly a German company that did not use slave and forced labor during World War II," conceded Count Otto Lambsdorff, the chief German government negotiator in the forced labor settlement.[680]About 1¼ million of these laborers were still alive in 2001.[681] The German government claimed it was not obligated to pay compensation since the slave labor was carried out by private German industry. German industry claimed that the German government, as successor of the Third Reich, is liable, because industry was forced to use slave labor for the wartime economy.[682]

B. Litigation

In March 1998 the first slave labor case was filed against German industry, *Iwanowa v. Ford Motor Company*.[683] In the ensuing months, close to 40 separate lawsuits were

676 MJ Bazyler, *Holocaust Justice: The Battle for Restitution in America's Courts* (New York University Press, New York 2003) at 320 et *seq.*

677 *Ibid.* at 61.

678 *Ibid.* at 61.

679 Y Eliach, B Gurewitsch and S Center for Holocaust, *The Liberators, Eyewitness Accounts of the Liberation of Concentration Camps: Oral History Testimonies of American Liberators from the Archives of the Center for Holocaust Studies* (Center for Holocaust Studies Documentation and Research, Brooklyn 1981); E Aroneanu, *Inside the Concentration Camps: Eyewitness Accounts of Life in Hitler's Death Camps* (Praeger, Conneticut 1996).

680 MJ Bazyler, *Holocaust Justice: The Battle for Restitution in America's Courts* (New York University Press, New York 2003) at 59.

681 MJ Bazyler and C Mesa, 'The Holocaust Restitution Movement in Comparative Perspective' 20 Berkeley Journal of International Law 11 (2002) at 21.

682 *Ibid.* at 22.

683 *Iwanowa v. Ford Motor Company*, 67 F Supp 2d 424, D.C.N.J. (1999).

filed in various courts throughout the United States against numerous German companies that used slave labor during the war.[684] The claims were based on: (1) the customary international law prohibition on the enslavement of conquered populations; and (2) the Nuremberg Principles that bar the commission of war crimes and crimes against humanity. Ed Fagan took American-style tactics to the heart of Germany in leading Holocaust survivors on a march through Frankfurt's financial district.[685]

The defendants argued that the claims founded on German law were barred by the two-year statute of limitations governing employment contracts and that the international law claims involved non-justiciable war reparations.[686] In September 1999, the claimants suffered a serious setback in the litigation. Two federal judges dismissed five of the lawsuits. First, Judge Joseph Greenaway, Jr. dismissed the lawsuit against Ford Motor Company.[687] In addition, Judge Dickinson R. Debevoise dismissed four separate lawsuits against German companies Degussa and Siemens.[688] Both judges held that the suits were non-justiciable, specifically that they were precluded by the "Two-Plus-Four Treaty."[689] Judge Greenaway also found some claims against Ford to be time-barred. The plaintiffs appealed, arguing that the fact that the treaty was silent on this issue cannot be construed as an intention to destroy the plaintiffs' claims.

Ultimately, the litigation became moot when the German government and German industry entered into a settlement in December 1999. The judicial persecution, the media attention and the settlement in the Swiss banks case, played a major role in persuading German industry to establish a German foundation to pay compensation to Holocaust victims.[690] The name of the foundation was "Remembrance, Responsibility, and the Future Foundation." The dismissal of some of the cases might have had the effect of reducing the final amount that was paid into the Foundation, but most of the other cases were still pending and the dismissals were appealed. Finally, the parties settled at 10 billion Deutsche Mark (approximately US$ 5 billion).[691] Each individual survivor will receive a lump sum payment of between

---

684 MJ Bazyler and C Mesa, 'The Holocaust Restitution Movement in Comparative Perspective' 20 Berkeley Journal of International Law 11 (2002) at 21.

685 J Weisman, 'Redress Sought in Nazi-Era Labor' *Baltimore Sun* (August 23, 1999) 1A.

686 B Neuborne, 'Preliminary Reflections on Aspects of Holocaust-Era Litigation in American Courts' 80 Washington University Quarterly 795 at 815.

687 *Iwanowa v. Ford Motor Company*, 67 F Supp 2d 424, D.C.N.J. (1999).

688 *Burger-Fischer v. Degussa AG*, 65 F Supp 2d 248, D.C.N.J. (1999).

689 Treaty on the Final Settlement with Respect to Germany Sept 12, 1990, FRG-GDR-Fr-USSR-UK-US, BGBl II S1317, 29 ILM 1186 (1990).

690 B Neuborne, 'Preliminary Reflections on Aspects of Holocaust-Era Litigation in American Courts' 80 Washington University Quarterly 795 at 815.

691 *Ibid.* at 815.

US$ 2,500 and $ 7,500.[692] In June 2007 € 4.32 billion (approximately US$ 5.1 billion) has been paid out to 1,66 million survivors.[693]

The German government and German industry only agreed to the settlement on the condition that it included "legal peace" that is, an indemnity from all current and future litigation.[694] The indemnity from future litigation proved to be a difficult undertaking to enforce, as US judges are independent and do not take "marching orders" even from their own government.[695] The governments entered into an unprecedented executive agreement that compels the US government to issue statements of interest in cases relating to slave labor in Germany. The legal character and the obligation of courts pursuant to these agreements have not been definitively determined and remain controversial. It is not possible for the executive branch to prevent all future litigation.[696] The agreements do not, however, purport to terminate the litigation of their own force, but instead obligate the State Department to file "Statements of Interest" requesting that courts dismiss the cases based on the foreign policy interests of the United States. To date, the agreement has been successful in preventing further claims.

The assistance from government, this time from both sides, was of great importance to the final settlement of this case.[697] US President Bill Clinton and German Chancellor Gerhard Schröder personally intervened and accelerated the settlement various times. They nominated two powerful government negotiators, US Undersecretary of Treasury Stuart Eizenstat and the former Secretary of Commerce, Count Otto Lambsdorff. The cooperation between the two governments was harmonious and successful.[698]

---

692 MJ Bazyler and C Mesa, 'The Holocaust Restitution Movement in Comparative Perspective' 20 Berkeley Journal of International Law 11 (2002) at 23.

693 M Marek, 'Zwangsarbeiter-Stiftung zieht Bilanz' *Handelsblatt* (December 28, 2005) 6; Stiftung Erinnerung Verantwortung und Zukunft, 'Website' (2007) <http:// www.stiftung-evz.de/> (December 10, 2007).

694 MJ Bazyler, *Holocaust Justice: The Battle for Restitution in America's Courts* (New York University Press, New York 2003) at 83; In greater detail: G O'Donoghue, 'Precatory Executive Statements and Permissible Judicial Responses in the Context of Holocaust-Claims Litigation' 106 Columbia Law Review 1119 (2006).

695 MJ Bazyler, *Holocaust Justice: The Battle for Restitution in America's Courts* (New York University Press, New York 2003) at 84.

696 Further information- see IB Wuerth, 'The Dangers of Deference: International Claim Settlement by the President' 44 Harvard International Law Journal 1 (2003).

697 B Neuborne, 'Preliminary Reflections on Aspects of Holocaust-Era Litigation in American Courts' 80 Washington University Quarterly 795 at 815.

698 MJ Bazyler, *Holocaust Justice: The Battle for Restitution in America's Courts* (New York University Press, New York 2003) at 71.

C. Analysis

This case proves that huge class actions against corporations for human rights violations can be won when judiciary, government, media and other institutions work together. "The idea that the new Volkswagen Beetle might have to compete for media attention with protesting Holocaust survivors was not something shareholders or corporate executives would allow to happen."[699] The judiciary plays a crucial role. In the end it was fear of American litigation that finally brought German business to the bargaining table.[700] Chancellor Schröder explicitly acknowledged in February 1999, when the German Foundation was first announced, that he was doing this "to counter lawsuits, particularly class action lawsuits, and to remove the basis of the campaign being led against German industry and our country."[701]

The outcome of approximately US$ 5 billion possibly represents the biggest settlement of any judicial litigation in history. In the light of the torments that were endured during the slave labor, an individual payment of approximately US$ 5000 per person for sometimes many years of forced labor is certainly nowhere near "fair compensation."[702] Nevertheless, the compensation represents an important symbol. More than 50 years after the end of the most horrific event of the 20th century, American courts enabled a settlement that might stand as a symbol for reconciliation and justice. The settlement might also stand as an example for future reconciliation processes for historical wrongs.[703] According to the Jewish expert on Holocaust justice Bazyler the case stands as an important victory for human rights and as a triumph of the US judicial system for making it possible.[704]

---

699 S Kreindler, 'History's Accounting: Liability Issues Surrounding German Companies for the Use of Slave Labor by their Corporate Forefathers' 18 Dickinson Journal of International Law 343 (2000) at 364.

700 MJ Bazyler and C Mesa, 'The Holocaust Restitution Movement in Comparative Perspective' 20 Berkeley Journal of International Law 11 (2002) at 25.

701 MJ Bazyler, *Holocaust Justice: The Battle for Restitution in America's Courts* (New York University Press, New York 2003) at 83.

702 *Ibid.* at 101 (As one Holocaust survivor put it: "I think the whole thing is a terrible scandal that one has to wait fifty years to be paid. And naturally there is no relation [between the compensation and] what we had to suffer.")

703 See M Ellinikos, 'American MNCs Continue to Profit from the Use of Forced and Slave Labor Begging the Question: Should America Take a Cue from Germany?' 35 Columbia Journal of Law and Social Problems 1 (2001).

704 MJ Bazyler and C Mesa, 'The Holocaust Restitution Movement in Comparative Perspective' 20 Berkeley Journal of International Law 11 (2002) at 12 ("The Holocaust did not occur in the United States, but in Europe. Most Holocaust survivors reside outside of the United States. It is the United States legal system, however, that has taken the lead in delivering some measure of long-overdue justice to aging Holocaust survivors. As with all transnational litigation today, the highly-developed and expansive system of American justice makes the United States the best, and in most instances, the only, legal forum for the disposition of such claims." According to Bazyler some of the progressive elements of the American legal culture are American-style discovery, expansive jurisdiction, the possibility to obtain large awards, punitive damages, class action suits, American attorneys as 'greater risktakers', contingency fees, losing party

IV. Japanese forced labor litigation – an example of failure

A. Material facts

Japan's use of slave labor during World War II appears to have equaled or possibly exceeded that of Nazi Germany. It is estimated that around 15 million Chinese and between four and six million Koreans were slave laborers during the war.[705] Among the Japanese companies that profited from slave labor are now some of the largest concerns in the world: Mitsubishi, Mitsui, Nippon Steel, Kawasaky Heavy Industries and others.[706] Japan's government and Japanese corporations continue to resist legal and moral responsibility.[707] Japanese courts have admitted that Korean and Chinese workers were forced to work without pay, but dismissed suits because the relevant statutes of limitation have expired.[708]

In California, one of Japan's largest construction companies, Kajima, was the target of a tireless campaign for compensation and an apology. In November 2000, it agreed to pay US$ 4.6 million to the families of the 986 slave laborers. It was the first Japanese company to have "broken ranks" and accepted responsibility for wartime injuries it caused to forced laborers.[709]

B. Litigation

In July 1999, California enacted a law, the California Code of Civil Procedure (CalCCP), Section 354.6 of which enabled "prisoners-of-war of the Nazi regime, its allies or sympathizers" to recover compensation for labor performed as a Second World War slave victim [...] from any entity or successor in interest thereof, for whom that labor was performed."[710] In the ensuing months, more than 30 lawsuits were filed in California courts. Plaintiffs included civilian American, Chinese, Filipino, and Korean forced laborers, former US and allied prisoner of war, and so-called "comfort women."[711]

In June 2000, most of the California litigation was consolidated by transfer orders to the courtroom of federal judge Vaughn Walker of the Northern District of California. In September 2000, the Court dismissed all claims brought by US civilians and

does not pay the attorneys' fees and last but not least ATCA.)

705 J Haberstroh, 'The Alien Tort Claims Act & Doe v. Unocal: a Paquete Habana approach to the rescue' 32 Denver Journal of International Law and Policy 231 (2004) at 255.

706 MJ Bazyler and C Mesa, 'The Holocaust Restitution Movement in Comparative Perspective' 20 Berkeley Journal of International Law 11 (2002) at 26.

707 J Haberstroh, 'The Alien Tort Claims Act & Doe v. Unocal: a Paquete Habana approach to the rescue' 32 Denver Journal of International Law and Policy 231 (2004) at 256.

708 *Ibid.* at 257.

709 *Ibid.* at 258.

710 *Ibid.* at 258.

711 *Ibid.* at 260. "Comfort women" is a euphemism referring to women who were forced into sexual servitude to gratify members of the Japanese armed forces.

prisoners of war on the ground of the 1951 Peace Treaty.[712] In the treaty, the United States waived all claims arising out of actions by the Japan government, Japanese nationals, or private Japanese corporations that were taken "in the course of the prosecution of the war;"[713] however, it is questionable if the use of slave labor can be seen as prosecution of the war.[714] In September 2001, the Court also dismissed the claims brought by the Korean, Chinese, and Filipino plaintiffs.[715] It stated that, as the Philippines Government signed the treaty, the claims by Filipinos must also be dismissed. The claims by the Chinese and Korean victims could not be dismissed on the ground of the Peace Treaty since those countries never signed it. The Court instead dismissed those claims on other grounds. It held that the CalCCP was unconstitutional, since it infringes the exclusive foreign affairs power of federal government.[716] Moreover, it held that the claims based on the ATCA were statute-barred.[717] The Court gave "significant weight" to a Statement of Interest that was given by the US government. It asserted that the claims of the Allied prisoners of war were barred by the Peace Treaty and the Californian law CalCCP was an intrusion into the federal government's exclusive responsibility for foreign relations.[718]

C. Analysis

The material facts and claims of the Nazi slave labor cases and the Japanese slave labor cases were very similar. The vastly different outcome of the Japanese slave labor cases is, therefore, striking. One of the reasons for the different outcome is the influence of the United States government. Still under Clinton's administration it supplied the first Statement of Interest in August 2000 asking for a dismissal of the Japanese forced labor claims.[719] On the other hand, in the Nazi forced labor claims, the same Clinton administration was eager to push the settlement through and achieve some compensation for the victims.

---

712 *In re World War II Era Japanese Forced Labor Litigation*, 114 F Supp 2d 939, D.C. N.D. Cal. (2001) at 942.

713 Treaty of Peace with Japan Sept 8, 1951, 3 UST 3169 (1951); it states in full in Article 14(b): "Except as otherwise provided in the present Treaty, the Allied Powers waive all reparations claims of the Allied Powers, other claims of the Allied Powers and their nationals arising out of any actions taken by Japan and its nationals in the course of the prosecution of the war, and claims of the Allied Powers for direct military costs of occupation."

714 U.S. Senate Committee on the Judiciary, 'Former U.S. World War II POW's: A Struggle for Justice, 106th Congress, 2nd Session' (2000) <www.aiipowmia.com/testimony/slvlbr1.html> .

715 *In re World War II Era Japanese Forced Labor Litigation*, 114 F Supp 2d 939, D.C. N.D. Cal. (2001).

716 *Ibid.* at 1164.

717 *Ibid.* at 1165.

718 United States Department of State, 'In re World War II Era Japanese Forced Labor Litigation (2001), Brief of the United States as amicus curiae in support of petitioners, Court of Appeal of the State of California Second Appelate District, Division Eight, 2d Civ. No. B155736' (2001) *at* 14.

719 *Ibid.* at 14.

The administration plays a considerable role in human rights class actions. It used its power in a discriminating fashion. The remarks of acting assistant attorney general David W Ogden before the Senate Judiciary Committee do not really enlighten the differing approaches taken.[720] From a victim's point of view it would seem unjust that the victims of slave labor in Europe could claim reparations and that they received some form of apology, whereas the victims of Japanese slave labor could not. To this day the Japanese forced labor claims remain unresolved.

V. *Wiwa v. Royal Dutch Petroleum* – US forum for human rights claims?

A. Material Facts

Ogoni is a densely populated area in southern Nigeria with vast oil resources. Shell began oil production in the Ogoni region in about 1958. Shell appropriated land though coercion and misrepresentation without adequate compensation to the owners.[721] Nigerian oil provided a considerable amount of Shell's yearly revenue. Shell still pumps about 500,000 barrels a day from the eastern delta region and from several large offshore platforms.[722] The company has previously outlined plans to resume operations in the delta, but there is no guarantee that it will succeed this time. Shell's profit in 2006 was US$ 22.4 billion, the third largest ever corporate profit in the world.[723] Oil revenues provide 80% of Nigeria's federal government budget.[724] Shell's oil exploration has contaminated the local water supply and agricultural land in Ogoni. The major part of the natural gas produced during the exploration has been flared, which causes persistent air and noise pollution.[725]

Since 1990 the Ogoni people have engaged in peaceful protests against Shell's operations. By 1993, more than half of the population of Ogoni supported the Movement for the Survival of Ogoni People (MOSOP), a Nigerian human rights organization designed to protect the rights of the Ogonis. In 1994, the Nigerian

720 DW Ogden, 'Statement of David W. Ogden, Acting Assistant Attorney General Civil Division before the Committee on the judiciary United States Senate concerning compensation for Bataan POWs' (2000) <www.usdoj.gov/ civil/ speeches/ ogden.htm or www.aiipowmia.com/ testimony/ slvlbr1.html>.

721 Center for Constitutional Rights and Earth Rights International, 'Wiwa v. Royal Dutch Petroleum Company, Complaint for Wiwa v. Anderson' (2001) <http:// www.earthrights.org/ files/ Legal% 20Docs/ Wiwa% 20v%20Shell/ Wiwa-v-AndersonComplaint.pdf> (December 12, 2006) at 3, Nr. 14.

722 J Mouawad, 'Shell expects full output from Nigeria' *New York Times* (April 5, 2007) C1.

723 C Krauss, 'Exxon and Shell Report Record Profits for 2006' *New York Times* (February 2, 2007).

724 See The World Bank Group, 'Nigeria at a glance' (2006) <http://devdata.worldbank.org /AAG/ nga_aag.pdf> (May 2, 2007).

725 Center for Constitutional Rights and Earth Rights International, 'Wiwa v. Royal Dutch Petroleum Company, Complaint for Wiwa v. Anderson' (2001) <http:// www.earthrights.org/ files/ Legal% 20Docs/ Wiwa% 20v% 20Shell/ Wiwa-v-AndersonComplaint.pdf> (December 12, 2006) at 3, Nr. 15.

government instigated violent raids in at least 60 towns and villages in Ogoni to punish entire communities for their support of MOSOP. During these raids, several hundred Ogoni people were tortured, flogged, raped, detained and at least 50 were killed.[726] Other sources speak of 2000 deaths.[727] Shell and the Nigerian military allegedly worked together in suppressing the Ogoni people. Shell paid Nigerian military forces, supplied logistical support and provided surveillance and monitoring information.[728] They transported troops via helicopter, boat and other means.[729] According to sources from the *New York Times*, Shell frequently called for assistance from security forces, which led to numerous deaths.[730] The security forces were locally known as the "kill-and-go-mobs."[731]

Ken Saro-Wiwa and John Kpuinen were the leaders of MOSOP. They were detained because of their non-violent opposition to the activities of Shell and the Nigerian government with fabricated murder charges.[732] In November 1995, they were sentenced to hang by a special tribunal, the Civil Disturbances Special Tribunal, thereby violating numerous norms of customary international law. The death penalty was given retroactive effect, the judgment was not subject to review by a higher court and it violated other procedural guarantees of due process of law, including the right to counsel and the right to know the charges against one. Several others were also detained and charged in front of the Civil Disturbance Special Tribunal and one died in detention.

Shell and the government worked closely together during the trial of Saro-Wiwa and Kpuinen. They allegedly held regular meetings – for example, one was held on March 16, 1995 in London.[733] On March 18, 1995 the Civil Disturbances Special Tribunal assumed jurisdiction. Shell allegedly promised bribes to at least two key witnesses to give false testimony against Saro-Wiwa.[734] There was a huge public outcry during the trial of Saro-Wiwa and Kpuinen, but Shell and its chairmen refused

---

726 *Ibid.* at 4, Nr. 27.

727 K Maier, 'Nigerian Dissident Faces Death Penalty' *The Independent* (October 29, 1995) World 12; A Rowell, 'Sleeping With the Enemy' *Village Voice* (January 23, 1996) World 23.

728 Center for Constitutional Rights and Earth Rights International, 'Wiwa v. Royal Dutch Petroleum Company, Complaint for Wiwa v. Anderson' (2001) <http:// www.earthrights.org/ files/ Legal% 20Docs/ Wiwa% 20v% 20Shell/ Wiwa-v-AndersonComplaint.pdf> (December 12, 2006) at 5, Nr. 20.

729 D Cassel, 'Corporate Initiatives: A Second Human Rights Revolution?' 19 Fordham International Law Journal 1963 (1996) at 1965.

730 P Lewis, 'Blood and oil: A special report; After Nigeria represses, shall defends its record' *New York Times* (February 13, 1996) 1.

731 *Ibid.*

732 Center for Constitutional Rights and Earth Rights International, 'Wiwa v. Royal Dutch Petroleum Company, Complaint for Wiwa v. Anderson' (2001) <http:// www.earthrights.org/ files/ Legal% 20Docs/ Wiwa% 20v% 20Shell/ Wiwa-v-AndersonComplaint.pdf> (December 12, 2006) at 4, Nr. 20g.

733 *Ibid.* at 5, Nr. 33.

734 *Ibid.* at 5, Nr. 38.

to intervene, even though they knew that an intervention could have prevented the death penalty, because of the strong interdependence of Shell and the Nigerian government.[735]

B. Litigation

Defendants in this case are the Royal Dutch Petroleum Company of the Netherlands and the Shell Transport and Trading Company plc of the United Kingdom, who jointly operate a vast international integrated network of affiliated but formally independent oil and gas companies (this network will be referred to as "Shell"). Among these affiliated companies is Shell Petroleum Development Company of Nigeria Ltd, a wholly owned Nigerian subsidiary of the defendants. The plaintiffs, through their surviving next of kin, alleged that they were imprisoned, tortured and executed by the Nigerian government for their peaceful opposition to the defendants' oil exploration activities. The action commenced in November 1996.

The plaintiffs based their claims on ATCA and RICO (the Racketeer Influenced and Corrupt Organizations Act). The defendants moved to dismiss on the grounds of lack of personal jurisdiction over Shell, *forum non conveniens*, and lack of subject matter jurisdiction. They argued that ATCA did not apply to a corporation and that the claim was precluded by the political question doctrine and the Act of State doctrine. In September 1998 the District Court for the Southern District of New York decided that the case should be dismissed on the grounds of *forum non conveniens*, ruling that England was a more convenient forum.[736] Furthermore, the Court held it lacked personal jurisdiction, because the defendant lacked "minimum contacts" with New York.[737]

In September 2000 the Court of Appeals for the Second Circuit overruled this decision and decided that the United States was a proper forum.[738] The US had an interest in seeing that claims for violations of international law were litigated in a US forum. It said that greater weight should be given to the choice of forum by the plaintiffs, since some of the plaintiffs were US nationals. It stated that the defendant had sufficient contact with New York on account of its maintenance of an investor relations office.[739] In February 2002 the District Court denied the motions to dismiss on virtually all of the plaintiff's claims. Judge Wood found that the plaintiff's allegations constituted participation in crimes against humanity, torture, summary

---

[735] D Cassel, 'Corporate Initiatives: A Second Human Rights Revolution?' 19 Fordham International Law Journal 1963 (1996) at 1966.

[736] *Wiwa v. Royal Dutch Petroleum Co.*, No 96 Civ 8386, 1998 US, Dist LEXIS 23064 D.C. S.D. N.Y. (1998).

[737] *Ibid.* at 10.

[738] *Wiwa v. Royal Dutch Petroleum Co.*, 226 F3d 88, C.A.2 (2000).

[739] *Ibid.* pages 94-99.

execution, arbitrary detention, cruel, inhuman and degrading treatment and other violations of international law.[740]

C. Analysis

Shell's exploitive and inhuman business methods in Nigeria might stand as one of the most blatant corporate violations of human rights after World War II. The *Wiwa* decision stands as a precedent for human rights accountability of TNCs.[741] The Court of Appeals for the Second Circuit acknowledged the importance of international law and human rights law for the US legal system. The Court also made a number of crucial findings in relation to *forum non conveniens*. It put more weight on the considerations of the poorer party in recognition of the difficulty of their moving to another jurisdiction.[742] The most important implication of this case is that it reduces the capacity of human rights violators to dismiss the case on the grounds of *forum non conveniens* and personal jurisdiction. In other words, the forum doors for human rights cases in the US were opened up a little more. The *Wiwa* case affirmed that US courts are willing to hear international human rights claims.

VI. *Bowoto v. Chevron* – Chevron's ties to Nigerian human rights abuses

A. Material facts

Chevron was the first oil corporation that came to Nigeria in 1956, it found oil in 1963.[743] It has explored oil in vast amounts from the Niger Delta for many decades. Because of their exploitive policies, environmental pollution and brutal military interventions they faced increasing resistance, beginning in the late 1990s.[744] In 1998 the Ijaw Youth Council (IYC) stated in a ten point declaration, the Kaiama declaration,[745] that, among other things, all natural resources in the Ijaw land belong

---

740 *Wiwa v. Royal Dutch Petroleum Co.*, No 96 Civ 8386, 2002 US, Dist LEXIS 3293, US D.C. S.D. N.Y. (2002).

741 L Wick, 'Human rights violations in Nigeria: Corporate Malpractice and state acquiescence in the oil producing deltas of Nigeria' 12 Michigan State Journal of International Law 63 (2003) at 88.

742 See also AX Fellmeth, 'Wiwa v. Royal Dutch Petroleum Co.: a new standard for the enforcement of international law in US courts?' 5 Yale Human Rights and Development Law Journal 241 (2002) at 254.

743 K Howe, 'Human Rights Group Investigates Chevron - 2 Nigerian Killed in Offshore Protest' *San Francisco Chronicle* (November 19, 1998) A1.

744 S Bräuer, 'Shell gefährdet Ölförderung' *Die Zeit* (June 28, 2006) ("Wer verstehen will, woher der Hass der Menschen auf Shell und die anderen in Nigeria aktiven Ölkonzerne kommt, muss sich vor Augen führen, wie sehr sich ihr Leben durch die Präsenz dieser Unternehmen verändert hat. 'Die Leute in der Region lebten traditionell von Fischfang und Landwirtschaft', sagt der nigerianische Politikwissenschaftler Thomas Imobighe. Doch nun hat ausgelaufenes Öl das Grundwasser verseucht. Viele Menschen haben keinen Zugang mehr zu sauberem Trinkwasser. 'Die Leute sind zu Bittstellern erniedrigt worden und von Gaben der Ölkonzerne abhängig, die ihre Umgebung zerstört haben.'")

745 IJAW Youths of the Niger Delta, 'The Kaiama Declaration' (1998) <http://

to the Ijaw people and is the basis of their survival.[746] They argued further that they would cease to recognize all undemocratic decrees, which rob them of the right to ownership and control of their resources and demanded the withdrawal of military forces of occupation from Ijaw land. The Kaiama declaration also demanded that all oil companies cease their operations in Ijaw land. Initially, the IYC protested peacefully for their cause.[747]

The subsequent military deployment after the Kaiama declaration and peaceful demonstrations was massive. Tanks, armored personnel carriers, artillery pieces, amphibious and fast attack crafts, warships and hundreds of combat ready soldiers were deployed. Many military checkpoints were installed. The creeks were patrolled by naval ships. Soldiers were posted to oil installations. The police stations were closed down.[748] On January 4, 1999, in the Ikenyan incidents, a helicopter flown by Chevron pilots and transporting Nigerian military opened fire on artless Nigerian villagers.[749] Chevron acknowledged that it paid the soldiers, but considered it a regulatory payment for the guarding of its facilities.[750] Since the incidents the situation in the Niger Delta region has increasingly deteriorated and militarized.[751] A human rights commission, installed by the Nigerian government, gives some insights on the responsibilities of the Nigerian military and the private corporations.[752]

B. Litigation

The plaintiffs, five Nigerians, filed an action in May 1999 alleging that Chevron violated human rights, including the rights to life and freedom of movement. The District Court for the Northern District of California held that (1) defendants could not be held directly liable for the alleged abuses; (2) genuine issues of material fact existed as to the extent to which defendants were integrally involved in the actions and structure of the company; and (3) defendants were not alter egos of the company.[753] In August 2007 the District Court granted Chevron's motion for

www.unitedijawstates.com/ kaiama.htm> (September 10, 2007).

746 A Ikelegbe, 'Encounters of Insurgent Youth Associations with the State in the Oil Rich Niger Delta Region of Nigeria' 22 Journal of Third World Studies 151 (2005).

747 *Ibid.*

748 *Ibid.*

749 *Bowoto v. Chevron*, 312 F Supp 2d 1229, D.C. N.D. Cal. (2004) at 1233.

750 *Ibid.* at 1242; See also A Gedicks, *Resource Rebels: Native Challenges to Mining and Oil Corporations* (South End Press, Cambridge, MA 2001) at 49 et *seq.*

751 J Iwori, 'Niger Delta: Still a Festering Sore' *This Day (Nigeria)* (January 29, 2006) ("Other security operatives in the sprawling complex of the multinational oil company [the Italian Agip] were not spared. In the gun battle that ensued later, not less than nine persons were killed. They include two civilians and seven mobile policemen."); E Amaize, 'Militants Threaten to Adopt New Tactics on Hostage Taking' *Vanguard Nigeria* (July 17, 2007).

752 Human Rights Violations Investigation Commission Nigeria, 'Human Rights Violations Investigation Commission Report (aka Oputa Report)' (2002) <http://www.dawodu.com/oputa1.htm> (September 10, 2007).

753 *Bowoto v. Chevron*, 312 F Supp 2d 1229, D.C. N.D. Cal. (2004).

summary judgment.[754] The case is still pending. The main legal issues in this case were the liability of a parent company for the acts of its subsidiary and whether the "corporate veil" can, in these circumstances, be pierced in order to hold a parent corporation liable for the actions of its subsidiary.

C. Analysis

The case confirms that TNCs aggressively engage in forum shopping and make use of lower regulatory standards concerning the protection of human rights. Chevron behaved like a moral free rider, since they voluntarily worked together with Nigeria's ruthless military government and restrained human and environmental rights to a large extent. Through the court proceedings the case attains a lot of attention and the legal battle in US courts over Chevron's responsibility for the human rights violations seems far from being resolved.

VII. *Bano v. Union Carbide* – A corporate environmental disaster

A. Material facts

Bhopal is a city of 1.5 million inhabitants in central India. In 1984, it became the site to one of the worst industrial disasters in recent history. On December 3, 1984, forty tons of lethal gasses leaked into the air over Bhopal from Union Carbide corporation's pesticide factory. Over 5,000 people were instantly killed and the current death toll from exposure-related conditions is estimated to be over 22,000 people.[755] The disaster was caused by corporate negligence and in 1989 Union Carbide agreed to settle with the Indian government on behalf of all victims for US$ 470 million to finalize all related civil litigation. [756]

Two decades after the original tragedy, another tragedy unfolds. When Union Carbide fled India after the disaster in 1984 it left behind tons of chemical wastes that have contaminated, slowly but steadily, the groundwater, thereby poisoning thousands of Bhopal residents.[757]

B. Litigation

In November 1999, one individual and three organizations brought a claim pursuant to the ATCA. It alleged that Union Carbide and its Chief Executive Officer (CEO) Warren Anderson, the defendants, violated human rights, as the rights to life, health and security of the person, and they were accused of cruel, inhuman and degrading

---

754 *Bowoto v. Chevron*, WL 2349336, D.C. N.D. Cal. (2007) (Summary judgment is a legal term which means that a court has made a determination (a judgment) without a full trial. Such a judgment may be issued as to the merits of an entire case, or of specific issues in that case.)

755 Amnesty International, 'Clouds of Injustice: Bhopal disaster 20 Years on' <http:// web.amnesty.org/ pages/ ec-bhopal-eng> (December 7, 2005).

756 D Housego, 'Union Carbide Asks Indian Unit To Help Pay Victims' *Financial Times UK* (February 16, 1989) 4.

757 *Bano v. Union Carbide*, 361 F3d 696, C.A. 2 (2004) at 702.

treatment and violation of environmental rights.[758] In August 2000, Judge Keenan in the District Court for the Southern District of New York dismissed the class action suit mainly on the ground that the Indian Bhopal Act of 1985[759] prevented individuals or organizations outside of India from bringing an action.[760]

In November 2001, the Second Circuit Court of Appeals in part affirmed and partly overturned the decision.[761] Claims on seven counts regarding contamination of ground water and soil were reversed and discovery began. In March 2003, Judge Keenan dismissed the case again, this time because the plaintiffs' claims were untimely and directed at improper parties. Having sold its shares, Union Carbide could no longer be held legally responsible.[762]

In March 2004, the Second Circuit reversed Judge Keenan's dismissal. The Court held that Union Carbide could be ordered to clean up individual victims' property and the plant site itself if the Indian authorities requested such a cleanup. At first the Indian government was reluctant to submit such a statement to the New York District Court. But the threat of an indefinite hunger strike by Bhopal activists made the Government of India bow to the pressure and the site of the Bhopal disaster can now be cleaned up.[763] In October 2005, the District Court of the Southern District of New York denied a motion to certify the claim as class action for all private land owners who are affected by the contamination.[764]

In April 2006, leading Congressmen and other lawmakers filed an *amicus* brief stating that it is unacceptable to allow an American company to evade civil liability for environmental pollution and abuses committed overseas. "It is [...] a mandate of the US Congress to ensure that US corporations and companies investing abroad or undertaking activities overseas comply with local, national and international laws regarding the environment and do not engage in environmental abuses. [The Members of Congress] request that this Court...accord due consideration to the strong legal and public policy interests of the United States in affording redress to victims of environmental pollution and harm caused by American corporations." [765]

---

758 KF McCallion and HR Sharma, 'Bano v. Union Carbide, Amended Complaint' (2004) <www.bhopal.net/ oldsite/ documentlibrary/amendedplaint.html> .

759 Bhopal Gas Leak Disaster (Processing of Claims) Act (the Bhopal Act) Indian Parliament Act No 21 of 1985, Gazette of India (Extraordinary) pt 2, sec 2, Mar 29 (1985).

760 *Bano v. Union Carbide*, 2000 WL 1225789, D.C. S.D.N.Y. (2000) at 10 et *seq.*

761 *Bano v. Union Carbide*, 273 F3d 120, C.A. 2 (2001).

762 *Bano v. Union Carbide*, 2003 WL 1344884, D.C. S.D. N.Y. (2003).

763 Students for Bhopal, 'Timeline, court and other materials, Dow is liable' <http:// www.studentsforbhopal.org/ DowIsLiable.htm#Civil> (December 7, 2005).

764 *Bano v. Union Carbide*, 2003 WL 1344884, D.C. S.D. N.Y. (2003).

765 F Pallone, 'Eleven Members of Congress File Amicus Brief in Support of Bhopal Victims' Lawsuit' (2006) <http:// www.house.gov/ list/ press/ nj06_pallone/ pr_apr4_india.html> (September 10, 2007).

C. Analysis

This case deals with one of the worst industrial tragedies in history. It is an example of how an American company made use of "pollution havens" and neglected liability until they were legally forced to accept some responsibility. The ATCA was the peg on which to hang the litigation and was instrumental in bringing justice for the victims of the disaster. American companies can now be sued for civil damages in some cases where they have taken advantage of lax environmental regulation and this has harmed the local populace.

VIII. *Sarei v. Rio Tinto* – Another victory after *Sosa*

A. Material Facts

Papua New Guinea (PNG) is one of the largest countries in the South Pacific with abundant natural resources. Plaintiffs in this case were 21 individuals who lived on the island of Bougainville, which belongs to PNG. The plaintiffs alleged that the Rio Tinto corporation has violated human rights.[766] Specifically, their claim alleged crimes against humanity, war crimes, murder, violation of the rights to life and health, racial discrimination, cruel inhuman and degrading treatment, violation of international environmental rights and a consistent pattern of gross violations of human rights. The allegations are atrocious – including the rape and murder of innocent women and men – conducted with the assistance of Rio Tinto.[767]

Rio Tinto is an international mining group, composed of a British corporation, Rio Tinto plc, and an Australian corporation, Rio Tinto Limited. It operates in 6 product groups including aluminum, diamonds and gold, copper, energy, industrial minerals and iron ore worldwide.[768] During the 1960s, the Rio Tinto Group built a mine in the village of Panguna on Bougainville. Rio Tinto required the approval of the PNG government to remove a village and destroy massive portions of the rain forest for the world's largest open-cast copper mine, which is approximately 500 meters deep and 7 kilometers wide. Rio Tinto offered 19.1% of the mine's profits to the PNG government.[769] By 1972, the construction was complete and operations began. By the early 1980s, the Panguna mine was responsible for 23% of the Rio Tinto Group's profit.[770] The mine produced approximately 180,000 tons of copper concentrate and 400,000 ounces of gold annually.[771] 4,000 people were working in three eight-hour

---

766 *Sarei v. Rio Tinto PLC*, 221 FSupp2d 1116, D.C. C.D. Cal. (2002).

767 *Ibid.* at 1127.

768 Rio Tinto, 'Website' (2007) <http://www.riotinto.com/> (September 10, 2007); see also JG Holt, 'The International Law Exception to the Act of State Doctrine: Redressing Human Rights Abuses in Papua New Guinea' 16 Pacific Rim Law and Policy Journal 459 (2007).

769 *Sarei v. Rio Tinto PLC*, 221 FSupp2d 1116, D.C. C.D. Cal. (2002) at 1121.

770 *Ibid.* at 1123.

771 *Ibid.* at 1123.

shifts seven days a week.[772] The majority of the persons working at the mine were foreign, while the local workers received "slave wages."[773]

The environmental impact of the operations was enormous. Over a billion tones of toxic waste were dumped into the Jaba River, which has destroyed all aquatic life.[774] The water is no longer safe for drinking or bathing.[775] The pollution of land, water and air caused many Bougainvilleans to suffer health problems. The construction was met by resistance of the local Bougainvilleans from the inception of the project onwards. In 1988, Rio Tinto threatened to close the mine and withdraw all of its investments if the government did not quell the uprising so that the company could recommence operations.[776] When the local resistance to close the mine was successful, Rio Tinto and the PNG government brought troops to reopen the mine. They allegedly crushed several riots, and many people were killed.[777]

In 1990, the PNG government with the support and encouragement of Rio Tinto imposed a blockade to force the Bougainville revolutionaries to surrender. The blockade prevented medicine, clothing and other essential supplies from reaching the people. A top Rio Tinto official purportedly encouraged continuation of the blockade.[778] Overall approximately 15,000 people died in the civil war that was fought in Bougainville and which was initiated by the mining activities of Rio Tinto. The war crimes included: (a) aerial bombardment of civilian targets; (b) wanton killing and acts of cruelty; (c) burning of houses and villages; (d) outrages upon personal dignity, acts of rape, humiliating and degrading treatment; (e) perfidious use of the red cross emblem; and (f) pillage.[779]

B. Litigation

In November 2000, Alexis Holyweed Sarei, a current California resident, who lived in Bougainville between 1973 and 1987 and 21 individuals filed a putative class action.[780] In January 2001 the defendants filed a motion to dismiss, asserting that the Court lacked subject matter jurisdiction and on the ground of *forum non conveniens*. The defendants also raised the issue of non-justiciability under the Act of State and political question doctrines. Finally, they stated that the Court should not intervene in this case on the basis of the doctrine of international comity.

---

772 *Ibid.* at 1123.
773 *Ibid.* at 1124.
774 *Ibid.* at 1125.
775 *Ibid.* at 1124.
776 *Ibid.* at 1125.
777 *Ibid.* at 1122, 1126.
778 *Ibid.* at 1126.
779 *Ibid.* at 1127.
780 *Ibid.*

In July 2002, the District Court for the Central District of California decided the case.[781] On the one hand the Court found that the plaintiffs sufficiently alleged a violation of international law and sufficiently pleaded that the mining group was a state actor. On the other hand the Court placed great emphasis to a Statement of Interest by the State Department to the effect that continuance of the lawsuit would negatively affect the foreign policy of the United States, because a peace treaty was negotiated.[782] Therefore, the Court held that all claims were barred by the political question doctrine.

The United States Court of Appeals for the Ninth Circuit decided the appeal in August 2006.[783] By a 2:1 majority, the Ninth Circuit ruled, among other things, that: (1) all of the plaintiffs' claims, with the exception of the *UNCLOS* claim, assert *jus cogens* violations that are actionable under *Sosa*; (2) the *UNCLOS* claim, while not *jus cogens*, can provide the basis of an actionable ATCA claim given the widespread ratification of that treaty; (3) corporations can be vicariously liable for violations of *jus cogens* norms; (4) the State Department's Statement of Interest did not expressly request dismissal therefore there was no basis to dismiss the lawsuit on political question grounds; (5) *jus cogens* violations cannot be "official acts" under the Act of State doctrine; and (6) the ATCA does not require that claimants exhaust local remedies, the language regarding exhaustion in *Sosa* notwithstanding.

C. Analysis

Rio Tinto earned billions of dollars exploiting the natural resources of Bougainville, while destroying nature and turning large parts of the island into wasteland. They face strong allegations that they initiated and supported a civil war which killed thousands of people. It is unlikely that Rio Tinto will face trial in either the host country, PNG, or in either of their countries of incorporation, Australia or England. The Court of Appeals decision is a significant victory. It is the most important human rights case decided on the appellate level since *Sosa* and is very promising. It widened the scope of the ATCA to include environmental claims and made TNCs vicariously liable for violations of *jus cogens* norms and other norms of international law.

IX. *Flores v. Southern Peru Copper* – Environmental harms not litigated

A. Material Facts

Southern Peru Copper is Peru's second largest copper producer and is controlled by the Mexican mining corporation Group Mexico.[784] Peru earns half of its annual

---

781 *Ibid.*

782 *Ibid.* at 1190.

783 *Sarei v. Rio Tinto*, 456 F3d 1069, C.A. 9 (2006).

784 Reuters News Service, 'Southern Peru says will commit to Ilo upgrade in May, Planet Ark' (2003) <http:// www.planetark.org/ dailynewsstory.cfm/ newsid/ 20313/ story.htm> (December

export income from copper.[785] The mining business also caused a "culture clash" between the mining companies and the farmers who say that their livelihood is at risk.[786] The waters and the pasture land have been contaminated, the animals are dying and the people are suffering from asthma and lung diseases as a result of the pollution.

B. Litigation

The plaintiffs in this case are eight residents of Peru, who claim to suffer from respiratory diseases that were caused by the pollution from the defendant, Southern Peru Copper. They commenced a trial in December 2000 and claimed that the pollution violated their rights to life, health and sustainable development.[787] The defendants moved to dismiss for failure to state a claim under international law and alternatively on the ground of *forum non conveniens*. The United States District Court for the Southern District of New York granted the motion to dismiss on both grounds.

The District Court held that the plaintiffs failed to establish that the pollution and resultant injury violated well-established rules of customary international law.[788] The human health impact was of growing concern, but there was no general consensus among nations that a high level of pollution, causing harm to humans, is universally unacceptable.[789] The Court stated that it was not to be determined by judges which specific acts are so egregious that they become the subject of international law under the ATCA.[790] The right balance between economic development and environmental protection lies within the sound discretion of each state with respect to land within its borders.[791] International law is not violated by pollution occurring exclusively within a state's borders.[792]

The Court also held that the *forum non conveniens* objection applied. Even though often egregious human rights crimes are involved, the Court opined that the ATCA litigation is not immune from *forum non conveniens* analysis.[793] Although widespread

---

8, 2005).

785 T Cespedes, 'Peru peasants march to Lima, protest mining damage, Planet Ark' (2002) <http:// www.planetark.org/ dailynewsstory.cfm/ newsid/ 16767/ story.htm> (December 7, 2005).

786 *Ibid.*

787 *Flores v. Southern Peru Copper Corp.*, 253 F Supp 2d 510, D.C. S.D. N.Y. (2002).

788 *Ibid.* at 519.

789 *Ibid.* at 519.

790 *Ibid.* at 523 ("It is not for judges, however humane and sensitive or callous and unfeeling, to determine which specific acts injuring life or health are so 'egregious' that they become the subject of international law. The Law of Nations, as that phrase is used in 28 USC. 1350 [ATCA], is declared by the Parliament of Nations, and not by judges, trial or appellate, of a particular nation. Thus it is for the nations of the world to develop customary international law that identifies those horrific acts that should be universally prohibited.")

791 *Ibid.* at 521-522.

792 *Ibid.* at 522.

793 *Ibid.* at 529.

corruption is widely reported from Peruvian courts, the Court denied to issue a blanket *forum non conveniens* condemnation of Peruvian courts.[794] In balancing the interests, it found that the Peruvian courts are an adequate forum to decide this case. An important consideration was also that the principal witnesses and documents were in Peru.[795]

The plaintiffs appealed and the United States Court of Appeals for the Second Circuit issued its decision in August 2003.[796] After a detailed survey of ATCA and the sources of international law, the Court of Appeals affirmed the decision of the District Court. The pollution did not constitute a violation of the law of nations.[797] It denied the proposed standard of egregiousness to distinguish between violation of customary international law and mere violations of national law.[798] The motion to dismiss on the ground of *forum non conveniens* was granted.[799]

C. Analysis

The *Flores* case is mainly a claim that is concerned with environmental issues. The courts purported to set a standard defining a violation of international law actionable under the ATCA. The environmental harms of the mining company in the Ilo Valley of Peru are unsettling, but did not achieve the standard for an ATCA claim. The Court's decision may be acceptable insofar as it is impossible for United States courts to intervene in respect of every claim relating to gross environmental pollution.

It also appears correct to dismiss the claim on the ground of *forum non conveniens*. It could be seen as judicial imperialism if the Court had sweepingly condemned all Peruvian courts as corrupt and inadequate. The judgments of the District Court and Court of Appeals carefully considered the sources and limits of international law and international comity. Developments after the Court decision show that the Peruvian forum dealt with the environmental problem. The Peruvian government took regulatory steps and enforced them insistently in order to stop the pollution. In March 2003, Southern Peru agreed to comply with the three-month government deadline to improve its smeltering facilities and reduce the sulfuric gases by 92 percent.[800] Not every violation of international law, or as in this case, international environmental law ought properly to be addressed by American courts, especially in cases where the host state jurisdictions agree.

---

794 *Ibid.* at 539.
795 *Ibid.* at 541.
796 *Flores v. Southern Peru Copper Corp.*, 406 F3d 65, C.A. 2 (2003).
797 *Ibid.* at 88.
798 *Ibid.* at 84.
799 *Ibid.* at 98.
800 Reuters News Service, 'Southern Peru may boost copper smelter capacity, Planet Ark' (2003) <http://www.planetark.com/dailynewsstory.cfm/newsid/20369/newsDate/4-Apr-2003/story.htm> (December 9, 2005).

X. Sinaltrainal v. Coca-Cola – Coca-Cola kills?

A. Material Facts

On the morning of December 5, 1996, two paramilitary members shot Isidro Segundo Gil, a leader of the Sinaltrainal trade union.[801] He was shot within the Coca-Cola bottling plant in Carepa, Columbia, where he was working. Before and after the incident, the workers had been constantly intimidated by the paramilitary forces in order to drive the union out of the bottling plant.[802] Numerous trade unionists were also shot.[803] The paramilitary forces, which intimidated the workers and shot Gil, were hired by the manager of the bottling plant, Ariosto Milan Mosquera, who aggressively pursued the goal of destroying the trade union with inhuman, criminal means.[804] Mosquera was, in turn, responsible for a US citizen, Richard Kirby, who was the owner of Panamco Ltd. This corporation exists solely for the purpose of bottling and distributing Coca-Cola products in Colombia. Panamco is a wholly owned subsidiary of the Delaware corporation, Panamerican Beverages Inc, which was largely owned by the Coca-Cola corporation.

B. Litigation

Members of the bottling plant brought a suit in July 2001 alleging Coca-Cola was guilty of war crimes.[805] In turn, Coca Cola brought a motion to dismiss for lack of subject matter jurisdiction. The District Court for the Northern District of Alabama granted the motion to dismiss. It held that war crimes committed by private individuals are only actionable if they are "committed in the course of hostilities that are related to an ongoing war."[806] The murder in this case was motivated by private business interests and did not occur in the course of a conflict between the Colombian military and paramilitary or guerilla forces.[807] Nevertheless, the Court held that summary execution violates international law if it is committed by state officials or private individuals acting under color of law.[808] The Court held that the complaint sufficiently alleged significant assistance of the Colombian government. However,

801 *Sinaltrainal v. Coca-Cola Co.*, 256 F Supp 2d 1345, D.C. S.D. Fla. (2003) at 1350; see also G Marx, 'Coca-Cola Feels Heat on Killing - Union Activist's Death in Columbia Spurs US Campus Boycott Talks' *Chicago Tribune* (February 13, 2006) 15 (Already, about 20 colleges in the US and abroad have halted sales of Coke on campus, in part over the Colombia controversy.)

802 *Sinaltrainal v. Coca-Cola Co.*, 256 F Supp 2d 1345, D.C. S.D. Fla. (2003) at 1350.

803 LM Sixel, 'Union to Protest at Coke Annual Meeting' *Houston Chronicle* (April 16, 2003) (According to Amalgamated Bank LongView Collective Investment Fund, which owns 819,209 shares of Coke stock, Gil was one of more than 1,500 Colombia trade unionists killed during the past decade.)

804 *Sinaltrainal v. Coca-Cola Co.*, 256 F Supp 2d 1345, D.C. S.D. Fla. (2003) at 1350.

805 *Ibid.*

806 *Ibid.* at 1352.

807 *Ibid.* at 1352.

808 *Ibid.* at 1356.

the plaintiffs did not adequately establish a causal connection between the Coca-Cola entities and the actions of their alleged agents in Columbia.

C. Analysis

Columbia has been the site of massive labor rights violations in recent years. This case shows the difficulty of proving the requisite causal connection between the parent company and its subsidiary, even though there was an unbroken chain of agency relationships from the plant manager to the US parent Coca-Cola corporation.

XI. Presbyterian Church of Sudan v. Talisman Energy – Corporations and Sudan genocide

A. Material Facts

Sudan is the largest country of Africa. The government of Sudan is currently run by the fundamentalist National Islamic Front (NIF) and its human rights record remains abysmal.[809] In the past the Sudanese civil war in southern Sudan between 1983 and 2005 was purportedly aimed at the forced Islamization of the country and has resulted in approximately two million deaths and the displacement of four million people.[810] In the Darfur conflict the government and Janjaweed soldiers fight against tribes in

809 International Commission of Inquiry on Darfur, *Report of the International Commission of Inquiry on Darfur to the UN Secretary-General, Pursuant to Security Council Resolution 1564 of 18 September 2004* (2005) at paras 106, 112, 123, 126, 342 and especially 518 ("On the basis of the above observations, the Commission concludes that the Government of Sudan has not pursued a policy of genocide. Arguably, two elements of genocide might be deduced from the gross violations of human rights perpetrated by Government forces and the militias under their control. These two elements are: first, the *actus reus* consisting of killing, or causing serious bodily or mental harm, or deliberately inflicting conditions of life likely to bring about physical destruction; and, second, on the basis of a subjective standard, the existence of a protected group being targeted by the authors of criminal conduct. Recent developments have led to the perception and self perception of members of African tribes and members of Arab tribes as making up two distinct ethnic groups. However, one crucial element appears to be missing at least as far as the central Government authorities are concerned: genocidal intent. Generally speaking the policy of attacking, killing and forcibly displacing members of some tribes does not evince a specific intent to annihilate, in whole or in part, a group distinguished on racial, ethnic, national or religious grounds."); See also Amnesty International, 'Annual Report - Sudan' (2007) <http:// web.amnesty.org/ report2006/ sdn-summary-eng> (May 2, 2007); Human Rights Watch, 'World Report 2007- Sudan' (2007) <http:// hrw.org/ englishwr2k7/ docs/ 2007/ 01/ 11/ sudan14715.htm> (May 3, 2007); E Reeves, 'A Brutal Regime Persists in a Distracted World - Sudan's Civil War' *International Herald Tribune* (April 3, 2003) 9.

810 M Burr, *US Committee for Refugees, Quantifying Genocide in Southern Sudan and the Nuba Mountains 1983-1998* (1998).

the Darfur region.[811] In that conflict the death toll is estimated at 450,000 and more than 2.5 million displaced.[812]

The oil revenues were one of the decisive factors in all of the conflicts in Sudan in the 20th century. The revenues, which make up 70% of Sudan's export earnings, were used for military purposes.[813] According to the CIA Factbook estimates of Sudan's proven oil reserves are at 1.6 billion.[814] At a conservative price estimate of around US$ 60 per barrel, the value of these reserves is in the region around US$ 100 billion. The Sudanese government's oil revenues are at approximately US$ 1-2 million per day.[815] "The oil is taken from here and the cash goes to Khartoum to buy bombs that then kill our people," claimed Salva Mathoc, a local commander of the Sudan People's Liberation Army (SPLA).[816]

Oil companies began involvement in Sudan in 1979. The US petrochemical company, Chevron, withdrew its involvement in Sudan because of continued attacks on its workers. The Canadian petroleum company, Talisman, bought its stake from Arakis in 1992 for around US$ 250 million.[817] Talisman bought 25% of the consortium of oil companies called Greater Nile Petroleum Operation Co. (GNPOC). It jointly owned the largest of the oil fields of southern Sudan and, more importantly, a 1,610 km long pipeline to a port located by the Red Sea. Other stakeholders of GNPOC are China National Petroleum Corporation (CNPC), Petronas Carigali Overseas Sdn Bhd, Malaysia and Sudapet Ltd, Sudan.[818]

---

811 International Commission of Inquiry on Darfur, *Report of the International Commission of Inquiry on Darfur to the UN Secretary-General, Pursuant to Security Council Resolution 1564 of 18 September 2004* (2005) at paras 518-519.

812 E Reeves, 'Quantifying Genocide in Darfur' (2006) <http:// www.sudanreeves.org/ Article102.html> (May 3, 2007).

813 HRW, 'Sudan, Oil, and Human Rights' (2003a) <http:// www.hrw.org/ reports/ 2003/ sudan1103/ 5.htm> (February 20, 2006) at 523.

814 USA Central Intelligence Agency, 'The World Factbook - Sudan' (2007) <https:// www.cia.gov/ cia/ publications/ factbook/ geos/ su.html> (May 2, 2007).

815 A Bixler, 'Private enforcement of international human rights laws: could a small church group successfully combat slavery in the Sudan?' 3 Chicago Journal of International Law 511 (2002) at 513; South Sudanese Friends International, 'Oil in Sudan' (2000) <http:// southsudanfriends.org/ issues/ oil000614.html> (December 07, 2005).

816 G Katsh, 'Fueling Genocide, Talisman Energy and the Sudanese Slaughter' (2000) <http:// multinationalmonitor.org/ mm2000/ 00october/ corp2.html> (10) at subheading "Blood and Oil."

817 HRW, 'Sudan, Oil, and Human Rights' (2003a) <http:// www.hrw.org/ reports/ 2003/ sudan1103/ 5.htm> (February 20, 2006) at 170; SJ Kobrin, 'Oil and Politics: Talisman Energy and Sudan' 36 International Law and Politics 425 (2004) at 437.

818 South Sudanese Friends International, 'Oil in Sudan' (2000) <http:// southsudanfriends.org/ issues/ oil000614.html> (December 07, 2005).

The export of oil started in 1999. At first glance, the involvement of Talisman in Sudan seemed to have been a success.[819] The oil production was consistently described as exceeding expectations. However, the stock price did not reflect these "facts on the ground." The stock was priced at a 10-20% discount during the period Talisman was in Sudan and only recovered when Talisman announced it would pull out of its activities in Sudan.[820] Activists linked Talisman to the gross human rights violations that occurred during the government-backed genocide in southern Sudan and many institutional investors began divesting from Talisman.[821]

In March 2003, Talisman sold its 25% in GNPOC to India's national oil company, ONGC Videsh, for US$ 770 million. This left the Swedish company, Lundin, the only Western oil company with any equity in Sudanese oil extraction. The other Western companies, like Talisman, have left Sudan in recent years. In turn, companies from Asia – such as CNPC from China, Petronas from Malaysia and ONGC from India – have taken their place. In August 2003 ONGC also acquired stakes in two other Sudanese oil blocks from Austria's OMV.[822] Other companies that either operate or hold equity in companies that operate in Sudan are likely to face similar divestment campaigns as Talisman.[823]

The oil companies constructed transportation infrastructure, such as the airstrip in Heglig, which was used to conduct attacks on civilians.[824] The runway at Heglig has probably been used in many military offences, but it has been proven that they were used for military operations at least four times in the year 2000.[825] The military used its Antonov planes to expel people under machine gun fire from their property as soon as oil is found.[826] The methods to protect the oil companies were draconian and arbitrary. The Sudanese government expelled people from their land, robbed and burned their property and killed family members.[827] The consortium of international

819 SJ Kobrin, 'Oil and Politics: Talisman Energy and Sudan' 36 International Law and Politics 425 (2004).

820 *Ibid.* at 426.

821 *Ibid.*

822 HRW, 'Sudan, Oil, and Human Rights' (2003a) <http:// www.hrw.org/ reports/ 2003/ sudan1103/ 5.htm> (February 20, 2006) at 2 (Glossaries, The Concessionholders).

823 E Iritani, 'Effort to divest from Sudan picks up steam' *Los Angeles Times* (April 11, 2007); W Hawkins, 'China's Role in Genocide' *Washington Times* 2006) A16; P Sherwell and P Goff, 'Beijing Courts New Allies with 'Black Gold Diplomacy' US Scrambles to Match China as Battle for Access to World's Oil Reserves Becomes New 'Giant Game'' *Sunday Telegraph* 2006) 28; See also Yale Law School - The Allard K. Lowenstein International Human Rights Clinic, 'An Analysis of Select Companies' Operations in Sudan: A Resource for Divestment' (2005) <http:// www.inosphere.com/ sudan/ docs/ Yale_Lowenstein_Updated_Report.pdf> (July 19, 2007) at 31-36.

824 HRW, 'Sudan, Oil, and Human Rights' (2003a) <http://www.hrw.org/ reports/ 2003/ sudan1103/ 5.htm> (February 20, 2006) at 524.

825 *Ibid.* at 524.

826 J Arunga, *The devil's footpath (Film)* (2004).

827 HRW, 'Sudan, Oil, and Human Rights' (2003a) <http:// www.hrw.org/ reports/ 2003/

oil companies was aware that the Government was engaged in a campaign of "ethnic cleansing" to provide a *cordon sanitaire* to facilitate the exploration and extraction of oil.[828] A good account for the genocide and Talisman's involvement is the Harker Report, commissioned by the Canadian government and released in early 2000.[829]

B. Litigation

The case against Talisman commenced in November 2001. The plaintiffs alleged that Talisman conspired with, aided or abetted violations of international law in connection with their former interest in Sudan's oil fields.[830] The plaintiffs claimed that Arakis Energy Corporation and later its successor, Talisman, had a well-established relationship with the Sudanese military. Talisman brought a motion to dismiss for lack of jurisdiction, *forum non conveniens*, international comity and the political question doctrine. Talisman's motion to dismiss the case was denied by District Judge Schwartz in the United States District Court for the Southern District of New York in March 2003.

On the question whether corporations are capable of violating international law, the Court referred to various decisions of international tribunals and provisions of international treaties in affirming that corporations could be held responsible.[831] The test for whether the plaintiffs have satisfied the element of complicity is to ask whether the violation "most probably would not have occurred in the same way had not someone acted in the role that the accused in fact assumed."[832] Concerning *forum non conveniens*, the Court found that Sudan was not an alternative forum due to the government's complicity with the human rights violations.[833] The Court held that the Act of State doctrine is not applicable because world opinion unanimously condemns genocide, war crimes, enslavement and torture as *jus cogens* norms.[834]

---

sudan1103/ 5.htm> (February 20, 2006) at 523.

828 *The Presbyterian Church of Sudan, et. al. v. Talisman Energy, Inc.*, Case No 01CV9882, D.C. S.D. N.Y. (2001) at 10.

829 J Harker, 'Human security in Sudan: The report of a Canadian assessment mission; Prepared for the Minister of Foreign Affairs' (2000) <http:// www.reliefweb.int/ library/ documents/ cansudan2.pdf> .

830 *Presbyterian Church of Sudan et al. v. Talisman Energy, Inc.*, 244 F Supp 2d 289, D.C. S.D. N.Y. (2003) at 296.

831 *Ibid.* at 317-18.

832 *Ibid.* at 324.

833 *Ibid.* at 335-36.

834 *Ibid.* at 345 ("The more clear-cut the alleged violation of international law, the less deference is due to the acts of a foreign sovereign, and vice-versa. It should be apparent that the greater the degree of codification or consensus concerning a particular area of international law, the more appropriate it is for the judiciary to render decisions regarding it, since the courts can then focus on the application of an agreed principle to circumstances of fact rather than on the sensitive task of establishing a principle not inconsistent with the national interest or with international justice.")

In August 2005, the Court declined to dismiss the lawsuit in response to the filing of a Statement of Interest by the US Department of Justice, expressing the US Government's view that the lawsuit interfered with US-Canadian relations. In October 2005 the plaintiffs filed papers to appeal. Both parties are now engaged in the discovery phase.

C. Analysis

Even though the case is yet to be finally determined, this case already stands as a victory for the human rights movement. It shows that complicity with states that vigorously and persistently violate human rights can be prosecuted in US courts even if the company is not incorporated in the US. On the non-legal side, it shows that investments in operations that have close links to gross human rights violations can also be punished on the capital market by investors. These developments of liability of TNCs did not go by unnoticed in business media.[835] It is a moot question whether the investors took into consideration the financial cost of the judicial process for the company or if they divested for moral reasons. It is not possible to retrace definitively the reasons for the depreciation of the share price, but it can be detrimental for companies to have close ties to countries where there are grave human rights concerns.

XII. Other human rights cases involving TNCs

The caseload of human rights cases against TNCs is ever increasing. A small selection of those cases shall be presented here, also in chronological order.

A. Carmicheal v. United Technologies – Early case from 1986

A United Kingdom citizen brought this case pursuant to the ATCA in March 1986.[836] Sigma, a Dutch corporation owned and operated by the Saudi royal family and headquartered in the U.S revoked the plaintiff's exit visa after which he fled to Qatar. He was returned to Saudi Arabia, where he was imprisoned and tortured. He brought the case against the creditors of Sigma. He alleged that Sigma aided and abetted in his torture by refusing to provide for a timely release. The District Court for the Southern District of Texas held that the plaintiff was unable to demonstrate that the creditors were aware of this arrest and incarceration.[837] The Court of Appeal for the Fifth Circuit affirmed the District Court's dismissal in summary fashion. The plaintiff failed to demonstrate a causal connection between the creditors and his imprisonment and torture.[838] It is noteworthy that this ATCA case was filed in the mid-1980s, whereas most of the cases against TNCs have been brought since the mid-1990s.

---

835 See, e.g., S Elliot, 'Emerging Threat: Human Rights Claims' 81 Harvard Business Review 16 (2003); M Hamblett, 'Suit Alleging Canadian Oil Firm Aided Sudan Genocide Proceeds' 229 New York Law Journal 1 (2003); J Drimmer, 'Corporate Exposure Under the Alien Tort Claims Act' *Corporate Counsellor* (June 2007).

836 *Carmichael v. United Technologies Corp.*, 835 F2d 109, C.A. 5 (1988).

837 *Ibid.* at 115.

838 *Ibid.* at 115.

B. Hamid v. Price Waterhouse Coopers – ATCA not for tax treaties

Depositors of a failed international bank brought a claim in 1992 against 77 individuals, firms, and a foreign nation, Abu Dhabi.[839] The plaintiffs alleged that the defendants misused and misappropriated funds, misstated the bank's financial condition and breached their fiduciary duty. The District Court for the Central District of California dismissed the case and the Appellate Court for the Ninth Circuit affirmed the dismissal. It held that international law only regulates the behavior of states, not of corporations or of private individuals.[840] Claims in substance of fraud, breach of fiduciary duty and misappropriation of funds were not appropriately considered breaches of "law of nations" for purposes of the ATCA.[841] This case stands as one of the most obvious cases that the ATCA cannot embrace all obligations from international treaties given the multitude of different topics that are regulated on an international basis. If it were otherwise, every breach of a bilateral tax agreement, for example, would ascend to the ATCA jurisdiction.

C. *Jota v. Texaco* – US corporation in Ecuadorian court

In *Jota v. Texaco* and *Aguinda v. Texaco*, more than 55,000 Ecuadorian and Peruvian residents brought claims in November 1993 against Texaco, a United States-based oil company.[842] The complainants alleged environmental and personal injuries, especially the damage to the tropical rain forest habitats in the Amazon basin, arising out of the oil exploration and extraction operations by Texaco subsidiaries in the Oriente region between 1964 and 1992. The claims were based on theories of negligence, public and private nuisance, strict liability, medical monitoring, trespass, civil conspiracy, and violations of the ATCA.

Both, the *Jota* case and the *Aguinda* case were assigned to Judge Rakoff of the District Court for the Southern District of New York. He dismissed the claims on the ground of *forum non conveniens*.[843] He stated: "In short, plaintiffs' imaginative view of this Court's power must face the reality that United States district courts are courts of limited jurisdiction. While their power within those limits is substantial, it does not include a general writ to right the world's wrongs."[844] The Court of Appeals for the Second Circuit affirmed the decision, but only given Texaco's agreement to subject itself to the jurisdiction of the courts of Ecuador.[845] The trial in Ecuador is ongoing in

---

839 *Hamid v. Price Waterhouse Coopers*, 51 F3d 1411, C.A. 9 (1995).

840 *Ibid.* at 1418.

841 *Ibid.* at 1418.

842 *Jota v. Texaco, Inc.*, 157 F3d 153, C.A. 2 (1998); *Aguinda v. Texaco*, 1993 WL 13148394, D.C. S.D.N.Y. (1993).

843 Concerning the dismissal of the *Aguinda* case, see *Aguinda v. Texaco*, 945 FSupp 625, D.C. S.D.N.Y. (1996) at 627-628; Concerning the dismissal of the *Jota* case, see *Aguinda v. Texaco*, 945 FSupp 625, D.C. S.D.N.Y. (1996) at 628.

844 *Aguinda v. Texaco*, 945 FSupp 625, D.C. S.D.N.Y. (1996) at 628.

845 Gabriel Ashtanga Jota v. Texaco Corporation, 157 F.3d 153 (2d Cir. 1998) at 159.

the Supreme Court of Lago Agrio in Ecuador.[846] This case proves that accountability of TNCs in a globalized world is a daunting and difficult task, but progress is being made. It is notable that a US Court has forced an US corporation to appear and comply with a foreign judgment. It may be considered a trial on Globalization itself.

D. *Beanal v. Freeport-McMoran* – Environmental claims and ATCA

The *Beanal* case arose out of the operations of a mining company in Irian Jaya, Indonesia.[847] The plaintiff, a resident and tribal leader of Irian Jaya, asserted claims for environmental torts, human rights abuses, and "cultural genocide." He alleged that the mining company deposited approximately 100,000 tons of tailings per day in the local rivers. This pollution resulted in the destruction of the lowland rainforest and increased the risks of future floods and landslides. Lake Wanagon was turned into an acid lake with extremely high copper concentrations. Beanal based his claims on three recognized principles of international environmental policy: the "polluter pays" principle, the "precautionary principle" and the "proximity principle."[848] Furthermore, Beanal claimed that Freeport conducted "cultural genocide" because the tribe was forced to relocate, thereby extinguishing its culture and traditions.[849]

Freeport-McMoran challenged Beanal's standing and argued that the Court for the Eastern District of Louisiana had no subject matter jurisdiction. In April 1997 the Court found that "cultural genocide" and environmental claims were not actionable under the ATCA.[850] It found that the only environmental principle that is of sufficient legal substance to give rise to an international obligation is Principle 21 of the *Stockholm Declaration* and Principle 2 of the *Rio Declaration* – namely, that "states have sovereignty over their natural resources and the responsibility not to cause environmental damage."[851] The Court of Appeals for the Fifth Circuit affirmed the decision.[852] The United States cannot displace the environmental policies of sovereign governments.[853]

---

846 C Kolker, 'Jungle Warfare' 6 Corporate Counsel S21 (2006).

847 *Beanal v. Freeport- McMoran, Inc.*, 969 F Supp 362, D.C. E.D. La (1997).

848 *Ibid.* at 382 et *seq.*

849 *Ibid.* at 372 et *seq.*

850 *Ibid.* at 370-381.

851 *Ibid.* at 384; Principle 2, Rio Declaration on Environment and Development June 13, 1992, 31 ILM 874 (1992) and Principle 21 Stockholm Declaration of the United Nations Conference on the Human Environment UN Doc A/ CONF48/14/ Rev 1, at 3, 11 ILM 1416 (the Stockholm Declaration) (adopted June 16, 1972) (1972) ("States have, in accordance with the Charter of the United Nations and the principles of international law, the sovereign right to exploit their own resources pursuant to their own environmental policies, and the responsibility to ensure that activities within their jurisdiction or control do not cause damage to the environment of other States or of areas beyond the limits of national jurisdiction.")

852 *Beanal v. Freeport-McMoran, Inc.*, 197 F3d 161, C.A. 5 (1999).

853 *Ibid.* at 167.

E. *Eastman Kodak Co. v. Kavlin* – ATCA also for corporations

The *Eastman Kodak Co. v. Kavlin* case is a somewhat unusual case. Susana Kavlin was the executive Vice President of the exclusive distributor for Eastman Kodak Company in Bolivia. Kodak cancelled the exclusive distributorship because it was dissatisfied with Kavlin's distribution services and instead assigned exclusivity to Juan Carballo. Kavlin, having very close relations to the highest judicial institutions, filed a criminal complaint against Carballo alleging that he had not registered his company with appropriate Bolivian governmental authorities. Carballo was subsequently detained and imprisoned in inhumane conditions without bail. Kavlin only dropped the suit on Kodak's agreement to reinstate Kavlin as its distributor. Kodak brought an action in October 1996 pursuant to ATCA alleging that Kavlin violated international law, especially through arbitrary detention.

The main legal issues of this case related to *forum non conveniens* and subject matter jurisdiction. The District Court for the Southern District of Florida held the chosen forum by the plaintiff, Kodak, could not be disturbed, because the defendant, Kavlin, had the ability to manipulate the Bolivian judicial system.[854] On the question of subject matter, the Court decided with "deep reservations" that the plaintiff's complaint stated a cause of action pursuant to the ATCA.[855] It held that the law of nations prohibits a state to misuse its coercive power to detain an individual for the purpose of extortion for the benefit for a private entity.[856]

This case is interesting for three reasons. First, the ATCA can also be used by TNCs and not only against them. Second, it is surprising that the scope of the ATCA is understood to be so far-reaching. A detention of 10 days in inhumane conditions can be enough to state a cause of action pursuant to the ATCA. Third, the Court confirmed that US courts remain an open forum for human rights claims.

F. *Bigio v. Coca-Cola* – Complicity in expropriation?

In this case, the plaintiffs being several Jewish Egyptians claimed damages from the defendants, the Coca-Cola Company and the Coca-Cola Export corporation, for a seizure of their property in the 1960s, which allegedly was in violation of international and New York State law.[857] The plaintiffs filed a suit in April 1997 alleging that the original seizure was motivated by religious persecution under the former President of Egypt, Abdel-Nasser, and was therefore a breach of international law. The Federal District Court for the Southern District of New York dismissed the case for lack of subject matter jurisdiction. It concluded that the purchase of the real estate by Coca-Cola in 1993, knowing of the unlawful seizure of the property in the

---

[854] *Eastman Kodak Co. v. Kavlin*, 978 FSupp 1078, D.C. S.D. Fla. (1997) at 1087.
[855] *Ibid.* at 1094.
[856] *Ibid.* at 1094.
[857] *Bigio v. Coca-Cola*, WL 293990, D.C. S.D. N.Y. (1998).

1960s, was not a breach of international law.[858] It held that Coca-Cola was not complicit in the expropriation. It also granted a motion to dismiss on the grounds of the Act of State doctrine.[859]

The Court of Appeals for the Second Circuit affirmed the District Court's dismissal of the claim under the Alien Tort Claims Act but reversed its dismissal of the Common law claims pursuant to the act-of-state doctrine. It found the Act of State doctrine was inapplicable because "the resolution of this case by United States courts will not likely impact on international relations or embarrass or hinder the executive in the realm of foreign relations."[860] On remand, the District Court again dismissed the remaining claims, this time on the ground of international comity or, in the alternative, on the ground of *forum non conveniens*.[861] The plaintiffs appealed again. The Court of Appeals then held that (1) international comity did not require the District Court to dismiss action, and (2) the District Court failed to accord deference to the plaintiff's choice of forum in dismissing action on *forum non conveniens* grounds.[862] Therefore the case was reversed and remanded again in March 2006. The case is still pending.

G. *Bao Ge v. Li Peng* – Adidas prison labor

The plaintiffs in this case alleged that they were thrown into prison for their activities in support of China's free labor movement.[863] They alleged that during their incarceration they were forced to do work for the Adidas Company. They alleged that the prisoners "were coerced into waxing, stitching, sewing and making 'Adidas' soccer balls 14-18 hours a day under inhumane conditions."[864] The plaintiffs claimed they were subjected to "beatings with belts, tortures of various horrifying kinds, exposure of their bodies to mosquito bites and needle wounds, high voltage electrical prod shocks and other inhumane treatments such as malnutrition, no medical attention and lack of sleep."[865]

The factual allegation connecting Adidas to the forced labor is that the prisoners were forced to make soccer balls bearing the Adidas logo, but cannot provide a joint venture or licensing agreement.[866] The District Court of the District of Columbia decided that: (1) Adidas was not a *de facto* state actor, (2) forced labor was not such an extreme form of egregious conduct as to confer jurisdiction over a private

858 *Ibid.* at 2.
859 *Ibid.* at 3.
860 *Bigio v. Coca-Cola Co.*, 239 F3d 440, C.A. 2 (2001) at 452.
861 *Bigio v. Coca-Cola Co.*, No 97 Civ 2858, 2005 WL 287397, 2005 US Dist LEXIS 1587, D.C. S.D. N.Y. (2005).
862 *Bigio v. Coca-Cola*, 448 F3d 176, C.A. 2 (2006).
863 *Bao Ge v. Li Peng*, 201 FSupp2d 14, D.C. D.C. (2000).
864 *Ibid.* at 18.
865 *Ibid.* at 18.
866 *Ibid.* at 18.

corporation under the private actor limb of the ATCA. The claims against the other defendants - the Bank of China and the Chinese government -were also dismissed.

H. *Doe v. Exxon* – Exxon and torture

ExxonMobil corporation, the world's biggest corporation measured at its market capitalization, faced charges of complicity of murder, torture and genocide in Indonesia. Exxon operates one of the world's largest and most profitable oil fields in Aceh/Indonesia. The government of Indonesia earns revenues of over US$ 24 billion annually from the Exxon operation.[867] Exxon has extracted oil worth many billion US$ from Indonesia.[868]

In June 2001, 11 villagers from Aceh filed suit against ExxonMobil and its business partners in the District Court for Washington, D.C., pursuant to the ATCA. Some of them were brutally tortured or raped.[869] They alleged that ExxonMobil provided barracks where the military tortured civilians and that they lent machinery to the military, such as excavators that were then used to dig mass graves. Soldiers who were working for Exxon are accused of appalling torturous acts and murder.[870] The alleged behavior of the corporate defendant, as documented, is shocking.[871]

ExxonMobil moved to dismiss on several grounds, including *forum non conveniens*, personal jurisdiction and lack of subject matter jurisdiction. The US State Department filed a Statement of Interest to dismiss the case. The Government stated that adjudication of this lawsuit at this time would risk a potentially serious adverse impact on significant interests of the United States, including interests related directly to the on-going struggle against international terrorism.

In October 2005, the District Court for the District of Columbia granted the motion in respect to subject matter jurisdiction.[872] The other reasons for dismissal were denied. The decision was appealed and the appeal was dismissed. The Court of Appeals for the District of Columbia held that the: (1) District Court's denial of company's motion to dismiss on political question grounds was not an immediately appealable collateral order, and (2) The District Court did not clearly and indisputably exceed its

867 USA Central Intelligence Agency, 'The World Factbook - Indonesia' (2007) <https:// www.cia.gov/ cia/ publications/ factbook/ geos/ id.html> (May 2, 2007) (1.136 million bbl/day (2005 est.) at approx. US$ 60).

868 International Labor Rights Fund, 'ExxonMobil: How the Company is linked with Indonesian Military, Torture and other severe abuse in Aceh, Indonesia' (2007) <http:// lrights.igc.org/ projects/ corporate/ exxon> (September 10, 2007).

869 See S Doddamani, 'Fighting for the Right to Hold Multinational Corporations Accountable: Indonesian Villagers Battle Oil Giant ExxonMobil' 49 Wayne Law Review 835 (2003) at 835.

870 See T Collingsworth and N Thys, 'Complaint against Exxon Mobil(June 20, 2001)' (2001) <www.achehtimes.com/ news2001/ at062301.htm> (September 10, 2007).

871 See S Doddamani, 'Fighting for the Right to Hold Multinational Corporations Accountable: Indonesian Villagers Battle Oil Giant ExxonMobil' 49 Wayne Law Review 835 (2003) at 859.

872 *Doe v. Exxon Mobil Corporation*, 393 FSupp2d 20, D.C. D.C. (2005).

jurisdiction by refusing to dismiss case under the political question doctrine so as to warrant issuance of writ of mandamus.[873]

J. *Abdullahi v. Pfizer* – Drug testing

The plaintiffs in this case were Nigerian minors and their guardians, all Nigerian citizens. The defendant was Pfizer, the largest pharmaceutical company in the world. In 1996, the city of Kano in Nigeria was besieged by an epidemic of meningitis, measles and cholera. Pfizer wanted to test its newly developed antibiotic drug, Trovaflozacin Mesylate, also known by its brand name "Trovan." This drug was not approved yet and animal testing had shown that Trovan might cause significant side effects in children such as joint disease, abnormal cartilage growth (osteochondiosis, a disease resulting in bone deformation) and liver damage. At the same time, Medicin Sans Frontiers (Doctors Without Borders) offered free and effective treatment with safe medication in the same town.[874] Article 7 of the *ICCPR* provides: "No one shall be subjected to torture or to cruel, inhuman or degrading treatment or punishment. In particular, no one shall be subjected without his free consent to medical or scientific experimentation."[875] The Nigerian victims brought a suit pursuant to the ATCA for violation of their human rights in August 2001.[876]

The Court for the Southern District of New York held that the alleged action was not a universal concern for which private actors could be held liable. However, Pfizer and the government were joint actors in this case and so Pfizer was a state actor and could be held liable. After a lengthy consideration of the relevant issues, the Court granted the motion to dismiss on the ground of *forum non conveniens*. It weighed all different public and private interest factors. The court's decision was largely based on the fact that the witnesses necessary to establish causation, injury and damages were exclusively located in Nigeria.[877] The court's order was made contingent on Pfizer's consent to suit and acceptance of service of process in Nigeria, its waiver of any applicable statute of limitations defense, its agreement to make all documents and witnesses available for discovery and trial and assent to return of the case to the District Court if the Nigerian Federal High Court declined to exercise its jurisdiction.[878]

In November 2002 further plaintiffs brought a similar case and again the case was transferred to the District Court for the Southern District of New York. Again the

---

873 *Doe v. Exxon*, 473 F3d 345, C.A. D.C. (2007).

874 Gzedit, 'Deadly Tests Saving Money Costs Lives' *Charleston Gazette* (December 21, 2000) 4A.

875 International Covenant on Civil and Political Rights (ICCPR) GA Res 2200A (XXI), UN Doc A/6316, adopted and opened for signature, ratification and accession by General Assembly resolution 2200A (XXI) of 16 December 1966,entered into force Mar 23, 1976 (1966).

876 *Abdullahi v. Pfizer*, No 01 Civ 8118, 2002 US Dist LEXIS 17436, 2002 WL 31082956, D.C. S.D. N.Y. (2002).

877 *Ibid.* at pages 35-36.

878 *Ibid.* at page at 38.

case was dismissed. It held that: (1) court lacked subject matter jurisdiction under Alien Tort Statute; (2) Nigerian law applied, barring suit under Connecticut Unfair Trade Practices Act (CUTPA) and Connecticut Products Liability Act (CPLA); (3) in any event, dismissal would be warranted under the doctrine of *forum non conveniens*, to allow for suit in Nigeria.[879] In 2005 Nigerian courts started proceedings against Pfizer and the Nigerian state joined party with the plaintiffs.[880]

K. *Arias v. Dyncorp* – Side effects of US cocaine war

The war on drugs by the US government has inflicted severe harm on the environment and people of Colombia, Bolivia and Ecuador.[881] The US Government had contracted with the private security company DynCorp, a company with dubious reputation, who spray fumigants on coca plants in Colombia to eradicate a major source of the cocaine exported to the US.[882] These fumigants were also harmful to humans and livestock.[883] They also destroyed legitimate crops such as corn and yucca. DynCorp also sprayed the Ecuadorian side of the border with the same effect, even though no coca is cultivated in that area. A group of villagers who are all suffering from serious side effects from the fumigant brought the suit against DynCorp. They claimed the corporation was responsible for murder, wrongful death, crimes against humanity, and numerous other crimes. The case was filed in the District Court for the District of Columbia, on September 11, 2001, moments before the terrorist attacks on New York and Washington, D.C. The case is still pending. This case is another example of harsh human rights violations by a TNC and it will be interesting to see how US courts will decide this case.

L. *Mujica v. Occidental* – Protecting the oil

In December 1998, the Colombian air force carried out an aerial assault from a helicopter, known as the Santo Domingo Massacre, killing 17 people.[884] There is ample proof that this massacre was done at the request of, and with financing from, the US corporation, Occidental Petroleum, an international petroleum exploration and development company located close to Los Angeles.[885] The Colombian army receives

---

879 *Adamu v. Pfizer*, 399 FSupp 2d 495, D.C. S.D. N.Y. (2005).

880 B Condie, 'Pfizer is sued over Nigerian drug trials' *Evening Standardt* (October 1, 2007).

881 ZP Mugge, 'Plan Colombia: The Environmental Effects and Social Costs of the United States' Failing War on Drugs' 15 Colorado Journal of International Environmental Law and Policy 309 (2004) at 339.

882 *Arias v. Dyncorp*, 01-CV-1908, D.C. D.C. (2002). Concerning Dyncorp's human rights reputation, see Anonymous, 'Dirty Deeds' *Cityview, Des Moines, Iowa* (June 15, 2006) 13.

883 ZP Mugge, 'Plan Colombia: The Environmental Effects and Social Costs of the United States' Failing War on Drugs' 15 Colorado Journal of International Environmental Law and Policy 309 (2004) at 328 et *seq.*

884 International Labor Rights Fund, 'Lawsuit Filed Against Occidental Petroleum for Involvement in Infamous Colombian Massacre' <http://www.laborrights.org/press/oxy042403.htm> (June 21, 2006); L Galvis and D Kovalik, 'Santo Domingo Massacre in Colombia, A Testimony' (2005) <http:// www.zmag.org/ content/ showarticle.cfm?ItemID=8907> (June 21, 2006).

885 *Mujica v. Occidental Petroleum Corp.*, 381 F Supp 2d 1134, D.C. C.D. Cal. (2005) at 1138.

direct funding from Occidental in return for protecting the pipeline.[886] The coordinates for the bombing were received directly from the second defendant AirScan, Inc., which was working in its capacity as a security contractor and agent of the defendant, Occidental. Allegedly, there were three AirScan pilots on the helicopter accompanied by a Colombian military officer who at the time served as air force liaison to Occidental. This bombing, moreover, was planned by the Colombian Air Force and AirScan in Occidental's complex in Cano Limón, Colombia. The United States is also indirectly involved in these operations, since it specifically gave US$ 98 million to the Columbian military to protect Occidental's oil pipeline.[887]

In April 2003, the plaintiff Luis Alberto Galvis Mujica, who lost several family members in the assault, brought suit against Occidental Petroleum, Inc. and Airscan, Inc. in the US District Court for the Central District of California. The suit is supported by the International Labor Rights Fund (ILRF) and the Center for Human Rights at the Northwestern University School of Law. The Court found that Colombia was an inadequate forum and the doctrine of international comity did not bar the action.[888] Furthermore, it decided that the ATCA claims were not subject to dismissal due to practical consequences and the Act of State doctrine did not bar the action, but the political question barred the action.[889] The case is on appeal.

M. *Corrie v. Caterpillar* – Selling bulldozers a war crime?

The family of peace activist Rachel Corrie and five Palestinian families brought an action against the US company, Caterpillar, which manufacture bulldozers that are used in the demolition of houses in the Gaza strip.[890] Since 1967, the Israeli army has used Caterpillar equipment, including specially modified and armored D9 and D10 bulldozers to destroy over 12,000 houses in the West Bank, Gaza Strip and East Jerusalem, leaving tens of thousands of men, women and children homeless. Since September 2000, the Israeli Army allegedly destroyed 3,000 homes.[891] Many organizations, including the UN Special Rapporteur on the Right to Food, Jean Ziegler, and other individuals have written to Caterpillar to point out the harm and violations of international law done with Caterpillar bulldozers. In March 2003, one Caterpillar bulldozer operated by an Israeli soldier drove over peace activist and killed Rachel Corrie, when she, standing non-violently with a megaphone in her hand, positioned herself between a Palestinian's home and the bulldozer.

---

886 *Ibid.* at 1189.
887 K Penhaul, 'Protection for Oil Pipeline Raises US Profile in Colombia, New Policy Stirs Fears Bush Seeks to Widen War' *San Francisco Chronicle* (February 16, 2002).
888 *Mujica v. Occidental Petroleum Corp.*, 381 F Supp 2d 1134, D.C. C.D. Cal. (2005).
889 *Ibid.*
890 *Corrie v. Caterpillar, Inc.*, 403 F Supp 2d 1019, D.C. W.D. Wash. (2005).
891 Stop Caterpillar, 'Declaration Regarding Caterpillar Violations of Human Rights' (2004) <http:// www.catdestroyshomes.org/ article.php?id=242> (June 21, 2006).

Eyewitnesses stated that the operator saw Mrs. Corrie and there was no malfunctioning of the machine itself, as it was later found.[892]

In the first claim, the plaintiffs allege that the demolition of civilian homes constitutes a breach of the *Fourth Geneva Convention*.[893] The claim is based on the ATCA. Caterpillar knew or should have known that the bulldozers that they supply would be used to breach international law. In the second and third claim, the plaintiffs alleged that the defendant breached the TVPA and aided or conspired with the Israeli Army to commit cruel, inhuman, or degrading treatment or punishment. The defendant submitted that it did not participate in any of the abuses and that it did not act as a state actor. The District Court in Washington D.C. dismissed the claims and the case will now be heard on the appellate level.[894]

N. In Re South African Apartheid Litigation

In the case *In Re South African Apartheid Litigation* several distinct complaints filed throughout the United States were consolidated and brought before Judge Sprizzo in the Southern District of New York.[895] The defendants included numerous corporate defendants from all over the world including giants such as IBM, ExxonMobil and Daimler Chrysler. The claimants sought damages of up to US$ 400 billion. The claims involved allegations of *apartheid*-related race discrimination and other human rights abuses. Judge Sprizzo dismissed the claims in November 2004, saying that the charges "bordered on the frivolous." Judge Sprizzo decided that the Court did not have subject matter jurisdiction and that any decision by it would seriously impede the flow of international commerce.[896]

O. Estate of Rodriguez v. Drummond Co. – Trade unionist killed

The defendant in this case was an Alabama company that managed the daily operations of Drummond Co. coal operations in Colombia.[897] The plaintiffs were relatives and heirs of murdered Colombian trade union leaders. The plaintiffs alleged that the defendant was liable for the death of the trade union leaders, because the paramilitaries who shot them were agents of the defendant. The defendant allowed them to enter their mining facilities in Colombia, because the paramilitaries are "in a

---

892 E Schechter, 'Pro-Palestinian US Activist Killed by IDF Bulldozer in Gaza Strip' *Jerusalem Post* (March 17, 2003) 1; J Adcock, 'Rep Production Puts the Spotlight on Rachel Corrie and Her Causes' *Seattle Post* (March 16, 2007) 27.

893 Article 53 of the Geneva Convention Relative to the Protection of Civilian Persons in Time of War (Fourth Geneva Convention) 75 UNTS 287 (12 August 1949) (entered into force Oct 21, 1950) (1949) (Destruction of personal property is prohibited "except where such destruction is rendered absolutely necessary by military operations.")

894 *Corrie v. Caterpillar, Inc.*, 403 F Supp 2d 1019, D.C. W.D. Wash. (2005), appeal docketed, No. 05-36210 (9th Cir. Dec. 21, 2005).

895 *In re: South African Apartheid Litigation*, 346 FSupp2d 538, D.C. S.D. N.Y. (2004).

896 *Ibid.* at 553.

897 *Estate of Rodriguez v. Drummond Co.*, 256 F Supp 2d 1250, D.C. N.D. Ala. (2003) at 1256.

cooperative and symbiotic relationship with the regular [Colombian] military that are stationed on Drummond's property."[898]

The plaintiffs filed the lawsuit in March 2002. In April 2003, the United States District Court of the Northern District of Alabama decided the case.[899] The main legal issues were the violations of the law of nations, especially the right of association and the standing of the trade union. District Judge Bowdre held that the trade union lacked standing. The Court denied the motion to dismiss in most of the other claims. The trade unions sufficiently alleged that the mining company acted in conjunction with Colombian paramilitary forces by paying them to murder trade union leaders. The trade unions adequately alleged state action to state claims under the ATCA. The Court dismissed the genocide claim because the plaintiffs failed to allege that the murders were the result of "an intent to destroy, in whole or in part, a national, ethnical, racial or religious group."[900] It held that the rights to associate and organize are actionable as norms of international law, even though no other US court had recognized this in ATCA litigation.[901]

This case is yet another example of a corporate actor committing hideous violations of human rights, which can be directly linked to an US corporation. It is interesting that the District Judge in this case held that the right of association is an actionable right pursuant to the ATCA. Most of his judgment was centered on the question of whether the trade union had standing, whereas other crucial parts as the question of complicity were just briefly affirmed. Overall, it represents a human rights friendly decision, but it remains to be seen if compensation is going to be paid to the heirs and relatives of the victims.

P. *Ibrahim v. Titan* – The privatized war on terror

In *Ibrahim v. Titan*, decided in August 2005, several Iraqi national detainees and spouses of deceased detainees brought an action against two private government contractors who provided interrogators and interpreters to US military in Iraq, alleging claims under the ATCA, RICO, and government contracting laws, as well as claims for assault and battery, wrongful death, false imprisonment, intentional infliction of emotional distress, conversion, and negligence stemming from alleged acts of torture inflicted upon them at prison in Iraq.[902] The District Court of the District of Columbia held that the detainees' claims were not barred by the political question doctrine, but they did not have standing to pursue RICO claims.[903] The

898 *Ibid.* at 1254.
899 *Ibid.*
900 *Ibid.* at 1260.
901 *Ibid.* at 1264.
902 *Ibrahim v. Titan Corp.*, 391 F Supp 2d 10, D.C. D.C. (2005).
903 *Ibid.* at 19.

Court did not have diversity jurisdiction over claims against a private governmental contractor incorporated in the Netherlands.[904] Therefore the case was dismissed.

In *Ibrahim* five points from the *Sosa* decision were induced: (1) Common law judges in the past were seen as "discovering" law, but they are now seen as making or creating law; (2) since the Supreme Court decision *Erie v. Tompkins* the role of federal Common law has been dramatically reduced, and courts have generally looked for legislative guidance before taking innovative measures; (3) creating private rights of action is generally best left to the legislature; (4) decisions involving international law may have collateral consequences that impinge on the discretion of the legislative and executive branches in managing foreign affairs; and (5) there is no mandate from Congress encouraging judicial creativity in this area, and in fact there are legislative hints in the opposite direction.[905] The *Ibrahim* Court therefore found that violations of the law of nations do not apply to the contractors, as they were private, rather than official, actors.[906]

The *Ibrahim* Court could be influenced by the scholarly writings of Curtis Bradley and Jack Goldsmith in finding that the role of federal Common law has been dramatically reduced since *Erie*, as mentioned above. *Erie*, however, seems to be not applicable here since the ATCA is not based on diversity jurisdiction, but on federal question jurisdiction.[907] The *Ibrahim* decision relied on the decisions in *Sanchez-Espinoza* and *Tel-Oren*,[908] and ignored *Kadic*, *Unocal*, *Talisman* and a small, but decisive and often-discussed note in the *Sosa* decision itself. *Sosa* pointed at the development of ATCA litigation, which now comprises human rights violations by non-state actors.[909] Therefore the *Ibrahim* decision seems ill-founded.

Q. *El- Masri v. Tenet* – State secrets doctrine bars terror cases

In *El-Masri v. Tenet* a German citizen of Lebanese descent, brought an action pursuant to *Bivens*[910] and the ATCA, against former Director of the CIA, and others, including two corporations Premier Executive Transport Services and Keeler & Tate Management Group, LLC, Aero Contractors, Limited. El-Masri alleged that he was illegally detained as part of the CIA's "extraordinary rendition" program, tortured, and subjected to other inhumane treatment.[911] He was abducted in Macedonia by

---

904 *Ibid.* at 20.

905 *Ibid.* at 14.

906 *Ibid.* at 14-15.

907 See also in chapter VI below at subheading "C. International law and the US Supreme Court" at 226.

908 *Ibrahim v. Titan Corp.*, 391 F Supp 2d 10, D.C. D.C. (2005) at 14-15.

909 *Sosa v. Alvarez-Machain* (03-339) 542 US 2739, US S.Ct. (2004) at 2766.

910 *Bivens v. Six Unknown Named Agents*, 403 US 388, US S.Ct. (1971) (Case in which the US Supreme Court ruled that an implied cause of action existed for an individual whose Fourth Amendment freedom (from unreasonable searches and seizures) had been violated by federal agents.)

911 *El-Masri v. Tenet*, 437 FSupp2d 530, D.C. E.D. Va. (2006); See also S Shane, S Grey and M

Macedonian authorities, handed over to US authorities, flown to a Kabul detention centre, allegedly tortured over a period of one and half years, including sodomization, was not permitted to contact a lawyer or German officials or his family, only to find out that he was innocent and subject of a mistaken identity.[912]

El-Masri contends that the corporate defendants are liable for authorizing the use of aircraft they owned or operated for the transfer of suspected terrorists to detention facilities despite the corporate defendants' knowledge that the suspected terrorists, including El-Masri, would be detained incommunicado, tortured and subjected to other cruel treatment.[913] In his complaint, El–Masri alleges aviation documents show that late on the evening of January 23, 2004 a Boeing business jet owned by defendant Premier Executive Transport Services Inc. and operated by defendant Aero Contractors Limited flew from Skopje, Macedonia to Kabul, Afghanistan.[914]

The US Government's motion to intervene was granted, and it moved to dismiss or for summary judgment. The District Court held that (1) state secrets privilege was validly asserted, and (2) dismissal was required where plaintiff's claims could not be fairly litigated without disclosure of secrets absolutely protected by the United States' state secrets privilege.[915] The Court of Appeals, King, Circuit Judge, confirmed the decision.[916]

XIII. Concluding remarks to Chapter IV

The cases presented here are the most important human rights cases involving TNCs in US litigation.[917] These cases included shocking examples of corporate malfeasants. The record of these corporate violations of human rights is appaling, considering the historic examples of the Holocaust, the involvement of Talisman in the Sudanese atrocities, Coca-Cola's involvement in widespread violent suppression and murder of union leaders, the involvement of private security companies in the War on Terror

Williams, 'C.I.A. Expanding Terror Battle Under Guise of Charter Flights' *The New York Times* (May 31, 2005); M Rosen-Molina, 'Two alleged CIA rendition victims join ACLU lawsuit against Boeing subsidiary' *Jurist Legal News & Research* (August 1, 2007).

912 *El-Masri v. Tenet*, 437 FSupp2d 530, D.C. E.D. Va. (2006) at 534.

913 *Ibid.* at 534.

914 *Ibid.* at 533.

915 *Ibid.*

916 *El-Masri v. US*, 479 F3d 296, C.A. 4 (2007).

917 Other cases: 1. Saipan litigation: *Doe I et al. v. Gap, Inc. et al.* , Case No CV01-0031-948, D.C.N.Mar. (2002); CA Williams, 'Corporate Social Responsibility in an Era of Economic Globalization' 35 UC Davis Law Review 705 (2002) at 761; 2. *Jama v. U.S. I.N.S.*, 22 FSupp2d 353, D.C. N.J. (1998) ; 3.*Villeda, et. al. v. Fresh Del Monte Produce Inc., et al.*, Case No 01-CIV-3399, D.C. S.D. Fla. (2001); case summaries can also be found at MCaHR Castan Centre for Human Rights Law, 'Transnational Human Rights Litigation against Companies' (2004) <http:// www.law.monash.edu.au/ castancentre/ projects/ mchr/ trans-hr-litigation.html> (March 8, 2006).

and the war on drugs or Shell and ExxonMobil's exploitive suppression of the local Nigerian people is appalling.

Of the 27 cases[918] surveyed in this chapter, nine cases were lost, but still in terms of human rights litigation not all of the lost cases were unsuccessful. The cases lost were the Japanese forced labor litigation, the *Sinaltrainal* case, the *Carmichael* case, the *Hamid* case, the *Beanal* case, the *Bao Ge* case, the *Exxon* case, the *Ibrahim* case and the *El-Masri* case. What were the main hurdles? Three cases were dismissed because of missing subject matter jurisdiction.[919] A subject matter dismissal in case of a breach of some international financial agreements seems desirable, since the ATCA then would become too far-reaching.[920] *Ibrahim* was dismissed, because ATCA would according to that Court not reach private conduct.[921] The US courts were reluctant to accept international environmental principles as part of the law of nations and dismissed two cases for lack of subject matter jurisdiction on these grounds.[922] The political question doctrine and statements of interest by the US government were crucial for the dismissal in three cases.[923]

The absence of a causal connection was the decisive factors in dismissing the *Sinaltrainal* cases. A gauntlet of further challenges to a human right action against TNCs has to be passed in order to win a human rights claim versus a TNC. Those hurdles are for example personal jurisdiction, time limitation, standing, exhaustion of remedies, doctrine of state action, comity, failure to join necessary parties and practical hurdles, as financing legal counsel. However, thanks to the past litigation, many of the hurdles are clarified and the door for human right actions against TNCs seems to be still ajar. The growing importance of international human rights litigation can be witnessed, especially after *Sosa*.

Eight cases are still pending.[924] Even though the *Wiwa* case and the case concerning Talisman in Sudan are still pending, they brought about important developments for

918 The German Holocaust slave labor litigation is counted as one case, even though it included 40 cases on its own. Also the Swiss banks restitution claims included many cases.

919 *Flores v. Southern Peru Copper Corporation*, 343 F3d 140, C.A. 2 (2003); *Hamid v. Price Waterhouse Coopers*, 51 F3d 1411, C.A. 9 (1995); and *Beanal v. Freeport-McMoran, Inc.*, 197 F3d 161, C.A. 5 (1999).

920 *Hamid v. Price Waterhouse Coopers*, 51 F3d 1411, C.A. 9 (1995).

921 *Ibrahim v. Titan Corp.*, 391 F Supp 2d 10, D.C. D.C. (2005) at 14.

922 *Flores v. Southern Peru Copper Corporation*, 343 F3d 140, C.A. 2 (2003); *Beanal v. Freeport-McMoran, Inc.*, 197 F3d 161, C.A. 5 (1999).

923 *In re World War II Era Japanese Forced Labor Litigation*, 114 F Supp 2d 939, D.C. N.D. Cal. (2001); *Sarei v. Rio Tinto PLC*, 221 FSupp2d 1116, D.C. C.D. Cal. (2002) and *Doe v. Exxon Mobil Corporation*, 393 FSupp2d 20, D.C. D.C. (2005).

924 *The Presbyterian Church of Sudan, et. al. v. Talisman Energy, Inc.*, 374 FSupp2d 331, D.C. S.D. N.Y. (2005); *Estate of Rodriguez v. Drummond Co.*, 256 F Supp 2d 1250, D.C. N.D. Ala. (2003); *Bowoto v. Chevron*, 312 F Supp 2d 1229, D.C. N.D. Cal. (2004); *Arias v. Dyncorp*, 01-CV-1908, D.C. D.C. (2002); *Mujica v. Occidental Petroleum Corp.*, 381 F Supp 2d 1134, D.C.

human rights litigation against TNCs. They established that complicity with states that vigorously violate human rights can be prosecuted and that the *forum non conveniens* evasion is not applicable in those cases.

In five cases the US Court has forced the corporation to appear in front of a foreign court, which also be counted at least as a partial victory.[925] In *Doe v. Exxon*, Ecuador's indigenous movements were galvanized to action and this has led to immense public attention and scrutiny of the behavior of TNCs in the mineral industries as well as tougher laws in Ecuador.[926]

Six cases can be counted as successful. Those are the *Unocal* case, the Swiss banks case, the German forced labor case, the *Bano* case, the *Sarei* case and the *Kodak* case. A partial victory was reached in the *Bano* case, where Union Carbide was forced to clean up their abandoned plants in India. The three most outstanding successes for the cause of human rights were probably the German forced labor case, the Swiss bank accounts case and the *Unocal* settlement. All three of those most successful cases show that TNCs would strive for a settlement where they teeter on the brink of judicial defeat, because of the unflattering effect of the negative media coverage and public opinion.

Overall, there is a clear trend towards more scrutiny of corporate behavior for human rights issues. It is a moderate, but persistent trend, which really began in the mid-1990s. The fact that some cases were already successful and many threshold arguments as *forum non conveniens* are clarified is promising. One especially optimistic example is the *Sarei* case and the decision of the Court of Appeals for the Ninth Circuit in 2006.[927] First, it made a pending unsuccessful human rights claim at first instance to a successful one on the appellate court level. Second, it opened the door for egregious environmental claims. Third, it stated that not only *jus cogens* rules fall under the ambit of ATCA, but also further rules of customary international law. Fourth, it found that the political question doctrine, the Act of State doctrine, the doctrine of international comity and a statement of interest by the US government cannot bar violations of *jus cogens* norms. Fifth, it held that corporations can be vicariously liable for violations of *jus cogens* norms. Last, it is the first case on the appellate level after the *Sosa* decision and it opened the door for human rights

C.D. Cal. (2005); *Corrie v. Caterpillar, Inc.*, 403 F Supp 2d 1019, D.C. W.D. Wash. (2005); *Bigio v. Coca-Cola*, 448 F3d 176, C.A. 2 (2006) and *In re: South African Apartheid Litigation*, 346 FSupp2d 538, D.C. S.D. N.Y. (2004).

925 *Wiwa v. Royal Dutch Shell Petroleum Corp.*, 226 F3d 232, C.A. 2 (2001); *Bano v. Union Carbide*, 361 F3d 696, C.A. 2 (2004); *Flores v. Southern Peru Copper Corporation*, 343 F3d 140, C.A. 2 (2003); *Jota v. Texaco, Inc.*, 157 F3d 153, C.A. 2 (1998) and *Abdullahi v. Pfizer*, No 01 Civ 8118, 2002 US Dist LEXIS 17436, 2002 WL 31082956, D.C. S.D. N.Y. (2002).

926 Maxi Lyons, "A case study in multinational corporate accountability: Ecuador's indigenous peoples struggle for redress," 32 Denver Journal of International law and policy, Fall 2004 at 701 and 731.

927 *Sarei v. Rio Tinto*, 456 F3d 1069, C.A. 9 (2006).

litigation to a considerable degree. In US litigation TNCs from all over the world will be under growing scrutiny for violations of human rights.

Chapter V. Human rights responsibilities of TNCs in ATCA litigation

What is the scope of liability of TNCs for human rights in US law? This chapter approaches the question of the subject matter jurisdiction in ATCA litigation against TNCs. The question of subject matter jurisdiction includes the question of the international legal personality of TNCs and their human rights responsibilities. This chapter will first demonstrate the historical development of human rights responsibilities in the relevant case law and therefore in US law. Later this chapter briefly outlines some of the specific human rights responsibilities of TNCs in US law.

I. Restatement

Written in 1987, the Restatement of Foreign Relations Law (the Restatement) continues to reflect the current US law and somewhat anticipates the answer to the question of this chapter: "In the past it was sometimes assumed that individuals and corporations, companies or other juridical persons created by the laws of a state, were not persons under (or subjects of) international law. In principle, however, individuals and private juridical entities can have any status, capacity, rights, or duties given them by international law or agreement, and increasingly individuals and private entities have been accorded such aspects of personality in varying measures … corporations frequently are vehicles through which rights under international economic law are asserted."[928]

Even though providing for *state* violations of customary international law, Section 702 of the Restatement has been an important authority in finding the responsibilities of TNCs in ATCA litigation, such as in *Pfizer*, *Beanal* and *Flores*.[929] In *Sosa,* Section 702 has been used as starting point to clarify when an arbitrary detention is, in fact, a violation of customary law, even though *Sosa* also dealt with the behavior of private actors.[930] In Section 702 of the Restatement it is stated that international law is violated if a state, as a matter of state policy, practices, encourages, or condones any of the following: (a) *genocide*, (b) *slavery or slave trade*, (c) *the murder or causing the disappearance of individuals*, (d) *torture or other cruel, inhuman, or degrading treatment or punishment*, (e) *prolonged arbitrary detention*, (f) *systematic racial discrimination*, (g) *a consistent pattern of gross violations of internationally recognized human rights*. Section 702 of the Restatement includes customary law

928 Restatement (Third) of Foreign Relations Law (1987) at Introductory Note to part II (Persons in international law).

929 *Beanal v. Freeport- McMoran, Inc.*, 969 F Supp 362, D.C. E.D. La (1997) at 371; *Abdullahi v. Pfizer*, No 01 Civ 8118, 2002 US Dist LEXIS 17436, 2002 WL 31082956, D.C. S.D. N.Y. (2002) at 4; *Flores v. Southern Peru Copper Corp.*, 253 F Supp 2d 510, D.C. S.D. N.Y. (2002) at 522.

930 *Sosa v. Alvarez-Machain* (03-339) 542 US 2739, US S.Ct. (2004) at 2768.

whose status as customary law is generally accepted (as of 1987) and whose scope and content are generally agreed.[931] It is not necessarily complete, and human rights not listed in the Section may have achieved the status of customary law, while some rights might achieve that status in the future.[932] Thus, the Restatement does not foreclose the possibility that additional types of conduct may come to be recognized by the community of nations as violating international law.[933]

More important than Section 702 for the question of which responsibilities are to be accorded to private actors is Section 404 of the Restatement. Section 404 defines universal offenses for which universal jurisdiction exists: "a state has jurisdiction to define and prescribe punishment for certain offenses recognized by the community of nations as of universal concern, such as *piracy, slave trade, attacks on or hijacking of aircraft, genocide, war crimes,* and perhaps *certain acts of terrorism.*" In finding subject matter jurisdiction and the responsibilities of non-state actors the *Kadic* decision relied on Section 702 in combination with Section 404 and the introduction to the Restatement.[934] Since Section 404 includes hijacking of an aircraft and piracy, which are both usually non-state acts, it was obvious to the *Kadic* Court that private actors were also bound to the norms in Section 404. The bench found that genocide, torture, and slave trade represent violations, which private actors can also be held liable for.

The *Bigio* Court found "an international law violation exists for private actors when the particular misconduct "is either listed as an act 'of universal concern' in [Section] 404 or is sufficiently similar to the listed acts for us to treat them as though they were incorporated into [Section] 404 by analogy."[935]

II. Chronological development of TNCs human rights responsibilities

This main part of the chapter addresses the question of imposition of human rights responsibilities on TNCs in chronological order. Even though *Tel-Oren* and *Kadic* dealt with the status of *individuals* in international law, they are also used as important precedents for the status of TNCs in international law.[936] The two *Talisman* decisions contain the most detailed analysis of the status of TNCs in international law by US courts.[937]

---

931 Restatement (Third) of Foreign Relations Law (1987) at Section 702.

932 *Ibid.* at Section 702.

933 *Ibid.* at Section 702.

934 *Kadic v. Karadzic*, 70 F3d 232, C. A. 2 (1995) at 240.

935 *Bigio v. Coca-Cola Co.*, 239 F3d 440, C.A. 2 (2001) at 448.

936 *Tel-Oren v. Libyan Arab Republic*, 726 F2d 774, C.A. D.C. (1984); *Kadic v. Karadzic*, 70 F3d 232, C. A. 2 (1995).

937 *Presbyterian Church of Sudan et al. v. Talisman Energy, Inc.*, 244 F Supp 2d 289, D.C. S.D. N.Y. (2003); *The Presbyterian Church of Sudan, et. al. v. Talisman Energy, Inc.*, 374 FSupp2d 331, D.C. S.D. N.Y. (2005).

A. *Tel-Oren* – February 1985 – Laying the base for human rights responsibilities of non-state actors

In *Tel-Oren v. Libyan Arab Republic* the three judges on the panel of the Court of Appeals for the District of Columbia gave concurring decisions.[938] Judge Edwards addressed the problem of individual liability in international law. He describes an interesting development in international law concerning individual liability. At the time of enactment of the ATCA in the late 18th century, American jurists believed that international law also bound individuals. He refers to the earliest two cases, involving individual liability in international law that were decided in the United States.

Respublica v. DeLongchamps decided in 1784, the Court of Oyer and Termine in Delaware decided that an individual is liable for an assault on a French Consul-General as a breach of international law.[939] In *United States v. Smith* in 1820, the US Supreme Court held that an individual was liable for piracy, a clear case of violation of the law of nations at that time.[940] According to Judge Edwards, the view that only states are responsible in international law emerged later, in the 19th century. In support of this view, he refers to three academic publications by highly influential legal scholars, Marek Korowicz, Hersch Lauterpacht and Peter Pavel Remec.[941] In the 20th Century, Judge Edwards argues that a trend can be observed back towards the recognition of the individual as having international legal personality.[942]

Judge Edwards also introduces an interesting distinction between two different types of individual liability in international law. On one hand, individuals may be liable when acting under the color of state law. According to Judge Edwards, this liability has been well established since the Nuremberg trials. On the other hand, individuals may be liable when acting separately from any state's authority or direction.[943] Judge Edwards refers to an impressive list of authorities, all but one of which (the exception being *Filártiga*) deal with ATCA prior to *Tel-Oren*, to demonstrate that US courts

938 *Tel-Oren v. Libyan Arab Republic*, 726 F2d 774, C.A. D.C. (1984).

939 *Respublica v. DeLongchamps*, 1 US (1 Dall) 111, 1 LEd 59, US Court of Oyer and Terminer, Delaware (1784); The Court of Oyer and Terminer was a court for crimes punishable with death penalty and was abolished in Delaware in 1951.

940 *United States v. Smith*, 18 US (5 Wheat) 153, 5 LEd 57, US S.Ct. (1820b).

941 *Tel-Oren v. Libyan Arab Republic*, 726 F2d 774, C.A. D.C. (1984) at 794, referring to M Korowicz, 'The Problem of the International Personality of Individuals' 50 American Journal of International Law 533 (1956) at 541; H Lauterpacht, 'The Subjects of the Law of Nations ' Law Quarterly Review 438 (1947), at 439; PP Remec, *The position of the individual in international law according to Grotius and Vattel* (M. Nijhoff, The Hague 1960) at 38.

942 PP Remec, *The position of the individual in international law according to Grotius and Vattel* (M. Nijhoff, The Hague 1960) at 8-18; C Hill, 'International Affairs: The Individual in International Organization' 28 American Political Science Review 276 (1934) at 282; M Korowicz, 'The Problem of the International Personality of Individuals' 50 American Journal of International Law 533 (1956) at 537-539.

943 *Tel-Oren v. Libyan Arab Republic*, 726 F2d 774, C.A. D.C. (1984) at 792.

have found that individuals acting without state authority are also liable for breaches of international law. In the first ATCA case in 1795, *Bolchos v. Darrell*, an individual was held liable for a breach of an international treaty between the US and France.[944] *Adra v. Clift* in 1961 is a more recent example of where another individual was held liable for a violation of international law involving the misuse of passports and child custody.[945] Furthermore, there were three other ATCA cases that found that individuals are liable, even when the individual acted without state authority.[946]

Therefore, Judge Edwards found that individuals can be held liable in ATCA litigation, even without state action under international law. Finally, he concurred with the other judges hearing the case and dismissed the claim, because he only accepted individual liability for the handful of egregious human rights violations and declined to read ATCA to cover torture by non-state actors, absent guidance from the Supreme Court on the statute's usage of the term "law of nations."[947]

Overall, *Tel-Oren* contains a thorough analysis of the history of the ATCA jurisprudence dealing with individual liability up to the time of the case. It is very interesting that all seven cases referred to by Judge Edwards that were based on violations of international law involved action taken against individuals. The origins of ATCA can therefore be seen as having a strong foundation for holding individuals responsible. In *Tel-Oren*, only Judge Edwards held that individuals are liable for violations of international law. In *Kadic* ten years later, this opinion was affirmed.[948]

B. *United Technologies* – January 1988 – First decision

Carmichael v. United Technologies is the earliest ATCA decision involving action brought against a TNC. The Court of Appeals for the Fifth Circuit did not decide on the question of human rights responsibilities of individuals or corporations, but denied that it had subject matter jurisdiction, since there was no breach of international law.[949]

In the *Kodak* decision nine years later, the District Court for the Southern District of Florida held that the Court in *United Technologies* had assumed that it held jurisdiction over non-state actors, such as TNCs and used it as precedent.[950]

---

944 *Bolchos v. Darrell*, 3 F Cas 810 (No 1,607), US District of South Dakota (1795).

945 *Adra v. Clift*, 195 FSupp 857, D.C. Md. (1961).

946 *O'Reilly de Camara v. Brooke*, 209 US 45, 28 SCt 439, 52 LEd 676, US S.Ct. (1908); an Attorney General opinion in 26 Op. Att'y Gen. 250 (1907); *Nguyen Da Yen v. Kissinger*, 528 F2d 1194, C.A. 9 (1975).

947 *Tel-Oren v. Libyan Arab Republic*, 726 F2d 774, C.A. D.C. (1984) at 794.

948 *Kadic v. Karadzic*, 70 F3d 232, C. A. 2 (1995).

949 *Carmichael v. United Technologies Corp.*, 835 F2d 109, C.A. 5 (1988).

950 *Eastman Kodak Co. v. Kavlin*, 978 FSupp 1078, D.C. S.D. Fla. (1997) at 1092 ("assuming, but not deciding, that the Alien Tort Statute does confer subject matter jurisdiction over private parties who conspire in, or aid in abet, official acts of torture by one nation against the citizens of another nation.")

C. *Price Waterhouse* – April 1995 – Parting with the statist viewpoint?

The *Hamid v. Price Waterhouse* decision named several corporations as defendants, including Price Waterhouse, Bank of America, Ernst & Young and others.[951] It was claimed that the defendants violated international law by breaching fiduciary duties that represented international law. By making a bank appear to be in better financial condition than it really was, some defendants were alleged to have enabled it to attract deposits which it otherwise would have been unable to obtain. The decision briefly mentioned *Sanchez-Espinoza* , which was incorrectly cited as opposing general human rights responsibilities.[952] The Court in *Price Waterhouse* refrained from deciding on individual or corporate human rights responsibilities in international law.[953] The reason for this omission was that one of the defendants was the Emirate of Abu Dhabi, who is a state actor, so the case would not have been resolved by resolving the question of human rights responsibilities of TNCs. The case was dismissed since the Court found that claims of fraud, breach of fiduciary duty, and misappropriation of funds were not breaches of the "law of nations" for purposes of ATCA.[954] This case, therefore, does not give any new insights on the question of corporate human rights responsibilities.

Interestingly, it was nevertheless cited in the *Ford* decision to demonstrate that the *Price Waterhouse* Court distanced itself from a statist viewpoint and endowed private actors with human rights responsibilities.[955] However, the *Price Waterhouse* decision only mentioned human rights responsibilities of private actors in two sentences to the effect that: (a) the Court does not "need to reach the issue of whether the law of

---

951 *Hamid v. Price Waterhouse Coopers*, 51 F3d 1411, C.A. 9 (1995), the corporate defendants included Price Waterhouse U.K.; Price Waterhouse World Firm Ltd.; Price Waterhouse US; Ernst & Young; Bank of America Corporation, Bank America Corp.; Bank of America NT & SA; Hill & Knowlton; Concorde Finance & Investments, GRP; Investments; Interredec, Inc.; Interredec Southern Co.; et al.; First American Corp., First American Bankshares; Independence Bank; Clifford & Warnke.

952 *Sanchez-Espinoza v. Reagan*, 770 F2d 202 D.C. D.C. (1985) at 207 ("We are aware of no treaty that purports to make the activities at *issue* here unlawful when conducted by private individuals. As for the law of nations-so-called "customary international law," arising from "the customs and usages of civilized nations,[...] we conclude that this also does not reach private, non- state conduct *of this sort* [...] Assuming, however, that the Alien Tort Statute covers state acts *as well*, then it embraces this suit only insofar as the federal appellees are sued in their official, as opposed to their personal, capacities.") (emphasis added); See below at subheading "law „*at* 182.

953 *Hamid v. Price Waterhouse Coopers*, 51 F3d 1411, C.A. 9 (1995) at 1418.

954 *Ibid.* at 1418; citing *Filártiga v. Peña-Irala*, 630 F2d 876, C.A. 2 (1980) at 881.

955 *Iwanowa v. Ford Motor Company*, 67 F Supp 2d 424, D.C.N.J. (1999) at 445 ("Third, the Ninth Circuit later distanced itself from its statement in *In re Estate of Ferdinand E. Marcos* that only state actors are liable for violations of international law. In *Hamid v. Price Waterhouse*, the Ninth Circuit ignored its earlier comment in *In re Estate of Ferdinand E. Marcos* and merely stated that it did 'not need to reach the issue of whether the law of nations applied to private as opposed to governmental conduct.'")

nations applies to private, as opposed to governmental conduct;"[956] and (b) "Deciding whether private conduct is subject to the law of nations would not resolve the case, because the complaint alleges that the Emirate of Abu Dhabi and the Abu Dhabi Finance Department were among the wrongdoers."[957]

D. *Kadic* – October 1995 – Private responsibility for human rights violations without state action

In *Kadic v. Karadcic* the Court used *Tel-Oren* as the precedent to extend the scope of individual liability established in that decision. Whereas in *Tel-Oren* Judge Edwards did not extend the scope of individual liability to torture without the guidance of the Supreme Court, *Kadic* did exactly that.[958] The *Kadic* decision did not contradict *Tel-Oren*, rather complemented it. It followed the Judge Edwards concurrence in the *Tel-Oren* decision. In addition to the cases cited in *Tel-Oren*, the *Kadic* Court relied on further cases to prove that in ATCA litigation individuals have been deemed to be liable without the state action requirement.[959] The Court also cited the Restatement of Foreign Relations Law, which notes that "individuals may be held liable for offences against international law, such as piracy, war crimes, and genocide."[960] The Court referred to the Genocide convention, which unambiguously states that "[p]ersons committing genocide or any of the other acts enumerated in Article 3 shall be punished, whether they are constitutionally responsible rulers, public officials or private individuals."[961]

The defendant, Karadzic, argued that with the enactment of the TVPA, Congress intended that state action be a requirement for ATCA claims.[962] The TVPA allows for the filing of civil suits, in the US, against individuals who, acting in an official capacity for any foreign nation, committed torture or extra-judicial killing. The Court rejected Karadzic's argument that the TVPA was intended to extend the TVPA action to plaintiffs that are US citizens. Congress also noted that ATCA has other important uses and should not be replaced. Therefore, the Court held that a human rights violation by an individual does not need to meet the state action requirement. As in *Tel-Oren*, it is again interesting to note that the Court relied greatly on US precedents

956 *Hamid v. Price Waterhouse Coopers*, 51 F3d 1411, C.A. 9 (1995) at 1418.

957 *Ibid.* at 1418.

958 *Doe v. Unocal (Unocal I)*, 963 F Supp 880, D.C.C.D. Cal. (1997) at 891.

959 *Kadic v. Karadzic*, 70 F3d 232, C. A. 2 (1995) at 239, referring to *United States v. Smith*, 18 US (5 Wheat) 184, 196-97, 5 LEd 64, US S.Ct. (1820a); *Brig Malek Adhel*, 43 US (2 How) 210, 232, 11 LEd 239, US S.Ct. (1844).

960 Restatement (Third) of the Foreign Relations Law of the United States pt. 2 introductory note (1986).

961 *Kadic v. Karadzic*, 70 F3d 232, C. A. 2 (1995) at 242; Convention on the Prevention and Punishment of the Crime of Genocide December 9, 1948, 78 UNTS 277, approved and proposed for signature and ratification or accession by General Assembly resolution 260 A (III) of 9 December 1948, entered into force Jan 12, 1951 (Genocide Convention) (1948).

962 *Kadic v. Karadzic*, 70 F3d 232, C. A. 2 (1995) at 241.

and US sources, such as the Restatement of Foreign Relations Law. To a minor degree, it relied on sources of international law, such as the Genocide convention.

E. *Freeport McMoran* – April 1997 – Only limited set of duties

In *Beanal v. Freeport-McMoran*, the District Court for the Eastern District of Louisiana draws an interesting distinction in regards to the liability of non-state actors. The Court held that non-state actors can be held liable for violations for certain offenses in international law, such as piracy, hijacking, genocide, war crimes, and certain acts of terrorism.[963] It based this finding on the Third Restatement of Foreign Relations Law, the *Kadic* decision, the Genocide convention and the *Genocide Convention Implementation Act of 1987*. The *Genocide Convention* provides: "[p]ersons committing genocide [...] shall be punished, whether they are constitutionally responsible rulers, public officials, or private individuals."[964]

However, a non-state actor cannot be held responsible for violations of the three environmental principles, which are: (1) the Polluter Pays Principle; (2) the Precautionary Principle; and (3) the Proximity Principle. These principles apply only to the "members of the international community."[965] The Court held that a corporation may sign a treaty in order to follow those principles, but international customary law does not require compliance to those environmental principles for non-state actors, as they "do not constitute international torts for which there is universal consensus in the international community as to their binding status and their content."[966]

F. *Unocal I* – April 1997 – Watershed case

The first decision of *Doe v. Unocal, (Unocal I)* has been referred to as the watershed case establishing *corporate* liability in ATCA litigation.[967] Discussing human rights responsibilities of private actors, the *Unocal I* decision included references to the decisions in *Tel-Oren, Estate I, Estate II, Kadic* and *Price Waterhouse*.[968] In

963 *Beanal v. Freeport- McMoran, Inc.*, 969 F Supp 362, D.C. E.D. La (1997) at 371 and 372.

964 Article IV Convention on the Prevention and Punishment of the Crime of Genocide December 9, 1948, 78 UNTS 277, approved and proposed for signature and ratification or accession by General Assembly resolution 260 A (III) of 9 December 1948, entered into force Jan 12, 1951 (Genocide Convention) (1948).

965 *Beanal v. Freeport- McMoran, Inc.*, 969 F Supp 362, D.C. E.D. La (1997) at 384.

966 *Ibid.* at 384, citing *Xuncax v. Gramajo*, 886 FSupp 162, D.C. Mass. (1995) at 186.

967 DD Christensen, 'Corporate Liability for Overseas Human Rights Abuses After Sosa v. Alvarez-Machain' 62 Washington and Lee Law Review 1219 (2005) at 1258; compare also E Duruigbo, 'The Economic Cost of Alien Tort Litigation: A Response to Awakening Monster: The Alien Tort Statute of 1789' 14 Minnesota Journal of Global Trade 1 (2004) at 7.

968 *Tel-Oren v. Libyan Arab Republic*, 726 F2d 774, C.A. D.C. (1984); *In re Estate of Ferdinand Marcos Human Rights Litigation ("Estate I")*, 978 F2d 493 C.A. 9 (1992); *In re Estate of Ferdinand Marcos Human Rights Litigation (Estate II)*, 25 F3d 1467, C.A. 9 (1994); *Kadic v. Karadzic*, 70 F3d 232, C. A. 2 (1995); *Hamid v. Price Waterhouse Coopers*, 51 F3d 1411, C.A. 9 (1995).

considering whether individual actions without state action can constitute a breach of international law, the District Court referred to the *Tel-Oren* and *Kadic* decisions. Relying on *Kadic*, the *Unocal I* Court concluded that there are a handful of crimes for which individual liability without state action exists, such as slave trading.[969] The *Unocal I* case deals with a case alleging forced labor that, according to the *Unocal I* Court, was sufficient to constitute an allegation of participation in slave trading.[970]

The Court conferred human rights responsibilities on TNCs without discussing the differences between corporate and individual responsibility under international law. The Court simply stated, "The private actors may be liable for violations of international law even absent state action."[971] It simply put individual responsibility on par with corporate responsibility. In a few sentences, without significant analysis and only brief reference largely to two cases concerning the human rights responsibilities of individuals, namely *Tel-Oren* and *Kadic*, the *Unocal I* Court held that TNCs are also subject to human rights responsibilities.

G. *Kodak* – September 1997 – Constitutional interpretation in ATCA litigation

In *Eastman Kodak Co. v. Kavlin*, the District Court of the Southern District of Florida stated: "As a matter of initial impression, the Court believes that it would be a strange tort system that imposed liability on state actors but not on those who conspired with them to perpetrate illegal acts through the coercive use of state power. Although the negative prohibitions of our own Constitution generally extend only to state action, those who conspire with state actors to invade the constitutional rights of others may be held liable along with the state actors."[972]

It is interesting that constitutional interpretation was exerted in order to approach the question of human rights responsibilities in international law. Again, it is interesting that the Court relied primarily on US cases instead of international sources to support the finding of human rights responsibilities of TNCs. It referred to some ATCA cases, where individual and corporate liability were assumed, but often without

---

969 *Tel-Oren v. Libyan Arab Republic*, 726 F2d 774, C.A. D.C. (1984) at 791.

970 *Doe v. Unocal (Unocal I)*, 963 F Supp 880, D.C.C.D. Cal. (1997) at 892 ("The allegations of forced labor in this case are sufficient to constitute an allegation of participation in slave trading. Although there is no allegation that SLORC is physically selling Burmese citizens to the private defendants, plaintiffs allege that, despite their knowledge of SLORC's practice of forced labor, both in general and with respect to the pipeline project, the private defendants have paid and continue to pay SLORC to provide labor and security for the pipeline, essentially treating SLORC as an overseer, accepting the benefit of and approving the use of forced labor. These allegations are sufficient to establish subject-matter jurisdiction under the ATCA. Accordingly, the Court has jurisdiction over plaintiffs' supplemental state law claims pursuant to 28 U.S.C. § 1367 [ATCA].")

971 *Ibid.* at 891.

972 *Eastman Kodak Co. v. Kavlin*, 978 FSupp 1078, D.C. S.D. Fla. (1997) at 1091, citing *Dennis v. Sparks*, 449 US 24, 27-28, 101 SCt 183, 185-87, 66 LEd2d 185 US S.Ct (1980).

discussion. It mentioned the cases *Carmichael v. United Technologies*, *Unocal I* and *Hilao v. Estate of Marcos*.[973]

H. *Texaco* – October 1998 – *Sua sponte*

In *Jota v. Texaco*, no view was expressed on whether non-governmental entities bear human rights responsibilities. No party raised the question of corporate liability for breaches of international law. Accordingly, the Court stated: "We express no view on whether the plaintiffs have alleged conduct by Texaco that violates the law of nations, whether an ATCA suit for environmental misconduct, alleged to violate the law of nations, may be brought against a non-governmental entity under the ATCA, …"[974] The case was dismissed due to *forum non conveniens* and comity.[975]

Nevertheless, this case was influential in the later decisions of *Talisman I* and *Talisman II*. In the Talisman decisions, the District Court from the same Second Circuit noted that the Court has the duty to bring up this question *sua sponte* (that is, of their own accord). In *Talisman I*, the Court stated: "By reaching the merits in *Jota v. Texaco*, the Second Circuit tacitly acknowledged that subject matter lay in that case."[976]

J. *Ford* – October 1999 – Color of law

In *Iwanowa v. Ford Motor Company*, the District Court of New Jersey stated: "No logical reason exists for allowing private individuals and corporations to escape liability for universally condemned violations of international law merely because *they were not acting under color of law*."[977] The Court held that sole responsibility of states is inapposite. The Court then criticized the statist viewpoint. Statist viewpoint in this context means that only states are subjects of international law *and* private actors can be held liable for acts under color of law. Color of law includes acts done with the apparent authority of law but actually in contravention of law.

According to the *Ford* decision a statist viewpoint was adopted in *Sanchez-Espinoza and Estate I*.[978] In the *Estate I* decision, the Court of Appeals of the Ninth Circuit stated that "*only* individuals who have acted under official authority or under color of such authority may violate international law." This decision followed *Tel-Oren* in that it stands for the proposition that individuals can only be liable for violations of

---

973 *Carmichael v. United Technologies Corp.*, 835 F2d 109, C.A. 5 (1988); *Doe v. Unocal (Unocal I)*, 963 F Supp 880, D.C.C.D. Cal. (1997); *Hilao v. Estate of Marcos*, 103 F3d 767, 776, C.A. 9 (1996).

974 *Jota v. Texaco, Inc.*, 157 F3d 153, C.A. 2 (1998) at 159, footnote 6.

975 *Ibid.*

976 *Presbyterian Church of Sudan et al. v. Talisman Energy, Inc.*, 244 F Supp 2d 289, D.C. S.D. N.Y. (2003) at 312.

977 *Iwanowa v. Ford Motor Company*, 67 F Supp 2d 424, D.C.N.J. (1999) at 445.

978 *Sanchez-Espinoza v. Reagan*, 770 F2d 202 D.C. D.C. (1985) at 206 and *In re Estate of Ferdinand Marcos Human Rights Litigation ("Estate I")*, 978 F2d 493 C.A. 9 (1992) at 501.

international law when the individuals are acting under state authority. And in the *Sanchez-Espinoza decision*, it was stated that there are neither any international treaties nor is there customary international law that reaches private liability for the conduct *at issue*.[979] Therefore, the decision did not necessarily take on a statist viewpoint.

The *Ford* decision names a number of reasons why a statist viewpoint is inapposite. The *Ford* Court reasoned, based on *Filártiga* that international law has to be interpreted *as it is today*.[980] This finding in *Filártiga*, which refers back to the *Paquete Habana* decision, was originally meant to distinguish between the law of nations as it was in 1789 and the law of nations as it exists contemporaneously.[981] It is interesting, if not novel, to use that argument for the development of law between a much shorter period of time such as only 5-10 years, as in this case. The next question is whether international law has changed between the finding of Tel-*Oren* (1984), *Sanchez-Espinoza* (1985) and *Estate I* (1992) in comparison to *Ford* (1999). It can be argued that the establishment of the ICTY in 1993 and the ICTR in 1994 were significant in influencing the recognition of individual liability in international law.

Interestingly, no sources of international law were cited and the *Ford* decision referred solely to the *Kadic* decision in 1995 in order to hold that international law in 1999 imposed liability on individuals. *Kadic* only cites one single source of international law, the *Genocide Convention*, in order to establish a change in between those years of the early 1990s in comparison to the late 1990s. The *Genocide Convention* was adopted in 1948 and entered into force in 1951, so it cannot have had anything to do with a change of international law in the 1990s.

Therefore, the argument that the position of the individual in international law has changed within the 1990s seems flawed, since neither *Kadic* nor *Ford* referred to a change in international law. The recognition of the individual as a subject of international law would normally include references to the Nuremberg and Tokyo

---

979 *Sanchez-Espinoza v. Reagan*, 770 F2d 202 D.C. D.C. (1985) at 206-207.

980 *Kadic v. Karadzic*, 70 F3d 232, C. A. 2 (1995) at 238 ("Filártiga established that courts ascertaining the content of the law of nations 'must interpret international law not as it was in 1789, but as it has evolved and exists among the nations of the world today.'")

981 *Filártiga v. Peña-Irala*, 630 F2d 876, C.A. 2 (1980) at 881 ("Habana [*The Paquete Habana* decision] is particularly instructive for present purposes, for it held that the traditional prohibition against seizure of an enemy's coastal fishing vessels during wartime, a standard that began as one of comity only, had ripened over the preceding century into "a settled rule of international law" by "the general assent of civilized nations." Thus it is clear that courts must interpret international law not as it was in 1789, but as it has evolved and exists among the nations of the world today."); *The Paquete Habana*, 175 US 677, US S.Ct. (1900) at 686; see also *Iwanowa v. Ford Motor Company*, 67 F Supp 2d 424, D.C.N.J. (1999) at 444, citing *Kadic v. Karadzic*, 70 F3d 232, C. A. 2 (1995) at 238; *Tel-Oren v. Libyan Arab Republic*, 726 F2d 774, C.A. D.C. (1984) at 777.

Trials, Article 36 of the *Convention on Consular Relations* and the ICTY and the ICTR. But the sources of international law are often not considered in US ATCA case law. Therefore, it is even more astonishing that the Court in *Ford* did not even consider the discussion in *Filártiga* concerning the recognition of individuals as subjects of international law.

The next argument is that the Ninth Circuit has also changed its stance concerning its former statist stand. The *Ford* Court found that in *Price Waterhouse* the Ninth Circuit distanced itself from the statist standpoint.[982] The *Ford* Court held that *Price Waterhouse* parted with the statist viewpoint, which is hard to follow, since the Court in *Price Waterhouse* expressly refrained from reaching a firm finding on that question.[983] Also the change of international law between 1993 and 1999 was not proven, at least not based on sources of international law. Even in the attempt to interpret the "law of nations" in ATCA litigation, US courts often do not base their arguments on international law itself but rather on US law. Furthermore, it is striking that in all ATCA cases concerning TNCs to date, the courts did not differentiate between the human rights responsibilities of natural and juridical persons.

The *Ford* Court concluded that it was inclined to agree with the *Kadic* line of cases and the Court went on to argue that it is not necessary to determine the question of individual liability, since the Ford corporation acted as a *de facto* agent of the state. It is confusing that the *Ford* Court refers to the Ford Motor Company as a *de facto* state agent. This term is not clear. In international law, *de facto* state actors refer to forces or actors that are not recognized as a state (for example paramilitary forces or guerilla forces), but that exercise *de facto* authority over a territory.[984] The *Ford* Court referred to the fact that the Ford Motor Company was acting as an agent of the Nazi state by being a joint actor.

Overall, the *Ford* decision is important in holding corporations liable under international law even without acting under color of law. The decision was very important for the entire Holocaust slave labor restitution movement.[985] However, it is not very insightful as to the reasons why the US courts impose legal responsibility on corporate actors in international law, even without acting under color of law. The reasoning in *Ford* is somewhat flawed, as it relates to corporate liability and its legal foundations in international law. The decision stands as further evidence of the misconception of US courts as to international law and its evidentiary sources.

---

982 *Iwanowa v. Ford Motor Company*, 67 F Supp 2d 424, D.C.N.J. (1999) at 445.

983 See above in this chapter at subheading "D. Kadic – October 1995 – Private responsibility for human rights violations without state action" at 179.

984 See, e.g., A Carillo-Suarez, 'Hors de Logique: Contemporary Issues in International Humanitarian Law as Applied to Internal Armed Conflict' 15 American University International Law Review 1 (1999) at 22 et *seq*, 42, 83, 101 et *seq*.

985 See in chapter IV at subheading "III. German forced labor litigation succeeded" at 135.

K. *Freeport-McMoran* – November 1999 – Importance of *Kadic*

In the second decision in *Beanal v. Freeport-McMoran*, the Court of Appeals for the Fifth Circuit dismissed an ATCA case against a corporation on the ground that there was no violation of international law.[986] On the question of human rights responsibilities of TNCs, the Court relied again on the findings in *Kadic*.[987] The US courts, including in the *Kadic*, *Ford* and *Beanal* decisions, are careful to distinguish international law violations that require state action and those that do not. Regarding the imposition of human rights responsibilities of *corporate* actors and *individual* actors in general there has been no US decision that differentiated the two so far. This is astonishing, given that there have been more than two years of ATCA litigation against corporations.

L. *Coca-Cola* – January 2000 – Section 702 of the Restatement

In order to establish legal responsibility of corporate actors, in *Bigio v. Coca-Cola* the Court of Appeals for the Second Circuit referred to three sources: *Kadic*, *Tel-Oren* and the Third Restatement of Foreign Relations Law.[988] In Section 702 of the Restatement it is stated that international law is violated if a state, as a matter of state policy, practices, encourages, or condones any of the following: (a) genocide; (b) slavery or slave trade; (c) the murder or causing the disappearance of individuals; (d) torture or other cruel, inhuman, or degrading treatment or punishment; (e) prolonged arbitrary detention; (f) systematic racial discrimination; or (g) a consistent pattern of gross violations of internationally recognized human rights.

In this case, the claimants could not prove a violation of these provisions of international law, and so the question of corporate human rights responsibilities was not discussed. Nevertheless, three years later in *Talisman I*, the Court stated, with reference to the *Coca-Cola* decision and other precedent, that "the fact that the Second Circuit did not address an obvious jurisdictional question [human rights responsibilities of TNCs] *sua sponte* [without a prior motion or request from the parties] indicates that it had no reservations about the ATCA reaching the acts of corporations."[989]

M. *Banque Paribas*– August 2000 – TNCs have human rights responsibilities

In *Bodner v. Banque Paribas*, plaintiffs claimed damages arising from participation in a scheme to expropriate assets of customers during Nazi occupation. The District Court of New York held that subject matter jurisdiction was given.[990] It simply stated that the alleged looting, conversion, and continued withholding of assets that

---

986 *Beanal v. Freeport-McMoran, Inc.*, 197 F3d 161, C.A. 5 (1999).

987 *Ibid.* at 165.

988 *Bigio v. Coca-Cola Co.*, 239 F3d 440, C.A. 2 (2001) at 447.

989 *Presbyterian Church of Sudan et al. v. Talisman Energy, Inc.*, 244 F Supp 2d 289, D.C. S.D. N.Y. (2003) at 312.

990 *Bodner v. Banque Paribas*, 114 FSupp2d 117, D.C. E.D.N.Y. (2000) at 127-128.

rightfully belonged to plaintiffs clearly violated the Nuremberg Principles and longstanding principles of customary international law. The decision did not consider the question of human rights responsibilities of TNCs. It seems that by August 2000, the human rights liability of TNCs has become well established in US law, even though there has never been an analysis of international law concerning that question.

N. *Wiwa* – September 2000 – TNCs are liable for violations of *jus cogens* norms

The Court of Appeals for the Second District did not raise the question of human rights responsibilities of TNCs in *Wiwa v. Royal Dutch Petroleum*. It just referred to the *Kadic* decision. "More recently, we held in *Kadic v. Karadzic* that the ATCA reaches the conduct of *private* parties provided that their conduct is undertaken under the color of state authority or violates a norm of international law that is recognized as extending to the conduct of private parties."[991] Here again, it seems evident without any further discussion, evidence or explanation, that corporations bear the same duty as individuals. Later in *Talisman I*, the Court stated: "*Wiwa* clearly extended the decision in Kadic to apply the ATCA to the acts of corporations that constitute *jus cogens* violations."[992]

O. *Unocal III*– September 2002 – Using the US Constitution to interpret the law of nations

The Court of Appeals for the Ninth Circuit acknowledged the responsibility of TNCs in the *Unocal III* decision.[993] Relying on *Kadic* and *Tel-Oren*, it held that individuals can be held liable.[994] Furthermore, *Unocal III* puts forward another very interesting argument from the Thirteenth Amendment to the US Constitution (abolition of slavery). The Supreme Court held that the undoubted aim of that amendment was to maintain a system of completely free and voluntary labor throughout the United States.[995] The Thirteenth Amendment also reaches private action.[996] This, in turn, supports the view that forced labor by private actors gives rise to liability under the ATCA according to the Second Circuit Court.[997]

Statute 18 U.S.C.A. § 1583, provides that anybody who kidnaps any other person, or induces such other person to go anywhere, with the intent that such other person be sold into involuntary servitude or held as a slave, shall be fined or imprisoned as

---

991 *Wiwa v. Royal Dutch Petroleum Co.*, 226 F3d 88, C.A.2 (2000) at 104.

992 *Presbyterian Church of Sudan et al. v. Talisman Energy, Inc.*, 244 F Supp 2d 289, D.C. S.D. N.Y. (2003) at 312.

993 *Doe v. Unocal (Unocal III)*, 395 F3d 932, C.A. 9 (2002) at 946 et seq; Note that *Doe v. Unocal (Unocal II)*, 110 F Supp 2d 1294, D.C. C.D.Cal. (2000) did not give any new insights for the question of international legal personality.

994 *Doe v. Unocal (Unocal III)*, 395 F3d 932, C.A. 9 (2002) at 977.

995 *Ibid.* at 946, citing *Pollock v. Williams*, 322 US 4, 17, 64 SCt 792, 88 LEd 1095, US S.Ct. (1944).

996 *Jones v. Alfred H. Mayer Co.*, 392 US 409, 438-39, 88 SCt 2186, 20 LEd2d 1189, US S.Ct. (1968).

997 *Doe v. Unocal (Unocal III)*, 395 F3d 932, C.A. 9 (2002) at 946.

specified.[998] Inferring from these legal evaluations in the US Constitution and in the US statutes, the Court decided that a corporation is liable in international law. By now, it should be clear that US courts prefer to look at US law in order to interpret the "law of nations" from the ATCA. This might contradict the original intent of the legislators of the ATCA. They wished that international treaties and obligations to be followed. Seemingly the US courts developed their own interpretation of what they think international law might be and declared it as being international law.

P. *Pfizer* – September 2002 – Referring to *Kadic* and the Restatement

In *Abdullahi v. Pfizer*, the District Court in New York decided that TNCs have human rights duties in international law, relying on the *Kadic* decision, with reference also to the Third Restatement of Foreign Relations Law.[999] The corporation can only be held liable for torture and summary execution when committed under color of law or in the course of genocide or war crimes.[1000] The Court held that the corporation, Pfizer, acted as *de facto* participant and joint participants in the acts of medical experimentation, but it dismissed the action on the ground of *forum non conveniens*.

The *Pfizer* decision, therefore, is another example of the outstanding role of *Kadic*, which dealt with individual responsibility and not corporate legal responsibility. Again, no distinction is made between natural and juridical persons.

Q. *Al-Baraka* – July 2003 – ATCA *only* for violations of international law by non-state actors?

The decision of the District Court in the District of Columbia in *Burnett v. Al Baraka Inv. and Development Corp.* in July 2003 raises an interesting new argument for the discussion of corporate liability.[1001] It refers to *Sanchez-Espinoza* and *Tel-Oren* and posits that the ATCA may conceivably have meant to cover *only private, nongovernmental* acts that are contrary to international law.[1002] The content of

---

[998] United States Code Annotated- Title 18. Crimes and Criminal Procedure- Part I. Crimes- Chapter 77. Peonage, Slavery, and Trafficking in Persons- § 1583. Enticement into slavery 18 USCA § 1583 ("Whoever kidnaps or carries away any other person, with the intent that such other person be sold into involuntary servitude, or held as a slave; or whoever entices, persuades, or induces any other person to go on board any vessel or to any other place with the intent that he may be made or held as a slave, or sent out of the country to be so made or held - Shall be fined under this title or imprisoned not more than 20 years, or both. If death results from the violation of this Section, or if the violation includes kidnapping or an attempt to kidnap, aggravated sexual abuse or the attempt to commit aggravated sexual abuse, or an attempt to kill, the defendant shall be fined under this title or imprisoned for any term of years or life, or both.")

[999] *Abdullahi v. Pfizer*, No 01 Civ 8118, 2002 US Dist LEXIS 17436, 2002 WL 31082956, D.C. S.D. N.Y. (2002) at 5.

[1000] *Kadic v. Karadzic*, 70 F3d 232, C. A. 2 (1995) at 243.

[1001] *Burnett v. Al Baraka Inv. and Development Corp.*, 274 FSupp2d 86, D.C. D.C. (2003).

[1002] *Sanchez-Espinoza v. Reagan*, 770 F2d 202 D.C. D.C. (1985); *Tel-Oren v. Libyan Arab*

international law at the time of enactment of the ATCA was very different from its content now.

At the time of ATCA's enactment, the three principal violations of international law were: 1. Violation of safe-conduct; 2. Infringement of the rights of ambassadors; and, 3. Piracy.[1003] These violations would normally be committed by individuals and not by states. This seems to contradict its original purpose if it would now foreclose individual liability. *Al-Baraka* then referred to the decisions in *Kadic*, *Talisman*, *Bao Ge*, *Iwanowa*, *Unocal I*, *Beanal* and *Tel-Oren* to establish individual liability.[1004] Even though *Al-Baraka* brought a novel and strong argument concerning the international legal responsibility of non-state actors, it again did not differentiate between natural and juridical persons.

R. *Talisman I* – March 2003 – First analysis of international law

In US litigation, the first decision in *Presbyterian Church of Sudan, et. al., v. Talisman Energy, Inc.* in 2003 contains the most detailed discussion of the obligations of corporations in international law.[1005] It is the first case in ATCA litigation that differentiated between corporations and individuals in terms of international legal personality and their responsibilities. Holding corporations liable for breaches of international law has been a long-standing practice since the *Unocal I* decision in July 1997 and according to the *Ford* decision already since *Price Waterhouse* decision in 1995.[1006] The Court in *Talisman I* stated: "Clear and consistent Second Circuit precedent demonstrates that corporations may be held liable for *jus cogens* violations of international law."[1007]

It is interesting that the Court in *Talisman I* started with an analysis of US law and only in a second step analyzed international law. The decision looks at precedents in the Supreme Court, in their circuit (the Second Circuit) and in other circuits. In international law, it considers international tribunal decisions, international treaties and international organization precedents. The Court addresses the US precedents in eight pages and the international precedents in three pages. This reflects how US

Republic, 726 F2d 774, C.A. D.C. (1984).

1003 WS Dodge, 'The Historical Origins of the Alien Tort Statute: A Response to the 'Originalists'' 19 Hastings International and Comparative Law Review 221 (1996) at 226.

1004 *Burnett v. Al Baraka Inv. and Development Corp.*, 274 FSupp2d 86, D.C. D.C. (2003) at 100.

1005 *Presbyterian Church of Sudan et al. v. Talisman Energy, Inc.*, 244 F Supp 2d 289, D.C. S.D. N.Y. (2003).

1006 *Doe v. Unocal (Unocal I)*, 963 F Supp 880, D.C.C.D. Cal. (1997) at 891; See above at subheading "Unocal I decision– April 1997- watershed case establishing TNCs as subjects of international law with little analysis;" *Iwanowa v. Ford Motor Company*, 67 F Supp 2d 424, D.C.N.J. (1999) at 445; See above at subheading "Ford decision-October 1999 - Flawed argumentation;" *Hamid v. Price Waterhouse Coopers*, 51 F3d 1411, C.A. 9 (1995) at 1418; See above at subheading "Price Waterhouse - April 1995- Parting with the statist viewpoint?"

1007 *Presbyterian Church of Sudan et al. v. Talisman Energy, Inc.*, 244 F Supp 2d 289, D.C. S.D. N.Y. (2003) at 309.

courts tend to give more weight to the US precedents on international law questions, than on the international law precedents.

1. US precedents

The *Talisman I* District Court criticizes the defendant, Talisman Inc., because it fails to cite a single Supreme Court, Second Circuit, or even Southern District case holding that a corporation is "legally incapable of violating the law of nations." Similarly, Talisman's expert witnesses, James Crawford and Christopher Greenwood, while citing a variety of international law sources, fail to cite a single United States case upholding their position, namely that corporations cannot be held liable under general international law.[1008]

At first, the Court was looking for Supreme Court precedents. Up until now there has only been one ATCA case decided by the Supreme Court, which involved a corporation, but in that case the corporation had been the claimant *Argentine Republic v. Amerada Hess Shipping Corp* in 1989.[1009] The question of corporate responsibility was not brought up in that case. Subsequently, District Court Judge Schwartz looked at the decision on the circuit level. He carefully examined the *Kadic* decision that held individuals liable for violations of international law.[1010]

After establishing the general possibility that non-state actors, meaning individuals, can violate the law of nations, the decision took its most interesting turn. It looked at the preceding Circuit decisions involving ATCA claims brought against corporations, such as *Jota v. Texaco*, *Wiwa v. Royal Dutch Petroleum*, *Bigio v. Coca-Cola* and *Aguinda v. Texaco*.[1011] None of these cases discussed the question of international legal personality and human rights responsibilities of corporations; rather, it was assumed with a brief reference to the *Kadic* decision.

In *Jota v. Texaco*, no views were given on the question of whether non-governmental entities bear responsibilities in international law.[1012] The *Bigio v. Coca-Cola* and *the Aguinda v. Texaco* decisions were dismissed on the ground of lack of subject matter jurisdiction and no view have been expressed on human rights responsibilities of

1008 *Ibid.* at 308.

1009 *Argentine Republic v. Amerada Hess Shipping Corp.*, 488 US 428, 109 SCt 683, 102 LEd2d 818, US S.Ct. (1989).

1010 *Kadic v. Karadzic*, 70 F3d 232, C. A. 2 (1995).

1011 *Jota v. Texaco, Inc.*, 157 F3d 153, C.A. 2 (1998); *Wiwa v. Royal Dutch Petroleum Co.*, 226 F3d 88, C.A.2 (2000); *Bigio v. Coca-Cola Co.*, 239 F3d 440, C.A. 2 (2001); *Aguinda v. Texaco, Inc.*, 303 F3d 470, C.A. 2 (2002).

1012 *Jota v. Texaco, Inc.*, 157 F3d 153, C.A. 2 (1998) at 159 ("We express no view on whether the plaintiffs have alleged conduct by Texaco that violates the law of nations, whether an ATA suit for environmental misconduct, alleged to violate the law of nations, may be brought against a non-governmental entity under the ATA.")

corporations in international law. The *Wiwa* case was the only one out of the four cases that was not dismissed.

In *Wiwa*, there was just a very brief reference to the *Kadic* decision as follows: "we held in *Kadic v. Karadzic* [...] that the ATCA reaches the conduct of private parties provided that their conduct is undertaken under the color of state authority or violates a norm of international law that is recognized as extending to the conduct of private parties."[1013] Therefore, none of these cases mentioned by *Talisman I* included any discussion on the question of human rights responsibilities of *corporations*. They only discussed private actor responsibilities.

The *Talisman I* Court stated: "The fact that the Second Circuit did not address an obvious jurisdictional question *sua sponte* indicates that it had no reservations about the ATCA reaching the acts of corporations."[1014] According to the Court, the question of legal human rights responsibilities should be considered as part of subject matter jurisdiction. This means that the preceding decisions established human rights responsibilities of corporations because they discussed the merits of the case. It does not matter that the courts did not discuss the question of human rights responsibilities at all. Human rights responsibilities of corporations are established in US law.

The *Talisman* Court also dismissed the notion, that the preceding judgments solely discussed the merits because there was the "mere possibility of having subject matter jurisdiction."[1015] According to the *Talisman* Court, the question of subject matter jurisdiction represents the most fundamental part of any judgment and a court will not discuss the merits if it does not have subject matter jurisdiction. The court has the duty to dismiss a matter over which it has no subject matter jurisdiction, even when no party has questioned it.[1016] Therefore, all of the preceding decisions in the Second Circuit presumed that TNCs have human rights obligations in international law.

2. International precedents

a. International tribunal interpretation

The examination of international tribunal decisions in the *Talisman I* decision legally relied on an article by Stephen Ratner.[1017] In this article, Ratner analyzed the decisions of the Nuremberg prosecutions brought against German industrialists. In those judgments, reference was made to corporate responsibility. "Such action on the part of [the pharmaceutical company IG] Farben constituted a violation of the Hague

---

1013 *Wiwa v. Royal Dutch Petroleum Co.*, 226 F3d 88, C.A.2 (2000) at 104.

1014 *Presbyterian Church of Sudan et al. v. Talisman Energy, Inc.*, 244 F Supp 2d 289, D.C. S.D. N.Y. (2003) at 312.

1015 *Ibid.* at 312.

1016 *Endicott Johnson Corp. v. Liberty Mutual Ins. Co.*, 116 F3d 53, C.A. 2 (1997) at 58.

1017 SR Ratner, 'Corporations and Human Rights: A Theory of Legal Responsibility' 111 Yale Law Journal 443 (2001).

Regulations on the conduct of warfare."[1018] The Nuremberg Tribunal also stated: "The confiscation of the Austin plant [...] and its subsequent detention by the Krupp firm constitute a violation of Article 43 of the Hague Regulations [... and] the Krupp firm, through defendants [...] voluntarily and without duress participated in these violations."[1019] The *Talisman* Court inferred from these decisions that the Nuremberg precedents are significant not merely because they constitute a basis for finding corporate liability for violations of international law, but because the language ascribes to the corporations involved the necessary *mens rea* (guilty mind) for the commission of human rights violations.[1020]

It has to be noted, though, that these decisions were brought solely against individuals. These cases, *Krupp*, *Flick* and *IG Farben*, addressed the question of responsibility of individual members of the board of directors of these three companies that were closely connected to the atrocities of World War II. These decisions did not hold corporations liable. They may include some references to the conduct of the whole company, but these decisions were criminal trials of individuals and therefore cannot stand as precedent regarding corporate liability in international law.

The Nuremberg Charter provided that organizations may be declared to be a criminal organization in Article 9: "At the trial of any individual member of any group or organization the Tribunal may declare (in connection with any act of which the individual may be convicted) that the group or organization of which the individual was a member was a criminal organization."[1021] Article 10 stated: "In cases where a group or organization is declared criminal by the Tribunal, the competent national authority of any Signatory shall have the right to bring individual to trial for membership therein before national, military or occupation courts. In any such case the criminal nature of the group or organization is considered proved and shall not be questioned."

Only public organizations, such as the SS (*Schutzstaffel* – Protective Squadron) and the Gestapo (*Geheime Staats Polizei* – Secret State police), were declared to be criminal organizations; no private organizations were declared to be criminal

---

[1018] *The United States of America vs. Carl Krauch, et.*, Trials of War Criminals before the Nuernberg Military Tribunals Under Control Council Law no 10, Washington, DC, Microcard Editions, 1971, International Military Tribunal (1947) at 1081, 1140.

[1019] *The United States of America vs. Alfried Krupp, et. al.*, Trials of War Criminals before the Nuernberg Military Tribunals Under Control Council Law no 10, Washington, DC, Microcard Editions, 1971, International Military Tribunal (1947) at 1327, 1352.

[1020] *Presbyterian Church of Sudan et al. v. Talisman Energy, Inc.*, 244 F Supp 2d 289, D.C. S.D. N.Y. (2003) at 316.

[1021] Charter of the International Military Tribunal for the Trial of the Major War Criminals appended to Agreement for the Prosecution and Punishment of Major War Criminals of the European Axis, Aug 8, 1945, 59 Stat 1544, UNTS 279, as amended, Protocol to Agreement and Charter, Oct 6, 1945 (Nuremberg Charter) (1945).

organizations. Even though the Nuremberg Charter did not endow human rights responsibilities on TNCs, *Talisman I* held that corporations were held liable in international tribunals. The Court then went on to state that corporations can be held criminally and civilly liable in US law.[1022]

In his affidavit for the defendant, Talisman, Professor James Crawford differentiated between criminal and general civil responsibility.[1023] Examining the *Torture Convention*, the *Genocide Convention*, the *Geneva Conventions*, various other international agreements and the statutes of the ICTY, ICTR and ICC, Professor Crawford concluded that there is currently no regime of international corporate *criminal* responsibility.[1024] He then examined *civil* liability of non-state actors. He affirmed that states and interstate institutions have been held civilly liable in international law and that there have been tentative approaches to hold other non-state actors liable, such as insurgent or opposition groups, but he categorized this discussion as still being "embryonic."[1025] International law does not recognize the legal personality of TNCs.[1026]

b. International treaties

Secondly, the court relied on international treaties to find that there exist obligations of TNCs in international law.[1027] The *ILO Convention No. 98* provides that "workers shall enjoy adequate protection against acts of anti-union discrimination in respect of

---

1022 *Presbyterian Church of Sudan et al. v. Talisman Energy, Inc.*, 244 F Supp 2d 289, D.C. S.D. N.Y. (2003) at 316, citing *New York Cent. & Hudson River R.R. Co. v. United States*, 212 US 481, 493, 29 SCt 304, 53 LEd 613, US S.Ct. (1909) ("We think that a corporation may be liable criminally for certain offenses of which a specific intent may be a necessary element. There is no more difficulty in imputing to a corporation a specific intent in criminal proceedings than in civil.")

1023 J Crawford, *Declaration of James Crawford S.C. as Affidavit for defendant Talisman (at hand)* (2002) at 7.

1024 Convention Against Torture and Other Cruel Inhuman or Degrading Treatment or Punishment 10 December 1984, 1465 UNTS 85 (entered into force 26 June 1987) (1984); Convention on the Prevention and Punishment of the Crime of Genocide December 9, 1948, 78 UNTS 277, approved and proposed for signature and ratification or accession by General Assembly resolution 260 A (III) of 9 December 1948, entered into force Jan 12, 1951 (Genocide Convention) (1948); Geneva Convention Relative to the Protection of Civilian Persons in Time of War (Fourth Geneva Convention) 75 UNTS 287 (12 August 1949) (entered into force Oct 21, 1950) (1949); Protocol Amending the Convention to Suppress the Slave Trade and Slavery 7 December 1953, 182 UNTS 51 (entered into force 7 December 1953) (1953); Supplementary Convention on the Abolition of Slavery, the Slave Trade, and Institutions and Practices Similar to Slavery 226 UNTS 3 (entered into force 30 April 1957) (1956).

1025 J Crawford, *Declaration of James Crawford S.C. as Affidavit for defendant Talisman (at hand)* (2002) at 12.

1026 *Ibid.* at 12.

1027 *Presbyterian Church of Sudan et al. v. Talisman Energy, Inc.*, 244 F Supp 2d 289, D.C. S.D. N.Y. (2003) at 316 et *seq.*

their employment."[1028] The *Convention on Third Party Liability in the Field of Nuclear Energy* states that "*the operator* of a nuclear installation shall be liable" for, *inter alia,* "damage to or loss of life of any person" and damage to property.[1029] The *International Convention on Civil Liability for Oil Pollution Damage* holds that "*the owner* of a ship at the time of an incident [...] shall be liable for any pollution damage caused by oil which has escaped or been discharged from the ship as a result of the incident."[1030]There are further examples of holding individuals or corporations liable in international law as the *Vienna Convention on Civil Liability for Nuclear Damage.*[1031] Many other treaties do not distinguish between natural and juridical persons, such as the *Genocide Convention* or the *Geneva Convention on the Treatment of Prisoners of War.*[1032]

The Court held that it seems implausible that international treaties would protect TNCs that engaged in slave trade or other violations of human rights: "These regimes do not distinguish between natural and juridical individuals, and it is implausible that international law would protect a corporation that engaged in the slave trade or produced the contemporary equivalent of Zyklon B for the destruction of Jews in concentration camps."[1033]

c. International organization precedents

The third part of the District Court's analysis of corporate obligations in international law considered precedents in international organizations. The Court chose an interesting array of examples from the UN General Assembly, the UN Security Council and decisions of the ECJ. The *UDHR* states that "every individual and every organ of society, keeping this *Declaration* constantly in mind, shall strive by teaching and education to promote respect for these rights and freedoms and by progressive measures, national and international, to secure their universal and effective recognition and observance."[1034]

1028 Article 1 Convention Concerning the Application of the Principles of the Right to Organise and To Bargain Collectively 96 UNTS 257 (entered into force 18 July 1951) (1949).

1029 Article 3 Convention on Third Party Liability in the Field of Nuclear Energy 956 UNTS 251, reprinted in 55 AJIL 1082 (1960) (amended in 1964, 1968 & 1982) (Paris Convention) (1960).

1030 Article III International Convention on Civil Liability for Oil Pollution Damage 9 ILM (1970) 45 (entered into force June 19, 1975) (1969).

1031 Vienna Convention on Civil Liability for Nuclear Damage 1063 UNTS 265, reprinted in 2 ILM at 727 (1963).

1032 Convention on the Prevention and Punishment of the Crime of Genocide December 9, 1948, 78 UNTS 277, approved and proposed for signature and ratification or accession by General Assembly resolution 260 A (III) of 9 December 1948, entered into force Jan 12, 1951 (Genocide Convention) (1948); Convention Relative to the Treatment of Prisoners of War August 12, 1949, 6 UST 3316, 75 UNTS 135 (Third Geneva Convention) (1949).

1033 *Presbyterian Church of Sudan et al. v. Talisman Energy, Inc.*, 244 F Supp 2d 289, D.C. S.D. N.Y. (2003) at 316.

1034 Universal Declaration of Human Rights GA Res 217 A(III), UN Doc A/810 at 71 (1948).

In construing the term "individual," the Court referred to academic writing by the noted legal scholar on international law and Chief Reporter for the Third Restatement of Foreign Relations, Louis Henkin, who argued that juridical persons were also addressed by the *UDHR* as "organ of society."[1035] The Court did not venture further into the question of whether this sentence in the declaration means that individuals and corporations are really obliged to adhere to human rights, or whether they are only called upon to promote respect, which is distinctly different.

As further proof of the obligations of TNCs, the *Talisman* Court referred to resolutions by the UN Security Council and UN General Assembly. In an UN Security Council Resolution in 1995, the so-called oil-for-food resolution, the UN required corporations wishing to purchase oil from Iraq to follow certain procedures.[1036] Similarly, the UN condemned any further economic co-operation with South Africa in 1970, including "foreign economic interests."[1037] Finally, the District Court referred to decisions of the ECJ, where corporations were held to be bound to comply with human rights norms.[1038]

3. Analysis to the *Talisman I* decision

The *Talisman I* decision is the most detailed decision in defining human rights responsibilities of TNCs in US law. The Court concluded that there is substantive precedent in US and international law showing that corporations can be held liable under international law for gross human rights violations.[1039] It held that actions against corporations for "substantial violations of international law, including *jus cogens* violations, are the norm rather than the exception."[1040] It based its holding mainly on US law. The analysis of international law is rather cursory, but represents the first time that a US court has explored sources of international law concerning the question of responsibility of corporations in international law.

S. *Sosa* – March 2004 – Tentative affirmation of human rights responsibilities of TNCs

The *Sosa* decision of the Supreme Court was pivotal for the future of ATCA litigation and basically kept the "door ajar" for litigating breaches of international law, especially human rights law, in US courts. In this case, an individual sued other US and

---

[1035] L Henkin, 'The Universal Declaration at 50 and the Challenge of Global Markets' 25 Brooklyn Journal of International Law 1 (1999) at 25.

[1036] UN SC, *SC Res. 986, UN SCOR, U.N. Doc. S/RES/986 (Oil-for-food resolution)* (1995).

[1037] UN GA, *GA Res. 2671 F, UN GAOR, 25th Sess., Supp. No. 28, U.N. Doc. A/8028* (1970) at 33, 34.

[1038] *Walrave v Association Union Cycliste Internationale*, ECR 1405, 36/74, ECJ (1974) at 1419; *Defrenne v Societe Anonyme Belge de Navigation Aerienne Sabena*, ECJ Ruling Case 43/75, 1976 ECR 455, ECJ (1976) at 457.

[1039] *Presbyterian Church of Sudan et al. v. Talisman Energy, Inc.*, 244 F Supp 2d 289, D.C. S.D. N.Y. (2003) at 319.

[1040] *Ibid.* at 319.

foreign individuals, as well as state agencies of the US government. The question of individual or corporate liability was only mentioned briefly in a footnote.[1041] The footnote reads as follows: "A related consideration is whether international law extends the scope of liability for a violation of a given norm to the perpetrator being sued, if the defendant is a private actor such as a corporation or individual. Compare *Tel-Oren v. Libyan Arab Republic* [...] (C.A.D.C.1984) (Edwards, J., concurring) (insufficient consensus in 1984 that torture by private actors violates international law), with *Kadic v. Karadzic* [...] (C.A.2 1995) (sufficient consensus in 1995 that genocide by private actors violates international law)."[1042]

This footnote has been referred to on a number of occasions. The "footnote in the *Sosa* opinion highlights one of the most important yet unanswered questions in the continued debate concerning the scope of the ATCA."[1043] Beth Stephens commented that the *Sosa* Court has indicated general agreement with addressing corporate defendants.[1044] Saad Gul cautioned that federal courts should weigh the "practical consequences" when deciding on corporate liability.[1045] And Frank Olah noted that "footnote twenty is the only time the Court made explicit mention of corporations as possible ATCA defendants in its opinion. Unfortunately, the Court failed to approve of any particular standard of liability already being utilized by the federal courts in assessing MNC liability under the ATCA (e.g., "color of law" liability under 42 U.S.C. § 1983 or aiding & abetting liability). It does, however, seem to suggest that whatever liability standard is appropriate for a given norm should be derived from international law rather than domestic law. Disappointingly, the Court appeared in the footnote to implicitly *affirm the cognoscibility of ATCA claims against MNC defendants*."[1046]

Therefore, *Sosa* does not rule definitively on the question of corporate or individual liability. By referring to these two decisions, *Tel-Oren* and *Kadic*, the Supreme Court hints that there has been a development in that area. Whereas in the earlier days of ATCA litigation, such as for example in 1984 US courts did not recognize individual liability, they now do. However, this is a difficult assumption, since the two decisions refer to different kinds of human rights violations; torture in the *Tel-Oren* decision

---

[1041] *Sosa v. Alvarez-Machain* (03-339) 542 US 2739, US S.Ct. (2004) at footnote 20, page 2766.

[1042] *Ibid.* at 2766, footnote 20; citing *Tel-Oren v. Libyan Arab Republic*, 726 F2d 774, C.A. D.C. (1984) at 781; *Kadic v. Karadzic*, 70 F3d 232, C. A. 2 (1995) at 239.

[1043] HR Bornstein, 'The Alien Tort Claims Act in 2007: Resolving the Delicate Balance Between Judicial and Legislative Authority' 82 Indiana Law Journal 1077 (2007) at 1077.

[1044] B Stephens, 'Sosa v. Alvarez-Machain: 'The Door Is Still Ajar' for Human Rights Litigation in US Courts' 70 Brooklyn Law Review 533 (2004) at 557.

[1045] S Gul, 'The Supreme Court Giveth and the Supreme Court Taketh Away: An Assessment of Corporate Liability Under § 1350' 109 West Virginia Law Review 379 (2007) at 381.

[1046] FC Olah, 'MNC Liability for International Human Rights Violations Under the Alien Tort Claims Act: A Review & Analysis of the Fundamental Jurisprudence and a Look at Aiding & Abetting Liability under the Act' 25 Quinnipiac Law Review 751 (2007) at 771.

and genocide in the *Kadic* decision. The pivotal human rights decision in *Sosa* does not take a definite stand on human rights responsibilities of TNCs, but it affirmed human rights responsibilities of individuals, since the case of *Sosa v. Alvarez* concerned individuals. It is also arguable that *Sosa* puts individuals and corporations on a par and therefore indicates affirmation of human rights responsibilities of TNCs.[1047]

T. *Talisman II* decision – June 2005 –Affirmation of *Talisman I*

In US law, the decision *Presbyterian Church of Sudan, et. al., v. Talisman Energy, Inc. (Talisman II)* in 2005 includes, together with the *Talisman I* decision, the most detailed analysis of the question of human rights responsibilities of TNCs. The *Talisman II* decision clearly confirms that corporations have human rights responsibilities, especially in case of *jus cogens* norms.[1048]

The *Talisman II* decision is naturally based on the preceding decision, the *Talisman I* decision of 2003. In the 2005 decision, the Court stated that the 2003 Opinion meticulously demonstrated that corporations may be held liable under international law for violations of *jus cogens* norms by citing US law precedent, as well as a wide array of international law sources.[1049] No subsequent decision since that Opinion's issuance, including *Sosa* and *Flores* indicates that the Opinion's conclusions regarding corporate liability in international law were erroneous.[1050] Indeed, subsequent events only confirm the validity of its analysis. After that Opinion, the Second Circuit twice confronted ATCA cases with corporate defendants, and neither time did it hold that corporations cannot be liable under customary international law. Those two decisions were *Bano* and *Flores.*[1051]

The *Talisman II* Court pointed out the denial of direct liability of TNCs in customary international law rests on a misreading of the *Flores* decision.[1052] The *Talisman* Court stated that one has to look primarily at the formal lawmaking and official actions of states.[1053] On the question of how international law can change, *Talisman II* referred to an American law journal article by Phillip R. Trimble on the treatment of international law by the Supreme Court.[1054] Trimble explains that the only way to

1047 *Presbyterian Church of Sudan et al. v. Talisman Energy, Inc.*, 244 F Supp 2d 289, D.C. S.D. N.Y. (2003).

1048 *The Presbyterian Church of Sudan, et. al. v. Talisman Energy, Inc.*, 374 FSupp2d 331, D.C. S.D. N.Y. (2005) at 335-337.

1049 *Ibid.* at 335.

1050 *Ibid.* at 335.

1051 *Bano v. Union Carbide*, 361 F3d 696, C.A. 2 (2004); *Flores v. Southern Peru Copper Corporation*, 343 F3d 140, C.A. 2 (2003) at 69.

1052 *The Presbyterian Church of Sudan, et. al. v. Talisman Energy, Inc.*, 374 FSupp2d 331, D.C. S.D. N.Y. (2005) at 336.

1053 *Ibid.* at 336.

1054 PR Trimble, 'The Supreme Court and International Law: The Demise of Restatement Section 403' 89 American Journal of International Law 53 (1995).

change customary international law is "by one state's violating the old norm and other states' acquiescing in the violation."[1055] *Talisman II* states that one of the clearest means is to look at claims where competing interests of states are involved and look to whether the states have objected to the claims.[1056]

The Court then stated that the "natural place" to find such state behavior is looking at claims where foreign TNCs have been involved. It is not necessary for all states to follow that rule. Referring to the *Nicaragua* judgment of the ICJ, it is only necessary that the conduct of states, in general, should "be consistent with such rules, and that instances of state conduct inconsistent with a given rule should generally have been treated as breaches of that rule."[1057]

Following this rationale, the *Talisman* decision cited various cases where the US as well as foreign governments have objected to the ATCA cases in general or on policy grounds. However, even in those cases, governments have not objected to human rights responsibilities of TNCs. "Indeed, Talisman [as defendant] has not cited a single case where any government objected to the exercise of jurisdiction over one of its national corporations based on the principle that it is not a violation of international law *for corporations* to commit or aid in the commission of genocide or other similar atrocities. If this issue was a genuine source of disagreement in the international community, it would be expected that the assertion of such a rule as customary would provoke objections from states whose interests were implicated by the assertion of the rule in those cases against their nationals."[1058]

It is also interesting to note that while the EU's *amicus* brief stated that most national jurisdictions do not offer anything like the ATCA litigation, it also did not question human rights responsibilities of corporations in general. The *amicus* brief concluded by stating: "Courts should also recognize the exceptional conditions under which individuals and corporations may be held liable under international law." This is compelling evidence with which to uphold corporate liability in international law.[1059]

The Court in *Talisman II* stated that it cannot be inferred from the fact that the ICTY and ICTR did not mention the liability of corporations that it does not exist. The Court held that the statutes always need to be construed in the context in which they

---

1055 *The Presbyterian Church of Sudan, et. al. v. Talisman Energy, Inc.*, 374 FSupp2d 331, D.C. S.D. N.Y. (2005) at 337; citing PR Trimble, 'The Supreme Court and International Law: The Demise of Restatement Section 403' 89 American Journal of International Law 53 (1995) at 55.

1056 *Committee of US Citizens Living in Nicaragua v. Reagan*, 859 F2d 929, C.A. D.C. (1988) at 941; *United States ex rel. Lujan v. Gengler*, 510 F2d 62, C.A. 2 (1975) at 67.

1057 *Military and Paramilitary Activities in and Against Nicaragua (Nicaragua v. US) (Merits)*, ICJ 14, 98, ICJ (1986) at paragraph 191.

1058 *The Presbyterian Church of Sudan, et. al. v. Talisman Energy, Inc.*, 374 FSupp2d 331, D.C. S.D. N.Y. (2005) at 337.

1059 *Ibid.* at 337.

were written and the genocides in Rwanda and Yugoslavia were mostly carried out by individual perpetrators and not corporations. This shortcoming of these two statutes of international tribunals concerning TNCs would be like denying a rule of the law of the sea "just because some landlocked states did not agree to it."[1060]

The *Talisman II* decision is a very interesting and important decision for the examination of the question of human rights responsibilities of TNCs according to US law. Unlike most other US decisions it raises arguments from international law. It is very interesting to note that no home nation of a TNC that was affected by ATCA litigation has objected to the proposition that corporations can be held liable for human rights violations in general. Governments generally tend to dislike interference in their internal affairs and might refer to their sovereign rights, which, in the case of human rights violations, seems to be inappropriate. In some cases they also voiced objections, such as in relation to the establishment of a Truth and Reconciliation Committee in post-Apartheid South Africa. No government has completely rejected the notion of human rights responsibilities of corporations. Therefore the Talisman II decision concluded that human rights responsibilities of corporations in international law are accepted by now.

U. *Titan* – Aug. 2005 – No responsibilities for private actors

Ibrahim v. Titan was the first ATCA decision in US law that dealt with the US led invasion into Iraq in 2003. It was a case concerning torture by private contractors in Abu Ghraib and was decided by the District Court for the District of Columbia.[1061] Also it was the first decision to deny human rights responsibilities to corporations. It held that "alleged acts of torture inflicted upon Iraqi national detainees by private government contractors that provided interpreters and interrogators to US military in Iraq were not actionable under the ATCA as violations of the law of nations, although numerous treaties and other sources of international law condemned torture; the law of nations did not apply to the contractors, *as they were private, rather than official*, actors."[1062]

The *Titan* Court relied on the *Sanchez-Espinoza v. Reagan* decision and the Judge Edwards opinion in *Tel-Oren*, stating that the law of nations does not reach private, non-state conduct like execution, murder, abduction, torture, rape.[1063] However, in *Sanchez-Espinoza the* Court found that the ATCA does not reach private, non-state conduct such as support of forces bearing arms against foreign governments.[1064] The *Sanchez-Espinoza* Case has been misread by the *Titan* Court. The Edwards Opinion

1060 *Ibid.* at 336.
1061 *Ibrahim v. Titan Corp.*, 391 F Supp 2d 10, D.C. D.C. (2005).
1062 *Ibid.* at 14-15.
1063 *Ibid.* at 14-15.
1064 *Sanchez-Espinoza v. Reagan*, 770 F2d 202 D.C. D.C. (1985) at 207.

found that ATCA covers individual responsibility under color of law, but did not completely deny individual responsibility.[1065]

Furthermore, the Edwards Opinion also stated that international law is developing towards allocating duties to private actors absent color of law authority; he only refrained from imposing such duties on individuals without guidance by the US Supreme Court.[1066] Exactly the same imposition of such international duties was found in the *Kadic* decision for individuals and affirmed by the *Ford* decision for corporate actors.[1067] These US decisions have not been mentioned or were incorrectly represented. The *Titan* Court completely refrained from citing sources of international law. Therefore it is fair to say that the *Titan* decision lacks any analysis of either US law or international law on the subject of human rights responsibilities of TNCs. The *Titan* decision stands in stark contrast to the scope of liability established by the preceding ATCA litigation.

V. *Exxon* – Oct. 2005 – Another attempt to deny human rights responsibilities of TNCs

In the decision *Doe v. Exxon* in October 2005 and for a second time following the *Titan* decision a US court in ATCA litigation found against human rights responsibilities of TNCs. Again this was decided by the District Court for the District of Columbia. It interpreted the Supreme Court's decision in *Sosa* to mean that a decision has to involve an element of judgment about the practical consequences of making that cause available to litigants in the federal courts.[1068] Therefore, the *Exxon* Court held that it would be "highly unfair" to impose liability on corporate actors that do business in countries with problematic human rights records.[1069]

It is correct that a corporation cannot be held liable for human rights violations carried out by the state in which it is doing business. However, where a corporation directed, controlled, conspired or aided and abetted gross human rights violations, such as genocide or torture, it seems fair to make the corporation liable for these violations. It is necessary to differentiate and look closely at the case. This liability standard for aiding and abetting in gross violations of human rights is also imposed

---

1065 *Tel-Oren v. Libyan Arab Republic*, 726 F2d 774, C.A. D.C. (1984) at 791.

1066 *Ibid.* at 795 ("While I have little doubt that the trend in international law is toward a more expansive allocation of rights and obligations to entities other than states, I decline to read Section 1350 to cover torture by non-state actors, absent guidance from the Supreme Court on the statute's usage of the term "law of nations.")

1067 *Kadic v. Karadzic*, 70 F3d 232, C. A. 2 (1995) at 239; *Iwanowa v. Ford Motor Company*, 67 F Supp 2d 424, D.C.N.J. (1999) at 443 et *seq.*

1068 *Sosa v. Alvarez-Machain* (03-339) 542 US 2739, US S.Ct. (2004) at 2766 ("Actionable violations of international law must be of a norm that is specific, universal, and obligatory. And the determination whether a norm is sufficiently definite to support a cause of action should (and, indeed, inevitably must) involve an element of judgment about the practical consequences of making that cause available to litigants in the federal courts.")

1069 *Doe v. Exxon Mobil Corporation*, 393 FSupp2d 20, D.C. D.C. (2005) at 26.

on individuals by international law (as in the ICC and the complementary national jurisdiction), as well as in US law. This liability standard was also established by the preceding US judgments in *Kadic*, *Wiwa*, *Talisman* and others.[1070]

Moreover, the Court in *Exxon* stated that the *Sosa* decision suggested that only states, and not individuals or corporations could be held liable.[1071] This is wrong.[1072] The Supreme Court briefly and neutrally describes the current scope of liability of individuals and corporations. It mentioned the *Kadic* decision, where there was sufficient consensus to hold non-state actors liable for grave breaches of international law.[1073] Many decisions have read the *Kadic* decision to include the liability of TNCs and not only private individuals.[1074] The *Exxon* decision therefore does not produce any significant argument to deny human rights responsibilities of TNCs. This also clearly needs to be differentiated from imposing duties, such as human rights obligations, on TNCs.

W. Other US decisions

The Courts in *Southern Peru Copper* and *Drummond* relied on the *Kadic* decision in establishing corporate human rights responsibilities.[1075] Many ATCA cases brought against TNCs have not discussed human rights responsibilities and were denied for other reasons.[1076] In the *Rio Tinto* decision of 2002, the District Court for the Central District of California quoted a *Harvard Law Review* article to the effect that a corporation may be held liable if it commits piracy, slave trading, genocide, or war crimes even absent state action.[1077] In the *Rio Tinto* decision of 2006, one of the most recent ATCA decision in a case brought against a TNC, the Court of Appeals of the

---

1070 *Kadic v. Karadzic*, 70 F3d 232, C. A. 2 (1995) at 239; *Wiwa v. Royal Dutch Shell Petroleum Corp.*, 226 F3d 232, C.A. 2 (2001) at 104; *Presbyterian Church of Sudan et al. v. Talisman Energy, Inc.*, 244 F Supp 2d 289, D.C. S.D. N.Y. (2003) at 309.

1071 *Doe v. Exxon Mobil Corporation*, 393 FSupp2d 20, D.C. D.C. (2005) at 26.

1072 See above at subheading "S. Sosa – March 2004 – Tentative affirmation of international legal personality of TNCs" at 194.

1073 *Kadic v. Karadzic*, 70 F3d 232, C. A. 2 (1995) at 239.

1074 See e.g.; *Beanal v. Freeport- McMoran, Inc.*, 969 F Supp 362, D.C. E.D. La (1997) at 384; *Doe v. Unocal (Unocal I)*, 963 F Supp 880, D.C.C.D. Cal. (1997) at 892; *Bigio v. Coca-Cola Co.*, 239 F3d 440, C.A. 2 (2001) at 447; *Beanal v. Freeport-McMoran, Inc.*, 197 F3d 161, C.A. 5 (1999) at 371; *Wiwa v. Royal Dutch Shell Petroleum Corp.*, 226 F3d 232, C.A. 2 (2001) at 104; *Doe v. Unocal (Unocal III)*, 395 F3d 932, C.A. 9 (2002) at 977; *Abdullahi v. Pfizer*, No 01 Civ 8118, 2002 US Dist LEXIS 17436, 2002 WL 31082956, D.C. S.D. N.Y. (2002) at 5; *Burnett v. Al Baraka Inv. and Development Corp.*, 274 FSupp2d 86, D.C. D.C. (2003) at 100.

1075 *Flores v. Southern Peru Copper Corp.*, 253 F Supp 2d 510, D.C. S.D. N.Y. (2002) at 513; *Estate of Rodriguez v. Drummond Co.*, 256 F Supp 2d 1250, D.C. N.D. Ala. (2003) at 1260.

1076 *Bowoto v. Chevron*, 312 F Supp 2d 1229, D.C. N.D. Cal. (2004), *In re World War II Era Japanese Forced Labor Litigation*, 114 F Supp 2d 939, D.C. N.D. Cal. (2001) and *Bano v. Union Carbide*, 2003 WL 1344884, D.C. S.D. N.Y. (2003); *Bano v. Union Carbide*, 361 F3d 696, C.A. 2 (2004), *Aguinda v. Texaco, Inc.*, 303 F3d 470, C.A. 2 (2002) and *Deutsch v. Turner Corp.*, 317 F3d 1005, C.A. 9 (2003).

1077 *Sarei v. Rio Tinto PLC*, 221 FSupp2d 1116, D.C. C.D. Cal. (2002) at 1140.

Ninth Circuit held that it had subject matter jurisdiction and did not discuss the question of human rights responsibilities of TNCs at all.[1078] However, it also affirmed that corporations will be held liable for egregious human rights violations in US courts.

III. Setting the standard for ATCA claims

Having established the general proposition that TNCs have human rights responsibilities, the next question is: what is the precise nature of those responsibilities? In order to approach this question, it is important to look at the standard of deducing the responsibilities.

A. Egregiousness standard

In order to limit possible ATCA claims, the decision of *Villeda Aldana v. Fresh Del Monte Produce, Inc.* in 2003 by the District Court for the Southern District of Florida in the Eleventh Circuit referred to the "egregiousness standard." "What the Plaintiffs ask the Court to find was that an eight-hour kidnapping by a shadowy 'security force,' accompanied by threats of death, is actionable under the ATCA. Yet, this Court's review of other ATCA cases confirms that the added quality of egregiousness is what confers subject matter jurisdiction under the ATCA. Despite the Plaintiffs best efforts at characterizing the October 13th events, the essential facts as alleged do not rise to a level of conduct actionable under the ATCA."[1079]

The egregiousness standard was first used in *Zapata v. Quinn*, a 1983 decision by the Court of Appeals for the Second Circuit.[1080] However, the same Court disapproved of this standard in the 2003 decision of *Flores*.[1081] Basically, it "would displace the agreement of nations as the source of customary international law and substitute for it the consciences and sensibilities of individual judges."[1082] The egregiousness standard seems no longer to apply in respect of ATCA claims.

B. Specific, universal and obligatory standard

"Actionable violations of international law must be of norm that is *specific, universal,* and *obligatory.*" This test was formulated in *In re Estate of Ferdinand Marcos Human Rights Litigation* in 1994.[1083] It was based on the concurring opinion by Judge Edwards in *Tel-Oren*[1084] and was upheld in many later decisions, including the recent

---

1078 *Sarei v. Rio Tinto*, 456 F3d 1069, C.A. 9 (2006) at 1077.

1079 *Villeda Aldana v. Fresh Del Monte Produce, Inc.*, 305 F Supp 2d 1285, D.C. S.D. Fla. (2003) at 1296.

1080 *Zapata v Quinn*, 707 F2d 691, C.A. 2 (1983) at 692.

1081 *Flores v. Southern Peru Copper Corporation*, 343 F3d 140, C.A. 2 (2003) at 145.

1082 *Flores v. Southern Peru Copper Corp.*, 253 F Supp 2d 510, D.C. S.D. N.Y. (2002) at 523.

1083 *In re Estate of Ferdinand Marcos Human Rights Litigation (Estate II)*, 25 F3d 1467, C.A. 9 (1994) at 1475.

1084 *Tel-Oren v. Libyan Arab Republic*, 726 F2d 774, C.A. D.C. (1984) at 780.

decisions of *Sarei* and *Hereros*,[1085] and the Supreme Court decision in *Sosa*. In that case, the Court held that ATCA can only be used for a limited amount of human rights violations and that the test should be strict and based on the historical origins of the statute, which only supplied a basis for three violations of international law: (1) violation of safe-conduct; (2) infringement of the rights of ambassadors; and (3) piracy.

C. *Sosa* standard

In *Sosa*, the Supreme Court has found that a mandate for human rights litigation was given by the legislature to the US jurisdiction. It was of the opinion that the ATCA litigation may be ambiguous,[1086] but on the other hand all of the justices in this matter (including Justice Scalia) found that, according to the legislative history of ATCA, the jurisdiction was originally understood to be available to enforce a small number of international norms that a federal court could properly recognize as within the Common law enforceable without further statutory authority.[1087] Further, in *Sosa* it was found that the US Congress, has not only refrained from expressing disagreement with the ATCA litigation as to the proper exercise of the judicial power, but it has responded by enacting legislation supplementing the judicial determination such that US nationals may also sue for damages in case of torture.[1088] The legislative history to the TVPA includes the remark that ATCA should "remain intact to permit suits based on other norms that already exist or may ripen in the future into rules of customary international law."[1089]

Furthermore, in defining the standards for future ATCA litigation it referred to the *Filártiga* decision with the clear comment that the Supreme Court's standard to define an ATCA claim "is generally consistent with the reasoning of many of the courts and judges who faced the issue before it reached this Court."[1090] And in the cryptic footnote 20 that touches upon human rights responsibilities of individuals and corporations, the Supreme Court also touched upon certain human rights violations and seems to affirm their cognoscibility. Because of its importance the relevant part shall be quoted again: "A related consideration is whether international law extends the scope of liability for a violation of a given norm to the perpetrator being sued, if the defendant is a private actor such as a corporation or individual. Compare *Tel-Oren v. Libyan Arab Republic*, [...] (insufficient consensus [in 1984] that torture by private actors violates international law), with *Kadic v. Karadzic* [...] (sufficient consensus [in 1995] that genocide by private actors violates international law)."[1091]

[1085] *Sarei v. Rio Tinto, PLC*, 487 F3d 1193, C.A. 9 (2007) at 1202 and *Hereros ex rel. Riruako v. Deutsche Afrika-Linien Gmblt & Co.*, 2007 WL 1066949, C.A. 3 (2007) at 1.

[1086] *Sosa v. Alvarez-Machain* (03-339) 542 US 2739, US S.Ct. (2004) at 2763.

[1087] *Ibid.* at 2764.

[1088] *Ibid.* at 2765.

[1089] *Ibid.* at 2764.

[1090] *Ibid.* at 2765-2766.

[1091] *Ibid.* at 2766.

In other words, the Supreme Court stated that a standard must be derived by assessing the liability of private actors as individuals and corporations in international law. According to the Supreme Court, federal Common law should not provide for liability for violations of any international law norm with less definite content and acceptance among civilized nations than the historical paradigms familiar when § 1350 was enacted.[1092]

This limit upon judicial recognition is generally consistent with the reasoning of many of the courts and judges who faced the issue before it reached this Court. The Supreme Court decision then referred to *Filártiga*, *Tel-Oren* and *In re Estate of Marcos Human Rights Litigation*. Referring to the *Filártiga* decision, *Sosa* stated that "for purposes of civil liability, the torturer has become-like the pirate and slave trader before him – *hostis humani generis, an enemy of all mankind*."[1093]

Referring to the *Tel-Oren* decision, *Sosa* stated that the limits of ATCA are defined by "a handful of heinous actions – each of which violates *definable, universal and obligatory norms*."[1094] And from the *Marcos* decision, the Supreme Court upheld that "actionable violations of international law must be of a norm that is *specific, universal, and obligatory*."[1095] Lastly, the Supreme Court noted that "the determination whether a norm is sufficiently definite to support a cause of action should (and, indeed, inevitably must) involve an element of judgment about the practical consequences of making that cause available to litigants in the federal courts."[1096]

D. Analysis

Sosa has set the new standard for defining human rights responsibilities of non-state actors. These responsibilities must be specific, universal and obligatory. They must derive from international law and they must consider the historic origins of ATCA, which was meant to cover only a small specific set of violations of international law.

IV. Specific human rights responsibilities of TNCs

Having established the standard of responsibilities the specific human rights responsibilities of corporations in US law shall be discussed.

1092 *Ibid.* at 2744 and 2762.

1093 *Filártiga v. Peña-Irala*, 630 F2d 876, C.A. 2 (1980) at 890.

1094 *Tel-Oren v. Libyan Arab Republic*, 726 F2d 774, C.A. D.C. (1984) at 781 (Relying on Judge Edward's concurrence in *Tel-Oren v. Libyan Arab Republic*, 726 F2d 774, C.A. D.C. (1984) at 781.

1095 *In re Estate of Ferdinand Marcos Human Rights Litigation (Estate II)*, 25 F3d 1467, C.A. 9 (1994) at 1475.

1096 *Sosa v. Alvarez-Machain* (03-339) 542 US 2739, US S.Ct. (2004) at 2766.

A. Torture and extrajudicial killing

The reason why torture and extrajudicial killing are dealt with under one subheading is that the operation of the TVPA causes them to be treated very similarly in ATCA litigation.[1097] The TVPA is the statutory provision, which provides a cause of action in respect of torture and extrajudicial killing. It was intended to affirm the ATCA litigation and supplement it by providing a cause of action also for US citizens, since only aliens, meaning non-US citizens, can sue under the ATCA.[1098] *Sosa* has acknowledged that the TVPA clearly provides authority to establish an unambiguous and modern basis for federal claims of torture and extrajudicial killing.[1099]

That torture belongs to the actionable claims under ATCA appears to be well-established. Prior to the Supreme Court's decision in *Sosa*, TNCs have been held liable for complicity in torture like in *Wiwa v. Royal Dutch Shell Petroleum Corp* by the Court of Appeals for the Second Circuit. The Court held that "deliberate torture perpetrated under the color of official authority violates universally accepted norms of international human rights law, and that such a violation of international law constitutes a violation of the domestic law of the United States, giving rise to a claim under the ATCA whenever the perpetrator is properly served within the borders of the United States."[1100] Relying on *Xuncax v. Gramajo*, the Court in *Wiwa* held that it is well established that torture, summary execution, and arbitrary detention "constitute fully recognized violations of international law, because they are inconsistent with the inherent dignity and the equal and inalienable rights of all members of the human family."[1101]

Referring to the *Filártiga* decision, the "torturer has become ... *hostis humani generis*, an enemy of all mankind."[1102] Interestingly, this particular part of the *Filártiga* finding was also explicitly upheld in *Sosa*.[1103] The *Wiwa* Court went on to refer to Article 2 of the *Convention Against Torture and Other Cruel, Inhuman or Degrading Treatment or Punishment*: "No exceptional circumstance whatsoever ... may be invoked as a justification for torture."[1104] Moreover, each of the torture practices is

---

1097 *Wiwa v. Royal Dutch Petroleum Co.*, 226 F3d 88, C.A.2 (2000) at 105 (In this opinion, we use the word "torture" to include both torture and "extra judicial killing," except where the context makes clear the more limited meaning is intended.)

1098 U.S. House of Representatives, *P.L. 102-256, Torture Victim Protection Act of 1991, H.R. REP. NO. 102-367 (I), November 25* (1991)*Connelly v. RTZ, July 24, 1997*, 1998 Law Reports, Appeal Cases 854, U.K. House of Lords (1997).

1099 *Sosa v. Alvarez-Machain* (03-339) 542 US 2739, US S.Ct. (2004) at 2763.

1100 *Wiwa v. Royal Dutch Petroleum Co.*, 226 F3d 88, C.A.2 (2000) at 106.

1101 *Wiwa v. Royal Dutch Petroleum Co.*, No 96 Civ 8386, 2002 US, Dist LEXIS 3293, US D.C. S.D. N.Y. (2002) at 6.

1102 *Filártiga v. Peña-Irala*, 630 F2d 876, C.A. 2 (1980) at 890.

1103 *Sosa v. Alvarez-Machain* (03-339) 542 US 2739, US S.Ct. (2004) at 2766.

1104 *Wiwa v. Royal Dutch Petroleum Co.*, No 96 Civ 8386, 2002 US, Dist LEXIS 3293, US D.C. S.D. N.Y. (2002) at 6.

well defined. "Thus plaintiffs may allege violations of the international norm against summary execution, torture, and arbitrary arrest under the ACTA."[1105] After *Sosa*, TNCs have also been held liable for torture, as in the *Talisman* decision by the District Court for the Southern District of New York, also in the Second Circuit. It expressed that TNCs are also bound by *jus cogens* rules of international law, including torture.[1106] The Court held that torture has accrued the status of customary international law.[1107] Furthermore, the *Talisman* decision in 2005 affirmed the earlier 2003 *Talisman* decision in conceding that "international law recognizes theories of complicit liability."[1108]

1. Definition

For the purposes of the TVPA and also the ATCA, "extrajudicial killing" means "a deliberated killing not authorized by a previous judgment pronounced by a regularly constituted court affording all the judicial guarantees which are recognized as indispensable by civilized peoples. Such term, however, does not include any such killing that, under international law, is lawfully carried out under the authority of a foreign nation."[1109]

According to the TVPA, the term "torture" means "any act, directed against an individual in the offender's custody or physical control, by which severe pain or suffering (other than pain or suffering arising only from or inherent in, or incidental to, lawful sanctions), whether physical or mental, is intentionally inflicted on that individual for such purposes as obtaining from that individual or a third person information or a confession, punishing that individual for an act that individual or a third person has committed or is suspected of having committed, intimidating or coercing that individual or a third person, or for any reason based on discrimination of any kind. Mental pain or suffering refers to prolonged mental harm caused by or resulting from: (a) the intentional infliction or threatened infliction of severe physical pain or suffering; (b) the administration or application, or threatened administration or application, of mind altering substances or other procedures calculated to disrupt profoundly the senses or the personality; (c) the threat of imminent death; or (d) the threat that another individual will imminently be subjected to death, severe physical pain or suffering, or the administration or application of mind altering substances or other procedures calculated to disrupt profoundly the senses or personality."[1110]

1105 *Ibid.* at 6.

1106 *The Presbyterian Church of Sudan, et. al. v. Talisman Energy, Inc.*, 374 FSupp2d 331, D.C. S.D. N.Y. (2005) at 336.

1107 *Ibid.* at 337.

1108 *Ibid.* at 338.

1109 Torture Victim Protection Act (TVPA), Title 28, Part IV, Chapter 85, § 1350, Mar. 12, 1992, 106 Stat. 73(1992).

1110 *Ibid.* The definition of torture may be relevant for future cases concerning the incidents in Abu Ghraib or other breaches of international law committed during the War on Terror.

2. Participation

In *Doe v. Exxon*, the District Court for the District of Columbia rejected the proposition that TNCs can be held liable for torture under the ATCA.[1111] *Joint action* is a possible basis for applying ATCA. Joint action is only a viable basis for ATCA when the corporation has *approved or directed unlawful conduct.*[1112] According to the *Exxon* decision, joint action was not present where companies hired components of the Indonesian army to guard natural gas pipeline, and that army allegedly engaged in human rights abuses.[1113]

The *Bowoto* decision in 2006 only approves of private actor responsibility for torture "when committed by state officials or under color of law."[1114] It held that the aiding and abetting standard is not applicable for TNCs or other private actors. The Court grants subject matter jurisdiction for ATCA claims against individual perpetrators only for crimes against humanity. According to the Statutes of the ICTY and ICTR to which the Court refers, crimes against humanity include torture.[1115] According to those statutes, the acts defined as crimes against humanity, such as murder, torture, or rape, reach the threshold of crimes against humanity only if they are part of a widespread or systematic practice or in armed conflict. Isolated inhumane acts of this nature may constitute grave infringements of human rights or, depending on the circumstances, war crimes, but they may fall short of meriting the superadded stigma attached to the category of crimes against humanity.

3. Analysis

Outside of the District of Columbia, ATCA appears to be an undisputed basis for claims of torture or extrajudicial killing by TNCs when *joint actors* with a state. Also, the Eleventh Circuit has acknowledged torture and extrajudicial killing as being actionable in the *Sinaltrainal* decision.[1116] The Ninth District holds TNCs liable for involvement in *jus cogens* violations, which include torture, murder, genocide and slavery.[1117] The treatment of torture or extrajudicial killing directly committed solely by TNCs has not been addressed by US litigation, since all of the existing cases deal with corporations that are alleged to have cooperated with state actors, which were

---

1111 *Doe v. Exxon Mobil Corporation*, 393 FSupp2d 20, D.C. D.C. (2005) at 26.

1112 *Ibid.* at 26.

1113 *Ibid.* at 26.

1114 *Bowoto v. Chevron Corp.*, WL 2455752, D.C. N.D. Cal. (2006) at 5.

1115 Article 7 f of the Rome Statute of the International Criminal Court July 17, 1998, 2187 UNTS 90 (1998).

1116 *Sinaltrainal v. Coca-Cola Co.*, 256 F Supp 2d 1345, D.C. S.D. Fla. (2003) at 1353 ("[I]f the complaint alleges that the Defendants murdered Gil by acting together with the paramilitary unit who acted under color of law by acting in concert with Colombian officials or with significant aid from the Colombian government, then an international law violation is sufficiently stated for purposes of subject matter jurisdiction.")

1117 *Doe v. Unocal (Unocal II)*, 110 F Supp 2d 1294, D.C. C.D.Cal. (2000) at 1304; *Mujica v. Occidental Petroleum Corp.*, 381 F Supp 2d 1134, D.C. C.D. Cal. (2005) at 1183.

involved in torture or extrajudicial killing. Where a TNC has, in a case of torture or extrajudicial killing, acted as a joint actor or aider and abettor together with a state actor, precedent from the Second, Ninth and Eleventh District clearly suggests that the TNC will bear human rights responsibilities.

B. Genocide

Five circuits have addressed the question whether corporations can be held liable for the violation of genocide and all have answered it in the affirmative.

1. Second Circuit

The first decision concerning genocide and private actor liability was the *Kadic* decision from the Second Circuit in 1995.[1118] In *Kadic*, an individual, the President of the unrecognized Bosnian-Serb Republic Srpska was held civilly liable for planning and ordering a campaign of murder, rape, forced impregnation, and other forms of torture designed to destroy the religious and ethnic groups of Bosnian Muslims and Bosnian Croats. This amounted to a violation of the international law norm proscribing genocide, regardless of whether the alleged perpetrator Karadzic acted under color of law or as a private individual.[1119] In the Holocaust-related 2000 *Bodner* decision, a District Court of the Second Circuit affirmed the human rights responsibility of TNCs when aiding and abetting genocide.[1120]

Aside from the *Bodner* decision, the *Talisman* decisions were the first corporate decisions that actually involved allegations of aiding and abetting genocide. Both *Talisman* decisions affirmed that corporations bear responsibility for aiding and abetting genocide.[1121]

In *Talisman I*, the District Court for the Southern District of New York pointed out that for the purposes of the interpretation of a genocide claim, the ICTY and ICTR statutes and the decisions of the ICTY and ICTR Tribunals have great importance. These decisions affirmed that individuals may be responsible for perpetrations of international law, such as genocide. Referring to the pivotal footnote in the *Sosa* decision, the *Talisman II* Court found that it is this distinction, and not distinctions within the category of private actors (individuals and corporations), that the Supreme Court emphasized. According to *Talisman II*, there is no reason for contending that acts such as genocide are of mutual and not merely several concern to States, and

---

1118 *Kadic v. Karadzic*, 70 F3d 232, C. A. 2 (1995) at 241.

1119 *Ibid.* at 242.

1120 *Bodner v. Banque Paribas*, 114 FSupp2d 117, D.C. E.D.N.Y. (2000) at 134 ("The Court finds that plaintiffs have stated a cognizable claim under international law for the confiscation and plunder of private property, for aiding and abetting genocide, and for conspiracy to plunder and transact in plundered property, all violations of international law.")

1121 *The Presbyterian Church of Sudan, et. al. v. Talisman Energy, Inc.*, 374 FSupp2d 331, D.C. S.D. N.Y. (2005) at 336; *Presbyterian Church of Sudan et al. v. Talisman Energy, Inc.*, 244 F Supp 2d 289, D.C. S.D. N.Y. (2003) at 306.

there is no reason why one should preclude corporations from this liability.[1122] The decision referred to the Nuremberg Tribunals, also cited in the 2003 opinion, wherein the liability of corporations was allegedly recognized and corporate officers were prosecuted.[1123]

Also, the most recent decision in *Bowoto v. Chevron* from the same circuit held that corporations may be held liable for genocide, war crimes and crimes against humanity in their private capacity.[1124]

2. District of Columbia

Even the District of Columbia, which has taken a relatively restrictive approach towards human rights litigation, recognized, in *Doe v. ExxonMobil,* that genocide is actionable against TNCs. However, these claims would have required adjudication on whether the Indonesian military was engaged in a plan allegedly to eliminate segments of the population and this, according to the *Exxon* Court, would be an impermissible intrusion in Indonesia's internal affairs.[1125] The *Exxon* Court followed the precedent of *Doe v. Qi*, where the Court declined to adjudicate claims of genocide and crimes against humanity when those claims required the court to evaluate the policy or practice of the foreign state.[1126]

3. Other Circuits

Relying on the *Kadic* decision, the *Genocide Convention* and the Restatement of Foreign Relations Law, the Fifth Court also held a corporation liable for certain offenses in international law, including genocide in *Beanal*.[1127] At the appellate level, the *Beanal* Court decided that genocide is an actionable claim, but cultural genocide is not.[1128]

Even though the *Unocal* case did not involve allegations of genocide the Court also affirmed that TNC's have human rights responsibilities in respect of genocide, since it is a *jus cogens* norm.[1129] Other decisions from the Eleventh District also affirmed this corporate responsibility.[1130]

1122 *The Presbyterian Church of Sudan, et. al. v. Talisman Energy, Inc.*, 374 FSupp2d 331, D.C. S.D. N.Y. (2005) at 336.
1123 *Ibid.* at 336.
1124 *Bowoto v. Chevron Corp.*, WL 2455752, D.C. N.D. Cal. (2006) at 3.
1125 *Doe v. Exxon Mobil Corporation*, 393 FSupp2d 20, D.C. D.C. (2005) at 25.
1126 *Ibid.* at 25.
1127 *Beanal v. Freeport- McMoran, Inc.*, 969 F Supp 362, D.C. E.D. La (1997) at 373.
1128 *Beanal v. Freeport-McMoran, Inc.*, 197 F3d 161, C.A. 5 (1999) at 167 et *seq.*
1129 *Doe v. Unocal (Unocal II)*, 110 F Supp 2d 1294, D.C. C.D.Cal. (2000) at 1304.
1130 *Estate of Rodriguez v. Drummond Co.*, 256 F Supp 2d 1250, D.C. N.D. Ala. (2003) at 1262; *Flores v. Southern Peru Copper Corp.*, 406 F3d 65, C.A. 2 (2003) at 76.

4. Analysis

It is well-established that corporations may be liable for aiding and abetting genocidal activities. This has also been accepted by the courts in the District of Columbia, whereas they have excluded the adjudication of these claims, because it would require an intrusion into "internal affairs." Other circuits, especially the Second Circuit, did not refrain from adjudicating claims of genocide. A corporation is liable when aiding and abetting genocide.[1131]

C. Slavery and forced labor

In the *Kadic* decision in 1995, private actors were only responsible for acts of piracy, war crimes and genocide.[1132]A clear affirmation that slavery belongs to the actionable claims can be found in the 1999 *Ford* case. It found that the Ford motorcar company forced civilians to perform unpaid labor during World War II and violated the law of nations, including by participating in slave trading, which confers subject matter jurisdiction on federal courts under ATCA.[1133]

In the 2002 *Pfizer* decision, it was held that some violations are actionable when committed by a state, and a more limited set of violations are of "universal concern" for which a private actor may be held accountable.[1134] In *Talisman* in 2003 and 2005, corporations were held liable for violations of *jus cogens* norms, among which slavery is listed.[1135] The *Estate* Court in 2003 also referred to *Kadic* to find that certain forms of conduct, including slavery, bind non-state (as well as state) actors.[1136]

Possibly the clearest statement that slavery, slave trade and forced labor are actionable under ATCA was made in the *Unocal* decision.[1137] Slavery and its modern incarnation, forced or bonded labor, therefore seem to be included in the list of actionable claims under ATCA jurisdiction. The Court stated that "forced labor, like

---

1131 *Bodner v. Banque Paribas*, 114 FSupp2d 117, D.C. E.D.N.Y. (2000) at 134; *The Presbyterian Church of Sudan, et. al. v. Talisman Energy, Inc.*, 374 FSupp2d 331, D.C. S.D. N.Y. (2005) at 336; *Presbyterian Church of Sudan et al. v. Talisman Energy, Inc.*, 244 F Supp 2d 289, D.C. S.D. N.Y. (2003) at 306.

1132 *Kadic v. Karadzic*, 70 F3d 232, C. A. 2 (1995) at 240.

1133 *Iwanowa v. Ford Motor Company*, 67 F Supp 2d 424, D.C.N.J. (1999) at 439 et *seq.*

1134 *Abdullahi v. Pfizer*, No 01 Civ 8118, 2002 US Dist LEXIS 17436, 2002 WL 31082956, D.C. S.D. N.Y. (2002) at 4.

1135 *Presbyterian Church of Sudan et al. v. Talisman Energy, Inc.*, 244 F Supp 2d 289, D.C. S.D. N.Y. (2003) at 304 ("States practicing, encouraging, or condoning genocide, slavery or the slave trade, extrajudicial killings, torture, or systematic racial discrimination violate international law. See, e.g., Restatement (Third) of Foreign Relations § 702 (1987). Individuals committing such acts may also be liable under international law.")

1136 *Estate of Rodriguez v. Drummond Co.*, 256 F Supp 2d 1250, D.C. N.D. Ala. (2003) at 1260.

1137 *Doe v. Unocal (Unocal II)*, 110 F Supp 2d 1294, D.C. C.D.Cal. (2000) at 1308.

traditional variants of slave trading, is among the handful of crimes to which the law of nations attributes individual liability, such that state action is not required for liability under Alien Tort Claims Act (ATCA)."[1138] Even though no state action was required for establishing an actionable claim,[1139] the Court found sufficient proof that the Burmese state and the US company were joint venturers and worked in connection with each other, and that they had "conspired to commit violations of human rights in order to further interest of gas pipeline project."[1140]

D. War crimes

War crimes indisputably give rise to claims that are actionable against corporations. Section 404 of the Restatement of Foreign Relations Law includes war crimes among the offenses recognized by the community of nations that are of universal concern.[1141] This position was upheld in *Kadic*. The liability of private individuals for committing war crimes has been recognized since World War I and was confirmed after World War II at Nuremberg.[1142] According to *Kadic*, war crimes that violate international law include acts of murder, rape, torture and arbitrary detention of civilians committed in the course of hostilities.[1143] The fact that war crimes are actionable against private actors from *Kadic* was confirmed in *Mehinovic* and *Flores*.[1144]

In *Talisman*, for the first time plaintiffs successfully made out claims of war crimes against a corporation. The *Talisman* Court found that expropriation or property destruction committed as part of genocide or war crimes may violate the law of nations and therefore could be actionable under ATCA.[1145] It also found that the

---

1138 *Doe v. Unocal (Unocal III)*, 395 F3d 932, C.A. 9 (2002) at 946.

1139 *Ibid.* at 946.

1140 *Doe v. Unocal*, 963 F Supp 880 D.C. C.D.Cal. (1997) at 891; affirmed in *Doe v. Unocal (Unocal III)*, 395 F3d 932, C.A. 9 (2002).

1141 Section 404 of the Restatement (Third) of Foreign Relations Law (1987).

1142 *Kadic v. Karadzic*, 70 F3d 232, C. A. 2 (1995) at 243.

1143 *Ibid.* at 242.

1144 *Mehinovic v. Vuckovic*, 198 FSupp2d 1322, D.C. N.D. Ga. (2002) at 1350 ("Acts of torture, inhuman treatment, and arbitrary detention of civilians committed in the course of hostilities violate the international law of war as codified in the Geneva Conventions and, hence, are a proper basis for liability under the ATCA."); *Flores v. Southern Peru Copper Corp.*, 406 F3d 65, C.A. 2 (2003) at 76 ("In particular, it determined that acts of piracy, slave trading, war crimes, and genocide violate customary international law regardless of whether they are undertaken by state or private actors, whereas acts of official torture and "summary execution" constitute violations of customary international law only when committed by state officials or under color of law.")

1145 *Presbyterian Church of Sudan et al. v. Talisman Energy, Inc.*, 244 F Supp 2d 289, D.C. S.D. N.Y. (2003) at 325 ("While expropriation or property destruction alone may not violate the law of nations, the Court finds that expropriation or property destruction, committed as part of a genocide or war crimes, may violate the law of nations.")

complaint sufficiently alleged war crimes even if the company's actions were directed specifically at furthering its oil operations.[1146]

The second important case in confirming the applicability of war crimes responsibilities is the *Sarei* case. In that case, residents of PNG made out their claim under ATCA against the international mining group, Rio Tinto, based upon war crimes allegedly committed by the PNG government. The Court found that the PNG government acted as the agent of the mining corporation, that the corporation "controlled" its actions and that the corporation was a willful participant and conspirator in those actions and was therefore held accountable.[1147]

The findings of the District Court were confirmed by the Court of Appeals for the Ninth Circuit in August 2006 and April 2007.[1148] If Rio Tinto did not direct and/or encourage a military response, none would have been initiated, and Rio Tinto officials exercised control over the behavior of PNG forces with regard to the conflict around the mine.[1149]

E. Crimes against humanity

Crimes against humanity have also been found to be actionable under ATCA subject matter jurisdiction.[1150] The *Bowoto* Court held that the only international law norm included in the plaintiffs' complaint, which is applicable to private actors, is crimes against humanity.[1151] In defining "crimes against humanity" the Court refers to the *Statutes* of the ICTY and ICTR.[1152] In the *Sarei* decision, the Court named murder, extermination, enslavement, or persecutions on political, racial or religious grounds of entire racial, ethnic, national or religious groups.[1153] The *Bowoto* Court applied the following test to hold corporations liable under international law for aiding and abetting a state actor in the commission of crimes against humanity. In order to be held liable, the plaintiff must show: 1) that the defendant provided practical assistance, encouragement, or moral support which had a substantial effect on the

1146 *Ibid.* at 327 ("The fact that the desired end of Talisman's acts was the extraction of oil is irrelevant if it employed means that violated the law of nations. Plaintiffs, while noting that Talisman's primary interest was in oil extraction, not in "ethnic cleansing," allege that Talisman willingly worked with Sudan to commit acts of "ethnic cleansing" as a means of securing the oil supply: Defendants have collaborated in a joint strategy to deploy military forces in a brutal ethnic cleansing campaign.")

1147 *Sarei v. Rio Tinto PLC*, 221 FSupp2d 1116, D.C. C.D. Cal. (2002) at 1139.

1148 *Sarei v. Rio Tinto*, 456 F3d 1069, C.A. 9 (2006) at 1078 and *Sarei v. Rio Tinto, PLC*, 487 F3d 1193, C.A. 9 (2007) at 1208.

1149 *Sarei v. Rio Tinto*, 456 F3d 1069, C.A. 9 (2006) at 1078.

1150 *Kadic v. Karadzic*, 70 F3d 232, C. A. 2 (1995) at 240; Affirmed in *Flores v. Southern Peru Copper Corporation*, 343 F3d 140, C.A. 2 (2003) at 150.

1151 *Bowoto v. Chevron Corp.*, WL 2455752, D.C. N.D. Cal. (2006) at 4.

1152 *Ibid.* at 9.

1153 *Sarei v. Rio Tinto PLC*, 221 FSupp2d 1116, D.C. C.D. Cal. (2002) at 1149.

perpetration of the crime, and 2) that the defendant knew that the state actor intended to commit the crime.[1154] Another case where crimes against humanity were successfully claimed against a corporation was in the *Mujica* case, where the attacks on Santo Domingo were found to be part of widespread and systematic violence intended to result in the forced displacement of civilians.[1155] Also in the *Cabello* and the *Mehinovic* decision the court recognized "crimes against humanity" as customary international law."[1156]

F. Environmental claims

In *Beanal*, the District Court for the Eastern District of Louisiana held that non-state actors cannot be held responsible for violations of the three environmental principles, which are: (1) the Polluter Pays Principle; (2) the Precautionary Principle; and (3) the Proximity Principle. These principles apply only to the "members of the international community," meaning: to states.[1157]

These principles, standing alone, do not constitute international torts for which there is universal consensus in the international community as to their binding status. A corporation could be bound to such principles by treaty, but not as a matter of customary international law. Consistent with this conclusion, Sections 601-602 of the Restatement of Foreign Relations Law mentions only state obligations and liability in the area of environmental law.[1158] Similarly, the *Flores* Court has found that intranational pollution does not violate customary international law and accordingly is not actionable under ATCA.[1159] In *Sarei*, the District Court for the Central District of California found that it could not identify the parameters of the right created by the principle of sustainable development and, therefore, it concluded that it cannot form the basis of a claim under the ATCA.[1160]

However, also in *Sarei*, the District Court for the Central District of California and the Court of Appeals of the Ninth Circuit confirmed that the *UNCLOS* as a whole represents customary international law that can be used as a basis for ATCA claims. In that case, Rio Tinto was alleged to have chemically defoliated and bulldozed an entire mountainside of pristine rain forest in order to build a mine. During the years of the mine's operations, billions of tons of toxic mine waste was generated and dumped onto the land and into pristine waters, filling major rivers with tailings, polluting a major bay dozens of miles away as well as the Pacific Ocean.[1161] The

---

[1154] *Bowoto v. Chevron Corp.*, WL 2455752, D.C. N.D. Cal. (2006) at 4.
[1155] *Mujica v. Occidental Petroleum Corp.*, 381 F Supp 2d 1134, D.C. C.D. Cal. (2005) at 1183.
[1156] *Estate of Winston Cabello v. Armando Fernandez-Larios*, 157 FSupp2d 1345, US S.D.Fla. (2001) at 1360; *Mehinovic v. Vuckovic*, 198 FSupp2d 1322, D.C. N.D. Ga. (2002) at 1352;
[1157] *Beanal v. Freeport- McMoran, Inc.*, 969 F Supp 362, D.C. E.D. La (1997) at 384.
[1158] Section 601- 602 of the Restatement (Third) of Foreign Relations Law (1987).
[1159] *Flores v. Southern Peru Copper Corp.*, 406 F3d 65, C.A. 2 (2003) at 87.
[1160] *Sarei v. Rio Tinto PLC*, 221 FSupp2d 1116, D.C. C.D. Cal. (2002) at 1160-1161.
[1161] *Ibid.* at 1162.

Court concluded that the plaintiffs adequately stated a claim for violation of the customary international law reflected in *UNCLOS*. It held that the ratification of the *UNCLOS* by at least 149 nations was sufficient for it to codify customary international law so as to provide the basis of an ATCA claim.[1162]

G. Other actionable human rights claims against corporations

1. Airplane hijacking

The District Court for the District of Columbia, which has proven rather dismissive with regard to ATCA litigation against corporations in the latter *Titan* and *Exxon* cases,[1163] found in *Al-Baraka* that the hijacking of four airplanes was a violation of the law of nations for the purpose of ATCA.[1164] The victims of the 9/11 terrorist attacks could hold accountable the persons and entities that funded and supported al Qaeda, since aircraft hijacking was generally recognized as a violation of international law of a type that gave rise to individual liability. Although no defendant in this case was sued as a direct perpetrator of the torts committed, they were sued as accomplices, aiders and abettors, or co-conspirators.

2. Arbitrary detention

Prolonged arbitrary detention may also give rise to an actionable claim against private actors. There have been two important cases on this question. In *Sosa*, the Supreme Court held that customary international law, so well defined as to support the creation of a federal remedy, is not violated by a single illegal detention of less than a day, followed by the transfer of custody to lawful authorities and a prompt arraignment.[1165] If the opposite were true, this would mean that US courts were competent to review the legality of any arrest, anywhere in the world.[1166] However, the Supreme Court did not rule out the possibility that arbitrary detention may rise to the level of being cognizable under ATCA litigation and the situation may differ if somebody were unlawfully detained for a longer period.[1167]

Pre-*Sosa* there was one ATCA decision concerning arbitrary detention. In *Eastman Kodak*, the Court found that the ATCA makes responsible anyone who conspires with state actors to achieve an unlawful arbitrary detention.[1168] It needs to be a substantial detention, which cannot solely be measured by the length of detention (in this case eight to ten days), but also by the intention and circumstances. In that case, it was not a standard pre-trial incarceration, but a calculated, extortionate imprisonment under

---

1162 *Sarei v. Rio Tinto*, 456 F3d 1069, C.A. 9 (2006) at 1078.

1163 *Ibrahim v. Titan Corp.*, 391 F Supp 2d 10, D.C. D.C. (2005); *Doe v. Exxon Mobil Corporation*, 393 FSupp2d 20, D.C. D.C. (2005).

1164 *Burnett v. Al Baraka Inv. and Development Corp.*, 274 FSupp2d 86, D.C. D.C. (2003) at 100.

1165 *Sosa v. Alvarez-Machain* (03-339) 542 US 2739, US S.Ct. (2004) at 2769.

1166 *Ibid.* at 2769.

1167 *Ibid.* at 2768.

1168 *Eastman Kodak Co. v. Kavlin*, 978 FSupp 1078, D.C. S.D. Fla. (1997) at 1094.

very harsh circumstances motivated solely by an extortionate desire for economic gain.[1169]

3. Other actionable human rights violations

According to the 2006 *Sarei* decision, systematic racial discrimination constitutes a *jus cogens* violation and may make corporations liable under ATCA litigation.[1170] In that case, the plaintiffs maintained that Rio Tinto used racially discriminatory policies in the operation of the mine, and that race was a motivating factor in several of the other alleged abuses. Furthermore, Section 702 (c) of the Restatement of Foreign Relations Law provides for the prohibition of murder or disappearance of individuals, which may also be used against corporations in case of violation.[1171]

In *Bodner*, the District Court for the Eastern District of New York found that looting, conversion, and continued withholding of assets that rightfully belonged to plaintiffs clearly violate the Nuremberg Principles and longstanding principles of customary international law.[1172]

Sarei and *Mujica* denied cruel, inhuman and degrading treatment as actionable claims because, according to *Mujica*, "it would allow foreign plaintiffs to litigate claims in United States courts that bear strong resemblance to intentional infliction of emotional distress."[1173] According to *Sarei*, it is not sufficiently specific to be a claim under ATCA.[1174] However, in *Abebe*, the District Court for the Northern District of Georgia found that the violation of cruel and degrading treatment represents an actionable ATCA claim."[1175]

In the *Fresh Del Monte* decision, the District Court for the Southern District of Florida found that the right to associate and organize was not a universally recognized norm of international law, and therefore alleged violation of that right was not actionable under ATCA.[1176] On the other hand in the decision *Estate of Rodriguez v. Drummond Co.* the District Court of the Northern District of Alabama held that these rights are actionable.[1177]

1169 *Ibid.* at 1094.
1170 *Sarei v. Rio Tinto*, 456 F3d 1069, C.A. 9 (2006) at 1085.
1171 Section 702 of the Restatement (Third) of Foreign Relations Law (1987).
1172 *Bodner v. Banque Paribas*, 114 FSupp2d 117, D.C. E.D.N.Y. (2000) at 127.
1173 *Mujica v. Occidental Petroleum Corp.*, 381 F Supp 2d 1134, D.C. C.D. Cal. (2005) at 1183.
1174 *Sarei v. Rio Tinto PLC*, 221 FSupp2d 1116, D.C. C.D. Cal. (2002) at 1163.
1175 *Abebe-Jiri v. Negewo*, Not reported in FSupp, 1993 WL 814304, D.C. N.D. Ga. (1993).
1176 *Villeda Aldana v. Fresh Del Monte Produce, Inc.*, 305 F Supp 2d 1285, D.C. S.D. Fla. (2003) at 1296.
1177 *Estate of Rodriguez v. Drummond Co.*, 256 F Supp 2d 1250, D.C. N.D. Ala. (2003) at 1264

H. Non-actionable human rights claims against corporations

In the *Price Waterhouse* decision, the Court found that fraud, breach of fiduciary duty and misappropriation of funds were not breaches of the law of nations and therefore not actionable in ATCA litigation.[1178]

In *Beanal* the District Court for the Eastern District of Louisiana found that "cultural genocide" is an amorphous cause of action under international law that has failed to garner universal acceptance and accordingly is insufficient to be actionable under ATCA.[1179]

In the *Coca-Cola* decision the Court found that discriminatory expropriation, as such, does not represent a violation of international law.[1180] Similarly, the first *Talisman* decision confirmed that while expropriation or property destruction alone may not violate the law of nations, expropriation or property destruction committed as part of genocide or war crimes, may violate the law of nations.[1181]

The *Pfizer* Court found that medical experimentation is not actionable under ATCA. It found that medical experimentation, however reprehensible, falls short of constituting a violation of *universal concern*. It is neither listed as an act of universal concern in Section 404 of the Restatement nor is sufficiently similar to the listed acts.[1182] Also the *ICCPR*, without implementing legislation, cannot give rise to a claim under ATCA litigation.

In *Flores*, the Court of Appeals for the Second Circuit has found that the "right to life" and "right to health" are insufficiently precise to constitute rules of customary international law.[1183] The provisions from the *UDHR* were described as vague and amorphous.[1184] *Sarei* also confirmed this finding and held that the right to life does not give rise to a claim that is actionable under ATCA.[1185]

V. Concluding remarks to Chapter V

It is clearly established in US law that US courts assume jurisdictions if TNCs violate certain norms of international law, such as in the case of the most egregious human rights violations. This means that corporations have: (a) at least partial international

---

1178 *Hamid v. Price Waterhouse Coopers*, 51 F3d 1411, C.A. 9 (1995) at 1418.
1179 *Beanal v. Freeport- McMoran, Inc.*, 969 F Supp 362, D.C. E.D. La (1997) at 373.
1180 *Bigio v. Coca-Cola Co.*, 239 F3d 440, C.A. 2 (2001) at 448.
1181 *Presbyterian Church of Sudan et al. v. Talisman Energy, Inc.*, 244 F Supp 2d 289, D.C. S.D. N.Y. (2003) at 325.
1182 *Abdullahi v. Pfizer*, No 01 Civ 8118, 2002 US Dist LEXIS 17436, 2002 WL 31082956, D.C. S.D. N.Y. (2002) at 4.
1183 *Flores v. Southern Peru Copper Corp.*, 406 F3d 65, C.A. 2 (2003) at 86.
1184 *Ibid.* at 86.
1185 *Sarei v. Rio Tinto PLC*, 221 FSupp2d 1116, D.C. C.D. Cal. (2002) at 1156.

legal personality according to US law; and (b) bear human rights duties. Except the two recent and ill-founded decisions in *Doe v. Exxon* and *Ibrahim v. Titan*, both from the District of Columbia, no US ATCA decision against TNCs indicates that these findings were mistaken. Indeed, the large number of decisions clearly affirmed this position, as in *Unocal, United Technologies, Price Waterhouse, Freeport McMoran, Kodak, Texaco, Iwanowa, Bodner, Coca-Cola, Royal Dutch Shell, Pfizer, Al Baraka, Talisman, Sarei* and many others.

The most important sources were US precedents and the Restatement of Foreign Relations Law. The finding of the US courts originally relied mainly on the *Tel-Oren* and *Kadic* decisions. *Kadic* stated that the "law of nations, as understood in modern era for purposes of action brought under Alien Tort Claims Act, does not confine its reach to state action, in that certain forms of conduct violate law of nations whether undertaken by those acting under auspices of state or only as private individuals, such as piracy, slave trade, and war crimes."[1186] The second most important source has probably been the Third Restatement of Foreign Relations Law. The finding of human rights responsibilities was then later affirmed and substantiated by the thorough analysis in the *Talisman* decisions.

Even though the decisive part of ATCA litigation may be the interpretation of the term "law of nations" and its content, the cases barely refer to sources of international law. The question of legal personality in international law as such was only touched on in the *Talisman* decisions; other decisions went straight to the question of which duties are to be imposed. Without any substantial discussion as to the sources of international law, ATCA has developed human rights duties of TNCs, ostensibly derived from international law. The human rights obligations of corporations in the ATCA litigation are quite extensive and range from the prohibition of substantial involvement in egregious human rights violations such as war crimes and crimes against humanity, to the adherence of the *UNCLOS*.

The exact scope of ATCA human rights claims against corporations remains to be resolved. At the moment the involvement or participation in torture, genocide, forced labor, war crimes, airplane hijacking, arbitrary detention and egregious violations of environmental rights embody human rights responsibilities of corporations, whereas the extent differs among the different court circuits.

[1186] *Kadic v. Karadzic*, 70 F3d 232, C. A. 2 (1995) at 239.

Chapter VI. Status of international law in the US

For many the notion of "international law" and the US seem to be two incompatible concepts. Victims of the so-called "Global War on Terror," led by the administration of President George W Bush, have been detained in the Abu Ghraib prison and in Guantánamo Bay. They have been kept shackled and incommunicado, subject to sensory deprivation, humiliation and coercion, often without access to legal counsel. Many commentators maintain that this amounts to a clear violation of international law and the *Geneva Conventions* and the *Vienna Convention on Consular Relations*.[1187]

As in almost all other jurisdictions, the interaction between national and international law is contentious and subject to constant change. Chapter VI briefly examines what role international law plays in the US. Given that the most progressive approach to accountability of TNCs examined in this thesis is also taking place in US courtrooms, an examination of the US understanding of international law is imperative.

In the US the question of whether the executive, legislative or judicial branch interprets international treaties is contentious.[1188] In order to understand the ATCA

[1187] See e.g., P Sands, *Lawless World* (Penguin Group, London 2005) at 143 et *seq.*; P Sands, *Lawless World* (Penguin Group, London 2005)M Byers, *War Law: Understanding International Law and Armed Conflicts* (1st edn, Grove Press, New York 2005) at 129-134; B Falk, 'The Global War on Terror and the Detention Debate: The Applicability of Geneva Convention III' 3 Journal of International Law and International Relations 31 (2007) at 59 ("The overall approach of the US in the Global War on Terror has arguably contributed "to an organizational and political culture of disrespect for longstanding and widely-held humanitarian norms, thus making easier the willfully blind violation of such norms, as is evidenced by the now well-documented inhumane treatment of detainees at Guantánamo Bay and the Abu Ghraib prison torture and abuse scandal."); A Glashauser, 'Difference and Deference in Treaty Interpretation' 50 Villanova Law Review 25 (2005) at 25; Paust describes Guantánamo as a "legal no man's land," see JJ Paust, 'The Changing Laws of War: Do We Need a New Legal Regime after September 11?' 79 Notre Dame Law Review 1335 (2004) at 1346; Koh describes Guantánamo as a "rights-free zone," see HH Koh, 'On American Exceptionalism' 55 Stanford Law Review 1479 (2003) at 1509; Fletcher describes Guantánamo as a "black hole" and says that "here is no way out, except through the good grace of the military," see G Fletcher, 'Black Hole in Guantánamo Bay' 2 Journal of International Criminal Justice 121 (2004); Hope describes Guantánamo as a place "beyond the rule of law," see D Hope, 'Torture' 53 International and Comparative Law Quarterly 807 (2004); M Ratner and E Ray, *Guantanamo: What the World Should Know* (Chelsea Green Pub. Co., White River Junction 2004); A Tabuga, 'Article 15-6 Investigation of the 800th Military Police Brigade (March 9, 2004)' (2004) <http:// www.npr.org/ iraq/ 2004/ prison_abuse_report.pdf> (September 11, 2007); UN High Commissioner for Human Rights, 'Report of the High Commissioner for Human Rights - The Present Situation of Human Rights in Iraq' (2004) <http:// www.unhchr.ch/ html/ hchr/ docs/ iraq.doc> (September 11, 2007); M Kurnaz, *Fünf Jahre meines Lebens* (Rowohlt, Berlin 2007).

[1188] See e.g., A Glashauser, 'Difference and Deference in Treaty Interpretation' 50 Villanova Law

litigation it is important to understand the role of executive communications, for example, in the form of "statements of interests." This chapter outlines briefly the concept of international law before moving on to discuss the status of international law in the US.

I. The meaning of "international law" under international law

Wherever there is a social structure, you will find law. This is the ultimate explanation for any kind of law. The more interactions there are in that social structure, the more necessary it became to have generally accepted rules and guidelines. Since international relations and international interactions are of steadily growing importance, the importance of international legal regulations is too.

What is international law? The precise scope of the term "international law" has long been a matter of debate. It is beyond the scope of this dissertation to engage fully with this debate. For present purposes, this section shall only look briefly at three views, one from one of the fathers of international law, another from a current judge sitting on the ICJ and one current from a German scholar.

Hugo Grotius defined "international law" in 1625 as "that body of law ... which is concerned with the mutual relations among states or rulers of states, whether derived from nature, or established by divine ordinances, or having its origin in custom and tacit agreement."[1189] ICJ Judge Higgins views international law as a normative system harnessed to the achievement of common values.[1190]

According to Angelika Emmerich-Fritsche the basic principles of international law are: prohibition of the use of force, sovereignty of states, equality of states, *effet utile, pacta sunt servanda, principle of reciprocity,* principle of non-interference and state immunity.[1191] She argues in favor of a paradigmatic shift from international law to world law, which has slowly started to begin already. The paradigmatic shift is reflected in the orientation from the sovereignty of states towards the legal subjectivity of individuals and the precedence of the rule of law over the principles of sovereignty, reciprocity and efficiency.[1192] The paradigmatic shift can already be seen in the growing importance of *erga omnes* and *jus cogens* rules.[1193]

Review 25 (2005).

1189 H Grotius, *De Jure Belli ac Pacis Libri Tres* (Apud Nicolavm Bvon, Parisiis 1625) at 9,12-13, 15.

1190 R Higgins, *Problems and Process: International Law and How We Use It* (Clarendon Press; Oxford University Press, Oxford; New York 1994) at 1.

1191 A Emmerich-Fritsche, *Vom Völkerrecht zum Weltrecht* (Duncker & Humblot, Berlin 2007) at 150 et *seq.*

1192 *Ibid.* at 188 et *seq.*

1193 *Ibid.* at 435 et *seq.*

Overall, public international law, commonly referred to simply as international law, is the body of law that regulates the activities of entities possessing international personality. Undeniably, a state has such international legal personality, but the exact scope of other subjects having international legal personality is steadily growing. International law continues to reflect, first and foremost, the basic state-oriented character of world politics, but it has been expanding in different directions in order to address the complexities of state relations in the modern globalized era.[1194]

Aside from the growing number of subjects, the subject matters regulated by international law are also steadily growing. Whereas international law historically mainly treated questions such as the laws of war and peace, it now regulates territorial questions of states, space, world trade, the law of the sea, environment (climate change, biodiversity), human rights and many other subject matters. It cannot be denied however, that international law in its current form is not fully developed concerning its creation, task, scope, organs, and especially enforcement.[1195]

There are obvious differences between international law and municipal law. There is no highest legislative body to promulgate law. The legislative function of international law is largely left to international treaties.[1196] There is not a single central law or institution for the enforcement of international law.[1197] International law possesses a fragmented system of law enforcement, such as in the areas of WTO law, Chapter VII measures under the UN Charter, EU law, and international criminal law. There is not a highest judicial body to interpret international law. The ICJ is the highest judicial organ of the UN, but firstly it lacks access for non-state actors and secondly even the jurisdiction for state actors is based on the basis of consent.[1198]

A. Is "international law" law?

What is law? Law is a system of regulations that governs the conduct of a community. According to Kelsen a norm is a law, if it requires a person to behave in

---

1194 MN Shaw, *International law* (4th edn, Cambridge University Press, Cambridge; New York 1997) at 36.

1195 S Oeter, 'Chancen und Defizite internationaler Verrechtlichung: Was das Recht jenseits des Nationalstaates leisten kann' in B Zangl and M Zürn (eds) *Verrechtlichung- Baustein für Global Governance* (Dietz, Bonn 2004) at 54; A Emmerich-Fritsche, *Vom Völkerrecht zum Weltrecht* (Duncker & Humblot, Berlin 2007) at 148.

1196 A Emmerich-Fritsche, *Vom Völkerrecht zum Weltrecht* (Duncker & Humblot, Berlin 2007) at 112.

1197 R Wolfrum, 'Obligations Under Public International Law to Implement International Rules: Mechanisms to Monitor such Implementation' in BBv Maydell and A Nußberger (eds) *Social Protection by Way of international Law- Appraisal, Deficits and Further Development* (Duncker & Humblot, Berlin 1996) at 98.

1198 Article 36 of the Statute of the International Court of Justice June 26, 1945, UNTS 993 (1945). See also A Emmerich-Fritsche, *Vom Völkerrecht zum Weltrecht* (Duncker & Humblot, Berlin 2007) at 138-139.

a specific way.[1199] Law requires also for the possibility of enforcing the norm, since the nature of humans induces some to ignore some regulations.[1200] Enforcing means in its last resort using physical force as *ultima ratio*, but includes also other less intrusive forms of sanctions. Even today, some commentators argue that international law does not represent law. Some scholars, like Jack Goldsmith, base this view on Hart's philosophy.[1201]

In his examination of the question "What is law?" Hart argued that a legal system is the union of primary rules and secondary rules. The secondary rules address three issues: (1) the problem of uncertainty about what the law is; (2) the problem of allowing change; and (3) the problem of how to resolve legal disputes. Hart argued that international law lacks the three secondary rules and therefore cannot be seen as a legal, but rather a moral obligation.

Hart wrote his monograph, *Concept of law* in the 1950s. Today it seems doubtful that his finding that international law is solely a moral obligation can still be upheld, since international law has been the subject of momentous change. EU law or WTO law for example comply with all of the secondary rules of Hart's concept and are legally binding. Therefore, it becomes clear that international law does govern the conduct of nations.

The fact that international law has been breached on many occasions does not call into question the overall legitimacy of international law. There exists no municipal legal system on earth where all rules are universally enforced or enforceable. Consequently, rather than describing municipal law and international law as two completely separate and distinct species, it is now more accurate to recognize that, though they may differ from each other in a number of key respects, they share enough commonalities to view them both as sub-species of "law."

B. Changes in international law

According to Andreas Zimmermann, current international law is subject to five changes.[1202] First, it has become more fragmented. In other words, it can be differentiated into specific fields of law, such as international environmental law and

[1199] H Kelsen, *Reine Rechtslehre* (2 edn, Deuticke, Wien 1960) at 196.

[1200] T Hobbes, *Leviathan (1651), Erster und zweiter Teil, published by Malte Diesselhorst, translated by Jacob von Mayer* (Reclam, Stuttgart 1970) at 151; A Emmerich-Fritsche, *Vom Völkerrecht zum Weltrecht* (Duncker & Humblot, Berlin 2007) at 129.

[1201] See JL Goldsmith and EA Posner, *The Limits of International Law* (Oxford University Press, Oxford; New York 2005) *at*3 (international law "lacks a centralized or effective legislature, executive, or judiciary; that it favors powerful over weak states; that it often simply mirrors extant international behavior; and that it is sometimes violated with impunity."); HLA Hart, *The concept of law* (Clarendon law series, Clarendon Press; Oxford University Press, Oxford; New York 1961) at 213-237.

[1202] Lecture of Prof. Dr. Andreas Zimmermann, LL.M. (Harvard) at the Max-Planck-Institute in Heidelberg on February 6, 2007 about the subject "Future of international law in Germany."

international criminal law. Second, it has become more supranationalized.[1203] Examples include the EU, AU and other instruments such as Chapter VII measures under the UN Charter.

Thirdly, it is increasingly directed towards individual responsibility and enforceability, as in the international criminal law and the developing human rights litigation. Fourth, international law has been increasingly intensified and clarified by the decisions of international tribunals – including the ICJ, ECJ, ICC, ICSID, WTO DSB, as well as the various other tribunals and arbitration and mediation mechanisms. Fifth, international law has become increasingly important in domestic litigation. State governments and law firms are increasingly interested in international law expertise.

Interestingly, all of these developments in international law have also occurred at the EU level, which stands now as a supranational union of states.[1204] The legal integration of the EU has obviously advanced much more rapidly than the integration at the world level, but it may be seen as the way forward for international law in many regards, as for example the protection of human rights and economic liberties.[1205] "From the point of view of world global order the EU seems to me to represent the most promising way of creating some structure capable of checking the abuse of economic and social power, and of directing social activities towards overriding common ends. The EU seems to be making the most successful effort so far to cope with the problematic effects of Globalization and, perhaps it offers a model for new legal institutions to be created on a world-wide basis."[1206]

Furthermore, international law itself has become increasingly globalized. It was formerly strongly influenced by Western Europe and North America.[1207] This has changed rapidly in recent years. Improved access to the sources of international law via the internet and other databases means that the legal derivation of international law now takes place on a globalized stage and this enhances its breadth and legitimacy.

1203 For an analysis of the term "supranationality", its typical characteristics and the EU as supranational organization (in the Kantian sense), see A Emmerich-Fritsche, *Vom Völkerrecht zum Weltrecht* (Duncker & Humblot, Berlin 2007) at 818 et *seq*.

1204 *Ibid*. at 818 et *seq*.

1205 H Steiger, 'Geht das Zeitalter des souveränen Staates zu Ende?' 41 Der Staat 331 (2003) at 347.

1206 D Thürer, 'The Emergence of Non-Governmental Organizations and Transnational Enterprises in International Law and the Changing Role of the State' in R Hofmann and N Geissler (eds) *Non-State Actors as New Subjects of International Law - International Law - From the Traditional State Order Towards the Law of the Global Community* (Duncker & Humblot, Berlin 1998) at 92.

1207 M Sornarajah, 'The Asian Perspective to International Law in Asia' 5 Singapore Journal of International and Comparative Law in Asia 284 (2001) at 289; it is in this regard also interesting to note the fact that English, French and Spanish are the working languages of the General Assembly; English and French are the working languages of the Security Council.

II. International law in the US

"International law is part of our law," as the US Supreme Court famously stated in the *Paquete Habana* decision in 1900.[1208] However, the exact meaning of this exclamation is largely uncertain. Which norms of international law are US law? Which meaning does this have for extraterritorial issues? The treatment of international law diverts considerably between the three branches of government: the legislature, the executive and the judiciary. In order to determine the status of international law in the US the three branches of government are briefly examined, beginning with the impact of the US Constitution.

A. International law and the US Constitution

Monist legal systems are characterized by direct incorporation of ratified treaties into domestic law.[1209] In a monist legal system, international law is directly applicable in the national legal order.[1210] There is no need for any domestic implementing legislation. International law is immediately applicable within national legal systems.

The dualists, on the other hand, view international and national law as separate legal orders.[1211] For international law to be applicable in the national legal order, it must be transformed through an active process of domestic legislative implementation. It is only after such a transformation from the international to the national sphere that individuals within the state may benefit from, or rely on, international law, because only then does it represent national law.

The United States Supreme Court has never addressed the question where the US stands on the monist or dualist spectrum regarding the relationship between national and international law.[1212] "Not by reference to any theory, but principally by construction of the Supremacy Clause of the Constitution, the Supreme Court has established that treaties are subordinate to the Constitution."[1213] As with most Common law countries, the US can therefore be placed somewhere in the dualist camp, not supreme to the constitution, but supreme to domestic law. To the extent that it requires treaties to be "executed," it is dualistic, but courts' acknowledgment of

---

[1208] "International law is part of our law, and must be ascertained and administered by the courts of justice of appropriate jurisdiction, as often as questions of right depending upon it are duly presented for their determination," see *The Paquete Habana*, 175 US 677, US S.Ct. (1900) at 700.

[1209] A Emmerich-Fritsche, *Vom Völkerrecht zum Weltrecht* (Duncker & Humblot, Berlin 2007) at 93.

[1210] M Herdegen, *Völkerrecht* (5th edn, Beck, München 2006) at 153.

[1211] *Ibid.* at 152; A Emmerich-Fritsche, *Vom Völkerrecht zum Weltrecht* (Duncker & Humblot, Berlin 2007) at 98.

[1212] L Henkin, 'The President and International Law' 80 American Journal of International Law 930 (1986) at 932.

[1213] *Ibid.* at 932.

"self-executing" treaties is a monistic view.[1214] It is beyond the scope of this dissertation to consider further the theoretical approach of monism and dualism. Instead, consideration is given to the US legal treatment of international law in the specific human rights situations.

Concerning international treaties the US Constitution states: "This Constitution, and the Laws of the United States which shall be made in Pursuance thereof; and all Treaties made, or which shall be made, under the Authority of the United States, shall be the supreme Law of the Land; and the Judges in every State shall be bound thereby, any Thing in the Constitution or Laws of any State to the contrary notwithstanding."[1215] First, these treaties must be negotiated, signed, and ratified. The Constitution gives the President the power to conduct foreign relations, but requires that the Senate ratify the treaty with a majority two thirds vote according to Article II, Section 2, Clause 2 of the Constitution. By these terms, treaties that are signed by the President and ratified by the Senate are the law of land and directly applicable in US courts.[1216]

US law differentiates between self-executing and non self-executing treaties. A self-executing treaty is one where "no domestic legislation is required to give [... it] the force of law in the United States."[1217] The distinction between non-self-executing and self-executing treaties is the subject of some debate.[1218] An example of a non-self executing treaty is the *Genocide Convention*. In Article V, it requires that the contracting parties enact "necessary legislation to give effect to the provisions of the Convention and, in particular, to provide effective penalties for persons guilty of genocide." The vast majority of international treaties are non-self-executing. All human rights treaties signed by the United States are non-self-executing.[1219] Examples of self-executing treaties are found in the area of economic law, including Friendship, Commerce, and Navigation Treaties, as well as the more recent bilateral investment treaties and their lineal descendants.[1220]

1214 See MW Janis, *An Introduction to International Law* (3rd edn, Aspen Law & Business, Gaithersburg 1999) at 98-99. Concerning self-executing and non-self-executing see below under this same subheading.

1215 US Constitution, Article IV, Clause 2.

1216 *Reid v. Covert*, 354 US 1, US S.Ct. (1957); *De Geofrey v. Riggs*, 133 US 258, US S.Ct. (1890).

1217 *Trans World Airlines, Inc. v. Franklin Mint Corp.*, 466 US 243, US S.Ct. (1984) at 252.

1218 See, e.g., CM Vázquez, 'The Four Doctrines of self-executing treaties' 89 American Journal of International Law 695 (1995).

1219 D Sloss, 'The Domestication of International Human Rights: Non-Self-Executing Declarations and Human Rights Treaties' 24 Yale Journal of International Law 129 (1999) at 131.

1220 RE Dalton, 'National Treaty Law and Practice: United States' in M Leigh, MR Blakeslee and B Ederington (eds) *National Treaty Law and Practice* (American Society of International Law, Washington, D.C. 1999) at 12.

B. Interpretation of international treaties

This small section on the interpretation of international treaties solely touches on the question who, meaning which branch of government, is competent to interpret international treaties and not how these treaties should be interpreted.

Under the US Constitution, the executive branch has the exclusive power to *make* or *enter into* treaties. However, there is debate as to whether the executive or the judiciary is responsible for *interpreting* international treaties. At one end of the spectrum, Professor John Yoo advocates absolute deference to the executive branch.[1221] Yoo argued that the treaty power is fundamentally executive and the President should have the last say, or perhaps even the only say, in interpreting treaties, since it is placed in Article II of the Constitution.[1222] In his view, the President should be able to interpret, reinterpret, and violate treaties as he or she sees fit, deciding when it would be appropriate to incur the international political costs of violation.[1223]

Professor Yoo acknowledges that interpretations of a certain treaty might evolve over time, but stresses that the interpreter is solely the President.[1224] He finds the notion that a treaty might have one meaning internationally, as interpreted by the President, and another meaning domestically, as interpreted by courts, to be "bizarre."[1225] It makes little sense constitutionally and "makes for unacceptable foreign policy."[1226]

Most scholars favor a more modest form of deference that preserves an independent role for the judiciary in treaty interpretation and application.[1227] First, the suggestion

---

1221 See J Yoo, 'Politics as Law?: The Anti-Ballistic Missile Treaty, the Separation of Powers, and Treaty Interpretation' 89 California Law Review 851 (2001) at 882-83; J Yoo, 'Treaty Interpretation and the False Sirens of Delegation' 90 California Law Review 1305 (2002) at 1315; For more information on John Yoo, see below at subheading "International law an US academics".

1222 See J Yoo, 'Politics as Law?: The Anti-Ballistic Missile Treaty, the Separation of Powers, and Treaty Interpretation' 89 California Law Review 851 (2001) at 882-83; J Yoo, 'Treaty Interpretation and the False Sirens of Delegation' 90 California Law Review 1305 (2002) at 1315.

1223 See J Yoo, 'Politics as Law?: The Anti-Ballistic Missile Treaty, the Separation of Powers, and Treaty Interpretation' 89 California Law Review 851 (2001) at 874-77 (arguing that it is within President's executive power to interpret, abrogate, and violate treaties, if necessary, just as it is in President's power to conduct day-to-day task of managing international relations).

1224 See *Ibid.* at 881 (comparing courts' continued interpretation of evolving statutes with President's ongoing interpretation of evolving treaties).

1225 See *Ibid.* at 862 (noting that if treaties can have two meanings, then they could impose differing legal obligations in different settings).

1226 *Ibid.* at 862.

1227 See, e.g., DJ Bederman, 'Deference or Deception: Treaty Rights as Political Questions' 70 University of Colorado Law Review 1439 (1999) at 1460-61, 1480-81; MPv Alstine, 'Federal Common Law in an Age of Treaties' 89 Cornell Law in an Age of Treaties 892 (2004) at 953; D Sloss, '"Constitutional Implications of the War on Terror" - Symposium held at the New

that the President has the exclusive authority to interpret treaties disregards the express description of the "judicial Power" in Article III of the Constitution.[1228] Article III, Section 1, provides that "the judicial Power of the United States, shall be vested" in the federal courts. Second, the mere fact that the treaty power is situated in Article II does not mean that this judicial power is somehow transferred to the executive.[1229] If that reasoning were followed, then Congress would have the exclusive power to interpret statutes merely because the authority to create this form of federal law appears in Article I.

However, the Supreme Court has found that the interpretive opinions of a later Congress are of "very little, if any, significance."[1230] Finally, although treaties come into being through a constitutional process that the President formally initiates, Article II also requires the consent of a legislative institution, the Senate, before treaties acquire the force of domestic law. To suggest that the President has exclusive authority to reinterpret the force of self-executing treaties would render the Senate's mandatory participation in the creation of Article II treaty law irrelevant.[1231] Pursuant to these considerations, the Supreme Court has repeatedly affirmed that the determination of individual rights under a self-executing treaty is fundamentally judicial, rather than an executive, responsibility.[1232]

Even though the Supreme Court theoretically regards itself as competent to interpret international law, it has mostly adhered to the statement of interests by the government. Interpreting the Constitution, the Supreme Court has repeatedly stated that "the meaning attributed to treaty provisions by the Government agencies charged with their negotiation and enforcement is entitled to great weight."[1233] The Court

---

York University School of Law, February 3, 2006' 62 New York University Annual Survey of American Law 497 (2007) at 522.

1228 MPv Alstine, 'The Judicial Power and Treaty Delegation' 90 California Law Review 1263 (2002) at 1275-1280.

1229 MPv Alstine, 'Federal Common Law in an Age of Treaties' 89 Cornell Law in an Age of Treaties 892 (2004) at 952.

1230 *United States v. Southwestern Cable Co.*, 392 US 157, US S.Ct. (1968) at 170 (quoting *Rainwater v. United States*, 356 US 590, US S.Ct. (1958) at 593; see also *South Dakota v. Yankton Sioux Tribe* 522 US 329, US SCt. (1998) at 355 ("We have often observed... that 'the views of a subsequent Congress form a hazardous basis for inferring the intent of an earlier one."' (quoting *United States v. Phila. Nat'l Bank*, 374 US 321, US S.Ct. (1963) at 348-349)); see further references in MPv Alstine, 'Federal Common Law in an Age of Treaties' 89 Cornell Law in an Age of Treaties 892 (2004) at footnote 329.

1231 MPv Alstine, 'Federal Common Law in an Age of Treaties' 89 Cornell Law in an Age of Treaties 892 (2004) at 953.

1232 See *Japan Whaling Ass'n v. Am. Cetacean Soc'y*, 478 US 221, US S.Ct. (1986) at 230 (holding that "the courts have the authority to construe treaties"); *Kolovrat v. Oregon*, 366 US 187, US S.Ct. (1961) at 194 (observing that "courts interpret treaties for themselves"); and further footnotes in MPv Alstine, 'Federal Common Law in an Age of Treaties' 89 Cornell Law in an Age of Treaties 892 (2004) at footnotes 325-328.

1233 See *El Al Israel Airlines, Ltd. v. Tsui Yuan Tseng*, 525 US 155, US S.Ct. (1999) at 168 (Respect

often adds that executive branch views on treaty interpretation questions are, however, "not conclusive."[1234] Professor Bederman reviewed Supreme Court decisions in treaty interpretation cases between 1986 and 1999. He found that, "of the twelve treaty interpretation cases considered so far by the Rehnquist Court, in all but one the holding followed the express wishes of the executive branch of the government."[1235]

C. International law and the US Supreme Court

1. Chronological development of the treatment of international law

US law derives its roots in English law and international law was already incorporated into the domestic law in the 18th century in English law.[1236] Especially for the first twenty years after the adoption of the US Constitution, the US judiciary left little doubt that both treaty-based and customary international law could be incorporated directly into US law.[1237] In 1793, Chief Justice Jay stated it was the interest as well as the duty of the United States to respect and obey international law.[1238]

In 1804, the US Supreme Court decided in the *Charming Betsy* case that statutory interpretation shall never violate international law.[1239] A few years later, in the famous *Paquete Habana* decision, the Supreme Court found that international law is part of US law: "International law is part of our law, and must be ascertained and administered by the courts of justice of appropriate jurisdiction as often as questions of right depending upon it are duly presented for their determination. For this purpose, where there is no treaty and no controlling executive or legislative act or judicial decision, resort must be had to the customs and usages of civilized nations."[1240]

---

is ordinarily due the reasonable views of the Executive Branch concerning the meaning of an international treaty. Quoting *Sumitomo Shoji Am., Inc. v. Avagliano*, 457 US 176, US S.Ct. (1982) at 184-85). See also *United States v. Stuart*, 489 US 353, US S.Ct. (1989) at 369 (also quoting *Sumitomo*); *Kolovrat v. Oregon*, 366 US 187, US S.Ct. (1961) *at*194 ("While courts interpret treaties for themselves, the meaning given them by the departments of government particularly charged with their negotiation and enforcement is given great weight.")

1234 *El Al Israel Airlines, Ltd. v. Tsui Yuan Tseng*, 525 US 155, US S.Ct. (1999) at 168 (quoting *Sumitomo Shoji Am., Inc. v. Avagliano*, 457 US 176, US S.Ct. (1982) at 184); *United States v. Stuart*, 489 US 353, US S.Ct. (1989) at 369; see also *Kolovrat v. Oregon*, 366 US 187, US S.Ct. (1961) at 194.

1235 DJ Bederman, 'Deference or Deception: Treaty Rights as Political Questions' 70 University of Colorado Law Review 1439 (1999) at 1465.

1236 *Barbuit's Case*, 25 Eng Rep 777 (Ch), English Court of Chancery (1735).

1237 JJ Paust, *International Law as Law of the United States* (2nd edn, Carolina Academic Press, Durham 2003) at vii and 7-8.

1238 *Chisholm v. Georgia*, 2 US (2 Dall) 419, US S.Ct. (1793) at 474.

1239 *Murray v. The Schooner Charming Betsy*, 6 US (2 Cranch) 64, 118, US S.Ct. (1804).

1240 *The Paquete Habana*, 175 US 677, 700 (1900).

In 1942, the Supreme Court stated: "From the very beginning of its history this Court has recognized and applied the law of war as including that part of the law of nations which prescribes, for the conduct of war, the status, rights and duties of enemy nations as well as of enemy individuals."[1241]

In 1977, in *Coker v. Georgia*, the US Supreme Court held that international standards were important for evolving US standards.[1242] Even though it is an example from international comparative law, it is still interesting to note that the Supreme Court referred to the law in England, India and Canada, when it out ruled the death penalty for felony murder.[1243]

In the 1988 *Thompson v. Oklahoma case*, the Supreme Court had to decide on the question of juvenile death penalties.[1244] It made reference to Article 4(5) of the *American Convention on Human Rights*,[1245] Article 6(5) of the *International Covenant on Civil and Political Rights*,[1246] and Article 68 of the *Geneva Convention Relative to the Protection of Civilian Persons in Time of War.*[1247]

The question of the juvenile death penalty came before the Court in two other cases: *Stanford v. Kentucky* in 1989 and *Roper v. Simmons* in 2005.[1248] Again, the Supreme Court looked to international law to confirm its findings, but solely as secondary sources.[1249] However, it must be said that at this time every country has either abolished the death penalty for juveniles or made public disavowal of the practice, and that the US stood alone in the world in allowing execution of juvenile offenders. As a sarcastic quip in *Roper v. Simmons*, Justice Scalia in a dissenting opinion to the majority asserted that "[t]hough the views of our own citizens are essentially irrelevant to the Court's decision today, the views of other countries and the so-called international community take center stage."[1250]

1241 *Ex Parte Quirin*, 317 US 1, US S.Ct. (1942) at 27-28.

1242 *Coker v. Georgia*, 433 US 584, 596 n10, US S.Ct. (1977).

1243 *Enmund v. Florida*, 458 US 782, 796 n22, US S.Ct. (1982).

1244 *Thompson v. Oklahoma*, 487 US 815, 830, US S.Ct. (1988).

1245 American Convention on Human Rights November 22, 1969, 9 ILM 673 (entered into force July 18, 1978) (1969b).

1246 International Covenant on Civil and Political Rights (ICCPR) GA Res 2200A (XXI), UN Doc A/6316, adopted and opened for signature, ratification and accession by General Assembly resolution 2200A (XXI) of 16 December 1966,entered into force Mar 23, 1976 (1966).

1247 Geneva Convention Relative to the Protection of Civilian Persons in Time of War (Fourth Geneva Convention) 75 UNTS 287 (12 August 1949) (entered into force Oct 21, 1950) (1949).

Stanford v. Kentucky, 492 US 361, US S.Ct. (1989) and *Roper v. Simmons*, 543 US 551, 125 SCt 1183 (Mar 1), US S.Ct. (2005).

1249 MA Weisburd, 'Roper v. Simmons and International Law' 45 Virginia Journal of International Law 798 (2005) at 798.

1250 *Roper v. Simmons*, 543 US 551, 125 SCt 1183 (Mar 1), US S.Ct. (2005) at 1225.

In 2004, the ICJ ruled that American courts must review the cases of 51 Mexicans who had been sentenced to death in the United States.[1251] According to the ICJ, the prisoners had been denied their rights under the 1963 Vienna *Convention on Consular Relations* to meet with representatives of the Mexican government following their arrests, or at least to be informed of their right to do so.[1252] Although the United States is a signatory to the *Vienna Convention* and acknowledges the ICJ's jurisdiction over the matter, the Court of Appeals denied that the diplomatic protection under the *Vienna Convention* created individual rights.[1253] The US Supreme Court confirmed the judgment.[1254]

In their dissenting opinion to the case Justices Breyer and Stevens argued that the United States Courts should view Article 36 of the *Vienna Convention* as directly enforceable for various reasons. "First, the [US] President has decided that state courts should follow *Avena*. […] And that fact permits [the defendant] Medellín to argue in the Texas courts that the President's determination – taken together with (1) the self-executing nature of the treaty, (2) the Nation's signature on the Optional Protocol, (3) the ICJ's determination that the United States give Medellín (and 50 other Mexican nationals) 'judicial,' i.e., court, 'review and reconsideration' of their Convention-based claims, 'by means of [the United States'] own choosing,' and (4) the United States' 'undertak[ing]' in the United Nations Charter to comply with ICJ judgments-requires Texas to follow the *Avena* decision in Medellín's case."[1255]

The self-attested appreciation for international law was upheld in *Sosa v. Alvarez-Machain*: "For two centuries we have affirmed that the domestic law of the United States recognizes the law of nations."[1256]

2. *Erie* decision and federal Common law

In order to understand the status of international law in the US judiciary and ATCA litigation in particular, it seems indispensable to have an understanding of the *Erie* decision from the US Supreme Court in 1938. In *Erie Railroad v. Tompkins*,[1257] the Court held that federal courts could not establish *federal Common law*, when hearing claims under diversity jurisdiction. "Diversity jurisdiction" describes the situation, when the parties to a dispute are "diverse," meaning they come from different states. Before *Erie*, claimants went "forum shopping," in that they would choose to sue in a state with favorable *federal* Common law rules. After *Erie*, the Federal Court was

---

[1251] *Case Concerning Avena and Other Mexican Nationals (Mexico v. US)*, ICJ 128, ICJ (2004).
[1252] Vienna Convention on Consular Relations Apr 24, 1963, 596 UNTS 261 (entered into force Mar 19, 1967) (1963).
[1253] *United States v. Jimenez-Nava*, 243 F3d 192, C.A. 5 (2004) at 195.
[1254] *Medellin v. Dretke*, 544 US 660, US S.Ct. (2005) at 666.
[1255] *Ibid.* at 693 et *seq.*
[1256] *Sosa v. Alvarez-Machain* (03-339) 542 US 2739, US S.Ct. (2004) at 2764.
[1257] *Erie Railroad Co. v. Tompkins*, 304 US 64, US S.Ct. (1938).

required to apply the *state* law of whichever state it was sitting in, as though it was a court of that state.

The critics of human rights litigation in the United States – including Justice Scalia and the academics Bradley and Goldsmith – argue that after *Erie* the federal courts lack authority to derive "general common law."[1258] However, *Erie* did not completely bar federal Common law rules. There remain several areas for federal Common law, particularly where the US Constitution gives the US Congress power to make laws in an area – for example, in areas such as admiralty law, antitrust, bankruptcy law, interstate commerce and civil rights. Furthermore, *Erie* seems inapplicable here since the ATCA suits enter federal courts under federal question jurisdiction and not diversity jurisdiction. After *Sosa*,[1259] even the critics seem to agree that international law is "part of our law."[1260]

3. Canadian Supreme Court and international law

Even though not from the US Supreme Court, an interesting Common law approach shall be briefly mentioned concerning the interplay between international law and domestic law. In *Baker v. Canada*,[1261] the Canadian Supreme Court rejected a lower court decision, because it did not give sufficient weight to the purpose of an international treaty that was ratified by Canada. In relation to the interpretation of international law, the Court found that international law is not directly binding, because it was not implemented by the Parliament. Nevertheless, domestic courts have to interpret domestic law consistently with international law.

It took an interpretative approach acknowledging the persuasive power of international law. This is a step forward moving away from the "all or nothing approach" to the effect of international law. It establishes that Canada's signing and ratification of a treaty indicates its adherence to the values of the treaty, which can then be used for domestic legislation in a purposive interpretation thereof.[1262] A similar point was also made by the High Court of Australia in *Minister for Immigration and Ethnic Affairs v Teoh*.[1263]

1258 *Sosa v. Alvarez-Machain* (03-339) 542 US 2739, US S.Ct. (2004), citing CA Bradley and JL Goldsmith, 'The current illegitimacy of international human rights litigation' 66 Fordham Law Review 317 (1997) at 824 and EA Young, 'Sorting out the Debate Over Customary International Law' 42 Virginia Journal of International Law 365 (2002) at 374.

1259 *Sosa v. Alvarez-Machain* (03-339) 542 US 2739, US S.Ct. (2004).

1260 CA Bradley, JL Goldsmith and DH Moore, 'Sosa, Customary International Law, and the Continuing Relevance of Erie' 120 Harvard Law Review 869 (2007).

1261 *Baker v. Canada (Minister of Citizenship and Immigration)*, 2 SCR 817, Canada S.Ct. (1999).

1262 Human Rights Internet, 'Case Studies from Canadian Jurisprudence: Applying International Law Domestically - Case Studies from the Supreme Court of Canada - Baker v. Canada' (1999) <http:// www.hri.ca/ fortherecordCanada/ vol3/ casebaker.htm> (March 21).

1263 *Minister for Immigration and Ethnic Affairs v Teoh*, 183 CLR 273, High Court of Australia (1995).

4. Analysis

The renowned international law professor Koh recently noted that "during the last two Supreme Court terms, promising signs have emerged that the American ostrich is finally starting to take its head out of the sand."[1264] Since the composition of the Supreme Court has altered following the retirements of Chief Justice Rehnquist and Justice O'Connor. This finding, possibly partially based on the decision *Roper v. Simmons*, can possibly be questioned again. In particular, the replacement of the moderate Justice O'Connor with the conservative Justice Alito could possibly cause a change towards a sovereignist and traditionalist view that tends to overlook international law, but only time will tell.

The exceptionalism or isolationism can also be detected in this statement of William H. Rehnquist, who served as 16th Chief Justice of the United States between 1986 and 2005: "For nearly a century and a half, courts in the United States exercising the power of judicial review had no precedents to look to save their own, because our courts alone exercised this sort of authority. When many new constitutional courts were created after the Second World War, these courts naturally looked to decisions of the Supreme Court of the United States, among other sources, for developing their own law. But now that constitutional law is solidly grounded in so many countries, it is time that the United States courts begin looking to the decisions of other constitutional courts to aid in their own deliberative process."[1265] This quote in essence states that now that the judiciaries all over the world orientated themselves towards the US judiciary, the US may now start looking to the rest of the world as the rest of the world has fabricated legal material of value for their own system. Overall, the Supreme Court has in the past viewed sources of international law only obliquely and its relevance was rather supplementary.[1266]

D. International law and US executive

The US executive has had a considerable influence on ATCA litigation. The US government has issued numerous statements of interest in the ATCA cases pursuant to 28 U.S.C. § 517 – for example, in *Doe v. Unocal, In re South African Apartheid Litigation, In re World War II Era Japanese Forced Labor Litigation, Sarei v. Rio Tinto, Mujica v. Occidental Petroleum Corp., The Presbyterian Church of Sudan et. al. v. Talisman Energy, Inc* and most importantly in the *Sosa* litigation.[1267] A reason

1264 HH Koh, 'International Law as part of our Law' 98 American Journal of International Law 43 (2004) at 48.

1265 William H. Rehnquist, Constitutional Courts--Comparative Remarks (1989), reprinted in P Kirchhof and others, *Germany and its Basic Law: Past, Present, and Future - a German-American symposium* (1st edn, Nomos, Baden-Baden 1993).

1266 See also JJ Paust, 'International Law before the Supreme Court: A mixed record of recognition' 45 Santa Clara Law Review 829 (2005).

1267 *Doe v. Unocal (Unocal III)*, 395 F3d 932, C.A. 9 (2002): In its Statement, the State Department maintained that it "believes that adjudication of this lawsuit at this time would in fact risk a

suggested for this is that the ATCA litigation could seriously impede foreign relations and the "Global War on Terror."

The US executive can, on the one hand, be seen as the major force that has established the post-World War II system of international law and the United Nations. On the other hand, the US has ratified only four of the 14 human rights protocols in the aftermath.[1268] During the cold war and also thereafter international law was often subdued under US geopolitical interests. As one of many examples, the ICJ found that the US had violated international law in 1986 when they placed mines in Nicaragua's harbors.[1269] The following short abstract shall shine a light on the US executive behavior in recent years, especially since September 2001.

In order to understand the US executive position on international law it is invaluable to understand the interaction between the scholar John Yoo, US President George W. Bush, former US Attorney General John Ashcroft, former US Attorney General

---

potentially serious adverse impact on significant interests of the United States, including interests related directly to the on-going struggle against international terrorism."); *In re: South African Apartheid Litigation*, 346 FSupp2d 538, D.C. S.D. N.Y. (2004): The United States government has expressed its belief that the adjudication of this suit would cause tension between the United States and South Africa and would serve to hamper the policy of encouraging positive change in developing countries via economic investment; *In re World War II Era Japanese Forced Labor Litigation*, 114 F Supp 2d 939, D.C. N.D. Cal. (2001): The United States government argued that the 1951 Treaty of Peace with Japan did not leave open the possibility of future war reparations or other war-related claims; *Sarei v. Rio Tinto*, 456 F3d 1069, C.A. 9 (2006): The State Department indicated that the ATCA action against the international mining corporation would have adverse effect on government's relations with Papua New Guinea; *Mujica v. Occidental Petroleum Corp.*, 381 F Supp 2d 1134, D.C. C.D. Cal. (2005): The State Department filed a Supplemental Statement of Interest indicating that it opposes the pursuit of the instant litigation since it would severely impact this country's diplomatic relationship with Colombia. As part of that Supplemental Statement of Interest, the State Department attached a letter from the Colombian government indicating that it also opposed this litigation; *The Presbyterian Church of Sudan, et. al. v. Talisman Energy, Inc.*, 374 FSupp2d 331, D.C. S.D. N.Y. (2005): The United States Government has submitted a Statement of Interest expressing concerns regarding the impact of this litigation on this Nation's foreign affairs and on the Government of Canada's foreign policies towards Sudan; U.S. Department of Justice, *2004 WL 577654 - Reply Brief for the United States as Respondent Supporting Petitioner* (2004)Asking the Supreme Court to acknowledge that customary international law does not create a cause of action and does not apply extrarerritorraly.

1268 Convention on Genocide in 1989; the Covenant on Civil and Political Rights – with reservations – in 1992; the Convention on the Elimination of All Forms of Racial Discrimination in 1994; and the Convention Against Torture and Other Cruel, Inhuman, or Degrading Treatment or Punishment, also in 1994; In 2002 the United States ratified two of the optional protocols to the Convention on the Rights of the Child, but not the convention itself; The United States became a party to the International Convention Relating to the Status of Refugees by signing the protocol in 1968.

1269 *Nicaragua v. US*, ICJ (1986).

Alberto Gonzales and former Secretary of Defense, Donald Rumsfeld, on the one hand, and their effects on the victims of their "Global War on Terror."

The first years of the 21st century might create the impression that law, and especially international law, is failing in one of the primary purposes – the regulation of an ordered community where the weak are protected from arbitrary action by the strong. Some commentators have even suggested that we are witnessing the death of the subject of international law as a legal discipline and should now recognize it as having political and moral, but not legal force.[1270] The US executive has strongly contributed to this situation and has violated international law in numerous cases. Some of the examples since 9/11 include the prison in Guantánamo Bay, the Iraq war, ferocious war crimes such as those conducted in Haditha in November 2005, the Abu Ghraib prison, and also the enactment of the US PATRIOT Act.[1271] The U.S executive under President George W. Bush, in its effort to combat terrorism, has increased its emphasis on collective prevention, instead of protecting individual human rights and has been involved in a pattern of violations of international human rights.

The Turkish citizen, Murat Kurnaz, was innocently imprisoned in Guantánamo Bay Detention Center after he was captured while visiting Pakistan. For five years, Kurnaz was detained without charge or trial, was not convicted, was tortured and did not have any contact with his family or a lawyer. He lived in a prison where neon light was constantly switched on. Kurnaz was allowed to return to his home country, Germany, not because of an acquittal; rather, as a result of an "act of grace" by the US administration, because the German chancellor, Angela Merkel, imposed political pressure, after the preceding German government failed to ask for Kurnaz's return.[1272]

[1270] M Dixon, *Textbook on International Law* (5th edn, Oxford University Press, Oxford; New York 2005) at 1.

[1271] A Bhoumik, 'Democratic Responses to Terrorism: A Comparative Study of the United States, Israel and India' 33 Denver Journal of International Law and Policy 285 (2005) (Argues that the USA Patriot is one facet of a greater move of the US government away from the democratic principles in counterterrorist efforts. Most importantly the act increases the surveillance capabilities of the government, including e-mails and financial activities. The act also allows for the indefinite detention of aliens suspected of terrorism. The government has exerted this authority in several cases.); Other examples of torture of innocent people is the treatment of Canadian citizen Maher who was arrested on a stop over in New York, US, see *Arar v. Ashcroft*, 414 F Supp 2d 250, D.C. E.D. N.Y. (2006); M Arar, 'MaherArar.ca' <www.maherarar.ca> (January 12, 2006); or the German citizen El Masri who was detained in Macedonia, see *E-Masri v. Tenet*, 437 FSupp2d 530, D.C. E.D. Va. (2006); *El-Masri v. US*, 479 F3d 296, C.A. 4 (2007); 'They beat me from all sides' *The Guardian* (January 14, 2005); Concerning the situation of Guantánamo and international law, see in this chapter above at the outset.

[1272] It needs to be noted that in the case of Murat Kurnaz the German government of chancellor Schröder and the head of his office Frank Walter Steinmeier probably frustrated US government's attempts to deport Kurnaz to Germany. Nevertheless the US government kept on

The United States have used some torturous interrogation techniques which date back to the techniques of the infamous Spanish Inquisition in the 15th Century. These interrogation techniques included sexual humiliation, religious desecration and beatings.[1273] Many of them violate international law.[1274] Donald Rumsfeld has directly authorized many of these violations of international law.[1275] In a now-famous memorandum from December 2, 2002, Rumsfeld directly authorized the use of stress positions. His note on the side of the memorandum was: "I stand for 8-10 hours a day. Why is standing limited to 4 hours?" In November 2006, German and American lawyers reported a well-founded second criminal charge against Donald Rumsfeld on 384 pages.[1276] The first 170 page-long criminal charge was reported against Rumsfeld in 2004 but the German Attorney General refused to take the case, because he believed the US would investigate the case.[1277] This rebuttal of the first criminal charge is legally very contentious and gives rise to the impression that political considerations of the German government were given more weight than the legal intention of the German Code of Crimes against International Law (CCAIL).[1278]

In one of the numerous memoranda on international law and their applicability in the US, the United States government made very interesting observations concerning

---

ferociously violating Kurnaz' human rights, even though they knew of his innocence. See for example: *The Republic of Ireland v The United Kingdom*, Series A, No 25, ECtHR (1978); A Förster and D Fras, 'Im Schatten' *Berliner Zeitung* (Januar 24, 2007) at 3.

1273 E Bazelon, P Carter and D Lithwick, 'What is Torture? - Slate Magazine Interactive Primer on American Interrogation ' (2006) <http://www.slate.com/features/whatistorture/taxonomy.html> (June 5, 2006) (Showing the direct chain of command, the memorandums and the taxonomy of torture and their legal status in US law and in international law).

1274 See for example *The Republic of Ireland v The United Kingdom*, Series A, No 25, ECtHR (1978) ("(k) Since the five techniques were applied in combination, with premeditation and for hours at a time, causing at least intense physical and mental suffering and acute psychiatric disturbances, they amounted to inhuman treatment; (l) Since the five techniques were such as to arouse in the victims feelings of fear, anguish and inferiority capable of humiliating and debasing them and possibly breaking their physical or moral resistance, they were also degrading.")

1275 See for example J Simon, 'Einer gegen Rumsfeld' *DIE ZEIT* (November 9, 2006) 17.

1276 Republikanischer Anwältinnen- und Anwaltverein e.V., '2. Strafanzeige gegen Rumsfeld' (2007) <http://www.rav.de/rumsfeld2.html> D Jochum, 'Noch ist Bush immun' *Junge Welt* (Januar 6, 2007).

1277 For the docket of documents concerning the first criminal charge against Rumsfeld, see Center For Constitutional Rights, 'Docket: Center For Constitutional Rights Seeks Criminal Investigation in Germany into Culpability of US Officials in Abu Ghraib Torture ' (2006) <http:// www.ccr-ny.org/ v2/ legal/ september_11th/ sept11Article.asp? ObjID= 1xiADJOOQx &Content=472> (Januar 24).

1278 A Fischer-Lescano, 'Torture in Abu Ghraib: The Complaint Against Donald Rumsfeld Under the German Code of Crimes Against International Law' 6 German Yearbook of International Law 689 (2005); A Fischer-Lescano, 'Global Law v. Realpolitik - The German Complaint against Donald Rumsfeld Concerning Torture in Abu Ghraib' (2005) <http:// www.ccr-ny.org/ v2/ legal/ september_11th/ sept11Article.asp?ObjID= 1xiADJOOQx&Content=472> (Januar 24).

their understanding of international law in the opening statement: "The following discussion addresses the requirements of international law, as it pertains to the Armed Forces of the United States, as *interpreted* by the United States. As will be apparent in other sections of this analysis, other nations and international bodies may take a more restrictive view, which may affect our policy analysis and thus is considered elsewhere."

The authors of the memorandum were Jack Goldsmith and John Yoo, both well-known professors of international law at Harvard University and at the University of California, Berkeley. They doubted the importance of international law and questioned the illegality of torture. Goldsmith relied on the philosophical concepts of Hart, who stated that international law does not represent law.[1279] By arguing that international law is often violated with impunity and therefore is no law and does not need to be followed, Goldsmith tried to legitimize a circular argument. Goldsmith stands rather isolated with his revisionist approach towards international law in the US and international legal academia and his writing appears to be guided by the idea to deny any normative force to international law.[1280]

Yoo stands even more isolated and is of the opinion that the US is in a war and follows the path of American exceptionalism. He states that the US fights for the good and is therefore allowed to be exempted from international obligations.[1281] His memoranda set a high bar as to what constitutes torture and gave extraordinary powers to the US President, ignoring the Geneva conventions. The US President George W. Bush accepted the conclusion to suspend the Geneva Conventions as to Afghanistan. There is ample proof that there was a direct chain of command from the government of George W. Bush and the Secretary of Defense Donald Rumsfeld via the Combined Joint Task Force Commander Ricardo Sanchez down to the Abu Ghraib prison staff.[1282]

The international law skeptics, such as Alan Dershowitz, Jack Goldsmith and John Yoo broadened the scope of torture and created loopholes in international law by establishing new categories of person at international law such as "enemy

---

1279 See JL Goldsmith and EA Posner, *The Limits of International Law* (Oxford University Press, Oxford; New York 2005) at 3 (international law "lacks a centralized or effective legislature, executive, or judiciary; that it favors powerful over weak states; that it often simply mirrors extant international behavior; and that it is sometimes violated with impunity."); HLA Hart, *The concept of law* (Clarendon law series, Clarendon Press; Oxford University Press, Oxford; New York 1961) at 213-237.

1280 See for example: Av Aaken, 'To Do Away with International Law? Some limits to the 'The Limits of International Law'' 17 European Journal of International Law 289 (2006) at 317; OA Hathaway and AN Lavinbuck, 'Rationalism and Revisionism in International Law' 119 Harvard Law Review 1404 (2006) at 1415.

1281 See FRONTLINE, 'Interview John Yoo' (2005) (December 22).

1282 See the allegations of the claim by the Center for Constitutional Rights and the German lawyer Wolgang Kaleck, J Simon, 'Einer gegen Rumsfeld' *DIE ZEIT* (November 9, 2006) 17.

combatants." The memoranda or writings then became the legal clearance for the George W. Bush administration to commit many of the violations of international law that followed after 9/11. With arguments such as "the Global War on Terror is a new category" and the "ticking time bomb," the international framework was undermined. Based on a utilitarian philosophy, the US government and their cohorts often sacrifice the means at the altar of the ends.[1283] By using such arguments, these scholars and politicians would be well-advised to think about the consequence that, in their thinking, they do not differ from the people they are fighting.

E. International law in US legislation

One important step of the US legislature incorporating international law into domestic statute was the Torture Victim Protection Act (TVPA) of 1992. This statute allows for the filing of civil suits in the United States against individuals who, acting in an official capacity for any foreign nation, committed torture and/or extrajudicial killing.

The United States became the first country to offer foreign torture victims the legal right to sue their oppressors for civil damages. But the enactment of the TVPA also served another purpose, as its legislative history shows that it was intended to confirm the ATCA human rights litigation. The House Report of the House of Representatives states: "The TVPA would establish an unambiguous and modern basis for a cause of action that has been successfully maintained under an existing law, section 1350 of the Judiciary Act of 1789 (the ATCA), which permits Federal district courts to hear claims by aliens for torts committed 'in violation of the law of nations.' [...] Section 1350 has other important uses and should not be replaced."[1284]

The Democratic member of the US House of Representatives, Gus Yatron, began the House hearings by explaining: "International human rights violators visiting or residing in the United States have formerly been held liable to money damages under the Alien Tort Claims Act. It is not the intent of the Congress to weaken this law, but to strengthen it."[1285] The House Report concluded that the TVPA "should remain intact to permit suits based on other norms that already exist or may ripen in the future into rules of customary international law." Every Circuit Court decision that has examined the influence of the legislative intent of the TVPA on the ATCA has come to the same conclusion.[1286]

1283 AM Dershowith, *Why Terrorism Works: Understanding the Threat, Responding to the Challenge* (Yale University Press, New Haven 2002) at 131 et *seq.*

1284 U.S. House of Representatives, *P.L. 102-256, Torture Victim Protection Act of 1991, H.R. REP. NO. 102-367 (I), November 25* (1991) at 3.

1285 The Torture Victim Protection Act: Hearing on H.R. 1417 Before the Subcomm. on Human Rights and International Organizations of the Comm. on Foreign Affairs, 100 Cong., 2d Sess. 1 (1988) (statement of Re. Yatron).

1286 See for example *Abebe-Jira v. Negewo*, 72 F3d 844, C.A. 11 (1996),*at* 848; *Wiwa v. Royal Dutch Petroleum Co.*, 226 F3d 88, C.A.2 (2000) at 105; *Kadic v. Karadzic*, 70 F3d 232, C. A. 2

Aside from the TVPA, there are numerous acts that incorporate international law. A number of US federal statutes provide for a particular type of response when a foreign nation acts in a way that violates international law. The Hickenlooper Amendment requires the suspension of foreign aid to countries that have expropriated property of US nationals or US corporations. The Hickenlooper Amendment may also deprive a country of the advantage of the Act of State doctrine.[1287] Another statute authorizes the President to prohibit the importation of fishery products or wildlife from countries that violate international fishery or endangered species programs.[1288] The US provides for effective enforcement of international law in many fields, including for international cultural property protection, such as the *Convention on Cultural Property*.[1289]

On the other hand, the US PATRIOT Act[1290] creates a broad definition of "domestic terrorism" that may impinge on the freedoms of expression and association, which are given voice in the *ICCPR*. The PATRIOT Act infringes the right of privacy, which is also recognized by the *ICCPR*. The PATRIOT Act allows non-citizens to be detained without charge and held indefinitely once charged, which is inconsistent with the rights in the *Vienna Convention on Consular Relations*, as some scholars argue.[1291]

Overall, it can be argued that the treatment of international law in US legislation is quite contradictory. This can even be noticed in the enactment of the TVPA, which was fairly progressive from an internationalist point of view. The TVPA provides a remedy for victims of torture only by foreign nations, not for those who have been

(1995) at 241. Further detailed references can be found in SJ Dubbin, 'Brief of Amici Curiae Alien Friends Representing Hungarian Jews and Bougainvilleans Interests in Support of Respondent' (2004) at 15.

1287 US Code Title 22 (Foreign Relations and Intercourse) - chapter 32- § 2370 Prohibitions against furnishing assistance (e) (e) Nationalization, expropriation or seizure of property of United States citizens, or taxation or other exaction having same effect; failure to compensate or to provide relief from taxes, exactions, or conditions; report on full value of property by Foreign Claims Settlement Commission; act of state doctrine.

1288 US Code Title 22 (Foreign Relations and Intercourse) - chapter 25 - § 1978 Restriction on importation of fishery or wildlife products from countries which violate international fishery or endangered or threatened species programs.

1289 Title 19- chapter 14- § 2600 Convention on cultural property.

1290 Uniting and Strengthening America by Providing Appropriate Tools Required to Intercept and Obstruct Terrorism Act of 2001 (USA PATRIOT Act) 115 Stat 272 (2001).

1291 Under Article 36 of the Vienna Convention on Consular Relations, foreign nationals must be notified of their right to communicate with consular officials "without delay" when they are detained, and if they request communication, competent authorities of the receiving state must inform the consular post "without delay." See also SM Akram and M Karmely, 'Immigration and Constitutional Consequences of Post 9/11 Policies Involving Arabs and Muslims in the United States: Is Alienage a Distinction Without a Difference?' 38 UC Davis Law Review 609 (2005) at 657; C Powell, 'The Role of Transnational Norm Entrepreneurs in the US "War on Terrorism"' 5 Theoretical Inquiries in Law 47 (2004) at 75.

tortured by US nationals. The US clearly and openly establishes a double standard. They forbid others to do something that they permit themselves to do.

F. International law and US academics

Even though clearly not a branch of state power, the views of US academics should also be briefly examined, because their views are often recited in US court decisions,[1292] and certain scholars have had an important influence on the US executive branch as well. International law appears to split US academia into warring camps. On one side are the anti-internationalists, such as Curtis A. Bradley, Alan Dershowitz, Jack L. Goldsmith, Eric Posner and John Yoo.

Bradley and Goldsmith are critics of international human rights. They can be seen as sovereignists.[1293] Bradley and Goldsmith question the value of international law in US courts and are critical towards international law in general and specifically international human rights litigation.[1294] Before the *Sosa* decision, they tried to question the ATCA as a basis for international human rights litigation, but now appear to agree that international law does have an increasing role in US law. In *The Limits of International Law*, Goldsmith and Posner question the normative authority of international law. Posner is more critical of international law and seeks to legitimize coercive interrogation techniques.[1295]

[1292] As one significant example from opposition of ATCA litigation, see Scalia in *Sosa v. Alvarez-Machain* (03-339) 542 US 2739, US S.Ct. (2004) at 749 ("The notion that a law of nations, redefined to mean the consensus of states on *any* subject, can be used by a private citizen to control a sovereign's treatment of *its own citizens* within *its own territory* is a 20th-century invention of internationalist law professors and human-rights advocates."); and in defense of ATCA litigation see *Presbyterian Church of Sudan et al. v. Talisman Energy, Inc.*, 244 F Supp 2d 289, D.C. S.D. N.Y. (2003) at 315 et *seq* (Examining if corporation are capable of violating international law the court draws its sources and opinions from SR Ratner, 'Corporations and Human Rights: A Theory of Legal Responsibility' 111 Yale Law Journal 443 (2001)). However there reamains some doubt on the importance of academic writing. See i.e. Thomas Ernst (2004); Und die Wahrheit starb im Fussnoten-Massaker; Zur Sprache der Wissenschaft im Zeitalter ihrer Delegitimation; ("Unter den Talaren der Muff von 1000 Jahren. Und in ihren Sätzen nur Fußnotengemetzel.")

[1293] PJ Spiro, 'The New Sovereignists: American Exceptionalism and Its False Prophets' 79 Foreign Affairs (2000).

[1294] See for example: CA Bradley and JL Goldsmith, 'The current illegitimacy of international human rights litigation' 66 Fordham Law Review 317 (1997); C Bradley and JL Goldsmith, 'Customary International Law as Federal Common Law: A Critique of the Modern Position' 110 Harvard Law Review 815 (1997) at 821 (The current attempts to domesticate international law through ATCA litigation are a "grotesque twist on the framers intent.")

[1295] "Our aim is not to praise coercive interrogation, which is a grave evil in any reasonable moral view. All we suggest is that law should treat coercive interrogation the way it treats other grave evils.", see EA Posner and A Vermeule, 'Should coercive interrogation be legal?' 104 Michigan Law Review 671 (2006) at 707.

The view that the US President stands above international law seems astonishing.[1296] The proposition that the President could stand above the law itself is reminiscent of absolutist monarchs or feudal lords from many centuries ago.[1297] The most saddening part is that the scholar Yoo, who has the most extreme views about international law that are beyond any reason and moral, is the authority that the US executive has sought legal advice from to legitimize grave breaches of international law.

Yoo is of the opinion that the US President has unlimited powers. He has even sought to uphold the legitimacy of torturing the juvenile relative of a terror suspect.[1298] Yoo co-authored the infamous torture memoranda that were the basis of the torture excesses in US detention centers in Guantánamo Bay and Abu Ghraib. The torture memoranda and his writings have been described as "blatantly wrong"[1299] and would be rejected by at least "98 per cent of the international lawyers in the world."[1300] A criminal charge was filed against Yoo in Berlin, Germany because of violations of international law based on his memoranda and further ample proof, such as military reports and a multitude of testimonies.[1301]

On the other hand, there are the proponents of binding the US to international law. Among many on the internationalist academic side are Philip Alston, Terry Collingsworth, William S. Dodge, Harold Honju Koh, John Haberstroh, Louis Henkin,

---

1296 This discussion has also been touched upon above under the subheading "Interpretation of international treaties".

1297 See for example the Danish Lex Regia from 1665, § 2 of which stipulates that the monarch shall from this day forth be revered and considered the most perfect and supreme person on the Earth by all his subjects, standing above all human laws and having no judge above his person, neither in spiritual nor temporal matters, except God alone. JE Nijman, *The Concept of International Legal Personality: An Inquiry into the History and Theory of International Law* (T.M.C. Asser Press, The Hague; New York 2004); www.danskekonger.dk, 'Kongeloven af 1665' (2007) <http://www.danskekonger.dk/biografi/andre/kongeloven.html> (April 27, 2007).

1298 Yoo is of the opinion that the US President has the power to interpret international treaties as part of the foreign affairs power; Yoo made the following statements during a December 1, 2005, debate in Chicago, Illinois, with Professor Doug Cassel; Cassel: "If the President deems that he's got to torture somebody, including by crushing the testicles of the person's child, there is no law that can stop him?;" "Yoo: No treaty." P Watts, 'John Yoo Argues Pres. George Bush Has Legal Power to Torture Children' (2005) <http://rwor.org/ johnyoo/ index.html> (March 14, 2007).

1299 A Liptak, 'Legal Scholars Criticize Memos on Torture' *New York Times* (June 25, 2004) A14.

1300 E Alden, 'US Interrogation Debate: Dismay at Attempt to Find Legal Justification for Torture: International Lawyers Call For Government Advisers behind Interrogation Memo to Face Professional Sanctions' *Financial Times UK* (June 10, 2004).

1301 Republikanischer Anwältinnen- und Anwälteverein e.V., 'Anzeige bei der Bundesanwaltschaft gegen Rumsfeld u.a. wegen Kriegsverbrechen in Abu Ghraib' (2006) <http:// www.rav.de/ 2006/ 141106_AbuGhraib.html> (March 14, 2007) and C-F Röhrs, 'Sie klagen an' (2006) <http:// archiv.tagesspiegel.de/ archiv/ 14.11.2006/ 2896394.asp> (March 14, 2007).

Paul Hoffman, Jordan J. Paust, Anita Ramasastry, Henry Steiner, Ralph Steinhardt and Beth Stephens. They generally argue that international law cannot be violated blatantly by the US executive or any other arm of government. They support the continuation of the ATCA international human rights litigation.

Overall, it can be noted that US legal academia in its vast majority promotes the view that the US is bound by international law and specifically by international human rights.

G. International law and the Restatement of Foreign Relations Law

A very interesting example of the treatment of international law in the US is the Restatement of Foreign Relations Law. It is used as one of the most important sources of international law in US litigation. The authoritativeness of the Restatement of Foreign Relations Law can be witnessed throughout the international human rights litigation and ATCA litigation. Aside from US precedents, the Restatement of Foreign Relations Law may stand as the most frequently cited source in the area of international law. In the most recent decision, the *Sarei* decision, the Restatement of Foreign Relations Law was cited 14 times, for example in finding the meaning of *jus cogens,*[1302] the exhaustion of remedies in the ATCA cases,[1303] and the treatment of international law in domestic litigation.[1304] The importance of the Restatement is also underlined by the fact that the Supreme Court frequently cited the Restatement in one of the most important decisions on international law of the last decades, *Sosa v. Alvarez*. In that decision, the Court referred to the Restatement seven times and additionally numerous times to the First Restatement of the Conflict of Laws.

In US law, restatements are secondary sources that seek to "restate" the legal rules that constitute the Common law in a particular area. They are not "the law" in and of themselves, but are used to find primary law. They are written by the American Law Institute (ALI), a prestigious legal organization composed of noted professors, judges and lawyers. In general, the statements in the Restatement reflect prevailing views and positions, and one can normally be sure that nothing is said that either does not meet the approval of the greater part of the legal community or is totally unacceptable.[1305]

The ALI has completed restatements in different areas of law including tort law, contract law, property law, conflict of laws, and foreign relations law. Section 1 of the Restatement of Foreign Relations Law defines its scope as: (a) international law as it applies to the United States; and (b) domestic law that has substantial

[1302] *Sarei v. Rio Tinto*, 456 F3d 1069, C.A. 9 (2006) at 8963.

[1303] *Ibid.* at 8967 et *seq.*

[1304] *Ibid.* at 9013.

[1305] D Vagts and others, 'Book Review Restatement of the Law Third: The Foreign Relations Law of the United States' 86 American Journal of International Law 608 (1992) at 609.

significance for the foreign relations of the United States or has other substantial international consequences.

This means that certain parts of international law are not of interest for the Restatement or Foreign Relations Law, because they have no application within the United States – for example, the question of jurisdiction of the ICJ. The Restatement presents US law impacting foreign relations. It discusses the sources of international law and its place in US jurisprudence. It is divided into nine main parts: I. International Law and its Relation to the United States; II. Persons in International Law; III. International Agreements; IV. Jurisdiction and Judgments; V. The Law of the Sea; VI. The Law of the Environment; VII. Protection of Persons (Natural and Judicial); VIII. Selected Law of International Economic Relations; IX. Remedies for Violations of International Law.

The Chief Editor of the Third Restatement on Foreign Relations Law from 1987 was Louis Henkin, who clearly stands on the rather internationalist side in US legal academia.[1306] According to the Restatement "international law is the law of the international community of states. It deals with the conduct of nation-states and their relations with other states, and to some extent also with their relations with individuals, business organizations, and other legal entities."[1307] It is surprising that in 1987 US law already clearly recognized that individuals and business organizations can be party to international law.[1308]

1306 See, e.g., L Henkin, 'Human Rights and State "Sovereignty"' 25 Georgia Journal of International and Comparative Law 31 (1995) at 43 ("Human rights have revolutionized the international system and international law. The law now reflects human values in addition to state values, or allows human values to modify state values. We have seen a revolution in the content of international law to include a growing field directly relevant to the lives of five billion people, every one of them now a 'subject' of international law.") or older L Henkin, 'International Law as Law in the United States' 82 Michigan Law Review 1555 (1984) („However, it is well-established that international law is " 'self-executing' and is applied by courts in the United States without any need for it to be enacted or implemented by Congress."); Commenting on the preamble during the 50th anniversary celebration of the *UDHR* in 1998, Professor Henkin emphasized that the *UDHR* applies to every individual, every company, every market and every actor. See L Henkin, 'The Universal Declaration at 50 and the Challenge of Global Markets' 25 Brooklyn Journal of International Law 1 (1999) at 25.

1307 Restatement (Third) of Foreign Relations Law (1987), part I, Introductory note ("In the past it was sometimes assumed that individuals and corporations, companies or other juridical persons created by the laws of a state, were not persons under (or subjects of) international law. In principle, however, individuals and private juridical entities can have any status, capacity, rights, or duties given them by international law or agreement, and increasingly individuals and private entities have been accorded such aspects of personality in varying measures. For example, international law and numerous international agreements now recognize human rights of individuals and sometimes give individuals remedies before international bodies. See § 703. Individuals may be held liable for offenses against international law, such as piracy, war crimes, or genocide. Corporations frequently are vehicles through which rights under international economic law are asserted.")

1308 Differing view in D Vagts and others, 'Book Review Restatement of the Law Third: The

III. Concluding remarks to Chapter VI

"Isolation from international tribunals has been an unwritten policy of US courts. Dependence on the executive branch has been a written one."[1309] The US executive had remarkable influence on the interpretation and application of international law. In recent years, the US government, especially under President George W. Bush has caused noteworthy damage to international law. It becomes increasingly clear that in order to achieve a more secure and peaceful world it is unacceptable to erode international law. The only avenue to achieve that goal is to strengthen international law in the US. In the words of their own courts, in *Filártiga*: "The requirement that a rule command the 'general assent of civilized nations' to become binding upon them all is a stringent one. Were this not so, the courts of one nation might feel free to impose idiosyncratic legal rules upon others, in the name of applying international law."[1310]

The US legal treatment of international law is quite erratic. On the one hand, they had a seminal role in founding the post World War II system of international law, especially for the protection of human rights. In the aftermath they did not abide by the rules they had established themselves. According to Ignatieff,[1311] this American exceptionalism has three facets:
(1) Exemptionalism – the US supports international treaties as long as they are exempt from them,
(2) Double standards – the US criticizes others for not complying with the findings of international human rights bodies, but ignores what these bodies say of the United States, and
(3) Legal isolationism – the tendency of US American judges to ignore other jurisdictions or comparative law.

Even though this conclusion on the status of international law in the US is rather disillusioning, it should be noted that the US also applies the most progressive approach in holding TNCs accountable to international human rights: ATCA. ATCA was created by the US legislation and executive branch in 1789, developed largely by the US judiciary since the 1980s, affirmed by the US legislation and executive branch in 1992 by enacting the TVPA[1312] and affirmed by the Supreme Court in 2004 in the *Sosa* case.[1313]

Foreign Relations Law of the United States' 86 American Journal of International Law 608 (1992) at 614.

1309 A Glashauser, 'Difference and Deference in Treaty Interpretation' 50 Villanova Law Review 25 (2005) at 84.

1310 *Filártiga v. Peña-Irala*, 630 F2d 876, C.A. 2 (1980) at 881 (quoting *The Paquete Habana*, 175 US 677, US S.Ct. (1900) at 694.

1311 For the general concept of American exceptionalism see HH Koh, 'On American Exceptionalism' 55 Stanford Law Review 1479 (2003).

1312 See above under subheading "International law and the US legislation".

1313 Concerning the *Sosa* affirmation see above in chapter III, subheading "VI. *Sosa* decision" at

Chapter VII. Role of international law in ATCA litigation

In the United States the championship series of the national baseball competition is called the "World Series," even though only US and a small number of Canadian teams can compete in that league. Is the same *Weltanschauung* reflected in the US perspective on the role of international law in ATCA litigation? Do US courts put the label "international law" on laws that are basically derived from US law? Is the US bound to follow international law? Is the US bound by international treaties that they have ratified or signed? Is the US bound by international customary law or other sources of international law? How should international law be determined?

This chapter examines how international law and the sources of international law are dealt with in ATCA litigation. It is a worldwide trend that domestic courts have to deal with questions of international public law.[1314] Largely due to ATCA litigation, questions concerning international law are increasingly reaching courtrooms in the United States.[1315]

Children in Nigeria were subjected to medical experimentation by the US corporation Pfizer.[1316] This may amount to a violation of Article 7 of the *ICCPR*, but what is the significance of this provision in treaty law in a US courtroom? It seems that international law does not behave in the same prescriptive manner as municipal law. The binding nature of international law is based on the consent of the states that are active members of the international community. States can interpret the law in accordance with their interests, they can attempt to change it, and they can choose to ignore it, so long as they are prepared to accept the political, economic and possibly even military consequences.

119.

1314 *Case concerning the arrest warrant of 11 April 2000 (Democratic Republic of the Congo v. Belgium)*, 2000 ICJ 182, ICJ (2000) at 232 ("States engaging in the domestic prosecution of such crimes as well as States called upon to co-operate with these States in extradition proceedings are confronted with applying norms of international criminal law. Increasingly, domestic courts are called upon to tackle difficult technical notions of public international law such as *jus cogens*, *erga omnes* obligations and the question what norms qualify as norms of customary international (criminal) law. The various Pinochet decisions (in Spain, Belgium, France and the United Kingdom) and the Dutch Bouterse case are examples of a growing number of national judicial decisions dealing with (different aspects) of the issues of international criminal law that are now before the International Court of Justice.")

1315 MA Weisburd, 'American Judges and International Law' 36 Vanderbilt Journal of Transnational Law 1475 (2003) at 1476.

1316 *Abdullahi v. Pfizer*, No 01 Civ 8118, 2002 US Dist LEXIS 17436, 2002 WL 31082956, D.C. S.D. N.Y. (2002).

Overall, it is not easy to construe international law, since there is no one body that has the ultimate power to make definitive determinations as to the interpretation of international law. This can be contrasted with the situation at the national level. Interpretation of international law will often have some degree of uncertainty.[1317] This chapter will look more specifically at the determination of international law and its authoritativeness in the ATCA litigation.

Some argue that the US courts do not employ a thorough analysis of international law in their decision making. The former US Supreme Court Justice, Sandra Day O'Connor, commented that even though American law still does not properly interpret international law, American judges are becoming more aware of their responsibilities to respect the law of nations.[1318] Bekker is of the opinion that the most fundamental problem underlying many ATCA rulings, especially in cases involving corporate defendants, is that "they lack a complete and consistent discussion or understanding of the sources and evidence of international law, especially in connection with 'soft-law' such as United Nations resolutions."[1319]

I. Sources of international law

Where do we find international law? Is a judgment of the ICJ a source of international law? A resolution by the UN General assembly? A convention ratified by 180 states? Diplomatic correspondence? The *UDHR*?

As noted above, a fundamental problem of international law is the absence of a single highest authority for the interpretation of international law. In municipal legal systems the sources – such as constitutions, statutes and precedents – are accepted and their structure or hierarchy is mostly well-defined. International law is determined using different sources and the structure and hierarchy of those sources is contentiously debated and uncertain. The sources of international law have a decentralized and non-hierarchical structure, meaning that the legislation and enforcement are largely assigned to the states. Jordan Paust stated that "international law is a complex and dynamic process profoundly interconnected with regional and domestic legal processes throughout the globe. There are no single sources or evidences of international law; no single set of participants and no single arenas or

---

1317 J Kammerhofer, 'Uncertainty in the Formal Sources of International Law: Customary International Law and Some of its Problems' 15 European Journal of International Law 523 (2004).

1318 PHF Bekker, *The Treatment of Evidentiary Sources of International Law in US Alien Tort Statute Cases (Europa Instituut of Leiden University)* (Kluwer, 2004) at 166; SD O'Connor, 'American Law Institute Speech May 15, 2002' (2002) <http://www.angelfire.com/ mi2/ aicap/ AmericanLawInstitute.html > (April 18, 2006).

1319 PHF Bekker, *The Treatment of Evidentiary Sources of International Law in US Alien Tort Statute Cases (Europa Instituut of Leiden University)* (Kluwer, 2004) at 157.

institutional arrangements for the creation, invocation, application, change or termination of such law."[1320]

Even though Article 38 of the *Statute of the International Court of Justice* is solely an expression of the sources that the ICJ uses for the interpretation of international law, it is generally accepted as the definitive statement of the sources of international law.[1321] Some scholars argue that Article 38 represents a *numerus clausus* of the sources of international law.[1322] This, however, should be repudiated. First, the *ICJ Statute* is itself an international agreement and can be further developed by the sources that are named in the *Statute*. Second, the *ICJ Statute* does not attempt comprehensively to regulate the question of the sources of international law, but only to lay down the organizational structure of the ICJ. Third, if the sources in Article 38 were exhaustive, this could preclude further development in international law.[1323]

Article 38 provides that international law has three primary sources: international treaties; customary international law; and general principles of law. In order to determine the content of international law, the Court is entitled to refer to judicial decisions and academic writing as subsidiary means. It is arguable that the practices of international organizations, most notably of the United Nations, are additional sources of international law, even though they are not mentioned in Article 38.[1324]

Which sources of international law are used in ATCA litigation? Section 102 of the Restatement of the Foreign Relations Law of the United States has the same content as Article 38 of the *Statute of the ICJ* and enumerates the sources of international law. Article 38 is also mentioned in many ATCA cases.[1325] In *Filártiga*, the Court stated: "we find the norms of contemporary international law by consulting the works of jurists, writing professedly on public law; or by the general usage and practice of nations; or by judicial decisions recognizing and enforcing that law."[1326]

[1320] JJ Paust, 'The Reality of Private Rights, Duties, and Participation in the International Legal Process' 25 Michigan Journal of International Law 1229 (2004) at 1229.

[1321] G Dahm, J Delbrück and R Wolfrum, *Völkerrecht* (2nd edn, De Gruyter, Berlin; New York 1989) at 44; I Brownlie, *Principles of Public International Law* (6th edn, Oxford University Press, Oxford; New York 2003) at 5.

[1322] See, e.g., K Doehring, *Völkerrecht* (2nd edn, Müller (C.F.Jur), Heidelberg 2004) at 284; I Seidl-Hohenveldern and T Stein, *Völkerrecht* (10th edn, Academia iuris and index, C. Heymann, Köln 2000) at 173.

[1323] K Nowrot, *Normative Ordnungsstruktur und private Wirkungsmacht - Konsequenzen der Beteiligung transnationaler Unternehmen an den Rechtssetzungsprozessen im internationalen Wirtschaftssystem* (BWV Berliner Wissenschafts-Verlag, Berlin 2006) at 141 et *seq.*

[1324] Krzysztof Skubiszewski, International Legislation, in R Bernhardt, *Encyclopedia of Public International Law, IV* (North-Holland Elsevier, Amsterdam 2000).

[1325] *Almog v. Arab Bank, PLC*, 471 FSupp2d 257, D.C. E.D.N.Y. (2007); *In re Agent Orange Product Liability Litigation*, 373 FSupp2d 7, D.C. E.D. N.Y. (2005); *Flores v. Southern Peru Copper Corporation*, 343 F3d 140, C.A. 2 (2003) and *Presbyterian Church of Sudan et al. v. Talisman Energy, Inc.*, 244 F Supp 2d 289, D.C. S.D. N.Y. (2003).

[1326] *Filártiga v. Peña-Irala*, 630 F2d 876, C.A. 2 (1980) at 880, quoting *United States v. Smith*, 18

Overall, it can be said that US courts in ATCA litigation theoretically refer to the same sources of international law used in international law. It is more interesting, however to look at the application of the sources of international law.

II. International treaties

The ATCA states: "The district courts shall have original jurisdiction of any civil action by an alien for a tort only, committed in violation of the law of nations or *a treaty of the United States*."[1327] It is important to understand that ATCA includes two alternatives, referred to as two prongs. The first prong is "violating the law of nations" and the second prong is "violating a treaty of the United States." The second prong – violating an international treaty – has been left largely unexamined and has not been a basis for a claim since ATCA was revived with the *Filártiga decision* in 1980.[1328]

On its face, this prong would mean that any violation of a treaty to which the United States is a party could be the base for an ATCA claim, but this is not so. In order to bring a claim under this prong – violating international treaties – the United States would have to be a party to the relevant treaty.

In addition, to invoke the treaty-prong of ATCA, the treaty must be either self-executing or has been implemented in the United States by domestic legislation. In the latter case, the claimant would pursue its claim under the national legislation. At this point in time self-executing treaties have not been the basis for an ATCA claim. This also explains why this dissertation deals with international treaties rather briefly, notwithstanding its importance in international law.

A. International treaties in international law

The first source of international law is international treaties. While the international community does not have a legislative body therefore no "international legislation," international treaties are the closest substitute.[1329] According to prevailing opinion,

---

US (5 Wheat) 153, 5 LEd 57, US S.Ct. (1820b) at 160-161.

1327 Aliens Tort Claims Act 1789, 28 U.S.C., § 1350(1789) (emphasis added).

1328 K Randall, 'Federal Jurisdiction over International Law Claims: Inquiries. into the Alien Tort Statute' 18 New York University Journal of International Law and Politics 91 (1985) at 46. See also S Zia-Zarifi, 'Suing Multinational Corporations in the US for Violating International Law' 4 UCLA Journal of International Law and Foreign Affairs 81 (1999) at footnote 31. There have been no cases relying on the violation of a treaty since 1999. The only exception of a claim based on a treaty signed by the United States has been the case of *Bolchos v. Darrell*, 3 F Cas 810 (No 1,607), US District of South Dakota (1795), see also K Randall, 'Federal Jurisdiction over International Law Claims: Inquiries. into the Alien Tort Statute' 18 New York University Journal of International Law and Politics 91 (1985) at 49 ff.

1329 G Dahm, J Delbrück and R Wolfrum, *Völkerrecht* (2nd edn, De Gruyter, Berlin; New York 1989) at 512; A Aust, *Handbook of International Law* (1st edn, Cambridge University Press, Cambridge; New York 2005) at 6.

international treaties represent the most important source.[1330] In international economic law, the most important are the Treaties of Friendship, Trade and Navigation, the bilateral investment treaties and also bilateral free trade agreements. Multilateral agreements are also important in international economic law, especially after World War II. These include, for example, the WTO treaties, the EU treaties, *NAFTA* and Mercosur.[1331] Lastly, there are the international treaties that set up international economic organizations, such as the Organisation for Economic Co-operation and Development (OECD), International Monetary Fund (IMF), Worldbank, International Labour Organization (ILO), Universal Postal Union (UPU), International Telecommunication Union (ITU) and World Intellectual Property Organization (WIPO).[1332]

Many people speak about human rights, but the sources of international human rights law are less settled. The sources of international human rights can be found in international treaties. The *UDHR* is widely recognized as articulating a common definition of human dignity and values.[1333] The *UDHR*, together with the *ICESCR*,

---

1330 T Oppermann and E-U Petersmann, *Reforming the International Economic Order: German Legal Comments* (Tübinger Schriften zum internationalen und europäischen Recht; Bd 1, Duncker & Humblot, Berlin 1987) at 194 ("Without doubt, the international treaty, inclusive of the statues setting up organizations, is the primary legal instrument on which the current international economic order is based."); G Dahm, J Delbrück and R Wolfrum, *Völkerrecht* (2nd edn, De Gruyter, Berlin; New York 1989) at 49; Tietje in A Zimmermann, R Hofmann and H Goeters, *Unity and Diversity in International Law: Proceedings of an International Symposium of the Kiel Walther Schücking Institute of International Law, November 4-7, 2004* (Veröffentlichungen des Walther-Schücking-Instituts für Internationales Recht an der Universität Kiel, 157, Duncker & Humblot, Berlin 2006) at 190.

1331 Agreement Establishing the World Trade Organization (Marrakesh Agreement) 33 ILM 1143; April 5, 1994 (entered into force January 1, 1995) (1994); Treaty Establishing the European Community Mar 25, 1957, 298 UNTS 11, as amended by Treaty of Amsterdam, Oct 2, 1997, 1997 OJ (C 340) 1, as amended by Treaty of Nice, Feb 26, 2001, 2001 OJ (C 80) 1, consolidated version reprinted in 2002 OJ (C 325) 33 (1957); North American Free Trade Agreement, US-Can.-Mex. Dec 17, 1992, 32 ILM 289 (1993); Treaty Establishing a Common Market between the Argentine Republic, the Federative Republic of Brazil, the Republic of Paraguay and the Eastern Republic of Uruguay 30 ILM 1044 (1991).

1332 Convention on the Organisation for Economic Co-operation and Development Dec 14, 1960, 12 UST 1728 (1960); Articles of Agreement of the International Monetary Fund July 22, 1944 (entered into force December 27, 1945), last amended effective November 11, 1992, 31 ILM 1307 (1944); Revised Constitution of the International Labor Organization 9 October 1946, 15 UNTS, 35 (1946); Constitution of the Universal Postal Union July 10, 1964, 611 UNTS 7 (1964); Constitution of the International Telecommunication Union Oct 14, 1994, 1996 WL 569887 (1994); Convention Establishing the World Intellectual Property Organization July 14, 1967, 828 UNTS 3 (1967); See also K Nowrot, *Normative Ordnungsstruktur und private Wirkungsmacht - Konsequenzen der Beteiligung transnationaler Unternehmen an den Rechtssetzungsprozessen im internationalen Wirtschaftssystem* (BWV Berliner Wissenschafts-Verlag, Berlin 2006), with further references.

1333 Universal Declaration of Human Rights GA Res 217 A(III), UN Doc A/810 at 71 (1948). See *United States v. Iran (May 24)*, 1980 ICJ Reports 3, ICJ (1980) at para 90 ("Wrongfully to deprive human beings of their freedom and to subject them to physical constraint in conditions

the *ICCPR* and the two Optional Protocols can be used as a yardstick by which to measure the degree of respect for, and compliance with, international human rights standards everywhere.

Additionally, there are many important international conventions, such as the *Genocide Convention* of 1948,[1334] the *Convention on the Elimination of all Forms of Discrimination against Women* from 1979,[1335] *Convention against Torture* from 1984[1336] and many others.[1337] These conventions are the main treaty-based sources for international human rights law.

B. International treaties in ATCA litigation

As a small introductory side note on the historical context, it should be noted that at the time of the enactment of the ATCA in 1789, the United States was party to fewer treaties than it is today. It had treaties of "Amity and Commerce" with France, the Netherlands, Sweden, and Prussia.[1338] Each of those treaties contained provisions guaranteeing safe-conducts to aliens, agreeing to the mutual defense of vessels from attack by enemies and pirates, and agreeing to provide immunity to dignitaries.[1339]

There have been one case and one Attorney General advisory opinion concerning the treaty-violation-prong of ATCA. The case being *Bolchos v. Darrell* in 1795 and the Attorney General advisory opinion of 1907.[1340] *Bolchos* and the Attorney General's opinion broadly interpreted the treaty element of the ATCA. Interestingly, both

---

of hardship is in itself manifestly incompatible with the principles of the Charter of the United Nations, as well as with the fundamental principles enunciated in the Universal Declaration of Human Rights."); P Alston, 'The Universal Declaration at 35: Western and Passé or Alive and Universal' 31 International Commission of Jurists Review 60 (1982) at 69; See H Hannum, 'The Status of the Universal Declaration of Human Rights in National and International Law' 25 Georgia Journal of International and Comparative Law 287 (1995) at 323-339 with many further references.

1334 Convention on the Prevention and Punishment of the Crime of Genocide December 9, 1948, 78 UNTS 277, approved and proposed for signature and ratification or accession by General Assembly resolution 260 A (III) of 9 December 1948, entered into force Jan 12, 1951 (Genocide Convention) (1948).

1335 Convention on the Elimination of All Forms of Discrimination against Women 1249 UNTS 13, adopted and opened for signature, ratification and accession by General Assembly resolution 34/180 of December 18, 1979, entered into force September 3, 1981 (1979).

1336 Convention Against Torture and Other Cruel Inhuman or Degrading Treatment or Punishment 10 December 1984, 1465 UNTS 85 (entered into force 26 June 1987) (1984).

1337 Office of the High Commissioner for Human Rights, 'International Human Rights Instruments' <http://www.unhchr.ch/html/intlinst.htm> (March 21, 2007).

1338 K Randall, 'Federal Jurisdiction over International Law Claims: Inquiries. into the Alien Tort Statute' 18 New York University Journal of International Law and Politics 91 (1985) at 49.

1339 *Ibid.* at 46.

1340 *Bolchos v. Darrell*, 3 F Cas 810 (No 1,607), US District of South Dakota (1795), see K Randall, 'Federal Jurisdiction over International Law Claims: Inquiries. into the Alien Tort Statute' 18 New York University Journal of International Law and Politics 91 (1985) at 49-50.

opinions found that the ATCA provides plaintiffs with a private cause of action for a treaty violation and, accordingly, that an individual or private party can sue and be sued for such treaty violations.[1341]

In *Sosa*, the US Supreme Court found that the *UDHR* held little weight, since it does not, in and of itself, impose obligations as a matter of international law.[1342] The United States ratified the *ICCPR* on the express understanding that it was not self-executing and did not itself create obligations enforceable in the federal courts.[1343] As noted above, a self-executing treaty is one where no domestic legislation is required to give it the force of law in the United States.[1344] The vast majority of international treaties, including all human rights treaties, are not self-executing. Examples of self-executing treaties come from the area of economic treaties, as Friendship, Commerce, and Navigation Treaties, as well as the more recent bilateral investment treaties and their lineal descendants.[1345]

Therefore, the plaintiff in *Sosa* could not rely on the *UDHR* to prove a violation of international law. Similarly, the Court of Appeals for the Second Circuit in *Flores v. Southern Peru Copper* found the *ICESCR* to be "vague and aspirational, and there is no evidence that the states parties have taken significant uniform steps to put it into practice."[1346]

In *Mehinovic v. Vuckovic*, *Estate of Winston Cabello v. Armando Fernandez-Larios*, *Ralk v. Lincoln County, Ga.* the courts have relied on the violations of the *ICCPR* in finding the applicable law in ATCA cases.[1347] These decisions, in turn, were based on the decision in *Abebe- Jiri v. Negewo*.[1348] In *Abebe*, the District Court for the Northern District of Georgia found that the violation of cruel and degrading treatment "is found in all of the major international human rights treaties, including the *ICCPR* ratified by the United States in September 1992 and the *Convention Against Torture and Other Cruel, Inhuman and Degrading Treatment or Punishment*."[1349]

1341 K Randall, 'Federal Jurisdiction over International Law Claims: Inquiries. into the Alien Tort Statute' 18 New York University Journal of International Law and Politics 91 (1985) at 50.

1342 *Sosa v. Alvarez-Machain* (03-339) 542 US 2739, US S.Ct. (2004) at 734.

1343 *Ibid.* at 734.

1344 *Trans World Airlines, Inc. v. Franklin Mint Corp.*, 466 US 243, US S.Ct. (1984) at 252. See chapter VI, subheading "A. International law and the US Constitution" at 222.

1345 RE Dalton, 'National Treaty Law and Practice: United States' in M Leigh, MR Blakeslee and B Ederington (eds) *National Treaty Law and Practice* (American Society of International Law, Washington, D.C. 1999) at 12.

1346 *Flores v. Southern Peru Copper Corporation*, 343 F3d 140, C.A. 2 (2003) at 90.

1347 See *Mehinovic v. Vuckovic*, 198 FSupp2d 1322, D.C. N.D. Ga. (2002); *Estate of Winston Cabello v. Armando Fernandez-Larios*, 157 FSupp2d 1345, US S.D.Fla. (2001); *Ralk v. Lincoln County, Georgia*, 81 FSupp2d 1372, D.C. S.D.Ga. (2000).

1348 *Abebe-Jira v. Negewo*, 72 F3d 844, C.A. 11 (1996) at 844.

1349 *Abebe-Jiri v. Negewo*, Not reported in FSupp, 1993 WL 814304, D.C. N.D. Ga. (1993).

In the *Ralk* decision of 2000, the District Court for the Southern District of Georgia found plaintiffs could bring a claim under the ATCA for violations of the *ICCPR*. It took notice of the reservations of the US to the *ICCPR*, but found that the allegations at hand fell outside the US reservations to the Treaty.[1350] In the *Cabello* decision of 2001, the District Court for the Southern District of Florida found that Article 6 of the *ICCPR* represents customary international law, violations of which may be remedied by suits filed under the ATCA.[1351] In the *Mehinovic* decision of 2002, the District Court for the Northern District of Georgia cited the *ICCPR* and the *Convention Against Torture and Other Cruel, Inhuman and Degrading Treatment or Punishment* as authority for the proposition that torture violates obligatory norms of customary international law.[1352]

In the *Talisman* decision in 2005 the Court found that the *Rome Statute* of the ICC could be considered as authority for the proposition that there existed liability for aiding and abetting under international law sufficient to sustain claim under ATCA, even though it had been only ratified by 100 of 191 United Nations member states.[1353] The accordance of authority to the *Rome Statute* is especially interesting in light of the fact that the United States did not sign the *Rome Statute*.[1354]

In summary, treaties may not have the same importance in ATCA litigation now in comparison with the first years of ATCA. Previously, it appears that all treaties to which the United States is a party are held to be self-executing. However, treaties ratified by the US are, in some decisions, given considerable weight in ATCA litigation even today. Strictly speaking, they are not applied as a breach of treaty under the ATCA but under the prong of representing customary international law.

The scope for violations of treaties was broadened by the *Sarei* decisions.[1355] The scope of the ATCA also encompasses treaties that have not been ratified, but only signed by the US, as in the case of the *UNCLOS*. According to *Sarei*, *UNCLOS* represents customary international law and a breach of the *UNCLOS* may lead to an ATCA claim.[1356]

1350 *Ralk v. Lincoln County, Georgia*, 81 FSupp2d 1372, D.C. S.D.Ga. (2000) at 1381. The US ratified the *ICCPR* with the reservation that "Art. 7 protections shall not extend beyond protections of the 5th, 8th and 14th Amendments of the US Constitution." Senate Comm. on Foreign Relations Report on the International Covenant on Civil and Political Rights, S. Exec. Rep. No. 23, 102nd Cong., 2d Sess. (1992), reprinted in 31 I.L.M. 645, 646 (1992).

1351 *Estate of Winston Cabello v. Armando Fernandez-Larios*, 157 FSupp2d 1345, US S.D.Fla. (2001) at 1361.

1352 *Mehinovic v. Vuckovic*, 198 FSupp2d 1322, D.C. N.D. Ga. (2002) at 1345.

1353 *The Presbyterian Church of Sudan, et. al. v. Talisman Energy, Inc.*, 374 FSupp2d 331, D.C. S.D. N.Y. (2005) at 339.

1354 Rome Statute of the International Criminal Court July 17, 1998, 2187 UNTS 90 (1998).

1355 *Sarei v. Rio Tinto PLC*, 221 FSupp2d 1116, D.C. C.D. Cal. (2002) at 1161, 1187 and 1190; *Sarei v. Rio Tinto, PLC*, 487 F3d 1193, C.A. 9 (2007) at 11.

1356 *Sarei v. Rio Tinto PLC*, 221 FSupp2d 1116, D.C. C.D. Cal. (2002) at 1161.

C. Analysis to international treaties

It is interesting to note that whereas treaties pertaining to international economic law are found to be self-executing, human rights treaties and international environmental treaties are not. However, it seems that breaches of human rights treaties and international environmental law treaties are increasingly taken into consideration as a basis for an ATCA claim. Breaches of those treaties are, according to ATCA litigation, breaches of the "law of nations." By enforcing non-self-executing treaties through customary international law, the difference between non-self-executing and self-executing treaties becomes less important. On one view, therefore, the US resembles more closely a monistic system or, at least, it cannot be said that it is strictly dualistic. International treaties are increasingly important in ATCA litigation. The "threshold question" remains, however, whether the conduct alleged falls under the first prong of ATCA and violates the law of nations, meaning customary international law.[1357]

III. Customary international law

As noted previously, the ATCA gives jurisdiction in respect of "any civil action by an alien for a tort only, committed in violation of *the law of nations* or a treaty of the United States."[1358] Since most international treaties of the US, especially human rights treaties, are not self-executing, it is necessary to have recourse to the first prong of ATCA "law of nations," which in this context refers to customary international law.

Some say that customary international law is epiphenomenal, in that it cannot and does not influence state behavior.[1359] There is no legislative body that enacts customary international law. There is no book, commentary nor judicial body which can be seen as authoritative source for stating, interpreting or applying customary international law. There is no sovereign to control the enforcement of international customary law.[1360] Likewise, there is no court with compulsory jurisdiction over states. The subjects of international law are also the law enforcers. The subjects of international law may also alter the rules of international law simply by their behavior. This leads to an especially peculiar difference between it and municipal law: a violation of customary international law may not only lead to a sanction, but also to a change of the law.

1357 *Filártiga v. Peña-Irala*, 630 F2d 876, C.A. 2 (1980) at 880.

1358 Aliens Tort Claims Act 1789, 28 U.S.C., § 1350(1789)(emphasis added).

1359 JL Goldsmith and EA Posner, *The Limits of International Law* (Oxford University Press, Oxford; New York 2005) at 13 for example; see also Av Aaken, 'To Do Away with International Law? Some limits to the 'The Limits of International Law'' 17 European Journal of International Law 289 (2006) at 291.

1360 MA Weisburd, 'American Judges and International Law' 36 Vanderbilt Journal of Transnational Law 1475 (2003) at 1478.

A. Customary international law in international law

Customary international law is the second source of international law. Hans Kelsen defined customary international law to mean that states ought to behave in such a manner as the others usually or customarily behave.[1361] Customary international law includes three elements: (a) Widespread repetition by states of similar international acts over time (state practice); (b) Acts must occur out of a sense of obligation (*opinio juris*); and (c) Acts must be taken by a significant number of states and not be rejected by a significant number of states.[1362] In other words, customary international law must be derived from a clear consensus among states, as exhibited both by widespread conduct and a discernible sense of obligation. A state can deny a rule of customary international law though, by showing that it has persistently objected to it.

Practice of states means official governmental conduct reflected in a variety of acts, including diplomatic correspondence, press releases, the opinions of official legal advisors, executive decisions and practices, comments by governments on drafts by the ILC and state legislation. In addition, decisions of national courts may in themselves be evidence of state practice on a particular topic. In an important early case, *The Lotus* case of 1927, the Permanent Court of International Justice (PCIJ) examined decisions of French national courts in order to discover what the state practice of France was on the subject at hand.[1363] Also, according to the ICJ customary law can evolve within a short period of time.[1364]

Opinio juris, short for *opinio juris sive necissitatis* is the belief that the behavior was done because it was a legal obligation. The precise meaning of *opinio juris* has been much debated. An insightful explanation comes from the ICJ: "Not only must the acts concerned amount to a settled practice, but they must also be such, or be carried out in such a way, as to be *evidence of a belief that this practice is rendered obligatory by the existence of a rule of law requiring it.* The need for such a belief, i.e., the

1361 H Kelsen, *Pure Theory of Law* (University of California Press, Berkeley 1967) at 216.

1362 See, e.g., *North Sea Continental Shelf (F.R.G. v. Den., F.R.G. v. Neth.)*, ICJ 3, ICJ (1969) at 41 et seq ; *Asylum Case (Columbia v. Peru)*, ICJ Reports 1950, 266, ICJ (1950) at 276 et *seq.*; MB Akehurst, 'Custom as a Source of International Law' 47 British Yearbook of International Law 1 (1974) at 1 et *seq.*; G Dahm, J Delbrück and R Wolfrum, *Völkerrecht* (2nd edn, De Gruyter, Berlin; New York 1989), I/1, pages 56 et *seq.*

1363 *Lotus*, PCIJ Ser A, No 10, PCIJ (1927) at 18 ("The rules of law binding upon states...emanate from their own free will as expressed in conventions or by usages generally accepted as expressing principles of law.")

1364 *North Sea Continental Shelf (F.R.G. v. Den., F.R.G. v. Neth.)*, ICJ 3, ICJ (1969) at para 74 ("Although the passage of only a short period of time is not necessarily, or of itself, a bar to the formation of a new rule of customary international law on the basis of what was originally a purely conventional rule, an indispensable requirement would be that within the period in question, short though it might be, State practice, including that of States whose interests are specially affected, should have been both extensive and virtually uniform in the sense of the provision invoked; -and should moreover have occurred in such a way as to show a general recognition that a rule of law or legal obligation is involved.")

existence of a subjective element, is implicit in the very notion of the *opinio juris sive necessitatis*. The states concerned must therefore feel that they are conforming to what amounts to a legal obligation.

The legal philosopher, Finnis, argues that this finding is paradoxical, since it proposes that a customary law can only come into existence in the event of an erroneous belief that it is already in existence.[1365] A possible solution might be that *opinio juris* emerges when states regularly start treating a behavior as legally required.[1366]

The frequency or even habitual character of the acts is not in itself enough. There are many international acts, e.g., in the field of ceremonial and protocol, which are performed almost invariably, but which are motivated only by considerations of courtesy, convenience or tradition, and not by any sense of legal duty."[1367]

Customary law might best be understood by looking at an example. One of the most interesting examples of evolving customary law may be the delimitation of territorial seas.[1368] At the turn of the 18th Century, the Dutch jurist Bynkershoek formulated the "cannon-shot" rule, declaring that the territorial domain of the state extends as far as projectiles could be thrown from onshore cannon.[1369]

This rule was adopted by the United States in 1793, gained widespread and rapid acceptance, and the limitation survived throughout the 19th century.[1370] However, the dramatic improvements to distant-water fishing techniques led to a massive increase in fish takings. This amounted to overfishing, especially by developed naval nations, in the coastal waters of less developed nations. Both the First United Nations Conference on the Law of the Sea (*UNCLOS* I) from 1958 and the Second United Nations Conference on the Law of the Sea (*UNCLOS* II) from 1960 failed to fix a uniform breadth for the territorial sea or establish consensus on sovereign fishing rights. The failure of the conferences to reach agreement provoked states to take matters into their own hands and resulted in a proliferation of divergent state practices.

1365 J.M.Finnis in JE Raz, *Authority* (B. Blackwell, Oxford 1990) at 180.

1366 BD Lepard, 'Is the United States Obligated to Drive on the Right? A Multidisciplinary Inquiry into the Normative Authority of Contemporary International Law Using the Arm's Length Standard as a Case Study' 10 Duke Journal of Comparative and International Law 43 (1999) at 162, citing FR Tesón, *A Philosophy of International Law* (New perspectives on law, culture, and society, Westview Press, Boulder 1998) at 86.

1367 *North Sea Continental Shelf (F.R.G. v. Den., F.R.G. v. Neth.)*, ICJ 3, ICJ (1969) at 44.

1368 See also ML Lee, 'The Interrelation between the Law of the Sea Convention and Customary International Law' 7 San Diego International Law Journal 405 (2006) at 412 et *seq.*

1369 See SA Swarztrauber, *The Three-Mile Limit of Territorial Seas* (Naval Institute Press, Annapolis 1972) at 2.

1370 RR Churchill and AV Lowe, *The Law of the Sea* (Manchester University Press, Manchester; New York 1988) at 65.

While most Western nations maintained the three-mile limit, newly-independent African states began to claim much wider territorial seas.[1371] So too did the Latin American countries. The *Santa Domingo Declaration* was issued in 1972 and was adopted by Columbia, Costa Rica, Guatemala, Haiti, Honduras, Mexico, Nicaragua, Trinidad and Tobago and Venezuela.[1372] It provided for a 12 mile territorial sea, together with a 200 mile "patrimonial sea." Most states now claimed 12 miles territorial sea zone. Finally, the Third United Nations Conference on the Law of the Sea (*UNCLOS* III) from 1973 to 1982 included the definition of maritime zones: the territorial sea was set at 12 miles and the exclusive economic zone at 200 miles, which represents customary law today. *UNCLOS* entered into force in 1994. So, this is an example of customary international law being "codified" into an international treaty.

B. Customary international law in ATCA litigation

In the ATCA litigation, the term "law of nations" refers to the body of law known as customary international law.[1373] All ATCA claims since the *Filártiga* decision in 1980 have been based on customary international law. But what constitutes customary international law for the purposes of the ATCA litigation? In *Sosa* the Supreme Court warned the courts in the ATCA litigation that "when deciding whether alleged norm of international law is sufficiently definite that violation thereof will support cause of action that district may hear under the Alien Tort Statute (ATS), district court, in absence of any treaty, or of any controlling executive or legislative act or judicial decision, must resort to the customs and usages of civilized nations and, as evidence thereof, to works of jurists and commentators, not for their speculations as to what the law ought to be, but for trustworthy evidence of what the law really is."[1374]

In *Flores v. Southern Peru Copper*, the Court of Appeals for the Second Circuit held that it was not a simple task to determine what offenses violate customary international law. "Customary international law is discerned from myriad decisions made in numerous and varied international and domestic arenas.

Furthermore, the relevant evidence of customary international law is widely dispersed and generally unfamiliar to lawyers and judges. These difficulties are compounded by the fact that customary international law – as the term itself implies – is created by the general customs and practices of nations and therefore does not stem from any

---

1371 NS Rembe, *Africa and the International Law of the Sea: A Study of the Contribution of the African States to the Third United Nations Conference on the Law of the Sea* (Sijthoff publications on ocean development, Sijthoff & Noordhoff, Alphen aan den Rijn; Germantown 1980).

1372 L Galvis and D Kovalik, 'Santo Domingo Massacre in Colombia, A Testimony' (2005) <http://www.zmag.org/content/showarticle.cfm?ItemID=8907> (June 21, 2006).

1373 *Villeda Aldana v. Fresh Del Monte Produce, Inc.*, 305 F Supp 2d 1285, D.C. S.D. Fla. (2003).

1374 *Sosa v. Alvarez-Machain* (03-339) 542 US 2739, US S.Ct. (2004) at 2767.

single, definitive, readily-identifiable source."[1375] The District Court of the Southern District of Florida held that citing sources of international law that merely refer to a general sense of responsibility and state abstract rights and liberties devoid of articulable or discernible standards and regulations to identify practices that constitute international abuses or torts is insufficient to support a claim that particular conduct is universally proscribed by the law of nations.[1376]

Flores is the ATCA decision that most explicitly deals with the subject of customary international law. It states that, in theory, the method for deriving the content of customary international law is similar to that of international law more generally. For customary international law to develop it needs to have both of the following elements: objectively assessed state practice and subjectively assessed *opinio juris*. Of primary significance are the formal lawmaking and official actions of states. Acts and practices of states constitute the essential evidence of whether states follow a rule as a legal obligation. This investigation into state practice is the decisive part of determining international law. Obviously, not all states need to follow customary international law, since then there would be no need for customary international law.[1377] The practice of states, in turn, "embraces not only their external conduct with each other, but is also evidenced by such internal matters as their domestic legislation, judicial decisions, diplomatic dispatches, internal government memoranda, and ministerial statements in Parliaments and elsewhere."[1378]

A principle of customary international law only exists if states accede to it out of a sense of legal obligation; this is what is meant by opinio *juris*.[1379] Citing the ICJ *North Sea Continental Shelf* case, the Court in *Villeda Aldana v. Fresh Del Monte* noted that customary international law does not include practices that states have adopted for moral or political reasons.[1380] Courts ought to proceed with extraordinary care and restraint in determining what offenses violate customary international law.[1381]

ATCA litigation also requires that the matter be *of mutual concern* in order to represent customary international law. The mere fact that every nation's municipal law may prohibit theft does not incorporate the Eighth Commandment "Thou Shalt not steal" into the law of nations.[1382] Offenses that may be purely intra-national in

---

1375 *Flores v. Southern Peru Copper Corporation*, 343 F3d 140, C.A. 2 (2003) at 80.
1376 *Villeda Aldana v. Fresh Del Monte Produce, Inc.*, 305 F Supp 2d 1285, D.C. S.D. Fla. (2003).
1377 *Flores v. Southern Peru Copper Corporation*, 343 F3d 140, C.A. 2 (2003) at 80.
1378 *Ibid.* at footnote 22 (quoting L Oppenheim, RY Jennings and A Watts, *Oppenheim's International Law* (9th edn, Longman, Harlow 1992) at 26).
1379 *Flores v. Southern Peru Copper Corporation*, 343 F3d 140, C.A. 2 (2003) at 80, cited from the Restatement (Third) of Foreign Relations Law (1987) § 102 (2).
1380 *Flores v. Southern Peru Copper Corporation*, 343 F3d 140, C.A. 2 (2003) at 80.
1381 *Ibid.* at 80.
1382 *Filártiga v. Peña-Irala*, 630 F2d 876, C.A. 2 (1980) at 888.

their execution, such as official torture, extrajudicial killings, and genocide, do violate customary international law because the "nations of the world" have demonstrated that such wrongs are of "mutual concern," and capable of impairing international peace and security. This finding was backed by materials from the Nuremberg tribunals that held that the "force of circumstance" and the "grim fact of worldwide interdependence" dictated crimes against humanity are proscribed by customary international law.[1383] A rule of customary international law needs to be of mutual concern by means of express international accords.[1384] This holding goes back to a US Supreme Court decision from 1820, in which piracy was clearly differentiated from robbery, since the pirate as *hostis humani generis* commits hostilities upon the subjects and property of any or all nations.[1385]

In *Flores v. Southern Peru Copper*, the Court of Appeals for the Second Circuit found that international treaties that are self-executing or that have been executed through an Act of Congress provide greater evidence of the customs and practices of the United States than a treaty that has not been executed. "All treaties that have been ratified by at least two states provide *some* evidence of the custom and practice of nations. However, a treaty will only constitute *sufficient proof* of a norm of customary international law if an overwhelming majority of states have ratified the treaty, *and* those states uniformly and consistently act in accordance with its principles. The evidentiary weight to be afforded to a given treaty varies greatly depending on (a) How many, and which, states have ratified the treaty, and (b) The degree to which those states actually implement and abide by the principles set forth in the treaty."[1386]

C. Analysis to customary international law

Lawyers who deal most frequently with municipal law are often unfamiliar with the concept of customary international law. Customary international law is an enigma. It is not codified anywhere and some aspects are uncertain. It is produced by decentralized actions of states. Nevertheless, its existence is more or less undisputed and it is assuming an increasingly important role. In ATCA litigation, the standards to derive customary international law appear to comply, at least theoretically, with generally accepted international standards. However, in construing customary international law ATCA litigation varies greatly. For example in the *Fresh Del Monte* decision, the District Court for the Southern District of Florida found that the right to associate and organize was not a universally recognized norm of international law, and therefore alleged violation of that right was not actionable under ATCA,[1387] and

---

[1383] *Flores v. Southern Peru Copper Corp.*, 406 F3d 65, C.A. 2 (2003) at 82.
[1384] *Filártiga v. Peña-Irala*, 630 F2d 876, C.A. 2 (1980) at 888.
[1385] *United States v. Smith*, 18 US (5 Wheat) 153, 5 LEd 57, US S.Ct. (1820b) at 161.
[1386] *Flores v. Southern Peru Copper Corporation*, 343 F3d 140, C.A. 2 (2003) at 88.
[1387] *Villeda Aldana v. Fresh Del Monte Produce, Inc.*, 305 F Supp 2d 1285, D.C. S.D. Fla. (2003) at 1296.

in *Estate of Rodriguez v. Drummond Co.* the District Court of the Northern District of Alabama held that these rights represent actionable customary international law.[1388]

IV. General principles of international law

The third source of international law is the general principles of law. They are often used solely for the interpretation and completion of treaties and customary international law and are therefore often seen only as a subsidiary source of international law.[1389] Nevertheless, there are some general principles that are also important to international economic law, such as the principle of good faith, *venire contra factum proprium,* estoppel, *ultra alterum tantum*, *jura novit curia*, forfeiture, statute of limitation and the principle of unjust enrichment.[1390] In ATCA litigation, the general principles of international law are potentially relevant, but have never been the subject of an ATCA dispute so far.

V. International judicial decisions

Article 38(1) lit. d of the ICJ statute recognizes "judicial decisions and the teachings of the most highly qualified publicists" as subsidiary means for the determination of international law.[1391] Despite being only subsidiary means of determining the content of international law, for example ICJ "judicial decisions" enjoy a highly authoritative status of and can often be seen as evidence of the current status of international law.[1392] This applies equally to other international or national tribunals and courts.[1393]

The ICJ has been briefly mentioned in ATCA cases in relation to the following issues: the principle of exhaustion of remedies in *Sarei*; joint liability in *Unocal*; environment as human right in *Flores*; arbitrary detention in *Sosa*; state action in *Villeda*; and the definition of genocide in *Mehinovic* and in the *Sudan* case.[1394] Even

---

[1388] *Estate of Rodriguez v. Drummond Co.*, 256 F Supp 2d 1250, D.C. N.D. Ala. (2003) at 1264.

[1389] J Delbrück, 'Prospects for a 'World (Internal) Law?': Legal Developments in a Changing International System' 9 Indiana Journal of Global Legal Studies 401 (2002) at 414; WG Vitzthum, *Völkerrecht* (3rd edn, Gruyter, Berlin 2004) at 69; J Kokott, K Doehring and T Buergenthal, *Grundzüge des Völkerrechts* (3rd edn, C.F. Müller, Heidelberg 2003) at 23.

[1390] K Nowrot, *Normative Ordnungsstruktur und private Wirkungsmacht - Konsequenzen der Beteiligung transnationaler Unternehmen an den Rechtssetzungsprozessen im internationalen Wirtschaftssystem* (BWV Berliner Wissenschafts-Verlag, Berlin 2006) at 154 with further references.

[1391] Statute of the International Court of Justice June 26, 1945, UNTS 993 (1945).

[1392] M Herdegen, *Völkerrecht* (5th edn, Beck, München 2006) at 151.

[1393] T Stein and C von Buttlar, *Völkerrecht* (11th edn, Carl Heymanns Verlag, Köln 2005) at 60.

[1394] *Sarei v. Rio Tinto*, 456 F3d 1069, C.A. 9 (2006) at 1108; *Doe v. Unocal (Unocal III)*, 395 F3d 932, C.A. 9 (2002) at 973; *Flores v. Southern Peru Copper Corp.*, 253 F Supp 2d 510, D.C. S.D. N.Y. (2002) at 521; *Sosa v. Alvarez-Machain* (03-339) 542 US 2739, US S.Ct. (2004) at footnote 27; *Villeda Aldana v. Fresh Del Monte Produce, Inc.*, 305 F Supp 2d 1285, D.C. S.D. Fla. (2003) at 1304; *Mehinovic v. Vuckovic*, 198 FSupp2d 1322, D.C. N.D. Ga. (2002) at 1354; *The Presbyterian Church of Sudan, et. al. v. Talisman Energy, Inc.*, 374 FSupp2d 331, D.C.

in one of the most detailed analysis of international law in ATCA litigation, in the first *Talisman* decision the ICJ was not mentioned.[1395]

Mostly, the ICJ's findings have played a minor supporting role or were mentioned as part of the plaintiff's assertions. Other international or national decisions have been referred to only in rare cases in line with Justice Rehnquist's statement above that has expressed certain inattentiveness towards foreign court judgments.[1396]

VI. Scholarly writings

The work of international scholars can also be used as a subsidiary source to determine international law as it was already done in the *Lotus* case before the PCIJ.[1397] Of particular value are the works of international law commissions, such as the International Law Commission (ILC), the International Law Association (ILA), the Institut de Droit International (IDI) and the American Law Institute (ALI). The ALI may have the most prominent influence on ATCA litigation of any source whatsoever through the Restatement on Foreign Relations Law.[1398]

There remains some controversy in ATCA litigation in relation to the worth of the commentary of international jurists. On one hand, *Sosa* cited the US Supreme Court decision in *The Paquete Habana* in holding that "where there is no treaty, and no controlling executive or legislative act or judicial decision, resort must be had to the customs and usages of civilized nations; and, as evidence of these, to the works of jurists and commentators, who by years of labor, research and experience, have made themselves peculiarly well acquainted with the subjects of which they treat. Such works are resorted to by judicial tribunals, not for the speculations of their authors concerning what the law ought to be, but for trustworthy evidence of what the law really is."[1399] Also Judge Edwards in *Tel-Oren* referred to numerous international scholars.[1400]

On the other hand, in *Flores*, the Court of Appeals for the Second Circuit found that the works of scholars as a subsidiary of customary international law "suffers from an anachronism," because in the older days international law scholars "did the hard work of collecting international practices," whereas now international law scholarship is "characterised by normative rather than positive argument, and by idealism and

S.D. N.Y. (2005) at 336.

1395 *Presbyterian Church of Sudan et al. v. Talisman Energy, Inc.*, 244 F Supp 2d 289, D.C. S.D. N.Y. (2003) at 316.

1396 See chapter VI, subheading "A. International law and the US Constitution" at 222.

1397 *Lotus*, PCIJ Ser A, No 10, PCIJ (1927) at 26.

1398 Described above in chapter VI, subheading "G. International law and the Restatement of Foreign Relations Law" at 239.

1399 *The Paquete Habana*, 175 US 677, US S.Ct. (1900) at 700.

1400 *Tel-Oren v. Libyan Arab Republic*, 726 F2d 774, C.A. D.C. (1984) at 794.

advocacy."[1401] The Court then went on to appraise the Restatement of Foreign Relations law (1987), which was produced by a group of esteemed scholars without an eye to pending litigation, finding it to be of significant value in ascertaining the well-established, universally recognized rules of international law."[1402]

The work of the scholars in the Restatement of Foreign Relations law is used as one of the most authoritative sources on international law in ATCA litigation, including by the US Supreme Court.[1403] When the US refers to scholarly writings on international law, it prefers the Restatement, which was written solely from American scholars.

VII. Resolutions by international organizations

A. Resolutions by international organizations in international law

Even though not listed in Article 38 of the *Statute of the ICJ*, resolutions by international organizations can also be considered in determining the content of customary international law. The prevailing opinion categorizes them neither as international treaty law nor as a *sui generis* legal system, but as an independent source of international law.[1404]

Decisions of international organizations can have binding effect within the organization, but there are also examples of decisions of international organizations that are binding even outside of their organizational context. These are, for example, the decisions of the WTO Ministerial Conference according to Article IX (3) of the *Agreement Establishing the World Trade Organization*, the competence of the IMF Board of Governors according to Article VII (3) of the Articles of Agreement of the IMF, the competence of the organs of the EU in Article 249 of the Treaty

---

1401 *Flores v. Southern Peru Copper Corporation*, 343 F3d 140, C.A. 2 (2003) at 14. This rather derogatory tone goes back to Remarks of Jack Goldsmith, LF Damrosch, 'Scholars in the Construction and Critique of International Law, Panel Discussion' 94 American Society of International Law Proceedings 317 (2000) at 318.

1402 *Flores v. Southern Peru Copper Corp.*, 253 F Supp 2d 510, D.C. S.D. N.Y. (2002) at footnote 17.

1403 *Sosa v. Alvarez-Machain* (03-339) 542 US 2739, US S.Ct. (2004) at 737. For further information on the Restatement see in chapter VI, subheading "G. International law and the Restatement of Foreign Relations Law" at 239.

1404 See K Nowrot, *Normative Ordnungsstruktur und private Wirkungsmacht - Konsequenzen der Beteiligung transnationaler Unternehmen an den Rechtssetzungsprozessen im internationalen Wirtschaftssystem* (BWV Berliner Wissenschafts-Verlag, Berlin 2006) at 159; G Dahm, J Delbrück and R Wolfrum, *Völkerrecht* (2nd edn, De Gruyter, Berlin; New York 1989), I/1 at 69; C Tomuschat, 'Die internationale Gemeinschaft' 33 Archiv des Völkerrechts 1 (1995) at 11; K Skubiszewski, 'Enactment of Law by International Organizations' 41 British Yearbook of International Law 198 (1965) *at*198; JE Alvarez, *International Organizations as Law-Makers* (Oxford; New York 2005) at 258; Orrego-Vicuña in G Ress and J Bröhmer, *Internationale Gemeinschaft und Menschenrechte - Festschrift für Georg Ress zum 70. Geburtstag* (Carl Heymanns, Köln 2005) at 200.

Establishing the European Community and measures of the UN Security Council under chapter VII of the UN Charter.[1405]

Searching for a customary rule prohibiting recourse to nuclear weapons, the ICJ noted that UN General Assembly resolutions may sometimes have normative value even if they are not binding. "They can, in certain circumstances, provide evidence important for establishing the existence of a rule or the emergence of an *opinio juris*."[1406]

ICJ Judge Rosalyn Higgins, in her important study, *The Development of International Law through the Political Organs of the United Nations* in 1963, examined and affirmed the extent to which General Assembly resolutions have an influence on the law-creating process of customary international law.[1407] Resolutions of the Assembly are not binding *per se*. However, the rules of general international law, which they may embody, are binding on member states. Resolutions can be seen as indications of general customary law and provide a rich source of evidence for the creation of customary law.[1408]

1405 Articles of Agreement of the International Monetary Fund July 22, 1944 (entered into force December 27, 1945), last amended effective November 11, 1992, 31 ILM 1307 (1944), Article IX:3: In exceptional circumstances, the Ministerial Conference may decide to waive an obligation imposed on a Member by this Agreement or any of the Multilateral Trade Agreements, provided that any such decision shall be taken by three fourths of the Members unless otherwise provided for in this paragraph; Articles of Agreement of the International Monetary Fund July 22, 1944 (entered into force December 27, 1945), last amended effective November 11, 1992, 31 ILM 1307 (1944), Article VII para 3: If it becomes evident to the Fund that the demand for a member's currency seriously threatens the Fund's ability to supply that currency, the Fund, whether or not it has issued a report under Section 2 of this Article, shall formally declare such currency scarce and shall thenceforth apportion its existing and accruing supply of the scarce currency with due regard to the relative needs of members, the general international economic situation, and any other pertinent considerations; Treaty Establishing the European Community Mar 25, 1957, 298 UNTS 11, as amended by Treaty of Amsterdam, Oct 2, 1997, 1997 OJ (C 340) 1, as amended by Treaty of Nice, Feb 26, 2001, 2001 OJ (C 80) 1, consolidated version reprinted in 2002 OJ (C 325) 33 (1957), Article 249: In order to carry out their task and in accordance with the provisions of this Treaty, the European Parliament acting jointly with the Council, the Council and the Commission shall make regulations and issue directives, take decisions, make recommendations or deliver opinions. For more information, see also K Nowrot, *Normative Ordnungsstruktur und private Wirkungsmacht - Konsequenzen der Beteiligung transnationaler Unternehmen an den Rechtssetzungsprozessen im internationalen Wirtschaftssystem* (BWV Berliner Wissenschafts-Verlag, Berlin 2006) at 159 et *seq*.

1406 *Legality of the Threat or Use of Nuclear Weapons - Advisory Opinion 08.07.1996* ICJ Reports 1995, 226, ICJ (1996) at 254.

1407 R Higgins, *The Development of International Law through the Political Organs of the United Nations* (Oxford University Press, London 1963).

1408 *Ibid.* at 5.

When the UN General Assembly solely declares existing rules, then the problem of acknowledging the formal absence of legislative competence is more or less solved. It is very difficult, in the absence of a formal agreement, to determine when a rule of law exists in a system without effective central institutions of government. Every norm will be derived as a matter of degree, reflecting the expectations of states toward what is permissible and impermissible.[1409] In the search for customary international law, it is clear that the resolutions of the General Assembly play a crucial role, one independent of whether their status is to generate binding legal rules or to embody mere recommendations.[1410] "The degree of authoritativeness that a particular resolution will acquire depends upon a number of contextual factors, including the expectations governing the extent of permissible behavior, the extent and quality of the consensus, and the degree to which effective power is mobilized to implement the claims posited in a resolution. The degree of authoritativeness that the process of law-creating by Assembly action comes to enjoy depends upon the extent to which particular resolutions influence behavior and gain notoriety."[1411]

B. Resolutions by international organizations in ATCA litigation

How are resolutions by international organizations viewed in ATCA litigation? ATCA litigation mainly referred to UN resolutions. There is no clear picture of how UN resolutions are treated in ATCA litigation. The majority of US decision has referred to UN resolutions as a conclusive or authorative source for purposes of ATCA litigation. In the *Talisman* decision in 2005 the Court found that "United Nations statutes governing prosecution of atrocities and formation of international criminal court were authority for proposition that aider and abettor liability existed under international law, sufficient to sustain claim under Alien Tort Statute."[1412] The Court referred to the ICTR and ICTY statutes that were both based on UN Security Council resolutions.[1413]

In *Almog v. Arab Bank* in 2007, the District Court for the Eastern District of New York stated that UN resolutions cannot be relied on as a sole source of international law, but they help to inform the current state of international law.[1414] This finding relied on the *Filártiga* decision, where UN General Assembly resolutions served as

1409 R Falk, 'On the Quasi-Legislative Competence of the General Assembly' 60 The American Journal of International Law 782 (1966) at 786.

1410 *Ibid.* at 786.

1411 *Ibid.* at 785.

1412 *The Presbyterian Church of Sudan, et. al. v. Talisman Energy, Inc.*, 374 FSupp2d 331, D.C. S.D. N.Y. (2005) at 43.

1413 Statute of the International Criminal Tribunal for the Former Yugoslavia as adopted in UNSCR 827 and amended by UNSCR Resolutions 1166, 1329, 1411, 1431, 1481, 1597, 1660; See online at http://wwwunorg/icty/legaldoc-e/indexhtm (1993); Statute of the International Criminal Tribunal for Rwanda as adopted by UNSCR 955 and amended by UNSCR 977, 978, 1165, 1166, 1329, 1411, 1431, 1503, 1512, 1503, 1534, 1684, 1717; See online at http://wwwictrorg (August 23, 2007) (1994).

1414 *Almog v. Arab Bank, PLC*, 471 FSupp2d 257, D.C. E.D.N.Y. (2007) at 279.

evidence of binding principles of international law.[1415] The *Almog* decision also referred to UN resolutions and the work of the Nuremberg tribunals as further evidence of the content of customary international law and the Court finds that "such analogies have merit."[1416] The Court referred to UN resolutions on a number of occasions for the establishment of customary international law, such as for the definition of "genocide" and in order to establish that financing terrorist bombings violates international law.[1417]

Similarly other US courts have referred to UN resolutions in numerous decisions. The *Filártiga decision* in 1980, referred to the *UDHR*, a UN General Assembly resolution, stating that "although there is no universal agreement as to the precise extent of the 'human rights and fundamental freedoms' guaranteed to all by the Charter, there is at present no dissent from the view that the guaranties include, at a bare minimum, the right to be free from torture. [...] The General Assembly has declared that the Charter precepts embodied in this *Universal Declaration* constitute basic principles of international law."[1418]

In the *Tel-Oren* decision in 1984, the Court of Appeals for the District of Washington D.C. relied on a General Assembly resolution in finding that only torture by public officials would violate international law,[1419] but it also stated that the *UDHR* is not an international treaty and, therefore, not binding.[1420] In *Doe v. Karadzic* in 1994, the Court relied on UN resolutions in defining torture where it was intentionally inflicted by, or at the instigation of, a public official.[1421] This finding was followed by the District Court for the Southern District of New York in the *Presbyterian Church of Sudan* decision in 2003.[1422]

1415 *Filártiga v. Peña-Irala*, 630 F2d 876, C.A. 2 (1980) at 882.

1416 *Almog v. Arab Bank, PLC*, 471 FSupp2d 257, D.C. E.D.N.Y. (2007) at 279.

1417 Definition of genocide - *Ibid.* at 274 ("In 1946, the General Assembly of the United Nations declared that genocide is a crime under international law that is condemned by the civilized world, whether the perpetrators are private individuals, public officials or statesmen."); Terrorist bombings -*Almog v. Arab Bank, PLC*, 471 FSupp2d 257, D.C. E.D.N.Y. (2007) at 276 (International Convention for the Suppression of Terrorist Bombings GA Res 52/164, 1, UN Doc A/RES/52/164, Dec 15, 1997 (1997)) and International Convention for the Suppression of the Financing of Terrorism adopted by the UN General Assembly in GA Res 54/109, 1, UN Doc A/RES/54/109 (Dec 9, 1999) (1999), ratified by over 130 countries, including the United States (26 June, 2002). The United States implemented the Financing Convention via the Suppression of the Financing of Terrorism Convention Implementation Act of 2002. See18 U.S.C. § 2339C).

1418 *Filártiga v. Peña-Irala*, 630 F2d 876, C.A. 2 (1980) at 881.

1419 *Tel-Oren v. Libyan Arab Republic*, 726 F2d 774, C.A. D.C. (1984) at 795.

1420 *Ibid.* at 818.

1421 *Doe v. Karadzic*, 866 FSupp 734, D.C. S.D. N.Y. (1994) at 739 (General Assembly Resolution 3452, 30 U.N. GAOR Supp. (No. 34) 91, U.N. Doc A/1034 (1975)).

1422 *Presbyterian Church of Sudan et al. v. Talisman Energy, Inc.*, 244 F Supp 2d 289, D.C. S.D. N.Y. (2003) at 310.

In *Karadzic*, the Court of Appeals for the Second Circuit relied on UN General Assembly resolutions in finding that genocide is a crime under international law.[1423] In *Doe v. Unocal* in 1995, the Court of Appeals for the Ninth Circuit used General Assembly resolutions as evidence that human rights violations are conducted by the government of Myanmar.[1424] In the *Cabello* decision in 2001, the District Court for the Southern District of Florida recognized "crimes against humanity" as customary international law, relying on numerous UN resolutions and found that "US adoption of these *laws* affirms its legal obligation to condemning crimes against humanity."[1425]

In the *Mehinovic* decision in 2002, the District Court for the Northern District of Georgia also found that crimes against humanity are violations of international

---

1423 *Kadic v. Karadzic*, 70 F3d 232, C. A. 2 (1995) at 241 ("In 1946, the General Assembly of the United Nations declared that genocide is a crime under international law that is condemned by the civilized world, whether the perpetrators are 'private individuals, public officials or statesmen.' G.A.Res. 96(I), 1 U.N.GAOR, U.N. Doc. A/64/Add.1 at 188-89 (1946). The General Assembly also affirmed the principles of Article 6 of the Agreement and Charter Establishing the Nuremberg War Crimes Tribunal for punishing 'persecutions on political, racial, or religious grounds,' regardless of whether the offenders acted 'as individuals or as members of organizations,' ... The Convention on the Prevention and Punishment of the Crime of Genocide, 78 U.N.T.S. 277, entered into force Jan. 12, 1951, for the United States Feb. 23, 1989 provides a more specific articulation of the prohibition of genocide in international law. The Convention, which has been ratified by more than 120 nations, including the United States.")

1424 *Doe v. Unocal (Unocal III)*, 395 F3d 932, C.A. 9 (2002) at footnote 9 ("In 1995 the General Assembly of the United Nations 'strongly urged the Government of Myanmar ... to put an end to ... the practices of torture, abuse of women, forced labour ..., and ... disappearances and summary executions....'; in Situation of Human Rights in Myanmar, U.N. General Assembly, 50th Sess., Agenda Item 112(c), U.N. Doc. A/RES/50/194 (1995).")

1425 *Estate of Winston Cabello v. Armando Fernandez-Larios*, 157 FSupp2d 1345, US S.D.Fla. (2001) at 1360 ("Charter of the International Military Tribunal, Nuremberg, of August 8, 1945, confirmed by G.A. Res. 3, U.N. Doc. A/50 (1946) and G.A. Res. 95, U.N. Doc. A/236, 59 Stat. 1546 (1946). While the United States has not ratified the Rome Statute on the International Criminal Court, the US has approved the other United Nations General Assembly and U.N. Security Council resolutions, cited by Plaintiff Aldo Cabello as sources of law which Defendant's alleged commission of crimes against humanity violated. E.g., Convention on the Non-Applicability of Statutory Limitations to War Crimes and Crimes Against Humanity, Nov. 26, 1968, G.A. Res. 2391, U.N. GAOR, 23d Sess., Supp. No. 18 at 40, U.N. Doc. A/7218, 754 U.N.T.S. 73 (entered into force Nov. 11, 1970); Principles of International Co-Operation in the Detection, Arrest, Extradition and Punishment of Persons Guilty of War Crimes against Humanity, G.A. Res. 3074, U.N. GAOR 28th Sess., Supp. No.30A at 78, U.N. Doc. A/9039/Add.1 (1973); Statute of the International Tribunal for the Prosecution of Persons Responsible for Serious Violations of International Humanitarian Law Committed in the Territory of the Former Yugoslavia since 1991, Report of the Secretary General, pursuant to para. 2 of U.N.S.C. Res. 808 (1993), U.N. Doc. S/25704 at 36 (1993), adopted by U.N.S.C. Res. 827, U.N. Doc. S/Res/827 (1993), reprinted in 32 I.L.M. 1159, 1170 (1993); Statute for the International Tribunal for Rwanda, U.N. SCOR, 49th Sess., 3453rd mtg. at 1, U.N. Doc. S/Res/955 (1994).")

law.[1426] It relied on the Nuremberg Trials, on the *Tadic* decision by the ICTY, the ATCA decision in *Cabello* and UN resolutions.[1427]

On the other hand, there are two decisions in particular that question the authoritativeness of UN resolutions – namely, the *Flores* decision in 2003 and the *In re South African Apartheid* decision in 2004.[1428] The *Flores* decision discusses in greater detail the importance of General Assembly resolutions for US litigation. The Court held that the General Assembly was not intended to be and is not a world parliament and therefore it cannot impose binding decisions on states.

"General Assembly resolutions and declarations do not have the power to bind member states because the member states specifically denied the General Assembly that power after extensively considering the issue – first at the Dumbarton Oaks Conference, held in Washington in 1944, then at the Yalta conference in 1945, and finally at the United Nations' founding conference, held in San Francisco in 1945 [...] it was agreed that, apart from certain internal arrangements such as the Organization's budget and other internal and financial matters not pertinent here, the General Assembly's resolutions would not be binding on states. [...] Had the powers of the Assembly been extended that far, one can be sure that not only the US and Russia, but also France and England, and what are considered the 'Middle Powers' (e.g., Brazil and Canada) would have asked for a larger representation. For it is self-evident that they could not have agreed that on vital decisions their powers should be no greater than those, for example, of small states like Nicaragua and Saudi Arabia."[1429] Therefore, the Court concluded that General Assembly resolutions are "not proper sources of customary international law because they are merely aspirational and were never intended to be binding on member states of the United Nations."[1430]

The second ATCA decision that is skeptical towards the worth of UN resolutions as sources of international law is *In re South African Apartheid*. Decided by the District Court for the Southern District of New York[1431] And using the same sources as the

1426 *Mehinovic v. Vuckovic*, 198 FSupp2d 1322, D.C. N.D. Ga. (2002) at 1352.

1427 *Ibid.* at footnote 44. ("In 1946, the General Assembly endorsed the principles of international law recognized in the IMT Charter. See G.A. Res. 95, 1 U.N. GAOR at 1144, U.N. Doc. A/236 (1946); see also Convention on the Non-Applicability of Statutory Limits to War Crimes and Crimes Against Humanity, Nov. 26, 1968, Article 1(b), 660 U.N.T.S. 195, reprinted in 8 I.L.M. 68 (1969) (adopting Nuremberg definition of crimes against humanity except for in connection with aggressive war."))

1428 *Flores v. Southern Peru Copper Corporation*, 343 F3d 140, C.A. 2 (2003); *In re: South African Apartheid Litigation*, 346 FSupp2d 538, D.C. S.D. N.Y. (2004).

1429 The decision cited B Simma and others, *The Charter of the United Nations - A Commentary* (2nd edn, Oxford University Press, Oxford; New York 2002) at 269 and S Meisler, *United Nations - The First Fifty Years* (1st edn, Atlantic Monthly Press, New York 1995) at 10-14.

1430 *Flores v. Southern Peru Copper Corporation*, 343 F3d 140, C.A. 2 (2003) at 91.

1431 *In re: South African Apartheid Litigation*, 346 FSupp2d 538, D.C. S.D. N.Y. (2004).

Flores decision, it was held that the member states of the UN specifically denied the General Assembly the power to make binding decisions. It concluded that General Assembly resolutions are not valid sources of international law.[1432]

C. Analysis to resolutions by international organizations

Overall, it can be stated that mainly UN resolutions were referred to in ATCA litigation. The authoritativeness of UN resolutions in international law can be seen as indicative of customary international law. As stated in the *In re South African Apartheid* and the *Flores* decision, they are neither invalid sources of international law on the one extreme, nor could they be seen as constitutive sources of international law. They are important declaratory evidence in determining international law. As such they have also been used mostly in ATCA litigation. UN resolutions have plaid a more important role in interpreting the "law of nations" pursuant to ATCA, then international tribunal decisions.

VIII. Concluding remarks to Chapter VII

What role does international law have in ATCA litigation? The determination of international law in ATCA litigation theoretically relies on the same sources as those that are recognized in international law. Many ATCA cases referred to the sources of law that are enumerated in Article 38 of the *Statute of the ICJ*. Theoretically, ATCA litigation also uses the same method of state practice and *opinio juris* to derive customary international law.

The practice of the interpretation of international law differs considerably from international law. International treaties are referred to in the interpretation of international law, but to very differing extents. In the *Sarei* decision, it was held by the Court of Appeals for the Ninth Circuit that articles from the *UNCLOS* convention that were not ratified by the US, were sufficient to establish customary international law and this was used as a basis to establish far-reaching duties for TNCs in international environmental law, even though *UNCLOS* was meant to bind states.[1433] In a similar case heard by the Court of Appeals for the Second Circuit, the *Flores* decision, environmental claims that have also seriously affected the health of local people were not held to be actionable. The *ICCPR*, which was ratified by the US and approximately 160 other nations, was not deemed to codify international customary law.[1434]

International judicial decisions from international bodies play a less important role for the interpretation of international law in ATCA decisions. Precedents from US courts certainly play a very important role according to the principles of Common

[1432] *Ibid.* at 553.

[1433] *Sarei v. Rio Tinto, PLC*, 487 F3d 1193, C.A. 9 (2007) at paras 14 and 16; *Sarei v. Rio Tinto PLC*, 221 FSupp2d 1116, D.C. C.D. Cal. (2002) at 1161, 1187 and 1190.

[1434] *Flores v. Southern Peru Copper Corporation*, 343 F3d 140, C.A. 2 (2003).

law. "Teachings of the most highly qualified publicists of the various nations" are a subsidiary source for interpreting international law according to Article 38 of the *Statute of the ICJ* and they are important for the determination of international law in ATCA litigation, whereas so far US scholars have been almost exclusively consulted. The most important source of international law in ATCA litigation has been the Restatement of Foreign Relations Law, aside from US precedents. UN resolutions are also referred to in very differing degrees.

Conclusion

1. The need to recognize universal human rights is a matter of increasing importance worldwide. Corporations engaged in trade and commerce often possess a level of power that transcends the borders of national jurisdictions. TNCs are business corporations that are incorporated enterprises comprising a parent enterprise and its foreign affiliates. TNCs are the driving force behind Globalization. They often assume the powers that were originally assigned to states and sometimes they possess means and potential beyond those of states.

Especially in countries with weak governance and less developed protection for the principle of the rule of law, there have been appalling examples of corporate exploitation of humans and environmental resources. However, that does not mean that TNCs are generally malfeasant. Comparing the overall effect of TNCs on human rights to those of nation states, it may be said that there are positive and negative examples of both forms of incorporated juridical entities.

Nevertheless, it should be acknowledged that, over the course of history, the worst human rights violations have been committed by, or in the name of, nation states rather than TNCs. Of special concern are those situations where nation states and TNCs cooperate in violating human rights, as occurred during the Holocaust and in many conflicts around the world, including Nigeria and Sudan. There remain many cases where TNCs profit from slave labor or child labor, often through subcontractors. The history of enforcing corporate legal accountability for human rights is still rather thin and is largely reduced to some cases against German individual industrialists in the Nuremberg tribunals.

2. The question of enforcement of human rights is a multi-facetted process. In international law, the *UN Declaration of Human Rights* also addresses TNCs, but rather on a vague and aspirational notion. The UN Norms on the Responsibilities of Transnational Corporations provide a helpful guideline to create corporate codes of conduct. The UN Global Compact is an innovative tool created by the UN to train the corporate world on human rights concerns under the auspices of the UN. The UN Secretary General's Special Representative for Business and Human Rights, John Ruggie, has delivered informative reports on the status of TNCs in international law.

The UN Council on Human Rights and the General Assembly have adopted resolutions that also address violations of human rights by corporations. However, all of the above-mentioned instruments of international law are non-binding. The UN Security Council may issue binding decisions on its member states. Only more recently, especially in the Global War on Terrorism, has the UN Security Council issued resolutions that also cover private business entities. In any event, these decisions were to be implemented through states and only covered a very small number of corporate human rights violations.

The WTO has one of the most effective dispute settlement mechanisms in international law. However, its main focus is to further international trade and the WTO conceives human rights to be outside the scope of its current system. The World Bank increasingly adopts a rights-based approach and sometimes conditions its loan approvals to commitments on measures being adopted to democratic governance, fight against corruption and human rights. However, the World Bank does not provide for an all-encompassing mechanism to enforce human rights against TNCs.

In principle, the ICC provides a viable mechanism to address human rights violations by TNCs. Many states have proposed holding business entities liable under the *Rome Statute*. However, the states could not agree on the standards that should apply for criminal responsibility of corporations and they were also afraid that states could be held liable for the actions of state corporations.

The first problem with addressing human rights violations by TNCs through the mechanism of state responsibility is that there remains no settled test under international law to determine which country is the home state of a TNC. Comparing the international courts, such as the ICJ, the ICTY, the IACtHR, the ACtHPR and the ECtHR, one will find that so far only the last of these has been used to hold states accountable for the human rights violations of corporations. The ECJ has long developed EU law to provide for human rights responsibilities of private actors, including TNCs, even though the Charter of Fundamental Rights will only become binding through the EU Reform Treaty, which is likely to be signed in Lisbon in December 2007.

The vast majority of the business community now acknowledges responsibility for human rights and environmental issues. Corporations are developing an awareness of their responsibilities to their employees, their subcontractors and the communities in which they work. All of this represents very important progress. The Sullivan Principles were among the first instruments to articulate human rights responsibilities of commercial entities. Corporate law scholars have developed two different theories concerning corporate responsibilities: the shareholder view and the stakeholder view. Both concepts seem to accept that corporations have certain human rights responsibilities.

Most major TNCs have adopted a code of conduct. However, their quality differs widely. There are still many corporations that issue glossy brochures stating that they recognize and respect the human and other rights of the communities they work in, while simultaneously conspiring with governments that egregiously violate human rights, such as the Chinese oil exploration corporations in Sudan. Therefore, while the business approach provides a cornerstone of human rights implementation in the corporate world, it does not provide for an enforceable mechanism against moral free riders. Important trends in addressing human rights by business entities are third-party audited triple bottom line reporting and human rights assessments.

An important avenue to address human rights violations by corporations is through the work of NGOs. Some NGOs set up independent auditing and reporting mechanisms and perform important tasks as international watchdogs. Another important avenue to make corporations adhere to human rights is through ethical consumerism and socially responsible investment, both of which have experienced a strong surge in recent years and can be very powerful. Nevertheless, these phenomena cannot replace regulatory approaches that include the direct regulation of moral free riders.

In many countries, corporations can be held liable for human rights violations under instruments such as *Drittwirkung* or corporate criminal liability. Only very few mechanisms, however, have extraterritorial reach. The most potent of these is the ATCA.

3. The ATCA is a peculiar and interesting US law from 1789. It basically gives every non-US citizen (alien) the right to sue any individual or juridical person on earth in an US court for breaches of customary international law. Even though this seems very broad, there are numerous hurdles to the ATCA litigation.

One of the main intentions of enacting the ATCA was to bring justice also to non-US citizens residing in the US, especially ambassadors, so that the European nations would not wage a war on the ground that the rights of their representatives were not protected. Jurisdiction was accorded to the federal courts instead of the state courts. The "law of nations" at that time is said to have comprised principally of: (a) violation of safe-conducts; (b) infringement of the rights of ambassadors; and (c) piracy. The ATCA was rarely applied until the 1980s.

With the *Filártiga*, *Tel-Oren*, *Kadic* and *Unocal* decisions in the 1980s and 1990s, it emerged as a most important tool to hold individuals and corporations accountable for human rights violations. In the pivotal *Sosa* decision, the Supreme Court largely affirmed the earlier ATCA decisions and held that the ATCA provides for an actionable basis in respect of human rights claims.

4. The most important categories of US human rights litigation brought against TNCs include cases concerning: (a) the involvement of oil exploration corporations in securing their operations in developing countries; (b) the Holocaust; (c) environmental allegations; (d) the war on terrorism; (e) the killing of trade unionists; and (f) other cases.

(a) The ATCA cases that addressed human rights against corporations in securing their oil explorations were *Unocal*, *Talisman*, *Wiwa*, *Bowoto*, *Mujica* and *Exxon*. In *Doe v. Unocal,* the watershed case, corporations were held to be subjects of international law and have responsibilities in case the corporation together with the government vicariously violates human rights.

One of the worst sites of human rights violations worldwide during recent years were the atrocities that might have amounted to genocide in southern Sudan and in Darfur/Sudan. Both of these conflicts were substantially supported, if not led by, the current Sudanese government. Against this backdrop, *Presbyterian Church of Sudan v. Talisman Energy* is an important, but as yet unresolved, case concerning the role of foreign corporations. So far, the case has proven partially successful in so far as nearly all Western corporations removed their investments in oil explorations in Sudan, leaving Chinese and other Asian corporations as the remaining investors.

In *Wiwa v. Royal Dutch Petroleum*, the Court found that the participation in crimes against humanity, torture, summary execution, arbitrary detention, and cruel, inhuman and degrading treatment violated international law and the Court denied the motion to dismiss on *forum non conveniens* grounds. The case, *Bowoto v. Chevron*, is still pending and highlights another cruel example of how corporations have violated human rights. The heinous human rights violations in Aceh/Indonesia that were alleged in *Doe v. Exxon* were dismissed on grounds of the political question doctrine. However, in *Mujica v. Occidental*, the oil exploration company Occidental was held responsible for the murders in connection with the protection of the oil pipelines.

In *Unocal* and *Mujica,* the corporations were held responsible; in *Exxon*, the case was dismissed on the ground of the political questions doctrine. The matters of *Talisman*, *Wiwa* and *Bowoto* are still pending. Therefore, it can be concluded that while the scope of liability concerning the duties of corporations conspiring with governments that violate human rights remains imprecise, these cases have definitely put those corporations under increased scrutiny.

(b) In the Holocaust litigation against Swiss banks, it was shown that banks may also bear human rights duties for trading in assets looted from the Jews by the Nazis and in assets that were the product of slave labor. The banks paid US$ 1.25 billion to settle the case. The forced labor litigation against German TNCs reaffirmed that corporations bear human rights duties for using slave labor. The German corporations and the German government paid US$ 5 billion to settle the case. In contrast to the Holocaust litigation against European corporations, the forced labor litigation against Japanese corporations was a failure. The dismissal relied on the Peace Treaty with Japan and therefore the claim was time-barred. In the entire Holocaust-related ATCA claims, the media, civil society, and US federal and state governments all played a decisive role in pushing either for pursuance or dismissal of the claims.

(c) ATCA litigation involving environmental allegations against TNCs include the cases *Sarei*, *Bano* and *Flores*. *Sarei v. Rio Tinto* represents a huge human rights victory. It deals with the involvement of the Anglo-Australian corporation, Rio Tinto, in the enormous degradation of the environment and its involvement in the civil war involving the people of Bougainville. The case was litigated for five years and ended in an appellate court judgment that held Rio Tinto liable for violations of *jus cogens* norms and for violations of the *UNCLOS*.

Union Carbide caused one of the worst industrial disasters and in the ATCA case, *Bano v. Union Carbide*, the company was ordered to clean up the site of the disaster. In *Flores v. Southern Peru Copper* the US courts dismissed the case on ground of *forum non conveniens*. The case led to increased scrutiny of environmental pollution by TNCs in Peru. In 2003, Southern Peru Copper agreed to improve its smeltering facilities and reduce sulfuric gases by 92 percent. In *Jota v. Texaco* the case was dismissed, but the US corporation was forced to appear in Ecuadorian court and comply with the judgment. Therefore, of the cases concerning environmental allegations against TNCs, all of the cases had some success, at least in that the allegations were given greater scrutiny and, in case of a dismissal in US courts, the cases were then heard in the host states of the operations and led to stricter environmental regulations.

(d) A recent trend in ATCA litigation involves the cases concerning the US-led War on Terrorism. The two most important cases are *Ibrahim* and *El-Masri*. In *Ibrahim v. Titan*, the Court delivered an ill-founded decision that it did not have jurisdiction over private corporations and therefore dismissed the case. The reason for the dismissal of *El- Masri v. Tenet*, which included private aviation corporations as defendants, was the inadmissibility to reveal state secrets for the resolution of this case. Therefore, the cases concerning the War on Terrorism have been unsuccessful so far.

(e) In particular, Columbia has been the site of numerous murders of trade unionists, often in close connection to foreign corporate activities, such as on the bottling plant of Coca-Cola. The cases concerning the killing of trade unionists are *Sinaltrainal* and *Estate of Rodriguez*. In *Sinaltrainal v. Coca-Cola*, the Court could not assert the requisite causal connection to Coca-Cola in Atlanta, US. In *Estate of Rodriguez v. Drummond Co*, involving another murder of a trade unionist, the Court held the corporation liable. Here again, the exact scope of liability seems to be unresolved but a heightened awareness of corporate human rights violations was achieved.

(f) There have been numerous other ATCA decisions against corporations. In *Hamid v. Price Waterhouse*, fraudulent behavior of banks was not held to be actionable under the ATCA. In *Carmicheal v. United Technologies*, the requisite causal connection between Price Waterhouse and torture was unable to be established. In *Eastman Kodak v. Kavlin*, it was established that corporations can also use ATCA litigation to protect themselves against human rights violations. In *Bigio v. Coca-*

Cola, the US courts examine the validity of an expropriation, the case is still pending. In *Abdullahi v. Pfizer*, which involved allegations of illegal drug testing, the US courts have dismissed the case on grounds of *forum non conveniens*, but have forced Pfizer to appear in Nigerian courts and cooperate in the discovery process. In *Bao Ge v. Li Peng*, the US courts held that the forced labor in that case was not such an extreme form of egregious conduct as to confer jurisdiction over a private corporation under the private actor limb of the ATCA. The case of *Arias v. Dyncorp*, concerning the harsh human and environmental side effects of the US war against cocaine plantations in South America, is still pending. Also *Corrie v. Caterpillar*, concerning the cooperation of the US bulldozer company in the violations of international law by the Israeli army, is still pending. Finally, in the case concerning South African Apartheid, a District Court Judge found that to hold corporations liable for the human rights violations in South Africa during that period would seriously impede international commerce and, on this basis, the case was dismissed.

g.) The human rights cases against corporations include a wide array of human rights violations. The exact scope of liability remains rather uncertain and is often dependent on the circuit in which the case is heard. The most human rights friendly circuits seem to be the Second and the Ninth. The District of Columbia seems particularly opposed to the extension of human rights responsibilities. The cases concerning the Holocaust were very successful in terms of articulating the general human rights responsibilities of corporations in US law. Interestingly, environmental cases have also been rather successful. There have been a number of successful cases concerning the security of oil exploration, as in *Unocal*, and many cases are still pending. The cases concerning the involvement of corporations in the killing of trade unionists are yet to provide a clear line of authority. The cases for corporate involvement in the War on Terrorism have been less successful, but it is worth noting that both of these cases were heard in the District of Columbia.

In conclusion, although the US cases against corporations have had mixed outcomes, the fact itself that some of them were successful in terms of human rights responsibilities of corporations can be seen as a victory for international law and human rights. Furthermore, scrutiny of corporate violations of human rights has largely increased through the ATCA litigation.

5. The human rights responsibilities of TNCs in US law were briefly outlined in the 1987 US Restatement of Foreign Relations Law. The introductory note to Part II stated that corporations may be subjects of international law. In Section 404, it stated that universal jurisdiction exists for certain offenses, such as piracy, slave trade, attacks on or hijacking of aircraft, genocide, war crimes, and perhaps certain acts of terrorism. These often were often held to be clear violations of international law for which corporations may be held liable.

The chronological development of the human rights responsibilities of TNCs in ATCA litigation has shown that the foundation of human rights duties of corporations in international law was developed largely relying on US sources and not on sources of international law. The Restatement has played a crucial role. The cases of *Tel-Oren* in 1985 and *Kadic* in 1995, which both dealt with duties of individuals in international law, provide very important precedent in the imposition of human rights duties on corporations. *Tel-Oren* relied largely on the ATCA cases against individuals in the late 18th and early 19th centuries. *Kadic* relied on *Tel-Oren*, the Restatement and a brief reference to Article 3 of the *Genocide Convention*. Many early decisions against corporations, such as *Carmichael v. United Technologies*, *Hamid v. Price Waterhouse* and *Jota v. Texaco*, have simply presumed that corporations have human rights responsibilities with no discussion in the judgment on how these human rights responsibilities are derived. These decisions were later applied to prove that corporations have these duties in international law, since the court would need to examine it *sua sponte* (that is, of its own accord) as part of the question of subject matter jurisdiction, as argued in the *Talisman I* decision in 2003.

The successful watershed case establishing human rights responsibilities of corporations was the 1997 *Unocal I* decision. Interestingly, it only included brief reference largely to two cases concerning the international legal personality of individuals, *Tel-Oren* and *Kadic*. It simply put the status of individuals in international law on par with the status of corporations. A similar and even briefer approach was taken in both *Beanal v. Freeport McMoran* decisions in 1997 and 1999, in *Bigio v. Coca-Cola* in 2000 and in *Abdullahi v. Pfizer* in 2002. All these decisions mainly relied on *Kadic*. Possibly the briefest imposition of human rights duties on corporations was chosen in *Bodner v. Banque Paribas*. It simply stated that the alleged looting, conversion, and continued withholding of assets that rightfully belonged to plaintiffs clearly violate the Nuremberg Principles and longstanding principles of customary international law.

Two other interesting arguments were proffered for the imposition of human rights duties on corporations. In the 2002 *Unocal III* decision the Court argued that the undoubted aim of the 13th Amendment to the US Constitution was to maintain a system of completely free and voluntary labor throughout the United States and, since it also reaches non-state actors, the ATCA litigation does too. In the *Al-Baraka* decision, the Court held, after examining the legislative materials and the first ATCA cases in the early 18th century, that it is conceivable that the ATCA was intended to cover *only* non-state actors.

The first extended examination of the sources of international law concerning international legal personality and the human rights duties of corporations was included in the 2003 decision of *Presbyterian Church of Sudan, et. al., v. Talisman Energy, Inc.* on three pages. It looked at international tribunal decisions, especially the Nuremberg Tribunal. The *Talisman* Court found that corporations were held liable in the Nuremberg Trials, but it ignored the fact that in Nuremberg only individuals and not corporations were subjects of jurisdiction. The *Talisman* Court referred to some very specialized treaties, such as the *Convention for Civil Liability for Oil Pollution*. This treaty undeniably imposes an international duty directly on non-state actors, specifically private ship owners. It does not prove that TNCs have human rights duties. Proving human rights duties in international law, the *Talisman* Court very briefly referred to the *Genocide Convention* and the *Geneva Convention on the Treatment of Prisoners of War* without discussing how far these liabilities reach. The *Talisman* Court also examined an interesting array of UN General Assembly resolutions, UN Security Council resolutions and decisions of the ECJ and affirmed its finding of human rights duties of corporations in international law.

The *Talisman II* decision in 2005 affirmed the first *Talisman* decision and represents the second and also last ATCA decision against corporations that had a closer look at sources of international law. Since the home and host countries of the corporations affected by human rights litigation against corporations have never denied corporate human rights responsibilities *per se*, the *Talisman* Court held that customary law was thereby established.

The pivotal US Supreme Court decision in *Sosa v. Alvarez* tentatively affirmed the ATCA litigation against corporations in footnote 20, although it was more directly concerned with ATCA litigation against individuals, which was expressly affirmed for a limited set of human rights. The *Sosa* Court indicated that it views corporate liability on par with individual liability. Overall, all decisions of US courts have affirmed that corporations have human rights responsibilities in US law. The only two decisions that ventured to deny this were the two decisions in the District of Columbia in August and October 2005: *Ibrahim v. Titan* and *Doe v. Exxon*.

Having established that corporations are subjects of international law in US litigation, it is now necessary to analyze the scope of liability. There are five different standards for passing the test of being a duty of international law binding for corporations:
(a) the duties must be universal, obligatory and specific;
(b) only violations of *jus cogens* norms;
(c) the *Sosa* test – they must be similar to the historic violations of ATCA (such as piracy, violation of safe conduct and infringing the rights of ambassadors);
(d) duties accepted as being of universal concern as specified in Article 402 of the Restatement of Foreign Relations Law (such as piracy, slave trade, attacks on or hijacking of aircraft, genocide, war crimes, and perhaps certain acts of terrorism); and
(e) the actions need to pass the egregiousness test.

Specifically, a corporation may be held liable as a joint actor or aider and abettor, together with a state actor in cases of torture or extrajudicial killing. Corporations may be held liable for aiding and abetting, meaning providing practical assistance, encouragement or moral support, which had a substantial impact on the commission of crimes against humanity or as part of genocide or war crimes. For example, expropriation or property destruction committed as part of genocide or war crimes may violate the law of nations and is actionable under ATCA. Corporations may face ATCA claims when using forced or slave labor. Furthermore, corporations may face ATCA lawsuits based on conduct affecting the environment, especially in relation to violations of the *UNCLOS*. Further claims actionable under ATCA are prolonged arbitrary detention or conspiring in such a violation. Looting or continued withholding of looted assets is a breach of a corporate duty under international law according to ATCA litigation, as well as airplane hijacking or acts of terrorism. Finally, racial discrimination may violate the "law of nations" actionable under ATCA.

6. International law widens its scope in terms of the actors that are regulated and the scope of subjects that are regulated. Whereas it was concerned with the behavior of nations before, it now also regulates rights and duties of international organizations, international non-governmental organizations, transnational corporations and individuals. International organizations gain influence, such as the EU, UN, WTO and IMF. Increasingly, international law affects national law, as can be seen in the Pinochet trials and the growing importance of universal jurisdiction in national courts, such as in Belgium's Universal Jurisdiction Law and the German Völkerstrafgesetzbuch.

The US Constitution is neither monist, nor dualistic. The question whether international treaties are to be interpreted by the US President or the judiciary has been the subject of some debate in the US. Even though the majority of scholars argue that only the judiciary interpret international treaties authoritatively, the judiciary (including the US Supreme Court) often adheres to statements of interest by the executive branch. The executive branch has also issued numerous statements of interest in ATCA litigation against corporations. Whereas the Clinton administration often sided with those claiming to be the victims of human rights violations, as in the case of the Holocaust litigation, the George W. Bush administration has mostly sided with the accused corporate perpetrators. The executive branch, especially in recent years under the Presidency of George W. Bush, has had a rather deteriorative effect on the importance of international law in US law.

Even though the US Supreme Court often emphasized its commitment to international law, most famously in the *Paquete Habana* decision, it has also, from time to time, disregarded sources of international law. In *Medellin v. Dretke*, the US Supreme Court voted to ignore the *Vienna Convention on Consular Rights* and the ICJ decision in *Avena*.

Like the US executive, the US legislature has played differing roles in recent years. On the one hand, it affirmed the ATCA litigation through the enactment of the TVPA but, on the other hand, it has created the PATRIOT Act, which gives the US executive widened powers that arguably encroach on rights guaranteed in the *ICCPR*. In US legal academia, the prevailing opinion favors strong international law and is anti-sovereignist. A progressive and internationalist example of their views can also be found in the 1987 Restatement of Foreign Relations Law. However, there are some exceptions to the internationalist view, such as John Yoo, Curtis A. Bradley and Jack Goldsmith. Unfortunately, John Yoo's extreme views on international law and human rights have been especially influential in providing legal memoranda to the US executive under President George W. Bush.

7. The decisive part of ATCA litigation is construing the "law of nations" actionable under ATCA litigation. However, the sources of international law – international treaties, customary international law, international tribunal decisions and other sources of international law – have been less influential than US precedents.

Overall, there appears to be a large amount of discretion for the US judiciary in the assessment of different sources of international law. Most ATCA decisions do not include a thorough analysis of international law based on Article 38 of the *ICJ Statute*, determining customary law. For support of their findings concerning international law they tend to rely on the Restatement of Foreign Relations law or on academic writing, which are according to international law subsidiary sources at best.

The *Sosa* decision might herald a slightly greater importance to sources of international law. In *Sosa*, the Supreme Court reminded US Courts that an ATCA claim "must be gauged against the current state of international law."

8. ATCA has led to increased scrutiny of corporate behavior abroad. It can be seen as a huge success for human rights so far. Even though the US courts can be criticized for largely disregarding sources of international law while construing the term "law of nations" in ATCA, they still developed one of the most forceful mechanisms for the imposition of human rights duties on TNCs. According to ATCA litigation, TNCs are not only subjects of international law, they also bear duties to adhere to human rights standards and these duties are largely put on par with those of individuals. This is very progressive and shows the way ahead for international law. The exact scope of human rights duties in ATCA litigation seems as yet unresolved, just as it remains unresolved in international law. A possible solution may be to hold corporations liable for aiding and abetting violations of *jus cogens* norms of customary law. Holding non-state actors civilly liable for violations of international law is also a way forward in international law, which has so far, in the regulation of individuals, mostly resorted to criminal liability only.

It is the task of international law to find answers to these emerging problems and situations. Corporations have amassed considerable power and investment protection law provides comprehensive protection in respect of many of their activities outside their home jurisdictions. Their duties appear to be less developed and some corporations exploit this situation. Certainly, it would be favorable to provide for human rights duties of corporations in an international treaty, as occurred in the *Rome Statute for the ICC*. Until then, this lacuna in international law needs to be filled and transnational litigation against corporations, such as ATCA human rights litigation, is a viable mechanism to enforce human rights.

Bibliography

Books

JE Alvarez, International Organizations as Law-Makers (Oxford; New York 2005)

S Anderes, Fremde im eigenen Land- Die Haftbarkeit transnationaler Unternehmen für Menschenrechtsverletzungen an indigenen Völkern (Zürich 2001)

E Aroneanu, Inside the Concentration Camps: Eyewitness Accounts of Life in Hitler's Death Camps (Praeger, Conneticut 1996)

A Aust, Handbook of International Law (1st edn, Cambridge University Press, Cambridge; New York 2005)

ADJ Balfour, Application of the European Convention on Human Rights by the European Court of Justice (Harvard Law School Student Scholarship Series, Berkeley Electronic Press (bepress), Berkeley 2005)

RJ Barnet and J Cavanagh, Global Dreams: Imperial Corporations and the New World Order (Simon & Schuster, New York 1994)

MJ Bazyler, Holocaust Justice: The Battle for Restitution in America's Courts (New York University Press, New York 2003)

PHF Bekker, The Treatment of Evidentiary Sources of International Law in US Alien Tort Statute Cases (Europa Instituut of Leiden University) (Kluwer, 2004)

R Bernhardt, Encyclopedia of Public International Law, IV (North-Holland Elsevier, Amsterdam 2000)

R Blanpain, The OECD Guidelines for Multinational Enterprises and Labour Relations, 1982-1984: Experience and Review (Kluwer Law and Taxation Publishers, Deventer; Boston 1985)

PE Bondzi-Simpson, The International Regulation of Relationships between Transnational Corporations and Host States: Conceptual Analyses and an Inquiry into Attempts at Codification and Control (University of Toronto, Toronto 1991)

I Brownlie, Principles of Public International Law (6th edn, Oxford University Press, Oxford; New York 2003)

M Byers, War Law: Understanding International Law and Armed Conflicts (1st edn, Grove Press, New York 2005)

RR Churchill and AV Lowe, The Law of the Sea (Manchester University Press, Manchester; New York 1988)

RC Clark, Corporate Law (Little, Brown, Boston 1986)

R Conquest, The Harvest of Sorrow: Soviet Collectivization and the Terror-Famine (Hutchinson, London 1986)

G Craig and others, Contemporary slavery in the UK (Joseph Rowntree Foundation, York 2007)

G Dahm, J Delbrück and R Wolfrum, Völkerrecht (2nd edn, De Gruyter, Berlin; New York 1989)

M Darrow, Between Light and Shadow: The World Bank, the International Monetary Fund and International Human Rights Law (Hart Publishing, Oxford 2003)

AM Dershowith, Why Terrorism Works: Understanding the Threat, Responding to the Challenge (Yale University Press, New Haven 2002)

U Di Fabio, Das Recht offener Staaten: Grundlinien einer Staats- und Rechtstheorie (Mohr Siebeck, Tübingen 1998)

M Dixon, Textbook on International Law (5th edn, Oxford University Press, Oxford; New York 2005)

K Doehring, Völkerrecht (2nd edn, Müller (C.F.Jur), Heidelberg 2004)

T Donaldson and TW Dunfee, Ties That Bind: A Social Contracts Approach to Business Ethics (Harvard Business School Press, Boston 1999)

SE Eizenstat, Imperfect Justice: Looted Assets, Slave Labor, and the Unfinished Business of World War II (Public Affairs, New York 2003)

Y Eliach, B Gurewitsch and S Center for Holocaust, The Liberators, Eyewitness Accounts of the Liberation of Concentration Camps: Oral History Testimonies of American Liberators from the Archives of the Center for Holocaust Studies (Center for Holocaust Studies Documentation and Research, Brooklyn 1981)

A Emmerich-Fritsche, Vom Völkerrecht zum Weltrecht (Duncker & Humblot, Berlin 2007)

EA Engle, Alien Torts in Europe? Human Rights and Tort in European Law (Bremen 2005)

TL Friedman, The World is Flat: A Brief History of the Twenty-First Century (1st edn, Farrar Straus and Giroux, New York 2006)

A Gedicks, Resource Rebels: Native Challenges to Mining and Oil Corporations (South End Press, Cambridge, MA 2001)

JL Goldsmith and EA Posner, The Limits of International Law (Oxford University Press, Oxford; New York 2005)

WG Grewe and M Byers, The Epochs of International Law (Walter de Gruyter, Berlin; New York 2000)

H Grotius, De Jure Belli ac Pacis Libri Tres (Apud Nicolavm Bvon, Parisiis 1625)

C Hailer, Menschenrechte vor Zivilgerichten - die Human Rights Litigation in den USA (Duncker & Humblot, Berlin 2006)

HLA Hart, The concept of law (Clarendon law series, Clarendon Press; Oxford University Press, Oxford; New York 1961)

D Hauck, Two Decades of Debate: The Controversy Over US Companies in South Africa (Investor Responsibility Research Center, Washington, D.C. 1983)

A Heidbrink, Der Alien Tort Claims Act (28 U.S.C. § 1350), Schadensersatzklagen vor US-amerikanischen Gerichten wegen Verletzungen des Völkerrechts (München 1989)

L Henkin, How Nations Behave: Law and Foreign Policy (2nd edn, Published for the Council on Foreign Relations by Columbia University Press, New York 1979)

M Herdegen, Völkerrecht (5th edn, Beck, München 2006)

R Higgins, The Development of International Law through the Political Organs of the United Nations (Oxford University Press, London 1963)

R Higgins, Problems and Process: International Law and How We Use It (Clarendon Press; Oxford University Press, Oxford; New York 1994)

C Hillemanns, Transnationale Unternehmen und Menschenrechte- Eine Studie zu den ersten beiden Prinzipien des Global Compact (Zürich 2004)

T Hobbes, Leviathan (1651), Erster und zweiter Teil, published by Malte Diesselhorst, translated by Jacob von Mayer (Reclam, Stuttgart 1970)

R Hofmann, Grundrechte und grenzüberschreitende Sachverhalte (Springer Verlag, Berlin 1994)

J Hollender and S Fenichell, What Matters Most: How a Small Group of Pioneers is Teaching Social Responsibility to Big Business, and why Big Business is Listening (Basic Books, New York 2004)

GC Hufbauer and NK Mitrokostas, Awakening Monster: The Alien Tort Statute of 1789 (Policy analyses in international economics 70, Institute for International Economics, Washington, D.C. 2003)

N Jägers, Corporate Human Rights Obligations: In Search of Accountability (Intersentia, Antwerpen 2002)

MW Janis, An Introduction to International Law (3rd edn, Aspen Law & Business, Gaithersburg 1999)

P Jensen, The Garotte: the United States and Chile, 1970-1973 (Aarhus University Press, Aarhus 1988)

H Jonas, Das Prinzip Verantwortung - Versuch einer Ethik für die technologische Zivilisation (Suhrkamp, Frankfurt am Main 1984)

S Joseph, Corporations and Transnational Human Rights Litigation (Human rights law in perspective, Hart Publishing, Oxford 2004)

S Jung, Die Rechtsprobleme der Nürnberger Prozesse- Dargestellt am Verfahren gegen Friedrich Flick (Mohr, Tübingen 1992)

H Kelsen, Reine Rechtslehre (2 edn, Deuticke, Wien 1960)

H Kelsen, Pure Theory of Law (University of California Press, Berkeley 1967)

HM Kindred, International law, chiefly as interpreted and applied in Canada (6th edn, Emond Montgomery, Toronto 2000)

P Kirchhof and others, Germany and its Basic Law: Past, Present, and Future - a German-American symposium (1st edn, Nomos, Baden-Baden 1993)

JHv Kirchmann, Die Wertlosigkeit der Jurisprudenz als Wissenschaft (2nd edn, Manutius-Verl., Heidelberg 2000)

J Kokott, K Doehring and T Buergenthal, Grundzüge des Völkerrechts (3rd edn, C.F. Müller, Heidelberg 2003)

M Kurnaz, Fünf Jahre meines Lebens (Rowohlt, Berlin 2007)

T Levitt, The Globalization of Markets (Division of Research Graduate School of Business Administration Harvard University, Boston 1982)

S Meisler, United Nations - The First Fifty Years (1st edn, Atlantic Monthly Press, New York 1995)

CdS Montesquieu and others, The Spirit of Laws (Clarke, Cincinnati 1873)

JE Nijman, The Concept of International Legal Personality: An Inquiry into the History and Theory of International Law (T.M.C. Asser Press, The Hague; New York 2004)

K Nowrot, Normative Ordnungsstruktur und private Wirkungsmacht - Konsequenzen der Beteiligung transnationaler Unternehmen an den Rechtssetzungsprozessen im internationalen Wirtschaftssystem (BWV Berliner Wissenschafts-Verlag, Berlin 2006)

TJ Noyelle, New York's Financial Markets: The Challenges of Globalization (Conservation of Human Resources studies in the new economy, Westview Press, Boulder 1989)

K Ohmae, Triad Power: The Coming Shape of Global Competition (Free Press, New York; London 1985)

K Ohmae, The End of the Nation State: The Rise of Regional Economies (Free Press, New York 1995)

L Oppenheim, RY Jennings and A Watts, Oppenheim's International Law (9th edn, Longman, Harlow 1992)

T Oppermann and E-U Petersmann, Reforming the International Economic Order: German Legal Comments (Tübinger Schriften zum internationalen und europäischen Recht; Bd 1, Duncker & Humblot, Berlin 1987)

Organisation for Economic Co-operation and Development, Environment and the OECD Guidelines for Multinational Enterprises: Corporate Tools and Approaches (Organisation for Economic Co-operation and Development, Paris 2005)

Organisation for Economic Co-operation and Development., OECD Guidelines For Multinational Enterprises: Focus on Responsible Supply Chain Management (OECD, Paris 2002)

JJ Paust, International Law as Law of the United States (2nd edn, Carolina Academic Press, Durham 2003)

HS Pérez Loose, Changing the International Regime for Multinational Corporations through Codes of Conduct from Harsh words to "Soft Law"; Doctoral thesis, Harvard Law School (Cambridge 1988)

B Pieroth and B Schlink, Grundrechte, Staatsrecht II (C.F. Müller Heidelberg 2000)

F Pigido-Pravoberezhny, The Stalin Famine: Ukraine in the year 1933 (Ukrainian Youth Association in Great Britain, London 1953)

A Ramasastry and RC Thompson, Commerce, Crime and Conflict (Fafo New Security Programme, 2006)

M Ratner and E Ray, Guantanamo: What the World Should Know (Chelsea Green Pub. Co., White River Junction 2004)

JE Raz, Authority (B. Blackwell, Oxford 1990)

NS Rembe, Africa and the International Law of the Sea: A Study of the Contribution of the African States to the Third United Nations Conference on the Law of the Sea (Sijthoff publications on ocean development, Sijthoff & Noordhoff, Alphen aan den Rijn; Germantown 1980)

PP Remec, The position of the individual in international law according to Grotius and Vattel (M. Nijhoff, The Hague 1960)

AD Renteln, International Human Rights: Universalism versus Relativism (Sage, Newsbury Park 1990)

G Ress and J Bröhmer, Internationale Gemeinschaft und Menschenrechte - Festschrift für Georg Ress zum 70. Geburtstag (Carl Heymanns, Köln 2005)

RJ Rummel, "Demozid" - der befohlene Tod: Massenmorde im 20. Jahrhundert; Übersetzung aus dem Englischem (Lit Verlag, Münster 2003)

A Sampson, Weltmacht ITT: Die politischen Geschäfte eines multinationalen Konzerns (Rowohlt Verlag, Reinbek 1975)

P Sands, Lawless World (Penguin Group, London 2005)

MA Santoro, Profits and Principles: Global Capitalism and Human Rights in China (Cornell University Press, Ithaca 2000)

AM Scott, The Civil Law (The Central Trust Company, Cincinnati 1932)

I Seidl-Hohenveldern and T Stein, Völkerrecht (10th edn, Academia iuris and index, C. Heymann, Köln 2000)

I Seidl-Hohenveldern, C University of and L Research Centre for International, Corporations In and Under International Law (Hersch Lauterpacht memorial lectures 6, Grotius, Cambridge 1987)

K Sellars, The Rise and Rise of Human Rights (Sutton, Stroud 2002)

AK Sen, Choice, Welfare, and Measurement (Harvard University Press, Cambridge 1997)

AK Sen, Development as Freedom (Knopf, New York 2001)

MN Shaw, International law (4th edn, Cambridge University Press, Cambridge; New York 1997)

B Simma and others, The Charter of the United Nations - A Commentary (2nd edn, Oxford University Press, Oxford; New York 2002)

A Smith, An inquiry into the nature and causes of the wealth of nations (Whitestone, Dublin 1776)

T Stein and C von Buttlar, Völkerrecht (11th edn, Carl Heymanns Verlag, Köln 2005)

HJ Steiner and P Alston, International Human Rights in Context: Law, Politics, Morals (2nd edn, Oxford University Press, Oxford 2000)

JE Stiglitz, Globalization and its Discontents (W.W. Norton, New York 2002)

JE Stiglitz, Making Globalization Work (W.W. Norton, New York 2006)

SA Swarztrauber, The Three-Mile Limit of Territorial Seas (Naval Institute Press, Annapolis 1972)

FR Tesón, A Philosophy of International Law (New perspectives on law, culture, and society, Westview Press, Boulder 1998)

GD Triggs, International Law- Contemporary Principles and Practices (Butterworths, Chattswood 2006)

United States Department of State, Country Reports on Human Rights Practices for 1991 (U.S. Government Printing Office, Washington, D.C. 1992)

WG Vitzthum, Völkerrecht (3rd edn, Gruyter, Berlin 2004)

CD Wallace, Legal Control of the Multinational Enterprise: National Regulatory Techniques and the Prospects for International Controls (M.Nijhoff, The Hague 1983)

G Walter, Globales Netz und globale Politik: Politische Antworten auf Globalisierung am Beispiel des Internet (1st edn, Weltpolitik im 21 Jahrhundert Bd 12, Nomos, Baden-Baden 2005)

A Watson, The Making of the Civil Law (Harvard University Press, Cambridge 1981)

CCv Weizsäcker, Logik der Globalisierung (3rd edn, Vandenhoeck und Ruprecht, Göttingen 2003)

A Zimmermann, R Hofmann and H Goeters, Unity and Diversity in International Law: Proceedings of an International Symposium of the Kiel Walther Schücking Institute of International Law, November 4-7, 2004 (Veröffentlichungen des Walther-Schücking-Instituts für Internationales Recht an der Universität Kiel, 157, Duncker & Humblot, Berlin 2006)

T Zülch, Völkermord an den Kurden - Eine Dokumentation der Gesellschaft für bedrohte Völker (Luchterhand Literaturverlag, Frankfurt am Main 1991)

Book sections

A Chan, 'The Culture of Survival: Lives of Migrant Workers through the Prism of Private Letters' in EP Link, R Madsen and P Pickowicz (eds) *Popular China: Unofficial Culture in a Globalizing Society* (Rowman & Littlefield Publishers, Lanham 2002)

Clapham, 'The Question of Jurisdiction Under International Criminal Law Over Legal Persons: Lessons from the Rome Conference on an International Criminal Court' in MT Kamminga and S Zia-Zarifi (eds) *Liability of Multinational Corporations under International Law* (Kluwer Law International, The Hague 2000)

RE Dalton, 'National Treaty Law and Practice: United States' in M Leigh, MR Blakeslee and B Ederington (eds) *National Treaty Law and Practice* (American Society of International Law, Washington, D.C. 1999)

G Fischer, 'Schadensersatzansprüche wegen Menschenrechtsverletzungen im internationalen Privat- und Prozessrecht' in Goydke (ed) *Vertrauen in den Rechtsstaat: Festschrift für Walter Remmers* (Heymann, Köln; Berlin; Bonn; München 1995)

P Fischer, 'Das transnationale Unternehmen als Phänomen in der Völkerrechtsgeschichte' in *Völkerrecht und Rechtsphilosophie, Internationale Festschrift für Stephan Verosta* (Duncker & Humblot, Berlin 1980)

J Galtung, 'What is Wrong with Transnational Corporations - And what can we do about it?' in W Däubler and K Wohlmut (eds) *Transnationale Konzerne und Weltwirtschaftsordnung* (Nomos, Baden-Baden 1978)

K Hailbronner, 'Der Staat und der Einzelne als Völkerrechtssubjekte' in WG Vitzthum (ed) *Völkerrecht* (de Gruyter, Berlin 2004)

R Higgins, 'The End of Sovereignty' in ASoI Law (ed) *ASIL Proceedings, Panel IV of the 88th Annual Meeting* (1994)

O Karitzki, 'Hinführung II: Auf dieHaltung kommt es an – über zu viel, zu wenig und falsches Vertrauen' in A Brink and O Karitzki (eds) *Unternehmensethik in turbulenten Zeiten Wirtschaftsführer über Ethik im Management* (Bern; Stuttgart; Wien 2004)

D Looschelders and D Olzen, '§ 242' in Jv Staudinger and others (eds) *BGB* (Sellier, Berlin 2005)

R Müller, 'The Multinational Corporation and the Exercise of Power: Latin America' in A Said and LR Simmons (eds) *The New Sovereigns - Multinational Corporations as World Powers* (Spectrum Books, Englewood Cliggs 1975)

S Oeter, 'Chancen und Defizite internationaler Verrechtlichung: Was das Recht jenseits des Nationalstaates leisten kann' in B Zangl and M Zürn (eds) *Verrechtlichung- Baustein für Global Governance* (Dietz, Bonn 2004)

KJ Partsch, 'Human Rights in General' in R Wolfrum and C Philipp (eds) *United Nations: Law, Policies and Practice* (Beck, München 1995)

RG Patman, 'International Human Rights' in RG Patman (ed) *Universal Human Rights?* (St. Martin's Press, New York 2000)

B Pischetsrieder, 'Konzernwerte als Grundlage ökonomischen Erfolgs – oder: Was hat Transparenz mit Ethik zu tun?' in A Brink and O Karitzki (eds) *Unternehmensethik in turbulenten Zeiten- Wirtschaftsführer über Ethik im Management* (Haupt, Bern; Stuttgart; Wien 2004)

H Ruh, 'Ethik und Erfolg verbünden sich: Ein neues Bündnis' in H Ruh and KM Leisinger (eds) *Ethik im Management: Ethik und Erfolg verbünden sich* (Orell Füssli, Zürich 2004)

T Rusche, 'Ethik und Wirtschaft im Dialog: Die Spannung von Moralität und Rentabilität in der kommunikativen Unternehmensethik' in H Ruh and KM Leisinger (eds) *Ethik im Management: Ethik und Erfolg verbünden sich* (Orell Füssli, Zürich 2004)

A Sen, 'Human Rights and Economic Achievements' in D Bell and JR Bauer (eds) *The East Asian Challenge for Human Rights* (Cambridge University Press, Cambridge; New York 1999)

D Thürer, 'The Emergence of Non-Governmental Organizations and Transnational Enterprises in International Law and the Changing Role of the State' in R Hofmann and N Geissler (eds) *Non-State Actors as New Subjects of International Law - International Law - From the Traditional State Order Towards the Law of the Global Community* (Duncker & Humblot, Berlin 1998)

R Wolfrum, 'Obligations Under Public International Law to Implement International Rules: Mechanisms to Monitor such Implementation' in BBv Maydell and A Nußberger (eds) *Social Protection by Way of international Law- Appraisal, Deficits and Further Development* (Duncker & Humblot, Berlin 1996)

Journal articles

'Multinational Business Enterprises' 12 Yearbook of International Organizations 1189

'Corporate Liability for Violations of International Human Rights Law' 114 Harvard Law Review 2025

'Symposium Program, Commentary by ambassadors to the United Nations' 4 Northwestern University Journal of International Human Rights 25

Av Aaken, 'To Do Away with International Law? Some limits to the 'The Limits of International Law'' 17 European Journal of International Law 289

A Afzal, 'Pakistan, the WTO, and Labor Reform' 29 Boston College International and Comparative Law Review 107

PC Aka, 'Prospects for IGBO human rights in Nigeria in the new century' 48 Howard Law Journal 165

MB Akehurst, 'Custom as a Source of International Law' 47 British Yearbook of International Law 1

SM Akram and M Karmely, 'Immigration and Constitutional Consequences of Post 9/11 Policies Involving Arabs and Muslims in the United States: Is Alienage a Distinction Without a Difference?' 38 UC Davis Law Review 609

MPv Alstine, 'The Judicial Power and Treaty Delegation' 90 California Law Review 1263

MPv Alstine, 'Federal Common Law in an Age of Treaties' 89 Cornell Law in an Age of Treaties 892

P Alston, 'The Universal Declaration at 35: Western and Passé or Alive and Universal' 31 International Commission of Jurists Review 60

P Alston, 'The Myopia of the Handmaidens: International Lawyers and Globalization' 8 (3) European Journal of International Law 435

P Arnold and T Hammond, 'The Role of Accounting in Ideological Conflict: Lessons from the South African Divestment Movement' 19 Accounting Organizations and Society 111

R Bahdi, 'Globalization of Judgement: Transjudicialism and the Five Faces of International Law in Domestic Courts' 34 The Geroge Washington Law Review 555

J Baker, 'The International Infant Formula Controversy: A Dilemma in Corporate Social Responsibility' 4 Journal of Business Ethics 181

MB Baker, 'Flying over the judicial hump: A human rights drama featuring Burma, the Commonwealth of Massachusetts, the WTO, and the federal courts' 32 Law and Policy of international business 51

MB Baker, 'Tightening the Toothless Vise: Codes of Conduct and the American Multinational Enterprise' 20 Wisconsin International Law Journal 555

E Barnert and N Doll, 'Conference Impressions: The persisting riddle of fundamental rights jurisprudence and the role of the Constitutional Court in a Democratic State' 4 (3) German Law Journal

MJ Bazyler and C Mesa, 'The Holocaust Restitution Movement in Comparative Perspective' 20 Berkeley Journal of International Law 11

DJ Bederman, 'Deference or Deception: Treaty Rights as Political Questions' 70 University of Colorado Law Review 1439

L Berat, 'Undoing and Redoing Business in South Africa: The Lifting of the Comprehensive Anti-Apartheid Act of 1986 and the Continuing Validity of State and Local Anti-Apartheid Legislation' 6 Connecticut Journal of International Law 7

MP Bergman, 'Montesquieu's Theory of Government and the Framing of the American Constitution' 18 Pepperdine Law Review 1

A Bhoumik, 'Democratic Responses to Terrorism: A Comparative Study of the United States, Israel and India' 33 Denver Journal of International Law and Policy 285

A Bixler, 'Private enforcement of international human rights laws: could a small church group successfully combat slavery in the Sudan?' 3 Chicago Journal of International Law 511

Av Bogdandy, 'Zweierlei Verfassungsrecht - Europäisierung als Gefährdung des gesellschaftlichen Grundkonsenses?' 39 Der Staat 163

HR Bornstein, 'The Alien Tort Claims Act in 2007: Resolving the Delicate Balance Between Judicial and Legislative Authority' 82 Indiana Law Journal 1077

C Bradley and JL Goldsmith, 'Customary International Law as Federal Common Law: A Critique of the Modern Position' 110 Harvard Law Review 815

CA Bradley and JL Goldsmith, 'The current illegitimacy of international human rights litigation' 66 Fordham Law Review 317

CA Bradley, JL Goldsmith and DH Moore, 'Sosa, Customary International Law, and the Continuing Relevance of Erie' 120 Harvard Law Review 869

DD Bradlow, 'The World Bank, the IMF, and human rights' 6 Transnational Law & Contemporary Problems 47

E Bucher, 'Drittwirkung der Grundrechte?- Überlegungen zu "Streikrecht" und "Drittwirkung" i.S. von BGE 111 245-259' 83 Schweizerische Juristen-Zeitung 37

A-M Burley, 'The Alien Tort Statute and the Judiciary Act of 1789: A Badge of Honor' 83 American Journal of International Law 461

A Carillo-Suarez, 'Hors de Logique: Contemporary Issues in International Humanitarian Law as Applied to Internal Armed Conflict' 15 American University International Law Review 1

H Carney, 'Prosecuting the Lawless: Human Rights Abuses and Private Military Firms' 74 George Washington Law Review 317

D Cassel, 'Corporate Initiatives: A Second Human Rights Revolution?' 19 Fordham International Law Journal 1963

S Chesterman, 'Oil and Water: Regulating the Behavior of Multinational Corporations Through Law' 36 New York University School of Law - Journal of International Law and Politics 265

DD Christensen, 'Corporate Liability for Overseas Human Rights Abuses After Sosa v. Alvarez-Machain' 62 Washington and Lee Law Review 1219

L Claus, 'Montesquieu's Mistakes and the True Meaning of Separation' 25 Oxford Journal of Legal Studies 419

T Collingsworth, 'The Key Human Rights Challenge: Developing Enforcement Mechanisms' 15 Harvard Human Rights Journal 183

AA D'Amato, 'Judge Bork's Concept of the Law of Nations is Seriously Mistaken' 79 American Journal of International Law 92

AA D'Amato, 'The Alien Tort Statute and the Founding of the Constitution' 82 American Journal of International Law 62

LF Damrosch, 'Scholars in the Construction and Critique of International Law, Panel Discussion' 94 American Society of International Law Proceedings 317

WK Davis, 'The International View of Attorney Fees in Civil Suits: Why is the United States the 'Odd Man Out' in How it Pays its Lawyers' 16 Arizona Journal of International and Comparative Law 361

J Delbrück, 'Prospects for a 'World (Internal) Law?': Legal Developments in a Changing International System' 9 Indiana Journal of Global Legal Studies 401

S Deva, 'Global Compact: A Critique of the U.N.'s "Public-Private" Partnership for Promoting Corporate Citizenship' 34 Syracuse Journal of International Law and Commerce 107

AA Dhir, 'Realigning the Corporate Building Blocks: Shareholder Proposals as a Vehicle for Achieving Corporate Social and Human Rights ' 43 American Business Law Journal 365

S Doddamani, 'Fighting for the Right to Hold Multinational Corporations Accountable: Indonesian Villagers Battle Oil Giant ExxonMobil' 49 Wayne Law Review 835

WS Dodge, 'The Historical Origins of the Alien Tort Statute: A Response to the 'Originalists'' 19 Hastings International and Comparative Law Review 221

MD Dubber, 'The German Jury and the Metaphysical Volk: From Romantic Idealism to Nazi Ideology' 43 American Journal of Comparative Law 227

E Duruigbo, 'The Economic Cost of Alien Tort Litigation: A Response to Awakening Monster: The Alien Tort Statute of 1789' 14 Minnesota Journal of Global Trade 1

M Ellinikos, 'American MNCs Continue to Profit from the Use of Forced and Slave Labor Begging the Question: Should America Take a Cue from Germany?' 35 Columbia Journal of Law and Social Problems 1

S Elliot, 'Emerging Threat: Human Rights Claims' 81 Harvard Business Review 16

D Everett, 'New Concern for Transnational Corporations: Potential Liability for Tortuous Acts Committed by Foreign Partners' 35 San Diego Law Review 1123

W Ewald, 'Comparative Jurisprudence (I): What was it like to Try a Rat?' 143 University of Pennsylvania Law Review 1889

B Falk, 'The Global War on Terror and the Detention Debate: The Applicability of Geneva Convention III' 3 Journal of International Law and International Relations 31

R Falk, 'On the Quasi-Legislative Competence of the General Assembly' 60 The American Journal of International Law 782

AX Fellmeth, 'Wiwa v. Royal Dutch Petroleum Co.: a new standard for the enforcement of international law in US courts?' 5 Yale Human Rights and Development Law Journal 241

J Fielding, 'Enforcing International Labor Standards through the Use of the Alien Tort Claims Act' 17 New York International Law Review 77

E First Baron and Lord Chancellor Thurlow, 'The Oxford Dictionary of Quotations 550 (3d ed. 1979).'

A Fischer-Lescano, 'Torture in Abu Ghraib: The Complaint Against Donald Rumsfeld Under the German Code of Crimes Against International Law' 6 German Yearbook of International Law 689

J Fitzpatrick, 'The Future of the Alien Tort Claims Act of 1789: Lessons from In re Marcos Human Rights Litigation' 67 St John's Law Review 491

G Fletcher, 'Black Hole in Guantánamo Bay' 2 Journal of International Criminal Justice 121

S Fohn, 'Do DEA Field Agents Have the Power to Unilaterally Execute a Trans-Border Abduction?: The Ninth Circuit's Take on Alvarez-Machain v. United States' 27 Houston Journal of International Law 221

C Forcese, 'Deterring "Militarized Commerce": The Prospect of Liability for "Privatized" Human Rights Abuses' 31 Ottawa Law Review 171

J Frowein, 'Solange II' 25 Common Market Law Review 201

S Gardbaum, 'The "Horizontal Effect" of Constitutional Rights' 102 Michigan Law Review 387

R Geiss, 'Humanitarian Safeguards in Economic Sanctions Regimes: A Call for Automatic Suspension Clauses, Periodic Monitoring, and Follow-Up Assessment of Long-Term Effects' 18 Harvard Human Rights Journal 167

A Glashauser, 'Difference and Deference in Treaty Interpretation' 50 Villanova Law Review 25

S Gul, 'The Supreme Court Giveth and the Supreme Court Taketh Away: An Assessment of Corporate Liability Under § 1350' 109 West Virginia Law Review 379

J Haberstroh, 'The Alien Tort Claims Act & Doe v. Unocal: a Paquete Habana approach to the rescue' 32 Denver Journal of International Law and Policy 231

C Hailer, 'Die US-amerikanische Human Rights Litigation' 44 Archiv des Völkerrechts 76

M Hamblett, 'Suit Alleging Canadian Oil Firm Aided Sudan Genocide Proceeds' (New York) 229 New York Law Journal 1

H Hannum, 'The Status of the Universal Declaration of Human Rights in National and International Law' 25 Georgia Journal of International and Comparative Law 287

H Hansmann and R Kraakman, 'The End of History for Corporate Law' 89 Georgetown Law Journal 439

R Harrison, 'The rise and rise of ethical consumerism' 50 Ethical consumer magazine

OA Hathaway and AN Lavinbuck, 'Rationalism and Revisionism in International Law' 119 Harvard Law Review 1404

L Henkin, 'International Law as Law in the United States' 82 Michigan Law Review 1555

L Henkin, 'The President and International Law' 80 American Journal of International Law 930

L Henkin, 'Human Rights and State "Sovereignty"' 25 Georgia Journal of International and Comparative Law 31

L Henkin, 'The Universal Declaration at 50 and the Challenge of Global Markets' 25 Brooklyn Journal of International Law 1

RL Herz, 'Litigating Environmental Abuses Under the Alien Tort Claims Act: A Practical Assessment' 40 Virginia Journal of International Law 545

C Hill, 'International Affairs: The Individual in International Organization' 28 American Political Science Review 276

C Hillemanns, 'UN Norms on the Responsibilities of Transnational Corporations and Other Business Enterprises with regard to Human Rights' 4 German Law Journal 10

JG Holt, 'The International Law Exception to the Act of State Doctrine: Redressing Human Rights Abuses in Papua New Guinea' 16 Pacific Rim Law and Policy Journal 459

D Hope, 'Torture' 53 International and Comparative Law Quarterly 807

S Howald, 'Globale Gerechtigkeit – Apartheid-Klagen gegen Konzerne, Vortrag an der Kantonschule Trogen AR vom 23. November 2005'

P-Y Hsu, 'Should Congress Repeal the Alien Tort Claims Act?' 28 Southern Illinois University Law Journal 579

A Ikelegbe, 'Encounters of Insurgent Youth Associations with the State in the Oil Rich Niger Delta Region of Nigeria' 22 Journal of Third World Studies 151

International Council on Human Rights Policy, 'Beyond Voluntarism, Human Rights and the Developing International Legal Obligations of Companies'

International Law Committee of the Association of the Bar of the City of New York, 'The Making of Filártiga v. Peña: The Alien Tort Claims Act after Twenty-Five Years' 9 New York City Law Review 249

MW Janis, 'Jeremy Bentham and the Fashioning of "International Law' 78 American Journal of International Law 405

F Johns, 'The Invisibility of the Transnational Corporation: An analysis of International Law and Legal Theory' 19 Melbourne University Law Review 893

S Kabel, 'Our Business Is People (Even If It Kills Them): The Contribution of Multinational Enterprises to the Conflict in the Democratic Republic of Congo' 12 Tulane Journal of International and Comparative Law 461

S Kadelbach, 'Ethik des Völkerrechts unter Bedingungen der Globalisierung' 64 Zeitschrift für ausländisches öffentliches Recht und Völkerrecht 1

J Kahn, 'Russian Compliance with Articles Five and Six of the European Convention of Human Rights as a Barometer of Legal Reform and Human Rights in Russia' 35 University of Michigan Journal of Law Reform 641

J Kammerhofer, 'Uncertainty in the Formal Sources of International Law: Customary International Law and Some of its Problems' 15 European Journal of International Law 523

S Kingah, 'Protecting African People against private violators of human rights: What can the new African Court of Human and Peoples' rights do to check the activities of Transnational corporations (TNCs)?'

D Kinley and J Tadaki, 'From Talk to Walk: The Emergence of Human Rights Responsibilities for Corporations at International Law' 44 Virginia Journal of International Law 931

R Klein, 'Cultural Relativism, Economic Development and International Human Rights in the Asian Context ' 9 Touro International Law Review 1

SJ Kobrin, 'Oil and Politics: Talisman Energy and Sudan' 36 International Law and Politics 425

HH Koh, 'Transnational Public Law Litigation' 100 Yale Law Journal 2347

HH Koh, 'Transnational Legal Process' 75 Nebraska Law Review 181

HH Koh, 'On American Exceptionalism' 55 Stanford Law Review 1479

HH Koh, 'International Law as part of our Law' 98 American Journal of International Law 43

K Kolben, 'Integrative Linkage: Combining Public and Private Regulatory Approaches in the Design of Trade and Labor Regimes' 48 Harvard International Law Journal 203

C Kolker, 'Jungle Warfare' 6 Corporate Counsel S21

E Kontorovich, 'Implementing Sosa v. Alvarez-Machain: What Piracy Teaches About the Limits of the Alien Tort Statute ' 80 Notre Dame Law Review 111

M Korowicz, 'The Problem of the International Personality of Individuals' 50 American Journal of International Law 533

S Kreindler, 'History's Accounting: Liability Issues Surrounding German Companies for the Use of Slave Labor by their Corporate Forefathers' 18 Dickinson Journal of International Law 343

H Lauterpacht, 'The Subjects of the Law of Nations ' Law Quarterly Review 438

LJ Lee, 'Barcelona Traction in the 21st Century: Revising its Customary and Policy Underpinnings 35 Years Later' 42 Stanford Journal of International Law 237

ML Lee, 'The Interrelation between the Law of the Sea Convention and Customary International Law' 7 San Diego International Law Journal 405

BD Lepard, 'Is the United States Obligated to Drive on the Right? A Multidisciplinary Inquiry into the Normative Authority of Contemporary International Law Using the Arm's Length Standard as a Case Study' 10 Duke Journal of Comparative and International Law 43

W-Y Leung, 'What can be done for the largest but deadliest manufacturing center in the world?' China Labour Bulletin

RB Lillich, 'Invoking International Human Rights Law in Domestic Courts' 54 University of Cincinnati Law Review 367

D McGoldrick, 'Sustainable Development and Human Rights: An Integrated Conception ' 45 International and Comparative Law Quarterly 796

D Monsma and T Olson, 'Muddling through Counterfactual Materiality and Divergent Disclosure: The Necessary Search for a Duty to Disclose Material Non-Financial Information' 26 Stanford Environmental Law Journal 137

PT Muchlinski, 'Holding Multinational to Account: Recent Developments in English Litigation and the Company Law Review' 23 Company Lawyer 168

ZP Mugge, 'Plan Colombia: The Environmental Effects and Social Costs of the United States' Failing War on Drugs' 15 Colorado Journal of International Environmental Law and Policy 309

SD Murphy, 'The ELSI Case: An Investment Dispute at the International Court of Justice' 16 Yale Journal of International Law 391

SD Murphy, 'Supreme Court Interpretation of Alien Tort Claims Act' 98 American Journal of International Law 845

B Neuborne, 'Preliminary Reflections on Aspects of Holocaust-Era Litigation in American Courts' 80 Washington University Quarterly 795

LH Newton, 'Truth is the Daughter of Time: The Real Story of the Nestle Case' 104 Business and Society Review 367

G O'Donoghue, 'Precatory Executive Statements and Permissible Judicial Responses in the Context of Holocaust-Claims Litigation' 106 Columbia Law Review 1119

FC Olah, 'MNC Liability for International Human Rights Violations Under the Alien Tort Claims Act: A Review & Analysis of the Fundamental Jurisprudence and a Look at Aiding & Abetting Liability under the Act' 25 Quinnipiac Law Review 751

F Orrego Vicuña, 'Changing approaches to the nationality of claims in the context of diplomatic protection and international dispute settlement' 15 ICSID review 340

W Osiatynski, 'Human Rights for the 21st Century' 2000 Saint Louis-Warsaw Transantlantic Law Journal 29

JJ Paust, 'The Changing Laws of War: Do We Need a New Legal Regime after September 11?' 79 Notre Dame Law Review 1335

JJ Paust, 'The Reality of Private Rights, Duties, and Participation in the International Legal Process' 25 Michigan Journal of International Law 1229

JJ Paust, 'International Law before the Supreme Court: A mixed record of recognition' 45 Santa Clara Law Review 829

J Pauwelyn, 'WTO Compassion or Superiority Complex?: What to make of the WTO Waiver for "Conflict Diamonds"' 24 Michigan Journal of International Law 1177

J Perez-Lopez, 'Promoting International For Workers Rights Through Business Codes of Conduct' 17 Fordham International Law Journal 1

P Pillai, 'From Corporate Social Responsibility to International Legal Responsibility-An Overview' 7 Faculteit der Rechtsgeleerdheid, Vrije Universiteit Amsterdam, Griffin's View 97

EA Posner and A Vermeule, 'Should coercive interrogation be legal?' 104 Michigan Law Review 671

I Poullaos, 'The Nature of the Beast: Using the Alien Tort Claims Act to Combat International Human Rights Violations' 80 Washington University Law Quarterly 327

C Powell, 'The Role of Transnational Norm Entrepreneurs in the US "War on Terrorism"' 5 Theoretical Inquiries in Law 47

A Ramasastry, 'Corporate Complicity: From Nuremberg to Rangoon An Examination of Forced Labor Cases and Their Impact on MNC Liability' 20 Berkeley Journal of International Law 91

K Randall, 'Federal Jurisdiction over International Law Claims: Inquiries. into the Alien Tort Statute' 18 New York University Journal of International Law and Politics 91

K Randall, 'Further Inquiries into the Alien Tort Statute and a Recommendation' 18 New York University Journal of International Law and Politics 473

SR Ratner, 'Corporations and Human Rights: A Theory of Legal Responsibility' 111 Yale Law Journal 443

P Redmond, 'Transnational Enterprise and Human Rights: Options for Standard Setting and Compliance' 37 International Lawyer 69

JM Rogers, 'The Alien Tort Statute and How Individuals "Violate" International Law' 21 Vanderbilt Journal of Transnational Law 47

SA Rosenberg, 'The Theory of Protective Jurisdiction' 57 New York University Law Review 933

BR Roth, 'Sosa v. Alvarez-Machain; United States v. Alvarez-Machain. 124 S.Ct. 2739. United States Supreme Court, June 29, 2004' 98 American Journal of International Law 798

AP Rubin, 'Professor D'Amato's Concept of American Jurisdiction is Seriously Mistaken' 79 American Journal of International Law 105

J Sarkin, 'Reparation For Past Wrongs: Using Domestic Courts Around The World, Especially The United States, to Pursue African Human Rights Claims' 32 International Journal of Legal Information 426

EJ Schrage, 'Judging Corporate Accountability in the Global Economy' 42 Columbia Journal of Transnational Law 13

P Sethi, 'Investing in Socially Responsible Companies is a must for Public Pension Funds - Because there is no Alternative' 56 Journal of Business Ethics 99

J-M Simon, 'The Alien Tort Claims Act: Justice or Show Trials?' 11 Boston University International Law Journal 1

K Skubiszewski, 'Enactment of Law by International Organizations' 41 British Yearbook of International Law 198

D Sloss, 'The Domestication of International Human Rights: Non-Self-Executing Declarations and Human Rights Treaties' 24 Yale Journal of International Law 129

D Sloss, '"Constitutional Implications of the War on Terror" - Symposium held at the New York University School of Law, February 3, 2006' 62 New York University Annual Survey of American Law 497

M Sornarajah, 'The Asian Perspective to International Law in Asia' 5 Singapore Journal of International and Comparative Law in Asia 284

GC Spencer, 'Her body is a battlefield: The applicability of the alien tort statute to corporate human rights abuses in Juarez, Mexico' 40 Gonzaga Law Review 503

PJ Spiro, 'The New Sovereignists: American Exceptionalism and Its False Prophets' 79 Foreign Affairs

H Steiger, 'Geht das Zeitalter des souveränen Staates zu Ende?' 41 Der Staat 331

RG Steinhardt, 'Fulfilling the Promise of Filártiga: Litigating Human Rights Claims Against the Estate of Ferdinand Marcos' 20 Yale Journal of International Law 65

B Stephens, 'The Civil Lawsuit as a Remedy for International Human Rights Violations Against Women' 5 Hastings Women's Law Journal 143

B Stephens, 'The Amorality of Profit: Transnational Corporations and Human Rights' 20 Berkeley Journal of International Law 45

B Stephens, 'Human Rights Accountability: Congress, Federalism and international law' 6 ILSA Journal of International and Comparative Law 277

B Stephens, 'Taking Pride in International Human Rights Litigation' 2 Chinese Journal of International Law 485

B Stephens, "Translating Filártiga: A Comparative and International Law Analysis of Domestic Remedies for International Human Rights Violations' ' 27 Yale Journal of International Law 1

B Stephens, 'Sosa v. Alvarez-Machain: 'The Door Is Still Ajar' for Human Rights Litigation in US Courts' 70 Brooklyn Law Review 533

B Stephens, 'Upsetting Checks and Balances: The Bush Administration's Efforts to Limit Human Rights Litigation' 17 Harvard Human Rights Journal 169

JM Sweeney, 'A Tort Only in Violation of the Law of Nations' 18 Hastings International and Comparative Law Review 445

A Taylor, 'The UN and the Global Compact' 17 New York Law School Journal of Human Rights 975

W Tetley, 'A Canadian Looks at American Conflict of Law Theory and Practice, Especially in the Light of the American Legal and Social Systems' 38 Columbia Journal of Transnational Law 299

C Tomuschat, 'Die internationale Gemeinschaft' 33 Archiv des Völkerrechts 1

S Toor, 'Child Labor in Pakistan: Coming of Age in the New World Order' 575 Annals of the American Academy of Political and Social Science 194

PR Trimble, 'The Supreme Court and International Law: The Demise of Restatement Section 403' 89 American Journal of International Law 53

United States Department of State, 'In re World War II Era Japanese Forced Labor Litigation (2001), Brief of the United States as amicus curiae in support of petitioners, Court of Appeal of the State of California Second Appelate District, Division Eight, 2d Civ. No. B155736'

D Vagts and others, 'Book Review Restatement of the Law Third: The Foreign Relations Law of the United States' 86 American Journal of International Law 608

D Vagts and DL Donoho, 'Book Review: International Human Rights. Universalism versus Relativism. By Alison Dundes Renteln' 85 American Journal of International Law 416

CM Vázquez, 'The Four Doctrines of self-executing treaties' 89 American Journal of International Law 695

CM Vázquez, 'Direct vs. Indirect Obligations of Corporations Under International Law' 43 Columbia Journal of Transnational Law 927

CD Wallace, 'The Legal Framework for Regulating the Global Enterprise Going Into the New WTO Trade Round--A Backward and a Forward Glance' 16 Transnational Lawyer 141

MJ Watts, 'Righteous Oil? Human Rights, the Oil Complex, and Corporate Social Responsibility' 30 Annual Review of Environmental Resources 373

MA Weisburd, 'American Judges and International Law' 36 Vanderbilt Journal of Transnational Law 1475

MA Weisburd, 'Roper v. Simmons and International Law' 45 Virginia Journal of International Law 798

D Weissbrodt, 'Business and Human Rights' 74 University of Cincinnati Law Review 55

M Weschka, 'Human Rights and Multinational Enterprises: How can Multinational Enterprises be Held Responsible for Human Rights Violations Committed Abroad?' 66 Zeitschrift für ausländisches öffentliches Recht und Völkerrecht 625

L Wick, 'Human rights violations in Nigeria: Corporate Malpractice and state acquiescence in the oil producing deltas of Nigeria' 12 Michigan State Journal of International Law 63

CA Williams, 'Corporate Social Responsibility in an Era of Economic Globalization' 35 UC Davis Law Review 705

D Williams, 'Reforming Human Rights Treaty Bodies' 1999 Australian Journal of Human Rights 30

IB Wuerth, 'The Dangers of Deference: International Claim Settlement by the President' 44 Harvard International Law Journal 1

J Yoo, 'Politics as Law?: The Anti-Ballistic Missile Treaty, the Separation of Powers, and Treaty Interpretation' 89 California Law Review 851

J Yoo, 'Treaty Interpretation and the False Sirens of Delegation' 90 California Law Review 1305

EA Young, 'Sorting out the Debate Over Customary International Law' 42 Virginia Journal of International Law 365

NE Zelman, 'The Nestle Infant Formula Controversy: Restricting the Marketing Practices of Multinational Corporations in the Third World' 3 Transnational Lawyer 697

S Zia-Zarifi, 'Suing Multinational Corporations in the US for Violating International Law' 4 UCLA Journal of International Law and Foreign Affairs 81

Newspaper articles

'Klare Regeln, Wer trägt in globalisierten Unternehmen die Verantwortung?; Antworten von Ulrich Steger, Professor am IMD in Lausanne und früher selbst Manager' *Brand Eins Online Magazin* (October 2004)

'They beat me from all sides' *The Guardian* (January 14, 2005)

J Adcock, 'Rep Production Puts the Spotlight on Rachel Corrie and Her Causes' *Seattle Post* (March 16, 2007) 27

E Alden, 'US Interrogation Debate: Dismay at Attempt to Find Legal Justification for Torture: International Lawyers Call For Government Advisers behind Interrogation Memo to Face Professional Sanctions' *Financial Times UK* (June 10, 2004)

E Amaize, 'Militants Threaten to Adopt New Tactics on Hostage Taking' *Vanguard Nigeria* (July 17, 2007)

Anonymous, 'Dirty Deeds' *Cityview, Des Moines, Iowa* (June 15, 2006) 13

S Bergius, 'Banken entdecken die Moral' *Handelsblatt* (December 6, 2005) 30

S Bergius, 'Dachfonds entdecken Nachhaltigkeit' *Handelsblatt* (February 8, 2006) 33

S Bergius, 'Investoren fordern Nachhaltigkeit' *Handelsblatt* (February 8, 2006) 27

RH Bork, 'Judicial Imperialism' *Wall Street Journal* (July 12, 2004) A16

S Bräuer, 'Shell gefährdet Ölförderung' *Die Zeit* (June 28, 2006)

H Buchter, 'Der gute Mensch und der Völkermord' *Financial Times Deutschland* (April 23, 2007) 1

B Condie, 'Pfizer is sued over Nigerian drug trials' *Evening Standardt* (October 1, 2007)

J Drimmer, 'Corporate Exposure Under the Alien Tort Claims Act' *Corporate Counsellor* (June 2007)

B Egelko, 'Nike settles suit for $ 1,5 million: Shoe giant accused of lying about workers' treatment' *San Francisco Chronicle* (September 13, 2003) B1

M Esterl and D Crawford, 'Why Siemens Bribery Probe Slogs On' *The Wall Street Journal* 2007) A12

A Förster and D Fras, 'Im Schatten' *Berliner Zeitung* (Januar 24, 2007) 3

M Friedman, 'The Social Responsibility of Business is to increase its Profits' *New York Times (Magazine)* (September 13, 1970) 32

P Gogoi, 'Wal-Mart's Organic Offensive' *Business Week* 2006)

B Grill, 'Wir sitzen im Glashaus- Der deutsche Antikorruptionskämpfer Peter Eigen über seine Initiative für Entwicklungsländer, den G8-Gipfel und seine große Enttäuschung über Siemens' *DIE ZEIT* 2007)

Gzedit, 'Deadly Tests Saving Money Costs Lives' *Charleston Gazette* (December 21, 2000) 4A

W Hawkins, 'China's Role in Genocide' *Washington Times* 2006) A16

D Housego, 'Union Carbide Asks Indian Unit To Help Pay Victims' *Financial Times UK* (February 16, 1989) 4

K Howe, 'Human Rights Group Investigates Chevron - 2 Nigerian Killed in Offshore Protest' *San Francisco Chronicle* (November 19, 1998) A1

E Iritani, 'Effort to divest from Sudan picks up steam' *Los Angeles Times* (April 11, 2007)

J Iwori, 'Niger Delta: Still a Festering Sore' *This Day (Nigeria)* (January 29, 2006)

D Jehl, 'Who Armed Iraq? Answers the West Didn't Want to Hear' *New York Times* (July 18, 1993) E 5

D Jochum, 'Noch ist Bush immun' *Junge Welt* (Januar 6, 2007)

J Karliner and B Kenny, 'The United Nations Sits In Suspicious Company' *International Herald Tribune* 2000)

S Kirchgaessner, 'World News: Darfur activists target US investors' *Financial Times Europe* (September 6, 2007) 6

C Krauss, 'Exxon and Shell Report Record Profits for 2006' *New York Times* (February 2, 2007)

DH Lamparter, 'Im Visier der Justiz; Siemens, Daimler, VW: In Deutschlands Konzernen werden immer mehr Korruptionsfälle aufgedeckt' *DIE ZEIT* (November 23, 2006) 27

DH Lamparter, '"Verpfeifen kommt zuletzt"; Gegen Korruption hilft nur ein radikaler Bruch in der Kultur des Unternehmens, sagt Wirtschaftsethiker Josef Wieland' *DIE ZEIT* (November 23, 2006) 27

P Lewis, 'Blood and oil: A special report; After Nigeria represses, shall defends its record' *New York Times* (February 13, 1996) 1

A Liptak, 'Legal Scholars Criticize Memos on Torture' *New York Times* (June 25, 2004) A14

J Lobe, 'Shell under fire from greens, shareholders' *OneWorld US* (December 23, 2004)

K Maier, 'Nigerian Dissident Faces Death Penalty' *The Independent* (October 29, 1995) World 12

M Marek, 'Zwangsarbeiter-Stiftung zieht Bilanz' *Handelsblatt* (December 28, 2005) 6

G Marx, 'Coca-Cola Feels Heat on Killing - Union Activist's Death in Columbia Spurs US Campus Boycott Talks' *Chicago Tribune* (February 13, 2006) 15

J Mouawad, 'Shell expects full output from Nigeria' *New York Times* (April 5, 2007) C1

E Ng, 'Fidelity sells down ADR holding in PetroChina' *South China Morning Post* (May 17, 2007)

T Niles, 'The Very Long Arm of American Law' *Financial Times* (November 6, 2002) 15

V Noce, 'L'«Adele» de Klimt bat le «Garçon à la pipe» de Picasso; Son portrait d'Adele Bloch-Bauer, à l'histoire tourmentée, est devenu la toile la plus chère au monde' *Liberation* (June 23, 2006) 24

M Nyberg, 'At Risk from Complicity with Crime' *Financial Times,* (July 28, 1998)

T Paterson, 'Leaked Report Says German and US Firms Supplied Arms to Saddam ' *The Independent* (December 18, 2002)

K Penhaul, 'Protection for Oil Pipeline Raises US Profile in Colombia, New Policy Stirs Fears Bush Seeks to Widen War' *San Francisco Chronicle* (February 16, 2002)

E Reeves, 'A Brutal Regime Persists in a Distracted World - Sudan's Civil War' *International Herald Tribune* (April 3, 2003) 9

M Rosen-Molina, 'Two alleged CIA rendition victims join ACLU lawsuit against Boeing subsidiary' *Jurist Legal News & Research* (August 1, 2007)

A Rowell, 'Sleeping With the Enemy' *Village Voice* (January 23, 1996) World 23

A Salpukas, 'Burma Project Tests Unocal Resolve' *New York Times* (May 22, 1997) D1

J Scahill, 'A Very Private War' *Guardian* (August 1, 2007)

E Schechter, 'Pro-Palestinian US Activist Killed by IDF Bulldozer in Gaza Strip' *Jerusalem Post* (March 17, 2003) 1

S Shane, S Grey and M Williams, 'C.I.A. Expanding Terror Battle Under Guise of Charter Flights' *The New York Times* (May 31, 2005)

P Sherwell and P Goff, 'Beijing Courts New Allies with 'Black Gold Diplomacy' US Scrambles to Match China as Battle for Access to World's Oil Reserves Becomes New 'Giant Game'' *Sunday Telegraph* 2006) 28

J Simon, 'Einer gegen Rumsfeld' *DIE ZEIT* (November 9, 2006) 17

P Singer, 'Outsourcing War' *Foreign Affairs* (March 1, 2005)

LM Sixel, 'Union to Protest at Coke Annual Meeting' *Houston Chronicle* (April 16, 2003)

M Smith and D Voreacos, 'The Secret World of Modern Slavery' *Bloomberg Markets December* 2006) 46

U Sommer, 'Konzerne wachsen stark im Ausland' *Handelsblatt* (December 27, 2006) 1

J Stephens, 'Panel Faults Pfizer in '96 Clinical Trial in Nigeria' *Washington Post* 2006) A01

K Sullivan, 'El Salvador Scarred by Child Labor, Subsistence Work in Sugar Cane Leads to Injuries, Continuing Poverty' *Washington Post* (June 10, 2004) A08

C Vogel, 'Lauder Pays $ 135, a Record for a Klimt Portrait' *New York Times* (June 19 2006) 12

P Waldmeir, 'An Abuse of Power: US Courts Should not Punish Companies for Human Rights Violations Committed Overseas' *Financial Times* (March 14, 2003) 12

J Weisman, 'Redress Sought in Nazi-Era Labor' *Baltimore Sun* (August 23, 1999) 1A

R Weissman, 'Victories! Justice! The People's Triumphs Over Corporate Power' *Multinational Monitor* (July 1, 2005) 35

M Wolf, 'Countries still rule the world' *Financial Times* (February 6, 2002)

Cases

Abdullahi v. Pfizer No 01 Civ 8118, 2002 US Dist LEXIS 17436, 2002 WL 31082956, D.C. S.D. N.Y.

Abebe-Jira v. Negewo 72 F3d 844, C.A. 11

Abebe-Jiri v. Negewo Not reported in FSupp, 1993 WL 814304, D.C. N.D. Ga.

Adamu v. Pfizer 399 FSupp 2d 495, D.C. S.D. N.Y.

Adra v. Clift 195 FSupp 857, D.C. Md.

Aguinda v. Texaco 1993 WL 13148394, D.C. S.D.N.Y.

Aguinda v. Texaco 945 FSupp 625, D.C. S.D.N.Y.

Aguinda v. Texaco, Inc. 303 F3d 470, C.A. 2

Al Odah v. United States 321 F3d 1134, C.A. D.C.

Almog v. Arab Bank, PLC 471 FSupp2d 257, D.C. E.D.N.Y.

Amerada Hess Shipping Corp. v. Argentine Republic 830 F2d 421, C.A. 2

Amerada Hess Shipping Corp. v. Argentine Republic 488 US, 109 SCt 683, 102 LEd2d 818, US S.Ct.

Arar v. Ashcroft 414 F Supp 2d 250, D.C. E.D. N.Y.

Argentine Republic v. Amerada Hess Shipping Corp. 488 US 428, 109 SCt 683, 102 LEd2d 818, US S.Ct.

Arias v. Dyncorp 01-CV-1908, D.C. D.C.

Asylum Case (Columbia v. Peru) ICJ Reports 1950, 266, ICJ

Attorney-Gen. of the Government of Israel v. Eichmann 36 ILR 277, Sup. Ct. Israel

Baker v. Canada (Minister of Citizenship and Immigration) 2 SCR 817, Canada S.Ct.

Bananenmarktordnung BVerfGE 102, 147, German Constitutional Court (Bundesverfassungsgericht)

Bano v. Union Carbide 2000 WL 1225789, D.C. S.D.N.Y.

Bano v. Union Carbide 273 F3d 120, C.A. 2

Bano v. Union Carbide 2003 WL 1344884, D.C. S.D. N.Y.

Bano v. Union Carbide 361 F3d 696, C.A. 2

Bao Ge v. Li Peng 201 FSupp2d 14, D.C. D.C.

Barbuit's Case 25 Eng Rep 777 (Ch), English Court of Chancery

Barcelona Traction, Light and Power Co. (Belgium v. Spain) ICJ Reports 1970, 3, ICJ

Baustahlgewebe ECR I-8417, C-185/95, ECJ

Beanal v. Freeport- McMoran, Inc. 969 F Supp 362, D.C. E.D. La

Beanal v. Freeport-McMoran, Inc. 197 F3d 161, C.A. 5

Bernard Connolly ECR I-1611, ECJ

Beschluss vom 21.6.1954 2/3 OH 12/54, German Regional Court (Landgericht)

Bigio v. Coca-Cola WL 293990, D.C. S.D. N.Y.

Bigio v. Coca-Cola 448 F3d 176, C.A. 2

Bigio v. Coca-Cola Co. 239 F3d 440, C.A. 2

Bigio v. Coca-Cola Co. No 97 Civ 2858, 2005 WL 287397, 2005 US Dist LEXIS 1587, D.C. S.D. N.Y.

Bivens v. Six Unknown Named Agents 403 US 388, US S.Ct.

Bodner v. Banque Paribas 114 FSupp2d 117, D.C. E.D.N.Y.

Bolchos v. Darrell 3 F Cas 810 (No 1,607), US District of South Dakota

Bowoto v. Chevron 312 F Supp 2d 1229, D.C. N.D. Cal.

Bowoto v. Chevron WL 2349336, D.C. N.D. Cal.

Bowoto v. Chevron Corp. WL 2455752, D.C. N.D. Cal.

Brig Malek Adhel 43 US (2 How) 210, 232, 11 LEd 239, US S.Ct.

Burger-Fischer v. Degussa AG 65 F Supp 2d 248, D.C.N.J.

Burnett v. Al Baraka Inv. and Development Corp. 274 FSupp2d 86, D.C. D.C.

Carmichael v. United Technologies Corp. 835 F2d 109, C.A. 5

Case Concerning Avena and Other Mexican Nationals (Mexico v. US) ICJ 128, ICJ

Case concerning the arrest warrant of 11 April 2000 (Democratic Republic of the Congo v. Belgium) 2000 ICJ 182, ICJ

Chisholm v. Georgia 2 US (2 Dall) 419, US S.Ct.

Coker v. Georgia 433 US 584, 596 n10, US S.Ct.

Committee of US Citizens Living in Nicaragua v. Reagan 859 F2d 929, C.A. D.C.

Connelly v. RTZ, July 24, 1997 1998 Law Reports, Appeal Cases 854, U.K. House of Lords

Corrie v. Caterpillar, Inc. 403 F Supp 2d 1019, D.C. W.D. Wash.

Costa v. ENEL ECR 585, 6/64, ECJ

Criminal Proceedings against X ECR I-6609, C-74 and 129/95, ECJ

Dagi v BHP 1 VR 428, Australia Supreme Court of Victoria

De Geofrey v. Riggs 133 US 258, US S.Ct.

Defrenne v Societe Anonyme Belge de Navigation Aerienne Sabena ECJ Ruling Case 43/75, 1976 ECR 455, ECJ

Dennis v. Sparks 449 US 24, 27-28, 101 SCt 183, 185-87, 66 LEd2d 185 US S.Ct

Deutsch v. Turner Corp. 317 F3d 1005, C.A. 9

Deutsche Milchkontor GmbH and others v Federal Republic of Germany 1983 ECR 2633, ECJ

Doe I et al. v. Gap, Inc. et al. Case No CV01-0031-948, D.C.N.Mar.

Doe v. Exxon 473 F3d 345, C.A. D.C.

Doe v. Exxon Mobil Corporation 393 FSupp2d 20, D.C. D.C.

Doe v. Karadzic 866 FSupp 734, D.C. S.D. N.Y.

Doe v. Unocal 963 F Supp 880 D.C. C.D.Cal.

Doe v. Unocal 27 F Supp 2d 1174, D.C. C.D. Cal.

Doe v. Unocal 248 F 3d 915 D.C. C.D. Cal.

Doe v. Unocal 2002 US App LEXIS 19263, C.A. 9

Doe v. Unocal 2003 WL 359787, C.A. 9

Doe v. Unocal (Unocal I) 963 F Supp 880, D.C.C.D. Cal.

Doe v. Unocal (Unocal II) 110 F Supp 2d 1294, D.C. C.D.Cal.

Doe v. Unocal (Unocal III) 395 F3d 932, C.A. 9

Eastman Kodak Co. v. Kavlin 978 FSupp 1078, D.C. S.D. Fla.

EC - Selected Customs Matters (16 June) WT/DS315/R, WTO DSB

El Al Israel Airlines, Ltd. v. Tsui Yuan Tseng 525 US 155, US S.Ct.

El-Masri v. US 479 F3d 296, C.A. 4

E-Masri v. Tenet 437 FSupp2d 530, D.C. E.D. Va.

Endicott Johnson Corp. v. Liberty Mutual Ins. Co. 116 F3d 53, C.A. 2

Enmund v. Florida 458 US 782, 796 n22, US S.Ct.

Erie Railroad Co. v. Tompkins 304 US 64, US S.Ct.

Estate of Rodriguez v. Drummond Co. 256 F Supp 2d 1250, D.C. N.D. Ala.

Estate of Winston Cabello v. Armando Fernandez-Larios 157 FSupp2d 1345, US S.D.Fla.

Ex Parte Quirin 317 US 1, US S.Ct.

Factortame Ltd. v Secretary of State for Transport (No. 2) 1 AC 603, U.K. House of Lords

Filártiga v. Peña-Irala 630 F2d 876, C.A. 2

Filártiga v. Peña-Irala 577 F Supp 860, D.C. E.D.N.Y.

Flexi-Van Leasing, Inc. v. Islamic Republic of Iran 12 Iran- United States Claims Tribunal Report 335, Iran- United States Claims Tribunal

Flores v. Southern Peru Copper Corp. 253 F Supp 2d 510, D.C. S.D. N.Y.

Flores v. Southern Peru Copper Corp. 406 F3d 65, C.A. 2

Flores v. Southern Peru Copper Corporation 343 F3d 140, C.A. 2

Frontini v. Ministero delle Finanze 2 CMLR 372, Corte Costitutionale Italy

GIRCA v. IBM http://jumpcgibgerch/cgi-bin/JumpCGI?id=14082006_4C113/2006, Federal Supreme Court of Switzerland

Grant v South West Trains ECR I-621, C-249/96, ECJ

Gulf Oil Corp. v. Gilbert 330 US 501, 67 SCt 839, 91 LEd 1055, US S.Ct.

Hamid v. Price Waterhouse Coopers 51 F3d 1411, C.A. 9

Hauer v Rheinland-Pfalz ECR 3727, 44/79, ECJ

Hereros ex rel. Riruako v. Deutsche Afrika-Linien Gmblt & Co. 2007 WL 1066949, C.A. 3

Hertzberg et al. v. Finland UN GAOR Human Rights Comm, 37th Sess, Supp No 40 at 161, para 103, UN Doc A/37/40, Human Rigths Committee

Hilao v. Estate of Marcos 103 F3d 767, 776, C.A. 9

Hoechst AG v Commission of the European Communities, September 21, 1989, 46/87 and 227/88 1989 ECR 2859, ECJ

Ibrahim v. Titan Corp. 391 F Supp 2d 10, D.C. D.C.

IIT v. Vencap, Ltd. 519 F2d 1001, C.A. 2

In re Agent Orange Product Liability Litigation 373 FSupp2d 7, D.C. E.D. N.Y.

In re Estate of Ferdinand Marcos Human Rights Litigation ("Estate I") 978 F2d 493 C.A. 9

In re Estate of Ferdinand Marcos Human Rights Litigation (Estate II) 25 F3d 1467, C.A. 9

In re Holocaust Victim Assets Litigation 105 FSupp2d 139, D.C. E.D.N.Y.

In re Pinochet 38 ILM 430, U.K. House of Lords

In re World War II Era Japanese Forced Labor Litigation 114 F Supp 2d 939, D.C. N.D. Cal.

In re: South African Apartheid Litigation 346 FSupp2d 538, D.C. S.D. N.Y.

International Technical Products Corp. v. Islamic Republic of Iran 9 Iran- United States Claims Tribunal reports 206, Iran- United States Claims Tribunal

Internationale Handelsgesellschaft, 1970 ECR 1125, Case 11/70

Iwanowa v. Ford Motor Company 67 F Supp 2d 424, D.C.N.J.

Jama v. U.S. I.N.S. 22 FSupp2d 353, D.C. N.J.

Japan Whaling Ass'n v. Am. Cetacean Soc'y 478 US 221, US S.Ct.

Jones v. Alfred H. Mayer Co. 392 US 409, 438-39, 88 SCt 2186, 20 LEd2d 1189, US S.Ct.

Jota v. Texaco, Inc. 157 F3d 153, C.A. 2

Kadic v. Karadzic 70 F3d 232, C. A. 2

Kasky v. Nike 24 Cal 4th 939, US SCt. Cal.

Ken Saro-Wiwa ACoHPR

Kolovrat v. Oregon 366 US 187, US S.Ct.

Krombach v Bamberksi ECR I-1935, C-7/98, ECJ

Legality of the Threat or Use of Nuclear Weapons - Advisory Opinion 08.07.1996 ICJ Reports 1995, 226, ICJ

Lopez Ostra v Spain Ser A No 303-C, ECtHR

Lotus PCIJ Ser A, No 10, PCIJ

Lubbe v. Cape plc 4 All ER 268 (HL) 277, U.K. House of Lords

Lüth BverfGE 7, 198 German Constitutional Court (Bundesverfassungsgericht)

Maastricht BVerfGE 89, 155, German Constitutional Court (Bundesverfassungsgericht)

Maria V. Altmann et. al. v. Republik Österreich Schiedsspruch vom 15. Januar 2006 http://wwwadeleat/Schiedsspruch/Schiedsspruchpdf, Arbitration Panel Austria (Schiedsgericht Österreich)

Medellin v. Dretke 544 US 660, US S.Ct.

Mehinovic v. Vuckovic 198 FSupp2d 1322, D.C. N.D. Ga.

Military and Paramilitary Activities in and Against Nicaragua (Nicaragua v. US) (Merits) ICJ 14, 98, ICJ

Minister for Immigration and Ethnic Affairs v Teoh 183 CLR 273, High Court of Australia

Mujica v. Occidental Petroleum Corp. 381 F Supp 2d 1134, D.C. C.D. Cal.

Murray v. The Schooner Charming Betsy 6 US (2 Cranch) 64, 118, US S.Ct.

National Panasonic (U.K.) Limited v Commission of the European Communities 1980 ECR, Case 136/79, ECJ

New York Cent. & Hudson River R.R. Co. v. United States 212 US 481, 493, 29 SCt 304, 53 LEd 613, US S.Ct.

Nguyen Da Yen v. Kissinger 528 F2d 1194, C.A. 9

Nicaragua v. US, ICJ

North Sea Continental Shelf (F.R.G. v. Den., F.R.G. v. Neth.) ICJ 3, ICJ

O'Reilly de Camara v. Brooke 209 US 45, 28 SCt 439, 52 LEd 676, US S.Ct.

P v S and Cornwall County Council ECR I-2143, C-13/94, ECJ

The Paquete Habana 175 US 677, US S.Ct.

Piper Aircraft Co. v. Reyno 454 US 235, US S.Ct.

Pollock v. Williams 322 US 4, 17, 64 SCt 792, 88 LEd 1095, US S.Ct.

Portugal v Council (Opinion by Advocate General La Pergola) ECR I-6177, 268/94, ECJ

Presbyterian Church of Sudan et al. v. Talisman Energy, Inc. 244 F Supp 2d 289, D.C. S.D. N.Y.

The Presbyterian Church of Sudan, et. al. v. Talisman Energy, Inc. Case No 01CV9882, D.C. S.D. N.Y.

The Presbyterian Church of Sudan, et. al. v. Talisman Energy, Inc. 374 FSupp2d 331, D.C. S.D. N.Y.

Prosecutor v. Jean-Paul Akayesu Case No ICTR-96-4-T, Summary available at 37 ILM 1399, ICTR

Rainwater v. United States 356 US 590, US S.Ct.

Ralk v. Lincoln County, Georgia 81 FSupp2d 1372, D.C. S.D.Ga.

Raoul George Nicolo 1 CMLR 173 Conseil d'Etat

Reid v. Covert 354 US 1, US S.Ct.

Report of the Panel, Thailand--Restrictions on Importation of and Internal Taxes on Cigarettes GATT BISD (37th Supp), WTO

The Republic of Ireland v The United Kingdom Series A, No 25, ECtHR

Respublica v. DeLongchamps 1 US (1 Dall) 111, 1 LEd 59, US Court of Oyer and Terminer, Delaware

Roper v. Simmons 543 US 551, 125 SCt 1183 (Mar 1), US S.Ct.

Roquette Freres SA v Directeur General de la Concurrence, de la Consommation et de la Repression des Fraudes ECR I-9011, C94/00 ECJ

Sanchez-Espinoza v. Reagan 770 F2d 202 D.C. D.C.

Sarei v. Rio Tinto 456 F3d 1069, C.A. 9

Sarei v. Rio Tinto PLC 221 FSupp2d 1116, D.C. C.D. Cal.

Sarei v. Rio Tinto, PLC 487 F3d 1193, C.A. 9

SEDCO, Inc. v. National Iranian Oil Co. 15 Iran-United States Claims Tribunal Report 23, Iran-United States Claims Tribunal

Sinaltrainal v. Coca-Cola Co. 256 F Supp 2d 1345, D.C. S.D. Fla.

Situation in Darfur, Sudan in the Case of The Prosecutor v. Ahmad Muhammad Harun ("Ahmad Harun") and Ali Muhammad al Abd-Al-Rahman ("Ali Kushayb") Pre-Trial Chamber I, No ICC-02/05-01/07, ICC

Smith Kline & French Labs Ltd. v. Bloch 1 WLR 730 Ct. App. (England)

Solange I BVerfGE 37, 271, German Constitutional Court (Bundesverfassungsgericht)

Solange II BVerfGE 73, 339, German Constitutional Court (Bundesverfassungsgericht)

Sosa v. Alvarez-Machain (03-339) 542 US 2739, US S.Ct.

South Dakota v. Yankton Sioux Tribe 522 US 329, US SCt.

Spiliada Maritime Corp v. Cansulex AC 460 U.K. House of Lords

Stanford v. Kentucky 492 US 361, US S.Ct.

Sumitomo Shoji Am., Inc. v. Avagliano 457 US 176, US S.Ct.

Tachiona et al. v. Mugabe et al. 169 FSupp2d 259, D.C. S.D. N.Y.

Tachiona et al. v. Mugabe et al. WL230860, D.C. S.D.N.Y.

Tel-Oren v. Libyan Arab Republic 517 F Supp 542, D.C. D.C.

Tel-Oren v. Libyan Arab Republic 726 F2d 774, C.A. D.C.

Thompson v. Oklahoma 487 US 815, 830, US S.Ct.

Trans World Airlines, Inc. v. Franklin Mint Corp. 466 US 243, US S.Ct.

Trials of Bruno Tesch and two others March 1-8, 1946, British Military Court Hamburg

United States - Section 211 Omnibus Appropriations Act of 1998 (US - Section 211 Appropriations Act) (1 February) WT/DS176/AB/R, WTO DSB

United States ex rel. Lujan v. Gengler 510 F2d 62, C.A. 2

The United States of America vs. Alfried Krupp, et. al. Trials of War Criminals before the Nuernberg Military Tribunals Under Control Council Law no 10, Washington, DC, Microcard Editions, 1971, International Military Tribunal

The United States of America vs. Carl Krauch, et. Trials of War Criminals before the Nuernberg Military Tribunals Under Control Council Law no 10, Washington, DC, Microcard Editions, 1971, International Military Tribunal

The United States of America vs. Friedrich Flick, et. al. Trials of War Criminals before the Nuernberg Military Tribunals Under Control Council Law no 10, Washington, DC, Microcard Editions, 1971, International Military Tribunal

The United States of America, the French Republic, the United Kingdom of Great Britain and Northern Ireland, and the Union of Soviet Socialist Republics v. Hermann Wilhelm Göring, et al.- Opening Statement http:// www.roberthjackson.org / Man/theman2-7-8-1/, International Military Tribunal

United States v. Iran (May 24) 1980 ICJ Reports 3, ICJ

United States v. Jimenez-Nava 243 F3d 192, C.A. 5

United States v. Phila. Nat'l Bank 374 US 321, US S.Ct.

United States v. Smith 18 US (5 Wheat) 153, 5 LEd 57, US S.Ct.

United States v. Southwestern Cable Co. 392 US 157, US S.Ct.

United States v. Stuart 489 US 353, US S.Ct.

United States v. von Weizsaecker (Ministries Case) Trials of War Criminals before the Nuernberg Military Tribunals Under Control Council Law no 10, Washington, DC, Microcard Editions, 1971, International Military Tribunals, XIV Trials of War Criminals

Van Gend en Loos v Nederlands Administatie der Belastingen ECR I, 26/62, ECJ

Velásquez Rodriguez Case Inter-AmCtHR (Ser C) No 4, Inter-American Court of Human Rights

Vereingte Familiapress v Heinrich Bauer Verlag 3 CMLR 1329, C-368/95, ECJ

Villeda Aldana v. Fresh Del Monte Produce, Inc. 305 F Supp 2d 1285, D.C. S.D. Fla.

Villeda, et. al. v. Fresh Del Monte Produce Inc., et al. Case No 01-CIV-3399, D.C. S.D. Fla.

Voth v Maildra Flour Mill 171 CLR 538, High Court of Australia

Walrave v Association Union Cycliste Internationale ECR 1405, 36/74, ECJ

Wiwa v. Royal Dutch Petroleum Co. No 96 Civ 8386, 1998 US, Dist LEXIS 23064 D.C. S.D. N.Y.

Wiwa v. Royal Dutch Petroleum Co. 226 F3d 88, C.A.2

Wiwa v. Royal Dutch Petroleum Co. No 96 Civ 8386, 2002 US, Dist LEXIS 3293, US D.C. S.D. N.Y.

Wiwa v. Royal Dutch Shell Petroleum Corp. 226 F3d 232, C.A. 2

WTO Appellate Body Report, European Communities -Measures Affecting Asbestos and Asbestos-Containing Products (Mar. 12) WT/DS135/AB/R, WTO DSB

WTO Appellate Body Report, United States--Standards for Reformulated and Conventional Gasoline (May 20) WT/DS2/AB/R, WTO DSB

X v. Ireland, (App. 4125/69) 14 Yearbook European Convention on Human Rights 198, European Commission on Human Rights

Xuncax v. Gramajo 886 FSupp 162, D.C. Mass.

Zapata v Quinn 707 F2d 691, C.A. 2

Electronic sources

Amnesty International, 'Clouds of Injustice: Bhopal disaster 20 Years on' <http:// web.amnesty.org/ pages/ec-bhopal-eng> (December 7, 2005)

Amnesty International, 'Human Rights Principles for Companies' (1998) <http:// web.amnesty.org/ library/ index/ engACT700011998? open&of= eng-398> (February 10, 2006)

Amnesty International, 'Annual Report - Sudan' (2007) <http://web.amnesty.org/ report2006/ sdn-summary-eng> (May 2, 2007)

S Anderson, 'Corporate vs. Country Economic Clout, The Top 100' (2003) <http:// www.ips-dc.org/ global_econ/ top_100.pdf>

S Anderson and J Cavanagh, '"Top 200- The rise of corporate global power", Institute for Policy Studies' (2001) <http:// www.ips-dc.org/ downloads/ Top_200.pdf>

K Annan, 'Secretary-General Calls for Efforts to Unleash African "Third Wave" Based on Democracy, Human Rights, and Sustainable Development; Address given on June 2, 1997 by Secretary-General Kofi Annan to the Annual Assembly of Heads of State and Government of the Organization of African Unity (OAU) in Harare.' (1997) <http:// www.un.org/ ecosocdev/ geninfo/ afrec/ vol11no1/ sgoau.htm> (December 1, 2007)

K Annan, 'Remarks of the UN Secretary-General on the occasion of the Human Rights Day 2006' (2006) <http:// www.un.org/ events/ humanrights/ 2006/ sg-remarks.shtml> (May 23, 2007)

M Arar, 'MaherArar.ca' <www.maherarar.ca> (January 12, 2006)

As you sow, 'Current Initiatives, Human rights abuses by US companies overseas Unocal Corp.' <http:// www.asyousow.org/ unocal.htm> (February 14, 2006)

Asia-Pacific Human Rights Network, 'Associating with the Wrong Company, Rio Tinto's Record and the Global Compact' (2001) <http:// www.minesandcommunities.org/ Company/ rio8.htm> (January 25, 2006)

W Baue, 'Social investment forum trends report tracks rises and falls of socially responsible investing' (2006) <http:// www.socialfunds.com/ news/ article.cgi/ 1913.html> (February 14, 2006)

E Bazelon, P Carter and D Lithwick, 'What is Torture? - Slate Magazine Interactive Primer on American Interrogation ' (2006) <http:// www.slate.com/ features/ whatistorture/ taxonomy.html> (June 5, 2006)

BBC News, 'BBC Global 30' (2007) <http:// news.bbc.co.uk/ 1/ hi/ business/ 3701740.stm> (September 6, 2007)

British Petroleum (BP), 'Code of Conduct' (2007) <http:// www.bp.com/ liveassets/ bp_internet/ globalbp/ STAGING/ global_assets/ downloads/ C/ coc_en_full_ document.pdf> (September 6, 2007)

K Brix, B Bromma and J Jaenisch, 'Nachhaltiges Unternehmertum- Diskussion des Konzeptes an Unternehmensbeispielen vom Bionier bis zum sustainable

Enterpreneur' (2006) <http:// www.uni-lueneburg.de/ fb4/institut/ ustrat/ management/ pdf-dateien/ csm_studien/ CSM_Studie_Nachhaltiges_ Unternehmertum.pdf> (July 18, 2007)

G Brodnig, 'The World Bank and Human Rights: Mission Impossible' (2005) <http:// www.ksg.harvard.edu/ cchrp/ Web% 20Working% 20Papers/ BrodnigHR& WorldBank.pdf> (May 25, 2007)

DK Brown, AV Deardorff and RM Stern, 'The Effects of Multinational Production on Wages and Working Conditions in Developing Countries' (2002) <http:// www.econ.kuleuven.be/ internationale.economie/ home/ WorkingGroup-Seminars/ Files/ Deardorff.pdf>

J Browne, 'Climate Change Speech' (1997) <http:// www.preen.org/ bpspeech.htm> (May 9, 2007)

Bundesrecht, 'Gesetz über Ordnungswidrigkeiten' (2007) <http:// bundesrecht.juris.de/ owig_1968/ __30.html> (June 5, 2007)

A Cantisano, 'Wal-Mart Plans to Move More Aggressively into Organics, Now Its Fastest Growing Category' (2005) <http:// www.organicconsumers.org/ organic/ walmart.cfm> (August 11, 2006)

Carbon Dioxide Information Analysis Center, 'Global CO2 Emmissions from Fossil-Fuels and Cement - Production in million metric tonnes of carbon' (2007) <http:// cdiac.ornl.gov/ trends/ emis/ glo.htm> (May 9, 2007)

MCaHR Castan Centre for Human Rights Law, 'Transnational Human Rights Litigation against Companies' (2004) <http:// www.law.monash.edu.au/ castancentre/ projects/ mchr/ trans-hr-litigation.html> (March 8, 2006)

Caterpillar, 'Our Values in Action, Caterpillar's Worldwide Code of Conduct' (2005) <http:// www.cat.com/ cda/ files/ 89286/ 7/ worldwide_code.pdf>

Center For Constitutional Rights, 'Docket: Center For Constitutional Rights Seeks Criminal Investigation in Germany into Culpability of US Officials in Abu Ghraib Torture ' (2006) <http:// www.ccr-ny.org/ v2/ legal/ september_11th/ sept11Article.asp?ObjID=1xiADJOOQx&Content=472> (Januar 24)

Center for Constitutional Rights and Earth Rights International, 'Wiwa v. Royal Dutch Petroleum Company, Complaint for Wiwa v. Anderson' (2001) <http:// www.earthrights.org/ files/ Legal% 20Docs/ Wiwa% 20v% 20Shell/ Wiwa-v-AndersonComplaint.pdf> (December 12, 2006)

Center for Justice and Accountability, 'Legal Documents, State Dep. Briefs' <www. cja.org/ legalResources/ StateDepartmentBriefdocs.shtml> (March 15, 2006)

T Cespedes, 'Peru peasants march to Lima, protest mining damage, Planet Ark' (2002) <http:// www.planetark.org/ dailynewsstory.cfm/ newsid/ 16767/ story.htm> (December 7, 2005)

SM Chelsey and others, 'Sosa v. Alvarez-Machain, US Supreme Court No. 03-339, Brief for the world Jewish Congress and the American Jewish Committee as Amici Curiae in support of respondents' (2005) <www.nosafehaven.org/ _legal/ atca_pro_ wrldJwshCongress.pdf>

S Chen and M Ravallion, 'How did the wold's poorest fare since the early 1980's' (2001) <http://www.worldbank.org/ research/ povmonitor/ MartinPapers/ How_ have_ the_ poorest_ fared_ since_ the_ early_ 1980s.pdf> (August 18, 2007)

China National Offshore Oil Corporation (CNOOC), 'Sustainable Development Report' (2007) <http:// www.cnooc.com.cn/ zhybg/ %BF% C9% B3% D6% D0% F8% B7% A2% D5% B9% B1% A8% B8% E6% D3% A2% CE% C4% B0% E6% A3% A82005% C4% EA% A3% A9.pdf> (September 6, 2007)

C Chiomenti, 'Corporations and the International Criminal Court; Global Law Working Paper 01/05, Symposium - 'Transnational Corporations and Human Rights', Hauser Global Law School Program' (2005) <http:// nyulawglobal.com/ workingpapers/ GLWP0105Chiomenti_000.rtf> (September 7, 2007)

Y-J Choi, 'Post-Mao Institutional Transformation and SOE Reform in China' (2003) <http:// journals2.iranscience.net: 800/mcel.pacificu.edu/ mcel.pacificu.edu/ easpac/ esterline.php3> (September 4, 2007)

Citigroup, 'Code of Conduct' (2007) <http:// www.citigroup.com/ citigroup/ corporategovernance/ codeconduct.htm> (September 6, 2007)

CNPC, 'Corporate Social Responsibility' (2004) <http://www.cnpc.com.cn/ Resource/ eng/ img/ 04AnnualReport/ Corporate_Social.pdf> (September 6, 2007)

T Collingsworth and N Thys, 'Complaint against Exxon Mobil(June 20, 2001)' (2001) <www.acehtimes.com/ news2001/ at062301.htm> (September 10, 2007)

E Consumer, 'Boycotts list' <http:// www.ethicalconsumer.org/ boycotts/ boycotts_ list.htm> (February 13, 2006)

S Danailov, 'The Accountability of Non-State Actors: the Special Case of Transnational Corporationa' (1998) <http:// www.humanrights.ch/ cms/ upload/ pdf/ 000303_danailov_studie.pdf> (January 12, 2006)

P De Grauwe and F Camerman, 'How big are the big Multinational Companies?' <http:// www.econ.kuleuven.be/ ew/ academic/ intecon/ Degrauwe/ PDG-Publications_ abstracts.htm>

Der Tagesspiegel Online, 'ExxonMobil und Shell 2006 erneut mit Rekordgewinnen' (2007) <http:// www.tagesspiegel.de/ wirtschaft/ nachrichten/ exxonmobil-shell/ 90604.asp>

DL Donoho, 'Human Rights Enforcement in the 21st Century' (2006) <http:// law.bepress.com/ cgi/ viewcontent.cgi? article= 6113&context= expresso> (March 14, 2007)

G Draffan, 'Endgame Directory of Transnational Corporations' (2006) <http:// www.endgame.org/ dtc/ e.html> (July 27, 2006)

SJ Dubbin, 'Brief of Amici Curiae Alien Friends Representing Hungarian Jews and Bougainvilleans Interests in Support of Respondent' (2004)

Earth Rights International, 'Historic advance for universal human rights: Unocal to compensate Burmese villagers' (2005) <http:// www.earthrights.org/ legalfeature/ historic_ advance_ for_ universal_ human_ rights_ unocal_ to_ compensate_ burmese_ villagers_2.html> (September 9, 2007)

Earthrights, 'In Our Court; ATCA, Sosa and the triumph of human rights; A report about the Alien Tort Claims Act' (2004) <http:// www.earthrights.org/ files/ Reports/ inourcourt.pdf > (March 14, 2006)

Earthrights, 'Final Settlement Reached in Doe v. Unocal' (2005) <http:// www.earthrights.org/ legalfeature/ final_ settlement_ reached_ in_ doe_ v._ unocal.html> (September 9, 2007)

ENEL, 'Code of Ethics' (2007) <http:// www.enel.com/ en/ our_company/ code_ of_ ethics/> (September 6, 2007)

EU, 'European Commission - Employment & Social Affairs - Corporate Social Responsibility: National public policies in the European Union' <http:// europa.eu.int/ comm/ employment_ social/ emplweb/ csr- matrix/ csr_ topic_ allcountries_ en.cfm? field=7> (February 10, 2006)

EU, 'ABC of the main instruments of Corporate Social Responsibility' (2004) <http:// ec.europa.eu/ employment_ social/ publications/ 2005/ ke1103004_ de.html> (March 1, 2006)

EU Commission, 'Brief of Amicus Curiae The European Commission in Support of Neither Party' (2004) <www.nosafehaven.org/ _legal/ atca_ oth_ EurComSupporting Sosa.pdf> (May 15, 2007)

ExxonMobil, 'Corporate Citizenship Report' (2007) <http://www.exxonmobil.com/ Corporate/ Citizenship/ CCR6/ index.asp> (September 6, 2007)

FAFO, 'Business and International Crimes, Category II: Forced Labor/ Enslavement' <http:// www.fafo.no/ liabilities/ part_ II-2forc-lab.htm> (January 20, 2006)

FAO, 'The State of Food Insecurity in the world- Eradicating World Hunger - Taking Stock Ten Years after the World Food Summit' (2006) <ftp:// ftp.fao.org/ docrep/ fao/ 009/ a0750e/ a0750e00.pdf> (September 3, 2007)

D Feinstein, 'Senator Feinstein Seeks to Clarify Adjudication of Foreign Lawsuits in US Federal Court' (2005) <http:// feinstein.senate.gov/ 05releases/ r-alientort.htm> (August 23, 2007)

A Fischer-Lescano, 'Global Law v. Realpolitik - The German Complaint against Donald Rumsfeld Concerning Torture in Abu Ghraib' (2005) <http:// www.ccr-ny.org/ v2/ legal/ september_11th/ sept11Article.asp? ObjID= 1xiADJOOQx& Content= 472> (Januar 24)

Five Winds International, 'Policy Framework for Environmental Sustainability Project: Case Studies' (2004) <http:// www.pollutionprobe.org/ whatwedo/ PFR/ casestudies.pdf> (July 18, 2007)

C Forcese, 'A definition of militarized commerce: Invitation to join new Coalition on Militarized Commerce (CMC), May 15, 2000,' (2000) <http:// www.peace.ca/ invitationtojoinnewcoalition.htm> (January 18, 2006)

Forum citoyen pour la responsabilité sociale des entrerprises, 'Increasing corporate social and environmental reporting in France' (2005) <http:// forumcitoyenpourlarse.org/ article.php3? id_article=42> (February 10, 2006)

Frontline, 'Interview John Yoo' (2005) < http:// www.pbs.org/ wgbh/ pages/ frontline/ torture/ interviews/ yoo.html> (December 22)

L Galvis and D Kovalik, 'Santo Domingo Massacre' (2005) <http://www.zmag.org/ content/ showarticle.cfm? ItemID=8907> (June 21, 2006)

General Electric, 'Citizenship Report' (2007) <http:// www.ge.com/ company/ citizenship/ index.html> (September 6, 2007)

Gesellschaft für deutsche Sprache, 'Wörter des Jahres' (2007) <http:// www.gfds.de/ index.php? id=11> (June 30, 2007)

Global Reporting Initiative, 'Homepage' (2007) <http:// www.globalreporting.org/ Home> (September 9, 2007)

Greenpeace, 'Press Releases and Diaries from the Brent Spar Occupation' (1996) <http:// archive.greenpeace.org/ comms/ brent/ diary.html> (February 7, 2006)

A Hamilton, 'The Federalist No. 80, The Powers of the Judiciary' (1788) <http:// www.constitution.org/ fed/ federa80.htm> (September 5, 2007)

J Harker, 'Human security in Sudan: The report of a Canadian assessment mission; Prepared for the Minister of Foreign Affairs' (2000) <http:// www.reliefweb.int/ library/ documents/ cansudan2.pdf>

M Hickmann, 'U.K. market for organic & fair trade clothes & other products growing rapidly' (2005) <http:// www.organicconsumers.org/ btc/ market121205.cfm> (February 13, 2006)

E Hoffmann, 'Environmental Reporting and Sustainability Reporting in Europe - An Overview of Mandatory Reporting Schemes in the Netherlands and France' (2003) <http:// www.iges.or.jp/ en/ phase2/ be/ pdf/ report7.pdf> (July 18, 2007)

HRW, 'Sudan, Oil, and Human Rights' (2003) <http:// www.hrw.org/ reports/ 2003/ sudan1103/> (September 8, 2007)

HSBC, 'CSR Report' (2007) <http:// www.hsbc.com/ 1/ PA_1_1_S5/ content/ assets/ csr/ 2006_hsbc_cr_report.pdf > (September 6, 2007)

Human Rights Internet, 'Case Studies from Canadian Jurisprudence: Applying International Law Domestically - Case Studies from the Supreme Court of Canada - Baker v. Canada' (1999) <http:// www.hri.ca/ fortherecordCanada/ vol3/ casebaker.htm> (March 21)

Human Rights Violations Investigation Commission Nigeria, 'Human Rights Violations Investigation Commission Report (aka Oputa Report) ' (2002) <http:// www.dawodu.com/ oputa1.htm> (September 10, 2007)

Human Rights Watch, 'Small Change- Bonded Child Labor in India' (2003) <http:// www.hrw.org/ reports/ 2003/ india/ India0103-03.htm> (May 15, 2007)

Human Rights Watch, 'Turning a Blind Eye- Hazardous Child Labour in El Salvador's Sugarcane Cultivation' (2004) <http:// hrw.org/ reports/ 2004/ elsalvador0604/> (May 28, 2007)

Human Rights Watch, 'The Curse of Gold' (2005) <http:// hrw.org/ reports/ 2005/ drc0505.> (May 28, 2007)

Human Rights Watch, 'Child Labor' (2007) <http:// hrw.org/ children/ labor.htm> (May 15, 2007)

Human Rights Watch, 'Human Rights and Business Reports' (2007) <http:// hrw.org/ doc/ ?t=corporations_pub> (May 28, 2007)

Human Rights Watch, 'World Report 2007- Sudan' (2007) <http:// hrw.org/ englishwr2k7/ docs/ 2007/ 01/ 11/ sudan14715.htm> (May 3, 2007)

Icelandic Human Rights Centre, 'International Supervisory Mechanism for Human Rights' (2007) <http:// www.humanrights.is/ the-human-rights-project/ human rights cases and materials/ human rights concepts ideas and fora/ theconceptsof human rights anintroduction/ international supervisory mechanism for human rights/> (May 29, 2007)

IJAW Youths of the Niger Delta, 'The Kaiama Declaration' (1998) <http:// www.unitedijawstates.com/ kaiama.htm> (September 10, 2007)

INFACT Canada, 'Examples of Nestlé's International Code Violations' (2005) <http:// www.infactcanada.ca/ The% 20Nestle% 20Boycott.pdf> (May 25, 2007)

Interface Inc., 'Homepage' (2007) <http:// www.interfaceinc.com> (June 5, 2007)

International Labor Rights Fund, 'Lawsuit Filed Against Occidental Petroleum for Involvement in Infamous Colombian Massacre' <http:// www.laborrights.org/ press/ oxy042403.htm> (June 21, 2006)

International Labor Rights Fund, 'Give 'em an inch, and they'll take a mile.' (2006) <http:// www.unionvoice.org/ campaign/ ChongWon> (November 5, 2006)

International Labor Rights Fund, 'Wal-Mart speaking tour' (2006) <http:// www.unionvoice.org/ laborrights/ notice-description.tcl? newsletter_id= 1571224> (August 25, 2006)

International Labor Rights Fund, 'ExxonMobil: How the Company is linked with Indonesian Military, Torture and other severe abuse in Aceh, Indonesia' (2007) <http:// lrights.igc.org/ projects/ corporate/ exxon> (September 10, 2007)

International Law Commission, 'Commentary on Articles on Responsibility of States for International Wrongful Acts' (2001) <http:// www.un.org/ law/ ilc/ texts/ State_ responsibility/ responsibility_commentaries(e).pdf> (January 30, 2006)

J Jay, 'The Federalist No. 3' (1787) <http:// www.constitution.org/ fed/ federa03.htm> (September 5, 2007)

G Katsh, 'Fueling Genocide, Talisman Energy and the Sudanese Slaughter' (2000) <http:// multinationalmonitor.org/ mm2000/ 00october/ corp2.html> (10)

J Kokott, 'Interim Report on "The Role of Diplomatic Protection in the Field of the Protection of Foreign Investment," International Law Association: Second Report of the Committee on Diplomatic Protection of Persons and Property' (2002) <http:// www.ilahq.org/ pdf/ DiplomaticProtection/ DiplomaticProtectionSecondReport2002.pdf> (June 6, 2007)

DA Levy, 'The Opium Trade' (2000) <http:// www.maritimeheritage.org/ newtale/ opium.html> (July 25, 2006)

Lifeonline, 'The Seattle Syndrom' <http:// www.tve.org/ lifeonline/ index.cfm? aid=1206> (February 8, 2006)

London Stock Exchange, 'European socially responsible investment reaches €1 trillion' (2006) <http:// www.londonstockexchange.com/ en-gb/ pricesnews/ investnews/ article.htm? ArticleID= 17643852> (September 26, 2006)

B Markesinis, 'Institute of Global Law - German Translated Decisions- BVerfGE 7, 198' <http:// www.ucl.ac.uk/ laws/ global_law/ german-cases/ cases_ bverg.shtml? 15jan1958> (February 1, 2006)

KF McCallion and HR Sharma, 'Bano v. Union Carbide, Amended Complaint' (2004) <www.bhopal.net/ oldsite/ documentlibrary/ amendedplaint.html>

C McCrudden, 'The Future of the EU Charter of Fundamental Rights, Jean Monnet Working Paper No.10/01' (2001) <http:// www.jeanmonnetprogram.org/ papers/ 01/ 013001.html> (September 6, 2007)

J McNulty, 'Consumers eager to know more about the environmental and social impacts of food, January 24, 2005, available at ' (2005) <http:// www.ucsc.edu/ news_events/ press_releases/ text.asp?pid=629> (February 13, 2006)

Microsoft, 'Citizenship Report' (2007) <http:// download.microsoft.com/ download/ 7/ 5/ 4/ 7548d2a2-9d22-4d2d-8c13-2521f6a1c148/ citizenship2006.pdf> (September 6, 2007)

C Morris, 'The Triple Bottom Line- A talk with Alyson Slator, Communications Director at the Global Reporting Initiative' (2007) <http:// www.heise.de/ tp/ r4/ artikel/ 24/ 24531/ 1.html> (March 2, 2007)

C Murphy, 'The Profitable Correlation Between Environmental and Financial Performance: A Review of the Research' (2002) <http:// www.lightgreen.com/ files/ pc.pdf> (July 19, 2007)

I Nadisan, 'Comments on Baia Mare Pollution- Flagelul poluare la Baia Mare, Evenimentul AURUL, Vasile Gordis University Press ' (2001) <www.zpok.hu/ cyanide/ baiamare/ nadisan.htm>

Nestlé, 'Corporate Principles' (2007) <http:// www.nestle.com/ Resource.axd? Id=70014B84-A4FC- 4F82-BFA0-23939DC52E9D> (September 6, 2007)

NewsCorp, 'Standards of Business Conduct' (2007) <http:// www.newscorp.com/ corp_gov/sobc.html> (September 6, 2007)

No Safe Haven, 'Legal Documents, Briefs supporting and opposing ATCA' <http:// www.nosafehaven.org/ legal.html> (March 16, 2006)

Nokia, 'Sustainability Summary' (2007) <http:// www.nokia.com/ A4359260> (September 6, 2007)

J Norberg, 'Globalization and the poor' (2004) <http:// medienbibliothek.fnst.de/ uploads/ medienbibliothek/ occasional1.pdf>

Novartis, 'Corporate Citizenship' (2007) <http:// www.corporatecitizenship.novartis.com/ managing-cc/ governance/ code-policies-guidelines.shtml> (September 6, 2007)

D O'Brien, 'Integrating Corporate Social Responsibility with Competitive Strategy' (2001) <http:// www.angelfire.com/ journal2/ comunicarse/ IntegratingCorporate.pdf>

SD O'Connor, 'American Law Institute Speech May 15, 2002' (2002) <http:// www.angelfire.com/ mi2/ aicap/ AmericanLawInstitute.html > (April 18, 2006)

Office of the High Commissioner for Human Rights, 'International Human Rights Instruments' <http:// www.unhchr.ch/ html/ intlinst.htm> (March 21, 2007)

Office of the UN High Commissioner for Human Rights, 'Status of ratifications of the principal international human rights treaties, As of 09 June 2004' (2004) <http:// www.unhchr.ch/ pdf/ report.pdf> (March 24, 2006)

DW Ogden, 'Statement of David W. Ogden, Acting Assistant Attorney General Civil Division before the Committee on the judiciary United States Senate concerning compensation for Bataan POWs' (2000) <www.usdoj.gov/ civil/ speeches/ ogden.htm or www.aiipowmia.com/ testimony/ slvlbr1.html>

Otto, 'Homepage' (2007) <http://www.otto.de> (June 5, 2007)

Oxfam GB, 'Nongovernmental Organizations Welcome the New UN Norms on Transnational Business' (2003) <http://www.humanrightsfirst.org/ workers_rights/ issues/ norms/ wr_press_st_081303.htm> (May 5, 2007)

F Pallone, 'Eleven Members of Congress File Amicus Brief in Support of Bhopal Victims' Lawsuit' (2006) <http:// www.house.gov/ list/ press/ nj06_pallone/ pr_apr4_india.html> (September 10, 2007)

Pew Global Attitudes Project, 'World publics approve increased international trade, But concern for problems of global economy' (2003) <http:// pewglobal.org/ commentary/ display.php?AnalysisID=68>

Pfizer, 'Corporate Responsibility Report' (2007) <http:// www.pfizer.com/ files/ corporate_citizenship/ cc_report_2005.pdf> (September 6, 2007)

B Powell and D Skarbeg, 'Sweatshop and Third World Living Standards: Are the Jobs Worth the Sweat?' (2004) <http:// www.independent.org/ pdf/ working_papers/ 53_sweatshop.pdf>

Procter and Gamble, 'Global Sustainability and Philanthrophy Report' (2007) <http:// www.pg.com/ content/ pdf/ 01_about_pg/ corporate_citizenship/ sustainability/ reports/ sustainability_summary_2006.pdf> (September 6, 2007)

Program on International Policy Attitudes (PIPA), 'Americans on Globalization: A Study of US Public Attitudes' (2000) <http:// www.pipa.org/ OnlineReports/ Globalization/ executive_summary.html> (February 13, 2006)

S Raman, 'Wal-Mart workers critique labor conditions' (2006) <http:// media.www.browndailyherald.com/ media/ storage/ paper472/ news/ 2006/ 02/ 08/ CampusNews/ WalMart. Workers. Critique. Labor. Conditions- 1603789.shtml? sourcedomain= www.browndailyherald.com& MIIHost= media. collegepublisher.com> (August 25)

A Ramasastry, 'A Swiss Court decides to allow Gypsies' Holocaust Lawsuit to proceed' (2004) <http:// writ.news.findlaw.com/ ramasastry/ 20040708.html> (March 6, 2006)

E Reeves, 'Quantifying Genocide in Darfur' (2006) <http:// www.sudanreeves.org/ Article102.html> (May 3, 2007)

Registry of the European Court of Human Rights, 'Survey of Activities 2006 of the European Court of Human Rights' (2007) <http:// www.echr.coe.int/ NR/ rdonlyres/ 69564084- 9825- 430B- 9150- A9137DD22737/ 0/ Survey_2006.pdf> (July 17, 2007)

Republikanischer Anwältinnen- und Anwälteverein e.V., 'Anzeige bei der Bundesanwaltschaft gegen Rumsfeld u.a. wegen Kriegsverbrechen in Abu Ghraib' (2006) <http://www.rav.de/ 2006/ 141106_ AbuGhraib.html> (March 14, 2007)

Republikanischer Anwältinnen- und Anwaltverein e.V., '2. Strafanzeige gegen Rumsfeld' (2007) <http:// www.rav.de/ rumsfeld2.html>

Reuters News Service, 'Southern Peru may boost copper smelter capacity, Planet Ark' (2003) <http:// www.planetark.com/ dailynewsstory.cfm/ newsid/ 20369/ newsDate/ 4-Apr-2003/ story.htm> (December 9, 2005)

Reuters News Service, 'Southern Peru says will commit to Ilo upgrade in May, Planet Ark' (2003) <http://www.planetark.org/ dailynewsstory.cfm/ newsid/ 20313/ story.htm> (December 8, 2005)

Rio Tinto, 'Website' (2007) <http://www.riotinto.com/> (September 10, 2007)

C-F Röhrs, 'Sie klagen an' (2006) <http://archiv.tagesspiegel.de/ archiv/ 14.11.2006/ 2896394.asp> (March 14, 2007)

Royal Dutch Shell plc., 'Alternative Energy' (2007) <http:// www.shell.com/home/ Framework? siteId= envirosoc-en& FC2=/ envirosoc-en/ html/ iwgen/ leftnavs/ zzz_lhn5_4_0.html& FC3=/ envirosoc-en/ html/ iwgen/ environment/ alternative_energy/ dir_alternative_energy_13042007.html> (May 9, 2007)

Royal Dutch Shell plc., 'Investor Centre Quarterly Results' (2007) <http:// www.shell.com/ home/ Framework? siteId= investor-en& FC2=/ investor-en/ html/ iwgen/ leftnavs/ zzz_lhn4_1_0.html& FC3=/ investor-en/ html/ iwgen/ quarterlyresults/ 2006/ dir_2006_qresults_index.html> (May 9, 2007)

JG Ruggie, 'National Roundtable on Corporate Social Responsibility and the Canadian Extractive Industry in Developing Countries, Montreal, November 14, 2006, Remarks at Public Session' (2006) <http:// www.ksg.harvard.edu/ m-rcbg/ CSRI/ publications/ other_Ruggie_Montreal.pdf> (August 17, 2007)

JG Ruggie, 'Speech at a Forum on Corporate Social Responsibility in Bamberg/Germany' (2006) <http:// www.reports-and-materials.org/ Ruggie-remarks-to- Fair- Labor- Association- and- German- Network- of- Business- Ethics- 14-June- 2006.pdf> (May 24, 2007)

JG Ruggie, 'Prepared Remarks at Clifford Chance, London, 19 February' (2007) <http:// www.reports-and-materials.org/ Ruggie-remarks-Clifford-Chance-19-Feb-2007.pdf> (May 24, 2007)

J Sabatini, 'Shareholder Activism, New York City funds push Freeport McMoran to improve human-rights policy' (2003) <http:// www.minesandcommunities.org/ Action/ press108.htm> (February 14, 2006)

J Sarra, 'Corporate Social Responsibility in the Global Economy: Canadian Domestic Law and Legal Processes as a Vehicle for Creating and Enforcing International Norms' (2003) <http:// www.ciaj-icaj.ca/ english/ publications/ J-Sarra.pdf > (February 7, 2006)

JJ Savitzky and SJ Burki, 'Globalization and the multinational corporation' <http:// www.iadb.org/ int/ jpn/ English/ support_files/ GLB% 203% 20Glob.and% 20Multinational% 20Corporation.pdf>

F Schreier and M Caparini, 'Privatizing Security: Law, Practice and Governance of Private Military and Security Companies' (2005) <http:// www.dcaf.ch/ _docs/ op06_privatising- security.pdf> (August 21, 2007)

Siemens, 'Responsibility Performance' (2007) <http:// w1.siemens.com/ en/ corporate-responsibility/> (September 6, 2007)

Social Accountability International(2007) <http:// www.sa-intl.org> (June 5, 2007)

South Sudanese Friends International, 'Oil in Sudan' (2000) <http:// southsudanfriends.org/ issues/ oil000614.html> (December 07, 2005)

Stiftung Erinnerung Verantwortung und Zukunft, 'Website' (2007) <http:// www.stiftung-evz.de/> (December 10, 2007)

Stop Caterpillar, 'Declaration Regarding Caterpillar Violations of HR' (2004) <http:// www.catdestroyshomes.org/ article.php? id=242> (June 21, 2006)

Students for Bhopal, 'Timeline, court and other materials, Dow is liable' <http:// www.studentsforbhopal.org/ DowIsLiable.htm#Civil> (December 7, 2005)

Sudan Divestment Task Force, 'PetroChina, CNPC, and Sudan: Perpetuating Genocide' (2007) <http:// www.sudandivestment.org/ docs/ PetroChina_ CNPC_ Sudan.pdf> (September 6, 2007)

A Tabuga, 'Article 15-6 Investigation of the 800th Military Police Brigade (March 9, 2004)' (2004) <http:// www.npr.org/ iraq/ 2004/ prison_ abuse_ report.pdf> (September 11, 2007)

Tagesschau.de, 'Noch mehr Geld verschwunden als gedacht?' (2006) <http:// www.tagesschau.de/ aktuell/ meldungen/ 0,,OID6175366_ REF1,00.html> (May 25, 2007)

The World Bank Group, 'Nigeria at a glance' (2006) <http:// devdata.worldbank.org/ AAG/ nga_aag.pdf> (May 2, 2007)

H Thie, 'Verlogene Argumente, vergiftete Köder- Hermann Scheer im Gespräch' (2006) <http:// www.freitag.de/ 2006/ 14/ 06140301.php> (May 9, 2007)

R Thompson, 'A Comparative Survey of Private Sector Liability for Grave Violations of International Law in National Jurisdictions, Surveys of Canada, France, Norway, the United Kingdom, and the United States' (2003) <http:// www.fafo.no/ liabilities/ nat_surv.htm>

HJ Tolley and A Lawrence, 'Doe v. Unocal: Forced Labor and Corporate Liability' (2002) <http:// homepages.uc.edu/ thro/ doe/ doe-unocal.htm> (December 9, 2005)

U.S. Senate Committee on the Judiciary, 'Former U.S. World War II POW's: A Struggle for Justice, 106th Congress, 2nd Session' (2000) <www.aiipowmia.com/ testimony/ slvlbr1.html>

USA Central Intelligence Agency, 'The World Factbook - Indonesia' (2007) <https:// www.cia.gov/ cia/ publications/ factbook/ geos/ id.html> (May 2, 2007)

USA Central Intelligence Agency, 'The World Factbook - Sudan' (2007) <https:// www.cia.gov/ cia/ publications/ factbook/ geos/ su.html> (May 2, 2007)

Vital Statistics: Oil Companies Operating in Sudan(2001) <http:// www.moles.org/ ProjectUnderground/ drillbits/ 6_02/ vs.html> (January 16, 2006)

P Watts, 'John Yoo Argues Pres. George Bush Has Legal Power to Torture Children' (2005) <http:// rwor.org/ johnyoo/ index.html> (March 14, 2007)

J Wise, 'Baby Milk Companies Accused of Breaching Marketing Code' (1997) <http:// www.bmj.com/ cgi/ content/ full/ 314/ 7075/ 165/ e> (July 18, 2007)

Women & the economy (A project of UNPAC), 'Ethical consumption' <http:// unpac.ca/ economy/ ethicconsumption.html> (February 13, 2006)

World Bank, 'World Bank Sanctions Lahmeyer International for Corrupt Activities in Bank-Financed Projects, Press Release No 129/2007/INT' (2006) <http:// web.worldbank.org/ WBSITE/ EXTERNAL/ NEWS/ 0,,contentMDK: 21116129~pagePK: 34370~ piPK: 34424~ theSitePK:4607,00.html>

WTO, 'Members and Observers' (2007) <http:// www.wto.org/ english/ thewto_e/ whatis_e/ tif_e/ org6_e.htm> (September 7, 2007)

www.danskekonger.dk, 'Kongeloven af 1665' (2007) <http:// www.danskekonger.dk/ biografi/ andre/ kongeloven.html> (April 27, 2007)

Yale Law School - The Allard K. Lowenstein International Human Rights Clinic, 'An Analysis of Select Companies' Operations in Sudan: A Resource for Divestment' (2005) <http:// www.inosphere.com/ sudan/ docs/ Yale_ Lowenstein_ Updated_ Report.pdf> (July 19, 2007)

D Yunhu, 'Inclusion of human rights in the Constitution- An Important Milestone in China's Human Rights Development' <http:// www.humanrights.cn/ zt/ magazine/ 20040200492110121 5.htm> (March 24, 2006)

Zyklon B, 'Website' (2007) <http://www.zyklon-b.info> (April 18, 2007)

UN sources

UN Special Representative of the Secretary-General on human rights and transnational corporations and other business enterprises, 'E/CN.4/2006/97- Interim report of the Special Representative of the Secretary-General on the issue of human rights and transnational corporations and other business enterprises' (2006) <http:// daccess-ods.un.org/ access.nsf/ Get? Open& DS=E/ CN.4/ 2006/ 97& Lang=E> (May 23, 2007)

UN Special Representative of the Secretary-General on human rights and transnational corporations and other business enterprises, 'A/HRC/4/35/Add.3- Human Rights Policies and Management Practices of Fortune Global 500 Firms: Results of a Survey' (2006) <http:// daccess-ods.un.org/ access.nsf/ Get? Open& DS=A /HRC/ 4/ 35/ Add.3&Lang=E> (May 23, 2007)

UN Special Representative of the Secretary-General on human rights and transnational corporations and other business enterprises, 'A/HRC/4/35- Report of the Special Representative of the Secretary-General on the issue of human rights and transnational corporations and other business enterprises' (2007) <http:// daccess-ods.un.org/ access.nsf/ Get? Open& DS=A/ HRC/ 4/ 35&Lang=E>

UN Special Representative of the Secretary-General on human rights and transnational corporations and other business enterprises, 'A/HRC/4/35/Add.1- State responsibilities to regulate and adjudicate corporate activities under the UN core human rights treaties: an overview of treaty body commentaries' (2007) <http:// daccess-ods.un.org/ access.nsf/ Get?Open& DS= A/ HRC/ 4/ 35/ Add.1& Lang=E>

UN Special Representative of the Secretary-General on human rights and transnational corporations and other business enterprises, 'A/HRC/4/35/Add.2- Corporate Responsibility under International Law and issues in Extraterritorial Regulation: Summary of Legal Workshops' (2007) <http:// daccess-ods.un.org/ access.nsf/ Get? Open& DS= A/ HRC/ 4/ 35/ Add.2&Lang=E>

UN Special Representative of the Secretary-General on human rights and transnational corporations and other business enterprises, 'A/HRC/4/35/Add.4- Business recognition of human rights: Global patterns, regional and sectoral variations' (2007) <http:// daccess-ods.un.org/ access.nsf/ Get? Open& DS=A/ HRC/ 4/ 35/ Add.4& Lang=E>

UN Special Representative of the Secretary-General on human rights and transnational corporations and other business enterprises, 'A/HRC/4/74- Report of the Special Representative of the Secretary-General on the issue of human rights and transnational corporations and other business enterprises' (2007) <http:// daccess-ods.un.org/ access.nsf/ Get? Open& DS= A/ HRC/ 4/ 74& Lang=E>

UN Commission on Human Rights, 'E/CN.4/Sub.2/2003/12/Rev.2 - Norms on the Responsibilities of Transnational Corporations and Other Business Enterprises with Regard to Human Rights' (2003) <http:// www1.umn.edu/ humanrts/ links/ norms- Aug2003.html>

UN Commission on Human Rights, 'E/CN.4/Sub.2/2003/12/Rev.2 - UN Norms on the Responsibilities of Transnational Corporations and Other Business Enterprises with Regard to Human Rights' (2003)

UN Committee on Trade and Development, 'Multinational corporations (MNCs) in least developed countries (LDCs) ' <http://www.globalpolicy.org/ reform/ 2002/ modelun.pdf>

UN GA, 'Observance of the International Day for the Eradication of Poverty - Report of the Secretary-General' (2006) <http://www.un.org/ esa/ socdev/ poverty/ documents/ SG_Poverty_2006_final.pdf>

UN Global Compact, 'Global Compact Note on Integrity Measures' (2006) <http:// www.unglobalcompact.org/ AboutTheGC/ gc_integrity_mesures.pdf> (September 21, 2007)

UN Global Compact, 'Issues- Human Rights' (2006) <http:// www.unglobalcompact.org/ Issues/ human_rights/ index.html> (July 27, 2006)

UN Global Compact(2007) <http:// www.unglobalcompact.org> (September 7, 2007)

UN Global Compact, 'Communication on Progress (COP)' (2007) <http:// www.unglobalcompact.org/ CommunicatingProgress/index.html> (September 23, 2007)

UN High Commissioner for Human Rights, 'Report of the High Commissioner for Human Rights - The Present Situation of Human Rights in Iraq' (2004) <http:// www.unhchr.ch/ html/ hchr/ docs/ iraq.doc> (September 11, 2007)

UN High Commissioner for Human Rights, 'Workshop on Attributing Corporate Responsibility for Human Rights under International Law- Summary Report' (2006) <Workshop on Attributing Corporate Responsibility for Human Rights under International Law- Summary Report> (March 13, 2007)

UN Human Rights Council, 'Press Release- Council Discusses Human Rights and Transnational Corporations, Right to Health and Human Rights Defenders' (2007) <http:// www.unhchr.ch/ huricane/ huricane.nsf/ view01/ 19207DD 921EE5D22 C12572AC00702E2C? opendocument> (May 23, 2007)

UN Millennium Development Summit, 'UN Millennium Development Goals' (2000) <http:// www.un.org/ millenniumgoals/ background.html> (August 18, 2007)

UN SC, 'UN Security Council Sanctions Committees' (2007) <http:// www.un.org/ sc/ committees/ dfp.shtml> (June 6, 2007)

UN Secretary General, 'A more secure world: Our shared Responsibility, Report of the Secretary-General's High-Level Panel on Threats, Challenges and Change' (2004) <www.un.org/ secureworld> (December 1, 2006)

UNCTAD, 'UNCTAD World Investment Report 2005, Transnational corporations and the Internationalization of R&D' (2005) <http:// www.unctad.org/ Templates/ WebFlyer.asp? intItemID=3489&lang=1>

UNCTAD, 'World Investment Report' (2006) <www.unctad.org/ en/ docs/ wir2006_en.pdf > (September 4, 2007)

UN GA, GA Res. 2671 F, UN GAOR, 25th Sess., Supp. No. 28, U.N. Doc. A/8028 (1970)

UN SC, SC Res. 986, UN SCOR, U.N. Doc. S/RES/986 (Oil-for-food resolution) (1995)

Other sources

J Arunga, The devil's footpath (Film) (2004)

M Burr, US Committee for Refugees, Quantifying Genocide in Southern Sudan and the Nuba Mountains 1983-1998 (1998)

J Crawford, Declaration of James Crawford S.C. as Affidavit for defendant Talisman (at hand) (2002)

International Commission of Inquiry on Darfur, Report of the International Commission of Inquiry on Darfur to the UN Secretary-General, Pursuant to Security Council Resolution 1564 of 18 September 2004 (2005)

Senate Commerce Science and Transportation, Congressional Testimony via FDCH by Charles Kernaghan, 2007 WLNR 3068941 (2007)

D Venkateswarlu, OECD Watch, Deutsche Welthungerhilfe, India Committee of the Netherlands, Eine Welt Netz NRW, International Labor Rights Fund, Seeds of Change- Impact of Interventions by Bayer and Monsanto on the Elimination of Child Labour on Farms Producing Hybrid Cottonseed in India (2007)

Statutes and conventions (sorted by year)

Treaty of Amity and Commerce, Feb 6, 1778, United States-France, 8 Stat 12, TS No 83 (1778)

Aliens Tort Claims Act 1789, 28 U.S.C., § 1350(1789)

Convention (IV) respecting the Laws and Customs of War on Land and its annex: Regulations concerning the Laws and Customs of War on Land. The Hague October 18, 1907, 36 Stat 2277, TS No 539 (1907)

International Convention to Suppress the Slave Trade and Slavery 25 September, 1926, ATS 11 (entered into force 9 March 1927) (1926)

International Bank for Reconstruction and Development (IBRD) Articles of Agreement Articles of Agreement of the International Bank for Reconstruction and Development, July 22, 1944, 60 Stat 1440, 2 UNTS 134, amended Dec 16, 1965, UST 1942, 606 UNTS 294 (IBRD Articles of Agreement) (1944)

Articles of Agreement of the International Monetary Fund July 22, 1944 (entered into force December 27, 1945), last amended effective November 11, 1992, 31 ILM 1307 (1944)

Charter of the UN 1945 1 UNTS xvi (1945)

Charter of the International Military Tribunal for the Trial of the Major War Criminals appended to Agreem. f. Prosecution and Punishment of Major War Criminals of the European Axis, Aug 8, 1945, 59 Stat 1544, UNTS 279, as amended, Protocol to Agreement and Charter, Oct 6, 1945 (Nuremberg Charter) (1945)

Statute of the International Court of Justice June 26, 1945, UNTS 993 (1945)

Revised Constitution of the International Labor Organization 9 October 1946, 15 UNTS, 35 (1946)

General Agreement on Tariffs and Trade (GATT 1947) October 30, 1947, 55 UNTS 194 (1947)

Universal Declaration of Human Rights GA Res 217 A(III), UN Doc A/810 at 71 (1948)

Convention on the Prevention and Punishment of the Crime of Genocide December 9, 1948, 78 UNTS 277, approved and proposed for signature and ratification or accession by General Assembly resolution 260 A (III) of 9 December 1948, entered into force Jan 12, 1951 (Genocide Convention) (1948)

Grundgesetz - German Basic Law (1949)

Geneva Convention Relative to the Protection of Civilian Persons in Time of War (Fourth Geneva Convention) 75 UNTS 287 (12 August 1949) (entered into force Oct 21, 1950) (1949)

Convention Concerning the Application of the Principles of the Right to Organise and To Bargain Collectively 96 UNTS 257 (entered into force 18 July 1951) (1949)

Convention Relative to the Treatment of Prisoners of War August 12, 1949, 6 UST 3316, 75 UNTS 135 (Third Geneva Convention) (1949)

European Convention of Human Rights and Fundamental Freedoms ETS No5 (1950)

Treaty of Peace with Japan Sept 8, 1951, 3 UST 3169 (1951)

Protocol Amending the Convention to Suppress the Slave Trade and Slavery 7 December 1953, 182 UNTS 51 (entered into force 7 December 1953) (1953)

Supplementary Convention on the Abolition of Slavery, the Slave Trade, and Institutions and Practices Similar to Slavery 226 UNTS 3 (entered into force 30 April 1957) (1956)

Treaty Establishing the European Community Mar 25, 1957, 298 UNTS 11, as amended by Treaty of Amsterdam, Oct 2, 1997, 1997 OJ (C 340) 1, as amended by Treaty of Nice, Feb 26, 2001, 2001 OJ (C 80) 1, consolidated version reprinted in 2002 OJ (C 325) 33 (1957)

Convention on Third Party Liability in the Field of Nuclear Energy 956 UNTS 251, reprinted in 55 AJIL 1082 (1960) (amended in 1964, 1968 & 1982) (Paris Convention) (1960)

Convention on the Organisation for Economic Co-operation and Development Dec 14, 1960, 12 UST 1728 (1960)

Vienna Convention on Civil Liability for Nuclear Damage 1063 UNTS 265, reprinted in 2 ILM at 727 (1963)

Vienna Convention on Consular Relations Apr 24, 1963, 596 UNTS 261 (entered into force Mar 19, 1967) (1963)

Constitution of the Universal Postal Union July 10, 1964, 611 UNTS 7 (1964)

International Convention on the Elimination of All Forms of Racial Discrimination (adopted December 21, 1965, entered into force January 4, 1969) 660 UNTS 195 (1965)

International Covenant on Civil and Political Rights (ICCPR) GA Res 2200A (XXI), UN Doc A/6316, adopted and opened for signature, ratification and accession by General Assembly resolution 2200A (XXI) of 16 December 1966,entered into force Mar 23, 1976 (1966)

International Covenant on Economic, Social and Cultural Rights (ICESCR) GA Res 2200, UN Doc A/6316, adopted and opened for signature, ratification and accession by General Assembly resolution 2200A (XXI) of 16 December 1966, entered into force Jan 3, 1976 (1966)

Convention Establishing the World Intellectual Property Organization July 14, 1967, 828 UNTS 3 (1967)

American Convention on Human Rights November 22, 1969, OASTS No 36, 1144 UNTS 123, 9 ILM 673 (entered into force July 18, 1978) (1969)

International Convention on Civil Liability for Oil Pollution Damage 9 ILM (1970) 45 (entered into force June 19, 1975) (1969)

Stockholm Declaration of the United Nations Conference on the Human Environment UN Doc A/ CONF48/14/ Rev 1, at 3, 11 ILM 1416 (the Stockholm Declaration) (adopted June 16, 1972) (1972)

Tripartite Declaration of Principles concerning Multinational Enterprises and Social Policy Nov 16, 1977, 17 ILM 422 (1977)

Convention on the Elimination of All Forms of Discrimination against Women 1249 UNTS 13, adopted and opened for signature, ratification and accession by GA res. 34/180 of December 18, 1979, entered into force September 3, 1981 (1979)

WHO International Code of Marketing of Breastmilk Substitutes WHA Res 3422 Annex, WHO ocl A34/VR/15 (1981)

United Nations Convention on the Law of the Sea December 10, 1982, 1833 UNTS 3 (entered into force November 16, 1994) ("UNCLOS") (1982)

Convention Against Torture and Other Cruel Inhuman or Degrading Treatment or Punishment 10 December 1984, 1465 UNTS 85 (entered into force 26 June 1987) (1984)

Bhopal Gas Leak Disaster (Processing of Claims) Act (the Bhopal Act) Indian Parliament Act No 21 of 1985, Gazette of India (Extraord.) pt 2, sec 2, Mar 29 (1985)

Restatement (Third) of Foreign Relations Law (1987)

UN Draft Code of Conduct on Transnational Corp. UN Doc E/1988/39/Add1 (1988)

Convention on the Rights of the Child November 20, 1989, UNGA Res 44/25 (entered into force 2 September 1990) (1989)

Treaty on the Final Settlement with Respect to Germany Sept 12, 1990, FRG-GDR-Fr-USSR-UK-US, BGBl II S1317, 29 ILM 1186 (1990)

Treaty Establishing a Common Market between the Argentine Republic, the Federative Republic of Brazil, the Republic of Paraguay and the Eastern Republic of Uruguay 30 ILM 1044 (1991)

U.S. House of Representatives, P.L. 102-256, Torture Victim Protection Act of 1991, H.R. REP. NO. 102-367 (I), November 25 (1991)

Treaty on the European Union, adopted February 7, 1992, entered into force on November 1, 1993 (Maastricht Treaty) ILM 247, 256 (1992)

Rio Declaration on Environment and Development June 13, 1992, 31 ILM 874 (1992)

Torture Victim Protection Act (TVPA), Title 28, Part IV, Chapter 85, § 1350, Mar. 12, 1992, 106 Stat. 73(1992)

Vienna Declaration and Programme of Action, U.N. GAOR, World Conference on Human Rights, 48th Sess., U.N. Doc. A/Conf.157/24(1993)

North American FTA, US-Can.-Mex. Dec 17, 1992, 32 ILM 289 (1993)

Statute of the International Criminal Tribunal for the Former Yugoslavia as adopted in UNSCR 827 and amended by UNSCR Resol. 1166, 1329, 1411, 1431, 1481, 1597, 1660; See online at http://wwwunorg/icty/legaldoc-e/indexhtm (1993)

The Labour Law of the People's Republic of China adopted at the Eighth Meeting of the Standing Committee of the Eighth National People's Congress of the PRC on July 5, at http://wwwacftuorgcn/ labourlawhtm (September 4, 2007) (1994)

Agreement Establishing the World Trade Organization (Marrakesh Agreement) 33 ILM 1143; April 5, 1994 (entered into force January 1, 1995) (1994)

Constitution of the International Telecommunication Union Oct 14, 1994, 1996 WL 569887 (1994)

Statute of the International Criminal Trib. F. Rwanda as adopted by UNSCR 955 and amended by UNSCR 977, 978, 1165, 1166, 1329, 1411, 1431, 1503, 1512, 1503, 1534, 1684, 1717; See online at http://wwwictrorg (August 23, 2007) (1994)

International Convention for the Suppression of Terrorist Bombings GA Res 52/164, 1, UN Doc A/RES/52/164, Dec 15, 1997 (1997)

Protocol to the African Charter on Human and Peoples' Rights on the Establishment of an African Court on Human and Peoples' Rights June 10, 1998, OAU Doc CAB/LEG/63/3rev 5 (1998)

Rome Statute of the ICC July 17, 1998, 2187 UNTS 90 (1998)

International Convention for the Suppression of the Financing of Terrorism adopted by the UN General Assembly in GA Res 54/109, 1, UN Doc A/RES/54/109 (Dec 9, 1999) (1999)

OECD Guidelines for Multinational Enterprises June 27, 2000, ILM 40 (2000), 237 (2000)

Charter of Fundamental Rights of the European Union 2000-12-18 EN Official Journal of the European Communities C 364 (2000)

Voluntary Principles on Security and Human Rights, Welcome available at http://wwwvoluntaryprinciplesorg/ (September 8, 2007) (2000)

Articles on Responsibility of States for International Wrongful Acts Report of the International Law Commission on the work of its Fifty-Third Session, UN GAOR, 6th Comm, 56th Sess, Supp No 10, at 43-44, UN Doc A/56/10 (2001)

Uniting and Strengthening America by Providing Appropriate Tools Required to Intercept and Obstruct Terrorism Act of 2001 (USA PATRIOT Act) 115 Stat 272 (2001)

Protocol of the Court of Justice of the African Union adopted during the 2nd Ordinary Session of the Assembly of the African Union, Assembly/AU/Dec 25 (II), 2nd Sess, Doc/EX/CL/59 (III) (not yet in force), available at http://wwwafrica-unionorg (2003)

Foreign Assets Control Regulations for Importers and Exporters (Office of Foreign Assets Control) (2007)

Schriften zum Internationalen und zum öffentlichen Recht

Herausgegeben von Gilbert Gornig

Band 1 Michael Waldstein: Das Asylgrundrecht im europäischen Kontext. Wege einer europäischen Harmonisierung des Asyl- und Flüchtlingsrechts. 1993.

Band 2 Axel Linneweber: Einführung in das US-amerikanische Verwaltungsrecht. Kompetenzen, Funktionen und Strukturen der "Agencies" im US-amerikanischen Verwaltungsrecht. 1994.

Band 3 Tai-Nam Chi: Das Herrschaftssystem Nordkoreas unter besonderer Berücksichtigung der Wiedervereinigungsproblematik. 1994.

Band 4 Jörg Rösing: Beamtenstatut und Europäische Gemeinschaften. Eine Untersuchung zu den gemeinschaftsrechtlichen Anforderungen an die Freizügigkeit der Arbeitnehmer im Bereich des öffentlichen Dienstes. 1994.

Band 5 Wolfgang Wegel: Presse und Rundfunk im Datenschutzrecht. Zur Regelung des journalistischen Umgangs mit personenbezogenen Daten. 1994.

Band 6 Sven Brandt: Eigentumsschutz in europäischen Völkerrechtsvereinbarungen. EMRK, Europäisches Gemeinschaftsrecht, KSZE – unter Berücksichtigung der historischen Entwicklung. 1995.

Band 7 Alejandro Alvarez: Die verfassunggebende Gewalt des Volkes unter besonderer Berücksichtigung des deutschen und chilenischen Grundgesetzes. 1995.

Band 8 Martin Thies: Zur Situation der gemeindlichen Selbstverwaltung im europäischen Einigungsprozeß. Unter besonderer Berücksichtigung der Vorschriften des EG-Vertrages über staatliche Beihilfen und der EG-Umweltpolitik. 1995.

Band 9 Rolf-Oliver Schwemer: Die Bindung des Gemeinschaftsgesetzgebers an die Grundfreiheiten. 1995.

Band 10 Holger Kremser: "Soft Law" der UNESCO und Grundgesetz. Dargestellt am Beispiel der Mediendeklaration. 1996.

Band 11 Michael Silagi: Staatsuntergang und Staatennachfolge: mit besonderer Berücksichtigung des Endes der DDR. 1996.

Band 12 Reinhard Franke: Der gerichtliche Vergleich im Verwaltungsprozeß. Auch ein Beitrag zum verwaltungsrechtlichen Vertrag. 1996.

Band 13 Christoph Eichhorn: Altlasten im Konkurs. 1996.

Band 14 Dietrich Ostertun: Gewohnheitsrecht in der Europäischen Union. Eine Untersuchung der normativen Geltung und der Funktion von Gewohnheitsrecht im Recht der Europäischen Union. 1996.

Band 15 Ulrike Pieper: Neutralität von Staaten. 1997.

Band 16 Harald Endemann: Kollektive Zwangsmaßnahmen zur Durchsetzung humanitärer Normen. Ein Beitrag zum Recht der humanitären Intervention. 1997.

Band 17 Jochen Anweiler: Die Auslegungsmethoden des Gerichtshofs der Europäischen Gemeinschaften. 1997.

Band 18 Henrik Ahlers: Grenzbereich zwischen Gefahrenabwehr und Strafverfolgung. 1998.

Band 19 Heinrich Hahn: Der italienische Verwaltungsakt im Lichte des Verwaltungsverfahrensgesetzes vom 7. August 1990 (Nr. 241/90). Eine rechtsvergleichende Darstellung. 1998.

Band 20 Christoph Deutsch: Elektromagnetische Strahlung und Öffentliches Recht. 1998.

Band 21 Cordula Fitzpatrick: Künstliche Inseln und Anlagen auf See. Der völkerrechtliche Rahmen für die Errichtung und den Betrieb künstlicher Inseln und Anlagen. 1998.

Band 22 Hans-Tjabert Conring: Korporative Religionsfreiheit in Europa. Eine rechtsvergleichende Betrachtung. Zugleich ein Beitrag zu Art. 9 EMRK. 1998.

Band 23 Jörg Karenfort: Die Hilfsorganisation im bewaffneten Konflikt. Rolle und Status unparteiischer humanitärer Organisationen im humanitären Völkerrecht. 1999.

Band 24 Matthias Schote: Die Rundfunkkompetenz des Bundes als Beispiel bundesstaatlicher Kulturkompetenz in der Bundesrepublik Deutschland. Eine Untersuchung unter besonderer Berücksichtigung natürlicher Kompetenzen und der neueren Entwicklung im Recht der Europäischen Union. 1999.

Band 25 Hermann Rothfuchs: Die traditionellen Personenverkehrsfreiheiten des EG-Vertrages und das Aufenthaltsrecht der Unionsbürger. Eine Gegenüberstellung der vertraglichen Gewährleistungen. 1999.

Band 26 Frank Alpert: Zur Beteiligung am Verwaltungsverfahren nach dem Verwaltungsverfahrensgesetz des Bundes. Die Beteiligtenstellung des § 13 Abs. 1 VwVfG. 1999.

Band 27 Matthias Reichart: Umweltschutz durch völkerrechtliches Strafrecht. 1999.

Band 28 Nikolas von Wrangell: Globalisierungstendenzen im internationalen Luftverkehr. Entwicklung der Regulierung und Liberalisierung unter Berücksichtigung strategischer Allianzen und des Code-Sharing. 1999.

Band 29 Marietta Hovehne: Ein demokratisches Verfahren für die Wahlen zum Europäischen Parlament. Legitimation gemeinschaftlicher Entscheidungsstrukturen im europäischen Integrationsprozeß. 1999.

Band 30 Nina Kaden: Der amerikanische Clean Air Act und das deutsche Luftreinhalterecht. Eine rechtsvergleichende Untersuchung. 1999.

Band 31 Brigitte Daum: Grenzverletzungen und Völkerrecht. Eine Untersuchung der Rechtsfolgen von Grenzverletzungen in der Staatenpraxis und Folgerungen für das Projekt der International Law Commission zur Kodifizierung des Rechts der Staatenverantwortlichkeit. 1999.

Band 32 Andreas Fürst: Die bildungspolitischen Kompetenzen der Europäischen Gemeinschaft. Umfang und Entwicklungsmöglichkeiten. 1999.

Band 33 Gilles Despeux: Die Anwendung des völkerrechtlichen Minderheitenrechts in Frankreich. 1999.

Band 34 Michael Reckhard: Die rechtlichen Rahmenbedingungen der Sanktionierung von Beitragsverweigerung im System der Vereinten Nationen. 1999.

Band 35 Carsten Pagels: Schutz- und förderpflichtrechtliche Aspekte der Religionsfreiheit. Zugleich ein Beitrag zur Auslegung eines speziellen Freiheitsrechts. 1999.

Band 36 Bernhard Mehner: Die grenzüberschreitende Wirkung direktempfangbaren Satellitenfernsehens aus völkerrechtlicher Sicht. 2000.

Band 37 Karl-Josef Ulmen: Pharmakologische Manipulationen (Doping) im Leistungssport der DDR. Eine juristische Untersuchung. 2000.

Band 38 Jochen Starke: Die verfassungsgerichtliche Normenkontrolle durch den Conseil constitutionnel. Zum Kompetenztitel des Art. 61 der französischen Verfassung. 2000.

Band 39 Marco Herzog: Rechtliche Probleme einer Inhaltsbeschränkung im Internet. 2000.

Band 40 Gilles Despeux: Droit de la délimitation maritime. Commentaire de quelques décisions plutoniennes. 2000.

Band 41 Christina Hackel: Der Untergang des Landes Braunschweig und der Anspruch auf Restitution nach der Wiedervereinigung Deutschlands. 2000.

Band 42 Peter Aertker: Europäisches Zulassungsrecht für Industrieanlagen. Die Richtlinie über die integrierte Vermeidung und Verminderung der Umweltverschmutzung und ihre Auswirkungen auf das Anlagenzulassungsrecht der Bundesrepublik Deutschland. 2000.

Band 43 Karsten Bertram: Die Gesetzgebung zur Neuregelung des Grundeigentums in der ersten Phase der Französischen Revolution (bis 1793) und deren Bedeutung für die deutsche Eigentumsdogmatik der Gegenwart. 2000.

Band 44 Ulrike Hartmann: Die Entwicklung im internationalen Umwelthaftungsrecht unter besonderer Berücksichtigung von *erga omnes*-Normen. 2000.

Band 45 Thomas Jesch: Die Wirtschaftsverfassung der Sonderverwaltungsregion Hongkong. Eine Darstellung vor dem Hintergrund der Wiedereingliederung in die Souveränität der Volksrepublik China. 2001.

Band 46 Sven Gottschalkson: Der Ausschluß des Zivilrechtsweges bei Eigentumsverlusten an Immobilien in der ehemaligen DDR. 2002.

Band 47 Gilbert Hanno Gornig/Gilles Despeux: Seeabgrenzungsrecht in der Ostsee. Eine Darstellung des völkerrechtlichen Seeabgrenzungsrechts unter besonderer Berücksichtigung der Praxis der Ostseestaaten. 2002.

Band 48 Andreas Zühlsdorff: Rechtsverordnungsersetzende Verträge unter besonderer Berücksichtigung des Umweltrechts. 2003.

Band 49 Katja Schmitz: Durchgriffswirkung von Maßnahmen der UN und ihrer Sonderorganisationen unter besonderer Berücksichtigung von Resolutionen des UN-Sicherheitsrates - Die Entwicklung supranationaler Strukturen. 2003.

Band 50 Stefanie Rothenberger: Die angemessene Nutzung gemeinschaftlicher Ressourcen am Beispiel von Flüssen und speziellen Ökosystemen. Eine vergleichende Betrachtung zum modernen Verständnis eines klassischen völkerrechtlichen Nutzungsprinzips. 2003.

Band 51 Christoph von Burgsdorff: Die Umsetzung der EG-Datenschutzrichtlinie im nicht-öffentlichen Bereich. Möglichkeit einer zukunftsorientierten Konzeption des Datenschutzes in der Privatwirtschaft unter besonderer Berücksichtigung des BDSG. 2003.

Band 52 Frank Reinhardt: Powerline. Verfassungs-, verwaltungs- und telekommunikationsrechtliche Probleme. 2003.

Band 53 Chie Sato: Immunität Internationaler Organisationen. 2004.

Band 54 Johannes Thoma: EU-Recht und Schranken hoheitlicher Staatstätigkeit. 2004.

Band 55 Wolf Peterhoff: Rechtsansprüche enteigneter Volksgruppen und ihre Durchsetzbarkeit. 2004.

Band 56 Do-Hyub Kim: Das deutsche parlamentarische Regierungssystem als mögliches Modell für Korea. 2004.

Band 57 Alexander Koberg: Die Exilregierung im Völkerrecht. Eine Untersuchung ihrer rechtlichen Klassifikation. 2005.

Band 58 Nils Christian Carstensen: Das Verhältnis des Seerechtsübereinkommens der Vereinten Nationen von 1982 zu fischereirechtlichen Übereinkommen und deren Streitbeilegungsvorschriften. 2005.

Band 59 Oliver Franz: Osttimor und das Recht auf Selbstbestimmung. Eine Untersuchung zur Anwendung des Selbstbestimmungsrechts der Völker am Beispiel Osttimors. 2005.

Band 60 Michael Kadgien: Das Habsburgergesetz. 2005.

Band 61 Felix Wolf: Terrorversicherungen und europäisches Wettbewerbsrecht. Verschiedene Modelle staatlicher Beteiligung an einer Terrorversicherung für Wirtschaftsbetriebe und ihre Vereinbarkeit mit dem europäischen Wettbewerbsrecht. 2005.

Band 62 Heiko Bertelmann: Die Europäisierung des Staatshaftungsrechts. Eine Untersuchung zum Einfluss des Europäischen Gemeinschaftsrechts auf das deutsche Staatshaftungsrecht unter besonderer Berücksichtigung der Haftung für judikatives Unrecht. 2005.